THE JUDGE A

DAVID ROBERTSON

The Judge as Political Theorist

Contemporary Constitutional Review

PRINCETON UNIVERSITY PRESS

Princeton and Oxford

Published by Princeton University Press, 41 William Street, Princeton, New Jersey 08540
In the United Kingdom: Princeton University Press, 6 Oxford Street, Woodstock, Oxfordshire OX20 1TW
press.princeton.edu

Library of Congress Cataloging-in-Publication Data

Robertson, David, 1946–
The judge as political theorist : contemporary constitutional review / David Robertson.
p. cm.
Includes bibliographical references and index.
ISBN 978-0-691-14403-0 (hardcover : alk. paper)
ISBN 978-0-691-14404-7 (pbk. : alk. paper)
1. Judicial review. 2. Political questions and judicial power. 3. Constitutional courts. I. Title.
K3175.R63 2010
347'.012—dc22 2009040518

British Library Cataloging-in-Publication Data is available

This book has been composed in Minion
Printed on acid-free paper. ∞
Printed in the United States of America
10 9 8 7 6 5 4 3 2 1

For Clare

CONTENTS

PREFACE

Those who write long books cannot quite forget Pascal's apology to his friend for writing a long letter, on the grounds that he did not have time to write a short one. Unfortunately, I have had quite long enough for that excuse not to work. Had I had longer, the book would have grown beyond any publisher's interest. Perhaps the material is just too complex for a shorter work, because I am far more conscious of what I have had to leave out. The book really ought to have had chapters on Australia, India, and Israel at the very least. Or perhaps I am just verbose?

I am a rarity nowadays, not because I am a political scientist writing about courts—there are now quite a lot of us—but because my approach is much nearer than most to the old style of political scientists, often dismissed scornfully by my more hard-edged colleagues as "doctrine scholars." Comparative work on judicial review is extraordinarily difficult unless one does adopt the methods of modern political science, measuring and seeking quantitative generalizations about external patterns of judicial behaviour. I do not do that here. Nor do I adhere to the currently dominant "rational choice" perspective in analysis. Neither of these methodological failings stems from incompetence. I was, still am, a political sociologist, and most of my work has been quantitative, including the first piece I ever wrote on courts. As for rational choice, I was a fully paid-up member of the gang from my doctoral days. I do not disrespect either quantitative methodology or rational choice theory; they just do not offer answers to the questions that interest me about constitutional review.

No political scientist writing about seven or eight jurisdictions, as I do here, can possibly know as much law as a real lawyer will know about any one of them. Or at least he will not "know the law" as a lawyer knows it. So this book is not one a lawyer is likely to write, nor is it that of a political scientist—it is not political science, and it is not truly a doctrine study. It is an attempt to understand the core nature of the business of doing judicial review by reading a lot of judicial opinion writing. And it is a speculation about how such activity fits into modern liberal democracy. I believe in judicial review. I have often noticed at conferences that the lawyers trust parliaments, and the political scientists trust the courts. I hope my ultimate trust in constitutional courts is not simply a case of preferring the evil one is familiar with. In the end the book is as it is because I am truly fascinated by constitutional argumentation. I hope some readers may become equally entranced.

A note on errors. There are errors in the book, quite inevitably given its range and my limitations. Sometimes, though, apparent errors are choices of emphasis, and apparent lacunae—a missing caution or shading of argument—are filled in elsewhere in the book. In a study of this size some things need saying more than once, and I may not always have spotted these desirable repetitions. Other apparent errors will turn out to be matters of interpretation. There are, after all, very few actual facts in legal doctrine. Though I have not consciously striven for originality in doctrinal exposition, I must at times have given sincere interpretations that others disagree with. These occasions are not necessarily errors or mistakes.

In writing this big book with a wide scope I have, as all authors admit, benefited from far more people than I can name or properly identify, even to myself. I owe a real debt to the lawyers in my own college—Andrew Burrows, Josh Getzler, Mike McNair, and Derek Wood—who have treated me more courteously than I deserve, talked to me at great length, treated me like an honorary lawyer. Apart from them, I owe many thanks to a perhaps unlikely helper, Peter McDonald, Fellow and Tutor in English, who over many lunches has shared his knowledge of South Africa. I would like to thank the two readers to whom Princeton University Press gave the manuscript for review. I have never really credited authors' expressions of gratitude for such reports, but these two reviewers' supportive but highly acute criticism has been both vital and a real pleasure to receive.

The Oxford scholar who has most influenced my thinking is the late Geoffrey Marshal. I have not achieved his wonderful down-to-earthness, nor managed to retain my Yorkshire accent as well as he did. The biggest of all my debts is owed to my wife Liz, not just for wifely support, but because as a practising corporate lawyer qualified in both the United Kingdom and United States she has been a constant intellectual influence. Finally, an apology to my daughter to whom this book is dedicated. I'm sorry you had to wait longer than your sister to get your book, but it is longer than the one Ellen got.

David Robertson
Oxford
May 2009

THE JUDGE AS POLITICAL THEORIST

CHAPTER ONE

The Nature and Function of Judicial Review

Le Conseil constitutionnel est une jurisdiction, mais il ne sait pas; mon rôle est de lui faire prendre conscience de sa nature.

—Robert Badinter, president of the Conseil constitutionnel, 1986–95[1]

The theme of this book is that modern constitutional review cannot always be adequately understood if seen through the traditional categories of the separation of powers. Constitutional courts do more than can be fitted into the domain allowed to courts exercising the judicial function. Much of what they do in what I call "transforming societies" involves spreading the values set out in the constitution throughout their state and society. Indeed, their idea of what a constitution is does not always fit well with the orthodox idea of a liberal constitution. I try to show that constitutional judges often come near to being applied political theorists, carrying out a quite new type of political function. This first chapter develops some of these concepts and sets out the plan of the book, offering technical information and definitions to be filled out in the substantive chapters.

A few examples always help in setting out a general approach. Though this book is primarily about "new" constitutional review in countries undergoing some form of transformation, I begin with a different sort of example. It is chosen not from a new constitutional court, or one involved in transformative jurisprudence, but from the oldest court doing constitutional review, what is beyond doubt the model court, the US Supreme Court. There are two reasons for this. First, the Supreme Court is familiar—if the reader knows anything about constitutional review, it is likely to be about America's experience. Second, I hope to show that the patterns and ideas that are relevant in newer jurisdictions have their counterparts even in this oldest and most familiar territory.

[1]D Rousseau, *Sur le Conseil constitutionnel: La doctrine Badinter et la démocratie* (Paris: Descartes & Cie, 1997), 19.

In 2003 the Supreme Court overturned one of its own precedents, a precedent that had only stood for seventeen years. The case was *Lawrence v Texas*, which challenged a state law criminalizing some homosexual practices.[2] The ruling precedent, *Bowers v Hardwick* from 1986, ought to have made the case unnecessary.[3] In *Bowers* a Georgia state law that made sodomy punishable by up to twenty years' imprisonment was challenged. Hardwick had been arrested for committing sodomy when a police officer had entered his house and found him with another man. In the end he was not prosecuted, but undertook a civil suit against the state claiming the law was unconstitutional. Though the federal appeals court agreed with Hardwick, the Supreme Court ruled that Georgia was entitled to use the criminal law to impose the majority's moral code.[4]

The Supreme Court is not totally forbidden to overturn its own previous decisions, but puts a very strong value on *stare decisis*, the rule of precedent. Certainly it is rare for the court to change its mind so soon after a major ruling, even one as controversial as that in *Bowers v Hardwick*. That case had raised a huge protest because it clashed with liberalising trends in American society during the 1970s and 1980s. When *Lawrence v Texas* overruled *Bowers*, there was an equivalent uproar from political and judicial conservatives.[5] When major courts do overturn their own precedents, they usually do so because they think an earlier decision has become inappropriate for a later society. Or they at least shade their disagreement with the past decision. The US Supreme Court of 2003 was much blunter. The majority opinion says outright, "*Bowers* was not correct when it was decided, and it is not correct today. It ought not to remain binding precedent."[6] This really was a choice by the Supreme Court—it could have held for Lawrence without overruling *Bowers*. The majority opinion explicitly says that the justices rejected an alternative approach that would have disallowed the Texas statute on narrower grounds. In fact Justice O'Connor, who voted along with the majority to overturn the Texas law, had been part of the majority in *Bowers* and still thought it correct. To find the law under which Lawrence was prosecuted unconstitutional, she used an ap-

[2] *Lawrence v Texas*, 539 US 558 (2003) (US Supreme Court).

[3] *Bowers v Hardwick*, 478 US 186 (1986) (US Supreme Court).

[4] The court's own summary of this point is this: "Sodomy laws may not be invalidated under the due process clause of the Fourteenth Amendment on the theory that there must be a rational basis for the law and that majority sentiments about the morality of homosexual sodomy are not an adequate basis." *Bowers v Hardwick*, 3.

[5] There is an extensive journal literature on both cases. As a selection, EM Maltz, "The Court, the Academy, and the Constitution: A Comment on *Bowers v. Hardwick* and Its Critics," 1989 *Brigham Young University Law Review* 59–95, gives a good account of both the first case and its reception, while J Weinstein and T DeMarco, "Challenging Dissent: The Ontology and Logic of *Lawrence v. Texas*," 2003 10 *Cardozo Women's Law Journal* 423–67, is a useful analysis of the judicial logic in the second case. The two cases and intervening decisions are treated together in R Turner, "Traditionalism, Majoritarian Morality, and the Homosexual Sodomy Issue: The Journey from *Bowers* to *Lawrence*," 2004 53 *University of Kansas Law Review* 1–81.

[6] *Lawrence v Texas*, 12. The nine justices on the court were split. Five signed the majority opinion, with a sixth judge concurring in the result but using a quite different approach. The main dissent, joined by two other justices, was by Justice Scalia. Even by the standards of the Supreme Court, it is bitter and confrontational towards the majority.

proach quite different from that offered in the majority opinion. But if the court in 2003 did not have to overrule *Bowers*, the court in 1986 did not have to rule on the constitutionality of the Georgia statute at all—it would have been perfectly possible to overturn the court of appeals by simply ruling, as the Supreme Court was invited to, that the case was moot. Right at the beginning, the first Georgia court to hear the case had ruled that Bowers had no cause of action because he had not actually been prosecuted.

The first point to make is that courts sometimes really do set out deliberately to make major legal statements. No one can avoid the fact that two US Supreme Courts, only seventeen years apart, felt so strongly about the issue of criminalizing homosexual behaviour that they took up challenges that could have been avoided. Both courts, though radically opposed to each other, felt it their duty to make law in this way. The second point to make at this stage is how much personnel changes matter. Since the 1930s the US Supreme Court has always had nine justices; though this number is not prescribed in the constitution and has not always been mandated by law, it may have hardened into a "constitutional convention." Of the nine men and women who heard *Lawrence*, only three survived from the *Bowers* court, and one of them, O'Connor, effectively changed tack. The six new appointments split four to two against the ruling in *Bowers*. On such minor things as judicial death and retirement can depend something as fundamental as a shift in a nation's public morality. (The route by which people become judges is commented on later, especially, as an example, in chapter 4 on France.)

In other ways this relatively ordinary piece of constitutional adjudication shares many of the features to be discussed at length in this book. The ruling in *Lawrence* is a self-conscious "modernization" of values, and an imposition of them. Much of the disagreement about the case revolves round the question of whether or not public disapproval of private behaviour can justify legal restrictions, but discussion is always admixed with matters of what I have called elsewhere "judicial methodology"—the rules to be applied in deciding such cases.[7] So those who wanted to overturn the Texas law claimed that there was no important and legitimate government aim served by it. Their opponents said that the law needed no such aim, because that test applies only to rights that are "deeply rooted in this Nation's history and tradition." Much of what will follow in this book is about what tests are applicable in what circumstances.

Part of the disagreement over *Lawrence* is factual—the two sides differ on the history of legal constraints on homosexuality—and we will see frequent use and misuse of claims to empirical knowledge in other jurisdictions. Much of the disagreement over *Bowers* and *Lawrence* is disagreement over what the cases are actually about. For both sides the issues have little to do with homosexuality in itself. For the majority in *Lawrence* the issue is the right of the citizen to be left alone in private. For the other side, the cases are about the right of the state governments to reflect majority feeling within their territories with no federal intervention. Sociol-

[7] D Robertson, *Judicial Discretion in the House of Lords* (Oxford: Clarendon Press, 1998), especially chapters 3 and 4.

ogists might call this the "framing" of the issues. A matter of framing or perception is the "What is this all about?" question, asked at a lower level. What is it about for the actual people caught up in the legislation? To the majority in *Bowers*, it is only a matter of their sexual activities. To the majority in *Lawrence*, it is a deep matter of human dignity, and the consequences for those liable to be prosecuted are far more onerous than the actual sentences. Indeed, where the protection of dignity is concerned, it does not matter that such laws as the Georgia and Texas statutes are hardly ever invoked. Not only will such framing issues occur in several contexts later in the book, but the concept of dignity will prove to be the most important single value in modern judicial review.

Lawrence, if not *Bowers*, raises the question of whether legal and constitutional thinking outside the United States counts in US courts. The majority in *Lawrence* attach great importance to, inter alia, decisions of the European Court of Human Rights, because they regard moral opinion across developed democracies as an important measure. To the minority, such matters are utterly irrelevant, because only aspects of American moral history are relevant or can legitimately be cited. (The extensive use of foreign judgements, so that a sort of international constitutional law is rapidly developing, will be discussed several times in this book.) These cases are about, and are examples of, what has come to be called "legal culture." They have to do with the way different generations and groups of judges are socialised or have their "professional formation." Justice Scalia makes this abundantly clear in one of his harshest condemnations of the *Lawrence* majority. I quote him at length to make this point (lengthy quotations from the judges are a major part of my technique throughout the book):

> Today's opinion is the product of a Court, which is the product of a law-profession culture, that has largely signed on to the so-called homosexual agenda, by which I mean the agenda promoted by some homosexual activists directed at eliminating the moral opprobrium that has traditionally attached to homosexual conduct. I noted in an earlier opinion the fact that the American Association of Law Schools (to which any reputable law school *must* seek to belong) excludes from membership any school that refuses to ban from its job-interview facilities a law firm (no matter how small) that does not wish to hire as a prospective partner a person who openly engages in homosexual conduct. . . . One of the most revealing statements in today's opinion is the Court's grim warning that the criminalization of homosexual conduct is "an invitation to subject homosexual persons to discrimination both in the public and in the private spheres." . . . It is clear from this that the Court has taken sides in the culture war, departing from its role of assuring, as neutral observer, that the democratic rules of engagement are observed. Many Americans do not want persons who openly engage in homosexual conduct as partners in their business, as scoutmasters for their children, as teachers in their children's schools, or as boarders in their home. They view this as protecting themselves and their families from a lifestyle that they believe to be immoral and destructive. The Court views it as "discrimination"

> which it is the function of our judgments to deter. So imbued is the Court with the law profession's anti-anti-homosexual culture, that it is seemingly unaware that the attitudes of that culture are not obviously "mainstream."[8]

Scalia may well be unfair, but the fact remains that matters like a profession's own rules crucially shape the way constitutional law develops. I shall often refer to this idea of a legal, or politico-legal, culture.[9]

Finally, there is one thing that neither *Bowers* nor *Lawrence* is really about. Neither case depends on interpretation of the US Bill of Rights, or any other part of the constitution—or not in any sense of textual interpretation that one would find outside law, and especially constitutional law. Nowhere in the constitution is homosexuality or sodomy mentioned. Indeed, nowhere in that document is any matter of sexual rights or behaviour mentioned. The whole of the more apparently "legal" parts of the opinions in *Bowers* and *Lawrence* are about previous judicial glosses on the constitution. This practice, as the book will show, is true to a large extent everywhere in adjudication. As soon as constitutional issues arise and are given judicial consideration, a rich body of interlinked judicial thought develops. This body of judicial material, part of what the French Conseil constitutionnel calls the *bloc de constitutionnalité*, is both the result of, and a constraint on, judicial review. Judges often decide on constitutionality by relying on what other judges have said more than on the document that is supposed to be controlling.

Introductory Definitions and the Plan of the Book

What is constitutional review? At one level this question is a technical matter of constitutional law. Constitutional review is a process by which one institution, commonly called a constitutional court, has the constitutional authority to decide whether statutes or other decrees created by the rule-making institutions identified by the constitution are valid given the terms of the constitution. It is a highly reflexive process. Such a definition tells us nothing about the purpose of constitutional review in the political system; it tells us nothing about the impact of constitutional review on the governance of the society; it does not describe constitutional review as a functional element in the political complex we usually call a state. Some liberal democracies, probably most by now, have some form of constitutional review, but not all, so it is not just a definitional element of democracy.[10] As long as impeccably democratic nations-states like the Netherlands do without judicial review, its presence and functioning in other countries must invite seri-

[8] *Lawrence v Texas*, 578.

[9] Certainly the *Lawrence* decision has provoked some anxiety about judicial bias: TA Sparling, "Judicial Bias Claims of Homosexual Persons in the Wake of *Lawrence v. Texas*," 2004 *Southern Texas Law Review* 255–309.

[10] One count gives 128 countries with judicial review: FR Romeu, "The Establishment of Constitutional Courts: A Study of 128 Democratic Constitutions," 2006 2 *Review of Law and Economics* 1, 104–35. A detailed analysis of such courts can be found at http://www.concourts.net/comparison.php.

ous inquiry. Only a very subtle argument would suggest that Norway, which has judicial review, is more democratic than the rest of Scandinavia, which does not. This whole book is really dedicated to answering one question—what does constitutional review *do* for the countries that have it? Ostensive definition can get us started. Constitutional review answers questions like these:

- Can a state pass legislation prohibiting floor-crossing by those elected to its legislature?[11]
- Can a state forbid a wide range of state officials to join political parties?[12]
- Can the new democratic parliament of a former Communist state pass a law characterising the previous regime as a state of "lawlessness"?[13]
- Can a state decriminalize the actions of doctors and patients involved in terminating a pregnancy?[14]
- Can an education authority ban teaching material that treats homosexual partnerships as equivalent to heterosexual families?[15]
- Can a state nationalise its banking sector?[16]

Yet these are only questions where something exists to make them questions—obviously states can, and do, do all of these things. They become real questions only where two conditions apply: there must be a constitution purporting to restrict what a state can do, and there must be a body independent of the legislature and executive empowered to test state action against that constitution. Where a parliament is entitled itself to decide whether or not its laws satisfy constitutional limitation, the constitution, in this respect at least, cannot be more than advisory or aspirational. There is a rich and complex literature in political theory considering whether a system of independent oversight on parliamentary legislation is fully compatible with democracy.[17] This book will not do more than touch tangentially on some aspects of that debate. It is not, however, irrelevant to the debate, because my concern here is to give a much fuller characterization of what exactly happens in judicial review than the theoretical literature normally concerns itself with. However, my concerns are also much narrower than those of the theoretical debate. I have chosen to concentrate almost entirely on constitutional review mechanisms in societies that have undergone major change, where constitutional review of legislation has been added to an ongo-

[11] *United Democratic Movement v The President of the Republic of South Africa* CCT 23/02 (South African Constitutional Court).

[12] *Statutory Prohibitions of Political Party Membership*, K26/00 (2000) (Polish Constitutional Tribunal).

[13] *Lawlessness*, Pl. US 19/93 (Czech Republic Constitutional Court). All citations are from the website of the court, which is http://angl.concourt.cz/angl_verze/cases.php.

[14] *Abortion Case No 1*, 39 BVerfGE 1 (1975) (German Federal Constitutional Court).

[15] *Chamberlain v Surrey School District No. 36*, 4 SCR 710 (2002) (Canadian Supreme Court).

[16] *Nationalizations*, 81-132 DC (1982) (Conseil constitutionnel).

[17] As examples, only, of the debate, consider the issues and citations in FI Michelman "The Constitution, Social Rights, and Liberal Political Justification," 2003 1 *International Journal of Constitutional Law* 1, 13–34. Perhaps the main writer associated with an anticonstitutional review position is Jeremy Waldron. See his classic essay "A Rights Based Critique of Constitutional Rights," 1993 13 *Oxford Journal of Legal Studies* 18–51.

ing society, either in a new constitution or as something grafted on to a continuing constitutional tradition. In essence I am looking to see what constitutional review tries to do, and how it does it, in societies undergoing a form of political transformation. This focus is not new. For example, Bruce Ackerman's seminal study of the international development of constitutional review is based on two general scenarios. One is federalism; the other is what he calls "new beginnings." The latter

> operates with a different logic, dealing in expressive symbols, not functional imperatives. Under this scenario a constitution emerges *as a symbolic marker of a great transition in the political life of a nation*.[18]

Most of the jurisdictions I talk about hereafter are also covered by Ackerman.

This choice is made for two reasons. First, it is intrinsically important to see how constitutional review functions in such societies, as compared with states, like the United States, where review was built in at the beginning of the constitutional epoch. Second, such transforming constitutional arrangements help me focus on what I take the main function of constitutional review to be. My claim is that constitutional review is a mechanism for permeating all regulated aspects of society with a set of values inherent in the constitutional agreement the society has accepted. This position is developed seriatim throughout the rest of this book. The idea embraces various subthemes. One crucial idea is that modern societies lack other all-embracing moral or ideological commitments as a result of religious secularization, on the one hand, and the victory of a middle-of-the-road political consensus around a form of liberalism, on the other. Consequently, constitutionalism reigns supreme. If a politician wants to attack another politician's policies in a way that seems nonpartisan, the claim that the policy is unconstitutional is the best bet. If constitutionalism is the main overarching value, it is also true that one specific constitutional value often seems to dominate constitutional discourse—the value of nondiscrimination. This is the legal equivalent to saying that equality is the one prime value: in a liberal secular society no value code exists to justify inequality. Equality of opportunity is a requirement for the legitimating of a secular, individualistic, liberal society. Thus constitutional interpretation takes centre stage whoever does it, and where it is done by special courts or tribunals, constitutional review becomes a process of throwing a net of logically derived values over legislation, creating a mesh policies must pass through.

These and related ideas are developed in the following chapters. The plan of the book is simple. There are five case studies of constitutional jurisdictions, chosen to represent different examples of transformative constitutions. There follows a long comparative theme chapter on particular problems in constitutional adjudication. The aim of this chapter is to demonstrate the variance, but also the limitations to variance, in the ways jurisdictions deal with issues none can avoid. The jurisdiction chapters are essentially descriptive. Very little has been published that seeks to describe several jurisdictions side by side, so there ought to be no sense that description is somehow a less valuable academic pursuit. These

[18] B Ackerman, "The Rise of World Constitutionalism," 1997 83 *Virginia Law Review* 4, 771–97, at 784.

accounts are sketches of the state of constitutional review in each jurisdiction, not up-to-date accounts of the exact body of law currently valid within them. As sketches, they highlight what seems to me most importantly characteristic of each jurisdiction's approach to constitutional review. This is the more so because of the methodology I embrace. To call it a methodology is overgrand, but the point is that my descriptions are concerned almost entirely with the actual cases decided, and above all with the judicial argument in them. Far too little attention is paid to what judges actually say in judging, as opposed simply to the decisions they reach. Because I see these courts as involved in the explication of constitutional values, in the making of low-level political theory, I attach huge importance to the arguments crafted by judges. An alternative title for this book would indeed have been "Constitutional Judging as Political Theorising: A Comparative Analysis." The nature of modern democracy is such that governments engage in justification, and judicial opinions constitute an important aspect of what is sometimes called "deliberative democracy."[19]

The same sorts of issues substantive and procedural occur in all these societies with judicial review, though with emphases that differ according to national politico-legal culture and the pathways that have brought the courts to importance. Finding out what variety of answers seem possible, and why some are chosen over others, should tell us a great deal about the nature of this obscure activity of judicial review. The first jurisdiction chosen is Germany because of its enormous importance as the first postwar constitutional court with real power, which has given it great influence over later courts. I follow that discussion with a composite chapter that describes judicial review in three of the new Eastern European democracies, Poland, the Czech Republic, and Hungary, which face similar problems in (re)establishing democracy and the rule of law. The differences in their approaches are as revealing as the similarities, and the apparently anodyne concept of the "rule of law" turns out to be richly complicated and various. These chapters are followed by one other European example, the French experience in the Fifth Republic. The most important aspect of the French story is that constitutional review came for the first time in the Fifth Republic, against a background of long-term historical antipathy to the courts in politics. What my sketch highlights here is summed up in the quotation heading the chapter: France really does have a body of complex and thought-out constitutional law, and the Conseil constitutionnel has not merely responded to issues in an ad hoc, partisan way.

Canada follows, vital as an example of a country where a decision was made to import constitutional review into a common-law-based political system with parliamentary supremacy. Canada had previously had constitutional review, but of a limited kind. How its judges coped with the new Charter of Rights and Freedoms,

[19] The idea of deliberative democracy has been used and developed by a host of major political theorists, including Elster, Habermas, and Rawls. It probably originated in an article by Joseph M. Bessete, who worked it out most fully in *The Mild Voice of Reason: Deliberative Democracy and American National Government* (Chicago: University of Chicago Press, 1994).

which expanded constitutional review, is an important topic in its own right, but is also worth examination because the problems they faced tell us a good deal about the special nature of the activity and the political role of constitutional review. The final jurisdiction treated is South Africa, the country that has most openly embraced the idea of "transformative jurisprudence," yet where constitutional review was grafted onto a long history of judicial passivity and a common-law background. Throughout these sketches several concepts occur and reoccur. The best example is the role of "dignity" as a touchstone for constitutionality, which can be found in very nearly every jurisdiction.

After the case studies there are two chapters, one rather long, taking themes in a directly comparative perspective. (I make a good deal of effort to draw useful comparisons within the jurisdiction chapters as well, to illuminate approaches to similar problems.) The longest chapter in the book, and probably the most demanding, is chapter 7. It is long because it offers a comparative study of how the most common and unavoidable issue in the whole of rights enforcement has been handled in different jurisdictions. The problem is simple to state. Whatever a constitution says about rights, it is virtually impossible to guarantee that any right will be absolute; there must always be some circumstances when a right will have to give in to the needs of the state. But how is this restriction of rights to be handled? Above all, what sort of analysis must a constitutional court go through to decide when a right can be trumped by social need? This chapter is unlike the others in that a good part of it considers the constitutional jurisprudence of the United States. The US Supreme Court has the longest experience in the world of dealing with just this question, made all the more difficult because the US Bill of Rights, unlike other statements of rights, does not on the face of it accept that the rights it guarantees cannot be absolute. Chapter 7 is thus, more than other chapters, about the sorts of arguments that can carry respect inside a deliberative democracy. It is also where I give my most sustained discussion of problems rising from antidiscrimination rights, the core value in modern constitutional thinking. The arguments for limiting rights are of the same logical form as those for allowing forms of discrimination between citizens where this allowance is necessary for policy. These themes and considerations are brought together in the concluding chapter, where I sketch a justification for judicial review of constitutionality in light of the fears some express about its lack of democratic legitimacy. In so doing I offer a characterisation of the constitutional judge as a professional political theorist.

The Forms of Judicial Review

There are two basic types of constitutional review. The first type involves questions about how authority to act is distributed by the constitution to various parts of the state, and with federal constitutions, how it is distributed between the national and component unit levels. The case that tradition claims began American judicial review, *Marbury v Madison*, was about such an issue, as were nearly all the major

US Supreme Court decisions until after the Civil War.[20] Virtually any constitution that involves a separation-of-powers doctrine, a federal structure, or both, requires some entity to police these boundaries. Although individual decisions by constitutional review bodies on the distribution of authority may be controversial, few observers object to the exercise of this function in general. The exception is perhaps where the reflexive nature of constitutional review is most apparent—where the review body acts to increase its own authority at the expense of other actors. This was the problem with *Marbury* and has been the source of most objections to the activities of the European Court of Justice. The newer constitutions are, on the whole, simpler than the old federal constitutions as far as boundary maintenance is concerned, but major problems have nonetheless required solutions. (In this book this issue is most clearly covered in the first part of the chapter on South Africa, and in some contexts from the Eastern European jurisdictions.) These instances have typically involved separation-of-powers clashes between the legislature and the executive—the power of the constitutional courts themselves has usually been unchallenged.

The second type of constitutional review concerns not who can do something, but what limits may be placed by the constitution on doing certain things, regardless of the actor. This is largely the domain of bills, charters, and declarations of fundamental, human, or citizens' rights. Although the American constitution had a Bill of Rights from its earliest days, it was not until the Fourteenth Amendment, passed after the Civil War in 1868, that it came to apply to the states as well as the federal government. The British North America Act, a nineteenth-century act of the UK Parliament that served as the Canadian constitution until 1982, did not have a binding bill of rights, and the Australian constitution, which came into force in 1900, still does not have one. Nor were equivalent limitations on what could be done found in continental Europe. (Interestingly, Kelsen himself thought it inappropriate to have such limitations enforced by a constitutional court.) The constitutions created after World War II nearly all contain bills of right, and they are often very extensive. The latest wave of constitution writing, in Eastern and Central Europe and South Africa, has added a further complication. The most recent constitutions contain provisions for "social" rights, under which the constitutional courts can order the government or parliament to do something, rather than merely to desist from doing something illiberal. (This problem is discussed mainly in the chapters on Eastern Europe, Canada, and South Africa.)

This distinction between types of review is often more clear in principle than in practice; it is somewhat of an ideal type. It is easy to come up with examples of constitutional adjudication that can be seen as either boundary maintenance, rights enforcement, or both. Boundary cases can be triggered or motivated by

[20] *Marbury v Madison*, 5 US 137 (1803) (US Supreme Court). So famous is the case that commentators on any region that is developing judicial review look to find the equivalent case, for example, HK Prempeh, "*Marbury* in Africa: Judicial Review and the Challenge of Constitutionalism in Contemporary Africa," 2005 80 *Tulane Law Review* 1239–1323. American legal historians do not see *Marbury* in such a clear architectonic light, but it has come down to modern constitutional commentators worldwide in this way.

disagreement on substantive political or policy goals. An interesting example that conflates all of these considerations is the famous Australian bank nationalisation case.[21] This case came about when the Labour government tried to make all private banking illegal and give a monopoly to the Commonwealth Bank. Losing the case was a factor in Labour's subsequent electoral defeat, which kept them out of power for over twenty years. As noted above, the Australian constitution has no bill of rights, but does have clauses that can be used as an equivalent if the High Court is so inclined. Where these provisions have applied to ordinary civil rights, they have been largely ignored by the High Court, but one in particular that touches on economic rights was brought to bear on the banks' challenge to the Labour government. This was Section 92, which provided that "trade, commerce, and intercourse among the states should be absolutely free." This constitutional provision can be regarded as, and was surely meant to be, essentially structural—it aimed at preventing trade barriers because a major part of the plan for the whole constitution was the creation of a free trade area. The High Court had previously developed out of it the doctrine that the clause protected the laisser-faire rights of individuals. Using this doctrine, which was not fully overturned until 1988, the High Court found any nationalisation to be completely unconstitutional. In a similar way the US Supreme Court has at times used the apparently structural Interstate Commerce Clause to achieve substantive political goals.[22] Although there are many other ways of categorising different forms of judicial review, several of which will be canvassed in this book, this simple distinction will be helpful in discussions in this chapter on why some writers have reservations about courts interpreting constitutions.

Types of Constitutional Courts

New methods of constitutional review developed in stages in the second half of the twentieth century. Some of the differences from earlier adjudication are structural; though some of the newly important constitutional review bodies, above all the Canadian Supreme Court, are general courts like that of the United States, most are purpose-built constitutional courts, often so labelled. These courts, like the German Federal Constitutional Court, arguably the most important of all, are often referred to as "Kelsen" courts. Hans Kelsen, an Austrian jurist, was the architect of the earliest purely constitutional court, set up in Austria between 1920 and the rise of the Nazi state in 1934. In jurisprudence he is best known for his idea of

[21] *Bank of New South Wales v Commonwealth*, 76 CLR 1 (1948) (Australian High Court). For a general account of the court and of this case, see B Galligan, *Politics of the High Court: A Study of the Judicial Branch of Government in Australia* (St. Lucia: University of Queensland Press, 1987).

[22] As an example of how "political" some commentators see judicial interpretation of such structural matters, see MV Tushnet, "Scalia and the Dormant Commerce Clause: A Foolish Formalism," 1990 12 *Cardozo Law Review* 1717–43. A more general discussion of the way the clause has been used is given in SG Gey, "The Political Economy of the Dormant Commerce Clause," 1989 1 *New York University Review of Law and Social Change* 17–97.

the *Grundnorm*, the highest element in a hierarchy of rules that gives legitimacy to all further derived norms.[23] Kelsen saw the constitution as functioning rather like a *Grundnorm* and argued that a special body, separate from the ordinary hierarchies of courts, should be created to interpret the implication this ultimate rule had for legislation passed under its auspices. Kelsen courts share typical features. First, they deal only with constitutional issues and are not, in theory at least, appellate courts. By this is meant that a case fully decided in one court is not passed up to the constitutional court for a final answer, in which all the arguments are re-heard. Second, they are not staffed by professional judges promoted up the hierarchy but by politically appointed, though legally qualified, people from other sectors. The judges are typically a mixture of academic lawyers and professional politicians with legal experience, though there is usually also a contingent who have come from, or been appointed by, the higher ordinary courts.[24] The varied background of judges came from the idea that much more creativity and political nuance was going to be needed in judgements than could be expected from a continental-style professional judiciary used to narrow interpretations of a code. Perhaps the most important difference from the US model is the ways in which issues can come before a constitutional court. Under the US system and those like it, constitutional issues arise in the process of ordinary litigation, usually in the public law or criminal law domains, where one of the litigants is the state. Any of the inferior courts through which the case has risen can have, and probably will have, made its own judgement on the constitutionality of relevant law. The Supreme Court is thus acting as a court of ultimate appeal. The "new" routes to constitutional adjudication vary a good deal between countries, but they include the following, not all of which will be found in all countries; nor is this list exhaustive.

1. A reference from an ordinary court trying a case that appears to involve an issue of constitutional law. This is more nearly like the US-style systems because the issues do arise in the process of ordinary litigation. The constitutional court, however, is limited to answering the constitutional question posed by the referring court, and does not actually decide the case. Once the constitutional court has given its ruling, the original proceedings recommence with the constitutional law applied as now defined by the original judge. This process is the one used by the European Union's Court of Justice when questions of EU law interpretation are referred to it from a national court.

[23] His views on constitutional review are encapsulated in H Kelsen, "Judicial Review of Legislation: A Comparative Study of the Austrian and the American Constitution," 1942 4 *Journal of Politics* 2, 183–200. The general theory of the *Grundnorm* is best described in H Kelsen, *The Pure Theory of Law* (Berkeley: University of California Press, 1967).

[24] This sort of detail for most European countries is covered in C Guarnieri and P Pederzoli, *The Power of Judges: A Comparative Study of Courts and Democracy*, Oxford Socio-Legal Studies (Oxford: Oxford University Press, 2002). Subsequent chapters deal with important structural aspects for the various countries studied.

2. A direct request by a citizen to say whether or not a rule under which the citizen has suffered a purported infringement of rights, or the act of some state agent, is constitutionally valid.
3. A reference from some state body or officer to give an a priori or abstract assessment of the constitutionality of a law, without there being any context of litigation or actual complaint. Such referrers can be groups of legislators, prime ministers or presidents, governments of federal subordinate units, public officers like an ombudsman, and various other actors who are deemed to have a special role in seeing that the constitution is observed.

These arrangements make the process of constitutional review much more obvious. The third route, that of a priori or abstract review, in particular makes it very clear that a power relationship exists between the legislative body and some other entity authorised to forbid the legislators to do what they wish to do. This is especially so because abstract review has frequently been a matter of high-profile political conflict. The most common pattern is for a parliamentary minority, having lost the debate and vote in its legislative chamber, to refer the statute to the constitutional court as a last resort. So, for example, in France in the last twenty years it is often claimed that almost all important bills have been referred to the Conseil constitutionnel by the parliamentary minority.

Constitutional Review and Political Science

Political science has real problems with constitutional review, of which it is often deeply sceptical, even when, rarely, it bothers to notice the process at all.[25] The scepticism and uncertainty displayed by political science probably stems in large part from the unavoidable reflexivity of the formal definition, combined with the usual political science categorisation of political institutions according to the classic separation-of-powers doctrine. How can a body be authorised by a document to measure the product of another equal ranking body set up by the same document against the document itself? The core problem is this: in the separation-of-powers model all three functions, the legislative, executive, and judicial, are the proper

[25] The political science literature on the United States is huge. The political science, as opposed to legal, literature on other courts is sparse, often amounting to one or two books and a handful of articles and chapters. I cite these where relevant in subsequent chapters. Modern comparative work is dominated by the writings of one man, Alec Stone Sweet, and his collaborators. While we take very different positions on many matters, and particularly on France, I note and cite these works in subsequent chapters. To a large extent we simply assess and evaluate the same phenomena differently, and are concerned with different questions. I have no doubt of his scholarship, or of the fact that, without his work, this subfield would hardly exist. I cite one of his most influential books, *Governing with Judges: Constitutional Politics in Europe* (Oxford: Oxford University Press, 2000) at places in this chapter because he epitomises at its best the political science paradigm on constitutional review. I do not mean to use it as a stalking horse or straw man. To criticise it in detail would take too long and essentially be a waste of space in a book that has quite large enough a territory to cover. For what it matters, my critique emerges throughout. The bibliography attempts to cover all the other main comparative work.

provinces of independent and equal ranking entities: parliaments, governmental administrations, and courts. The only way constitutional review can be compassed within that trichotomy is by assuming that constitutional review of legislation is just like any other act of the judiciary. From this perspective constitutional review bodies, whether or not called courts, are just courts. But they are not really very much courts when serving in the constitutional review function. Furthermore, constitutional review bears only superficial similarity to judicial interpretation of legislation or common-law development. The differences are noted by the constituting courts themselves (a point discussed at great length later, especially in the chapter on Canada).

Ignoring both these caveats makes it easy to characterise a constitutional review body as acting "out of role." Hence much political science and politicians' rhetoric denounces the misbehaviour of constitutional "courts," only because the critics make an inappropriate analogy. Theories are developed explaining that these bodies are something else—third chambers of legislatures, for example. Statistical analyses are mounted to "explain" decisions on the premise that these "courts" are motivated not by "legal" factors but by "political values," that they do not neutrally give "legal answers" but "make" policy.

However valuable some of these analyses and analogies may be, they only work by assuming a tripartite division-of-power model. In other words, they do not ask the fundamental question posed here—just what *is* constitutional review? Political scientists should not be blamed too severely for this failure to take a sharp look at the very nature of judicial review. Those charged with the function—we can call them judges for convenience—have assiduously cultivated the myth that constitutional review and ordinary judging are alike. To do otherwise would be to take a dangerous risk, given that constitutional review can easily seem illegitimate according to theories of liberal democracy.

Contributing to the misapprehension of judicial review is the impact of the United States Supreme Court. Until very recently this was the only well-studied entity that carried out the constitutional review function. The Supreme Court is a court of general appellate jurisdiction, which does constitutional review as well as handle other things. (The Canadian Supreme Court and Australian High Court are even more fully general appellate courts. The nature of American federalism removes much of the nonconstitutional work on civil and criminal law from the federal courts.) Thus the US Supreme Court has had both a need to make its constitutional review activities look like ordinary judging, and the possibility of doing so. At the same time there is sometimes a stark discrepancy between ordinary judging mandated by the Supreme Court's place in a division of powers, and its constitutional review function. This has encouraged political scientists and politicians to see the latter as a stepping out of role, even, to use an evocative barbarism, as "mission creep." The problem goes all the way back to the origin of the US Supreme Court's jurisdiction. As any beginning student of US constitutional history knows, the constitution does not, in any clear words, give the court the power of judicial review. The court recognized that it gave such power in the famous *Marbury v Madison* case of 1803. It was argued then by Chief Justice Marshall, and the argument has never been successfully countered, that the power to strike down a congressional statute that violated the constitution was necessarily implied by the constitution.[26] But the full nature of what was implied was not articulated then and has not been since. Had it been spelled out in the constitution, the logical problem of reflexivity might still not have been noticed; there are plenty of modern constitutions that do explicitly grant constitutional review authority to constitutional courts without facing up to the issue. Furthermore, there are several modern examples of courts deciding cases hailed by commentators as their local equivalents to *Marbury* that have come no nearer to discussing what exactly is the power found implicit in the constitutional order. The early cases decided by the European Court of Justice, especially *Van Gend en Loos* and *Costa v ENEL*[27] still tend to shelter behind the analogy between "ordinary judging" and constitutional review. These modern examples—the French Conseil constitutionnel's decision in 1971[28] is another—have, however, been a good deal more controversial, though the controversy has revolved round the claim that courts in question have exceeded their authority. Little recognition has been given to what they are actually doing.[29] The strategy of simply denouncing these cases as "political" rather than "legal" has avoided the need to question the nature of constitutional review. The dominance of American constitutional review, both in actuality and in academic study, has not well prepared analysts to think about constitutional review as it appears at the beginning of the twenty-first century. Not only is the Supreme Court a common-law court of general jurisdiction, unlike the important constitutional courts of continental Europe, but its jurisprudence, that is, its dominant legal doctrines and intellectual methodology, is notably different from most of the review bodies that have recently become important. Yet these latter have often been viewed through lenses adapted for looking at their American antecedent.

Of course decisions courts make pursuant to their constitutional review function are "political" rather than "purely legal," and of course they involve "policy" arguments. So do a great many decisions falling into what I have called "ordinary judging." It has been argued, for example, that an act of judging is political, or at least legislative, whenever precedents allow for more than one result in a case. Thus Rosenfeld, claiming that constitutional judges in a common-law country are more constrained than in a civil-law country, argues that

[26] A good short coverage of the scholarly literature on *Marbury* is given in a review article on two recent books, J O'Neil, "*Marbury v Madison* at 200: Revisionist Scholarship and the Legitimacy of American Judicial Review," 2002 *Modern Law Review* 792–802.

[27] *Van Gend en Loos* (Case 26/62) (1963) ECR 1; *Costa v ENEL* (Case 6/64) (1964) ECR 585. A good survey of EU law often from a political angle is given in P Craig and G De Búrca, eds., *The Evolution of EU Law* (Oxford: Oxford University Press, 1999). The chapter by Martin Shapiro on the European Court of Justice is one of the best general essays on comparative constitutional courts I am aware of.

[28] *Associations Law*, 71-44 DC (Conseil constitutionnel).

[29] Very occasionally a judge will throw some light on this question in nonbench writings. One of the more interesting is the US appeals court judge and legal theorist Richard Posner: *How Judges Think* (Cambridge: Harvard University Press, 2008). His views are not commonly supported by his brethren, however.

> Both civil law and common law adjudication thus involve a legal as well as a political component—where "legal" means the application of a pre-existing rule or standard and "political" means choosing one from among many plausible principles or policies for the purposes of settling a constitutional issue.[30]

Rosenfeld's comparative argument takes far more seriously than I do the real binding effect of precedent in common-law countries (and its absence in the civil-law world). This point I have elsewhere argued at length as far as the United Kingdom is concerned.[31] His position also implies that continental constitutional judges are much less concerned to follow their earlier decisions than in fact they are. This point is considered seriatim throughout the rest of this book. But certainly the idea of a necessary "political" element in all judging is only recently accepted. At one stage judges everywhere tried to deny this element, and judges in the code law world still tend to. But "policy" considerations are openly canvassed in much "ordinary" judicial debate, with appropriate self-warnings about not trespassing on the legislative function. The separation-of-powers categories have never been watertight, and the whole American idea of a healthy "check and balance" conflict between the separated powers is predicated on their not being watertight. There can easily be constitutional review decisions that are actually much nearer to being nonpolitical and policy neutral than many routine decisions made by courts in jurisdictions that allow no constitutional review process.

On December 28, 2000, the French Conseil constitutionnel struck down as incompatible with the constitution the Finance Act for 2001.[32] By any standards this decision must count as a major act of political power—yet the reasons the court presented were nearer to apolitical, value-neutral argument than much that goes on in the UK courts, and the United Kingdom does not have constitutional review. The French constitution specifies in detail what procedures parliament must use to pass certain types of legislation, especially financial legislation. The French parliament, as is its wont, had disregarded these rules. Earlier that year parts of a law governing hunting, always a tender subject in France, had also been struck down on the ground of irregularities of parliamentary procedure.[33] Both these decisions are full examples of constitutional review by a body that, perhaps more than any other, has been held to be a court functioning in a nonlegal manner: it has been accused of being some sort of legislative "Third Chamber," and it experiences little but hostility in the academic press. Compare these two cases with *Phelps v London Borough of Hillingdon*,[34] also from 2000, a case before the English House of Lords that had at that time not even the circumscribed review power given by the Human Rights Act of 1998.[35] In *Phelps* the Law Lords made a massive change

[30] M Rosenfeld, "Constitutional Adjudication in Europe and the United States: Paradoxes and Contrasts," 2004 2 *International Journal of Comparative Law* 4, 633–68, at 637.

[31] Robertson, *Judicial Discretion*, especially chapters 3 and 4.

[32] *Loi de finances pour 2001*, 2000-442 DC (Conseil constitutionnel).

[33] *Loi relative à la chasse*, 2000-434 DC (Conseil constitutionnel).

[34] *Phelps v London Borough of Hillingdon*, 2 AC 619 [2001] (House of Lords).

[35] The act was passed in 1998 but did not take full effect for several years.

in the extent to which educational authorities, schools, even individual teachers could be liable for negligence in educating pupils. In so doing they overturned a major and fairly recent precedent that had firmly established the immunity of local government against such suits; the decision reversed an important series of decisions from the Court of Appeal, and opened up local authority finance to possible extensive damage claims. In the most useful senses of the word it was a political decision; it was certainly not an inevitable legal conclusion. Yet it was an "ordinary" piece of common-law judging. Ironically it could have been conducted as something close to constitutional judging, because there had shortly before been a ruling from the European Court of Human Rights on an appeal from English courts that many observers thought would determine *Phelps*. Lord Slynn, who gave the leading opinion, went out of his way to insist that the ECHR case, *Osman v UK*,[36] had nothing to do with *Phelps*, and that his argument was based purely on English common law. Had it come up only a few moths later the Lords would have faced an argument under the Human Rights Act in which *Osman* might be thought to be binding.

The point is that even though *Phelps* is political, expansive of state duties, and probably costly to the treasury, no one would suggest that it fell outside the usual separation of powers. The French cases, purely technical and virtually automatic, what lawyers have sometimes called "slot machine jurisprudence," are irrefutably examples of constitutional review. The UK parliament could reverse *Phelps* (though not *Osman*), but the French parliament had no choice but to obey *Décision n° 2000-434 DC* and *Décision n° 2000-442 DC*. The latter are exercises of hierarchical power under the constitution. That characteristic, though vital, is not all that separates ordinary judging and constitutional review. For there are real differences between constitutional review, on the one hand, however "innocent" some of its decisions are, and the interpretation and incremental development of statutory, code, or common-law rules by ordinary courts, however expansive. One of the best statements of this distinction comes from an English Law Lord who had been forced to interpret a constitution while sitting on the Privy Council. Lord Wilberforce insisted that a constitution was

> sui generis, calling for principles of interpretation of its own, suitable to its character, [and requires] . . . a generous interpretation avoiding what has been called "the austerity of tabulated legalism," suitable to give individuals the full measure of the fundamental rights and freedoms referred to.[37]

In the Canadian Supreme Court, Wilberforce was quoted to make the point of how different constitutions are.

Of course the real difference between interpreting an ordinary law and a constitution is irreversibility—a parliament can re-pass an ordinary statute if it does not like the way courts have interpreted it. But it takes a constitutional amendment to

[36] *Osman v UK*, 5 BHRC 293 (1998).

[37] *Minister of Home Affairs v Fisher*, AC 319 [1980] (Privy Council) The case arose under the constitution of Bermuda, which at that date used the Privy Council as its final appeal court.

undo a constitutional court's interpretation based on that constitution, and such changes are hard to achieve politically. Indeed some parts of some constitutions cannot be amended at all, so a country may be stuck for a very long time with a constitutional doctrine imposed by a court. The chapter on Germany demonstrates one use its constitutional court has made of the irreversibility of part of the constitution.

Constitutional review has developed in such a way as does not fit easily into the division-of-powers doctrine. There is a simple and fundamental reason why constitutional review cannot be just seen as "political" ordinary judging from courts guilty of engaging in policymaking. The liberal-democratic constitutions of the second half of the twentieth century are, in some respects, notably different from the classic constitutions of the eighteenth and nineteenth centuries. If constitutions differ, reviewing them will be a different process. Constitutional review at its most controversial and theoretically problematic occurs in two cases. The first, though relatively rarer, is where the review body strikes down a statute, or forbids executive action aimed at achieving something the reviewer says is forbidden by the rights component of the constitution.

More common, but still controversial, and certainly more theoretically difficult to characterise, is a case in which a statute is struck down not because its overt aim is forbidden, but because it employs means that are seen as constitutionally impermissible. In this latter case some right is being infringed in pursuit of an otherwise acceptable end. The reasons this latter case is the most complex include the fact that as few rights are absolute, the reviewing body is forced to decide just how much of a right can acceptably be trampled on to gain the statute's aim; the court has to weigh and balance goods, rather than protect goods from evil. (This is the domain of chapter 7, on rights limitations.) Perhaps the most intensely troublesome situation is where the right affected by an otherwise acceptable statute is the right not to suffer discrimination or unequal treatment. If I had to select one problem that raises all that is theoretically difficult and politically controversial in constitutional review, it would be this one—measuring the degree and type of discrimination acceptable in furtherance of a goal. This issue comes at the intersection of the logical structure of legislation and a fundamental social fact of modern life. The point about logical structure is simple—nearly all policy requires discrimination. The social fact is that nondiscrimination is possibly the most widely shared and passionately held value in modern secular societies, because, as already suggested, liberal democracy is also, and crucially, egalitarian.

Much of the contrast in the literature between political and policy-oriented adjudication, on the one hand, and purely legal adjudication, on the other, does not work very well. It is not that judges sometimes make politically motivated decisions, or that they sometimes consider policy matters. Most decisions are probably politically motivated in some sense or other, and policy considerations crop up in the law everywhere and are often inevitable.[38] It is necessary to look very carefully at the different ways in which a piece of constitutional adjudication may

[38] J Bell, *Policy Arguments in Judicial Decisions* (Oxford: Clarendon Press, 1983).

be called "political." In the Australian bank case personal laisser-faire ideology almost certainly explains why a terribly vague constitutional provision came to be interpreted the way it was (and possibly why the human rights articles in the Australian constitution have not been developed very far).[39] A purist could continue to believe that the decision was improper and politically motivated, and that there could have been, in some abstruse way, a purely "legal" interpretation of Article 92. Such a view would get its credibility from the fact that it is fairly easy to demonstrate that the Australian Constitutional Convention did mean the clause to be about free trade, but for political reasons underdefined it.[40] This alternative decision only seems to be a neutral "legal" solution because the choice of judicial methodology is itself a value choice. Some argue, of course, that one choice, that of sticking strictly to the language of the text, constitutional or statutory, does allow for "neutrality." This position is most commonly found amongst judicial conservatives in the United States. Most scholars would, however, agree that such a "textualist" position is no more neutral, if indeed it is possible, than any other.[41] It is entirely proper for a constitutional judge to make such a decision, but the idea that it is neutral is false. Methodologies may not inevitably tend to favour one set of policies over another, though that is likely, but to choose one way of interpreting a constitution over another is to opt for one constitutional design rather than another. One might make a distinction between choosing a judicial methodology just to get a certain end, and choosing it for its own sake. In the former case there is a double value choice, in the latter a single one, but both are judicial impositions of values on the state.

In the end, the most important reason constitutional adjudication is different from ordinary judging lies not in the fact that political factors are involved, but in the fact that it is the job of constitutional adjudication to choose and impose values. The chapters on Germany and South Africa bring out this aspect of a court's role most clearly, but it is a view no constitutional court can really avoid, however quiet it may be about its actions. Of course judges make choices all the time when interpreting statutes, but there is a huge difference between the narrow and specific sense of value choice in deciding what a phrase in a statute means, constrained as this decision is by countless rules of statutory construction, and the much broader choice of major social value involved in constitutional interpretation.

As to political motivations for decisions, these can be teased out at times. One might guess that Mr. Justice McTiernan, who dissented on Article 92, was in favour of nationalisation (he was a former Labour Party MP), and was therefore motivated to make a different interpretation of the interstate trade clause. In contrast, none of the councillors in the French hunting case could be accused of choosing to rule that the 1789 Declaration of the Rights of Man, and its protection of pri-

[39] Galligan, *Politics of High Court*.

[40] M Coper, *Freedom of Interstate Trade under the Australian Constitution* (Sydney: Butterworths, 1983).

[41] See the many discussions of the issue in modern American legal scholarship, well summarised in K Roosevelt, *The Myth of Judicial Activism: Making Sense of Supreme Court Decisions* (New Haven: Yale University Press, 2005).

vate property, applied to the law, because that had been established as early as the mid-1980s; the view that the Declaration's property protection clause applied to modern French legislation was, as lawyers say, a *res adjudicata*. But this would not rule out the choice to find the restriction on private property was excessive simply because a councillor liked hunting. Any such analysis goes to exploring individual motivations, and much of the political science approach to constitutional review is concerned precisely with such motives. This is a perfectly respectable academic endeavour, though neither strikingly successful nor addressed to the fundamental questions that concern me here. For various reasons that will become apparent as the book proceeds, seeking private motivations tends to direct attention away from something I regard as crucial—the study of the role of judicial argument, methodology, and logic. This investigation requires, and this book unashamedly relies on, actually reading cases rather than looking at judicial votes alone. I seek a general characterisation of what function constitutional review has come to play, and how it works, rather than an account of individual motivations. In the same way that one can study the nature and function of parliaments and leave aside the public and private motivations of parliamentarians, I seek to study constitutional courts.

A Note on My Approach

It is hard to locate my approach within the schools of political science. I regard it as falling within the general approach known as "new institutionalism." More specifically, I adhere to the subgroup of those sometimes called "value" institutionalists. That is, I think that a political actor is usually best studied as a role incumbent, subject to what has aptly been called "a logic of appropriateness." I cannot put this position better than in the words of the leaders of the new institutionalist movement, James March and Johan Olsen:

> The simple behavioral proposition is that, most of the time humans take reasoned action by trying to answer three elementary questions: What kind of a situation is this? What kind of a person am I? What does a person such as I do in a situation such as this?[42]

This means that I regard judicial self-perception as crucial: on the whole, judges try to be good judges, or, at least, constitutional judges try to do the job of creating constitutional jurisprudence according to their understanding of their role. The best way to see what this means is to read the reflections of a thoughtful judge. The most powerful I know in this field is a book by Aharon Barak, a recently retired president of the Supreme Court of Israel.[43] His account of how he has thought through the process of being a constitutional judge is not only illuminating in

[42] JG March and JP Olsen, "The Logic of Appropriateness," in M Moran, M Rein, and RE Goodin, eds., *Oxford Handbook of Public Policy* (Oxford: Oxford University Press, 2006).

[43] A Barak, *The Judge in a Democracy* (Princeton: Princeton University Press, 2006). It should be said that I came across this book belatedly. Had I read it earlier it would be more often cited in my own analysis.

its own right, but strong support for the thesis that a "logic of appropriateness" governs judicial behaviour to a great extent. Throughout my own book I refer to articles and speeches by constitutional judges for enlightenment about their perceptions of their role. (Barak's ideas form part of my concluding argument in chapter 8.)

This book is rather different from most work by political scientists on courts, not because I think other work wrongly conceived, but because I am much more concerned with judicial argument, which I take to be the core of judges' activity, and central to understanding the role courts play in complex societies. But I owe it to the reader to describe the more usual work, even if I leave it largely to others to decide whether my approach is compatible with such work, and if it is not compatible, which approach should be preferred. My method is to take judicial argument seriously as one of the major, if not the sole, determinant of the decisions courts make. I prefer my approach because it simply seems beyond credibility that so many thousands of professionally socialized and able men and women should be lying or deluding themselves in their arguments. They just cannot all, or even many of them, be like that. One thing seldom recognized is this: even if judges were bent on forcing into decisions their own ideological views, these are views honed by decades of professional legal "formation." Legal and constitutional values inevitably take a high priority for such people, even as political actors. In a previous book of mine I recount the way English Law Lords talk in terms of "not cheating," of being intellectually honest. One of those I interviewed said, in all seriousness, that in his entire career he had only come across one judge who personally believed in the legal realist model. It is an old dictum that "politicians bargain, judges argue." Of course judges bargain with each other to get majorities on multimember courts—but the currency they trade in is itself argument. However, my views of what judges are up to are not shared by most of the (very small) part of the political science profession that studies courts.

The first characteristic of most political science research on courts is that it is American. It is either written by Americans (about American courts—the largest single category by a long way—or about other courts) or, less common, written by non-Americans about other courts but in a way heavily influenced by American paradigms.[44] The opening sentence of a recent study of courts outside the United States highlights the dominance of scholarship on the American Supreme Court.

> Two decades ago, Martin Shapiro urged public law scholars to expand their horizons and begin studying "any public law other than constitutional law, any court other than the Supreme Court, any public lawmaker other than the judge, and any country other than the United States.[45]

[44] A fuller presentation on modern political science approaches to the courts is given in "Appeal Courts," my contribution to P Cane and B Kritzer, eds., *The Oxford Handbook of Empirical Legal Research* (Oxford: Oxford University Press, forthcoming 2010).

[45] T Ginsburg and T Moustafa, eds., *Rule by Law: The Politics of Courts in Authoritarian Regimes* (Cambridge: Cambridge University Press, 2008), 1.

In itself the prevailing scholarly orientation is a neutral fact, and it is easily explicable. Americans have lived for more than two centuries under a Supreme Court that no one has ever been able to claim was not a political institution. In the most obvious senses the courts of other countries have not seemed so much a part of the political system except in the last few decades (leaving aside the traditional sense of common-law courts making the law in the days before statutes became so extensive and important). Given that American political science has been the technical leader in the academic world of the discipline, and that it was attuned to courts, and that there are so many American political scientists, it was perhaps inevitable that studies of courts would end up being dominated by US paradigms and assumptions.

What are the assumptions? The first is that judges are primarily policy-oriented political actors in very much the same way that congressmen are; they vote for their preferred policy outcomes, constrained loosely by purely "legal" matters of doctrine and procedure. At the level of individual judges, therefore, the main efforts have been addressed to demonstrating this policy preference voting, characterizing it and measuring it. At the level of courts as institutions, this approach has led also to the study of what might be called judicial coalition making, an account of how individual judicial policy preferences lead to group decisions.

The second main assumption, which follows in part from the first, is that courts themselves as institutions are not different in important ways from other institutions in the policymaking world, be they congressional committees or bureaucratic offices. Courts are assumed to have and pursue collective interests in wielding influence and protecting their status and power. This assumption leads to studies of court decisions in terms of the court's strategic concerns. It is interesting to note that this approach has been highly influential in the literature on one court that has largely been written about by non-American political scientists, the European Court of Justice. Because the ECJ has inevitably been so influential in developing the European Union as a power, and in creating the legal framework within which it works, its political nature can hardly be denied. It does not follow, though, and it cannot be said to have been proved, that the decisions of the ECJ follow political imperatives other than those that derive from the court's conception of the nature and meaning of the relevant treaties. This is not cavilling—if the ECJ develops its jurisprudence because of such an understanding, it has severe restrictions on what it can do, even if only those set by itself. These argumentative restrictions and imperatives are the stuff of judicial argument, and of my book.

A further area of research has stemmed from these joint assumptions, the need to explain why, to what extent, and under what conditions the other actors in the political system will tolerate the policy role of courts. This question takes particular resonance in the American literature because it touches closely on a long-running normative concern of theorists of democracy, again especially those with a characteristic American conception of democracy. This is the problem of the legitimacy of courts as policymakers seen against a relatively simple conception of democracy as the rule of majority preferences, at least as articulated by democratically elected legislators. Indeed the most usual phrase for this is that politically influential courts are "counter-majoritarian" institutions. An American researcher is likely to find it problematic that the rest of the political system has put up with what can be seen as illegitimate power, a theme running through much of the work in what has come to be known as the study of "American political development." The same sense of puzzlement is transferred to other countries. Or the assumption is that courts will always try to act in this way, and the research question becomes how and when they can get away with it. An otherwise sensible extension of political science to the study of courts in authoritarian countries increases the tendency to think that courts are tolerated only to the extent that they are useful to other political institutions.[46] An alternative interpretation is that if even authoritarian rulers have to tolerate courts a little, democratic leaders may have no option about tolerating them.

The early literature on judicial behaviour was addressed to the first question—can it be shown that judges are policy-seeking actors? Originally, American political science studies of the Supreme Court were as much "doctrinal" and normative as were legal studies. As was the case in Europe, many political science departments began inside law schools—but they escaped their parents much earlier, and perhaps more completely, than was the case elsewhere. In any case in America the lawyers themselves, and not only academic lawyers, came to take a more sceptical stance towards the courts with the rise of legal realism in the early twentieth century, making it highly likely that political scientists could fail to treat the courts simply as political institutions not radically different from Congress, the presidency, or any other part of the political system. Authors like Karl Llewellyn, Felix Cohen, and Jerome Frank made assumptions about judges being result oriented and about rules and doctrine being "constructed" post hoc to reach results, assumptions of the sort that have since become common in political science. Books like Frank's *Law and the Modern Mind* "de-mystified" judicial argument; "rule scepticism" was almost an invitation to a certain social science model of judicial behaviour.[47]

This model is based on certain assumptions, not always well articulated: that judges are free to decide cases any way they wish; that they use this freedom to try to further their own ideological or policy preferences; that as a collectivity, courts are focused on maximizing their own power in conflict with other institutions in their political system; and (though this is not always assumed) that judges vote "strategically" according to the political context and in the light of these aims. What nearly all political science approaches reject is what they sometimes describe as "slot machine jurisprudence," the idea that a judge's job is, and a judge thinks his or her job is, merely to give a technical legally correct answer to a legal question of the sort the judge is technically trained to do. Some studies, for example, aim at demonstrating that a core aspect of the judicial craft, identify-

[46] See T Ginsburg, *Judicial Review in New Democracies: Constitutional Courts in Asian Cases* (Cambridge: Cambridge University Press, 2003); Ginsburg and Moustafa, *Rule by Law*.

[47] J Frank, *Law and the Modern Mind* (New York: Brentano, 1930).

ing and applying precedents, does not account for judicial decisions.[48] Segal and Spaeth, who carried out the first study purporting to show that precedent does not constrain judges, are leaders in one of the dominant American schools, using what is usually called the "attitudinal" model.[49] Even those who support the model for American courts are beginning to have doubts about its transferability to other countries, even one as ideologically and legally similar as Canada.[50] No one, to my knowledge, has ever convincingly applied such an attitudinal model to, for example, a European court, though in the early days some less than powerful analyses were carried out on Australia. Not all American political scientists, even those given to seeing judges as policy dominated, deny the importance of their role perceptions; important work of a considerably more nuanced nature was done as early as the 1970s and 1980s.[51] It is still the case that virtually no attention is paid to, nor credibility given to the importance of, the detailed arguments judges make to each other (other than in legal journals, of course). Since the advent of rational choice scholarship, in much of political science the focus has been on what is most usually called the "strategic model."[52] These studies still regard judges as free of anything like "legal" constraints, and still see them as in pursuit of their own policy goals, either as individuals or as collective actors. Scholars seek to understand courts as operating in complex political environments of other goal-directed rational actors such as legislatures, and their work can be subtle. Courts, in their eyes, do as much as they can get away with, but will at times make decisions to please or placate other actors so as to retain their power. This model has been applied outside the United States, perhaps best on the European Court of Justice.[53] In America something like this approach has been enthusiastically taken up by scholars working on "American political development." One of the questions they are concerned with, and echoed elsewhere in the political science fraternity,

[48] JA Segal and HJ Spaeth, "The Influence of Stare Decisis on the Votes of United States Supreme Court Justices," 1996 40 *American Journal of Political Science* 4, 971–1003. This, however, is severely criticized, even within the US public law fraternity, as in S Brenner and M Stier, "Retesting Segal and Spaeth's Stare Decisis Model," 1996 40 *American Journal of Political Science* 4, 1036–48.

[49] The best study I am aware of comparing precedent usage in US and UK courts does suggest that both systems take them seriously, but that the Law Lords are more deferential to legal authority: RP Caldarone, "Precedent in Operation: A Comparison of the Judicial House of Lords and the US Supreme Court," 2004 *Public Law* 759–87.

[50] ME Wetstein, CL Ostberg, DR Songer, and SW Johnson, "Ideological Consistency and Attitudinal Conflict: A Comparative Analysis of the U.S. and Canadian Supreme Courts," 2009 42 *Comparative Political Studies* 6, 763–92.

[51] JL Gibson, "Judges' Role Orientations, Attitudes, and Decisions: An Interactive Model," 1978 72 *American Political Science Review* 3, 911–24; HM Scheb, TD Ungs, and AL Hayes, "Judicial Role Orientation, Attitudes and Decision Making: A Research Note," 1989 42 *Political Research Quarterly* 427–35; L Baum, "What Judges Want: Judge's Goals and Judicial Behaviour," 1994 47 *Political Research Quarterly* 3, 749–68.

[52] This approach is not entirely new, of course—the seminal article was probably Robert Dahl's in 1957, discussed in L Epstein, J Knight, and AD Martin, "The Supreme Court as a Strategic National Policy Maker," 2001 50 *Emory Law Journal* 583–611.

[53] A good example is G Garrett, RD Kelemen, and R Schulz, "The European Court of Justice, National Governments, and Legal Integration in the European Union," 1998 52 *International Organization* 1, 149–76.

is how courts "get away with it," why politicians put up with reversal from the courts. As noted above, this is not a question felt with the same urgency outside the United States, probably because Europeans assume their politicians believe in the constitution as much as their judges. As has been said of democracy in the transition countries, but as is equally true elsewhere in Europe, "Democracy is the only game in town." And to a European, obeying a court is a democratic rule. But also, of course, non-American courts are much less obviously political actors, and much more cautious ones. Without doubt judges outside America take care not to flout clearly popular governments. *Fiat justitia ruat caelum*, "Let justice be done though the heavens fall," is nowhere an absolute in the judicial mind. Even decisions concerning quite ordinary pieces of legislation, interpreted by courts without the power of judicial review, are replete with judicial reminders to themselves not to trespass too far into overtly political domains.[54] Nonetheless, courts may gain self-confidence because they do not think of themselves as political actors in the same sense as, for example, elected politicians. How otherwise could the following judicial statement be relatively orthodox?

> The proper constitutional relationship between the courts and executive government is that the courts will respect all acts of the executive within its lawful province, and the executive will respect all decisions of the courts as to what that province is.[55]

And this from a case where the home secretary himself was held in contempt of court? The real problem with the idea of strategic decisions is that it is difficult to see that any particular case has been decided strategically. One can frequently come up with a plausible post hoc account of why a decision could have been strategic, whatever the judges claimed as their reasoning. *Dolphin Deliveries* in Canada was an early Charter case in which the Supreme Court declined to broaden its own power.[56] This decision might have been out of fear the government would oppose such an extension. That is not the reason the judges gave, which involved a traditionally limited theory of constitutional review. Why should political scientists privilege their own guess about motivation over the court's account? Such problems are well demonstrated in the more thoughtful work of the American political development scholars, as in Mark Graber's assessment of the US Supreme Court in the Civil War period.[57]

This book, however, stands apart from this tradition because it takes the existential position that if so many judges worldwide spend so much time arguing

[54] See, for example, the way Lord Millet cautions his colleagues to be careful of pushing the government too far in *R v Secretary of State for the Home Department, Ex parte Fire Brigades Union*, 2 AC 513 [1995] (House of Lords).

[55] Nolan in *M v Home Office*, QB 270 [1992] (Court of Appeal).

[56] *Retail, Wholesale and Department Store Union v Dolphin Delivery Ltd*, 2 SCR 573 (1986) (Canadian Supreme Court).

[57] M Graber, "Legal, Strategic, or Legal Strategy: Deciding to Decide during the Civil War and Reconstruction," in R Kahn and KI Kersch, eds., *The Supreme Court and American Political Development* (Lawrence: University Press of Kansas, 2006).

with each other, and act as though these arguments matter to them, they ought to be taken at face value. If I am simply wrong, then I can only say, along with Leonard Cohen, "Your vision is right, my vision is wrong / I'm sorry for smudging the air with my song."[58]

It is worth speculating a little on why the American model is so different from ones that apply elsewhere, because later in this book I do analyze some US opinions side by side with similar opinions from other jurisdictions. A host of factors in American political and legal practice and culture might account for American judges being more openly "political" in their behaviour, or indeed being forced into more obviously ideological decision-making. Political science models may more effectively apply to American than to non-American courts simply because those models are assessing a different reality. Therefore, they should be exported with care. Practitioners of the attitudinal model are sometimes prepared to say that their models may need to be more complex to deal with "courts that are not as ideologically polarized as the US Supreme Court."

> Indeed, our approach calls for a much greater degree of skepticism on the part of researchers and for a much greater degree of testing unidimensional assumptions in other cultural, legal, and political settings. If our Canadian findings from the high court illustrate a broader indictment of the unidimensional hypothesis, then comparative legislative, executive, and bureaucratic scholars, in addition to public law researchers, may find a much higher level of ideological complexity in the decisions of non-U.S. policymakers.[59]

While this is undoubtedly true, it might also be the case that the motivational and role conception differences are so great that even a common dimensionality would not make US-inspired models fit. Some of the possible factors that distinguish American from non-American courts are quite subtle, and could only be teased out with serious research. One good candidate is differences in professional socialization of lawyers all the way from law school to life as a partner in a US-style law firm. Another is both the extent and nature of political input into judicial selection.

A really obvious candidate to explain differences in judicial decision-making, however, is curiously understudied, seldom even commented on, and might be crucial even if there are no cultural, institutional, and practical differences between courts. The US constitution is unlike most of those interpreted by the constitutional courts studied in this book. Above all, it is shorter—the Bill of Rights runs to only 485 words. Interestingly, the all-important Fourteenth Amendment is almost as long at 437, reflecting perhaps a greater understanding of the problems of constitution writing in 1868 than in 1791. Overall, fewer than 1,000 words—the Bill of Rights plus the Fourteenth Amendment—provide the material on which a huge number of major constitutional cases hang. The Canadian Charter, itself a relatively nonverbose document, is more than two and a half times as long. It

[58] Leonard Cohen, "A Singer Must Die," from the album *New Skin for the Old Ceremony.*

[59] Wetstein et al., "Ideological Consistency," 786.

is the language of the US Bill of Rights as much as its terseness that may cause problems because, as I argue in a later chapter, it is absolutist in its depiction of rights, while modern constitutions accept the inevitability of limitations on rights. US judges therefore have to interpret a much more opaque and much older, pre-industrial, document. This certainly allows, and maybe requires, far more judicial creativity, and therefore allows, and may require, more intrusion of private judicial ideology.

The Nature of Modern Review

The nature of many modern constitutions, and the view their appointed review bodies take of their role, sometimes differs from the classic model in a further respect. Jurists in older courts have tended to express a modest notion of their job, and of the reach of constitutional rights. Rights are seen as a largely unconnected set of specific limitations that have to be applied seriatim to legislation when it is very clearly in breach of them. There is little or no sense, however, of the rights as instantiations of a broader ideology that it is the court's duty to develop. Typically such courts do not try to create a hierarchy of the rights, and may even be opposed to such a consideration. Where a case involves a clash of rights, they are prone to see no conflict, or to "balance" the rival claims in a pragmatic way that does not involve reference to an overall moral vision. Another way of saying much the same thing is that older courts seldom refer to the reason a right is protected—rights are taken as black-and-white restrictions on government, not as aspects of an articulated "good life." An example of this predilection is the difference in development of "free speech" rights in continental European jurisdictions compared with the United States and Australia.[60] Freedom of speech is well protected in the latter as a necessary aspect of competitive democracy. In the former, speech is equally well protected, but much more as a right involved in human self-development and personal dignity.

There is little sense, with the older courts, of the constitution as embodying values for the whole of society. Individual rules are strictly brought to bear on governments, or governments are excused obedience because of pressing national policy requirements. Never, though, are the constitutional values allowed to permeate legal relations between other legal actors. Yet one of the most pressing issues in many courts is the question of "horizontal effect"—the extent to which a constitution, if it forbids the government to do something, ought to also protect the individual from similar depredations by other private actors. While the German constitutional court since its earliest cases has talked about the "radiating effect" of constitutional values throughout society, the US Supreme Court still insists that the Bill of Rights applies only to federal and state governments, even in areas like

[60] I take up the Australian doctrine on speech rights again in the last chapter, with special reference to the most recent case, *Coleman v Power*, 220 CLR 1 (2004) (Australian High Court), where the whole question of the ideological justification for the right is hotly contested on the bench.

racial discrimination.[61] Again, the US Supreme Court has upheld a state law forbidding the religious use of drugs to members of the Native American Church on the grounds that a "religious exception" for such drug users is held by the state in question to be impossible to organise while admitting that several other states do allow precisely such an exception.[62] The German court, also working in a federal system, would never allow such diversity because its decision, whatever it might be, would be seen as drawing out the implications for the whole society of the complex of religious freedom rights in the constitution.

Almost every decision of the South African Constitutional Court is backed by an explication in terms of its mission in helping to build a new nonracist, nonsexist moral consensus in the society.[63] The French Conseil constitutionnel regularly refers to itself as developing "French Republican Principles" and building a "bloc de constitutionnalité."[64] Most of the courts in the former Soviet bloc are self-conscious about their role in creating a new rule of law that, again, must permeate society.[65] The post-Franco Spanish constitutional court, in a more muted way, talks about its role in the development of a democratic culture. Even the Canadian Supreme Court has begun to see itself as enunciating the values of the Charter rather than merely applying its rules as neutrally as possible.[66]

The actual texts of the respective constitutions facilitate this new approach, but hardly force the judges to adopt it; much depends on the interaction between the new groups of judges and the new contexts. Both the texts and the judicial will are necessary, and together they are sufficient to produce a form of constitutional review that is the focus of this book. The older courts and the older constitutions are not as innocent of this form of constitutional review as the description here might imply—but to the extent that a similar function is performed, it is less obvious.[67] The lack of obviousness has contributed to political scientists feeling comfortable treating constitutional review as fully within the judicial function of the classic division of powers.

[61] BS Markesinis, *Always on the Same Path: Essays on Foreign Law and Comparative Methodology* (Oxford: Hart 2001), chapters 7 and 8 for the German ideas. More generally, M Tushnet, "The Issue of State Action / Horizontal Effect in Comparative Constitutional Law," 2003 1 *International Journal of Constitutional Law* 1, 79–98.

[62] *Employment Div., Dept. of Human Resources of Oregon v Smith*, 494 US 872 (1990) (US Supreme Court). But compare: *Garreth Anver Prince v The President of the Law Society of the Cape of Good Hope*, 2002 (2) SA 794 (South African Constitutional Court).

[63] M Chanock, "A Post-Calvinist Catechism or a Post-Communist Manifesto? Intersecting Narratives in the South African Bill of Rights Debate," in P Alston, ed., *Promoting Human Rights through Bills of Rights* (Oxford: Oxford University Press, 1999), gives a good account of the surrounding ideology. A better sense of what I mean can be found by reading one of the early cases, for example, *Garreth Anver Prince*.

[64] J Bell, *French Constitutional Law* (Oxford: Clarendon Press, 1992).

[65] D Robertson, *Democratic Transitions and a Common Constitutional Law for Europe* (Oxford: Europaeum, 2001).

[66] P Beyer, "Constitutional Privilege and Constituting Pluralism: Religious Freedom in National, Global, and Legal Context," 2003 42 *Journal for the Scientific Study of Religion* 3, 333–39.

[67] See, for example, the perceptive account of all the functions the US Supreme Court carries out in P Bobbitt, *Constitutional Interpretation* (Oxford: Blackwell, 1991).

It is not modernity itself that has led to constitutional courts being willing and able to take up what can look like a wholly new function in society. More likely, constitutional and political change is the driver—above all transition from some form of autocracy to liberal democracy. It cannot be accidental that all of the countries mentioned above where constitutional courts see themselves as developing a culture of democracy are creatures of political change, though not always rapid and extreme. With most of the examples the transition is obvious, starting with the most influential of all such courts, the German Federal Constitutional Court, set up in the aftermath of the Nazi regime and the 1945 defeat. Others may seem less obvious; is the French Conseil constitutionnel the beneficiary of regime change? Can the Canadian Supreme Court be seen in this light? I would argue that the answer is yes, in both cases. The French Conseil constitutionnel is part of the Fifth Republic constitution, which was revolutionary in French republican history. That republic took more than a decade to become established, during which it was dependent on de Gaulle's leadership. Throughout that period the Conseil acted as the constitution's drafters intended—it kept parliament under check vis-à-vis the executive, and was otherwise passive. It began to be active in 1971 shortly after de Gaulle's demise, and thrust itself into French politics forcefully after a constitutional amendment in 1974 opened access to it to all parliamentarians. The whole period from the beginning of the Fifth Republic constitution for perhaps twenty years was a lengthy but major adaptation of French politics in a way never before experienced. It is hardly surprising that the historically unprecedented idea of allowing constitutional review of legislation should get out of the control of the drafters and become a new force in politics as part of this transition.

The argument on the Canadian case is weaker, but still real. Canada "repatriated" its constitution in a time of stress and near breakup; the Charter was without doubt a dramatic break from an English-style history of parliamentary supremacy. (Indeed, sixteen years after the Charter came into force, the Canadian Supreme Court had to rule on the legality of a possible secession by Quebec.)[68] It could have amounted to very little, but the combination of demand from diverse publics and eagerness on the part of the judiciary presented the opportunity for the growth of serious constitutional review of this new form in an uneasy society. There can be little doubt that merely introducing a form of legislative review absent a fully fledged national creation of a new constitution would have had much less impact. Canada already had a nonenforceable bill of rights; had the whole constitution not been re-created in the name of the national sovereignty of a disunited nation, the Charter itself might have been no more important than the New Zealand or United Kingdom's Human Rights Acts.[69] It is hardly surprising that some form of national remaking seems to have been crucial in the launching of serious constitutional review. After all, the US constitution and its Supreme Court were

[68] *Reference re Secession of Quebec*, 2 SCR 217 (1998) (Canadian Supreme Court).

[69] For a comparison of the New Zealand and UK experience of their Human Rights acts, which concludes that in New Zealand the judges have been far from activist, see P Butler, "Human Rights and Parliamentary Sovereignty in New Zealand," 2004 35 *Victoria University Wellington Law Review* 341–67.

themselves the product of a revolution. The classic eighteenth-century individualist liberalism that court helped entrench into American political culture was in its day as radical as anything a modern constitutional review body is doing in the twenty-first century. It is largely because the basic principles of that ideology are now so completely accepted in the United States that it is easy not to see the Supreme Court as anything but a routine practitioner of the judicial branch of the state. In fact it is precisely where that ideology still finds opposition in parts of the society that the US court most obviously carries out constitutional review in a full-blooded way—as for example where state-religion connections, or religiously loaded issues like abortion, arise. It is pertinent that the impact of the Canadian Charter has been criticised by some precisely for importing an American "rights culture" into a "communal" society.[70]

Transition status alone will not bring about the development of serious constitutional review. If it did, then the Italian Constitutional Court should have been as effective as the German court, for they were created at roughly the same time in very similar historical contexts. I referred earlier to judicial willpower; not a good phrase, but it connotes a desire and intention to pick up the burdens of constitutional review that may be missing for many reasons. The most common reason for review courts not to be eager to impose constitutional values is that the members may have much in common with sectors of society well entrenched in legislatures and executives—they may, that is, not strongly share the ideology that the constitution, or part of it, encodes. To some extent the Italian Constitutional Court in its earlier days shared with all other Italian political institutions one characteristic—domination by the Christian Democrats, whose interests were not well represented in either the structural or the "rights" aspects of the constitution despite their ability to dominate the actual politics carried out under it.[71] It is a measure of how that court has changed its orientation that its main political enemies are now on the right.

Again this fate of being staffed with people who shared the dominant values of those in control of both the executive and legislative powers befell the French Conseil constitutionnel in its first decade and a half. There was no reason why the Conseil could not have "discovered" the sources of constitutional doctrine it began to use so effectively from 1971 at any earlier date after 1958. As the political Right in France began to fragment after de Gaulle left power, and as regular replacements of councillors took effect, the Conseil was much readier in the early 1970s to take on a constitutional review role. In contrast one of the reasons some of the Central and Eastern European courts leapt immediately into quite passionate value enforcement through constitutional review was the fact that many of the first generation of judges had been members of the constitutional creation movements and were already eager exponents of the values they had fought for in these earlier arenas.

[70] See, for one example of a common complaint, WA Bogart, *Courts and Country: The Limits of Litigation and Social and Political Life of Canada* (Toronto: Oxford University Press, 1994).

[71] See ML Volcansek, *Constitutional Politics in Italy* (London: Macmillan, 2000). A comparative approach is given in A Stone Sweet, "Constitutional Courts and Parliamentary Democracy," 2002 25 *West European Politics* 1, 77–100.

Part of the French story has to do with the paucity of chances the early Conseil had to be effective, as it has been in Italy. One of the greatest concerns for the exponents of constitutional review in Eastern Europe was a fear that the institutional mechanisms inherited from the past, together with the attitudes of members of the judicial ancien régime would similarly starve the new courts of subject matter. Effects like this, including institutional restrictions on the review bodies, are a matter of detail—though crucially important detail—and must be left for later exposition. It should be clear, though, that effective constitutional review is no mere matter of a rich constitutional text and an eager court being combined.

Technical Aspects of Judicial Review

What constitutional review is cannot properly be described without some description of how it is done. The courts work on texts—initially the constitution itself and other sources identified by the constitution as having authority. Thus the French Conseil constitutionnel has used both the preamble to the constitution of the Fourth Republic and the 1789 Declaration of the Rights of Man as authorised by the text of the Fifth Republic constitution. Many of the East European courts have referred to the European Convention on Human Rights because their own constitutions tell them so to do. Secondarily, courts refer to their own previous decisions and, often prompted by their own constitutions, they consider the decisions of other similar courts. They may also consult more amorphous bodies of legal writing, especially things with titles like "principles of international law" or "general principles of law." Again, the French Conseil consults "general principles of French republican law."

The national constitution is the starting place. To say that these constitutional review bodies "interpret" the constitution is largely empty. It is easier to think in terms of their trying to answer questions posed to them by others by looking at these documents. There are at least two rather different sorts of problems the constitutional review bodies can be asked because of the various routes by which they can be directed to an issue. If it is a court to which issues arising in real litigation are referred or appealed, the context of the litigation forms the precise question. For example, can the state government prevent a retailer from opening his shop on a Sunday even though, being a devout Jew, he must also close on Friday, and given that there is a clause in the constitution forbidding the state to interfere with its citizens' freedom of religion (from the United States, Canada, and with variations, South Africa)?[72]

If the constitutional review is a priori or abstract, there is less of a context. The question may be quite precise in one sense, but lacking any story. So, from Hungary, are the provisions of the criminal code that provide for the death penalty unconstitutional given Article 54 of the constitution?[73] This case was brought

[72] A typical US case on this question is *Braunfeld v Brown*, 366 US 599 (1961) (US Supreme Court).

[73] *Decision of 31st October 1990 on Capital Punishment*, 23/1990 AB (Hungarian Constitutional Court). Much of the Hungarian argument was adopted by the South African Court in *S v Makwanyane and Another*, CCT 3/94 (South African Constitutional Court).

not by a condemned criminal on appeal, where his personal details and his crime could help narrow the focus, but by a pressure group, the League Against Capital Punishment. The various courts themselves seem unanimously to prefer, or would if allowed, to have cases arise under the first route. In an example like the Hungarian one it might not matter much, but often the absence of a context forces the court to make a decision that might be quite unsuitable to some highly specific real-life story. It is probably for this reason that some such review bodies, especially in France and Germany, are prone to add what they call "reservations of interpretation" in carrying out abstract review. These opinions have come under specific attack from political scientists as over much involvement in policy, but they are really attempts to prevent an overgeneral judgement of constitutionality. Such reservations are an attempt to prevent the law in question from being taken as constitutional if applied in a context that would have made the court unsure of the constitutionality of the legislation. Effectively it means the court is saying, "Law X conforms to the constitution *only if* it is taken to mean . . ." In a way the court is posing its own imaginary fact situation for want of a real one.

What these two examples have in common is, inevitably, that the constitutions do not, in so many words, answer the questions asked of the courts. There is no clause in the Hungarian constitution that forbids the death penalty, any more than Sunday closing is mentioned in the US Bill of Rights, the Canadian Charter, or the South African constitution. What one finds instead are general value statements that have to be brought to bear on the policy intention of the government. Bills of rights are not moral or even political philosophies. They are, at best, bullet points from such philosophies. Furthermore, because bills of rights are bargained lists, the outcome of committee warfare, they are not necessarily even bullet points from the same underlying philosophy. The bullet point for the US Supreme Court is simply the well-known First Amendment provision that "Congress shall make no law respecting an establishment of religion, or prohibiting the free exercise thereof." The Canadian Charter only provides, in Article 2, that "Everyone has the following fundamental freedoms: (a) freedom of conscience and religion . . ." In the Hungarian example, the nearest thing to a relevant bullet point is Article 54(1): "every human being has the inherent right to life and to human dignity, of which no one can be arbitrarily deprived."

The courts are required to answer a question something like this: is forcing someone to close on Sunday whose religion forbids him to work on a day other than Sunday also equivalent to prohibiting the free exercise of religion? Or something like this: is a human being arbitrarily deprived of life or dignity by a carefully constructed death penalty law? There are any number of ways one can go about building an answer. Did the writers of the constitution intend such and such an implication? Would the language of the document at its time of writing imply that? Does the language now imply it? Do other firmly held values in modern society require such and such an answer? These and other techniques are nothing but that—technical tricks to help a court. The judges are required to weave the bullet points into a coherent and cohesive ideology for their contemporary world. It is in this sense that constitutional judges are applied political theorists, and their job is unavoidably creative. If the job was just that, it would be difficult enough, but in fact it is much harder. By the time the Sunday closing law was challenged in the United States, there was more for the court to consider than the sixteen words of the First Amendment. There was by then a rich case law of attempts to work out what those sixteen words implied for concrete situations. Much of that case law deals with a latent problem in constitutional analysis. The First Amendment seems absolute: "Congress shall make *no law* . . ." In almost no real political context are rights actually treated as absolute, and when a constitutional court tries to do so it either creates huge problems for itself, or risks a legitimacy-weakening scorn from the other elites. The case law in the First Amendment is partially taken up by devising rules by which the court can accept that freedom of religion is being hindered, but in an acceptable way. The US court has had to create for itself the right to make such assessments. More modern constitutions build that capacity in to the texts the courts are provided with. Thus what the Canadian Charter actually says, in Article 1, is that it guarantees the rights it sets out "subject only to such reasonable limits . . . as can be demonstrably justified in a free and democratic society." The Hungarian problem required not only Article 54(1) but Article 8(2) which says that the rights and duties shall be determined by statute, "which, however may not limit the essential content of any fundamental right."[74]

Constitutions that recognise that rights need to be flexible and only rigorously imposed when necessary, present a further complexity—they actively require the courts to be policy analysts and to work out for themselves whether a government goal is sufficiently important to allow a proposed limitation on a right. So it is an *applied* political theory that judicial review bodies are required to construct. Only a political theory constructed by *someone* can tell us whether the French government can restrict hunting rights. Only an *applied* one can work out whether the restriction in the *Loi relative de la chasse* of 2000 can decide whether the text of the law infringes the right to property more than, to borrow the Canadian test, "can be demonstrably justified in a free and democratic society." The fact that this is not the test the French Conseil constitutionnel uses is part of the overall story of constitutional review. A great variety of tests has been invented by courts to assess whether legislation can override a constitutional right. One has even become the title of a thriller—the US legal test for abridging freedom of speech that requires a "clear and present danger."[75] Some require merely a "rational connection" between a legislative goal and its details; others impose tougher conditions, or require a degree of "proportionality" between the policy goal and the means. The trouble is that these legal formulae do not get the courts very far. As one scholar said of the interpretation acts that some countries pass to aid the court dealing with ordinary legislation, "The judge is not told how to decide; he is told how to state what he has

[74]The interim South African constitution had an equivalent "essential content" clause. The court expressed its relief when it was dropped from the final version, though the court still has a complicated test to apply.

[75]By Tom Clancy, dealing with the threat posed to the United States by the Colombian drug barons.

decided.[76]" However, this can be an overcynical position. It is a mistake to go the judicial realist route and insist that judicial argument is never anything more than a smokescreen to cover purely personal prejudice.[77]

It remains true there are numerous divided constitutional law decisions where judges differ only on whether or not legislation does pass the relevant test, as well as those where the disagreement goes to what the relevant test is. Such disagreements can be instructive for us in assessing the importance of the tests themselves. In one American religious exemption case the issue appeared to be whether it was even remotely feasible to give a particular religious sect an exception from the Social Security laws.[78] The majority applied a test that required the government to show that the tax law in question was "essential to accomplish an overriding governmental interest." This is a very tough test, and the majority could only find for the government by stressing that it would be inordinately difficult to run the tax system were the exception justified. One justice however, claimed it would be trivially easy to make the exception, but that the test was wrong—instead the complainant ought to have "to shoulder the burden of demonstrating that there is a unique reason for allowing him a special exemption from a valid law of general applicability." Justice Stevens admits this is "an almost insurmountable burden," which he clearly welcomes. Which is the more appropriate approach is not obvious. The example serves to show both the vital role these tests play, and the intrinsic difficulty of the quasi-empirical policy analysis that tests require. (These matters are discussed at length in chapter 7.) All in all, being a constitutional review judge is a really difficult job, and honest men and women disagree over the implications of policy and rights. The different tests do matter, but they are the product of judicial craftsmanship whether or not they are apparently spelled out in constitutional texts.

The judicial realist challenge is an old one, and one that cannot fully be resolved. In fact it turns out to matter rather little whether we conceive of constitutional judges as making up their minds quite independently of the reasons they give, or as genuinely trying to use their tests, formulae, and rules of constitutional interpretation to get answers. For a host of reasons, the arguments that can be given in any one case are restricted by past cases, restrict future ones, and need to be deployed with care and skill whether these arguments are the "real" reason for a decision or "merely" the ways a decision is expressed. Marx says, on the question of historical determinism, that men do make history, but they do not make it on their own terms. In a similar way judges determine themselves whether something is constitutional or not, but are only free to make this determination inside a complex web of legal and political restrictions. For our purposes the study of constitutional adjudication is the study of these constraints more than it is the study of any underlying motive. Another example from the Hungarian court should make this clear. The court's abortion decision of 1991 is one of the most complicated

[76] JH Merryman, *The Civil Law Tradition* (Stanford, Calif.: Stanford University Press, 1969).

[77] A useful discussion of the original ideas of the legal realist school, and the way those ideas have developed, is given in N Duxbury, "Jerome Frank and the Legacy of Legal Realism," 1991 18 *Journal of Law and Society* 2, 175–205.

[78] *US v Lee*, 455 US 252 (1982) (US Supreme Court).

in a field recognised for complicated constitutional jurisprudence.[79] It is also a good deal more conservative than most, apart from that of the German Federal Constitutional Court, and surprising given the overall liberal slant of most of the Hungarian cases from the period. It seems that the court was caught by its own earlier decision on capital punishment, which had set out so strong a doctrine of preservation of human dignity that it found itself with very little freedom of movement.[80]

This German influence on the Hungarian court is widely recognised and indeed admitted by its first president.[81] The court's attention to German precedents is only a particularly well-known example of a further aspect of constitutional jurisprudence that marks out how important the actual argument is to understanding the nature of constitutional review. Virtually all constitutional review bodies, with the exception of the US Supreme Court, make extensive reference to the decisions and arguments of other courts, and to the work of supranational bodies like the European Court of Human Rights and the European Court of Justice.[82] This process, which is leading to a marked standardisation of constitutional "answers," is neither accidental nor avoidable. There is a respected, if sometimes controversial, theory about legal development in general that argues that legal change is almost never entirely homegrown, but is, and has always been, dependent on import.[83] This is very clearly the case with constitutional law, in part because there is only one—or only one general—model of liberal democracy. Under the label of "constitutional borrowing" the process has begun to attract academic attention, much of it hostile.[84] To some extent the whole of chapter 5 can be read as a study of constitutional borrowing, because what Canada has done is to graft a very "foreign" idea—a fully established overarching bill of rights—onto an ongoing common-law legal world. Nonetheless, foreign decisions are not only a source of ideas for constitutional review bodies, they also act as a further discipline, making the arguments used on one issue sharply constraining on others, and furthering the way in which constitutional review has become a highly intellectual act of drawing out what may or may not be done in a modern society. For whatever reason, those who make up the courts and councils care a good deal about the opinion of their foreign brethren—

[79] A thorough coverage of abortion law worldwide is given in A Eser and H-G Koch, *Abortion and the Law: From International Comparison to Legal Policy* (The Hague: TMC Asser Press, 2005).

[80] J Kis, *Constitutional Democracy* (Budapest: Central European University, 2003), 250–70.

[81] C Dupré, *Importing the Law in Post-Communist Transitions: The Hungarian Constitutional Court and the Right to Human Dignity* (Oxford: Hart, 2003).

[82] Whether or not it is legitimate to use foreign judgements to interpret US constitutional law is a highly controversial matter. As I showed at the beginning of this chapter, this controversy came to a head in *Lawrence v Texas*. It and other cases are surveyed in J Yoo, "Peeking Abroad? The Supreme Court's Use of Foreign Precedents in Constitutional Cases," 2003 26 *University of Hawaii Law Review* 385–404.

[83] A Watson, *Legal Transplants: An Approach to Comparative Law* (Athens: University of Georgia Press, 1993).

[84] See particularly CF Rosenkrantz, "Against Borrowings and Other Nonauthoratative Uses of Foreign Law," 2003 1 *International Journal of Comparative Law* 2, 269–95. Useful also is Y Hasebe, "Constitutional Borrowing and Political Theory," 2003 1 *International Journal of Comparative Law* 2, 224–43. All the articles in this issue of the journal deal with the problem.

they meet a good deal, and clearly hope to exert as much influence as they accept. It is notable that one of the main concerns of Robert Badinter, the president of the French Conseil constitutionnel quoted at the beginning of this chapter, was to have the Conseil accepted as one of the world's constitutional courts and to lose its isolation.

The idea that constitutional review is a highly intellectual, and creatively intellectual, process helps formulate a first rough answer to our query, which will be refined as the book goes on to study both individual countries and subject areas. It is also a partial defence of constitutional courts against a common criticism. The criticism is that even if states unavoidably require this drawing out and articulating of constitutional values, it is wrong that an unelected group of judges should do this. Instead the elected part of the state itself can be trusted to work out what the constitution must mean.[85] Even those who believe in constitutional courts usually accept the description that they are "counter-majoritarian" institutions, simply accepting that populist majoritarian government requires a nondemocratic brake. This position is widely held amongst practising politicians; one of the main complaints against the French Conseil constitutionnel indeed is that it has arrogated to itself a role that French Republican tradition has always left to the Senate, which is, with arguable justification, proud of its record in this respect. In general the "counter-majoritarian" critique, whether unfavourable or not, is based on an unsophisticated assessment of how majoritarian, let alone democratic, modern political systems are. Kim Lane Scheppele, one of the shrewder commentators on the new Eastern European courts, has pointed out that, at best, the critique only works assuming parliaments are on their best, and courts on their worst, behaviour.[86] Parliaments are not machines for developing intellectually complex political theories that articulate and make coherent a society's values. They represent interests, and their executives aggregate these interests into programmes. There is a pithy truism to this point: "Judges argue, politicians bargain."

The idea that courts should "defer" to parliaments is commonly heard from the judges themselves—but always within limits. Parliaments have a duty to abide by the constitution as well. A quotation from the Canadian court makes this clear:

> While the courts are guardians of the Constitution and of individuals' rights under it, it is the legislature's responsibility to enact legislation that embodies appropriate safeguards to comply with the Constitution's requirements. It should not fall to the courts to fill in the details that will render legislative lacunae constitutional. Without appropriate safeguards legislation authorizing search and seizure is inconsistent with s. 8 of the *Charter*. As I have said, any law inconsistent with the provisions of the Constitution is . . . of no force

[85] Certainly the idea that the Supreme Court was not only the interpreter, but the only authoritative interpreter, of the US Constitution was not determined by *Marbury v Madison* but by *Cooper v Aaron*, 358 US 1 (1958) (US Supreme Court).

[86] KL Scheppele, "Constitutional Negotiations: Political Contexts of Judicial Activism in Post-Soviet Europe," 2003 18 *International Sociology* 1, 219–38.

> or effect. I would hold subss. 10(1) and 10(3) of the *Combines Investigation Act* to be inconsistent with the *Charter* and of no force and effect.[87]

Modern society needs two forces balanced—interest articulation and idea articulation; society requires both the force of citizens' demands for each individual's preferred good life, and the checking of these demands against a societal commitment to a communal good life. The constitutional review function is this working out of the meaning of the values hastily signed on to in constitutional conventions and referenda. Everywhere it exists, constitutional review presents a sort of theoretical sieve through which legislation must pass. What follows is not much concerned with the counter-majoritarian argument, because this book does not set out to make normative judgements about constitutional review, but only to characterise it. Despite this purpose, I would be remiss to ignore the charges of counter-majoritarianism entirely, and a section of the concluding chapter considers the arguments.

At this stage it is more relevant to note that whether or not they respect majority desires *in democracies*, constitutional courts are often clearly involved in furthering the degree of democracy in a country and take this responsibility very seriously. As the Canadian court said in one of its decisions involving the electoral system:

> it is precisely when legislative choices threaten to undermine the foundations of the participatory democracy guaranteed by the *Charter* that courts must be vigilant in fulfilling their constitutional duty to protect the integrity of this system.[88]

Against the criticism that the court was simply pitting its own social philosophy against that of the parliamentary majority, the court pointed out:

> This case is not merely a competition between competing social philosophies. It represents a conflict between the right of citizens to vote—one of the most fundamental rights guaranteed by the *Charter*—and Parliament's denial of that right. Public debate on an issue does not transform it into a matter of "social philosophy," shielding it from full judicial scrutiny. It is for the courts, unaffected by the shifting winds of public opinion and electoral interests, to safeguard the right to vote guaranteed by s. 3 of the *Charter*.[89]

At times this is part of the structural interpretation role described earlier. The sample question from the South African court on the constitutionality of floor-crossing is to the point. Courts are often forced to consider very deeply what the structural and institutional demands of democracy are. This was required of the French Conseil constitutionnel considering restrictions on the traditional French multiple mandate; of the Czech court deciding on the implications of party electoral pacts in electoral law; of the Hungarian court deciding on whether parlia-

[87] *Hunter v Southam Inc.*, 2 SCR145 (1984) (Canadian Supreme Court), 169.
[88] *Sauvé v Canada (Chief Electoral Officer)*, 3 SCR 519 (2002) (Canadian Supreme Court), par. 15.
[89] *Sauvé v Canada (Chief Electoral Officer)*, par. 13.

ment could reduce its hours of sitting, of the German court deciding on the constitutionality of party finance laws. As shown in chapter 2, the German court has often been solicitous of small parties potentially crushed by major ones. A second area courts have been active in, and where they perhaps have had to consider most deeply the practical requirements of competitive democracy, is that of broadcasting and media law. This area has occupied many courts, not only France, Italy, and Germany but Australia[90] and even the United Kingdom, where constitutional review does not as such exist.[91]

With some modern courts the process goes further than "filtering" legislation through a constitutional value net: the court may act as a moral leader, attempting to infuse the whole of society, or at least those aspects that are regulated by law, with a positive value orientation. If they are seen like this, one must accept that judicial review bodies are a fourth branch of government—a branch alongside the legislative, executive, and judicial.

I would argue further that the growth of this new function is directly related to the decline of ideological politics in modern societies. Ordinary political competition is no longer often competition between ideological camps. Instead, highly consensual societies have relatively little other than the values of the constitution against which to judge political initiatives. One consequence of this use of the constitution has been noted but possibly mischaracterised by political scientists. It is now commonplace that the growth of constitutional review has led to a "legalisation" of the parliamentary process; parliamentarians use the argument that a bill they oppose is unconstitutional, and majorities fear the court will find it so and suffer from what is sometimes called a legislative "freezing effect."[92] But might this practice not be at least as much because there is so little one can say in attacking the sort of legislation produced by governments in modern democracies other than (1) it is technically incompetent or (2) that it offends constitutional standards? The constitution is all many countries have as a setter of overarching values. On one case in Germany that attracted a good deal of criticism on these lines, the court went out of its way to welcome the concern members of the Bundestag had expressed about the constitutionality of a major statute. For them it was evidence that constitutionalism had become a major value in its own right in modern society.[93]

Appeals to patriotism, Christianity, socialism, tradition, have all faded away as generators of value. To some extent constitutional review is involved with (1) tech-

[90] *Australian Capital Television Pty Ltd v Commonwealth*, 177 CLR 106 (1992) (Australian High Court).

[91] The best UK example is *Derbyshire CC v Times Newspapers Ltd*, 1 All ER 1011 [1993] (House of Lords), where the Lords held that it was incompatible with the democratic need for press freedom to allow an elected body to sue for libel. See Robertson, *Judicial Discretion*, 284–88.

[92] Stone Sweet in his work on France was probably the first person to stress this phenomenon. A Stone Sweet, *The Birth of Judicial Politics in France: The Constitutional Council in Comparative Perspective* (Oxford: Oxford University Press, 1992).

[93] The academic comments they were thinking of were similar to those expressed in C Landfried, "Judicial Policy-Making in Germany: The Federal Constitutional Court," 1993 15 *West European Politics* 52–63.

nical incompetence, because of balancing tests of policy aims, and to a major extent it has the last word on (2) offences against constitutional standards. The following chapters attempt to put some flesh on the bones of the theoretical skeleton I have sketched so far. The next five chapters are each centred round a particular country or area—Germany, Eastern Europe, South African, Canada, and France. They are not single country "case studies" in the usual sense, however. In each chapter I take a country's predominant concerns to help a focus on different comparative questions. For this reason amongst others, there is no chapter on the United States per se. American jurisprudence comes into comparative perspective on virtually all issues. America is discussed particularly in the broad themes discussed in chapter 7, where I treat issues in comparative constitutional jurisprudence. Other important jurisdictions, especially Australia, are drawn in where they can provide a comparative or theoretical edge.

CHAPTER TWO

Germany: Dignity and Democracy

It is contrary to human dignity to make the individual the mere tool of the state. The principle that "each person must always be an end in himself" applies unreservedly to all areas of the law: the intrinsic dignity of the person consists in acknowledging him as an independent personality.

If this helps, well and good.

—David Currie, commenting on a Federal Constitutional Court ruling[1]

The General Imposition of Rights

The Structure of German Constitutional Review

If so distinguished a commentator on the German Federal Constitutional Court (FCC) as David Currie admits the court's ideas on human dignity are less than transparently clear, we can be sure that grasping what the German experience means for understanding constitutional review is a major task. It is an unavoidable task. The court's record is so huge, all-encompassing, and important that one can find examples of almost any aspect of constitutional review in it. Many other, younger constitutional courts openly admit the influence it has on them.[2]

The case Currie is commenting on came to the FCC from one of the three main sources of reference to constitutional courts, a criminal law case in which the trial court referred a question of constitutional law for guidance. The judge had doubts as to whether the mandatory sentence he would have to impose for murder was consistent with the constitution's values.[3] Though this is not a common route to major constitutional review decisions, it is not only important in its own right, but serves a valuable function in educating the ordinary judiciary into constitutional

[1]DP Currie, *The Constitution of the Federal Republic of Germany* (Chicago: University of Chicago Press, 1994); emphasis added.

[2]J Jones, "'Common Constitutional Traditions': Can the Meaning of Human Dignity under German Law Guide the European Court of Justice?" 2004 *Public Law* 167–87.

[3]*Life Imprisonment*, 45 BVerfGE 187 (1977) (German Federal Constitutional Court).

thinking. There are only about 100 such referrals per year to the FCC, which rejects two-thirds of them as unfounded. The judge who feels he or she cannot "reach an interpretive solution in conformity with the Constitution" must give a reasoned account of the problem to the FCC.[4] The most frequent route is from a procedure known as a "constitutional complaint." In this process, an individual who thinks one of his or her rights has been violated by the state can directly approach the constitutional court for redress, provided all the usual appeal remedies have been exhausted. It is important to know that the FCC's place outside the ordinary hierarchy of courts means that it is not an appeal court as such. If a constitutional complaint does get to the FCC from a decision of one of the other top courts, all the FCC can do is to remand the case with an instruction to rehear and come up with a solution compatible with its interpretation of the constitution. The ordinary appeal courts do not always jump to obey. So, for example, it took eight years and two constitutional complaints for Benetton to overcome a Federal Civil Court ruling that one of its adverts broke the law. The first hearing before the FCC, which Benetton won, was in 1995. The Federal Court of Justice reheard the case, considered the FCC's ruling, changed its own reasoning, and upheld the initial ban in 2000. Only in 2003 did the FCC stamp down hard and make it impossible for the other court to maintain the ban, which it interpreted as breaching Article 5 of the Basic Law, governing the freedom of the press.[5] So keen is the FCC to avoid usurping the role of the other supreme courts that it has set itself a very high standard before it will overrule them. As Smith says in his comment on the Benetton case:

> The Federal Constitutional Court . . . acknowledged that it lacks power to correct an interpretive error by the Federal Court of Justice unless that error has substantive weight in the case and rests on a fundamentally incorrect view of a basic right. This rule imposes a high threshold the Federal Constitutional Court must cross before it can reverse a decision of the Court of Justice. Nonetheless, the Federal Constitutional Court concluded that the Federal Court of Justice had again committed such a grave error, thereby unjustifiably restricting freedom of the press.[6]

The third route to review by the constitutional court, least common by far, is an "abstract review" procedure where state authorities ask the court for a ruling on the constitutionality of a piece of legislation. It is this route that marks the German court as a "Kelsen court" (as described in chapter 1), and most political science has been directed to this, the numerically least important, role. For simplicity I run together here a variety of different types of constitutional conflict. The category includes, for example, what the Germans call an *Organstreit*, by which the Federal Constitutional Court

[4] H Hausmaninger, "Judicial Referral of Constitutional Questions in Austria, Germany and Russia," 1997 12 *Tulane European and Civil Law Forum* 25.

[5] *Benetton II*, 1 BvR 426 (2003) (German Federal Constitutional Court).

[6] C Smith, "More Disagreement over Human Dignity: Federal Constitutional Court's Most Recent Benetton Advertising Decision," 2003 4 *German Law Journal* (e-journal) 6.

> decides on the interpretation of [the] Basic Law in the event of disputes concerning the extent of the rights and duties of a supreme Federal organ or of other parties concerned who have been endowed with independent rights by this Basic Law or by rules of procedure of a supreme Federal organ.[7]

This is the type of constitutional issue that I have described as one of "boundary maintenance"; they may cover, for example, federalism issues, or the rights of parliamentary parties or single parliamentarians, both at the federal level and in the Länder. They can be extremely difficult to deal with, and result in no little controversy. Often constitutions are fatally silent on highly technical matters of institutional description that suddenly become politically crucial. The FCC has certainly had its share of these cases. The government lost a vital new act on immigration reform in 2001 just because of a voting irregularity in the Bundesrat. The act went through and was signed by the federal president, but was referred to the FCC by the Bundesrat opposition on exceptionally technical grounds. The FCC had no choice but to give a decision, and though it was split six to two, few experts think it could have decided otherwise. No constitutional vision of any sort was either required or allowed in the case, and the substance of the act was never discussed. The most one can say about cases like this is that "someone has to do it," but it is unclear that one learns anything important about constitutional review from such examples.[8]

It is worth giving a capsule account of the decision to show that, in such cases, there is seldom a "right answer." The fate of the government's bill depended on the vote of one Land where, unusually, both the major national parties were in a regional coalition. The vote of each Länder has to be given as a bloc. Was the vote cast by the Brandenburg delegation split, and therefore invalid, and therefore to be treated as an abstention? If so, the government did not have a majority for the bill. Or was it, as the minority on the FCC argued, split and therefore not invalid but not a vote at all? And in that case, was the subsequent query by the president of the Bundesrat a legitimate second polling producing a single voice from Brandenburg, whose four votes thus gave the government what it needed?

Ironically, perhaps, it is cases like this that can be most at risk of being seen as "political" in a very simple partisan way, at least by journalists. Just as the US Supreme Court will take ages to recover from its decision on the legitimacy of the Florida vote in 2000, the FCC has recently been severely attacked for deciding not to overturn an election where political corruption was clearly proven in a Länder election in Hesse.[9] Yet as discussed in chapter 1, maintaining the democratic framework is, beyond contention, part of the court's job. From any profound level of analyses these are, at most, examples of pathology and hardly crucial for a characterisation of the true nature and work of the courts. This not to say that

[7] Article 93 of the Basic Law.

[8] N Arndt and R Nickel, "Federalism Revisited: Constitutional Court Strikes Down New Immigration Act for Formal Reasons," 2003 4 *German Law Journal* 2 (e-journal). The case is *Immigration Law Decision*, 2 BvF 1/02 (2002) (German Federal Constitutional Court).

[9] *Hesse Election Result*, 2 BvF 1/00 (2001) (German Federal Constitutional Court). See RA Miller, "Lords of Democracy: The Judicialization of 'Pure Politics' in the United States and Germany," 2004 61 *Washington & Lee Law Review* 587.

none of the boundary maintenance questions have theoretical import; we shall see the FCC struggling to develop a detailed theory of democracy through some of them later in this chapter.

More typically commented on by political scientists are the abstract reviews where the text of a law is referred by the parliamentary opposition, or some other state body that has lost the original battle in parliament. While some political scientists like Sweet Stone and Landfried may wish to concentrate on these "cases" as part of their attempt to argue for their own particular interpretation of constitutional politics, such instances of the FCC's work are no more important than others for my purposes.[10] Though some of the most important rulings have arisen through this latter route, the first two are the source of most of the court's work. As we have already seen in chapter 1, dealing with issues in the abstract rather than in the context of a real-life conflict is never the favourite approach by a court.

Membership, Structure, and Initial Legitimation

The other structural difference between the German constitutional court—indeed all Kelsen courts—and the more familiar ones of the common-law world is that of its membership. The FCC consists of two senates or chambers each of eight judges. In fact the court went through a series of changes in its early structure because the initially political negotiations were both difficult and hurried. The court originally had twenty-four members, with a provision for re-election that was brought down in stages to the current sixteen members elected for fixed and single twelve-year terms. As with most courts, the structural details are contained in ordinary legislation, which was amended with respect to size of the court in 1956. This amending statue also abolished the original duty of the court, sitting as a "Plenum" of both senates, to give an advisory opinion on potential legislation when asked to do so by the government. This responsibility had proved both politically and jurisprudentially awkward on the only important occasion it was tried.[11]

Originally each senate had a particular task. The first senate dealt largely with human rights issues, essentially the first nineteen articles in the constitution, the second with more "political" questions, mainly the ones I have described as structural or boundary maintaining. To a large extent this distinction has been amended away, though there is still some division of responsibilities. In part this restructuring was the result of very uneven caseloads: in its first four years the court had

[10] Stone Sweet, *Governing with Judges*; C Landfried, *Constitutional Review and Legislation: An International Comparison* (Baden-Baden: Nomos, 1989).

[11] This was the request of the government or an advisory opinion on the European Defence Force treaty that the government feared would not pass the Bundestag with a convincingly high majority. The Plenum issued a preliminary decision that any such advisory opinion would bind both senates even if they believed, when faced with actual litigation, that the Plenum's abstract answer was wrong. The ruling appears to have been a political move to prevent the government and opposition from "forum shopping" between the senates. E McWhinney, "Judicial Restraint and the West German Constitutional Court," 1961 75 *Harvard Law Review* 1, 5–38; JR Rogers and G Vanberg, "Judicial Advisory Opinions and Legislative Outcomes in Comparative Perspective," 2002 46 *American Journal of Political Science* 2, 379–97.

nearly 3,000 cases before the First Senate, and only 34 before the Second. The Second Senate was seen as likely to be more politically involved because it dealt with both federalism and conflicts between different branches of the state. The Second Senate was set up this way as part of a compromise between the Left and Right in the original constitutional convention. It was for some time known unofficially as the "Red" Senate. The First Senate, adopted under pressure from the Right, was ironically called the Black Senate. There seems little evidence that the senates ever were particularly "politically coloured" in this way, but even as a juridical folktale it reminds us of the impact of political election as a method of appointment.[12] The judges themselves denied any importance to such a pattern. Thus an FCC justice from the period, Konrad Zweigert (1951–1956) said:

> the popular talk of a Red and a Black Senate in the early years has never had any real basis, if it is taken to mean that a Justice's political background also determines his decisions. Rather, each Senate as well as the Plenum integrated itself with each decision to a body committed to the result required by the cause, i.e. the constitutional law, and common sense, behind which the party-political direction of the individual Justice became almost indiscernible.[13]

Thus from its origins no one was under any illusion that a body as powerful as the Federal Constitutional Court could be realistically seen as nonpolitical. The appointment mechanism recognises this. The Bundestag, the lower chamber of the federal parliament, and the Bundesrat, the higher chamber, each appoints one-half of each senate. The former does so via a committee on which parties are proportionately represented, ensuring that the major parties have rough parity in appointments. The Bundesrat, which elects directly, uses a two-thirds majority rule, enforcing a good deal of compromise. The end result, given the low intensity of German parliamentary conflict, is a court that allows genuine political sensitivity on the part of the judges with no great degree of partisan conflict.

Three judges in each senate must come from the career federal judiciary; all the rest must have the qualifications to have been such a judge, and they come mainly from academe. It should be noted here that academic lawyers in Germany have always had much more respect amongst actual judges than in many other jurisdictions, and their opinions have carried great weight. So in a real sense the entire FCC is staffed with similar people.[14] The appointments are for a fixed term of twelve years with no possibility of re-election, a condition that was part of the

[12] Writing after the first decade of its work, Edward McWhinney fully accepts that this was a popular conception—but his account of the court's early crucial decision on the EDC treaty stresses much more that the judges demonstrated collective solidarity against both Left and Right in the Bundestag. McWhinney, "Judicial Restraint."

[13] Cited in S Flemig, "Access to Justice—a Jurimetric Analysis of the Constitutional Complaint Admission to the German Federal Constitutional Court," MPhil, University of Oxford, 2008.

[14] Indeed in McWhinney, "Judicial Restraint," it is suggested that an initial lukewarmness to the court by the legal academic profession betokens a jealousy of loss of status by law professors as a result of its creation.

compromise in 1970 by which the court was authorised to issue dissenting opinions.[15] As time passed the political culture developed a pattern in which seats on the court were "owned" by different parties, so that there would be little challenge to the nominee of whichever party's turn it was to choose a candidate. Table 1 gives the membership and party affiliation for the court as of December 2007.

As the table shows, eleven of the sixteen had no formal party membership at the time of election. All but one were nominated by either the CDU/CSU (Christian Democratic Union / Christian Social Union) or the SPD (Social Democratic Party). The exception, Brun-Otto Bryde, was nominated by the more left-wing Green Party, but was himself nonpartisan. It has become common for the majority party in a coalition government to "lend" one of its nomination spots to its minor party allies.[16] Vanberg provides information and analysis on the question of political affiliation, coming to much the same conclusion as offered here, which is that the process of electing judges probably does what it was intended to do—to provide a bench more capable of the inherently political act of constitutional judging than ordinary courts, without creating anything like an automatic partisanship.[17] As the process of each party owning seats has developed, the consequence has been a more or less steady-state balance in both senates. Because the huge majority of decisions are, as far as the external world can know, consensual, any partisan impact is in any case very much moderated. The rarity of dissenting opinions to some extent speaks to this nonpartisanship.

It may surprise Anglo-Americans to know that dissenting opinions are seldom allowed in continental jurisdictions at any level. In Germany the decision to allow such dissents, taken in 1971, years after the beginning of the court, was a deliberate act to increase the ability of the FCC to engage in constructive constitutional debate. It is generally accepted that many crucial constitutional debates have been engendered by lone dissents that eventually win the day, rather than by firmly unanimous holdings. Dissents are crucial in the development of constitutional doctrine, and in this book they are often cited as much as the opinions of majorities. The US doctrine of substantive due process, for example, made law in the *Lochner* decision, was originated in Field's dissent in the famous *Slaughterhouse* case, and Holmes's dissent in *Lochner* itself became as famous as the majority opinion.[18] Dissents remain rare in Germany. Kommers estimates that 90 percent of judgements are, at least to the public's eye, unanimous. Each case is discussed in the relevant senate under the leadership of a single judge, the rapporteur, who

[15] The best short account of the setting up of the FCC is in chapter 1 of DP Kommers, *The Constitutional Jurisprudence of the Federal Republic of Germany*, 2nd ed. (Durham, N.C.: Duke University Press, 1997). Without this magisterial work, not only could this chapter not have been written, but several opinions of various constitutional justices worldwide could not have been pronounced. Technical details of the rest of the German court system are given in Guarnieri and Pederzoli, *The Power of Judges*.

[16] Source for tables is Flemig, "Access to Justice."

[17] G Vanberg, *The Politics of Constitutional Review in Germany* (Cambridge: Cambridge University Press, 2005), especially chapter 3.

[18] *The Slaughterhouse Case*, 16 Wall (83 US) 36 (1873) (US Supreme Court); *Lochner v New York*, 198 US 45 (1905) (US Supreme Court); see JH Ely, *Democracy and Distrust: A Theory of Judicial Review* (Cambridge: Harvard University Press, 1980).

Table 1
First and Second Senates

Name	Appointed in	Nominated by	Elected by	Party affiliation	Previous occupation
First Senate					
Hans-Jürgen Papier (president)	February 1998	CDU/CSU	Bundestag	CSU	Law professor/ judge
Christine Hohmann-Dennhardt	January 1999	SPD	Bundesrat	SPD	Minister (Hesse)
Wolfgang Hoffmann-Riem	December 1999	SPD	Bundesrat	Nonpartisan	Researcher/law professor
Brun-Otto Bryde	January 2001	Bündnis 90/ Die Grünen	Bundestag	Nonpartisan	UN/law professor
Reinhard Gaier	November 2004	SPD	Bundesrat	SPD	Bundesgerichtshof
Michael Eichberger	April 2006	CDU/CSU	Bundestag	Nonpartisan	Bundesverwal-tungsgericht
Wilhelm Schluckebier	October 2006	CDU/CSU	Bundestag	CDU	Bundesgerichts-hof/law professor
Ferdinand Kirchhof	October 2007	CDU/CS	Bundestag	Nonpartisan	Law professor
Second Senate					
Winfried Hassemer (vice-president)	May 1996	SPD	Bundesrat	Nonpartisan	Law professor/ civil servant
Siegfried Broß	September 1998	CDU/CSU	Bundestag	Nonpartisan	Bundesgerichts-hof
Lerke Osterloh	October 1998	SPD	Bundestag	Nonpartisan	Law professor
Udo Di Fabio	December 1999	CDU/CSU	Bundesrat	Nonpartisan	Law professor
Rudolf Mellinghoff	January 2001	CDU/CSU	Bundesrat	Nonpartisan	Bundesgerichts-hof/law professor
Gertrude Lübbe-Wolff	April 2002	SPD	Bundestag	Nonpartisan	Law professor
Michael Gerhardt	July 2003	SPD	Bundestag	Nonpartisan	Bundesverwal-tungsgericht
Herbert Landau	October 2005	CDU/CSU	Bundesrat	CDU	State secretary/ law professor

Note: All those listed as law professors were still practising while on the Federal Constitutional Court.

will most likely draft the opinion of the court, possibly even if the rapporteur has circulated a dissent in private. Great effort is expended on producing an opinion that all the judges can accept, and there is little doubt that dissent is frowned upon within the court.[19] It is unlikely that such a self-denying ordinance would survive

[19] Kommers, *Constitutional Jurisprudence*, 26ff. Flemig, "Access to Justice," on the basis of interview with judges, also argues that dissents are very unwelcome in the panels that do most of the work, and are seen more as a sign of the weakness of a judge forced to dissent than as an act of principle.

for over thirty years were the FCC to be riven along partisan lines. We do know that the court has begun to develop a more "precedential" approach than is usually in continental Europe. This is even written into the procedures because a panel is allowed to dispose of a matter without upward reference to its senate where it can point to a prior decision covering the matter. Furthermore, the full plenum must be called if one senate wishes to depart from a legal position already taken by the other senate. Such formal acknowledgement of a form of *stare decisis* in itself lessens the discretionary area required for highly politicised judicial behaviour.[20]

The workload of the court is so high that it could not possibly do its job if each case had to be discussed by the whole of a senate. (There are around 5,000 constitutional complaints per year, to take only one source of its workload.) Instead a winnowing process occurs whereby initial consideration is given by a chamber of three judges. The chamber can dismiss the case as unfounded, refer it to the full senate, or, where the court's precedents are clear, decide it then and there.

The lack of any overt partisanship can also probably be inferred from the very high levels of public support for the court. There are many indicators of this. Vanberg cites public opinion figures showing not only that the court is trusted and respected by a large majority of the population, but that it is the most trusted of all German institutions.[21] In 1999, for example its ranking was higher than even the Bundesbank, and very much higher than the Bundestag or Bundesrat. On the issue of public trust, a time series question regularly shows the court, along with the ordinary courts and the police, to be the only institution to have trust ratings much above 50 percent. Similarly a major comparative study of public attitudes about high courts in Europe shows the German constitutional court as one of the most trusted, ranking at the top with other courts that have no political role, and thus no danger of partisan orientation.[22]

The Nature of Rights and the Reach of German Constitutional Review

The constitutionality of life sentences for murder may seem the stuff of books on constitutional review, but a discussion of *Benetton*, on the legitimacy of adverts for clothing, might surprise readers. I shall come back to both, because they are both centred around the most important single concept in German constitutional law, and hence in German constitutional politics, the value of human dignity. But we need to start from a still less usual angle. Most political science commentary on Germany will focus, perhaps, on the famous abortion decisions, when a publicly acclaimed parliamentary statute was struck down. Alternative starting points might be the FCC's ruling about the Maastricht Treaty with its caution about erosion of sovereignty, or the decision about troop deployments outside NATO that accepted

[20] At least as far as constitutional complaints are concerned, the role of precedent is fairly obvious. M Singer, "The Constitutional Court of the German Federal Republic: Jurisdiction over Individual Complaints," 1982 31 *International and Comparative Law Quarterly* 2, 331–56.

[21] Vanberg, *Politics of Constitutional Review*, 97–99.

[22] JL Gibson, GA Caldeira, and VA Baird, "On the Legitimacy of National High Courts," 1998 92 *American Political Science Review* 2, 343–58.

a massive symbolic change in Germany's world role. Stone Sweet attaches huge importance to the co-determination case as an example of a left-wing government being restrained by a court. All of these are cases that raise very obvious political issues, and I shall have comments on several of them in due course. But all of them could come before a constitutional review body in any liberal democracy. (Even the Benetton advert could be litigated constitutionally in many jurisdictions where the law of freedom of expression has been fully developed.) Though political scientists may start their analyses with these cases, many comparative law texts would home in on a 1958 case, *Lüth*, instead.[23] We can benefit from following this approach because, in its own way, the case has some title to the label of the *Marbury v Madison* of Germany, the case that sets up the characteristic jurisdiction of the court.

The fastest way into what is really special about the German court's role is via a recent case in the *Lüth* tradition, which probably could not get to a constitutional review stage anywhere else, unless that other court had been closely influenced by German experience. The case, from 2001, presented this question: could a woman be bound by a prenuptial agreement not to ask for alimony when she later divorced, or did she have constitutional rights to financial support that she was simply not free to renounce?[24] *Lüth* opened up in Germany a debate, never quite completed, over the range of effect of a constitution. In technical language it raised the question of whether a constitution has "horizontal effect." (This is discussed later in the book, especially with reference to South Africa.) The usual idea of constitutional rights is that they are there to protect the individual from the state. But the German court has added two extra ideas to this. First, it is not only against the state that people may need protecting: imbalance of social and economic power between private citizens or between citizens and institutions like companies and corporations may call for similar protection. More fundamentally, rights have two dimensions: they are, on the one hand, "subjective," that is, they belong to an individual to protect him or her. But they also have an "objective" existence, as concrete values to which the whole society ought to be committed, and the furtherance of which is a duty of the state. (Such a conception is largely alien to the common-law-dominated legal culture of the Anglo-American legal world.)[25] This dual nature is evident at the very beginning of the Basic Law. Article 1(1), to which I shall return over and again, states that "Human dignity shall be inviolable. To respect and protect it shall be the duty of all state authority." To respect *and protect*, not merely not to offend *against* it. In *Lüth* this double nature of rights was spelled out clearly for the first time. First, the classic liberal definition of rights:

> The primary purpose of the basic rights is to safeguard the liberties of the individual against interference by public authority. They are the defensive rights of the individual against the state. This follows from the historical de-

[23] *Lüth*, 7 BVerfGE 198 (1958) (German Federal Constitutional Court).

[24] *Divorce Decision*, 2001 *Neue Juristiche Wochenschrift* 957 (German Federal Constitutional Court).

[25] The distinction in one way is age-old, but it has not been used in much Western legal thinking until recently. See A Pagden, "Human Rights, Natural Rights, and Europe's Imperial Legacy," 2003 31 *Political Theory* 171–99.

velopment of the concept of basic rights and from historical developments leading to the inclusion of basic rights in the constitutions of various countries. This also corresponds to the meaning of the basic rights contained in the Basic Law, and is underscored by the enumeration of basic right in the first section of the Constitution, thereby stressing the primacy of the human being and his dignity over the power of the state.

Then the extra dimension the FCC adds:

> It is equally true, however, that the Basic Law is not a value-neutral document. . . . Its section on basic rights establishes an objective order of values, and this order strongly reinforces the effective power of basic rights. This value system, which centers upon dignity of the human personality developing freely within the social community, must be looked upon as a fundamental constitutional decision affecting all spheres of law [public and private]. It serves as a yardstick for measuring and assessing all actions in the areas of legislation, public administration, and adjudication. . . . Every provision of private law must be compatible with this system of values.[26]

The apparent claim to "objective" values here is not a statement in moral philosophy. It only means, as above, a set of values held to be legislated for the society as a whole, and thus objective in contrast to being merely subjective, where subjective means pertaining to the individual. The *Lüth* story is simple enough to expound and should help us grasp what the FCC is doing with this judgement. Erich Lüth was the director of information for Hamburg and also a campaigner for a Christian-Jewish reconciliation society. He discovered that Veit Harlan, a notorious Nazi film director of, inter alia, the infamous *Jud Süss*, was attempting to resuscitate his reputation by releasing a new film. Lüth was incensed, fearing the impact on the international reputation of the German film industry, and publicly called for a boycott of its distribution. Harlan got an order for damages from the courts because they accepted his claim that Lüth's actions amounted to a breach of the civil code for causing him financial loss. Having lost in the ordinary courts, Lüth brought a constitutional complaint to the Federal Constitutional Court, claiming his Article 5 right to freedom of speech was being abridged by the courts themselves. Article 5 was slightly problematic for him. Section 1 provides a full and generous definition of the right:

> Every person shall have the right freely to express and disseminate his opinions in speech, writing, and pictures and to inform himself without hindrance from generally accessible sources. Freedom of the press and freedom of reporting by means of broadcasts and films shall be guaranteed. There shall be no censorship.

However, Section 2 says, inter alia, "These rights shall find their limits in the provisions of general laws." The lower courts had not made up the law they applied to the case—it was clearly within Article 826 of the civil code, and this was a gen-

[26] Kommers, *Constitutional Jurisprudence*, 363. All quotations from German cases are from translations in this book.

eral law, not some specially passed anti-free-speech law. In any case Harlan, who instigated the proceedings, was an individual with no connections to the state, asserting his ordinary civil law rights against another individual. Where does constitutional review come in?

Moments of creativity like this come to all constitutional review bodies, and unless rapidly retreated from, can form and mark the nature of constitutional review in the society. The FCC engaged in some complex manoeuvres that need not concern us to establish that "general law," which had appeared in the earlier Weimar constitution in a similar context, meant absolutely any legally enforceable rule of both public and private law. Thus in principle Article 826 could have legitimately restricted Lüth's freedom of speech. Why did it not? First, as in the quotation above, the Basic Law serves to assess "all actions in the areas of legislation, public administration and adjudication." Thus all actions of all courts must be compatible with Article 5, regardless of the nature of the litigants. This is the crucial step in establishing "horizontal effect." If courts in a country are forbidden to act against the constitutional code, then they can never render a verdict in favour of someone if that verdict is itself unconstitutional. Obvious though this may be to those who favour a very wide effect for a constitution, it is by no means a step always taken. A very similar argument was rejected initially by the South African Constitutional Court under the provisional constitution, with the consequence that the second draft of the constitution specifically orders them to act as the German FCC insisted German courts must. In Canada the same strategy was attempted early in the days of the new Charter of Rights and Freedoms. There the courts successfully refused flatly to accept the German argument—they were not to be seen as agents of the state in such a way as themselves to be bound to enforce the Charter values in every decision they made.[27] The argument for horizontal effect of the Human Rights Act in the United Kingdom, on the grounds that the act binds all "public authorities" and lists courts as amongst them, has yet to be fully decided. In the United States, where the relevant doctrine is called the "State Action" argument, the Supreme Court has been unwilling to give it effect. The case most frequently cited as showing that there may be the rudiments of horizontal effect in the United States is still highly controversial after half a century.[28] Thus one can see that it was a major step for the German court to give itself this power of using the court system to widen the range of a bill of rights further than simply protection against the state more narrowly conceived. In itself this should show how vital doctrine and doctrinal decisions are in understanding the nature of constitutional review.

Balancing and Limiting Rights

Still, what of the fact that Article 5(2) allows general law to circumscribe the right to free expression? Here again is a crucial moment in the development of constitu-

[27] Tushnet, "State Action / Horizontal Effect." The case was *Retail, Wholesale and Department Store Union v Dolphin Delivery Ltd*, 2 SCR 573 (1986) (Canadian Supreme Court).

[28] *Shelley v Kraemer*, 334 US 1 (1948) (US Supreme Court).

tional review. Everywhere such rights are accepted as not absolute—government could hardly function in a world where there could be no invasion of any right. As foreshadowed in chapter 1, the construction of tests or methods to allow but also to restrict such constraints on rights is a crucial part of the constitutional review armoury. Later in this book an entire chapter (chapter 7) is dedicated to this aspect of judicial review. The German method was not entirely initiated by *Lüth*, but is set out there with greater rigour than before. It is one of the hallmarks of the FCC's approach, and characterises the vast majority of its opinions. What the FCC called for in *Lüth*, (the approach was developed over the subsequent years), was a balancing of the ordinary law claim against the Basic Law right—neither trumps the other, and the court imagines an optimising process. In the instant case, because free speech is so crucial to democracy, the Basic Law certainly has the upper hand in the balancing process.

> The basic right to freedom of opinion is the most immediate expression of the human personality in society and, as such, one of the noblest of human rights. . . . It is absolutely basic to liberal-democratic constitutional order because it alone makes possible the constant intellectual exchange and the contest of opinions that form the lifeblood of such an order.[29]

The passage concludes with a famous quotation from Cardozo that freedom of speech is "the matrix, the indispensable condition of nearly every other form of freedom." The balance is the initial job of the courts below; they must

> Evaluate the effect of general laws which would limit the basic right in the light of the importance of the basic right. They must interpret these laws so as to preserve the significance of the basic rights: in a free democracy this process must assume that fundamentality of freedom of speech in all spheres, particularly in public life. . . . there is a mutual effect. . . . the general laws sets bounds to the basic right, but in turn, those laws must be interpreted in the light of the value-establishing significance of this basic right in a free democratic state, and so any limiting effect on the basic right must itself be restricted.

Although the FCC did not refer to it here, the Basic Law itself sets a limit to this interpretative procedure. Article 19(2) states, "In no case may the essence of a basic right be affected." Again a comparative note may help situate the German process of constitutional review: the provisional South African constitution had a similar rule that the judges thought was unworkable and that, to their pleasure, was dropped in the final version. On the other hand the Hungarian constitution also has the rule, and judges seem to find it useful. Nor should one think that Article 19 is the only rights limitation aspect of the constitution—that would seriously underrate the sophistication of the constitution. The German constitution shares with other European documents like the European Convention on Human Rights

[29] Kommers, *Constitutional Jurisprudence*, 365.

another technique. Many of the other articles of the constitution contain their own internal limitations clauses. Article 2 shows two versions of these limiting clauses:

> Article 2: Rights of liberty (1). Everyone has the right to the free development of his personality insofar as he does not violate the rights of others or offend against the constitutional order or the moral code. (2). Everyone has the right to life and to inviolability of his person. The freedom of the individual is inviolable. These rights may only be encroached upon pursuant to a law.

Article 2(1) protects free development of personality subject to relatively precise restrictions—not to "violate the rights of others or offend against the constitutional order or the moral code." Article 2(2) simply says, *ceteris paribus*, that individual freedom "rights may only be encroached upon pursuant to a law"—though this means more than it might in some countries, because no mere regulation, administrative order, or local by-law would count as "a law," which invariably means a full parliamentary statute. Furthermore a judge-made "proportionality test" (discussed comparatively and at length in chapter 7) usually comes into play before the limit in Article 19 needs to be considered.

Of course it is much easier to announce the need for such a balancing act than to prescribe how to do it. The process tends to be very ad hoc, and the balance the FCC draws often surprises. What is clear is that it is a largely empirical process. The FCC goes into very considerable contextual detail which, though it may deliver instant justice, does not make the legal community's task of deriving rules easy. In *Lüth* there was perhaps little problem—the moral case for his boycott that the FCC strongly supported compared very well with the purely economic interest claimed by Harlan. Indeed the court sketched a scale of values clearly indicating that "narrow" private economic interest would always weigh light in the scale against Basic Law values. This is all part of the crucial development of a test, endemic to constitutional review: when is it appropriate to enforce a constitutional prohibition? I shall argue throughout this book that the nature of the tests devised by constitutional courts goes a long way to accounting for how interventionist they are. The German doctrine on the tests to be applied will be further discussed.

Lüth is not substantively an interesting case because the free speech values it characterises are simple, and it did not require the FCC to develop much of a theory of free speech. Other speech cases described later involve a much richer theory about *why* freedom of speech is valuable; in *Lüth* a fairly standard "necessary for democracy" defence is used. This can be found even in countries not much used to judicial review of rights, as with cases in England and Australia. The judgements in *Lüth* do hint at one of the richer aspects of the FCC's jurisprudence, which can best be described as socio-psychological theory of human nature. For example, freedom of opinion is described as "the most immediate expression of the human personality in society." This, which is closely tied to the German stress on human dignity, lies at the heart of both the FCC's view of its mission, and its chosen constitutional review methodology. What we really must take from the case are two connected ideas. The first is that the court has a duty to ensure that the objective values of the constitution "radiate" throughout the legal part of society.

Radiate is the FCC's own word, and splendidly connotes the essence of their sense of purpose. The second is that the justification for radiation is that the enactment of the constitution was a once-and-for-all and deliberate moral act on the part of the German people, an affirmation of a whole value set. Other cultures may perhaps see a constitution as on the level of a political "table of organization," a bureaucratic wall chart for policymaking. For the FCC, as quoted above, the rights section of the Basic Law *must be looked upon as a fundamental constitutional decision*. The FCC is there to draw out the implications of that once-and-for-all decision.[30] How it does this can be very surprising, and it is worth looking quickly at another example of radiation to demonstrate this innovation. It is also easier to see the nature of the balancing act involved in the FCC's constitutional test if we turn to the recent divorce case mentioned earlier, which also serves to show how very far from a narrow definition of constitutional issues the Basic Law has come.

In 1976 a woman who already had one child from a previous marriage became pregnant by her new partner. He claimed subsequently that there had been an agreement not to have children. She persuaded her partner to marry, but he insisted in return that she sign a prenuptial agreement limiting the amount he would have to pay, in the event of a divorce, to a mere 150 DM monthly, for the upkeep of the new child. After the birth she had an office job that paid her substantially less than the new husband earned. They divorced in 1989 when the child, a boy, was thirteen, and he sued the father for adequate maintenance. Although the first court found for the son, on the grounds that the prenuptial agreement was "contrary to public policy," the father won on appeal to the Land Supreme Court. The woman thereupon lodged a constitutional complaint with the Federal Constitutional Court. Between *Lüth* in 1957 and this case in 2001 there had been several cases in which the FCC further established the doctrine of radiating effect, largely in the area of contract law, but it had never been held to apply in so purely individual circumstances as family law. The decisions in the contract cases, however, had depended on a highly "political" reading of the Basic Law that stressed egalitarian elements in its value code, and were surprisingly well suited to apply to this rather different sort of contract.[31] Initially, in the *Commercial Agent* case the FCC had concentrated on aspects of coercion in a business relationship that seemed to threaten the autonomy of one party. This had broadened in the *Bank Guarantee* case to cover other circumstances where unequal bargaining power allowed one side to impose its terms. According to the court, "the duty of the law is to reinforce the fundamental right positions of both parties in order to prevent the private autonomy of one of the parties being replaced by duress." Applying this idea to marriage, the FCC coupled it with another article of the Basic Law. Article 3(2) says, "Men and women shall have equal rights. The state shall promote the actual

[30] I stress the "once and for all" nature of the Basic Law because Article 79 (3) specifically treats Articles 1 and 20 as incapable of being amended. The dignity clause of Article 1 is the heart of all the basic rights. Article 20 includes, for emphasis if nothing else, the promise that "All Germans shall have the right to resist any person seeking to abolish this constitutional order, if no other remedy is available."

[31] *Commercial Agent Case*, 81 BVerfGE 242 (1990) (German Federal Constitutional Court); *Bank Guarantee Case*, 89 BVerfGE 214 (1993) (German Federal Constitutional Court).

implementation of equal rights for women and men and take steps to eliminate disadvantages that now exist." The court drew the conclusion that the state, and therefore the FCC, had a duty to limit the terms someone could agree to in order to ensure that this Basic Law equality provision could not be lost through the dominance of one party. (The court describes the situation as one of "disturbed contractual parity.")

In coming to this "balance" of rights—the right to freedom of contract against the rights to equality (and others the court considered)—the court demonstrated how reliant its arguments are on real factual contexts. The court quoted extensively, for example, from statistics about single mothers' welfare and the disparity between financial pressures on children in and out of marriages. Even more notably, the judges actually found the father in breach of his *duties* in the Basic Law, rather than just finding his ex-wife had suffered a restriction in her rights. The Basic Law is unlike many such documents in that it records duties as well as rights. Article 6(2) insists: "The care and upbringing of children is the natural right of parents and a duty primarily incumbent upon them. The state shall watch over them in the performance of this duty." This breach of duties existed even though the terms of the prenuptial agreement did not, legally, deny the father's duties. As far as the FCC was concerned, the reality that the mother's financial circumstances meant resultant insecurity for the child put the father in breach of this constitutional duty.

It is hard to keep in mind with a story like this that we are not reading the report of a family court applying a child protection statute—this is all constitutional law, enforcing between private individuals implications drawn from their defensive rights against the state. Furthermore, it is a derived constitutional doctrine sharply aware of economic inequality, and deeply grounded in empirical context. The decision is not uncontroversial, of course. None of the horizontal effect decisions have gone down well with the practising bar, which wishes to cling to its special expertises and defend its turf. And, of course, it is policymaking. But policymaking was afoot right at the beginning when the district court initially declined to implement the father's prenuptial agreement on the grounds that is was "contrary to public policy," a decision that a similar court in the United Kingdom might well have come to from its sense of the values of the common law. What is important here is to see a formal constitution being developed in this way. It is hard to see how a court behaving like this can be seen as anything but a new type of political institution carrying out a new function in the state.

The Centrality of Dignity

So far we have concentrated on the reach that constitutional review has in Germany. The cases discussed have only incidentally told us anything about the substance of the FCC's jurisprudence. In one way or another this substance is mostly built round one central organising concept, the dignity of man. This is the most powerful argument the court can ever use, because, if it treats a statute as violating human dignity, no balancing test of public interest may be applied, and no constitutional amendment can save the law, because Article 1(1) cannot ever be amended. This was discussed briefly in chapter 1, regarding the way the irreversibility of constitutional adjudication makes it different from even very "political" ordinary law. In a recent highly controversial case the FCC ruled out part of an antiterrorism law that would have allowed the Government to order the shooting down of a highjacked airliner whose captors intended to use it as a bomb. Such an action, by treating the lives of innocent passengers as a necessary sacrifice, regarded them as things and not as persons, and affronted the dignity clause. The FCC made this a separate argument from the passengers' right to life because the right to life, in Article 2(2) can be balanced against overwhelming state need.[32]

Perhaps the classic case, mentioned at the beginning of this chapter, is *Life Imprisonment* of 1977. The opening words of the Basic Law are "Human dignity shall be inviolable. To respect and protect it shall be the duty of all state authority." Not surprisingly such a rich but inchoate concept has required a good deal of highly theoretical expansion and has found its way into a mass of vastly different legal and policy contexts. Article 1 is, in fact, seldom relied on by itself, but more usually functions to flesh out and aid other more concrete rights, as with the airliner decision that could have been based merely on the right to life. Another parallel right is the almost equally general right granted by Article 2(1), usually called the "personality clause."

> Every person shall have the right to free development of his personality insofar as he does not violate the rights of others or offend against the constitutional order or the moral law.

These two articles came together in the *Life Imprisonment* case to produce a ruling that, like many from the FCC, did not actually strike down a law, but rather explained how it must be read in order to make it compatible with the constitution. This form of review, common in France as well as Germany and used elsewhere, attracts the opposition of many critics because it is seen as involving the courts even more in the legislative process. Courts that use the technique instead claim it is a matter of greater, rather than less, deference to the legislator.

A drug dealer shot to death one of his clients who had tried to get drugs with a threat to report him to the police; the drug dealer thus put himself firmly under the criminal code clause that prescribed a mandatory life sentence for murder committed to cover up other criminal activities. The judge he came before believed that this mandatory sentence, with no guaranteed limit, offended against the human dignity clause, and exercised his authority to suspend the trial while the issue was referred to the Federal Constitutional Court. (The top criminal court in Germany recorded itself, during the process of referral, as convinced there was no constitutional barrier to the sentence that was contained in a revision to the Code only a few years old.) The constitution itself forbids the death penalty (Article 102)

[32] O Lepsius, "Human Dignity and the Downing of Aircraft: The German Federal Constitutional Court Strikes Down a Prominent Anti-terrorism Provision in the New Air-Transport Security Act," 2006 7 *German Law Journal* 9, 762–76.

so the case is the most important challenge that could arise over criminal law in Germany. The ordinary court's argument, which the FCC considered very seriously, was that a sentence of imprisonment that held out no hope of re-entering society involved treating the murderer as no more than an object, stripped of all that made him a person.[33] This spoke to one of the better definitions of human dignity used by the FCC, a direct reference to Kantian philosophy, in which the idea of a human as always an end and never a means is central.

The first step in the FCC's judgement is of considerable importance as far as its methodology for constitutional interpretation goes. They had to take notice of the fact that the constitution's framers, less than twenty years earlier, had specifically decided that life imprisonment was an acceptable replacement for the death penalty. In many jurisdictions so recent a consideration of a matter at the core of an appeal would have foreclosed all further argument. One does not have to be an American "originalist," à la Bork, to think that the creators' intentions have some role to play when they are nearly contemporaneous. The FCC would not accept this, however, putting themselves on record for the future when the original intent will be less contemporaneous:

> [This] does not clearly decide the constitutional issue before us. Neither original history nor the ideas and intentions of the framers are of decisive importance in interpreting particular provisions of the Basic Law. Since the adoption of the Basic Law our understanding of content, function and effect of basic rights has deepened. Additionally the medical, psychological and sociological effects of life imprisonment have become better known. Current attitudes are important in assessing the constitutionality of life imprisonment. New insights can influence and even change the evaluations of this punishment in terms of human dignity and the principles of a constitutional state.

There are actually two different points here. The relevance of founders' intent is indeed doubted, as it has to be if my theory of constitutional interpretation is to be a good characterisation of how the German court behaves. "Our understanding of content, function and effect of basic rights has deepened" is bound to be true, more or less regardless of how long ago the constitution was written, because it has come into the hands of an agency, a constitutional review body, whose task is precisely to work out what the simple original commitment to a broad value actually means. The FCC does, as it happens, often refer to history, including the Weimar history, to interpret clauses in the constitution, just as German courts have always looked at the "travaux preparatoires" of ordinary legislation as one amongst many tools for interpretation. But the interpretative role is the job of the court, not of the complex political alliances that drafted the original. The second point is equally characteristic of the FCC's work. What Americans used to call "Brandeis Briefs," detailed social science reports on the problem addressed by the legislation in question, are routine in front of the FCC, which will carry out its own research wherever necessary. So the second reason for not being bound by any original intent

[33] Kommers, *Constitutional Jurisprudence*, 306–13.

is mentioned: "Additionally the medical, psychological and sociological effects of life imprisonment have become better known." Note the "additionally"—even absent scientific development, the court insists that an understanding of the practical meaning of human dignity as far as life imprisonment goes might change, but given the growth of scientific knowledge, this is even more the case. The court is keenly aware of the historical subjectivity of values like human dignity, which it refuses to see as some static idea. Noting that attitudes to criminal punishment have become gentler over the years, the court insists that "any decision defining human dignity must be based on our present understanding of it, and not on any claim to a conception of timeless validity," which further establishes the special role of constitutional adjudication.

The FCC referred to its own past cases to establish that the state has a duty "not merely to incarcerate but also to rehabilitate." Rehabilitation, it says, is actually "constitutionally required in any community that establishes human dignity as its centre piece and commits itself to the principle of social justice." This is to use the "objective value" aspect of the Basic Law that enforces positive duties on the state. "The condemned criminal must be given the chance, after atoning for his crime, to re-enter society. The state is obligated within the realm of the possible to take all measures necessary for the achievement of this goal." And this duty applies, if anything even more strongly, where life imprisonment is concerned. This is because the duty to rehabilitate comes from the combination of the dignity clause and the Article 2 right to free development of an individual's personality.

The decision is replete with the FCC's view both of constitutional principles and of the nature of man. "The Free human person and his dignity are the highest values of the constitutional order." The state's duty to protect these values is "based on the conception of man as a spiritual-moral being endowed with the freedom to determine and develop himself." But the German idea of freedom, at least in the eyes of the FCC, is never an atomistic or purely individualistic one, a view that runs through much of its caseload. Here it is stressed, for example, that the meaning of freedom in the Basic Law "is not that of an isolated and self-regarding individual but rather of a person related to and bound by the community." It is best here to do no more than give the flavour of this, not untypical, opinion. All the concepts quoted in this paragraph come themselves from just one paragraph of a long opinion.

In short, the FCC held that the destructive effect on this personality and its hopes for development that they see as protected by the Basic Law would be unbearable were even a murderer to know for sure that he could never be released. To treat someone like that would be to "turn the offender into an object of crime prevention to the detriment of his constitutionally protected right to social worth and respect"; that is, it would deny the Kantian imperative to regard people only as ends. Much of this assessment was based on careful study of criminological and sociological research. It comes as something of a surprise, after reading this opinion, to discover that the court did not, in fact, just strike down Section 211 of the criminal code. In fact the FCC has not struck down all that much legislation in its fifty-year history, preferring to achieve its ends by interpretation, by hinting to the government about its duty, by finding ways to make statutes constitutionally workable. What the court did instead of striking Section 211 was to suggest that it should not be, and need not be, read very strictly. As long as the courts actually refrained from passing the full life sentence, using their own powers of interpretation on the criminal code, the system was more or less acceptable. It is hard to make sense of a result like this unless one takes note of the very high degree of consensus and conflict avoidance that characterises the German political system throughout. In this case the court had noted a 1974 report from justice ministries throughout Germany that the then existing parole system was inadequate to protect the interests of such prisoners. Within a few years of the FCC's decision, though not formally as a consequence, the law was changed to avoid clashing with the court's ideas on human dignity. In the *Life Imprisonment* case the mere fact that the FCC did so sharply stress how important continued respect for Articles 1 and 2 was even when dealing with an out-and-out criminal was quite enough—the criminal code did not actually have to be struck down. In almost any other jurisdiction it would be unthinkable for a constitutional or any other top court to solve a problem by telling the lower courts to be relaxed in their interpretation of clear statute law.

It has been pointed out that many of the important civil liberties cases in the United States have been won on the backs of thoroughly unsavoury individuals. There is a sharp difference in tone between the German and US cases on criminal human rights, however. The essence of US decisions, like the famous *Miranda v Arizona* or *Gideon v Wainwright*, has been to control the police or the lower courts to protect the innocent from injustice.[34] What marks out the German cases is this stress on the continued humanity of the indisputably guilty. Typical of this concern for the personal autonomy of even the criminal is the decision in the *Lebach* case.[35] A man was coming to the end of a prison sentence for being an accessory to an armed robbery on an army barracks during which several soldiers were killed. A television company planned to make a documentary on his case, using his real name and an actor with a physical likeness. He complained that this infringed a privacy right stemming from the dignity and free development clauses. The ordinary courts argued that the freedom of broadcasting rights of the TV company in Article 5 of the Basic Law prevailed and found against him. The FCC analysed the same legal issues using a "proportionality" test through which, without denying the vital importance of such a documentary, the privacy rights triumphed. The Article 2 rights include the right "to remain alone, to be oneself within this sphere, and to exclude the intrusion of, or the inspection of, others." The FCC's statement of how a clash between constitutional rights should be handled is worth quoting extensively, particularly with reference to the use of the idea of a democratic order.

[34] *Gideon v Wainwright*, 372 US 335 (1963) (US Supreme Court), established the right to counsel in all criminal cases. See also A Lewis, *Gideon's Trumpet* (New York: Random House, 1966). *Miranda v Arizona*, 384 US 436 (1966) (US Supreme Court), established the need to warn suspects of all their civil rights on arrest.

[35] *Lebach Case*, 35 BVerfGE 202 (1973) (German Federal Constitutional Court). See Kommers, *Constitutional Jurisprudence*, 416–17.

Much the same language can be found in, for example, Canadian post-Charter jurisprudence.

> In resolving [this] conflict [one] must remember that both constitutional concerns are essential aspects of the free democratic order of the Basic Law, the result being that neither can claim precedence. . . . In case of conflict the court must adjust both constitutional values if possible; if this cannot be achieved the court must determine which interest will defer to the other in the light of the nature of the case and [its] special circumstances. In so doing the [court] must consider both constitutional values in their relation to human dignity as the nucleus of the Constitution's value system. . . . the freedom to broadcast may have the effect of restricting rights based on the claims to personality; however any damage to "personality" resulting from a public broadcast may not be disproportionate to the significance of the publication to free communication . . . [The court must also consider] the extent to which the [legitimate] interest served by the broadcast can be satisfied without such a far-reaching invasion of the intimate sphere.

Balancing Dignity, Freedom, and Abortion

Numerous cases deal with this intermix of dignity and personal freedom that becomes the right to the slightly mysterious concept of "personality." They cover such matters as the right not to answer questions in a census, the right to use one's name in broadcasting attacks on someone, the right not to have one's passport taken by the government, the protection of one's private "honour," even the right for religious sects not to be unfairly characterised in ministerial speeches. What they have in common, and what so much of the work of the FCC shows up, is this problem of balancing rival rights, and the idea of the proportionality of actions, whether the state's or an individual's. First we need to look at the most famous and controversial of all human dignity cases, the FCC's striking down twice of an abortion reform law. It is a prime example of something that is actually quite rare—intervention in legislation where a court directly strikes down something the government had intended, rather than some unforeseen or ignored secondary consequence of the law.

On June 18, 1974, the federal parliament passed the Abortion Reform Act. It was immediately sent to the Federal Constitutional Court as an abstract review proceeding by the Christian Democratic opposition in the Bundestag, and by five of the Länder governments. The court immediately suspended the operation of the new act, bringing the old act it replaced back into force until it could give judgement, which it did within a year. There are two major abortion cases, but I am primarily concerned with *Abortion I*,[36] the major ruling of which has been crucial outside of Germany as well as within the Federal Republic. With the possible partial exceptions of Hungary and Spain, no major court has denied a relatively

[36] *Abortion Case No 1*, 39 BVerfGE 1 (1975) (German Federal Constitutional Court).

automatic right to abortion at least within the earlier part of a pregnancy. The Hungarian court was certainly highly influenced by the German court, though probably more from its general constitutional jurisprudence than this actual decision, and the Spanish court certainly refers to the German example.[37] There is a voluminous literature on the abortion case, so the barest outline of the argument will suffice.[38] In many ways it is a curious case, because it was more about moral symbolism than actual practice. The existing legislation categorised abortion as a criminal offence and laid down prison sentences for both doctors and mothers involved in procuring an abortion. After the fall of the Nazi regime abortion became again regulated by the law as it had been declared in 1927 by the Weimar Republic's courts, this being given legislative form in the 1962 reform of the General Criminal Code. The essence of the old law was that abortion was always a criminal offence, but a woman would not be punished if abortion was the only way to save her life. In practise doctors had become more willing to certify to this—between 1968 and 1974 legal abortions rose from 2,858 to 17,814, while prosecutions for illegal abortions dropped from 596 to 94.[39] The proposed new law decriminalised abortion completely during the first twelve weeks of pregnancy, requiring only a counselling session and the consent of one doctor. This would have brought German abortion law into line with that in most Western countries, and is parallel to the rule set up by the major US case of *Roe v Wade*.[40] In a split decision, five of the eight judges held the law to be incompatible with the constitution and void. Their decision, though deeply unpopular, was accepted by the Bundestag, which rapidly passed a new act almost completely mirroring the terms suggested by the FCC. The argument of the majority ranges widely over constitutional values, some of which are highly specific and not usually to be found in constitutions. Article 6 of the Basic Law, for example, is a clear constitutional affirmation of the value of marriage and the family, including the idea that "every mother is entitled to the protection and care of the community." These and similar ideas only form the backdrop to the decision that turned on the obvious clash between the life and dignity protection that could be deduced for the foetus from Article 1, and the woman's freedom of personal development that is clear in Article 2. Most abortion decisions by courts have been reached by denying the foetus is capable of holding rights (or denying that is has "life," which amounts to the same thing). Once that step is taken, there is nothing to get in the way of the individual freedom claim for the woman. Few courts have wanted to assert very clearly that the foetus is alive and the bearer of rights but that these have to take second place to the woman's interest. Indeed the

[37] On Hungary, see Dupré, *Importing the Law*; and chapter 3 here. On Spain see R Stith, "New Constitutional and Penal Theory in Spanish Abortion Law," 1987 35 *American Journal of Comparative Law* 3, 513–58; and B Barreiro, "Judicial Review and Political Empowerment: Abortion in Spain," 1998 21 *West European Politics* 4, 147–62.

[38] The details of the case and analyses of judicial argument are given in Kommers, *Constitutional Jurisprudence*, 336–46; and Currie, *Constitution of Germany*, 310–14.

[39] U Werner, "The Convergence of Abortion Regulations in Germany and the United States: A Critique of Glendon's Rights Talk Thesis," 1996 18 *Loyola of Los Angeles International and Comparative Law Journal* 571.

[40] *Roe v Wade*, 410 US 113 (1973) (US Supreme Court).

old German law was cast in terms of the unbearable sacrifice involved in expecting a woman to give her life for her unborn child. The FCC relied, however, on the new conception of the constitution as providing not only defensive (subjective) rights for the individual, but as laying down an "objective" moral order for the society. Under this reading the mere fact that a foetus is in some sense alive couples with the duty of the state under Article 1 to protect life *tout court.* As Kommers says, the court can be seen as ruling that "the legal order exists to instruct its citizens in the moral content of the Basic Law, and that includes substantive values pertaining to the nature of life."[41] The proposed law had been based, as are most Western laws, on what has been called a "periodic" approach to abortion—dividing pregnancy up into stages and allowing more or less restricted abortion on this basis. The FCC opted instead to widen the approach of the old German law, often called the "indicative model": abortion is allowed only where certain factors indicate its necessity. These are the basic threat to the mother's life, but also others including pregnancy caused by rape and, most important, social conditions. For the FCC it was crucial that abortion in itself remain a criminal offence—both because nothing less could really ensure the protection of life, and because, symbolically, the state could not be seen to remove the moral evil of destroying life by failing to see this act as criminal. The language in which the majority allows the social condition "indicator" makes clear what the whole of the judgement was about:

> The general social situation of the pregnant woman and her family may produce conflicts of such gravity that sacrifices in favour of the unborn life cannot be extracted by the instrumentalities of criminal law. . . . the legislature must describe the statutory elements of the offence which will not be subject to punishment so that the gravity of the social conflict . . . is clearly recognized

The court was not content just to allow this exception; instead it spelled out the state's positive and precise duties. The court expects "the state to offer counselling and assistance so as to remind the pregnant woman of her fundamental duty; to respect the unborn's right to life, to encourage her to go through with the pregnancy, and to support her—particularly in the case of social need—with practical assistance."

As so often in German constitutional jurisprudence the dissent was on a narrow point—the dissenters did not doubt that the state must discourage abortion, and must take a moral stand against any destruction of life. They disagreed only on whether retaining ineffectual criminal sanctions was the only way to go about this, and concluded that the Bundestag had taken the matter seriously and formed a pragmatic decision that criminalising all abortion was not necessary to this end. More importantly for the theme of this book, the dissent was more about whether the constitutional court was trespassing on the legislative domain. Indeed, there may be no clearer example of the sort of "instructive reading" that critics dislike anywhere in modern constitutional experience. The dissenters argued that

[41] Kommers, *Constitutional Jurisprudence*, 346.

the "objective moral order" side of the constitution could, and here had, become an instrument to allow the FCC directly to legislate, rather than merely protect values. The distinction is one that may make abstract sense—in practise there is no clear difference, certainly not if one accepts the argument that constitutional courts are something other than ordinary courts. As long as constitutional courts are seen as courts within the classic division of power and separation of power, the minority claim is more forceful. It is much easier to understand the abortion decision, in the Weberian sense of understanding as *Verstehen*, when one remembers the period of German history to which the majority alludes throughout the decision. Simply remembering that one of the Nazi era abortion laws was called the law for "the destruction of unworthy life" goes a long way to explaining why the retention of criminality seemed to be the only way to entrench the importance of Article 1. It was crucial also to maintain the doctrine of the Basic Law as imposing a duty on the state always to respect constitutional values. The dissenters may have been right on the pragmatic question of what were the necessary steps in carrying out this duty. But that is only to say that the majority made a mistake of technical judgement. The subsequent history in the *Abortion II* decision shows them accepting that in a restricted way criminalization could be removed. But it remains true that *Abortion I* is the strongest evidence we have for the idea that when interpreting some aspects of constitutions, constitutional review bodies are carrying out a new function in society. (Another way for a court to do this and retain a respect for the legislator's duties is found in the Hungarian abortion case.)

Abortion I is often thought of as far more generally significant than the issue itself. The decision amounted to a recognition of a duty on the part of the state to protect rights of individuals against any trespasser, not just the state. Though it is impossible to trace the effect of this general understanding comprehensively in this book, it is important. Jurists do feel they are entitled to instruct the government to legislate to protect rights more fully, and the government often obeys. In some ways this plays into the problem, discussed at various stages later in the book, especially with South Africa, of "positive" rights.

Abortion II was brought about by the post reunification need to reconcile the previous law in East Germany, which effectively treated abortion as a form of birth control, with the 1975 court-approved law in the West. After lengthy negotiations a new law was passed through the newly united federal parliament in 1992. It was immediately challenged by all the Christian Democrat members of the Bundestag elected from the old West Germany, under the leadership of the chancellor himself. The new law retained much of the 1975 law but specifically allowed that abortions during the first twelve weeks, even if not indicated by the act but performed anyway, should not be illegal provided the women had undergone the counselling session. In other words, it allowed abortion on demand. Unsurprisingly this law was struck down for the same reasons as its predecessor, though the language had been tightened up in many ways, and the FCC now spoke directly of the foetus's subjective rights, not only of the objective state duty to protect life. This is a significant change because it demonstrates that judicial argument is not just window dressing around brute policy preference, but can have a constraining effect. The shift in emphasis was forced by the dissent in *Abortion I*. The dissenters' argument that the court was trespassing on parliamentary rights was predicated on the idea that "subjective" rights could not be used to insist on criminality; thus the "objective order" argument had had to be used to give the FCC its authority. By basing the need for criminality in *Abortion II* both on objective and on individual subjective or defensive rights, the court largely removed this criticism. It could now present the issue as, amongst other things, a straightforward clash between the rights, especially the Article 2 rights, of two individuals:

> This right to life, which is not given to the nasciturus through acceptance by his mother but is granted to the unborn solely because of its existence, is the most elementary . . . right that [stems] from the dignity of man.[42]

However the FCC did compromise in one respect. Though insisting that abortion remain a criminal offence, the court accepted that it was not necessary to insist on actually carrying out punishment on those who gained "nonindicated" abortions in the first trimester. Because of this stress on symbolism over practice, *Abortion II* may well be an even better example of the role of constitutional review bodies as "moral tutors." This form of "dialogue" whereby legislation gets tossed to and fro between court and parliament until some workable compromise between governmental policy preferences and constitutional review requirements is one more feature, increasingly commented on, of the new role of constitutional review. The idea is commonly referenced by the courts themselves in, for example, Canada.

Economics and Property Rights

The Constitutional Idea of Property

Given that the whole corpus of German constitutional law cannot be covered here, much has to be left out. Several vital areas are left for consideration in later comparative theme chapters. Why on earth, then, is an entire section dedicated to property and economic rights? The answer is that it is precisely by seeing how the FCC has interpreted property rights that one can best see the nature of the German constitution through the court's own eyes, and understand the court's function in German society.[43] Such rights are at the heart of much constitutional jurisprudence, of course, as chapter 4, on France, makes clear, and as the history of the US Supreme Court abundantly demonstrates. The German constitution protects private property, in so many words—not all constitutions do. The Canadian Charter makes no reference to property at all; the US Bill of Rights guarantees only due process and compensation for governmental "taking" of property. But it is the

[42] My amendment to a translation given in Werner, "Convergence of Abortion Regulations," 13.

[43] I discuss German property rights in the context of positive rights in D Robertson, "Thick Constitutional Readings: When Classic Distinctions Are Irrelevant," 2006 35 *Georgia Journal of International and Comparative Law* 277–331.

words themselves that count. The German constitution contains a simple property right, like, say, the French Declaration of the Rights of Man, whose Second Article actually defines the purpose of politics:

> The aim of every political association is the preservation of the natural and inalienable rights of man. These rights are liberty, property, security and resistance to oppression.

Article 14 of the Basic Law provides in part:

> Article 14 [Property, inheritance, expropriation]
> (1) Property and the right of inheritance shall be guaranteed. Their content and limits shall be defined by the laws.
> (2) Property entails obligations. Its use shall also serve the public good.

Nor is this all—elsewhere the Basic Law stipulates that Germany shall be "a republican, democratic, and *social* state governed by the rule of law, within the meaning of this Basic Law."[44] It has sometimes been declared by scholars that the Basic Law is neutral as regards the economic order, and some have claimed it is compatible with full-blown socialism, though this seems very doubtful. The Federal Constitutional Court itself has always upheld a much more nuanced view. In a very early case it argued that "the Basic Law's neutrality in economic matters consists merely in the fact that the 'constituent power' has not adopted a specific economic system. This omission enables the legislature to pursue economic policies deemed proper for the circumstances, provided the Basic Law is observed."[45] What is clearly not the case, in the eyes of the FCC, would be a claim that the Basic Law is compatible with a full-blown "devil take the hindmost" individualistic laisser-faire system. The reason the FCC would not accept the latter, and the reason the court's property jurisprudence is such a good example of the true nature of judicial review, is that it too involves the ever present human dignity and human personality arguments.

Typically the FCC, as in all areas of its work, has sought to solve problems about property by asking *why* property is constitutionally valued, rather than taking for granted that property and wealth are the same thing, and valuable only as a means to further an individual's private consumption preferences. Many quote Ernst Benda in this context, who is not only a leading legal scholar, but a former president of the Federal Constitutional Court's First Senate. For him, the Basic Law rejects the "individualistic conception of man derived from classical liberalism as well as the collectivist view."[46] Property is seen as crucial to self-realization and self-development, thus being vital for the crucial Article 1 and 2 values of dignity and personhood.[47] Property is required for individuals to develop fully as

[44] Article 28 (1); emphasis added.

[45] *Investment Aid I*, 4 BVerfGE 7 (1954) (German Federal Constitutional Court).

[46] Quoted in GS Alexander, "Property as a Fundamental Constitutional Right? The German Example," 2003 88 *Cornell Law Review* 733.

[47] Fittingly, this was a major argument developed by Hegel when writing about the Prussian state, especially in *The Philosophy of Right*.

moral actors and as useful community members. Property is needed to give the individual autonomy, not to make her rich. This theme can be seen throughout relevant cases—especially the cases that protect some forms of welfare benefit as forms of property. It is because of this stress on property as a matter of human development that only those welfare rights based in part on past contributions by the recipients are protected. The argument used the first time the issue arose was that a governmental attempt to reduce old people's health benefits was a deprivation of a property right that was, in itself, necessary to protect the Article 2 right to personhood.[48] Thus property became linked back into one of the two dominant rights. In the actual case the FCC held that there was no private property in the particular benefit involved, precisely because it lacked that element of personal contribution, but the principle was nonetheless accepted. The essence, as far as the court is concerned, is very much this Article 2 right; it sees the prime function of Article 14 as protecting freedom. This leads also to the setting of a subsistence level test—the FCC is not going to protect "welfare property" just for enrichment. Of course a German court's idea of subsistence level is rather more generous than in other countries—the FCC noted that the majority of Germans expect their subsistence level security to come from employment-related programmes, and not their own resources.

> Legal protection for social insurance interests is possible only in the event that their termination or reduction would vitally affect the freedom-assurance function of the constitutional guarantee of ownership.[49]

Other benefits, however, which both involve some aspect of contribution and pass this means test, have been found to be property, including unemployment insurance, and, crucially, retirement pensions. This latter causes considerable concern currently because the need to restructure the extensive and very expensive welfare programme in Germany has led to concentration on the pensions sector, yet some constitutional lawyers seriously doubt whether such restructuring would be found constitutional.[50] This approach to property also explains in part the way other rights, like that of Article 12's protection of freedom of occupation, all go together with Article 14 to make a coherent theory of the economic basis of dignity and freedom.

The Limitations on Property

What exactly does Article 14 protect? What the constitution has been held to protect is, specifically, property, the property itself. In one way this view contrasts, for example, with the United States. There property may be taken by the government for public benefit provided both an adequately strong public interest is shown and, following the Fifth Amendment, fair compensation is given. Someone who does

[48] *Personal Contributions Case*, 69 BVerfGE 272 (1985) (German Federal Constitutional Court).

[49] Translation taken from Alexander, "Property."

[50] M Herdegen, "Global Economy, Lean Budgets, and Public Needs," 2000 53 *Southern Methodist University Law Review* 543.

not want compensation but wants to hang on to his land will have no constitutional case. In Germany just compensation will certainly be required if a "taking" of property is allowed, but absent evidence that the taking is the least disruptive possible method of solving an adequately serious public problem, the owner will be allowed to keep the actual property.[51] This is not because the FCC puts private interests before public interests. It takes very seriously the public good definition of property in 14(2).

The leading case on private property in Germany is the *Co-determination* case.[52] To political scientists this has often been taken as the equivalent of nationalisation issues before the courts, as especially in France. As such, it has been criticised by writers like Stone Sweet and Landfried.[53] Perhaps unfairly, the decision has been criticised for two reasons, neither of which are to be found in the FCC's judgement. First, because the Bundestag evinced considerable concern that some versions of the reform might prove to be unconstitutional, it took great care, including asking for expert evidence from professors of constitutional law, to avoid such a judgement, and passed a less extreme version of the bill than some members of the Social Democrat Party might have preferred. The FCC specifically welcomed this development in legislative politics, making critics like Landfried concerned. This point has been addressed already in chapter 1, as bearing on the general idea of constitutionality in modern society. According to Landfried, this deference amounted to a disturbing example of "obedience in advance" and speaks to excessive power on the part of the court. It might be seen, alternatively, to be evidence for the general thesis that constitutionalism has become a major value in its own right in modern society. More generally the FCC is criticised for not going far enough in welcoming the act.

The Co-Determination Act, which caused the trouble, was an extension to large industrial corporations of worker representatives on boards of directors, as already existed in the iron and steel industries.[54] The original intention of the Social Democrats when in opposition had been to insist on parity representation, which was dropped from the final version—the junior member of the coalition, the FDP, is very friendly towards business and was unhappy about full parity. In any case the Bundestag contented itself with extending the model that had already applied to smaller firms since 1972. It was nonetheless a major reform of industry in a generally egalitarian direction. The case arose when several firms and employers' associations lodged constitutional complaints, claiming both an invasion of property rights under Article 14 and of several other rights. One of these was the claim that Article 2, the general freedom clause, contained the right to freedom of economic activity, which would now be abridged. The act was complex and the

[51] TR Draeger, "Property as a Fundamental Right in the United States and Germany: A Comparison of Takings Jurisprudence," 2001 14 *Transnational Lawyer* 363.

[52] *Co-determination Case*, 50 BVerfGE 290 (1979) (German Federal Constitutional Court).

[53] Landfried, "Judicial Policy-Making"; A Stone, "Judging Socialist Reform: The Politics of Coordinate Construction in France and Germany," 1994 26 *Comparative Political Studies* 443–69.

[54] A useful discussion of the legislation and the case is BA Streeter III, "Co-determination in West Germany—through the Best (and Worst) of Times," 1982 58 *Chicago-Kent Law Review* 981.

FCC judgement lengthy, but the core question was this: if shareholders are now only to account for roughly half of the voting power in the corporations they own, have they not lost half their property rights, in denial of Article 14? The FCC had no trouble in rejecting this suggestion, noting that the general idea of worker participation in enterprises had a lengthy German tradition, including recognition in the Weimar constitution. As to the act before it, it did not "infringe the property of shareholders nor that of enterprises." Instead it was an example of the power of the Bundestag to "define the contents and limits of property" that is specifically granted by Article 14(1). The basis of the court's support for the act is the social duty part of Article 14. After admitting that there is a restriction on shareholder power, the court argues:

> [The] restriction remains within the ambit of the commitments of property owners to society in general, and these commitments increase in scope as the relationship between the property in question and its social environment as well as its social function narrows. . . . these share holdings have far-reaching social relevance and serve a significant social function, especially since the use of this property always requires the cooperation of the employees whose fundamental rights are affected by such use.[55]

In this statement alone, and even more in the detail of a complex judgement, the FCC showed itself intent on digging below conceptual simplicity to examine the empirical reality. Property as a concept is unpacked to look at the actual nature of economic relations in question, at which stage the "public use" clause of Article 14 cannot but triumph. Most commentators have indeed picked simply on one phrase to show what the decision was all about: "especially since the use of this property always requires the cooperation of the employees." Shareholding just is not the same as owning a piece of physical property, and cannot be constitutionally protected the same way. There is a powerful idea contained in the first half of that sentence as well: "these share holdings have far-reaching social relevance and serve a significant social function." The criticism of the FCC, incidentally, is based on the idea that it specifically refused to speculate on what its answer would have been had full parity of representation been incorporated. Yet it is an unwritten, though often cited, rule of all constitutional courts that they will never decide more than they have to in a case—a sentiment to be heard in courts as different as the US Supreme Court and the Constitutional Court of South Africa.

In fact the FCC's record for supporting governmental acts against putative property claims where important social measures are concerned is very good, and usually consists of a definition that simply excludes the claimed right from the coverage of the property protection. A famous example is the *Groundwater* case, where the owner of a gravel pit sued the city of Münster for refusing him a permit to continue using the water extracted from below his pits because it was threatening the quality of the city's water supplies.[56] The Federal High Court, where his

[55] *Co-determination Case.*

[56] *Groundwater Case*, 58 BVerfGE 300 (1981) (German Federal Constitutional Court).

litigation had ended up, referred the case to the constitutional court. The FCC made just one, but a fundamental, step. It noted that the High Court had assumed that groundwater was the gravel pit owner's property because under the civil code "the right of an owner to a piece of land extends to the space above the surface and to the terrestrial body under the service." The FCC could have stuck with that and nonetheless found that the city was entitled to refuse him his use permit, but the simple step the court took was more typical, and continued the process of building a general constitutional morality in the society. What the court did was to say that the purely legal definition of property was irrelevant. Instead, "the concept of property as guaranteed by the constitution must be derived from the constitution itself." This idea, part of what I have meant by the "reflexivity" of constitutional jurisprudence, is found elsewhere, certainly in Canada and South Africa. The constitution is *the* source of *all law*, and its definitions prevail over all other sources.

> The Water Resources Act does not constitute expropriation by law . . . the law merely defines for the future and for the entire Federal Republic of Germany, as a matter of objective law, the content of property in groundwater. Such a change in objective law does not result in a deprivation of a concrete legal interest protected by the institutional guarantee of Article 14 (1) and thus does not constitute an expropriation of property.

Of course the FCC has often overturned the state's attempts to regulate. One fine example is known as the *Chocolate Candy* case. The sale of a candy bar made of puffed rice and covered with chocolate had been banned in case consumers thought it actually was a chocolate bar. That part of the consumer protection statute was struck down as being a disproportionately heavy weapon to use when merely insisting on proper labelling was enough. In fact this case is more important than it sounds. An equivalent case in the United States, where a ban was attempted on the sale of margarine in case people thought it was butter, is still seen as one of the major constitutional decisions in the realm of economic activities.[57]

Other Economic Rights

There is a huge a range of cases based on the right to choose and practise an occupation. The state can be seen here as invading an economic right through market restrictions.[58] This constitutional right, an essentially economic right, is as important as the simple Article 14 property right. Together they have been used to make the constitution's defence of economic rights much more far reaching in terms of social protection than might have been the case with a court that took a more limited view of its role. The right in question, Article 12(1), states:

[57] *Chocolate Candy Case*, 53 BVerfGE 135 (1980) (German Federal Constitutional Court). The US case is *Carolene Products v United States*, 323 US 18 (1944) (US Supreme Court).

[58] An early and influential example is *Pharmacy Case*, 7 BVerfGE 377 (1958) (German Federal Constitutional Court).

> All Germans shall have the right freely to choose their occupation or profession, their place of work, and their place of training. The practice of an occupation or profession may be regulated by or pursuant to a law.

It is, in itself, an interesting example of how a right can come to take on a role almost certainly not thought of by the constitution writers, because the rest of Article 12 shows the context the drafters were thinking within. The heading for the article, for example, is "Occupational freedom; prohibition of forced labour," and it goes on to give general protection against any form of civil conscription except for "traditional community service" or within a prison sentence. Despite this limitation, it has become a crucial economic constitutional right. (As noted above, it was even raised by employer organisations, to no avail, in the *Co-determination* case.) It is also the constitutional right invoked in a long series of cases where the FCC can be seen as going as far as the constitution allows to force the government into doing something positive, rather than preventing it from doing what it ought not to do. Germany seldom features in discussions of positive rights, unlike South Africa or even Canada, but this is one area that might be considered more often than it is. Certainly there are frequent hints in FCC decisions about how the government ought to act. In fact many argue that the 1975 abortion decision, based as it was on a duty of the government to protect rights against all attacks, is the basis for an approach much like that of positive rights.

An example is a gender equality case known as the *Night Work* decision in which the court upheld a constitutional complaint by a manager in a bakery who had been employing women on the night shift in defiance of a law that made it illegal to employ women in unskilled jobs during the night hours.[59] Though not technically an occupational freedom case, it serves to demonstrate aspects of the FCC's style, and leads into occupational freedom. The case revolved largely around the general equality requirement of Article 3(1) and its specific gender equality rule in 3(2), but the decision ranged widely. (This and related equality issues are mainly covered in chapter 7.) It was undeniable that the law imposed gender inequality. The FCC took apart the state's defence, which was that women needed protection both against the harmful effect of night work and against the dangers of being out at night. Indeed its language is almost derisory in places; "working at night is fundamentally harmful to everyone"; "the state may not escape its responsibility to protect women from being attacked in the public streets by restricting their occupational freedom in order to keep them from leaving their houses at night." The court finished by a clear instruction to the government that, by incorporating Article 2 freedom rights, shows how far from purely economic, or even simply egalitarian, the decision was—again showing the interconnectedness and cohesion of the FCC's view of the constitution it enforces.

[59] *Night Work Decision*, 85 BVerfGE 191 (1992) (German Federal Constitutional Court). See M Battacharyya, "From Nondifferentiation to Factual Equality: Gender Equality Jurisprudence under the German Basic Law," 1996 21 *Brooklyn Journal of International Law* 915.

> The legislature is under an obligation to adopt new rules to protect workers from the harmful effects of nocturnal employment. Such rules are necessary in order to satisfy the objective dimension of the fundamental rights, especially . . . [Article 2(2)]. This basic right imposes an affirmative duty of protection on the state. . . . The fact that night work is performed on the basis of voluntary agreements does not obviate the need for statutory protection. The principle of private autonomy that underlies the law of contract can afford adequate protection only to the extent that conditions permit the exercise of free will. When there is a gross inequality of bargaining power between the parties, contract law alone cannot ensure an appropriate accommodation of competing interests. . . . To leave [this] unregulated . . . would be contrary to the objective dimension of Article 2-2.

As in the first case discussed here, the divorce case, the FCC demonstrates its determination to take factual contexts into consideration, and to ensure, through the "objective" dimension, that the society as a whole upholds constitutional values like equality and physical safety as a basis for freedom. The German Federal Constitutional Court does not have the power to order the Bundestag to pass a law. The Hungarian Constitutional Court, under the doctrine of "constitutional omissions," does have such a power. It is an interesting speculation to consider what contemporary German statute law would look like had the FCC an equivalent authority.

As far as occupational freedom goes, the most famous case is the *Numerus Clausus* case, from 1972 (there is an ongoing set of linked cases on the subject).[60] It arose because the continental European tradition of allowing everyone who passes the state school leaving qualification to go to the university of choice and read for any degree had become impossible to maintain in medicine. Medical schools began applying competitive admissions standards, the constitutionality of which were challenged in a series of cases in the administrative courts. The FCC became heavily involved in policing the actual nature of the admission processes to ensure equal opportunities, but also to enforce rational utilisation of resources. The general background to their arguments again rests on the idea of the duty of the state to take note of objective values. The by now familiar phrases like "basic rights in their capacity as objective norms . . . establish a value order that represents a fundamental constitutional decision" abound in the opinions in all these cases. This position, that "basic rights are not merely defensive rights of the citizen against the state," leads to a full-blown demand for the state to make real the exercise of rights.

> The more involved a modern state becomes in assuring the social security and cultural advancement of its citizens, the more the complementary demand that participation in governmental services assume the character of a basic right will augment the initial postulate of safeguarding liberty from state intervention.

[60] *Numerus Clausus I Case*, 33 BVerfGE 303 (1972) (German Federal Constitutional Court).

This argument leads to the conclusion that the right to freely choose one's education is not worth much if there are not enough places in the universities. The FCC had to stop short of ordering the building of more medical schools, but the depth of its involvement in university selection systems and the closeness of its attention to empirical detail have earned it the nickname of the "Ministry of Education." Only perhaps in some areas of US constitutional law, as with the federal courts' involvement in desegregation plans, has a court anywhere taken so active a role in enforcing its own decisions. (To the horror of any academic, the FCC has even investigated university teaching loads to ensure that there is no spare capacity to take extra students.) Again, the FCC lacks the powers that some other courts have, or have given themselves, to order governments to provide resources. It is probably the case, however, that this freedom, as demonstrated in, inter alia, South Africa and Poland, is one that the later generation of constitutional courts could be expected to enjoy. Without the huge strides in developing the role of such courts pioneered by the German constitutional court, the later courts would not have been as free as they have been.[61]

Enforcing Democracy

Militant Democracy

As noted in chapter 1, constitutional review is frequently criticised as inherently undemocratic because constitutional courts may act in ways that are "countermajoritarian." I noted that there were several senses in which a court could be either pro- or antidemocracy, and being subservient to a supposed majority demand was only one. The German constitutional court has, from its beginning, been much concerned to foster democracy in a variety of ways that we need briefly to consider. Chapter 1 pointed out that it is a crucial role of a constitutional court, one for which it is uniquely equipped precisely because it is not connected to majoritarian politics, to be responsible for supervising the building blocks of a democratic state. This point arises in all the jurisdictions covered in this book. In Germany this is recognised by the constitutional doctrine that Germany must, after 1933—45, be a "militant democracy," the idea that a democracy cannot be completely tolerant of those who would threaten its values. The court is given this role directly in the Basic Law. The FCC is one of very few courts that have the right to outlaw an extremist political party, a right that it has exercised, though sparingly.

The actual phrase *militant democracy* was probably first used in 1956 when the FCC exercised its authority to ban the Communist Party at the request of the federal government.[62] It had first been used in the interwar years when the émigré

[61] In a very limited situation the FCC has in fact ordered the state to spend resources to satisfy a constitutional right, in the area of providing confessional secondary schools. This whole area of religion and the constitution I omit from this single country chapter, preferring to deal with it later in a general comparative discussion.

[62] *Communist Party Case*, 5 BVerfGE 85 (1956) (German Federal Constitutional Court).

Karl Lowenstein had complained that the American, more liberal, conception of democracy was what had caused such weakness in Germany.[63] The court recognised a possible contradiction at the heart of the Basic Law, while expressly denying that there was one. It claimed that the Basic Law represented a "synthesis between the principle of toleration with respect to all political ideas and certain inalienable values of the political system," but noted that experience had taught the founding fathers that the state could no longer "maintain an attitude of neutrality towards political parties." It described the Basic Law as having created a "'militant democracy,' a constitutional value decision that is binding on the Federal Constitutional Court." So we have again the idea of the constitution as being the creation of a once-and-for-all value set, part of which says that, amongst other things:

> Parties which, by reason of their aims or the behaviour of their adherents, seek to impair or abolish the free democratic basic order or to endanger the existence of the Federal Republic Germany shall be unconstitutional.[64]

Though it attracts a lot of attention, this aspect of the Basic Law probably is not really very important in itself. It has been used seldom, and initially anyway against parties with only tiny and waning support.[65] It is really part of Germany's version of the "problem of the past," with which we shall be much concerned later in relation to Central and Eastern Europe (and which arose again when the question of punishing members of the East German Border Guard came up after unification).[66] The most recent attempt by the Federal Parliament to have a party banned was the request in 2002 for the Federal Constitutional Court to ban the Neo-Nazi National Democratic Party. The FCC was about to start the process when it discovered that the party leadership was so heavily infiltrated by intelligence agents that there was, in the court's mind, no choice but to drop the proceedings as procedurally tainted. (The government would only admit that "not more than 15%" of the leadership were actually working for the intelligence services.)[67] It is, rather, the first part of Article 21 that really matters, because it makes the German constitution one of very few in the world positively to value political parties. So entrenched is the idea of the positive value of political parties, perhaps for the first time in German history, that political scientists in Germany created the label of *ParteienStaat* as a

[63] K Lowenstein, "Militant Democracy and Fundamental Rights," 1937 31 *American Political Science Review* 417. The debate over the problems with the concept continues in other jurisdictions. A particularly troublesome example is described in P Macklem, "Militant Democracy, Legal Pluralism, and the Paradox of Self-Determination," 2006 4 *International Journal of Constitutional Law* 3, 488–516.

[64] Article 21 (2).

[65] At the time it was banned, the German Communist Party's vote had dropped to 2.3 percent of the national vote and was going down. The first party to be banned, in 1949, was the Socialist Reich Party, whose clear Nazi identity would have led to its suppression in any country at the time, by one means or another. Kommers, *Constitutional Jurisprudence*, 222.

[66] MJ Gabriel, "Coming to Terms with the East German Border Guards Cases," 1999 38 *Columbia Journal of Transnational Law* 375–418; P Quint, "The Border Guard Trials and the East German Past—Seven Arguments," 2000 48 *American Journal of Comparative Law* 541–72.

[67] T Rensmann, "Procedural Fairness in a Militant Democracy: The 'Uprising of the Decent' Fails before the Federal Constitutional Court," 2003 4 *German Law Journal* (e-journal) 11.

rival to *Rechtsstaat* as a description of the new political order. It is the positive role foreseen for parties, that they participate in the "creation of the political will of the people," that has attracted the more creative jurisprudence of the FCC.

The Importance of *Rechtsstaat*

Before discussing this partisan dimension of democratic oversight, there is a simple but often overlooked point to be made about the FCC, and, *pari passu*, most constitutional courts in their relationship to democratic principles. If a political system is to be even remotely majoritarian, this must mean that major binding rules come, at least indirectly, from the duly elected majoritarian institution, parliament. Protecting this principle goes to the essence of a court's duty to police the democratic values of the society. German constitutional law is very firm on the principle that laws must emanate from the legislature, especially where any infringement on a basic right is concerned. Thus administrative discretion is restricted far more than in many countries. The point may not seem important to those who take their bearings from countries of the common-law world, where parliament has usually been the sole author of laws. But in continental Europe the right of the state to pass binding rules in the form of decrees has a long history, and one the post-Nazi state is especially eager to overcome. As a result the German doctrine of the legitimate justification for any intrusion into basic rights stresses very heavily the need for a parliamentary basis for any government action. It is not unique, of course. As chapter 1 notes and chapter 4 discusses, the French Conseil constitutionnel was originally intended to police the decree power of the executive, as well as the statute power of the legislature. In Germany it is a very high constitutional value, stemming mainly from the definition of the Federal Republic as a *Rechtsstaat* in Article 20 of the Basic Law. *Rechtsstaat* is usually translated as "a state under the rule of law," though there are any number of learned articles explaining that this is not really an adequate translation.[68] The FCC is exceptionally strong in policing any slippage, and an idea of how it insists on this most basic aspect of democracy can be given graphically. In 2002 two complaints were handled together by the FCC, both from organisations that claimed that mere statements by federal ministries and ministers had deprived them of constitutional rights. In one case some wine distributors were listed in a health warning about wine containing harmful additives. In the other a fringe religious group, the Osho or Bhagwan movement, complained about ministerial statements that had described them, inter alia, as a destructive and "pseudo religious" psycho sect. The first group claimed property rights and Article 12 freedom of occupation rights were involved, because members now could not sell any wine. In the second case, the crucial Article 4 right to religious freedom was supposedly at risk. The state was not going to do anything at all to either of these groups, but it had spoken without any statutory backing; there was no law allowing or requiring the government to give

[68] G Schram, "Ideology and Politics: The *Rechtsstaat* Idea in West Germany," 1971 33 *Journal of Politics* 1, 133–57.

such warnings about either physical or religious health. In the end the wine growers lost their case, and the religious group partially won. But in both cases the FCC had to invent a new doctrine to cover governmental authority, and one the court wished to curtail maximally, to allow the government to do something no minister in another country could ever find himself in court for. The doctrine the court invented has by no means been easily accepted by German constitutional lawyers,[69] based as it is on an imputed power to govern rather than the more traditional notion of the executive simply applying legislation. The critics probably do not have to worry—there is an extensive track record of the FCC holding the federal and Länder governments to have abridged a Basic Law right because of the lack of clear statutory authority to take action. To the common lawyer this may seem like a simple application of the *ultra vires* rule in administrative law. But these are cases where government actions went all the way through Germany's own very effective administrative law court hierarchy with no hindrance and still failed, at the constitutional level, to show a strong enough statutory backing.

Parties, Elections, and Finance

There are two areas where the FCC has most obviously been active in trying to build the bases of democracy: directly in its rulings on parties and elections, and indirectly in its rulings on broadcasting. As far as electoral politics goes, the court seems to have operated on two principles. The first, obviously derived from the constitution, has been a concern for equality of each citizen's chance of affecting politics. This primarily, but not only, means that each vote must count equally. The second principle is that of equal chances for all parties. While the first principle is, or ought to be, compatible with majoritarianism, the second is not necessarily so. Where constitutional courts are involved with electoral conflict there is no great logical difference from their general business of protecting minorities. Major parties seldom advocate policies that are blatantly against minority interests, but they will, given a chance, design electoral systems that penalise small parties. They also like to organise parliamentary life in ways that minimise the impact of small political parties, and the FCC has, usually, sprung to the defence of such parties in parliament. Most of the courts in the new Eastern European democracies have had to deal with this ever present phenomenon of party democracy, and they have not always been as sensitive to minority rights as the FCC has, on the whole, been. Admittedly the first time a new minor party challenged the major parties in the Bundestag it lost before the FCC, but the dissenting judgements were so powerful that the court has been more sensitive to such demands in later years. It has even protected a single member of the Bundestag who, having resigned his party mem-

[69] M Albers, "Rethinking the Doctrinal System of Fundamental Rights: New Decisions of the Federal Constitutional Court," 2002 3 *German Law Journal* (e-journal) 11; R Ruge, "Between Law and Necessity: The Federal Constitutional Court Confirms the Right of the Federal Government to Warn the Public," 2002 3 *German Law Journal* (e-journal) 12. The cases are Rogers and Vanberg, "Judicial Advisory Opinions," and R Rogowski and T Gawron, *Constitutional Courts in Comparison: The U.S. Supreme Court and the German Federal Constitutional Court* (Oxford: Berghahn Books, 2002).

bership, found himself deprived of all committee membership. Ironically, the same party was involved in both these cases. In 1986 the new Green Party was excluded from a select committee that controlled the intelligence agencies but lost its challenge before the FCC. In 1989 the Greens tried to prevent their own ex-member from sitting on committees, and he won.[70] In both cases, though, the FCC showed itself almost equally concerned with the need for efficient and stable government and with the equality of groups and individuals once elected. As an indication of the relations between parliament and the court, it should be noted that many of the latter's decisions on the rights of parliamentary minorities and of independent MPs have subsequently been written into the parliament's own procedural rules. Many of the decisions are aimed at preventing parliamentary majorities from freezing minorities out of debating time, or otherwise blunting their effectiveness. Very similar issues have been before the constitutional courts of Central and Eastern Europe, where the new party systems are vulnerable to such attempted manipulation. In one sense this is a clear example of a constitutional court being "counter-majoritarian"—but it is hardly one that most democrats would think inappropriate.[71]

Where it comes to the process of getting elected, minorities have faired even better. The classic case, perhaps, arose after reunification. Application of the old federal election law would undoubtedly have penalised parties in the new Länder from the former East Germany. Germany has always had a threshold rule to avoid the election of too many small and splinter parties. A party has to gain a minimum of 5 percent of the vote cast nationwide to gain its share of the 50 percent of seats allotted on a party list vote system. (The other 50 percent of seats are directly elected from constituencies.) The new and the remnant parties in the East had no chance of getting a national 5 percent, though they would poll well in the East itself. The initial solution suggested was precisely the sort of deal typically cooked up by existing parties to protect themselves. It would allow East German parties to enter alliances with the major traditional parties so that, as far as the list-based seats went, they would "piggyback" on the successes of the old parties. This would inevitably penalise parties that, like the PDS, a reformed eastern Communist party, would find no allies. It would also disadvantage existing minor parties who could get no helping hand. Thus both the SED from the East and the small far right Republican Party, along with the Green Party, went to the FCC. The FCC accepted that new rules could be made on a one-off basis for this first ever German-wide election because of the shortage of time some parties would have had to experience democracy. But it refused flatly to countenance a plan that so obviously denied its own equal chance principle, and the court insisted on a revision that the Bundestag ultimately complied with.[72]

[70] *Green Party Exclusion Case*, 70 BVerfGE 324 (1986) (German Federal Constitutional Court); *Wüppesahl Case*, 80 BVerfGE 188 (1989) (German Federal Constitutional Court).

[71] Source is a conference paper in my possession: P Cancik, "Making Parliamentary Rights Effective—the Role of the Constitutional Courts in Germany," (2004).

[72] *National Unity Election Case*, 82 BVerfGE 322 (1990) (German Federal Constitutional Court).

The most important cases on parties have been a whole series of party finance decisions, starting in 1957 and going on (at least) into the 1990s. Reviewing a series of Bundestag initiatives, the FCC has struggled to impose equality on federal funding, whether direct or through tax breaks to party contributors. The details are too complex to take on here, and are very well set out in Donald Kommers's massive study of German constitutional jurisprudence.[73] It is one of the very few areas in which the FCC has fundamentally changed its mind, with a major 1992 ruling in *Party Finance VII* that reversed most of its decisions in a series of related cases from *Party Finance II* in 1966 to *Party Finance VI* in 1986. There have been two core issues for the FCC: one is to ensure at least roughly equal chances to parties; the other is to find some way of constitutionally legitimating state funding while at the same time keeping the state itself from even the suspicion of controlling the political parties.[74]

Equality showed itself very early when the FCC agreed with a Social Democrat Party complaint that the original tax breaks for party contributors inevitably favoured parties with rich contributors. Similarly the court has been concerned at any plans that favoured large and well-established parties over new and small parties, without going so far as to say that electoral strength could not at all be a measure of how much finance a party deserved. The intertwining of state and party has caused the FCC much more trouble. It was this that the court backed away from in the 1992 ruling, with the effect that political parties are now rather less well financed from state funds than had at one time been the case.[75] The court had tried to erect a distinction between funding for the general activities of parties, and funding specifically for election campaigns. In this way the court could allow state support for the "forming the political will" function in fighting elections, without inculpating the state and the parties in an unhealthy relationship by allowing state funding of the very existence of the parties. The constitution sets out the main doctrine on parties in Article 21, which provides, inter alia, "Political parties shall participate in the formation of the political will of the people." But by 1992 this formulation had proved unworkable, and the FCC's retrenchment went even further, by slapping much tighter limits on individual tax breaks and denying them altogether to corporate supporters.

In some ways the FCC has made a burden for itself by its initial generous attitude towards the very status of political parties. So keen was it to make good on the Basic Law's idea that the parties helped "form political will" that it actually promoted political parties to the status of constitutional institutions in two very early decisions. In the *Socialist Reich* decision of 1952 the FCC argued that Article

[73] Kommers, *Constitutional Jurisprudence*, 181–216.

[74] Political scientists have become quite concerned about collusion between major parties and the state over funding, even suggesting a whole new type of party system is emerging. RS Katz and P Mair, "Changing Models of Party Organizations and Party Democracy: The Emergence of the Cartel Party," 1995 1 *Party Politics* 5–28, though this has been criticised for example in K Detterbeck, "Cartel Parties in Western Europe?" 2005 11 *Party Politics* 2, 173–91.

[75] Political scientists have been sufficiently concerned over the role of state financing to invent a new category of political party in some analytic schema, the "Cartel" party. See the preceding note.

21 "treats political parties as more than mere politico-sociological organizations; they are raised to the rank of constitutional institutions."[76] The seal was set on this promotion in a 1954 case when the FCC ruled that the crucial role of forming the political will during election campaigns entitled parties to the same status as other state organs, and that they could therefore bring cases to protect their rights directly to the constitutional court.[77] Although the FCC has never managed quite to solve the tensions involved in the *ParteienStaat*, it has certainly made political success more attainable to minorities.

It is assumed in this book that there can hardly be any doubt that one function of judicial review must be the construction of basic democratic institutions. The word *construction* is chosen because when the FCC strikes down part of a statute governing parties or elections, it is not in any normal sense "interpreting" the constitution, as an ordinary court might interpret a statute. The Basic Law is replete with references to democracy, but, perhaps understandably, nowhere defines it. There is no doubt that the FCC must undertake the job of building democratic institutions, if only because no other body can be trusted to do so. This is a recurrent problem in transforming societies, as will be seen particularly clearly in the chapters on Eastern Europe and South Africa. Yet working out what "democracy" requires in an electoral system or a regime of party financing cannot be anything but a highly creative job of making political theory on the run. In one way there is no formal difference between interpreting "property" and interpreting "democracy'; but the sheer blankness of the canvass in the latter case is the crucial difference that makes the creativity so much more obvious. As long as political parties are to be seen as "constitutional institutions," the task can be seen as equivalent to the structural or boundary-maintaining role I have previously identified as the less controversial aspect of constitutional review. But then, one has to remember that it was the constitutional court itself that promoted parties to this status.

Party "Speech" Rights

Equal attention has been paid by the FCC to protecting the "expressive rights" of unfashionable political parties. This is only briefly discussed here, because the general problem of free speech jurisprudence in Germany is retained for discussion in comparative perspective later in the book. Despite the FCC's attempt to do so, distinguishing between the legitimate constraints on an *individual's* speech, and what restrictions *parties* may have to live under in getting out their message, is probably futile. The court has made this attempt—most recently when refusing a constitutional complaint from someone prosecuted under a law that had banned a political association, the Kurdish Worker's Party (PKK). It was banned as a foreign association, not under the FCC's power to ban a political party, but under routine criminal law against extremist groups. The complainant had put up posters advocating the association, and claimed his criminal law prosecution contravened

[76] *Socialist Reich Party Case*, 2 BVerfGE 1 (1952) (German Federal Constitutional Court).
[77] *Plenum Party Case*, 4 BVerfGE 27 (1954) (German Federal Constitutional Court).

his Basic Law right to freedom of speech under Article 5. The FCC held, perhaps tenuously, that the law did not forbid individuals from supporting certain political goals, but only from pursuing them through the activities of a banned association.[78] It is again the problem of combining liberalism with "militant democracy." Usually, however, the FCC has supported the right of unpopular and minor parties to express themselves electorally. A good example is a case that displays all the tortured logic the FCC has found itself forced into by its pursuit of "militant democracy," and that contrasts well with the Kurdish activist's situation. The case, known as the *Radical Groups* case, was a constitutional complaint brought against decisions of the administrative courts that had supported TV and radio stations that had refused airtime to several extreme left-wing political parties, including the (by then reinvented and legal) Communist Party.[79] The FCC held that despite the clearly antidemocratic, antisystem content of the election adverts that the parties had submitted for broadcasting, the stations had no right to refuse them, given their general legal obligation to provide some amount of free airtime. What stands out is just how important it is to be a political party, and that only the FCC itself can rule that a party is unconstitutional. The mere fact that a party's programme might lead to such a ban were the court apprised of it does not prevent its having, until such a day, the protection of its party status. As long as something falls under the largely institutional definition of party, it is entitled to enjoy the equal opportunity rule the constitutional court has crafted. What is interesting, for the overall task of characterising constitutional review, is the openness with which the FCC admits that it is, itself, the author of this equality principle. As the court said in the *Radical Groups* case:

> While this right of all parties to equal opportunity is not expressly mentioned in the Basic Law, [it] may be inferred from the significance associated with the multiparty principle [sanctioned by the Basic Law] and the [guaranteed] freedom to establish political parties. . . . This basic right extends not only to the election itself but also, since elections are influenced by measures of public authority, to campaign propaganda . . . so necessary for electioneering in modern mass democracy.

The FCC is engaging in what is often called, in other legal contexts, "imputing" a right from the context of the whole constitution, or, much the same thing, deducing a structural principle. As long as the FCC has not acted—and it speaks specifically of its "jurisdictional monopoly" that "categorically precludes administrative action against the existence of a political party"—the court is clear that the Basic Law "tolerates the dangers inherent in the activities of such a political party." This is reminiscent of the NDP case mentioned earlier: parties are so precious that they are entitled to all the procedural protection the law can provide, even when,

[78] *PKK Case*, 1 BvR 98/97 (2002) (German Federal Constitutional Court). For an analysis of the case see D Wielsch, "Calibrating Liberty and Security: Federal Constitutional Court Rules on Freedom of Speech in PKK Case," 2002 3 *German Law Journal* (e-journal) 6.

[79] *Radical Groups Case*, 47 BVerfGE 198 (1978) (German Federal Constitutional Court).

as here, the parties in question have goals that, were they elected, would "constitute a political danger."

Whether the German constitutional court has been successful in squaring the circle between a *ParteienStaat* and a "militant democracy" is not relevant here. No one would try to argue that constitutional review bodies always succeed. What is clear is that the jurisprudence of the German court in this context demonstrates most clearly how special a function constitutional courts serve in any type of liberal democracy, but also how crucially constrained they are, even at their most imaginative, by the original document they start from.

In Conclusion

Much of what is important in the jurisprudence of the German Federal Constitutional Court has been passed over here in silence. Some of it, especially where equality and free speech rights are concerned, will be discussed in later comparative chapters. So important is this court that any synoptic discussion will depend on frequent mentions of the German approach. Other issues that might well have been discussed, for example the importance of the FCC's rulings on broadcasting[80] as part of building democracy, will come up when we tackle similar problems in other countries. The first of these discussions, in chapter 7, concerns two fundamental issues in rights discussion. Can "positive rights," sometimes called "socioeconomic rights," be made legally enforceable? New constitutions like those in Eastern Europe and South Africa clearly intend some degree of legal enforcement of such rights. But other, apparently more traditional jurisdictions like Canada have experienced demands for the courts to force governments to satisfy positive demands. Yet Canada is also a country where the other unorthodox "rights-demand" discussed in the chapter has been most resolutely refused by the courts. This is the question of whether or not the values of the constitution can be made to apply between nonstate actors, or whether they apply only in the relationship between the state and the private actor. These questions are crucial for the development of rights jurisprudence, and chapter 7 canvasses different approaches and answers in the various jurisdictions to come to some conclusion about the likely future for such rights.

What this chapter has attempted is a synthesis of some aspects of the jurisprudence to show, through looking at one country, the crucial elements of a constitutional review body's function, and how that role is carried out.

But there is another area, alluded to throughout this chapter, and signalled in chapter 1, which is largely left to a later chapter—the whole question of how specific decisions are reached; how a principle, once derived, is applied to generate an answer to a specific case. This comes under the basic idea of "constitutional tests," the formulae applied to get from principle, via facts, to decision. This topic,

[80] A good general survey of the issues is given in P Humphreys, "The Goal of Pluralism and the Ownership Rules for Private Broadcasting in Germany: Re-regulation or De-regulation?" 1998 16 *Yeshiva University Cardozo Arts & Entertainment Law Journal* 527.

nonetheless, I need to discuss very briefly here, because one problem of the cases discussed in this chapter, which must in all probability have struck readers, is how the decisions actually operate in later cases before ordinary courts, or how they can guide other state actors seeking to behave constitutionally. The methodology of constitutional jurisprudence, the moves a review body has to go through, can be divided in several ways. I will use a simple model here, and illustrate it with one of the more recent cases I cite above.

The case concerning public statements by government ministers about the religious group Osho was problematic for German constitutional lawyers because the classic test applied by the FCC to assess the constitutionality of intrusions into a protected right has had three elements. One, defining the scope of the right, we can ignore. The second is finding a legal basis on which the state can have acted. The importance of this was stressed earlier when talking about the way courts can serve democracy simply by ensuring that the actions of the government rest, directly or otherwise, on parliamentary authority in a statute. This was lacking for the Osho and contaminated wine cases, because though the individual Länder seem unambiguously to have such a power to warn the public, there is no equivalent statutory basis for the federal government to act. Thus the FCC had to invent a new authorisation to act, by creating a hitherto unheard-of public duty of "Governance" that entitles the federal government to issue public warnings. The court claimed this followed from the general provision in the Basic Law on the formation and tasks of the federal government. Controversial though this may be to academic constitutional lawyers in Germany, it is not the step that most concerns us here. The whole process of constitutional review is one of expanding or narrowing governmental activity, and difficult though it may be in many ways, it does not present the special problems I wish to draw attention to as peculiarly present inside the German model.

It is the largely uncontroversial final step that raises a fundamental problem, one mentioned, giving a French example, in chapter 1. In Germany the final step, after defining the scope of the right and identifying the authority to act, is to judge whether it is something that, in the extant case, the government should not do. To act constitutionally the measure has to be appropriate, necessary, and proportionate, and it must be aimed at a legitimate goal—the sort of thing the state should be concerned about. Most constitutional review bodies use tests with similar elements, and the range of such tests, which can vitally affect how intrusive a constitutional court is, will be canvassed thoroughly in chapter 7. The legitimate goal requirement does not provide many problems, at least in high-consensus societies like Germany. The trouble with the other three elements of the constitutionality test is that they have a rather odd epistemological character, neither purely normative nor entirely empirical. And to the extent that they are empirical, it is not clear how courts are to go about them. A governmental action will pass muster if it is

1. Appropriate because it is objectively suitable to achieve the task
2. Necessary in not going beyond what is necessary to achieve the task
3. Not disproportionate to the accomplishment of the task.

These tests are difficult and inevitably subjective, as are their counterparts in any jurisdiction. All three branches of the test inevitably involve matching the worth of the aim to the measures, which is a value judgement, as well as knowing whether there were other tools available, which might be an empirical matter, but equally might be one in which no one can engage without sheer guesswork. It is crucial to see that constitutional review requires these intellectual feats on a daily basis worldwide. The trouble with the German situation is that the FCC has set itself a task even harder by its overarching insistence that the Basic Law represents a unity, a cohesive moral philosophy, and not a set of discrete values to be checked off where a single one of them applies. Furthermore, because the judges have refused to set up a hierarchy of values, they are very frequently involved in applying these tests where two constitutional values—one might more properly call them two instantiations of the overall unified constitutional value choice—conflict. Take one of the first cases mentioned, *Benetton II*. This presented the following choice—was the objective protection of human dignity (the Benetton adds featured AIDS victims) to outbalance the freedom of expression of the magazine that published them, and was it appropriate to apply the Unfair Competition Act to suppress the adverts? In the *PKK* case was the infringement of freedom of speech the correct balance against the dangers to society, given the detailed factual context, and was a criminal conviction and fine appropriate to the situation? In several cases on religious freedom the FCC has had to decide not only whether an atheist's right not to have his child exposed to Christian influences should outbalance the religious preferences of other parents, but whether this outbalancing should lead therefore to a ban on prayer in a classroom. (In contrast the much simpler question for the US Supreme Court, which disapproves of balancing, is just whether or not school prayer implies government support for religion.) The problem is not that the FCC has to handle such difficult questions—it only has to blame itself for the shape of its tasks. The problem is whether or not its decisions can really ever be applied with any confidence by other courts or administrators later on with new fact situations. The FCC itself claims not to try to second-guess lower courts, but only to ensure that they have considered every relevant issue when they do their own balancing. But there is no obvious logical distinction between saying that undue weight was given to one or other element, which would allow overruling, and that a particular judge would balance them differently, which would not. *Benetton II* came to the FCC twice precisely because the highest civil court in the federation, told to think again and consider all the relevant values, did so, and returned their original answer.

So detailed and "factually" based are the decisions of the FCC that it is unclear to what extent it has really succeeded in deriving constitutional doctrine, as opposed to giving justice in the handful of cases it has time to hear. The balancing of the ex-husband's freedom of contract rights against his ex-wife and her son's rights to freedom and dignity rights was done against the background of a mass of statistical information on the earnings of single parents. Would a lower-paid ex-husband facing a wife with a better job have balanced out that way? There are plenty of critics of the way the FCC uses its vision of the Basic Law as a unified moral code with one supreme value of human dignity and a secondary one of the free development of personhood. Several of these critics are themselves former members of the court. What the more interesting critics have in common is a fear of the very vagueness of those two concepts. Given the huge importance of the Federal German Constitutional Court for other jurisdictions, it will be important to see to what extent these problems are replicated elsewhere. Has the FCC set itself, or perhaps, has it set the rest of Germany, just too rich an intellectual task? Has it set the rest of the world too difficult a goal to aspire to? But at least we now have a vision of what constitutional review can amount to to guide us in examining other jurisdictions.

CHAPTER THREE

Eastern Europe: (Re)Establishing the Rule of Law

Commonalities

The Need for Structural Constitutional Review

All the East and Central European new democracies after 1990 wrote constitutional courts into their constitutions. As far as one can tell, they did so with no hesitation, and with no sense that they were exercising choice; it seems that the idea of a constitution logically implied constitutional courts and judicial review.[1] But in fact it was a choice—and by no means the obvious one. The truth is that many indisputably democratic Western states do not have judicial review, or not full review. France, as shown later in this book, has a form of it, largely by accident, and in a way that most emphatically was not intended by the authors of the Fifth Republic constitution. The United Kingdom is beginning to edge marginally towards a very weak form. Even that weak form has run into government criticism, especially when the Law Lords have interfered with antiterrorist legislation.[2] Italy has a constitutional court, but one that has seldom been of importance in its politics, though over the last decade it has shown some signs of life.[3] Belgium

[1] For a general account of this process see H Schwartz, *The Struggle for Constitutional Justice in Post-Communist Europe* (Chicago: University of Chicago Press, 2000).

[2] *A and Others v Secretary of State for the Home Department; X and Another v Secretary of State for the Home Department*, 3 All ER 169 [2005] (House of Lords).

[3] For an account of the earlier days see V Vigoriti, "Italy: The Constitutional Court," 1972 20 *American Journal of Comparative Law* 3, 404–14. The main English-language treatment of the Italian court is M Volcansek, *Constitutional Politics in Italy* (London: Macmillan, 2000).

does not, nor the Netherlands, nor anywhere in Scandinavia except Norway.[4] New Zealand does not have full judicial review, and though Australia does, its High Court has no bill of rights to interpret and little interest in developing such powers.[5] This Central European enthusiasm occurred even though several countries, notably Poland and Hungary, were not to get fully fledged new constitutions until years after the courts were set up—and in Hungary's case, there is still no new purpose-built constitution. Clearly these countries believed a constitutional court could do something for them that they needed in their new situation.[6] (The Polish Constitutional Tribunal actually predates the end of the Communist era, but we can assume that the way it was fought for in the earlier days is itself symptomatic of this felt need for whatever it is that such a body can do.)[7]

There are in fact two answers to why a new democracy with a written constitution might think it needed a constitutional court, especially before any habits or rules of the game have had time to develop amongst political actors. This was discussed in chapter 1 at some length, but a brief recap here will help. Constitutions are, amongst other things, just big tables of organisation, saying who shall do what within the state. New political systems have highly permeable boundaries between functional roles, and the actors filling the roles can be guaranteed to wish to expand their remits.[8] Constitutional courts exist, particularly in the early days of a political system, to keep such actors firmly within their role definitions. This requirement is always present. American organizational experts have the evocative, if ugly, concept of "mission creep" that covers the inexorable process of ambition to take on more authority, and it applies to the most stable and developed of political systems. In the UK in 1995 for example a case between the Home Office and the Fire Brigades Union involved the home secretary trying to usurp Parliament's role in setting the level of compensation for victims of crime.[9] Only fairly recently have the Law Lords finally achieved the proper separation of powers in criminal sentencing when they managed to strip the home secretary of his involvement in setting the time a murderer would have to serve in prison, a clearly judicial func-

[4] C Smith, "Judicial Review of Parliamentary Legislation: Norway as a European Pioneer," 2000 *Public Law* 595–606.

[5] A study that shows how unwilling some of the Australian judiciary are to having anything like a bill of rights is JL Pierce, *Inside the Mason Court Revolution: The High Court of Australia Transformed* (Durham, N.C.: Carolina Academic Press, 2006). On New Zealand see KJ Keith, "Concerning Change: The Adoption and Implementation of the New Zealand Bill of Rights Act 1990," 2000 31 *Victoria University Wellington Law Review* 721–47. For a broader perspective on New Zealand's constitution and the courts, see G Palmer, "The New Zealand Constitution and the Power of Courts," 2005 15 *Transnational Law and Contemporary Problems* 551–79.

[6] An idea of how great the difficulties seemed in the early days can be gained from an article by Sajo, before he lost his faith in the Hungarian court. A Sajo, "On Old and New Battles: Obstacles to the Rule of Law in Eastern Europe," 1995 22 *Journal of Law and Society* 1, 97–104.

[7] MF Brzezinski, *The Struggle for Constitutionalism in Poland*, St Antony's Series (Basingstoke: Macmillan, 2000).

[8] My argument here is very similar to Shapiro's account of the origins of the European Court of Justice: M Shapiro, "The European Court of Justice," in Craig and Búrca, *Evolution of EU Law*.

[9] *R v Secretary of State for the Home Department, Ex parte Fire Brigades Union*, 2 AC 513 [1995] (House of Lords).

tion that the European Convention on Human Rights does not allow to elected politicians.[10] The clearest example of a form of judicial review being written into a new constitution to keep the institutions within new constitutional bounds is the existence of the Conseil constitutionnel in France. As discussed in a later chapter, no country has a history more hostile than France to judges being involved in politics. The very idea of a court-like body being able to strike down legislation has been anathema since the Revolution, yet de Gaulle had no doubt that he needed to create such an entity in 1958, because his new constitution required an unprecedented stripping of powers away from the parliament to the executive. French political culture was so strongly "legislature-oriented" that nothing else would do. The new democracies clearly had to have a similar restraining entity, particularly as the doctrine of the separation of powers seems to have appeared almost definitional of democracy to many of these constitution builders. (It was also later one of the conditions set by the European Union for membership, but the decisions to add a constitutional court to the new constitutions can hardly have been much influenced by assuming such a future requirement.)

From the earliest days of the new constitutions their constitutional review bodies were faced with questions like these:

- From Poland: The president has the power to appoint the chairman of the Television and Radio Commission—but can he fire him?
- From Hungary: Must the president appoint the nominees of the prime minister to certain posts, where he is the formal appointing officer, or is he merely required to consider the candidacies?
- From Bulgaria: Does the government or the president have the power to appoint the head of the National Intelligence Service and the ambassadors; can the government rather than the president take control of the National Guards Service?
- From Poland: A 1995 act of the Polish parliament gave itself the right to veto proposed sales under the privatisation programme. Was that a breach of the separation-of-powers doctrine?
- From the Czech Republic: Does the president require the agreement of the prime minister to appoint a governor of the Czech National Bank?

And, of course, in countries less ready for parliamentary democracy, these decisions were not always accepted, and were never easy.[11] It would be tempting, but a mistake, to assume that the need for this function withers away, may indeed

[10] *Regina (Anderson) v Secretary of State for the Home Department*, 1 AC 837 [2003] (House of Lords).

[11] The best study of the early days of the East European courts is Schwartz, *Struggle for Constitutional Justice*. There is now an extensive literature. See, for example, I Pogany, *Righting Wrongs in Eastern Europe*, Europe in Change (Manchester: Manchester University Press, 1997), as well as country-specific studies mentioned later. The now defunct *East European Constitutional Review* is a good source for most of the 1990s. A very thorough survey of the problems is W Sadurski, A Czarnota, and M Krygier, eds., *Spreading Democracy and the Rule of Law? The Impact of EU Enlargement on the Rule of Law, Democracy and Constitutionalism in Post-Communist Legal Orders* (Dordrecht: Springer, 2006).

already have largely withered away in the three Eastern European countries chosen for this study. If the United Kingdom is still having problems—and France certainly is, from politicians' "mission creep"—Eastern Europe can expect to need its constitutional courts for some considerable time yet. As recently as 2002, for example, the Czech Constitutional Court had to intervene to put a stop to a technique the lower house of its parliament had developed to prevent the Senate voting on matters its majority wanted to keep to themselves. The Czech constitution forbids the Senate to have any involvement in the budget process. Increasingly, therefore the majority in the lower house was passing nonbudgetary legislation in the guise of amendments to the budget. When finally the Senate went ahead and voted on the nonbudget element of such a hybrid measure, the matter went to the Constitutional Court on the grounds that it was the *Senate* that was acting unconstitutionally. The court was not having this, and very firmly stated:

> From the perspective of the Constitution, it is impermissible to tack on to a bill on the State budget a provision which in substance bears no direct connection to the substance of the State budget.

Apparently still not entirely trusting the lower house, the court goes on to insist:

> it does not suffice to limit oneself to consideration of the formal designation of such a bill. Such an approach would, in consequence, lead to the situation where the Senate could, in the case of certain important statutes, be excluded from the legislative process simply by designating that bill an act on the State budget, even if in fact that statute were to regulate substance having no direct connection with the State budget. On the other hand, the Constitutional Court considers it necessary to emphasize that the substantive conception of the term, "act on State budget," should not in practice lead to too broad an interpretation, since it is evident that practically every bill is related, either directly or indirectly, to the State budget.

The court even went so far as to cite the Irish constitution as a model of how to define a budget act. But this did not end the process, and in 2006 the court was still fighting to empower the Senate, this time on its right to have a say in election law.[12] (The Polish court has more than once had to come to the aid of its Senate too—it may be that the more directly elected lower houses, being more easily populist, are the main enemies of constitutional review.[13]) No doubt that other parliaments in other Eastern European countries will continue to generate business of this

[12] *Decision of 22 June 2005—Role of Senate in Election Law*, Pl. US 13/05 (Czech Republic Constitutional Court).

[13] *Inequality in Competences of Sejm and Senate Committees in Respect of EU Proposals*, K24/04 (2005) (Polish Constitutional Tribunal). I have used the names of cases given in the sources cited, though Polish cases do not routinely have names in the official reports. The sources are, up to 1997, a compilation of cases provided by the tribunal, J Oniszczuk, ed., *A Selection of the Polish Constitutional Tribunal's Jurisprudence from 1986 to 1999* (Warsaw: Polish Constitutional Tribunal, 1999); and, from 1997, the tribunal's website (http://www.trybunal.gov.pl). The latter are summaries, though very complete ones, and do not contain direct quotations. The cases reported in Oniszczuk are presented as direct quotations.

sort for a long time yet. It is nearly half a century since the French adopted their fifth constitution, yet each year there are two or three examples of impermissible boundary crossing.

The Need for the Rule of Law

Yet this function of constitutional courts, as boundary maintainers, is not what differentiates the new democracies from most of the old ones. It is when we come to look at the rights-protecting role of constitutional courts that the differences between East and West stand out most. In a nutshell, the Western tradition has been to see constitutions as essentially value-free documents. Of course they sometimes have bills of rights, but each "right" is taken alone, protected as a highly circumscribed restriction on government, and never seen as just an instantiation of a general set of values the constitution must enforce on the state. In other words, the German understanding of a constitution, discussed at length in the previous chapter, is not found in most jurisdictions. The most obvious area where this shows is with positive or socioeconomic rights. Certainly socioeconomic rights exist in Eastern Europe. Those who know nothing else about the courts in Poland and Hungary know that they have ruled parts of the national economic recovery strategies unconstitutional, because of a failure to protect welfare rights. One commentator has suggested in fact that in its first few years of activity after 1990 the Polish tribunal heard more social welfare cases than it did cases on more ordinary political rights.[14] (These issues are discussed both in the chapter on South Africa and more comparatively in chapter 8.) The interesting point about such rights, as handled by Eastern courts, is not just that they have been recognized, but the logic used to solve them. In South Africa recognizing rights to housing or health care has been a relatively straightforward matter of pointing to a very well specified entitlement in the constitution; the important arguments in South Africa happened during the process of ratifying the constitution itself. At that stage the Constitutional Court publicly accepted that positive rights were justiciable, and denied that they involved a breach in the separation of powers, or at least, that they involved a greater breach than many "negative" rights did. In Hungary and Poland, however, a further vital step has been added, by calling into play a core constitutional value that permeates much of the jurisprudence in these two countries, as in the Czech Republic and elsewhere. At one level this legal step may seem trivial, even obvious. But if it does, it will seem so only to an audience steeped already, perhaps without realizing it, in the expectations and hopes that lead to these courts being created. The concept in question is one for which the standard English translation is quite inadequate—the idea of "the rule of law." Naturally, one might think, constitutional courts must protect and further the rule of law. It is, apart from anything else, written into the very constitutional definition of the polities. In Poland, Article 2 of the constitution spells this out: "The Republic of Poland shall be a democratic state ruled by law and implementing the principles of social justice."

[14] Schwartz, *Struggle for Constitutional Justice*, 64, 232–34.

Similarly the Czech constitution stipulates in Article 1(1): "The Czech Republic is a sovereign, unitary, and democratic state governed by the rule of law, founded on respect for the rights and freedoms of man and of citizens." And in Hungary the constitutional act begins, "In order to facilitate a peaceful political transition to a state under the rule of law, realizing . . . a social market economy."

To a Western eye this reference to the rule of law, or to a state governed by law, is too obvious to stand out. It seems almost meaningless, trite, even window dressing. Yet of course it was the prime reason for the new constitutions, the one thing that made constitutional courts indisputably necessary. If one reads the opinions of the Polish tribunal, this phrase comes up over and again—that Poland is a state governed by law, or that such and such a decision is forced by the acceptance of a state ruled by law. To Western eyes, the rule of law is a positivist conception—it carries only procedural weight. It is not a value applied to test a law, merely the requirement to have a law.[15] Thus although a democracy does require that regulations and so on be passed in a way that has formal validity, there is no substantive content. In the courts discussed in this chapter, "the rule of law" is more of a "black box" into which judges can load constitutional values. The rule of law is, in H.L.A. Hart's famous terminology, a "rule of recognition." Were that all it was in the Polish or Hungarian courts, it would still be of vital importance. In many ways the horrors of the past came about because not even procedural constraints existed. If one gives a classic definition of the rule of law it is Aristotelian in origin: the "rule of law and not of men," *non sub homine, sed sub lege*. This is perhaps why so many substantively important constitutional court decisions in Eastern Europe depend on what seem at times relatively minor procedural failures. The first important decision of the Hungarian court on abortion, for example, depended on the fact that an instruction to doctors was given by ministerial ordinance, not statute law. The Polish court has perhaps been even more concerned than others to demand careful observance of procedure. The Czech court has several times directly addressed the positivist versus substantivist orientation to the idea of the rule of law, usually in terms such as these, taken, interestingly, from before the "Velvet Divorce":

> Thus, the concept of the law-based state does not have to do merely with the observance of any sort of values and any sort of rights, even if they are adopted in the procedurally proper manner, rather it is concerned first and foremost with respect for those norms that are not incompatible with the fundamental values of human society as they are expressed in the Charter of Fundamental Rights and Basic Freedoms.[16]

[15] Obviously there are exceptions to this generalisation. Interesting treatments of the idea are found, inter alia, in RH Fallon, "'The Rule of Law' as a Concept in Constitutional Discourse," 1997 97 *Columbia Law Review* 1; SL Esquith, "Toward a Democratic Rule of Law: East and West," 1999 27 *Political Theory* 3, 334–56; and, especially relevant to this discussion, S Coyle, "Positivism, Idealism and the Rule of Law," 2006 26 *Oxford Journal of Legal Studies* 2, 257–88.

[16] *Decision of 26 November 1992 on Lustration*, Pl. US 1/92 (Constitutional Court of the Czech and Slovak Federal Republic).

Exactly what values are inherent in the rule of law clearly varies from court to court, probably from judge to judge. What is crucial for my argument is that the application of a "rule of law" test *is* a value application, a substantive judgement as well as a positivist or procedural judgement. This is why it has had such utility and produced results that could not be produced in a West European or North American court. The Polish tribunal's decision to strike down the 1991 Pensions Act is one of the earliest of its cases to come to the eyes of the West, and it was only one of several cases where welfare entitlements were upheld. The main logic behind these decisions was not reference to a specific freestanding welfare entitlement in the constitution, as were similar cases in South Africa. The same is true for the Hungarian court's striking down of parts of the budget in 1995. Both these decisions, and many others in both countries, were actually justified under the doctrine of protection of legitimate expectations, which was said to be a part of the commitment to the rule of law.[17] Is it? Many Western commentators are more likely to argue that legal protection of legitimate expectations, or the more general legal value of certainty in the law, is one of the things that a state might commit itself to, but is not, cannot be, definitional of whether it is a state ruled by law. The claim is that any general level of pension entitlement, or even an entitlement to a pension at all, is logically entirety separable from the question of whether the rule of law is abided by. However, there are good reasons for taking the Polish, and even more, the Hungarian stance on this. The problem is that it is easy to argue that a constitutional court, in supporting socioeconomic rights, is breaching the separation of powers, is involving itself in policymaking in a way that is illegitimate. If it is true that boundary maintenance is at risk in a new democratic state, then it is just as important that the court stay on its side of the border as that the elected politicians and the executive stay on theirs. On the whole these courts have been careful to abide by such boundaries. The Hungarian court, for example, has regularly held that the state's obligation to provide social welfare is satisfied as long as it has a proper and worked-out welfare system; it is not for the court to investigate the actual levels of payment. This is fine, until the court wants to do just that. When the economic austerity package in 1995 involved major cuts in a series of welfare benefits, it had therefore to find a new argument. The argument used was that legal certainty was a prime value, being part of the indisputably vital rule of law, and the austerity programme was in breech of this certainty. The attraction of the strategy is obvious—no one can accuse a court of straying from its just remit when it is doing nothing more than imposing the rule of law, because the rule of law is absolutely its business.

The best test case for how flexible the idea of the rule of law must be is given in the hugely important "lustration" cases (an analysis of them forms the last section of this chapter). However, it is important to see that Eastern European courts do not just understand the idea of the rule of law differently than Western courts.

[17] A powerful counterargument to the idea that the rule-of-law concept is automatically a blessing is given in A Sajo, "How the Rule of Law Killed Hungarian Welfare Reform," 1996 *East European Constitutional Review* 31.

They also differ in their conception of their overall duty, and in this they are heavily influenced by the German court, where, of course, many of their judges studied. That court is very frequently cited elsewhere, as in South Africa, when a judge wants to typify a new way of looking at constitutions. In the words of the German court itself:

> The jurisprudence of the Federal Constitutional Court is consistently to the effect that the basic rights norms contain not only defensive subjective rights for the individual but embody at the same time an objective value system which, as a fundamental constitutional value for all areas of the law, acts as a guiding principle and stimulus for the legislature, executive and judiciary.

The Polish tribunal speaks less often in this way than others, but in Warsaw the ideas are just as rooted as they are in Prague. Perhaps the most coherent court on this sense of a mission to make the constitutional values radiate throughout society is the Hungarian court. In its first few years, above all, the idea of human dignity was, in the Hungarian version, "the mother right" from which all else flows.[18] But the Polish tribunal is just as prone to cite dignity, amongst other values. For example in February 2005 the tribunal struck down part of the 1984 press law because it appeared to give more protection to the dignity of a corporation or government department than to a human individual. The language is powerful:

> Human dignity, referred to in Article 30 of the Constitution, as a transcendent value, being supreme vis-à-vis all human rights and freedoms (since it constitutes the source thereof), is inherent and inalienable; it is intrinsic in human beings and may not be infringed by the legislator's activities or the actions of other entities. In this sense, a human being always retains their [*sic*] dignity and no action may deprive them thereof, nor constitute an infringement thereof. In its second meaning, human dignity appears in the guise of "personal dignity"—which may best be expressed as a right of personality, encompassing the values of the psychological life of each human being and all the values determining the position of the individual within society, which compose, within general opinion, the respect due to each person. Only dignity within this second meaning may be infringed by the actions of other persons and legal regulations.[19]

As argued in chapter 1, it may be when, and only when, a society gets a chance to rethink itself, and to put those thoughts down on paper, that one has the material on which a court can see itself in a new light—as, essentially, the moral guardian of the people. One can see this in less obvious cases as well. The French Conseil constitutionnel clearly sees itself nowadays as such a guardian, helping spread above all the values of nondiscrimination throughout legislation. Even better is the Canadian example. Up to 1982 the Canadian Supreme Court had no real role other

[18] An excellent treatment of the Hungarian importation of German ideas is Dupré, *Importing the Law*.

[19] *Public Prosecution of Offences Arising from Failure to Publish, Contrary to the Press Act, a Rectification or Response*, K10/04 (2005) (Polish Constitutional Tribunal), Summary Point 5.

than policing the boundaries inherent in Canada's federal structure. But once the Charter was in force, with a preamble very similar to that in many Eastern European constitutions, talk of human dignity became very common, and some of its decisions were, if not as supportive of positive rights as they might be, certainly very liberal. Above all we have the example of South Africa.

It is in part because they provide such a useful lens through which to see these other countries that Eastern European jurisprudence is a useful subject for this book. Concerns about length, as well as a relative paucity of English-language material, make it impossible to treat each of the major Eastern European courts at the level of detail it deserves. The second part of this chapter therefore gives very brief portraits of what strikes me as most characteristic of Poland, Hungary, and the Czech Republic. The third part, by giving a comparative analysis of their decisions on one common and vital theme, how to deal with the past, brings out more generally the lessons the area has for the rest of democratic constitutional jurisprudence. Before these sections, I will offer a two-country comparison on one issue that is often thought of as typical of jurisprudence in this region, the idea of positive or socioeconomic rights. The topic crops up in several places in this chapter, and the arguments intersect with others that also occur more than once. This is inevitable because even within one jurisdiction constitutional argument does not fall neatly into discrete blocks—and much less so when one is considering three jurisdictions whose differences are almost as important as their similarities.

A Look at Positive Rights in Poland and Hungary

A reliance on a rich concept of the rule of law has proved important where courts in this region tackle the idea of positive, or socioeconomic, rights.[20] There exist perfectly clearly stated socioeconomic rights in several of the constitutions of Central and Eastern Europe (CEE).[21] The Hungarian constitution, for example, provides in Article 70-E that "citizens of the Republic of Hungary have the right to social security; they are entitled to the support required to live in old age, and in the case of sickness, disability, being widowed or orphaned and in the case of unemployment through no fault of their own." It goes on to require that "The Republic of Hungary shall implement the right to social support through the social security system and the system of social institutions."

Similar double requirements, that a right be recognized and that the government set up machinery, exist for health and education. Poland has a whole chapter on Economic, Social and Cultural Freedoms and Rights, with articles like Article 67:

1. A citizen shall have the right to social security whenever incapacitated for work by reason of sickness or invalidism as well as having attained retire-

[20] South Africa, as described elsewhere in the book, has also found a link between the rule of law and positive rights. See *President of the Republic of South Africa v Modderklip Boerdery (PTY) Ltd.*, CCT 20/04 (South African Constitutional Court).

[21] Ideas similar to those in Poland and Hungary exist throughout the former Communist states, but the legal arguments are best exemplified in the cases from Poland and Hungary.

ment age. The scope and forms of social security shall be specified by statute.

2. A citizen who is involuntarily without work and has no other means of support, shall have the right to social security, the scope of which shall be specified by statute.

All the usual socioeconomic rights are covered in the same manner, and similar patterns are found throughout the CEE constitutions. Not surprisingly many of the early decisions of these courts were on socioeconomic rights, at least in part because the pro-capitalist revolutions produced inevitable uncertainty on the one area of strength in the socialist economies, the provision of relatively generous social expenditure.[22] There is a sense in which the Polish and Hungarian constitutions are less overtly aspirational than, for example, South Africa's constitution. One has to remember that because the respective histories are different, the salience of constitutional value commitments will be as well. No one in Eastern Europe had to stress the priority of welfare rights; rather the need was to find a way of maintaining them when quite other problems were in the forefront. For the Eastern Europeans, the "rule of law" is what transformation is all about, while in South Africa it has been the drive for equality that is all important. The social aspirations were already present for the Eastern Europeans, though they did indeed fear losing the historic priority of welfare. In both cases, and especially in Hungary, the jurisprudence of those constitutional guarantees themselves has not usually presented anything to disturb those dubious of the propriety of positive rights. The Hungarian court has regularly held that Article 70-E is satisfied as long as some form of welfare system is in place. Similarly there have been few challenges accepted in Poland that the statutes called for by articles like Article 67 as created by the Sejm are inadequate. Decisions otherwise would indeed have raised, fatally or not, the problem of separation of powers, a value the CEE countries, not least their courts, were strongly in favour of during this period because it was one of the conditions for entry into the European Union. Where welfare statutes were found at fault, it was more likely because they offended a different sort of value, especially unjustified or irrational discrimination, which is a far more "normal," perhaps a purely "negative," right entitlement.

A good example was a case in 1993 concerning problems in interpreting unemployment and social assistance legislation.[23] The Polish Constitutional Tribunal was clearly concerned that where the relevant act deals with provision of social assistance after the period when an unemployed person was entitled to an unemployment benefit, it "lacks a suitable normative content" because it appears to

[22] Schwartz, *Struggle for Constitutional Justice* (suggesting that the courts were heavily involved in such issues). There are counterclaims, notably Andras Sajo, who, at the time of writing, did not think the Hungarian court was as involved in such issues as might have been expected. A Sajo, "Reading the Invisible Constitution: Judicial Review in Hungary," 1995 15 *Oxford Journal of Legal Studies* 2, 253–67.

[23] *Decision of 13th July 1993—Unemployment Benefits*, in Oniszczuk, *Selection of Jurisprudence* (Polish Constitutional Tribunal), 103. Both the Polish and Hungarian cases I discuss are surveyed in B Bugaric, "Courts as Policy Makers: Lessons from Transition," 2001 42 *Harvard International Law Journal* 248–88.

leave the actual duties of social assistance institutions underdefined. Nonetheless, the tribunal's decision was to petition its own president to launch a tribunal investigation of the 1990 Social Assistance Act, rather than to strike down any part of the act under consideration, which was the 1991 Employment and Unemployment Act. The constitution, according to the tribunal, does contain a guarantee of social justice, and social justice requires that people not be left helpless after unemployment pay runs out. But, as the court says itself, "given its general and legally virtually undefined nature, the principle of justice does not, however, determine the legal form for the implementation of the justice formula with respect to the unemployed."[24] No negative rights theorist could object to such a description of the tribunal's approach. The court's concern was not that social justice requires any particular level of social assistance, or even any particular set of qualifications. Rather it argues the "function of the law requires that the right to such an allowance follow from a statute and the eligible person be entitled to make a claim, the satisfaction of which could be prosecuted in a court."[25] Where the court did act decisively was to strike down a part of the 1991 act, which differentiated between unemployed people depending on whether they had previously been involved in agricultural or nonagricultural sectors. The tribunal saw this distinction as simply an irrational and unjustified discrimination:

> No rational justification can be identified for the differentiation of citizens based on the form of their earlier professional activity. . . . matching the State's financial means to its obligations toward citizens cannot be achieved through differentiation that discriminates against legally defined groups of citizens.[26]

The thrust of both parts of this decision is the same, the overriding need for *legal* values: the proper justifications for unequal treatment, the proper concern for legally enforceable rights, as opposed to concern with the level of rights provision. In some ways it is reminiscent of French jurisprudence on discrimination, discussed later in the book. Very much the same attitudes coloured Hungarian jurisprudence through its great period of activism in the 1990s.[27] Over and again the court stressed that "the State has a wide margin of appreciation with respect to changes, regroupings and transformations within welfare benefits depending on economic conditions." All that is absolutely required is the provision of some welfare system:

> In [an earlier] decision, the Constitutional Court established as a general constitutional requirement that the right to social security contained in Article 70/E of the Constitution entails the obligation of the State to secure a

[24] *Unemployment Benefits*, 105.

[25] *Unemployment Benefits*, 107.

[26] *Unemployment Benefits*, 109.

[27] The best short account is by the court's first president, L Sólyom, "The Role of Constitutional Courts in the Transition to Democracy: With Special Reference to Hungary," 2003 18 *International Sociology* 1, 133–61.

> minimum livelihood through all of the welfare benefits necessary for the realisation of the right to human dignity.[28]

The state will be "deemed to have met its obligation specified in Article 70/E by organising and operating a system of social institutions including welfare benefits. Within this, the legislature can itself determine the means whereby it wishes to achieve its social policy objectives."

It seems that part of the court had struggled in early cases for a more intrusive role, but relatively early a compromise was struck whereby the margin of appreciation would be satisfied as long as total welfare provision did not fall below some notion of a minimum subsistence level.[29] So in the case from which the quotations are taken, proceedings were suspended to await a report on whether the challenged legislation would still "secure the minimum livelihood necessary for the realisation of the right to human dignity in line with the constitutional requirement specified in the holdings." How one reacts to this position depends largely on one's substantive political views. The president of the court at the time, who was on the losing side in the conflict, sees this as reducing socioeconomic rights to mere "state goals":

> This means that the ordinary test for (subjective) fundamental rights—necessity and proportionality—does not apply. This, in turn, amounts to a silent acceptance by the whole court of the understanding of social rights as being similar to "state goals," for which . . . only excessive infringements reach the level of constitutional significance.[30]

Others might more plausibly note that the strict negative liberty theory would not regard even excessive infringement of Article 70-E as entitling a court to strike down welfare legislation. They might also note that the minimum level is to be set by the court, and that it is tied, by the court itself, to the powerful but elastic conception of human dignity, a phrase that does not occur in the constitutional provisions for socioeconomic rights. More important, perhaps, is László Sólyom's arguably unwarranted description of a "real" right as one to which a specific limitation test applies. It may well be that a useful distinction between rights could be based on whether the proportionality/necessity limitation test applies, or some other. There are several alternative candidates, including the German conception of retaining the core meaning of a right, which would here be the implication of a minimum subsistence test.[31] But it by no means follows that the distribution of

[28] *Decision of 22 June 1998 on Unemployment Assistance*, 32/1998 (VI.25) AB (Hungarian Constitutional Court).

[29] KL Schepple, "Round Table Constitution-Making Process and the Rule of Law: Panel II, Constitutional Courts and the Rule of Law," 1997 12 *American University Journal of International Law and Policy* 85–115, 99.

[30] L Sólyom and G Brunner, *Constitutional Judiciary in a New Democracy: The Hungarian Constitutional Court* (Ann Arbor: University of Michigan Press, 2000), 37.

[31] In fact, the core minimum concept appears in the Hungarian constitution, as it did in the interim South African constitution, in both cases based on the German model, but has been little used.

rights into such categories would map closely onto the positive/negative rights or rights / state goals distinctions.

Despite this caution, these courts are nonetheless famous for really major intrusions into policy, to the point that any orthodox sense of the separation of powers becomes extremely weak. Both have struck down state retrenchment of social benefits, especially in the areas of pensions. In both cases, the government's policy was thought crucial to major economic reform, and in both cases, the decisions cost the state treasuries massive amounts of money. The crucial point is that both courts relied primarily not on specific socioeconomic rights, but on fundamental assumptions about the relationship between society and law. In Poland in 1992, the tribunal decided a complex of issues involving several interrelated statutes that were intended to cut pension benefits in multiple ways, especially the act of October 1991, On the Revaluation of Retirement and Disability Pensions. In all, the court found parts of these acts offended Article 67 (nondiscrimination), Article 7 (protection of personal property), and parts of Article 70. This latter is a more typical socioeconomic rights article, guaranteeing the right to health protection and to "assistance in the event of sickness or the inability to work." Article 70(2) states, "This right shall be implemented to an increasing degree by the development of social insurance to cover sickness, old age and inability to work, and enlargement of various forms of social assistance." These were used almost as additional arguments, however. The real work was done in the judgement by reliance on the very simple language of Article 1: "The Republic of Poland is a democratic state ruled by law and implementing the principles of social justice." Furthermore, Article 1 was applied twice, the tribunal finding most of the legislation in breach of both the conception of "a state ruled by law" and, separately, in breach of the idea that the state should implement "the principles of social justice."[32] Several of the many clauses struck down were found to be in breach of both limbs of this clause; the tribunal found it useful to make these separate attacks because it seems to have wished to mark the two lines of criticism as equally valid. The social justice arguments largely revolved round the expectation that pension and similar schemes would promote social solidarity by being redistributive, an aspect that the new legislation minimized. The tribunal does remind itself that "the velocity of change within the realm of economic and social relations, especially over a period of basic transformations . . . demands that the lawmaker be given a relatively broad range of freedom in moulding the law." It even cites German cases to support its admission that "as is the case in the constitutional legislation of other democratic states, the Constitutional Tribunal cannot test if, in detail, the lawmaker chooses the most expedient and appropriate solutions."[33] Nonetheless, in this area the tribunal gave quite detailed objections, citing expert opinion on, inter alia, the need for, and fail-

[32] The constitutional articles come from the 1952, i.e., Communist, constitution, relevant parts of which were kept in force by Article 77 of the 1992 constitutional act, usually called the "Small Constitution." Not until 1997 did Poland adopt an entirely new post-Communist constitution. The Polish Constitutional Tribunal is the only one of the CEE courts to predate the collapse of Communism.

[33] *Decision of 11th February 1992 (K. 14/91)—Pensions Laws*, in Oniszczuk, *Selection of Jurisprudence* (Polish Constitutional Tribunal), 63.

ure to provide, a "flattening" of the "benefit to contribution" ratios. Despite these words of caution, the Polish tribunal derived a very strong social justice restriction on the government's plans to deal with the economic problems of the state:

> retirement and disability rights cannot be restricted without agreeing that the criteria for selecting the types of resource financed by the State be socially justified and without an objective conviction that the State is undertaking sufficient actions to combat economic crisis. Furthermore, the concepts of social equality and justice signify that "the weights of economic crisis should encumber all social strata and not specifically affect only certain strata or groups," . . . especially if these were to have been pensioners.[34]

External Influences

Taking up a point from chapter 1, we note that these new courts are not lonely individuals. One of the most marked aspects of their jurisprudence is the widespread use of arguments and decisions from other constitutional courts. This was mentioned in chapter 1 and will be obvious in each jurisdiction chapter. I have discussed the phenomenon elsewhere and cannot to do more here than repeat my argument—that the effect of the intercitation of the newer constitutional courts is to begin to build an international constitutional common law.[35] One crucial question is pressing, and as yet unanswerable. What will be the impact on the development of these courts and their jurisprudence of their new membership of the European Union? In vital respects, the constitutional courts of Poland, Hungary, and the Czech Republic are no longer supreme—they owe deference to the Court of Justice of the European Union. Admittedly this is no different from the position of other European courts—even the English Law Lords must acknowledge the supremacy of EU law in some contexts. But the East European courts are in nations that have more recently had to satisfy the EU of their legal loyalties as the price of entry. How much deference do they really show, though? These courts are certainly good citizens of the newly developing commonwealth of constitutional courts. This can be shown by their concern, already well demonstrated, for the rulings of the European Court of Human Rights, and their willingness both to impose, and be influenced by, the European Charter on Human Rights. It is too early to know with any certainty how, for example, the Polish tribunal will orient itself to the ECJ. Certainly it will continue to be a good citizen, in part because the ECJ is as likely to be an ally against actions of other elements of the Polish state as an enemy of the court. The tribunal has indeed already handed down decisions in which it clearly relishes EU directives as an extra source of ammunition. A good example is a case in 2004 in which the Polish Bio Fuels Act was struck down, in part because rather than implementing an EU directive, the tribunal saw it as conflicting with that directive.[36] It is fairly clear

[34] *Pensions Laws*, 63.

[35] Robertson, *Democratic Transitions*.

[36] *Bio-Components in Gasoline and Diesel*, K33/03 (2004) (Polish Constitutional Tribunal).

Table 2
Past Careers of Constitutional Judges

Career	Hungary	Czech Republic	Poland	Total
Academic	8	5	6	19
Political		4	4	8
Civil servant	4	3	3	10
Judicial		3	2	5
Total	12	15	15	42

that the law would have been struck down as an unconstitutional interference with property and private enterprise anyway, but the EU was a convenient extra source of legitimacy. This is really the key—all the courts of the region have a legitimacy problem, and they have all sought to use international support. The very eagerness of the member states first to be accepted by the Council of Europe and then the EU has actually helped the national courts. Would the Hungarian public have so easily accepted the first controversial ruling of their court, abolishing the death penalty, had the European Convention on Human Rights not been just around the corner? Nonetheless, there are signs that the Polish tribunal has carefully positioned itself to protect its own rights against the ECJ, though it takes an equally careful reading of the tribunal's decision on the accession treaty to see that.[37] Again, similar positions do not make similar legal solutions inevitable. The European Arrest Warrant has been challenged before both the Polish and the Czech courts. The Poles found it in conflict with their constitution;[38] the Czechs found it compatible.[39] The constitutions are not very different textually.

Judicial Appointment

The individual political stories of how the courts in this region came to be set up are too complex to be gone into here. It is, though, worth briefly recounting the constitutional status and recruitment processes involved, all three countries having very similar arrangements, though rather different constitutional positions. In Hungary an existing constitution was amended; in the Czech Republic the current court, though it flows from the 1992 constitution, inherited from the equivalent court in the short-lived democratic Czechoslovakian constitution; and in Poland an existing Communist-era tribunal, modified, was already in place, to be altered

[37] *Poland's Membership in the European Union (the Accession Treaty)*, K18/04 (2005) (Polish Constitutional Tribunal).

[38] *Application of the European Arrest Warrant to Polish Citizens*, P105 (2005) (Polish Constitutional Tribunal).

[39] *Decision of 3d May 2006 European Arrest Warrant*, Pl. US 66/04 (Czech Republic Constitutional Court).

only marginally when the final 1997 Polish constitution came into being. Typically for such courts, the details of structure and appointment depend on ordinary legislation rather than being constitutionally specified—as was the case in Germany.

In Hungary the origin was a parliamentary resolution in January 1989, completed by a constitutional amendment writing in Article 32-A in October. The details were fleshed out in the same month in Act XXXII of 1989, with the court starting work in January 1990. But some time before the initial parliamentary resolution, much of the groundwork negotiations had taken place in the trilateral political roundtable negotiations that had cleared the path for full Hungarian democracy.

The "postdivorce" constitution of the Czech Republic, which was adopted in December 1992, required, in Chapter 4, the setting up of a constitutional court, though the details depend on a statute (Act No. 182/1993) that was passed in June 1993. The new court inherited the decisions and jurisprudence of its predecessor, and indeed at least one member of the new court had sat on the earlier version. (The extent to which some matters coming before the new court were *res judicata* in its predecessor's work has been a matter for some debate.)

In Poland the origin of the Constitutional Tribunal was the Communist-era Constitutional Tribunal Act of 29 April 1985. Though the tribunal was not without impact, the original act severely limited its competence, as well as allowing its decisions to be overruled by the Sejm (the lower house of parliament). In the initial agreements of 1989 and the "Small Constitution" of 1992, most limitations were removed, but not the role of the Sejm, and it was not until the full new constitution of 1997 that the tribunal became fully independent. The Constitutional Tribunal Act of 1 August 1997 set out the details of the new arrangements.[40]

The method of appointment in all three countries follows a similar pattern, with the parliament ultimately responsible for election to the court. The Hungarian system probably goes furthest in attempting to remove partisanship as decisive in curial election. The eleven members are elected to nine-year terms, nominated by a parliamentary committee with one member from each organized party group. Election requires a two-thirds vote of the entire parliament. Re-election to one further term is allowed, but has been very infrequent. The judges on the court elect their own president and vice president. Unusually, all of these details are in the constitution itself rather than in enabling legislation.

The Czech system appears modelled on America. The president appoints the fifteen judges "with the consent of the Senate" for ten-year terms, and also appoints, from their number, the chair and two vice chairs. In fact, because the Senate had not been established at the beginning of the court, the initial appointments

[40]The best accounts of these early days are given in Schwartz, *Struggle for Constitutional Justice*; Brzezinski, *Struggle for Constitutionalism*; and Dupré, *Importing the Law*. See also, for Poland, J Kurczewski, "Parliament and the Political Class in the Constitutional Reconstruction of Poland: Two Constitutions in One," 2003 18 *International Sociology* 1, 162–80; for Hungary, I Pogany, "Constitutional Reform in Central and Eastern Europe: Hungary's Transition to Democracy," 1993 42 *International and Comparative Law Quarterly* 2, 332–55; for the Czech Republic, Z Kuhn and J Kysela, "Nomination of Constitutional Justices in Post-Communist Countries: Trial, Error, Conflict in the Czech Republic," 2006 2 *European Constitutional Law Review* 2, 183–208.

had the consent instead of the Chamber of Deputies. Though this large court does much of its work through panels of three, the full "plenum" must sit for major decisions, which include not only annulling legislation, but also departing from its own precedents. At least ten members of the court are needed to constitute a plenum, and a supermajority of nine is required for annulment.

Poland, which also has a fifteen-person court, is slightly more open to partisanship, as any group of fifty deputies in the Sejm may nominate, but so also may the president of the Sejm acting alone, and election requires a simple majority, though at least half of the deputies must be present. Judges may not serve more than one term in office, and are expressly forbidden to be members of a political party or trade union.

Only a detailed study of the appointments to these courts could tell jut how partisan appointments actually are, but a glance at the current membership across the three countries suggests appointments are mainly given to established leading jurists, though, inevitably in continental Europe, such persons are more likely to have been academics than practising lawyers and judges—none of the three countries requires a quota of judges from the ordinary court system, as Germany and Italy do. This is hardly surprising because of the Communist Party background of most such people who would have been eligible at the beginning of the 1990s. Certainly there is a sprinkling of former professional politicians in the group. The Czech Republic and Poland both have four former politicians serving on their courts in 2008, though all of them were lawyers at some stage in their careers: all of these courts require such qualifications, unlike the French Conseil constitutionnel. (The Czech requirement is that justices have to "have been active for at least ten years in the legal profession," the Polish judges must have "the necessary qualifications to hold the office of a judge of a Supreme Court or the Supreme Administrative Court." Perhaps it is Hungary's rather more demanding requirement that only "jurists of outstanding theoretical knowledge or having at least twenty years of legal practice" can be elected that helps keep it more obviously a professional court—all its current members have been either academics of civil servants. A very rough breakdown of currently serving members is given in table 2. It is rough because many of these judges have had a complex career in several different fields, so that allocating them to any one "past" career is highly arbitrary. More to the point, these are all early appointments to courts, many made during or shortly after the democratic break, from within a relatively small non-Communist elite. How the courts will develop after a longer period of democratic consolidation cannot be predicted.

Poland

Procedural Propriety and the Rule of Law

Poland is unlike nearly all the new democracies of Eastern and Central Europe in one respect at least. Poland's constitutional review body, the Constitutional Tribunal, predates the collapse of the Communist state, being established in 1985 and starting work in January 1986.[41] The tribunal was one of the fruits of the slow pressure from Solidarity towards a reform of the state. Inevitably in its earlier incarnation it was very restricted in its powers, and even in the extent the judges were able to use the powers they did have. It is probably better to regard the tribunal in this first stage as more like a restricted administrative law court. Certainly no decisions before the collapse of the Communist regime are worth noting. The tribunal was reformed and enlarged after the full constitution came into force in 1997, but vital decisions were made under the several preceding constitutional settlements. These covered the periods December 31, 1989, to December 7, 1992, under a constitutional amendment to the old Communist constitution; December 8, 1992, to October 16, 1997, under what was called "the small constitution," and from October 17, 1997, when the full new constitution of the Polish republic came into force. (As for the issues we are concerned with in this chapter, there are few important differences between the small and full constitutions.) It is probably fair to say, however, that its origin as more or less an administrative law court has continued to affect the flavour of the tribunal's work, though it has not restricted either its acceptance of a fully constitutional role nor its courage in developing and enforcing constitutional values even when faced with a hostile parliament or executive. The effect is more in the terseness of its judgements and perhaps in the way it sometimes seems more concerned with procedure than either the Hungarian or Czech courts. Certainly there is none of the broad and overtly philosophical sweep one finds in Hungarian judgements, nor the rhetorical political engagement of the Czech court. The one argumentative strategy most commonly found in the tribunal's decisions, a move that it has shown can do a great deal of work, is the massive reliance on the idea of the rule of law, and the use of many subordinate values derived from it, often summarised as involving the idea of the "principle of correct legislation."

The tribunal's record in standing up to the government is at least as strong as those in the other countries covered in this chapter. The tribunal has been prepared to take on government economic policy in much the same way as, and possibly even more strongly than, the Hungarian Constitutional Court, as discussed in the earlier analysis of positive rights, and has stood up to governments of different political persuasions. One example is that within months of the election of a conservative and populist government in 2005, the tribunal struck down one of its first, and highly politically charged, policies.[42] In December 2005 the recently elected government rushed through a bill restructuring the National Broadcasting Council, and giving the president of the Republic the power to appoint the chairman. The NBC had been routinely criticised by the then opposition before and during the election. The bill in fact ended the life of the existing council even

[41] The best account of the early history of the Polish Constitutional Tribunal is given in Brzezinski, *Struggle for Constitutionalism*. An earlier article, written with a judge of the court, brings out some of the theoretical issues relevant here more closely: MF Brzezinski and L Garlicki, "Judicial Review in Post-Communist Poland: The Emergence of a *Rechtsstaat*?" 1995 31 *Stanford Journal of International Law* 13–60.

[42] *Modifications to the Composition and Functioning of the National Broadcasting Council*, K4/06 (2006) (Polish Constitutional Tribunal).

before a new council under the president's influence could be appointed. It also attempted to give the council disciplinary powers over journalists under the guise of the "protection of journalistic ethics." The law was challenged immediately on a host of different grounds in an abstract review procedure by groups of deputies from the new opposition and by the commissioner for citizens' rights.[43] The case, as well as establishing the continued independence of the tribunal, serves to demonstrate many of the traits of its jurisprudence. The tribunal is very careful to be sure of its grounds when it opposes parliament, and is in any case given to a "black letter" procedural precision in interpretation. Here this shows in its refusal to accept one of the grounds for dismissing the act, that it was carried out in a great hurry. There is a constitutional procedure for emergency legislation, with the restriction that such bills must have been countersigned by the Council of Ministers and cannot affect the structure of public authorities. Apart from speed, the emergency procedure allows for leaving out normally required readings of the bill. Yet the tribunal refused to accept that the act had fallen foul of this restriction, because though carried out without all normal procedural steps, and carried out very fast, the legislative proceedings at no time specifically referred to the Article 123 emergency provision. As the summary of the judgement says, "Rapidity in the case of legislative procedure is not *per se* unconstitutional." They acknowledge in general the parliament's right to alter its own proceedings except where the violations of procedure are so severe as to prevent parliamentarians functioning properly.

Irregularities appeared in the course of the legislative work leading to the adoption of the challenged 2005 act, inter alia in regard to the convening of sittings of Sejm committees. This exerted a negative influence upon the quality of the legislative process and the drafting of legal provisions. Nonetheless, in the present case, the breach of good customs and failure to reflect political and legal culture in the course of the legislative procedure did not amount to an infringement of the constitution. That said, the fact that the Constitutional Tribunal did not find unconstitutionality in that respect (cf. point 1 of the ruling) should not be taken to signify the tribunal's approval of such conduct.[44]

Such a ruling might be expected to preface a generally subservient approach to the Sejm (the Polish lower chamber of parliament), but it is quite normal for the tribunal. The insistence on the record's not referring to Article 123, and the refusal therefore to invalidate the act on that ground, is evidence simply of the tribunal's procedural orientation. The act was invalidated in several respects, and always in an impeccably strict procedural manner. The role of the National Council of Broadcasting in supervising journalistic ethics, for example, is thrown out because

[43] The commissioner acts *sua sponte* to protect rights and is not restricted to channelling complaints received from citizens. The constitution allows direct access by aggrieved citizens in a process of "constitutional complaint" similar to that in Germany. Abstract review may also be called for by a group of deputies or senators, and by the president before signing a bill into law. The constitution also provides for a constitutional reference from an ordinary court. It is not unusual for a case to arrive before the tribunal, as here, by more than one route at the same time. Details of the whole process of getting cases to the tribunal are given in Schwartz, *Struggle for Constitutional Justice*, chapter 3.

[44] *National Broadcasting Council*, Summary Point 4.

"The Polish legal system features no generally-binding and uniform catalogue of principles of journalistic ethics (professional ethics of journalists), which would serve as the source of legal norms addressed to journalists."[45] A right like that of freedom of speech cannot be abridged except by a statute. There is no such clear statute, and there cannot be a restriction on journalistic activity. Anything else would allow the National Council of Broadcasting to do something beyond its constitutional scope. The president's power to appoint and dismiss the chairman of the council is not within the list of prerogatives of the office in Article 144, which is of an exhaustive nature. Such a listing cannot be developed:

> the list of presidential prerogatives may not be statutorily broadened, neither according to the principle of the "continuation" of an act released from the countersignature requirement, nor according to the principle of analogical competences.[46]

Not all constitutional courts by any means would deprive themselves of interpretative powers by so bold a statement that aspects of the constitution cannot be broadened in such a way. Many would try to develop their own interpretative rules based on the constitution makers' intentions, if only to empower the court itself. But however active the tribunal may be, its commitment to a form of "strict construction" often exceeds the views even of American legal conservatives. Much of the act is ripped away in a similar vein. However, here, as in many cases, the tribunal is also capable of making much more substantive, and economically aware, judgements. So its reason for a striking out another aspect of the act, which would have made it easier for "social" broadcasters to have their licences renewed, is quite unlike the heavily procedural nature of those parts of the judgement so far mentioned. A social broadcaster is one that has no other economic activity and carries no paid advertisements. Yet to favour these broadcasters, according to the tribunal, is to breach a general equality principle forbidding discrimination under Article 32 of the constitution. The tribunal has developed a strong interpretation of discrimination that will be briefly discussed later. Most of the time it uses Article 32 rulings that do involve substantive judgement, as here:

> The launching of and engagement in broadcasting activity is connected with substantial financial and organisational outlays. A lack of certainty as to the ability to continue with broadcasting activities constitutes a real economic threat for all broadcasters. Under such circumstances, less-favourable treatment of those broadcasters who do not meet the social broadcaster criterion within the meaning of the Act, infringes Article 32, read in conjunction with Article 20, of the Constitution. Such discrimination against a certain group of broadcasters in economic life as may negatively affect their economic condition also serves to sustain the allegation regarding infringement of the principle of equal protection of ownership and property rights (Article 64(2) of the Constitution).[47]

[45] *National Broadcasting Council*, Summary Point 10.

[46] *National Broadcasting Council*, Summary Point 12.

[47] *National Broadcasting Council*, Summary Point 24.

Article 20 defines Poland as having a "social market economy" involving, inter alia, freedom of economic activity and private ownership, while Article 64(2) requires that "Everyone . . . shall receive equal protection regarding ownership and other property rights." The tribunal's jurisprudence is just as much involved in re-creating a free market economy as it is in ensuring the rule of law. It is almost as an afterthought that the tribunal also notes that discrimination in favour of one type of broadcaster also "implies unequal treatment with regard to enjoyment of the freedom of expression and the freedom to obtain and disseminate information."

To say that the tribunal is concerned with free market property rights might be taken to imply a degree of conservatism that is probably unfair. Nor is the distinction in the paragraph above between caring about proceduralism and about property rights quite fair, because the tribunal's jurisprudence would probably not fully accept the distinction, so firmly are its actual decisions dependent on a very complex and full idea of the rule of law. Much of this will become clearer when we consider the socioeconomic rights jurisprudence of Eastern European courts in chapter 8, but a useful insight into how the two ideas, commitment to procedural propriety and commitment to private property and market economics, interrelate can be gained by quickly looking at a concept essentially unknown to Anglo-American common law but common in the European tradition and beloved of the tribunal, the idea of a *vacatio legis*. The tribunal is concerned to develop a concept of the rule of law that is in some ways more prescriptive than is common in Western thinking. It is not just that there should be a clear law authorising state action, but that the laws should conform to several normative standards. Some of these are fairly routine, though perhaps more fiercely wielded by the tribunal than by some review bodies, such as the requirement for clarity and precision in statutes. Some standards are more or less universal, like the ban on retrospective law—though in common with other Eastern European countries this can cause problems with lustration legislation, as discussed in the last section of this chapter. Some are textually specific to Poland, though common in other European states with similar constitutions, especially Germany, such as the sharp requirement for full statutes rather than administrative edicts or decree legislation in many contexts. Perhaps what is most characteristic of the Polish view of the rule of law is the tribunal's sense, shared especially with Hungary but even more pronounced, that the rule of law requires "fairness" in the way laws act on people's life plans. This is sometimes described as a matter of trust in government, and often expressed in language such as the law "not taking people by surprise," or not "setting traps for people."

A very clear example is in a tax case where the public prosecutor himself raised the question about a change to the tax law that introduced a new higher level of tax (at 50 percent for those earning more than 600,000 zlotys). The problem was that the bill in question was only signed into law on December 13, 2004, and was to come into force on January 1, 2005. The tribunal had, in several earlier decisions, ruled that a minimum time gap of one month was the relevant *vacatio legis* for tax laws, combined with a general principle that it was never permissible to change the law relating to tax liability during the tax year to which it would apply. The tribunal did indeed throw out the new legislation—the only dissent was by a judge who thought its language not severe enough. This was no trivial matter—it effectively meant that the government could not raise the extra revenue for at least another year, and would have to reintroduce legislation. In the event, of course, a general election intervened. It was—though there is no reason to assume the tribunal to be intentionally a party to this—a tactical move by the president. The bill had finished its parliamentary process by November 18, but the president waited until the last legally possible day before signing it. Had he signed it earlier, there could have been a constitutionally acceptable *vacatio legis*. According to the summary, the tribunal's opinion starts from an impeccably democratic position: "In evaluating the constitutionality of tax legislation, the starting assumption is the legislator's relative freedom in shaping the State's income and expenditure."[48] But it rapidly qualifies this position by insisting that the legislator must nonetheless respect "the procedural aspects of the rule of law," which include "the principles of correct legislation." This is fleshed out in a way that characterises much of the tribunal's thinking, particularly in tax and property cases:

> As stemming from the rule of law principle, the principle of trust in the State and its laws (also known as the principle of the State's loyalty towards the addressees of legal norms) requires laws to be created and applied in such a manner that they do not create "traps" for citizens. Citizens should be entitled to conduct their affairs with confidence that they will not be exposed to legal consequences that were unforeseeable at the time the decision was taken and that their actions, being in accordance with the law operative at that time, shall continue to be recognised by the future legal order. New legal regulations should not surprise their addressees but, rather, should allow them time to adjust to the revised provisions and to thoughtfully decide as to their further actions.[49]

The clue to why this principle has been constitutionalized by the tribunal is probably given by the words "continue to be recognised by the future legal order" combined with the fact that the conclusion "derived from the rule of law principle whilst the previous Constitution was operative" remains valid. It is a general problem for courts in this area that the struggle for economic reform since the fall of Communism has destroyed much of the stability and certainty of prior social and economic life. Indeed there is, in each country, a major problem about the validity, or the requirements for validity, of predemocratic law. The situation is all the worse in Poland because of the changes in constitutional order that have followed each other since the fall of the old regime, but not entirely of its state, in 1989. The language of "the principle of trust in the State and its laws" is crucially important. The tribunal clearly sees itself as having to educate both a citizenry and its governments into how to behave to establish a difference between the old and the new regime, and this establishment of trust and predictability ranks

[48] *Insufficient Vacatio Legis When Introducing Higher Rate of Personal Income Tax*, K48/04 (2005) (Polish Constitutional Tribunal).

[49] *Insufficient Vacatio Legis When Introducing Higher Rate of Personal Income Tax*, Summary Point 2.

above direct government financial welfare. The whole idea of a *vacatio legis*, it is worth noting, is an empirical one—the tribunal is not to be satisfied with symbolic periods, but makes its own judgements about how long is long enough given the circumstances.

There is a rather different case where a feature of both European and British commercial law was incorporated into Poland, by which minority shareholders in a joint stock company could be removed following the purchase of their shares by majority shareholders. When this law was challenged the tribunal decided that the fifty-day *vacatio legis* involved in the act, though rather short, did just about comply with constitutional requirements.[50] What the tribunal will not do, however, is to tell the parliament how long a period is necessary. It is an important reflection of the narrowness with which the tribunal defines its scope at times that it uses the language of the original Kelsen theory of constitutional review, and insists that it is a purely "negative legislator." To the extent that this self-denying ordinance applies generally, it restricts quite seriously the tribunal's options, particularly if the law being challenged has actually gone into operation.[51]

> Where the Constitutional Tribunal finds that a given *vacatio legis* is excessively brief, it may (acting as a "negative legislator") only declare unconstitutional the statutory provision prescribing this period. It may not, however, usurp the legislator's role and decree a period which would, in its opinion, be sufficient. In the event of a finding of unconstitutionality, the Act would have to return to Parliament in order for a new date of its entry into force to be determined. Consequently, a long period of time would lapse between the date of entry into force originally planned by the legislator and the date on which the Act would actually acquire binding force. Where the substantive content of legal provisions and appropriateness of their adoption do not raise any doubts, such an excessive delay appears unjustified.[52]

What happened in this case shows the reason the tribunal values the doctrine at all. Because many cable television companies had in fact complied with the act, randomness and uncertainty would actually follow from a finding of unconstitutionality as much as might be said to have followed for others from its unconstitutionality:

[50] *Compulsory Purchase of Shares Held by Minority Shareholders (Squeeze-Out)*, P25/02 (2005) (Polish Constitutional Tribunal).

[51] The idea of courts as "negative legislators" is associated with Hans Kelsen. The original source for his ideas on constitutional review is a classic text in French, H Kelsen, "La Garantie Jurisdictionel de La Constitution," 1928 44 *Revue de Droit Public* 197. Kelsen also thought that courts should have no power to apply a bill of rights. Some political scientists think these ideas are linked, and that a jurisdiction that does allow courts to impose bills of rights cannot have "negative legislator" courts. This is claimed, for example, in M Shapiro and A Stone Sweet, *On Law, Politics and Judicialization* (Oxford: Oxford University Press, 2002). This is a mistake. Whatever Kelsen may have thought, the ideas are not incompatible.

[52] *Brief Vacatio Legis in Introducing the Requirement to Obtain a License for Cable Network Re-transmission*, K55/02 (Polish Constitutional Tribunal), Summary Point 3.

> The principle of the rule of law, from which stems the duty to protect trust in the State and its laws, precludes adverse consequences being imposed on the addressees of legal norms who have utilised the rights granted to them by a duly adopted and promulgated Act, even where the Act is not free of certain legislative flaws.[53]

The deep insecurity of citizens faced with a lawless state may well take some time to overcome, and undoubtedly the tribunal's jurisprudence will relax as this happens. In the cable case the tribunal does comment that it was only the 1997 constitution that actually stated that a law needed to be promulgated before it became legally effective—thus their need to derive such a rule from the mere reference to Poland's being "a democratic state governed by the rule of law" in the 1989 constitutional document, and the lack of such a need after 1997. It is to demonstrate this core concern with stability that what might seem unnecessarily recondite legal issues have been discussed here.

Social Issues and the Impact of History

The tribunal deals with an enormous range of issues, covering all the classic human rights problems faced by any constitutional court. But it does this always against the background of radical economic transformation. Thus there are inevitably far more cases involving apparently mundane matters like the nature of ownership in communal property, rules governing rent increases, and so on, than one would find in any Western court. Bit by bit the tribunal helps dismantle the Communist socioeconomic system, while trying to make the process as humane as possible. Indeed it must be remembered that the most important use of the *vacatio* principle, as discussed in chapter 8, was to protect welfare and pension recipients from an overfast economic transformation. The problems of housing continue to bedevil Poland, and the parliament's record is unimpressive, given its tendency to veer back and forth between free market and social housing. At times the tribunal is clearly exasperated, and certainly the bulk of its decisions lean towards free market solutions.

It is not in any other way a court that can be described as conservative, however. Across the whole range of more typical human rights issues its decisions usually conform with the liberalism of most constitutional review mechanisms. The exceptions are predictable given Poland's social history—it has been more supportive of religion in public life, including being less than enthusiastic about abortion rights, than most courts elsewhere. Always there is the problem of the past, a past whose legal legacy can be used against liberal as much as against economically conservative policies. Religion provides a good example of how the tribunal has tended to deal with the past—by outright and open reinterpretation of ideas. So when in the very early days of the new republic there was a challenge to the reinstatement of religious teaching in schools, from the commissioner for citizens' rights, it was

[53] *Brief Vacatio Legis in Introducing the Requirement to Obtain a License for Cable Network Re-transmission*, Summary Point 6.

cast in terms of a breach with an act from the Communist period, the Education Development Act of 1961. This act had demanded a secular education system, the last thing in the world the Solidarity-backed new republic was going to want. The tribunal defined secularity and religious neutrality as compatible with religious education in schools where parents wanted it. "A different interpretation of these concepts would not mean neutrality but interference by the state with freedom of conscience and religion." The tribunal went on to say outright that

> This understanding of secularity and neutrality follows from semantic premises and from a systematic interpretation which, in the contemporary Republic of Poland, obviously differs from the interpretation of secularity made in the times of the People's Republic of Poland.[54]

It is worth noting that the tribunal very much wanted to make this point, because it says itself that it could simply have said that later statutes overrule earlier ones, but that this is something "one may cite only as an auxiliary means of support" for the tribunal's decision.

Given that this chapter cannot deal at any length with the three countries covered, it must be stressed that the Polish tribunal covers the whole range of matters one might expect from a constitutional court. There is no single, not even a cluster, of values one can associate with its jurisprudence. Above all it has engaged in a careful spelling out of what is necessarily implied by the idea of a state under the rule of law, and, of all the three courts, is most committed to precise procedural argument. It may also, perhaps in keeping with the administrative court mode identified earlier, be the one most careful not to transgress the separation of powers, the court most likely to be self-restricting. We saw earlier, for example, its insistence on the role of "negative legislature." One aspect of its self-restriction is the high number of cases in which it denies it has competence to hear a case, especially where an applicant is trying to make a constitutional complaint and has not fulfilled all the requirements to exhaust other avenues. Most telling perhaps is the way in which it has narrowed the range under which a plaintiff may claim discriminatory treatment. In a fiercely contested case with no less than five dissents it ruled that a citizen could only claim unconstitutionality for unequal treatment where there was a specified right in the constitution that was being unequally protected—inequality of government action itself would not suffice.[55] In this, if in no other area, the Polish tribunal is behind many other constitutional review bodies. The case was decided by a full senate of the court precisely because of a lack of consistency in decisions by separate panels. If the decision is a fair representation of the majority view on the court, it stands as strong evidence that the Polish tribunal is indeed less likely to extend its reach than it might. It may well be the least ambitious to impose or develop fundamental values, certainly compared with both Hungary and the Czech Republic.

[54] *Decision Dated 30th January 1991 on Religious Instruction (K11/90)*, in Oniszczuk, *Selection of Jurisprudence* (Polish Constitutional Tribunal), 47.

[55] *Constitutional Complaint and the Principle of Equality*, SK10/01 (2001) (Polish Constitutional Tribunal).

The Czech Republic

Boundary Problems and Electoral Issues

The Constitutional Court of the Czech Republic naturally deals with the full range of issues that crop up anywhere, and with much the same emphases as the Polish tribunal. In particular, as suggested earlier, the Czech court is frequently called on to handle the boundary maintenance problems inherent in a new separation-of-powers state. These cases frequently involve relations between the lower and upper houses, but quite often, particularly in the earlier years, the clash was between the government, in the sense of the prime minister and Council of Ministers, and the presidency, a conflict found elsewhere in the region. Thus in 2001 the prime minister claimed a presidential appointment to be chairman of the National Bank required his consent as well, a claim struck down by the court.[56] Equally the court may get involved in clashes between local government and the national level. One feature of several of the new East European democracies has been a tendency for central government to increase the role of local authorities, only to find these moves opposed because of the extra financial burdens the reforms imposed on localities. In 2003 the court explained at length that the essence of democracy was indeed sound local government, but that such territorial autonomy was hindered, not helped, when the state handed over a whole set of functions and administrative departments to the localities, along with their attendant financial obligations, whether or not the territorial units wanted them.[57] A similar case occurred in Poland when the tribunal had to annul an apparently benign law that allowed property owners simply to relinquish their title to land, which then automatically went to the local government in question. This had the effect of dumping financial obligations and the costs like those involved in cleaning up environmental hazards on the local council without their consent.[58]

Inevitably the court has always been extremely vigilant about one aspect of the separation of powers, the independence of the judiciary. At least one decision on this shows the court in a less than good light—when it struck out judges from a list of state officials expected to accept salary reductions during a national financial crisis, leaving the other officials to suffer. What made this decision worse was that the court had to invent a rather specious argument for reversing itself, having earlier insisted that judges should be treated equally with others. The case elicited one of the rare dissents in the court's history, with four justices voting against the decision.[59] It is perhaps only because the court has throughout its history demon-

[56] *Decision of 26th June 2001 Czech National Bank*, Pl. US 14/01 (Czech Republic Constitutional Court).

[57] *Decision of 9 July 2003 on Territorial Self Government*, Pl. US 5/03 (Czech Republic Constitutional Court).

[58] *Relinquishing Ownership of Real Estate and Interests of Communes*, K9/04 (2005) (Polish Constitutional Tribunal).

[59] *Decision of 11th June 2003 on Judge's Salaries*, Pl. US 11/02 (Czech Republic Constitutional Court).

strated such courage and intellectual and ideological passion that this relatively predictable fall from grace stands out.

Rather more than other courts, the Czech court has been heavily involved with surrounding elections and the status of political parties, and especially the question of state support for political parties. There has been a good deal of conflict in the Czech Republic over alterations to electoral law as different governments have sought to solidify or improve on electoral gains, and this has inevitably become part of the court's business. In general the court has tried to keep out of major issues, but has not avoided its role in ensuring fairness within these laws. So the court rejected a complaint against the 5 percent threshold for political parties in the 1995 election act, and another claim, ten years later, that the vote threshold to qualify for state aid was too high.[60] But earlier the court had been adamant that state funding must not even give the appearance of allowing the state to control or influence political parties, and had struck down part of the original act allowing for state financial aid to parties.[61] Where it has seen electoral partisanship in a state body, the court has acted firmly. In an early case under a law that made it harder for a coalition of parties to succeed electorally than for a single unit party, the Central Election Commission had deemed a list produced by three parties to be such an electoral coalition. The court describes the commission's action very bluntly:

> The issue is that the Central Election Commission decided that the complainant, heretofore considered a political party, which needs 5% of votes to enter the first scrutiny, would in future be considered a coalition, which needs to receive 7% of votes to enter the first scrutiny. The complainant states that the Central Election Commission decided on this condition even though no provision of the Election Act authorizes it to do so, and decided in its own discretion. In view of the fact that this commission is composed of representatives of all political parties, it can in fact be said that representatives of political parties decided, completely outside the scope provided by law, to create more difficult conditions for another political subject to enter the Parliament of the Czech Republic.[62]

The court not only annulled the decision but stated,

> The Constitutional Court forbids the Central Election Commission to express an opinion on the question of whether the complainant's candidate list is or is not a candidate list of a coalition, or to pass resolutions about this. The Constitutional Court also orders the Central Election Commission to renew the status of the complainant in elections to the Chamber of Deputies of the Parliament of the Czech Republic so as to correspond to the status

[60] *Decision of 2nd April 1997 on the Principles of the Electoral System of the Czech Republic*, Pl. US 25/96 (Czech Republic Constitutional Court); *Decision of 19th January 2005—On Election Contribution*, Pl. US 10/03 (Czech Republic Constitutional Court).

[61] *Decision of 18th October 1995 on Financing of Political Parties and Inspection of Their Management*, Pl. US 26/94 (Czech Republic Constitutional Court).

[62] *Decision of 27 April 1996 on Election Coalitions*, US 127/96 (Czech Republic Constitutional Court).

> before the election commission's resolution. . . . further, in connection with the renewal of the complainant's status, within 24 hours after delivery of this judgment, to send to the CTK press agency a declaration that the complainant's candidate list will be considered a candidate list of a single political party in the 1996 parliamentary elections.

The Legitimacy of the New State

None of the cases mentioned above, however, touch on what has been the single most distinguishing characteristic of the Czech court, which is its passionate struggle to find a basis of legitimacy for its state, and, in doing this, to deal with the problem of the past. Much of this has to do with the struggles over lustration, which forms the subject of the last part of this chapter. These issues are so important for the Czech court, however, that some aspects must be touched on in this section as well. Apart from its substantive importance, the struggle to come to legal terms with the Communist and Nazi past is where the court's particular intellectual style shows most clearly. And a style of its own it certainly has—I know of no other court that frequently quotes Max Weber and other social theorists, including Hayek. It does so because throughout their jurisprudence, the members of the court have sought to base their legal decisions on a subtle sociological understanding of how modern democracies work. They have done so in part because they are continually aware of the need for the courts as much as other institutions to have a strong basis of public legitimacy.

An unusually sharp reprimand to a lower court in one of the vital cases concerning the past helps make this point:

> To overlook these norms of reference and principles does not merely render the Supreme Court's decision defective due to the infringement of the complainant's individual rights. In addition, and the Constitutional Court deems it necessary to make this observation outside of the strict confines of the case before it, it renders the decision incomprehensible for the society, for its legal, even constitutional, consciousness, and contributes to the existing lack of faith in the judiciary in the sense that Czech courts prove incapable of protecting the rights of citizens in relation to state power, when that manifests itself in an excessive manner. In this way, confidence in the substantive conception of the Czech Republic's character as a democratic law-based state is diminished. If the principle of legal continuity is not to have a destructive impact in relation to the Czech Republic's character as a constitutional state, when applying "old law" the value discontinuity with that law must consistently be insisted upon, and this approach must be reflected in judicial decisions.[63]

[63] *Decision of 26th March 2003 on Freedom of Conscience*, Pl. US 42/02 (Czech Republic Constitutional Court), section VII.

The intellectual problem thrown up by this and other cases is one that other courts in the region have considered, although it has never caused them as much angst as it has the Czechs. The problem is just how much a country can continue to respect laws passed before its overthrow of dictatorship. It is particularly troublesome for the Czechs because they have every reason to want to validate the relatively short-lived first republic, the post-1918 creation of Versailles. Thus they cannot as easily simply draw a line against the past. No country can in practice, of course, and the Hungarian court has been especially keen to present the onset of democracy there as an evolutionary, not revolutionary, move. The fear the Czech court has is well described in its own phrase above—can the "principle of legal continuity" be supported without "a destructive impact in relation to the Czech Republic's character as a constitutional state." This case is a rich example of much that makes the Czech court a particularly good example of the idea of a court as a developer of political theory, almost a moral guardian for its society, as well as showing clearly the problems of reapplying the rule of law. It involved a constitutional complaint by someone who had sought to have the ordinary courts of the Czech Republic rule that his conviction in 1965 by a military court of the old regime for refusing military service was invalid. One unusual feature of the case was that the minister of justice joined the complainant in opposing the Czech Supreme Court's decision against him.[64] The Supreme Court had argued that, as the offence was not listed in the 1990 Act on Judicial Rehabilitation, it had no choice but to judge his conviction in terms of the law as it stood in 1954, at which time the Communist constitution in force did not accept freedom of conscience as a ground for failing to carry out duties to the state. It turns out that the decision of the Supreme Court was by a wafer-thin majority—the chairman of the Supreme Court "expressed doubts as to whether the view which prevailed in the contested decision was sufficiently representative."[65]

The Constitutional Court went to great lengths to show that the Czech constitution of 1920, as well as the one now in force, would both have treated the matter differently than the law in 1954 would have, and that the Communist constitutions, of 1948 and 1960 were out of keeping with long-term democratic values. As often in its jurisprudence the court relied heavily on analogous cases before the European Court of Human Rights, citing not only the main decision in one case, but quoting at length from a minority concurring opinion that strengthened the reasoning of the majority.[66] The citation by the Czech court of Judge Levits's opinion is worth quoting here, representing as it does much of the thinking in Eastern and Western Europe on the problem:

> interpretation and application of national or international legal norms according to socialist or other non-democratic methodology (with intolerable

[64]The Czech constitution, in common with most jurisdictions in Eastern Europe, has copied the German idea of a constitutional complaint, as well as allowing abstract review at the behest of parliamentary or executive officeholders, and referrals from ordinary courts.

[65]*Decision of 26th March 2003 on Freedom of Conscience*, section III.

[66]*Streletz, Kessler and Krenz v Germany* (March 22, 2001) (European Court of Human Rights).

> results for a democratic system) should from the standpoint of a democratic system be regarded as wrong. In my view, that is a compelling conclusion, which derives from the inherent universality of human rights and democratic values, by which all democratic institutions are bound. At least since the time of the Nuremberg Tribunal, that conception of the democratic order has been well understood in the world and it is therefore foreseeable for everybody.[67]

This is the intellectual background courts like that of the Czech Republic come from, though it is more pronounced and important in the Czech Republic than elsewhere. Obviously it is of merely symbolic importance, to the complainant as much as the court, but symbols have tremendous political power, especially where countries need to reassure themselves of their national worth and to exorcise aspects of their past. In this case the Czech court argued that freedom of conscience historically was a legal trump in Czech law, and that Communism had interrupted this tradition, which is shared by the community of democratic nations:

> The fact that the Constitution of 9 May denied the freedom of conscience its character as an "absolute" right followed alone from the essence of the political regime enthroned in February, 1948. The new restrictions upon the freedom of conscience breached the continuity of the conception that the freedom of conscience is an absolute right, as it was protected by the Constitutional Charter of 1920. The post-1948 constitutional formulation of the freedom of conscience deviated, in terms of legal philosophy, from the development of fundamental rights which was begun by the Nuremburg Tribunal and continued with the adoption of the Universal Declaration of Human Rights.[68]

The problem the court has in finding a way to sanitise "old law" is more than symbolic, however, because legal continuity is crucial at a very practical level. And not any solution to a problem like this one will work. It is an important feature of the judgement that the court went to great length to find a definition of freedom of conscience that does not automatically promote any set of religious or ideological beliefs into a justification for civil disobedience. In so doing the court invents a theory of conscience that comes quite close to being one of psychological determinism, and that relegates beliefs to a secondary role. It is also highly context dependent—individuals must feel a sense of absolute lack of choice given the interaction of their beliefs and the situation they find themselves in:

> The freedom of conscience is manifested in decisions made by the individual in certain concrete situations, that is, "here and now," felt as a profoundly experienced duty. It is not a matter of the individual's attitude toward abstract problems, valid once and for all and in all situations. In the case of decisions

[67] *Freedom of Conscience*, in section VI, par. 2.

[68] *Freedom of Conscience*, in section VII. May 5, 1948, was the date the first of the two communist era constitutions came into force. The second, as the court notes, was even less friendly to the idea of freedom of conscience.

> dictated by conscience, it is the fusion for the individual of binding moral norms with the situation as evaluated by her. It is the integration of recognized norms with an assessment of the factual situation. A decision dictated by consciences is based on the existence of the conscience itself, and not on specific religious or ideological conceptions.

Following in part a German constitutional decision, the court goes on to describe the individual's position when faced with a conflict between law and conscience in fundamental moral terms. "What is fundamental is that it concerns a solemn moral decision oriented toward the category of good and evil which the individual experiences as a binding duty or an unconditional order to behave in a certain fashion."[69] A refusal to treat the citizen as a full moral agent offends against not just the values of democratic society, but its essence.

> The freedom of conscience has constitutive significance for the democratic law-based state which respects the liberal idea of the primacy of responsible and dignified human beings before the State, that is, the idea of esteem (respect and protection) by the state for the rights of persons and citizens. In contrast, it is characteristic of a totalitarian political regime that it does not respect the autonomy of the individual conscience, as it attempts, even with the aid of a repressive criminal policy, to suppress the freedom of conscience of the individual, and by this means to compel her to accept the will of the ruling elite, which claims recognition for its decisions as the sole good decisions and, in that sense, the sole ethical decisions.[70]

The court is not naïve or simple minded. It insists that such a recognition of freedom of conscience cannot automatically mean that the individual is not bound by it. It will always be a judgement required of a court, which, above all, would have to be sure that no one else's fundamental rights were being encroached on, and that no other fundamental constitutional value conflicted. And here a further problem arises for the Constitutional Court, which admits that it is not its task to make such first-order judgements. The task of the Constitutional Court essentially is to see if lower courts have interpreted the law and constitution correctly in reaching their decision. Here the court was safe because the Supreme Court had said, aloud, that it was not going to invoke current constitutional values but, effectively, to endorse the values of the 1948 constitution. To repeat the court's main concern, to do this might endanger the new constitution. What the court calls a "value discontinuity" between the Communist and modern periods must always be taken into account in judicial decisions. "It is only in this restrictive sense, that of value discontinuity, that one may conceive of continuity with 'old law.'" The decision is very similar to that of the Polish court in its religious freedom case, but the latter is a good deal less "theorised."[71] It ought to be noticed also that the problem of forcing the ordinary courts to abide by the constitution is not trivial—the

[69] *Freedom of Conscience*, section VI 2 a.
[70] *Freedom of Conscience*, section VI 2 a.
[71] *Religious Instruction.*

Constitutional Court has had repeatedly to insist that its interpretations are binding and must be applied widely and generously. One often feels the Czech court feels itself alone amongst all the political institutions of the Czech state.[72]

One crucial decision that set the tone for dealing with the question of continuity, and shows why it is of more than symbolic importance, was the court's retrospective validation of the 1945 Benes decree, from October 1945, "On the Confiscation of Enemy Property and the Funds of National Renewal." It might have helped the court had this come up even earlier. As it is, problems had already arisen, to be discussed in the last section of this chapter, regarding criminal liability in the past. The case arose because of a challenge to the legality of the confiscation of property belonging to German citizens and Czech sympathizers at the end of World War II. It could have been handled by a short and technical demonstration of the constitutional status of the interim government in 1945, and indeed the court did give such an answer. But far more of the judgement is dedicated to answering the plaintiffs' claim, hopeless in terms of positive law, that the Benes decree "violated the legal canons of civilized European societies and that, therefore, they must be considered not as acts of law but of force." In answering this claim the court made a series of assertions that characterize the way it looks at the past, and at the foundations of a democratic legal order. In particular the sense of the primacy of the political base for the legitimacy even of procedural law comes across clearly.

> The constitutional requirement laid down in the 1920 Constitutional Charter that the Czechoslovak state have a democratic character, is rather a concept of a political science character (and which is juristically definable only with difficulty) which, however, does not mean that it is a meta-legal concept, hence not legally binding. On the contrary, the constitutional principle mandating the democratic legitimacy of the governmental system was a basic characteristic feature of the constitutional system which as a result meant that, in the 1920 Constitutional Charter of the Czechoslovak Republic, this principle *was ranked above and prior to requirements of formal, legal legitimacy*.[73]

It is, of course, possible to make the argument that any court that does indeed think that any principle can rank above "formal, legal legitimacy" does not understand the rule of law, and it is arguable the Hungarian court, for one, would take that position. For the Czech court, the rule of law, or the idea of a "state under law," especially in a transition period, actually requires this politically informed depth of analysis. Much is made in this ruling of the nature of human political responsibility, in a way that is vital for the other decisions where the rule of law has to be interpreted in relation to dealing with the past.

[72] See most recently, *Decision of 25th January 2005 on Constitutionally Conforming Interpretation*, III. US 252/04 (Czech Republic Constitutional Court). Similar complaints have arisen from the court all through its history. The first and bluntest came some years after the court started work, in *Decision of 2nd April 1998 Binding Force of Constitutional Court Decisions*, III. US 425/97 (Czech Republic Constitutional Court).

[73] *8th March 1995 Benes Decree*, Pl. US 14/94 (Czech Republic Constitutional Court); emphasis added.

> This decree has a more general scope and can be considered as one of the documents reflecting the age-old conflict between democracy and totalitarianism. The dividing line was drawn according to which side of the conflict a person chose to support.

Similarly the very nature of human political society can be seen to be based on a human political and moral obligation:

> It is mankind's fate that human beings are placed into power relations, and this situation gives rise to their responsibility to champion the forces which will make human rights a reality. The grounds for social, political, moral, and in some cases even legal, responsibility is thus precisely the person's neglect to make a contribution in the structuring of power relations, his failure, during the struggle for power, to act in the service of right.

A court that thinks in this way is unlikely to produce the sort of formalistic application of the idea of the rule of law that might please some. It is equally a court that cannot easily be accused of indifference to the deepest moral and political questions of legal legitimacy. It is indeed a court, as this book argues all constitutional courts are in truth, that deals with concepts "of a political science character," but which nonetheless insists, as most would not admit, that this "does not mean that it is a meta-legal concept, hence not legally binding."

Hungary

An Evolutionary Court?

Hungary's Constitutional Court, set up like most of the others in the region after the fall of Communism in 1990, was the first to gain attention and a major reputation. This was partly because of the intellectual drive of the first president, László Sólyom, partly because the relatively calm pathway to democracy in Hungary allowed the court to act from the beginning as a legitimate entity essentially involved in "normal" constitutional politics. The first few years of its existence showed a strongly activist court, overturning not only laws inherited from the past, but a remarkable amount of legislation stemming from the new regime. At one stage it looked as though Hungary's glory days in constitutional review were over. All the original judges, who serve eight-year terms, were out of office by the end of the decade, and the second president of the court made it clear that no great activism was to be expected. Much of this seems to have been a matter of appearance, and perhaps of style, rather than of substance. A casual glance at the court's decisions in the last few years does not back up the idea of a submissive court giving in to the politicians.[74]

[74] Indeed the fact that Sólyom was elected president in 2005 suggests that the political elite could hardly have objected that strongly to what his court did.

What makes the Hungarian court in many ways different from its fellow constitutional review bodies in Eastern Europe is a sense of normality. Studying its decisions is much more like following those of a well-established, if unusually active, Western court, though it would be hard to say exactly which court it resembles. At times there is a look of the US Supreme Court, though its debt to the German constitutional court is both well established in the literature and openly acknowledged by its members. Perhaps a better analogue is that of the South African Constitutional Court, and indeed there is a distant analogy in the way both came into being, and in their relationship to the preexisting legal cultures they have had to fit into. The German connection shows most of all in the way the jurisprudence of the Hungarian court has centrally developed the idea of "human dignity" as what it likes to call "the mother right."[75]

A second aspect of the Hungarian court's jurisprudence that makes it seem like a long-standing Western court is that from the very beginning it attached great importance to its own precedents, and as the court has now had fifteen years to build up its cases, they have come to play an important part in its work. Even before it had much of a case list of its own, the court's determination to find authority for its decisions led to an approach that depended heavily on reference to foreign decisions, and above all to the decisions of the European Court of Human Rights. Sometimes this determination to view constitutional law internationally can seem contrived. There is far more citation of US cases than perhaps anywhere outside Canada. Yet the number of times the court actually has found the US case helpful is low—in part because, as the court points out, American understanding of the nature or value of some rights is often radically different. An interesting example is a case from 2001 in which legislation would have provided a "right of reply." The act provided that if the press "publishes or disseminates false facts or distorts true facts about a person, the person affected shall be entitled to demand, in addition to other actions provided by law, the publication of an announcement identifying the false or distorted facts and indicating the true facts." The Hungarian court initially cited with approval the pro-press ruling in *Sullivan*, which sought to prevent defamation law from crushing journalistic comment.[76] But the court went on to lament the way the US court had understood freedom of speech in some decisions:

> However, the European legal approach shows significant differences in comparison with the American one, as the Convention expressly provides for various cases of restricting the freedom of expression and the freedom of the

[75] A good survey of the first few years of the court's existence and of its early jurisprudence is Sajo, "Reading the Invisible Constitution." The idea of an "invisible constitution" is an important part of the court's own doctrine, though Sajo uses it more generally. The reliance on German constitutional doctrine is well argued for in Dupré, *Importing the Law*, though it should be noted that Sólyom himself suggests a rather less automatic reception of the German positions in recent articles, for example, "Role of Constitutional Courts," and in his vital monograph, Sólyom and Brunner, *Constitutional Judiciary*. This latter is also the only real source for English texts of decisions before about 1996. Thereafter a good selection is published by the court on its website, http://www.mkab.hu/en/enpage3.htm. Unless otherwise indicated, my case references are to the latter.

[76] *New York Times Co. v Sullivan*, 376 US 254 (1964) (US Supreme Court).

> press. . . . in the American practice there are elements no longer found in the decisions of the Court. This way, it is related to the principle of the freedom of expression as enforced in the American practice that the courts did not deem it possible to prevent a Nazi demonstration in a neighbourhood where persons who had been victims of the holocaust lived, and that they did not see any possibility for action against the burning of a cross reminiscent of the Ku-Klux-Klan in front of the house of an Afro-American family.[77]

More important in building up the caseload for purposes of supportive citation, however, have been two doctrines of the court's own, introduced from an early date. The first of them is the idea that the change of regime in 1990 did not produce any radical break in the legal system—the laws of Hungary, both before and during the Communist era, remain valid in general, though individual aspects may prove to be unconstitutional when and if tested. Though both Poland and the Czech Republic inevitably retain such validity, they do so much more cautiously, especially the latter. In Hungary the doctrine of the crucial importance of legal certainty has led to a much more wholesale acceptance of prior law. There is in addition the idea of the "living law"—attention paid to what has actually been the practice of Hungarian courts in the past, rather than to, and at times in contradistinction to, the letter of the law. This latter technique was introduced in 1991 and was criticised then as an attempt to move in on the territory of the ordinary courts, but the Constitutional Court continues to rely on it.[78] According to Sólyom, the court has not "reviewed the language of the law itself as determining the contents of the norm, but rather the meaning and the content that can be attributed to it from the constant and uniform practice of applying the law."[79] The court claimed that because the way a law had been consistently (mis)interpreted was unconstitutional, the law itself was unconstitutional. The main dissent in the case made the obvious counterargument forcefully:

> If the Constitutional Court accepts the theory of the "living law," the necessary repercussion of that will be that practically it can never decide on the basis of a published statutory text but will always be compelled to examine the application of the law in practice, at the very least with the view to determine whether or not such an application is "permanent and uniform." The court has neither competence nor technical resources for this purpose.[80]

Though interpretation of the "living law" would seem to give the court extra discretion, it continues as a working doctrine even in recent cases, suggesting again that the demise of activism after 1998 is much exaggerated.

[77] *Decision of 4th December 2001 on Right of Reply*, 57/2001 (XII.5) AB (Hungarian Constitutional Court). The cases the court refers to are *National Socialist Party v Village of Skokie*, 432 US 43 (1977) (US Supreme Court) and *RAV v City of St. Paul, Minnesota*, 505 US 377 (1992) (US Supreme Court).

[78] *Decision of 8th November 1991 on Legal Guardians and on the Family Act*, 57/1991 (Hungarian Constitutional Court), 171–77.

[79] Sólyom and Brunner, *Constitutional Judiciary*, 4.

[80] Dissent by Kilényi and Schmidt, *Legal Guardians*, 177.

The idea of the continuity of past law was inherent from the beginning but was given its clearest exposition in the first of what elsewhere would be called "lustration decisions." This case is discussed from that perspective later in this chapter. Here it is enough to say that the decision crystallised the court's sense that, though the rule of law meant previous law must be made to conform to the new constitution,

> The change of system has been carried out on the basis of legality. . . . The politically revolutionary changes adopted by the Constitution and all the new fundamental laws were enacted in full compliance with the old legal system's procedural laws on legislation, therefore gaining their binding force. The old law retained its validity. With respect to its validity there is no distinction between "pre-Constitution" and "post-Constitution" law. The legitimacy of the different (political) systems during the past half century is irrelevant from this perspective.[81]

While other East European systems may be able to claim some degree of procedural continuity, none of them describe their legitimacy in quite this way. It is in striking contrast even to debates in the United States on exactly how the constitution can be seen as legitimately following from the Confederation, or even how legitimacy carries over from the Civil War system to the post–Fourteenth Amendment system.[82] There were no dissents in this case. This is a point worth making, because yet another feature of Hungarian Constitutional Court practise that makes it seem more Western is the open acceptance of dissent. No exact figure can easily be given, but evidence suggests a very high rate of dissent. Of the thirty-two cases since 1998 that are reported on the court's website, 50 percent contained at least one dissent. Naturally only the more important cases are reported, and importance, equating with difficulty, is likely to lead to dissent, but a 50 percent rate is high even given that caveat. What is not open to doubt is that twenty-five of these thirty-two cases involved a finding of at least partial unconstitutionality. Given that they are all taken from after 1998, this ratio again suggests that claims the court has become supine or inactive with its second generation of judges must be exaggerations.

A Theoretically Ambitious Court

If the Hungarian court is activist, at least in one respect it cannot be blamed for its practices. The constitution empowers the court more fully than most of its fellow constitutional review bodies—there is hardly any route for bringing a matter before a constitutional court known in the democratic world that does not appear in the Hungarian constitution. And there is one route, the idea of a "constitutional exception," which is probably unique to Hungary. An example of how this

[81] *Decision of 5th March 1992 on Retroactive Criminal Legislation*, 11/92 (Hungarian Constitutional Court).

[82] As, for example, in the arguments centring round Ackerman, *We the People*.

works is given in a case where the court intervened in parliamentary investigations of former Soviet-era security officers involved in politics.[83] Like some other such bodies, including the French Conseil constitutionnel, one of the Hungarian court's duties is to police parliamentary procedure. It has been quite strict in this role, not entirely to the liking of parliament, on the grounds that it is incumbent on the court not only to make the parliament obey the general list of constitutional rights, but also to perform its role in the separation of powers. In 2003 the court found an unconstitutional omission to act where the parliament had inadequately controlled its own investigative committee, going so far as to actually annul the existence of one such committee, and even to do so retroactively.[84] This idea of a constitutional omission has been used relatively sparingly by the court, for it is a potentially powerful weapon for any review body. The constitutional definition is relatively clear but intentionally wide, set out in the 1989 act creating the court:

> an unconstitutional omission of legislative duty may be established if the legislature has failed to fulfil its legislative duty mandated by a legal norm, and this has given rise to an unconstitutional situation. The Constitutional Court shall establish an unconstitutional omission if the guarantees necessary for the enforcement of a fundamental right are missing, or if the omission of regulation endangers the enforcement of a fundamental right.[85]

The first major use of the technique, very effectively, was in a most difficult political clash early in the new republic over the extent of the government's control of state-run media channels.[86] Of course the aim of using the technique in the *Parliamentary Investigative Committees* case was as much to protect the civil rights of those accused by the committee as it was to control the role of these committees more generally. It is not up to the court itself to find a constitutional omission—it cannot just survey Hungarian politics and decide, *sua sponte*, that something ought to be done that has not been done. As much as any other review body, the Hungarian Constitutional Court is passive until someone else presents a case to it. But few cases come up where the plaintiff might possibly argue for an omission and has not done so, with the court preferring to decide the case on other grounds wherever possible.

The real function of the omission technique in the hands of the court is to allow analogical argument between rights. Thus if right X is protected effectively by legislation, but another right Y lacks adequate legislative backing, the court can find that this constitutes an omission to act—the technique cannot in itself found a right. But whether the court will or will not accept the invitation to notice such an omission seems to be almost entirely discretionary. Thus in 2003 plaintiffs asked for such a finding in a case concerning the legislative law on the right to die.[87] The

[83] *Decision of 2003 on Procedure of Parliamentary Investigative Committees*, 50/2003 (XI.5) AB (Hungarian Constitutional Court).

[84] *Procedure of Parliamentary Investigative Committees.*

[85] Section 49(1) of Act XXXII of 1989 on the constitutional court.

[86] *Decision of 10th June 1992 on the Media*, 37/1992 (VI.10) AB (Hungarian Constitutional Court).

[87] *Decision of 28th April 2003 on Physician Aided Termination of Life*, 22/2003 (IV.28) AB (Hungarian Constitutional Court).

legislation attacked had in fact considerably eased the treatment of those with terminal illnesses, allowing amongst other things the right to refuse treatment. The dignity-in-death movement thought this did not go far enough, and claimed, inter alia, that in not amending the law to remove physician-aided death from possibly counting as murder, the legislature had failed to protect the right to dignity. The whole case caused the Constitutional Court enormous trouble because even more than other national constitutional review bodies it has imported enthusiastically the German constitutional court's jurisprudence on human dignity. Article 54 of the constitution reads: "every human being has the inherent right to life and to human dignity, of which no one can be arbitrarily deprived." The problem is that in early decisions the court had taken this to be one unitary right—"life and human dignity"—especially in its earliest controversial case abolishing the death penalty. Not surprisingly, there had never been a situation where, if taken as two rights, life and dignity might clash. In fact the entire "right to life" jurisprudence of the court is complex and full of possible internal contradictions.[88] This particular case threw up a host of the more intractable questions that the court's already rich constitutional thinking has raised. For example, the constitution contains a rule that has plagued the German court, and at one stage existed in the South African constitution in a way that caused those justices much trouble: the idea that even allowable legislative restrictions on a right must not "limit the essential content of any fundamental right." This is a bar, when it can be deployed, against proportionality arguments, and against countervailing rights or duties. One particular previous ruling of the court on the right to life was involved, as controversial in 2003 as it had been when it surfaced in the abortion ruling of 1991.[89] Although the argument, both in 1991 and 2003, may seem curious to many schooled in a common-law tradition, it in fact follows from basic principles of constitutional law as developed in Germany. The idea is that that state's duty to protect life is not simply a duty held towards someone whose life might be at risk, but to life in general. This was used in the abortion case to insist that there was at least a minimum sense of life involved with a foetus, and the state had to protect that, protect the absolute existence of life, even if the individual life bearer, the foetus, may have no interest in it. Here the argument becomes one that the state has a generalised duty towards life separate from any interest a terminally ill person might have in his or her own life prolongation. This was in the end a trump card for the court in failing to find a constitutional omission, but it had to be held against the essential content argument proffered by the death-with-dignity lobby.

The court cited the plaintiff's argument thus:

> Self-determination is the core of the right to human dignity, relating to the free development of one's personality as well as to realising one's personal freedom on the basis of self-determination. In this respect, the State's obliga-

[88] Dupré, *Importing the Law*, gives a particularly acute analyses of these problems, though her book predates this decision.

[89] *Decision of 17th December 1991 on the Regulation of Abortion*, 64/1991 (Hungarian Constitutional Court).

> tion of institutional protection—and the constitutional definition thereof—is nothing else but ensuring self-determination that follows from human dignity. All other obligations of the State would violate the essence of the fundamental right to human dignity, i.e. personal self-determination, and as such, they would be contrary to the guarantee for protecting the essence of the fundamental right granted in Article 8 para. (2) of the Constitution. Therefore, one should conclude that human dignity may not be protected by violating the right to self-determination, which represents the essence thereof.[90]

It should be noted that in the plaintiff's argument "dignity" has been translated into "self-determination"—but this is itself a borrowing from other cases where the court itself has used this translation in order to derive from dignity some other more precise right.[91] It is a feature of the "mother right" status attributed to dignity by the court that it can be used to derive other rights not actually mentioned in the constitution, and as such has been a major engine of constitutional interpretation and judicial discretion. Ultimately, and despite much agonising, the court held firmly that there was no constitutional omission, though the arguments are less than totally persuasive:

> In contrast, the desire of a terminally ill patient to have his death induced by a physician, for example, by supplying or administering an appropriate substance is—as indicated by the Constitutional Court in point IV.6.2—beyond that part of the patient's right to self-determination that is unrestrictable, both in part or in whole, by the law, as in such cases, death is actively induced by another person, i.e. the physician. Therefore, the possibility of a physician actively inducing the death of a terminally ill patient at the patient's request cannot be deduced from the general right to self-determination enjoyed by all patients. Thus, in the opinion of the Constitutional Court, in view of the significant differences between dispensing with an intervention necessary for sustaining the life of a terminally ill patient and actively inducing with the aid of a physician the death of such a patient, the fact that the former act is allowed by the law does not impose a constitutional obligation on the legislature to allow the latter one as well.[92]

Many other arguments were deployed, and an exhaustive analysis of case law and legislation elsewhere in the world was undertaken. But there is no escaping the sense that the Hungarian court has by now an overrich conceptual apparatus, one that rather than making it easy to answer problems, has in fact forced ever more sophisticated attempts to escape initial sweeping and ambitious doctrine. Certainly this case, which is not atypical, demonstrates a wide variety of legal and constitutional tropes being deployed by both sides. There were after all four power-

[90] *Physician Aided Termination of Life*, Section 1.

[91] For example another crucial early case *Decision of 13th April 1991 on Use of Personal Data*, 15/1991 (Hungarian Constitutional Court).

[92] *Physician Aided Termination of Life*, Section 6.

ful and lengthy dissents, as well as a separate concurring opinion, all out of a court of eleven. What has happened is that a combination of constitutionally mandated rules, like those of constitutional omission and essential content, have interacted with sweeping value creation (dignity, for example), methodological preferences (the living law), and a deeply litigious culture to produce a confusing if admirable legal culture where judicial discretion is maximised. Much of this work, for good or evil, was done in the very first years of the court. It is perhaps an attempt to be less intellectually adventurous in order to leave fewer hostages to fortune that has taken over the court in the last few years and has been mistaken for a lack of preparedness to use discretion or to work hard for constitutional values.

The Rule of Law and the Problem of the Past

The best way to understand the differences and similarities of East European attempts to reimpose the rule of law is by comparison. It happens that most of the courts in the region have had to cope, in their own ways and subject to their local political contexts, with one common problem. Furthermore, this problem lies at the heart of almost anything that might be meant by the tendentious phrase *the rule of law*. The problem is that the precursor polities were conspicuous for not abiding by the rule of law. As a result the new political systems have had to find ways of dealing with the offences of the past, in ways that do not themselves replicate the lawlessness of the past. In this section we will look at some typical approaches, mainly from Hungary, Poland, and the Czech Republic (and, marginally, from Czechoslovakia before the divorce).

The idea of the rule of law is very rich and deep, allowing much legitimate variation in its implication. We can see ourselves as asking, in a way, what precise rules or constitutional court decisions are necessarily implied by the avowed preference *non sub homine, sed sub lege*. There is no simple and uniform definition being applied everywhere in the area—it is indeed the differences that are most revealing. Such doctrines constitute further building blocks in the constructive writing of democratic political theory by courts as they move towards an international constitutional common law.[93] What the Hungarian, Czech, Polish, Slovenian, Lithuanian, and Estonian high courts have thought when asked about the constitutional validity of some methods of dealing with the problems of the past could be of enormous value in this long-term endeavour. At the very least their difficulties draw our attention to how little worked out are many of our legal assumptions and icons in this area.

[93] I have discussed the idea that the CEE courts are working towards a *common* constitutional law in Robertson, *Democratic Transitions*. It is clear that at least some of the leading CEE jurists themselves have an idea very close to this, and an ambition to share in developing such an international approach. See, especially, L Sólyom, "Opening Address, 10th Conference of European Constitutional Courts," in *Bulletin on Constitutional Case Law* (Budapest: Council of Europe, 1996).

The Nature of the Case Law

The way in which concepts like "the rule of law," "a state under the rule of law" and so on are worked out and used in Central and East European (CEE) court decisions needs to be understood in terms of the very nature and context of the case law, which is often very different from that of established Western courts, as demonstrated in the previous three subsections. The material comes from the very early years of the development of curial authority in CEE jurisdictions. The consequence of this history is that these courts did not assess the constitutionality of, for example, lustration statutes against a background of well-established constitutional rights doctrine, or even of well-established structural constitutional doctrine. Rather the lustration cases were, inter alia, precisely part of the material used by the courts to develop their doctrines on *vires* and rights. It was not quite a matter, in other words, of asking whether a section on retrospective punishment of an act passed by the Czech parliament breaches guarantees of legal certainty that are of vital constitutional importance, as it might be in a longer established court. It is much more a matter of using reflection on this section to work out what legal certainty means and how important such legal certainty is to a democratic constitution and the rule of law. The difference is that to a large extent a Western court analyses a troubling statute against a relatively well-established definition of a constitutional right to see if it passes scrutiny. There is, as it were, only one puzzle. Here there is a double puzzle: the statute needs to be analyzed, but the right has to be as well, for they are interdefined. There is thus a self-reflexivity in the process of constitutional jurisprudence over this period and in these countries that is highly unusual and crucial. Although chapter 1 argues that constitutional review is always self-reflexive, it is never as clear elsewhere as in these countries. From our point of view the great advantage is that there is far more, more thoughtful, and less formulaic discussion of absolutely core questions than one finds anywhere except in similar transition states.[94] This cannot be stressed enough. This idea of reflection on complex problems is crucial, though its relative frequency between countries is also one of the keys to the differences in constitutional understanding one finds on the rule of law.

Decisions of the Czech court are perhaps the best examples. As suggested earlier, there is frequently a depth of reflection on democracy and on the relationship between law and core sociopolitical values that one could never find in an established Western court—indeed that no Western court *has ever* undertaken. One good example is the case on the constitutionality of the statute Regarding

[94] Transitions need not be dramatic to be useful to us in this way—not only does the South African court give us similar original reflection, but so does the Canadian court on receiving its Charter. On the latter see C L'Heureux-Dubé, "Realising Equality in the Twentieth Century: The Role of the Supreme Court of Canada in Comparative Perspective," 2003 1 *International Journal of Constitutional Law* 1, 35–57; for a South African case exhibiting the degree of open and flexible thought typical in some CEE cases, consider *Grootboom and Others v Government of the Republic of South Africa and Others*, CCT 11/00 (South African Constitutional Court). The rival constitutional theories behind the South African Bill of Rights are well depicted in Chanock, "Post-Calvinist Catechism."

the Lawlessness of the Communist Regime and Resistance to It,[95] to be discussed later.[96] We considered earlier the famous decision on the Benes decree, which culminated in the statement that the democratic principle ranked above "formal, legal legitimacy." It is, of course, possible that a court that thinks any principle can rank above "formal, legal legitimacy" does not understand the rule of law, and it is arguable the Hungarian court, for one, would take that position. Others might argue, with the Czech court, that the rule of law, or the idea of a "state under law," especially in a transition period, actually requires this politically informed depth of analysis. A court that thinks in this way is unlikely to produce the sort of formalistic application of the idea of the rule of law that might please some. It is equally a court that cannot easily be accused of indifference to the deepest moral and political questions of legal legitimacy.

It must be said as a general comment that it would be odd if the jurisprudence of the CEE courts was deficient in respect for the rule of law, however nuanced and regionally specific their rulings might be. These courts all show very considerable commitment to a comparative methodology. It is important to each of them that the solutions used elsewhere to the special problems of transition states be taken into account. But equally, constitutional law from a wide range of countries is cited in aid of developing the local rule—not only other CEE states and Germany but other Western countries, for example France, and when possible common-law constitutional jurisprudence from North America.[97] The exact way in which the courts use external jurisprudence is more controversial. Some commentators seem to think there was more automaticity about the process than do the leading jurists themselves. We have, for example, the powerful and detailed analysis of the Hungarian court's debt to Germany given by Catherine Dupré that only partially coincides with the account the court's chief legal architect, László Sólyom, himself gives. Sólyom is more prone to stress the differences in actual results, Dupré the reliance on German reasoning.[98] Sólyom is, however, also our best source for how influential foreign law in general and German law in particular has been for other CEE national constitutional courts.[99] If a developing constitutional law so heavily influenced by Western Europe is deficient in respect for the rule of law, something very strange must have happened in the process of legal borrowing. From their beginnings all of these courts have shown every sign of working towards a comparatively constructed common understanding of democratic constitutionalism.

A final important characteristic may only be noteworthy to those used to looking through common-law eyes, and with an Anglo-American perspective on con-

[95] Act No 198/1993 Sb.

[96] This has been very ably analysed by J Priban, "Moral and Political Legislation in Constitutional Justice: A Case Study of the Czech Constitutional Court," 2001 8 *Journal of East European Law* 1.

[97] The mere fact that Germany allowed a potentially retroactive prosecution in its *Border Guards* case might lead one to wonder why the CEE countries were peculiarly thought to lack respect for the rule of law. For a good discussion of this issue in the context of transition law, see Gabriel, "East German Border Guards." A more theoretical treatment is Quint, "Border Guard Trials."

[98] Dupré, *Importing the Law*. Contrast the account given by Sólyom, "Role of Constitutional Courts."

[99] See also Sólyom's address in "Opening Address."

stitutional rights. This feature is the extent to which at least some courts spin a coherent web of rights jurisprudence, rather than treating each case and each issue as largely freestanding. There is a surprising degree of reference to a court's own decisions wherever analogies can be made even though at such an early stage in curial history there are seldom other cases so directly relevant that they must be brought to bear. Even where precedent-like references are not made, much of what shapes an interpretation of what "the rule of law" requires is the use a court hopes, or needs, to put the concept to in some likely future application to a different question. One way to interpret the Hungarian court's narrow and positivistic interpretation of "legal certainty" on the retrospective punishment issue is to note the far from narrow and positivistic use it made of the concept in striking down social security reductions, as discussed later. In the same way, the entire Czech "methodology of constitutional interpretation" in the Benes degree case is clearly connected to the approach in an earlier lustration case before the Czechoslovakian court and the later decision on retroactivity of the Czech court. Again the Hungarian court, in the eyes of its interpreters,[100] was very conscious of shaping tools of general utility in its constitutional interpretations.

I proceed by examining three sets of cases, covering different aspects of the problems of dealing with the past.

Retroactivity, Legal Certainty, and Substantive Justice

I have used, and largely continue to use, the word *lustration* in a rather broad sense, mainly to avoid the cumbersome but more appropriate "problems arising from dealing with the past." What is not often fully appreciated is that these cases, whether they be technically lustration, or retroactive punishment or property compensation or whatever, are about the past in two rather different ways. They are, as is obvious, about the constitutionality of attempts to deal with injustices past and present arising from the previous ruling political ideology and system. But they involve questions of the *legal* impact of the past, and indeed generally of the passing of time in a more abstract sense.[101] This is because courts have chosen to deal, or been unable to avoid dealing, with these issues partly in terms of the doctrine of legal certainty. It is a question of some interest whether this route was avoidable. Certainly the insistence of all the courts, but especially the Hungarians, that legal certainty is at the very core of the idea of "a state governed by law" involves a stance that in many eyes marks their doctrine out as a very "legalistic" approach. To many, "legal certainty" is the lawyer's value par excellence, and too often used by conservative judges to restrict innovations by their brethren. It is also the hallmark of a constitutional jurisprudence favouring procedural over substantive values, favouring a traditional continental European formalism. Yet to the extent that a major problem of the past regimes in Central and Eastern Europe

[100] This is a major theme in Dupré, *Importing the Law*.

[101] The best analysis I know of the entire nature of the problem of the past is J Priban, *Dissidents of Law* (London: Ashgate, 2002), especially chapter 4.

was not the imposition of cruel law but the failure to obey existing law, a common theme in the judicial arguments in these cases, it may not be possible to take a more relaxed attitude to legal certainty.[102]

Compounding this problem is the difficulty arising from the story the new regime tells about its birth. New CEE regimes vary in how much they wish to see their origins in a revolution. It is no accident that the court that most stresses legal certainty as the cornerstone of a democratic constitution, the Hungarian, is the one that has tried most ardently to tell a story about the essentially unrevolutionary and *legal* nature of the transition. László Sólyom makes a strong defence of the Hungarian decision about retroactive punishment, which rested on making "legal certainty" a prime constitutional virtue under the aegis of rule of law. His claim is that Hungary before the revolution had been a very mild regime in which much freedom was allowed to citizens. To mark the difference under the new regime, where "permissions" were replaced by "rights," required a firm commitment to procedural values in order to establish that the constitution now really was the sole source of legal authority.[103] If this was really the motivation, the presumed contrast with the Czech Republic must be that Czechs, because they had had a rougher experience of the last days of Communism, could be trusted to value their new constitution highly enough to allow it to be interpreted in a more substantively just manner. Oddly, one country with good institutional grounds for such an account, the only one whose constitutional court predates transition, Poland, is much less likely to tell itself that story and to cite legal certainty as core.

The issue above all in which legal certainty has mattered most is that of retroactive punishment. One of the problems of comparative constitutional law is finding cases from two or more jurisdictions sufficiently similar to make comparison effective. We are thus very lucky that this issue has arisen in so similar a way in two countries, the Czech Republic and Hungary—sufficiently similiar to be, in old lawyer language, on all fours with each other. We are even luckier that the two constitutional courts gave opposed decisions, and luckiest of all that they discussed almost exactly the same issues in coming to radically different understandings of how to deal with the past under democratic constitutions.[104] The cases both involved an attempt by the respective legislatures to make open to prosecution people who had committed crimes under the Communist regime but had not been prosecuted precisely because their criminal behaviour was carried out on behalf of the regime. Many such offenders were, by the early 1990s, immune from prosecution because the statute of limitation written into the law at the time of the commission of their crimes, had run its course. In both cases the statutes attempted to treat such offenders as though the clock had stopped for the whole or part of the

[102] I have discussed this in D Robertson, "The Role of Constitutional Courts in the New Eastern European Democracies," Public Lecture, Jagellonian University, Kraków, October 3, 2005.

[103] Sólyom, "Role of Constitutional Courts."

[104] The Czech Republic: *Decision of 21st December Regarding the Lawlessness of the Communist Regime*, Pl. US 19/93 (Czech Republic Constitutional Court). For Hungary, *Decision of 5th March 1992 on Retroactive Criminal Legislation*. This is reported in Sólyom and Brunner, *Constitutional Judiciary*.

period of the previous regime, thus giving the new regime time to deal with the cases. But also in both countries it was decided not to make all alleged criminals from that period who had not been tried face renewed legal vulnerability. Instead only those whose prosecutions had not taken place for "political reasons" were to be vulnerable to a restarted clock.

The Hungarian president declined to promulgate the act[105] (On the Prosecution of Serious Criminal Offences Not Previously Prosecuted for Political Reasons) and addressed a series of questions to the Constitutional Court. Essentially these questions suggested that a recommencement of the statute of limitations "conflicted with the rule of law, an essential component of which was legal certainty"; second, that it was based on "overly general provisions and vague concepts," which also offended against legal certainty; and finally, that distinguishing "between perpetrators of the same offence on the basis of the State's reason for prosecuting such offences" was in violation of a constitutional prohibition on arbitrariness and of the equal protection clause of Article 70-A-1 of the constitution.

The Hungarian court did find the act unconstitutional on all of these grounds; in doing so it developed further the doctrine it had enunciated since its beginning, commented on above. The change of system in Hungary in 1989 had been fully legal by the predecessor system's own law, and this very fact, according to the court, imposes an even stronger obligation to obey the new constitution than might otherwise have been the case.[106]

> The change of system has been carried out on the basis of legality. The principle of legality imposes on the state under the rule of law the requirement that legal regulations regarding the legal system itself should be abided by unconditionally. The politically revolutionary changes adopted by the Constitution and all the new fundamental laws were enacted, in full compliance with the old legal system's procedural laws on legislation, thereby gaining their binding force. The old law retained its validity. With respect to its validity there is no distinction between "pre-Constitution" and "post-Constitution" law.[107]

This sense of legal continuity is somehow or other found compatible with a clear sense of how the new system differs from the past. "The Republic of Hungary is an independent democratic state under the rule of law" is taken to have "conferred on the State its law and the political system a new quality, fundamentally different from that of the previous regime." But this difference is seen as potentially fragile, requiring great purity of legal purpose to preserve it:

> That Hungary is a state under the rule of law is both a statement of fact and a statement of policy. A state under the rule of law becomes a reality when the Constitution is truly and unconditionally given effect. For the legal system the change of system means, and the change of the legal system is possible

[105] Act (IV/1991).

[106] Though Priban makes the point that the continuity of the pre- and post-transition Hungarian system is largely a legal fiction. Priban, *Dissidents of Law*.

[107] Sólyom and Brunner, *Constitutional Judiciary*, 220.

> only in that sense, that the whole body of law must be brought into harmony—and new legislation kept in harmony—with the new Constitution. Not only must the legal provisions and the operation of state organs comply strictly with the Constitution but the Constitution's values and its conceptual culture must permeate the whole of society. This is the rule of law, and this is how the Constitution becomes a reality. The realization of the rule of law is a continuous process.[108]

This is, in effect, a legal equivalent to the oft-heard cry from those inside CEE countries who are opposed to lustration: "We are not like them!" The need to be perfectly consistent in following the rule of law arises simultaneously from the fact that the old system was not law-abiding, and that the new system has its origin in abiding by the old procedural laws. It does not follow from any of this, of course, that legal certainty is quite so crucial an element of the rule of law, but this second move is stated more than justified. Having defined legal certainty as requiring, inter alia, the protection of vested rights, and noninterference with legal relations already executed, the primacy of legal certainty is made almost tautologous—and a very powerful tautology at that:

> individual legal relations and legal facts become independent of the statutory sources from which they emerge and do not automatically share their fate. Were this otherwise, a change in the law would necessitate in every instance a review of the whole body of legal relations. Thus from the principle of legal certainty, it follows that already executed or concluded legal relations cannot be altered constitutionally by enactment of a law or by invalidation of a law by either the legislature or the Constitutional Court.[109]

Whether the court really believes the last sentence, there is no doubt left about the role of legal certainty in constitutional definitions of the rule of law. Citing an earlier case,[110] the court insists "the consequences of the unconstitutionality of a law must be evaluated primarily with reference to their impact on legal certainty."

The court was fully aware of the pragmatic arguments from the political nature of the pretransition crimes, and develops here an almost chillingly formalistic view of the constitution. (This occurs quite frequently, notably in the economic compensation cases.) Shortly after these statements, the court says quite bluntly

[108] Sólyom and Brunner, *Constitutional Judiciary*, 219.

[109] Sólyom and Brunner, *Constitutional Judiciary*, 223.

[110] *Decision of 25th February 1992 on Powers Ex Nunc*, 10/1992 (Hungarian Constitutional Court), reported in Sólyom and Brunner, *Constitutional Judiciary*, 209. This case occurred after the first two "compensation" cases, *Decision of 4th October 1990 Compensation Case I*, 21/1990 (Hungarian Constitutional Court) and *Decision of 20th April 1991 Compensation Case II*, 16/1991 (Hungarian Constitutional Court) in which past legal relationships had been protected and before the Social Security case, *Decision of 30th June 1995 on Social Security Benefits*, 43/1995 (Hungarian Constitutional Court), where legal certainty was used to strike down benefit reductions. This latter is discussed later in the book. The cases are reported in Sólyom and Brunner, *Constitutional Judiciary*, 108, 151, 322. One can see the way in which a concept can take on an unavoidable constitutional importance in some contexts, beyond the point, perhaps, the court might wish, because of its importance as a tool in other contexts.

that "the unjust result of legal relations does not constitute an argument against the principle of legal certainty"; this develops into "the requirement of the rule of law as to substantive justice may be attained within the institutions and guarantees ensuring legal certainty. The Constitution does not and cannot confer a right for substantive justice," and finally:

> The basic guarantees of the rule of law cannot be set aside by reference to historical situations and to justice as a requirement of the state under the rule of law. A state under the rule of law cannot be created by undermining the rule of law. Legal certainty based on formal and objective principles is more important than necessarily partial and subjective justice.[111]

The arguments go on like this, and further quotation would add very little to the point. Throughout a fierce commitment to procedural principle is shown, often in language making the demands of this principle greater than the justices themselves can really have believed. We are told that legal guarantees can *never* be denied by a state under the rule of law, that criminal law constitutional provisions cannot even be restricted or suspended in "a state of national crisis, a state of emergency or a state of danger." There is real fear throughout the judgement of law being misused. While admitting that the criminal law is not merely an instrument but "protects and embodies values," it turns out that the values it protects are "the principles and guarantees of constitutional criminal law." More importantly, "though criminal law protects values, as a guarantee of freedom it cannot become an instrument for moral purges in the process of protecting values." Quite simply, under the law in place at the time, ruthless criminals killing people to serve the political masters of the state were entitled to become free of risk of prosecution a set number of years after their crime, and the constitution of the new republic would be put at risk denying them their entitlement.

It must be stressed that this supremacy of legal certainty has been extensively used by the Hungarian court, often in quite brave ways—it was the basis, for example, on which it struck down important budgetary policies that trimmed too far, in the court's eyes, legitimate expectations of welfare payments, as discussed in a later chapter on "positive rights." It may be for this reason that the court refused to look at the logic of limitation rules, and consider whether the values the court sought to protect were in fact the sort that legal certainty is actually intended to promote. Statutes of limitations are rather low on the scale of basic human rights; they vary enormously from jurisdiction to jurisdiction, and have their main justification from the fact that a long-delayed criminal trial may produce evidentiary problems. It would have been an easy task to support the challenged legislation on the grounds that the normal reasons for such limitations did not apply, and that evidentiary questions could always be handled by trial judges. But to open up the question of why and when legal certainty needed to be seen as a high constitutional value would have weakened the court's ability to use it in other contexts.

[111] Sólyom and Brunner, *Constitutional Judiciary*, 221.

It might not be worth spending as much time on the nature of the thought processes in this judgement, which is, in its own way, a flawless development of a purely procedural orientation to constitutional law, but for one fact. The fact is that another court in another country with a similar history looked at the same issue and came out in the other direction. But before discussing the Czech case, a further chapter in the Hungarian story is worth mentioning, because it underscores the formalism of the court. A year later the parliament, still determined to wield substantive justice in this area, took another and highly creative tack. It passed an act, On the Procedure of Certain Criminal Offences Committed during the 1956 October Revolution and Freedom Struggle,[112] which got round the statute of limitations problem by applying international laws against war crimes and crimes against humanity, which by a 1968 agreement to which Hungary was signatory, had no statute of limitations. This act was also found to be unconstitutional, largely because of bad draftsmanship. But the court was so eager to show that Hungary now *had* found a way to proceed against some of the worst offenders of the past regime in a way that was procedurally proper that it not only set out how the act could be remedied, but went even further and essentially announced that the relevant international law had direct effect in Hungary and did not need statutory support! What this does to legal certainty in a substantive sense is anyone's guess.[113] Nonetheless, the decision, based on a strong interpretation of the constitution's recognition of the supremacy and automatic incorporation of international law, demonstrates the typical openness of the new democracies' constitutional judiciary to foreign and international jurisprudence. It would certainly have been possible to avoid granting direct effect that, given the failure of the parliament to draft adequately, would have continued the immunity of Communist-era criminals.[114]

Hard Lustration

The contrast between the Czech and Hungarian approaches—as in general with lustration issues—is enormous. To start with, the context within which the Czech case arises is vastly different. The issue of extending the date at which prosecutions become time-barred was buried in a very strange statute, probably unique amongst CEE nations. The statute itself, Regarding the Lawlessness of the Communist Regime and Resistance to It[115] was primarily concerned with making a statement about collective moral and political guilt for the past, and condemning the Communist Party and its members. By the terms of the act itself, most of the

[112] *Decision of 13th October 1993 on War Crimes and on Crimes against Humanity*, 53/1993 (Hungarian Constitutional Court).

[113] This case is described, with commentary, in Sólyom and Brunner, *Constitutional Judiciary*, 283–83.

[114] One interpretation of why the court decided the second version of the limitations issue this way is that throughout the 1990s it was involved in a negotiation process with the Hungarian parliament so that it usually gave the legislature part of what it wanted in return for the legislature accepting the court's authority by demanding less a second time around. See Schepple, "Constitutional Negotiations."

[115] Act No 198/1993 Sb.

language, even when cast in pseudo-legal terms of criminal law, was not intended to create any criminal liability, though it was attacked as doing just this, as well as for many other things. However the court used its answer to objections about the general unconstitutionality of such a statement to set a context within which it became much easier to uphold the really controversial aspect, which was the prolongation of the prosecution period for politically protected crime. So completely different is the Czech view on legal continuity that one wonders whether it was in part written with an eye to the Hungarian case that had been decided a year earlier—though there is no reference at all to that case in the court's opinion.[116]

This section of the opinion requires explication because it is at least as important in helping us draw conclusions about our topic as the more legally concrete later section. The group of forty-one Czech deputies who brought the action claimed that the statement in Section 2 of the act whereby the previous regime was declared illegitimate must be unconstitutional because the new republic was a successor state in which inherited statutes, rules, and other legal obligations remained in force. As the court put the claimants' case, "this 'substantive continuity of domestic and international rights' is . . . an indication of the legitimacy of the governmental and political regime during the period 1948—1989." In fact the claimants' argument in part could have been taken directly from the Hungarian judgement:

> If the statutory statement concerning the illegitimacy of the government and political system during the period . . . were correct and remained in effect, then the legal acts adopted during the stated period would no longer have been valid as of 1st August 1993; naturally this did not occur, for legal certainty is one of the basic characteristics of a law-based state, and that certainty depends on the constancy of legally expressed principles in particular areas of the law, on the constancy of legal relations.

The Czech court clearly had a problem in answering this account, but it was a problem it seems to have relished, and the answer, which depends on a trenchant rejection of some forms of legal formalism, has real implications for constitutional law throughout Europe. The court asserts that the positivistic legal tradition that predated the early development of post-1918 democracies in Central Europe, though it had strengthened legal certainty and the stability of laws, had in its later development "many times exposed its weaknesses. Constitutions enacted on this basis are neutral with regard to values." The court argued such positivism led directly to Hitler's ability to claim legality for his destruction of Weimar. In a resounding paragraph, it cast early post-1945 Czechoslovak history as the victim of such legal positivism:

> After the war this legalistic conception of political legitimacy made it possible for Klement Gottwald to "fill up old casks with new wine." Then in 1948 he was able, by the formal observance of constitutional procedures, to "legitimate" the February Putsch. In the face of injustice, the principle that

[116] *Regarding the Lawlessness of the Communist Regime.*

"law is law" revealed itself to be powerless. Consciousness of the fact that injustice is still injustice, even though it is wrapped in the cloak of law, was reflected in the post-war German Constitution and, at the present time, in the Constitution of the Czech Republic.[117]

But note the way, as we saw earlier, this historically informed style of argument was used to legitimise the Benes decrees, which occurred in the brief period between Nazi and Communist regimes. It is certainly a fine line one walks if one is to pick and choose between substantive and procedural constitutional legitimacy. The court goes on to spell out in what way the Czech constitution is not value neutral, is not "merely a demarcation of institutions and processes," but is suffused with the core values of democracy that must be used in legal interpretation. It becomes an important interpretative point—one initially developed earlier in the first lustration case, as I shall go on to discuss. Here the point is made in words that require full quotation:

> The Czech Constitution accepts and respects the principle of legality as a part of the overall basic conception of a law-based state; positive law does not, however, bind it merely to formal legality, rather the interpretation and application of legal norms are subordinated to their substantive purpose, law is qualified by respect for the basic enacted values of a democratic society and also measures the application of legal norms by these values. *This means that even while there is continuity of "old laws" there is discontinuity in values from the "old regime."* (Emphasis added)

In other words, the old laws must be interpreted via the new values, and not as a value-free procedural system. We have already discussed these intellectual moves applied in different cases earlier in this chapter. What this ends up as is the idea that in order to be faithful to the values of a modern democratic state, something akin to a "piercing of the corporate veil" (in the terminology of commercial law) is required. Ironically, it is the specifically Hungarian stress, borrowed from the Italians, on looking at the "living law" (though here the living law of the past) that is needed and used. This has to be the case because, as both the complainant deputies here and the Hungarian court point out, mere anarchy would follow from a generalised removal of legal certainty. This becomes clearer when the Czech court turns to the issue of stopping the clock on the statute of limitations for the whole duration of the previous regime. Doing so in general is justified by the now statutory illegitimacy of the past, but it is necessary to show that no real violence is done to legal certainty, but rather, a very ambitious aim, legal certainty actually *requires* such a move. The argument the court uses is essentially one of empirical

[117] The fact that Germany has allowed a similar prolongation of the statue of limitations for East German, alleged politically protected, criminals is important later in the court's argument. But it is noteworthy that the Hungarian court, usually close to German thinking, does not cite the German court at all, whereas the Czech court gives this distinctly nonpositivistic reading to the German constitution. An extremely interesting account of the German situation, which also suggests some ways of squaring the circle between the Hungarian and Czech positions, is AJ McAdams, *Judging the Past in Unified Germany* (Cambridge: Cambridge University Press, 2001).

common sense. No one really believes that the state had any intention of prosecuting its own agents for illegal behaviour—"Political power founded on violence should, in principle, take care not to rid itself of those who carry out its violence." The court then defines the actual legal condition for a statute of limitations—it depends on the state actually wishing and trying to prosecute. Without this proviso, the concept of limitation is empty and the very purpose of the legal institution is beyond fulfilment. A statute of limitations can only exist

> if there has been a long-term interaction of two elements: the intention and the efforts of the state to punish an offender and the ongoing danger to the offender that he may be punished, both giving a real meaning to the institution of the limitation of actions.

Courts must always have the last word, so it is hardly surprising that the Czech court makes the ultimate move, which is that legal certainty requires this analysis: the orthodox application of the idea, treating the situation as the running of a limitation period that was not permitted to run, would produce "a quite paradoxical interpretation of a law-based state," the validation of a different legal certainty, the certainty the perpetrators originally had that they were safe. More fully:

> This "legal certainty" of offenders is, however, a source of legal uncertainty to citizens (and vice versa). In a contest of these two types of certainty, the Constitutional Court gives priority to the certainty of civil society.

Indeed, the court argues, any other answer would legitimate a dictatorship *as law based*, giving a sign that "crime may become non-criminal." In competition with the Hungarian idea that strict application of traditional legal certainty is vital for the health of the new democracy, the Czech judges argue instead that such an approach would mean "the loss of credibility of the present law-based state." In fact it would infringe Article 9(3) of the constitution, "legal norms may not be interpreted so as to authorise anyone to do away with or jeopardize the democratic foundations of the state."

Further to demonstrate this technique of showing that formal legal values may better be protected by doing the opposite of what they seem to require, it is well to point out how very briefly the court dealt with the discrimination argument. In both Hungary and the Czech Republic it had been argued that removing time-barring only for one sort of offender, the politically protected, but not others who happened to have escaped prosecution, involved unequal treatment. The Hungarian court had agreed that this was unjust discrimination. The Czech answer is short and characteristic. This differentiation is not unjust; actually "this is the way to rectify their inequality with those who had already faced the possibility of being put on trial because, not only were they not under special political protection, but it was the state's wish and in its political interest to prosecute them."

As the interpretative methodology of the Czech approach is so different from the Hungarian and potentially so important to our assessment of the CEE in this area, it is worth looking at what is probably its origin, in the first Lustration case. Here I am now using *lustration* in the more technical sense of investigating the past records of people in the public life of the new democracies. It is, of course, well known that Czechoslovakia was the first CEE country to carry out such a policy with any rigour.[118] Considering that the Czech policy, though rather milder and affecting far fewer people than often thought, is one of the strongest, it may alarm some how easily the statute got through the Constitutional Court of the Republic of Czechoslovakia. The opinion, which, again, contains an instant history of the past regime, to act as an empirical justification, starts with a very clear statement of the court's overall attitude to constitutional adjudication. It describes the setting up of the new constitution in ambitious words: "thus an entirely new element of the renaissance of natural human rights was introduced into our legal order." The court also stressed that the new constitution was not to be value free, in language already familiar from the limitations case, dismissing the merely procedurally legitimate: "the concept of the law-based state does not have to do merely with the observance of any sort of values and any sort of rights, even if they were adopted in the procedurally proper manner." But it is when the court talks directly of legal certainty that the determination to produce a novel form of constitutional adjudication becomes clear, all the more strongly because legal certainty as an argument hardly appears in the judgement once the court turns to the issues rather than to introductory noises. Indeed it is not very clear, in the bulk of the argument, why legal certainty needs to be discussed at all. Nonetheless:

> not even the principle of legal certainty can be conceived in isolation, formally and abstractly, but must be gauged by those values of the constitutional and law-based state which have a systematically constitutive nature for the future.

This is spelled out with an early version of the concern for the public legitimacy of the new state found in the statute of limitations case, and needs to be quoted in full:

> As one of the basic concepts and requirements of a law-based state, legal certainty must, therefore, consist in certainty with regard to its substantive values. Thus the contemporary construction of a law-based state which has for its starting point a discontinuity with the totalitarian regime as concerns values may not adopt a criteria [*sic*] of formal-legal and material-legal continuity which is based on a different value system, not even under the circumstances that the formal normative continuity of the legal order makes possible. Respect for continuity with the old value system would not be a guarantee of legal certainty but, on the contrary, by calling into question the values of the new system, legal certainty would be threatened in society and eventually the citizens' faith in the creditably of the democratic system would be shaken.

[118] Although the decision of the unified Czechoslovakian court remained good law in post-divorce Slovakia for some years, the policy was never implemented, and the statute was ultimately repealed. See Schwartz, *Struggle for Constitutional Justice*.

The purpose of the statement in the context of the arguments that follow on the legitimacy of the Czechoslovakian lustration policy is logically unclear, but symbolically vital, because the main proposition embraced is that the new state is entitled to be sure that those in leadership positions fully share the new values. When it comes to discussing the technical constitutionality of the statute, the court actually takes refuge in highly definitional moves. The Czech lustration system required citizens to present a certificate proving that they had no unacceptable connections to the old security regime before they could hold a position above a certain level in a variety of institutions. For the court there was no question of retroactivity, no question of discrimination, no breach of any international obligations under employment law. All that was happening was that the state was setting an extra qualification for holding a post. This requirement was future oriented, hence no retroactivity, it was equally applicable to all, so no discrimination, and was equivalent to similar practices elsewhere, even where it involved taking membership in a group as determinative of unsuitability without individuation of judgement.[119] And the state's entitlement to set such a qualification was the paramount need to ensure the elite of the new republic fully held to its new democratic values. The dismissal of merely "formal" rights from the past is acknowledged and dismissed:

> If compared with the preceding legal order, these conditions might appear to be, from a formal perspective, a restriction on civil rights; however, in the current legal order the basic criteria which will serve as the guide for our actions in the future are those found in the charter.

Just as the realities of actual safety from prosecution of those working for the state had been cited to show that the statute of limitations had never been running, here the partisan employment practises of the old regime are cited as justification. But the connection is, of course, a very different one, and the court's argument is weak on this point despite the impressive rhetoric of the new meaning of legal certainty. The lustration policy was revisited much later because parliament removed the time restriction—the original act had been intended to lapse in 1996—and the court of the Czech Republic decided an appeal, again by parliamentarians opposed to the act, in 2001. A large part of the judgement was involved in working out the status of the previous decision—did it mean the issue was *res judicata*, and if not, to what extent could the court of the Czech Republic still follow the ruling of the court of the Czech and Slovak Federal Republic? It was an issue that had to be dealt with precisely because of the earlier court's stress on the irrelevance of formal continuity, but one easily enough handled because of the same stress on value continuity. The doctrine enunciated was a form of common-law *stare decisis*—to the extent that the world had changed, so could the ruling. But, and this was crucial, the world was judged not to have changed enough, and the second court was careful to limit the extent that the first court had relied, as it had, on the short-term nature of the original lustration restrictions. It derived a form of

[119] Again the court cites Germany, though the only example it could find was a prohibition on some people who been involved with the Stasi working in advanced armaments firms.

"political question" doctrine to insist that it was for the legislature, not the court, to solve the sociological question of when a state was secure enough to do without lustration. Instead the court emphasised the right of a democracy to defend itself, usefully relying on ECHR rulings on the notion of "a democracy capable of defending itself."[120] The new court did regard the external legal environment as, if not decisive, certainly vitally important. It notes that no international court has decided the question of the legitimacy of lustration laws and that they are thus forced to use other "indicators," leaving no doubt that any future case arising after such an international decision might be handled very differently. As it is, the court recites the usual list of similar measures elsewhere, taking especial care to note the 1996 Resolution of the Council of Europe legitimising lustration as long as it is not punishment but protection of democracy.[121] The temper of the second decision is much more even, with greater acknowledgement of the problem of passing time from the old days, and, as noted, with very careful reference to the external legal world. However no single doctrinal aspect of the first decision is doubted, and we are left unsure quite what Czech law does think about the role of legal certainty in a state ruled by law.

There are two forms of lustration. One, the Czech model, restricts access to positions of power directly. The other, the Hungarian and Polish models, operates essentially by "name and shame" policy—all that is formally at risk is that, if an individual does not resign, his past will be made public (Hungary) or if a citizen is found to have lied in his account of his past, he will be debarred from office for ten years (Poland). Other states have used the Czech model, and nowhere has a constitutional court banned it. Lithuania, for example, banned anyone who had worked for the KGB from a wide list of offices and employment sectors, taking much the same line as the Czechs. No discrimination is involved, because it is simply a matter of a legitimate technical qualification for a post applied prospectively.[122] Nor was the challenge, also found elsewhere, under the right to freely choose an occupation seen as relevant. Lithuania did object to the machinery of adjudication as not providing an adequate appeal mechanism, but in fact the original Czech decision had done the same.

Some more far-reaching cases about the past that are not lustration but fit in no obvious category have been dealt with by a different attitude to the continuity of the past, one more in keeping, perhaps with the formalism of the Hungarians. Thus Ukraine's Constitutional Court overturned legislation banning the Communist Party by finding that the current party was legitimately registered in 1991 and had no institutional continuity with its predecessor. Given this, the ban on it breached the freedom-of-association clause of the constitution. But, neatly, as

[120] In particular the court cited *Glasenapp v Germany*, 1986 4/1984 (European Court of Human Rights); *Vogt v Germany* 7/1994 (1994) (European Court of Human Rights).

[121] Resolution No. 1096 (1996).

[122] "On the Assessment of the USSR Committee of State (NKVD, NKGB, MGB, KGB) and Present Activities of the Regular Employees of This Organization," Decision of the Constitutional Court of the Republic of Lithuania, Vilnius, March 5, 1999, from the court's website.

there was no institutional continuity, the party had no claims over its predecessor's property either, thus giving the government much of what it wanted.[123] It is fairly clear that this case had as much to do with asserting the court's authority within the separation of powers as solving the substantive rights claim—something that, as noted earlier, characterises much of the litigation. A powerful example of this was the Polish case on retroactivity in punishing judges who had, in their words, "transgressed against the duty of issuing independent and impartial decisions in political trials conducted before 1989."[124] The tribunal struck down the legislation because of procedural improprieties. However, it saw the procedural lapse in question, failing to consult the National Judiciary Council as required by legislation, as extremely important. We saw earlier the enormous importance the Polish tribunal places on procedure. It developed a complex and far-reaching doctrine covering such consultation rights, based on a scale of constitutional importance of the issues in question, which is itself of major constitutional importance. There is no reason, therefore, to disregard what they did say about the substantive issue, in which the court made it clear that the crucial necessity of an impartial judiciary did justify such retroactivity in this case. The could should, therefore, be seen as on the Czech side of a robust preparedness to deal with past injustices regardless of legal formalism. It might be thought this is even more remarkable given that judiciaries tend to be protective of their brethren. In making my point about the fact that the cases discussed here are seldom only about the issue we look at, it might be thought particularly powerful that it was procedural propriety that stopped the court overruling a concern for procedural propriety. This is not some undisciplined court bowing to political pressure and likely to be indifferent to human rights—it is a court delicately balancing conflicting rights demands, albeit an unusual version of such a clash.

There are other examples of cases on what one might call the Czech end of the lustration spectrum, often dealing specifically with the judiciary,[125] but nowhere has the basic principle been found unconstitutional, nor has such a detailed argument about the nature of legal continuity and its relation to value discontinuity been developed.

Soft Lustration

The first decision on what I have called "soft lustration," systems involving simply publicising some individuals' past records, was rendered in Poland on the ill-fated and politically transparent attempt in May 1992 that ultimately caused the fall of the prime minister. The case is almost infamous, and could not have got through

[123] The case is reported by A Trochev, "Ukraine: Constitutional Court Invalidates Ban on Communist Party," 2003 1 *International Journal of Constitutional Law* 3, 534–40.

[124] Judgement K. 3/98, delivered June 24, 1998, website of the Constitutional Tribunal.

[125] For example, the Slovenian case in which assessment of whether or not a judge had been guilty of favouritism to the old authorities was made a condition for his promotion or confirmation in office. Constitutional Court of the Republic of Slovenia, U-I-83/94, 1994.

even the laxest of constitutional reviews.[126] It is important to us because it is perhaps the best example, even more than the Polish case on retroactivity for punishing judges, to show the interaction between structural constitutional decisions and more obviously human rights issues. It is part of my thesis here that the alertness of the CEE courts to structural power in their constitutional jurisprudence is as much a contribution to a united Europe as would be a simple "good" and "liberal" approach to issues of individualised rights. These two aspects, attention to structural concerns and a liberal position on individual rights, have tended to go hand in hand. In this case the Sejm gave an ill-defined instruction to the minister of internal affairs to provide "complete information regarding government officials from the level of voivode upwards, deputies, senators, prosecutors, barristers, township councillors and members of township management boards who collaborated with the UB Security Bureau and SB Security Services." This instruction was issued as a resolution of the parliament, rather than a statute or any more normal form of regulatory instrument. Whether the format had been chosen to avoid judicial review or for other reasons is unclear, but the Constitutional Tribunal was incensed when the parliament tried to argue the tribunal had no right of review over such motions. The tribunal produced an immediate and wide interpretation of its overview powers in what the tribunal described as an "all encompassing interpretation of the provisions of the Constitution and the Constitutional Tribunal Act." The opinion effectively said that if anything is done purporting to be a legally enforceable norm, then the tribunal gets to review it. In fact the tribunal produced what was almost a tautology, and one that certainly empowers it. In a democratic state under the rule of law—a state founded on the separation of powers—legal norms cannot be established whose conformity with the constitution is not evaluated in a manner facilitating the removal of any inconsistencies. The tribunal describes nonreview as literally "unthinkable." In a word, anything the Sejm wanted to do important enough to worry the tribunal was, by definition, a fit subject for the tribunal.

Casting the instruction as a resolution was fatal to the Sejm, because the tribunal went on to take the position that any such intrusion into private life was a breach of constitutional rights, given that protection "of one's honour" was crucial to human dignity. This form of "personal interest" is "inseparably coupled with the essence of a human being." It follows from the fact that this is a major intrusion on human rights that it could not be carried out by anything less than a full statute, and, of course, the statute itself would have to pass constitutional review. It was also cause to annul the resolution, in the tribunal's eyes, that there had been procedural irregularities in the process of passing it as a resolution, irregularities that prevented its proper debate in the Sejm. This accords with the style of objection in the judicial discipline case cited above—the tribunal is very concerned about the actual working of the institutions it supervises. It is notable that Poland uses the form "a *democratic* state under the rule of law," not merely "a state under . . ."

[126] *Decision of 19th June 1992 on Lustration*, U/92, in Oniszczuk, *Selection of Jurisprudence* (Polish Constitutional Tribunal), 71–80.

As to the substance, it is unconstitutional because of vagueness—collaboration was not even defined—and, most important, because the vagueness prevented the natural assessment of whether the intrusion authorised was proportional to the good it might do—hinting at a strong rational connection test that would have been applied.[127]

This recognition of the human dignity aspect is stronger than anything found even in Hungary, and fully in keeping with the best standards of any Western European state. It is noteworthy that the tribunal cites legal textbooks in French, Italian, and German on the "inalienability of human rights" as well as international human rights documents. It is also at least in part a pragmatic understanding of the cost to anyone listed in the sort of search the Sejm was calling for, building that into the understanding of the right itself by stressing that "not only the subjective feelings of the person . . . should be taken into account, but also the objective reaction of public opinion." In rendering this opinion the tribunal was keen to buttress it with earlier opinions of its own, mainly on the structural aspect. It was typical of the decision on the Hungarian form of lustration that it should demonstrate very well one of my initial points—the new courts' concern to weave a coherent rights jurisprudence by self-reference wherever possible.

It is also a valuable sign of how varied the concerns identified by CEE courts can be that the Hungarian court worried a good deal less about the affront to the dignity of those exposed than about an aspect of these old secret police records that no other court appears to have noticed.[128] The records are, they say, unconstitutional in themselves, and always have been. Thus part of the problem for the constitutionality of the statute is that it failed to accept that those records not made public had to be dealt with in some other way—they could not simply be kept under lock and key. In doing this the court was relying heavily on its own, already by then extensive, jurisprudence on what is called, in the Hungarian constitution, "informational self determination."[129] The act as a whole was declared unconstitutional for a variety of reasons, though none went to the basic question of disclosing the past of those in public life. The court relies on an American-style concept of those in public life necessarily having a restricted "scope of private life." This is made all the more pressing by the fact of the transition and the need for transparency in public life. The court indeed regards the general thrust of the act as exhibiting "a confluence of the moral obligation that remained in the wake of the transition: the unveiling of deceit, publicity rather than punishment, and the value system normal to a state under the rule of law." The court does, however, have con-

[127] It would be a mistake to think the lustration issue has vanished from Polish constitutional review. Cases still occur, and still produce powerful dissents. See, for example, *Amendment to the Definition of "Co-Operation" within the Lustration Act*, K44/02 (2003) (Polish Constitutional Tribunal), especially the dissent by judge Bohdan Zdziennicki. The tribunal cites no less than eight previous rulings it has made on the 1997 Lustration Act.

[128] Decision 60/1994, December 24, 1994.

[129] The key early decision that laid down very strong personal rights to control data collected by the government was *Decision of 13th April 1991 on Use of Personal Data*, on the use of personal data and PIN numbers.

cern about the way the legislation makes the government arbiter of what may be made public, not because the court fears unfair publicity, but because of the rights of everyone to control data about themselves. Unusually, for this court, it comes close to recognising an American-style "political question" doctrine in admitting that there is much room for policy latitude in the details of this act, but the court notes, in an apt phrase, that "This political decision could not be based on the Constitution but rather on the constitutional certainty that the records can neither be kept secret not brought entirely to light." As discussed earlier, the Hungarian court has the probably unique power of ruling that the legislature has allowed or created a state of "constitutional omission." Here it ruled that failure to provide for citizens to see and destroy those secret service records that were *not* going to be disclosed as part of the lustration process was such an omission that had to be dealt with by statute:

> The fundamental rights to the protection of personal data and to access to information of public interest shall be interpreted in light of each other. This is natural, for informational self-determination and the freedom of information are two complementary preconditions for individual autonomy. . . . when freedom of information conflicts with the protection of personal records it cannot simply be said that the latter must always be strictly interpreted and must take precedence. In the light of the subject of the Act at issue, the Constitutional Court has established a hierarchy of these two basic rights.

The other problem the court found with the act related to the charge that unconstitutional discrimination was involved in the categorisation of who would be vulnerable to these background checks. The approach here does not fit the idea that the court is happy to allow a margin to legislatures. In keeping with much of its work during the nineties, the judgement might actually be seen in many ways as an illegitimate intrusion into policymaking at the micro level, à la Stone Sweet.[130] The discrimination argument was upheld on the grounds that the categories used in the act were variously too broadly or too narrowly defined to "establish consistent constitutional criteria to distinguish between public and private data." Just what these criteria would look like the court did not say. But the judges were quite certain that records of university and college officials and top business executives of state enterprises "were not information of public interest since such people neither exercised public authority nor took part in (public) political affairs." This can only be regarded as a bizarre judgement, and even if the claim that circulation figures were no basis to decide when a newspaper editor might have political influence was not bizarre, it was equally no business of a court to so judge. Indeed, excluding academics as opinion formers went ill with the other objection, that restricting such checks to the press corps but not to other opinion formers such as church leaders, trade union leaders, and political parties produced too narrow a group. We need

[130] See his general criticisms of European constitutional courts usurping the legislative function, particularly in *Governing with Judges*.

not, perhaps, be concerned by this tendency of the court. Human rights can probably only be strengthened, if other aspects of policy are weakened, by overactive courts who verge on legislation—behaviour commonly found in Western Europe. For example, a large number of judgements of unconstitutionality rendered by the French Conseil constitutionnel are based on detailed objections to categories used in legislation, thus arguably producing discriminatory problems.[131]

Conclusions

One thing above all stands out at least at the level of rhetoric, and surely much more—the idea of the state governed by law, or the democratic state governed by law, is central to the way the CEE courts have responded to their legislatures' attempts to deal with the past. The concept is the starting point of all these judicial discussions, and it is usually analysed with considerable care, if not always to the same conclusion. Whatever may be allowed or forbidden, it is filtered through this intellectual sieve. Only if one is prepared to be an extreme judicial realist and discount the language of decisions completely could one doubt that the conceptual framework used is at least as thoroughly imbued with constitutional values as those of older courts. It is equally important to see that assessments via this check relate as much to how a proposed accounting with the past is made as with its substance. Had the CEE courts simply ruled out particular proposals that Western liberals might dislike, without being overconcerned by procedure, we would have nothing but the happenstance that, in certain specified cases, policies were measured against relatively inchoate values. It is precisely the great care taken over other constitutional matters that reassures us for the future. A state ruled by law is, at least in the eyes of Central and Eastern European constitutional justices, a state abiding strictly by the separation of powers and careful to ensure that legislative procedure is abided by.

There is one serious question to resolve, however. It arises primarily in the contrast between Hungary and the Czech Republic. What are we to make of the radically different approach to assessing the requirement that a policy satisfy the standards of a state ruled by law? One knows, of course, that the political background to transition sharply affects the context within which a court as well as a legislature has to come to terms with the past. Were it simply a matter of accounting for why the Czechs did, and the Hungarians did not, allow an extension of the statute of limitations, it might be enough to point to their respective histories in the decades before transition.[132] As already noted, much of the difference comes about through the story the two countries choose to tell about themselves. What is problematic is the fact that both courts claimed to be doing the same thing—abiding by the requirements of a state ruled by law *where legal certainty is a major part of the definition of such a state*. It simply cannot be the case that legal certainty is compatible

[131] See D Rousseau, *Droit du contentieux constitutionnel*, 6th ed. (Paris: Montchrestien, 2001), especially 409–27.

[132] Sólyom, "Role of Constitutional Courts," comes very close to using this form of argument to account for differences between various CEE states.

both with allowing and forbidding the extension of time during which someone can be tried for a crime. It cannot be the case, for that matter, that selecting only some such criminals, those who were protected by political forces, both is and is not discrimination against one group. This demonstrates, more perhaps than any example in the whole of this book, that there is an ultimate core of deep discretion in judicial review, with which constitutional theory and comparative political science must come to terms. It is not for me to choose between the formalism of the Hungarians or the determination to ensure substantive justice of the Czechs. Must anyone make that choice? There are those who would have preferred the Czech court, if they felt obliged to allow the prosecution of political offenders from the past, to simply say that during a period of transition exceptions had to be made to the normal standards of a state governed by law, rather than to try to show that no breach of the standards was being tolerated. There will be others who very much take the Czech point of view, and regard Hungarian formalism as dangerous because it insufficiently couples the values of the new state to the formal idea of a law-governed state. Which is the greater problem for the theory of liberal democracy? An overfacile demonstration that something rather dubious is not only acceptable but characteristic of the new values, or an overwilling acceptance that constitutions cannot be expected to provide substantive justice? Or does it not, in fact, matter? Perhaps the dichotomies set up above are false—maybe two conflicting definitions of legal certainty can be contained within one legal universe. Maybe that is what the classic "margin of appreciation" of the European Court of Human Rights is all about. As long as courts face and have to answer problems like this, the idea of constitutional courts as part of the orthodox three-branch separation of powers will not work. That type of decision does require a whole fourth branch. Bernhard Schlink has likened the writing of legal opinions to the writing of a series of mysteries or love stories:

> Format, printing, and layout remain the same, the blurbs above the authors' names look similar, and the covers are designed to match. Some novels have the same author, and the reader recognises the same writing. Some obviously belong to the same tradition or follow the same pattern. Others could hardly be more different from each other. Each novel tells a different mystery or love story. But all of the novels preserve the law of the genre.[133]

Perhaps this is as good a model for the fourth branch as any other.

[133] B Schlink, "Hercules in Germany," 2003 1 *International Journal of Constitutional Law* 4, 610–20.

CHAPTER FOUR

France: Purely Abstract Review

> Let us not remove this fundamental acquisition [the Conseil constitutionnel], because the guarantee of democracy and of citizens rests on this recognition of a legal order emanating from the Conseil constitutionnel that is higher than the parliamentary order.
>
> —Raymond Barre in *Le Monde*, January 27, 1987[1]

The Nature of the Conseil Constitutionnel and Its Decisions

The Political Context

There is no judicial review mechanism that can so easily be characterized as a purely political, policymaking interloper into executive and parliamentary arenas as the French Conseil constitutionnel. Nor has any been so often and so widely thus accused. Perhaps the most important single thing to keep in mind in assessing the Conseil constitutionnel is that it is young, and that it has changed a good deal during its life. Coming as it did into a political culture so totally bereft of the idea of constitutional review, it would be hardly surprising if some of its early decisions were not, perhaps, ill judged. It would be frankly amazing if it had not originally been highly controversial politically. It is also vital to grasp the realities of French politico-legal culture that form the backdrop for any assessment. There is one simple fact that helps to bring some of this background and history into focus. Many of the Conseil's decisions have been fiercely opposed, and some have been seen as massive attacks on the programmes of the government of the day. Mostly the Conseil has been seen as favouring the Right, or at least the classic French bourgeoisie (which is not quite the same). In any political system, the ultimate way around an awkward constitutional court is to amend the constitution. If you change the constitution to require what your act was struck down for doing, the court has no recourse. Only twice has a French government amended the constitution in order

[1]Quoted in Bell, *French Constitutional Law.*

to get its way. This was done first by a conservative government, as part of a drive to tighten up immigration procedures for political asylum seekers. The second time it was a Socialist government acting to enforce gender equality laws on elections. Technically the constitution is not hard to change—it requires a three-fifths majority in the two houses combined, sitting as the Constituent Assembly, or a text agreed by majorities in both houses and passed by a referendum. But to have such a majority of the combined Assembly and Senate is usually beyond any plausible hope for the Left in France because the Senate is elected indirectly by a system that notably overrepresents conservative rural France. In fact the Left has not had a majority in the Senate in the last three republics. Even the 2008 conservative majority under a newly elected president only managed to get its constitutional reforms through, some of which affect the Conseil constitutionnel, by one vote.

This brute political fact has another consequence, incidentally, for the Conseil constitutionnel. One-third of its membership is chosen by the president of the Senate, every one of whom has been a conservative of one sort or another since the inception of the Conseil in 1959. The point is that French politics is, by many European standards, conservative. The state has a long history of being run by a technocratic elite largely independently of the parliament; the electorate has been riven by cross-cutting political and religious cleavages that have militated against any long-term coherent radical majority developing. The most common attack on the Conseil constitutionnel as a reactionary intrusive body thwarting popular policy desires centres round its decision on the nationalisation of industries by the 1981—1986 Socialist government during Mitterrand's presidency. This decision is carefully reviewed later, but at this stage I wish merely to point out that in any long-term view of French politics what is surprising is not that the Conseil interfered with these plans, but that they were ever put into operation at all.[2] The crux of the arguments was about the right to private property. It would take a very strong sociological thesis indeed to hold up the one electoral victory of the Left in 1981 as evidence that French political ideas had collectively swung against this most deeply rooted French obsession entrenched in the history of at least three republics and indeed all regimes since the Revolution, itself a deeply proprietarian event. Despite the attempts of some critics to argue otherwise, there is no parallel at all between this decision and the infamous lengthy period during which the US Supreme Court held up Roosevelt's New Deal.[3] In some senses the Conseil constitutionnel is conservative, but saying this is saying little more than that it is an institution of the French state. To say that it is counter-majoritarian, which is what the criticism of its actions over nationalisation implies,

[2]It is worth noting that there is something anachronistic indeed in a modern state embarking on a nationalisation drive as late as 1982, which was, elsewhere, about the beginning of the international return to a deregulated market. The fact that the government's policy reflected a commitment of nearly a century by the French Left says more about the stagnation of French left-wing thought than the problems the bill had says about the Conseil constitutionnel.

[3]FL Morton, "Judicial Review in France: A Comparative Analysis," 1988 36 *American Journal of Comparative Law* 1, 89–110; J Keeler, "Confrontations juridico-politiques: Le Conseil constitutionnel face au gouvernement socialiste comparé à la Cour Suprême face au New Deal," 1985 35 *Pouvoirs* 133–48.

is to say no more than that it carries out the job it was designed for, the job most of the constitution was written to achieve. It was the considered opinion of those who wrote the fifth constitution, under de Gaulle's guidance, that the problem of the previous two republics had been an oversensitivity to majority opinion as that was represented (or misrepresented) in overpowerful legislative assemblies. The greatest parliamentary vote the combined parties of the French Left gained during the 1980s amounted to 40 percent of the electorate, and this includes the Communist Party, which, while doubtless in favour of nationalisation, was also opposed to the republic itself. In contrast the constitution itself was carried in 1958 by an unprecedented 66 percent of the entire electorate. But the Senate has never been controlled by the Left—which is why nationalisation could not be carried by constitutional reform. Only one man has ever won the presidency for the Left; all others who have tried have been beaten convincingly.[4] Against this background there now follows a sketch of the important points of the Conseil constitutionnel's history.

The Constitutional Context

The Conseil constitutionnel of the Fifth Republic was from the beginning a huge breach with French democratic theory. Ever since the Revolution France has had a horror of the involvement of courts and judges in politics. There was no choice, however, when Michel Debré and others drafted de Gaulle's constitution, because they wanted to shift power away from parliament to the executive, itself something that the previous republics would have found almost as objectionable as politically influential judges. To do this, Article 37 of the constitution limited the areas in which parliament could legislate, and increased the scope of purely decreed legislation directly under the control of the government. The constitution further allows for the "deregulation" of parliamentary acts so that they can be developed further by decree. These provisions present immediate issues someone has to decide—has either the parliament or the executive overstepped the boundaries of its competence? Has an act properly or legitimately been deregulated? It was to answer these questions, and in truth, to answer them in the interests of the executive, that the Conseil constitutionnel was created. No one at that stage thought other aspects of the constitution would be the source of a future, much more invasive role for the Conseil. In fact the case law on this boundary maintenance problem is very complex, and it may be that the massive change from previous practice has not really materialized. As the whole idea was to protect insecure governments against irresponsible parliamentary behaviour, the development in the Fifth Republic of secure majoritarian governments has rendered the need for independent executive rule-making much less important.[5] It is neither possible nor useful to go into this question in this book.

[4]Probably the best recent general political history of France, against which my summary can be judged, is M Larkin, *France since the Popular Front: Government and People, 1936–1996*, 2nd ed (Oxford: Oxford University Press, 1997).

[5]Bell, *French Constitutional Law*, chapter 3. A first-rate account of the French legal system in comparative perspective is given in J Bell, *Judiciaries within Europe* (Cambridge: Cambridge University Press, 2006).

What is worth noting is that several of the Conseil's decisions actually favoured the Socialist government of 1981—1986 rather than the conservative minority in the National Assembly.[6] These other aspects amount to a bill of rights, otherwise notably lacking in the constitution of France's Fifth Republic. In fact, and this has been a source of irritation to the Conseil's critics but often of strength to the Conseil, this constitution with no bill of rights actually enforces not one, but at least two and arguably three, rights charters, none entirely compatible with the others.

The constitution starts with a preamble, the first paragraph of which has turned out to be crucial in the work of the Conseil constitutionnel:

> The French people solemnly proclaims its attachment to the rights of man and to the principles of national sovereignty such as are defined by the Declaration of 1789, confirmed and completed by the Preamble to the 1946 Constitution.

The preamble to the fourth republican constitution is too long to quote here. It is a loose set of rights, many of which might better be described as national aspirations, a political compromise cobbled together by a highly divided constitutional convention that had already seen its first draft decisively rejected by the electorate. In tone, and sometimes in detail, it clashes with the 1789 Declaration; the real contrast is that the 1789 document was the work of a rising property-owning bourgeoisie, the 1946 document a compromise between that social class, by then long in power, and a socialist movement that had never seriously held power.[7] This earlier preamble "solemnly reaffirms" the Declaration of Rights, but also "the fundamental principles set out by the Laws of the Republic." This has proved to be a gold mine for the Conseil constitutionnel, in part because, by not listing the principles in question, it has been left up to the Conseil to cherry-pick across the whole history of French republicanism. It seems largely to have been intended to refer to basic human rights values established by the Third Republic. This was an odd constitution in that it consisted essentially of a handful of ordinary acts of parliament, not even as marked as, for example, the Basic Laws that protect rights in Israel, another constitution-less society.[8] (There are also a few specific rights scattered elsewhere in the Fifth Republic's constitution.)

Membership

These other aspects of the constitution have been the real growth sources, but before they could become important, two things had to happen. The Conseil had to become willing to use them, and it had to be given a chance to show that it was.

[6]The first such decision, rolling back executive dominance in an area, was *Price and Salaries Freeze*, 82-143 DC (Conseil constitutionnel).

[7]Both these documents, with commentary, can be found in D Robertson, *A Dictionary of Human Rights* (London: Europa Publications, 1997).

[8]R Hirschl, "Israel's 'Constitutional Revolution': The Legal Interpretation of Entrenched Civil Liberties in an Emerging Neo-liberal Economic Order," 1998 46 *American Journal of Comparative Law* 3, 427–52.

The first point goes to the appointment process. The appointment process for the Conseil constitutionnel is one of the more overtly political among constitutional review bodies. The nine members are appointed in thirds every three years to a nine-year term. Each generation consists of one appointment by the president of the Republic and one each by the presidents of the two parliamentary chambers. The president of the Republic has the further right to appoint one of the members of the Conseil as its president, a post that has often been highly influential in forming the body's jurisprudence. Presidential influence is all the greater because until the presidential election of 2000, presidents had been elected to a seven-year term, while the Assembly was elected only for five years. There have only been five presidents of the Fifth Republic, and only one of them, Mitterrand, was from the Left. There are no qualifications for membership on the Conseil, and no checks on the pure discretion of the individual who appoints. As a consequence the early appointees were all staunch and unquestioning allies of President de Gaulle and his regime. This was not important so much in terms of the political colour of decisions, which were few, but in the way the Conseil accepted the drafters' narrow view of its role. There was no doubt about the councillors' subservience to the regime, though this is neither surprising nor to be deprecated given the conditions in which the Conseil was hurriedly designed and ushered in. This was best demonstrated in 1962 when de Gaulle used an entirely unconstitutional referendum to amend the constitution by changing the rules for presidential election—to his own advantage. He claimed to have consulted the Conseil, omitting to say it had advised against the process. When the matter was officially referred to the Conseil by the president of the Senate, the Conseil essentially abdicated responsibility, claiming it had no authority to review the matter. At this time the president of the Conseil, Léon Noel, who had been appointed by de Gaulle, went so far as to say that the Conseil could hardly challenge the president's interpretation of the constitution, given that he had written it.[9] The people appointed to the Conseil in its early years were predominantly political figures: of the forty-eight appointed up to 1992, twenty-four had been in parliament if not also in governments, and at least another half dozen had civil service or ministerial cabinet experience. Not more than eight had no obvious political history, apart from party activism.

Much of this has changed, if slowly. That first cohort had, with only six exceptions, been appointed by conservative politicians.[10] Steadily appointments became more frequently influenced by a sense of technical competence, if not strictly legal professionalism. While appointees can be expected to share the political position of the appointer, at least roughly, they are much less likely to be former elected politicians. And the changes in incumbency of modern French politics have produced more political balance in the Conseil. Thus the current councillors include two unambiguously left appointments, those made by the presidents of the National Assembly in 1998 and 2001, and four clearly conservative appointments,

[9] The story is widespread. The most authoritative source, as for most of the early history of the Conseil, is J Boudéant, "Le Président du Conseil constitutionnel," 1987 *Revue de droit public* 443. The comment is attributed also to others, and the actual veracity is hardly important.

[10] Bell, *French Constitutional Law*, 35–41.

three by President Chirac in 1998, 2001, and 2004 and one by the conservative president of the National Assembly in 2004. Yet two of Chirac's appointees are former civil servants, both of them graduates of the École Nationale d'Administration, one whose career was predominantly in the Conseil d'Etat, and the other from the Corps Prefectoral. The man appointed in 2004 by the conservative Assembly president had made his whole career in the Assembly's own civil service. There are only two former deputies, both former ministers, one a former minister of the interior appointed by the Left, and one appointed by President Chirac in 1998 and made president of the Conseil in 2004. The latter, Pierre Mazaud, has a doctorate in law and has been involved in legal aspects of legislation throughout his career. It is very hard indeed to characterize the other three councillors in any simple sense as left- or right-wing appointments. All three were appointed by the president of the Senate, who is a member of the main Gaullist party. One is, however, Simone Veil, former president of the European Parliament, an Auschwitz survivor, and famous in France for pushing forward the legalization of abortion when minister of health under President Giscard D'Estaing. One is an academic sociologist and former member of various government commissions on matters like the drug problem and educational reform. The third is a former practising lawyer, magistrate, and legal civil servant. All three are women; Christian Poncelet, the president of the Senate in question, has appointed three of the five women ever to sit in the Conseil. All in all, the modern Conseil looks a lot more like a body suited to review the constitutionality of laws than the early councils. It has never followed, of course, that because someone is appointed by a politician and appointed in the expectation that he or she will exercise the judicial role according to the appointee's general ideological preferences, this necessarily works out. Constitutional history is full of disappointment for politicians who have made this mistake. The classic case is Earl Warren, the liberal chief justice of the US Supreme Court who pushed through, amongst other things, school desegregation; when he was the Republican governor of California, he was appointed by the Republican president, Eisenhower. Testimony to the ability of members of the French Conseil constitutionnel to transcend their political past is given very powerfully in a rare book written by a former member who as a left-leaning professor of law had advised the Socialist government that the original draft of the nationalisation bill was entirely constitutional.[11]

The First Chance at Activism

The irrelevance of much of the expectation of conservatism on the part of the Conseil is shown by turning to the question of its needing an opportunity to become a creative interpreting body, because the very first chance it was given, it jumped at. Yet this was in 1971, long before modern-style appointments had really started. The reason the Conseil had no chance before 1971 to demonstrate its potential for constitutional creativity is that even more than most review bodies, it is entirely passive

[11] J Robert, *La Garde de la République: Le Conseil constitutionnel raconté par l'un de ses membres* (Paris: Plon, 2000).

and reactive. The Conseil constitutionnel only has the right to exercise a priori and abstract judicial review if a law (and only a law, not an administrative decree) is referred to it by the three presidents. Boundary disputes between parliament and the executive can occur easily enough even when all three of these are from the same political tendency, as was the case until the early seventies. But why would any of them refer a substantive issue for external adjudication? Such fights are carried on inside the party or coalition, not in public. In 1971 the Senate, thought controlled by the Right, was not Gaullist dominated, and disagreed strongly with the details of a bill that would have given the state more control over the formation of political groups, part of the legislation arising from the shock the authorities experienced with the *evénements* of 1968. The president of the Senate, Alain Poher, was a leader of the centre-right who had been a major player in organizing the "Non" vote in the referendum that destroyed de Gaulle's political dominance, and had been meant largely to destroy the Senate. He had even run against Pompidou, the ultimately successful Gaullist candidate to replace de Gaulle as president. Through this political chink a substantive law was at last referred to the Conseil constitutionnel. In a very short decision, only one paragraph of which does the work, one article of the law was ruled to be "not in conformity with the constitution." The law would have allowed a prefect to refer the objectives of any would-be civil association to a court for a ruling on their legality before registering it: without registration the association would have no legal standing or indeed existence. The Conseil began here the construction of what it has itself come to call the *bloc de constitutionnalité*, the concatenation of bits and pieces of doctrine and sources that make up the Conseil's constitutional review armoury. Nothing in the text of the fifth or fourth constitutions, or the Declaration of 1789 forbids the state to put such a restriction on the formation of groups. Instead the Conseil used the clause, sometimes described as the "in case we've forgotten anything" clause, of the Fourth Republic's preamble, which refers to the "fundamental principles recognized by the laws of the Republic." This is an invitation to a constitutional shopping trip—any law passed by any republic can be used as evidence that there is such and such a fundamental principle. The one the Conseil found on this first occasion was a 1901 law of the Third Republic, which had required a prefect to issue a registration certificate automatically on application. Consequently the bill was deemed to be partially nonconforming, but, as this article was severable from the rest, the truncated bill, which fitted the Senate's preference but not that of the Gaullist-controlled Assembly, could go ahead. It is important to see just how powerful a tool the drafters of the Fourth Republic's constitution have given the Conseil constitutionnel in this short phrase. It is undisputed constitutional doctrine almost everywhere that a parliament cannot, by ordinary legislation, bind its successors. Laws can, perhaps, be entrenched by special mechanisms, but though a law may be unconstitutional judged against some externally given document, it cannot be unconstitutional simply because an earlier parliament had legislated in a contrary way. To hold this would be to make parliamentary government logically impossible. So, absent the idea that some fundamental principles were "recognized" by the laws of the Republic, all that could have been said about the 1971 bill was that parliament now thought differently from one two republics earlier, hardly a surprising matter. The Conseil, however, has the right in effect to decide, years later, that what parliamentarians of the day saw as ordinary legislation was in fact entrenched legislation. Only the Conseil can do this, and there are no rules it must apply in deciding when a law contains such a principle. What this has turned out to mean is that it can apply a sort of ratchet effect, by which once a step has been taken along a civil liberty line, it cannot be taken back. Exactly this version of the doctrine was indeed announced some years later.

Limitations on the Conseil Constitutionnel

Thus by 1971 we can see that the Conseil constitutionnel had the will and competence, and was beginning to amass the armoury, to be an effective, perhaps an unusually powerful, constitutional review body despite its odd origins. It would have remained a very occasional body had it continued to require this special "chink" in the constellation of political forces before it received referrals. This is because, being allowed only to review bills a priori, and only the once, before they are promulgated, it is totally dependent on elected politicians falling out with each other. There was originally some suggestion of allowing some sort of reference to the Conseil by the French courts, as happens in virtually all other constitutional review jurisdictions. This was rejected before the Consultative Committee on the constitution right at the beginning; Debré, one of the primary drafters said outright, "It is neither in the spirit of a parliamentary regime, nor in the French tradition, to give to the courts, that is to say, to each litigant, the right to examine the validity of a law."[12] The French fear evoked by the idea of courts in politics was summarized later before the same body by a government spokesman who, admitting that a full constitutional court "would be tempting intellectually," went on to denounce it in practice because to give the Conseil constitutionnel more power would "risk leading us into a kind of government by judges, would reduce the role of Parliament, and would hamper government action in a harmful way."[13]

Despite this early opposition, many on the Conseil have continued to hunger for such an enlarged role, including the most influential of all its presidents, Robert Badinter. In fact his close friend Mitterrand, as president, tried as early as 1990 to get a constitutional amendment to allow the two top courts, the administrative Conseil d'Etat and the civil law Cour de Cassation, to make such referrals. This plan was torpedoed by the Senate, though the Assembly had no problem with it. The Senate has long been jealous of its self-proclaimed role as the older guardian of the constitutions.[14] It is worth noting, en passant, that at least one French president from the Left feared the supposed conservative nature of the Conseil so little that he favoured this reform, as did his prime minister, and that it was the right-wing Senate that claimed that the Conseil was already too powerful. In the summer of 2008 President Sarkozy, by one vote, managed to get a reform package through the Constituent As-

[12] Bell, *French Constitutional Law*, 20.

[13] Janot, *Commissaire du gouvernement*, cited in Bell, *French Constitutional Law*, 27.

[14] Robert, *Garde de la République*, 205, 211. See also L Favoreu, "Sur l'introduction hypothétique du recours individuel direct devant le Conseil constitutionnel," 2001 10 *Cahiers du Conseil constitutionnel*.

Table 3
Caseload of the Conseil Constitutionnel 1958–2004

Period	Ordinary laws	Organic laws, etc.	Total
1964–1973	5	22	27
1974–1983	80	33	113
1984–1993	118	46	164
1994–2003	112	46	158
1958–2004	330	171	501

sembly. Amongst other measures the reforms include a restricted right of appeal to the Conseil constitutionnel from litigants in lower courts, which will hold against any legislation at any time in the history of the legislation after it is promulgated. A new paragraph, 61(1), is added to the constitution providing that, "When in the course of a controversy before a judicial court, it is claimed that statutory disposition infringes over the rights and liberties that the constitution safeguards, the constitutional Council may be requested to judge on the issue." These referrals may only be made by the senior courts, the Conseil d'Etat for administrative law, and the Cour de Cassation for other laws. Ordinary courts cannot themselves make such a reference. If the Conseil constitutionnel does make such a ruling, the statutory disposition in question is repealed from the date of that ruling. As yet no one has any idea of how much this new process will affect French constitutional law and practise. Given this restricted appeal route, often called a "double filter," it will inevitably take some time before it is possible to answer these questions; thus the rest of this chapter will proceed as though the reforms had not taken place.[15]

With whatever justification, the role of the Conseil is thus limited, and the effect of this limitation we shall see shortly in the nature of its review work. At this point the limitation goes to the fact that one further change was necessary before the real history of constitutional review in France could begin. The breakthrough was a constitutional amendment authored by the first non-Gaullist president, Giscard d'Estaing, in 1974 that gave the right to refer bills before promulgation to any group of at least sixty deputies or senators. Since 1974 the parliamentary opposition has been able to have, as it were, a second bite of the cherry. Having lost the fight and vote on the floor of one or both chambers, they can still hope that the Conseil constitutionnel will see the matter their way. If it is politically expedient, and there is a shadow of a constitutional doubt about a bill, it will most probably be referred under this authority. Table 3 shows what an explosion there has been since 1974 in the number of chances the Conseil has had to develop constitutional rules. Between 1958 and 1974 there was, on average, less than one referral of an ordinary

[15] Details can be found in F Fabbrini, "Kelsen in Paris: France's Constitutional Reform and the Introduction of A posteriori Constitutional Review," 2008 9 *German Law Journal* 10, 1298–1312. The translation of Article 61(1) is taken from this article.

law per year. Since 1974 this has multiplied nearly eighteen-fold, to an average of nearly eleven per year, while the number of references of treaties and organic laws, which is automatic, has done no more than keep up with the worldwide trend to more legislation.

French Judicial Style

So, some sixteen years after it was set up, the Conseil constitutionnel began to develop its constitutional jurisprudence, to weld the various sources of argument and value together into this *bloc de constitutionnalité*. Quite a complex conceptualization has developed around these sources, not all of which is necessary to grasp how the Conseil works. What follows is a simplified account, in a form that a constitutional lawyer might not approve of. Nonetheless, some vital aspects need documenting. First, though, because it affects the intellectual methodology of constitutional review, we must consider the implication of the purely "abstract review" system in France. A bill, after all parliamentary stages have been completed but before its promulgation by the president, may be sent to the Conseil constitutionnel for a decision on its "conformity" with the constitution. The Conseil has very little time to render this judgement—a month under ordinary conditions, eight days if the president of the Republic certifies it is a matter of urgency. The reference comes with the referrers' arguments for why all or some part of the bill is unconstitutional, and other bodies may offer supporting or counterarguments. The proceedings are entirely written. One member of the Conseil is appointed as a rapporteur, and may take absolutely any matters or documentation into account. In particular, rapporteurs often consult the Conseil d'Etat, which will already have given initial advice to the government on the likely constitutionality of early drafts. His recommendation is taken before the whole Conseil, which discusses it and votes. The vote is by majority, and there are no dissenting judgements—a single statement, in the typically formulaic and laconic style of the French courts, is issued. Confidentiality is almost perfect—we know very little indeed about the actual voting on any case in the Conseil's history. The style of judgement means that no lengthy justifications are given for the decisions, and the arguments of the parties are seldom addressed, though the core of their complaint will be stated. Even the famous nationalisation decision runs to less than 6,000 words, a mere thirteen A4 pages; the decision that started it all, on the freedom to establish associations, is 572 words long. To put this in context, a relatively uncontroversial South African case from 2004 ran to 14,000 words, a major Canadian case from 1988 to 55,000, and a US case from 2004 that resulted only in the Supreme Court ruling that it had no jurisdiction took 17,000 words. (Even then, the Conseil constitutionnel is almost loquacious by the usual standard of French courts.)[16] The point is that the abruptness of the French style,

[16] A sample of cases from the top administrative court, the Conseil d'Etat, taken from 2004 shows them running an average of less than 1,500 words per decision. Yet the Conseil d'Etat has an international reputation as a leader of administrative law thinking, the only European court whose opinions are regularly tracked, for example, by the English journal *Public Law*.

consisting mainly in simply stating a decision rather than arguing it, makes any reasoned account of French constitutional doctrine almost as much a matter for the analyst as for the Conseil.

An example should suffice to demonstrate this abruptness of intellectual style. The Conseil constitutionnel has been in conflict with the parliament on and off for several years about its attempts to do what amounts to setting gender quotas for elective offices. This led in 1999 to a constitutional amendment, though not one that actually overruled any prior decision of the Conseil. In 2001 an act reorganizing the judiciary and its governing council was referred to the Conseil, as it had to be because it was what the French call a *loi organique*, an "institutional act." One clause only was found to be in breach of the constitution, where the method of election to the High Council of the Judiciary involved gender restrictions in the election process. The quotation below, taken from the Conseil constitutionnel's own English translation, is the whole of the discussion on this point:

> The rules enacted to govern the drawing up of lists of candidates for election to high offices, public positions and employments other than those of a political nature may not, with respect to the principle of equal access stated by Article 6 of the Declaration of 1789, involve any distinction between candidates on the basis of their sex; consequently, the provisions of section 33 of the Institutional Act which introduce a distinction according to the sex in the composition of the lists of candidates for election to the High Council of the Judiciary, are unconstitutional.[17]

So short a judgement might be less problematic if there was a long trail of complex reasoning in earlier cases to point to. This is not so. The first major case in the area, identified by the Conseil itself as one of its "Grande décisions," was in 1982, when the Socialist government reformed the ordinary electoral law for municipal elections.[18] A list system was imposed, and section L260b required that no list could have more than 75 percent of its members from the same sex. After simply quoting Article 3 of the Fifth Republic constitution and Article 6 of the Declaration of Rights, the Conseil simply states:

> It is clear from a combined reading of these provisions that citizenship confers the right to vote and stand for election on identical terms on all those who are not excluded on grounds of age, incapacity or nationality, or on any ground related to the preservation of the liberty of the voter or the independence of the person elected; these constitutional principles preclude any division of persons entitled to vote or stand for election into separate categories; this applies to all forms of political suffrage, in particular to the election of municipal councilors. . . . It follows that the rule whereby, for the establishment of lists presented to voters, a distinction is made between candidates on grounds of sex, is contrary to the constitutional principles set forth above.

[17] *High Council of the Judiciary*, 2001-455 DC (Conseil constitutionnel).

[18] *Quotas par sexe I*, 82-146 DC (Conseil constitutionnel).

Unfortunately neither quoted article really addresses the question of whether parties can be required to have a certain quota of candidates from each sex. Article 3, referring only to voting rights, does not obviously apply at all. Article 6, which was used in the 2001 decision, gets a bit further, but leaves plenty of room for argument. "All citizens, being equal in its eyes, shall be equally eligible to all high offices, public positions and employments, according to their ability, and without other distinction than that of their virtues and talents." It is irrelevant that some hold that the Conseil's decision was untenable. There are probably several arguments that would make its decision follow from its premises. But that is the trouble—there are several arguments against its conclusion. The problem is not what any academic critic thinks of the decision—it is that we simply do not know what sort of theory of democracy lies behind the decision, and are thus left, in a fundamental sense, not knowing what French constitutional doctrine on the matter is.

A greater contrast to the German situation, to take one example, let alone constitutional review in the common-law world, is hard to imagine. As mentioned earlier, this is not something unique about constitutional adjudication in France—it is a method directly modelled on the culture of ordinary French courts. There is a reason for the real courts acting in this way—the French fear of judicial involvements in politics historically led them to believe in courts as passive enunciators of the code, in Montesquieu's words, merely "the mouth of the law." The nearer law could seem to come to a syllogistic process where an appeal court just set out the correct legal premise and the result followed, the less judicial creativity there would appear to be. To the extent that the early members of the Conseil constitutionnel, predominantly figures from the legislatively dominated Fourth Republic, actually shared this approach to constitutional adjudication, it is unsurprising that the model was followed. But as the Conseil constitutionnel indisputably is now a creator of substantive constitutional law, the mask hinders more than it helps. The left-wing deputies who were outraged by the decision in *Quotas par sexe* were not mollified by the absence of a reasoned explanation why the terse commitment of the 1789 Declaration must obviously cover the rules on electoral lists—they were further outraged by the Conseil appearing to take no notice of the views of the act's legislative supporters. The criticisms by the Left are pointless, though understandable. When academic commentators echo them, they are paying inadequate attention to the role of a society's legal culture.[19] Thus Stone Sweet, commenting on *Quotas par sexe*, says, "What was not said was deafening. The Conseil ignored altogether the constitutional command, contained in the 1946 Social Principles *and cited constantly by the left during the legislative debates* that equal rights between men and women should be guaranteed by statute."[20] It is just no part of the tradition to cite matters that the court or council in question does not regard as the essential legal basis for a decision. He also objects to the fact that the quota aspect was not part of the complaint made by those referring the bill. The Conseil has always held that it is entitled to look at any aspect of a bill referred—indeed it could not carry out its duty to assess conformity with the constitution otherwise. Criticisms like these come from too fixed an assumption, however

[19] Or "cultures"—see J Bell, *French Legal Cultures* (London: Butterworths, 2001).

[20] Stone Sweet, *Governing with Judges*, 107; emphasis added.

unconscious, that constitutional law rulings are to be seen in the adversarial mode of common-law adjudication. Arguably this is never an appropriate frame of reference for constitutional review—it certainly ill fits a body like the Conseil constitutionnel that is not only an inheritor of the inquisitorial rather than adversarial notion of judicial action, but restricted in any case to abstract and a priori review.

There is a strong case to be made that external interpreters of the French legal tradition seriously mistake the extent to which it lacks argumentation, because we ignore the special role of academic lawyers, and the way their comments on cases are regarded by all concerned, including the courts, as essentially part of the development of doctrine. This is put very forcibly in a fascinating study of French courts by Mitchel Lasser.[21] He adds that the internal working papers of the judge appointed as rapporteur, and of others involved in the process, some of which can be found, demonstrate a much more common-law-like process of argument and doctrinal development. Effectively, Lasser argues, there is a "bifurcation" in the French process, whereby only the results of the process are publicly issued by the courts, but a rich debate goes on behind this screen. It is unclear to what extent this may also apply to the Conseil constitutionnel. Certainly there is reason to believe that the rapporteur is important, and it is also known that the equivalent to law clerks, mainly on secondment from the Conseil D'Etat, are crucially involved. Furthermore, it may be significant that the Conseil constitutionnel takes note of the fact that a formally private publication, *Les grandes decisions du Conseil constitutionnel*, selects a small number of cases to be annotated and printed as *grandes décisions*, comparable to the historically important *grandes arrêts* of civil law.[22] It seems that the doctrinal notes published in the Conseil's own *Cahiers du Conseil constitutionnel* have much the same role that Lasser attributes to similar doctrinal writings in civil law. However even if something like Lasser's model applies to constitutional review, it is no help, because far more than ordinary law, constitutional law needs to be argued in public.

Réserves d'Interprétation

This basic fact of the restriction of the Conseil constitutionnel's remit leads to more fundamental difficulties. Difficulties in pulling together French constitutional doctrine are aggravated by a technique forced on it by dealing only with abstract review. Known as the *réserve d'interprétation*, this technique, hotly criticized by some, especially Stone Sweet, is also used extensively in Italy and Germany, though arguably without the same necessity, given that abstract review is rarer in Germany and missing

[21] M Lasser, *Judicial Deliberations: A Comparative Analysis of Judicial Transparency and Legitimacy*, Oxford Studies in European Law (Oxford: Oxford University Press, 2004). Details of how the rapporteur system works can be found in Robert, *Garde de la République*, and Bell, *French Constitutional Law*, the latter also describing the links with the Conseil d'Etat.

[22] L Favoreu and L Philip, *Les grandes décisions du Conseil constitutionnel*, 12th ed. (Paris: Dalloz 2003). Each of the fifty-three (up to 2003) decisions so treated in this book are marked as such in the Conseil constitutionnel's own listing of its decisions.

in Italy.[23] The Conseil is unwilling to render a decision of nonconformity where it is possible to avoid doing so, and these réserves d'interprétation are a means to reduce the incidence of nonconformity findings. What happens is that the Conseil considers whether some part of a bill might in practice lead to a result that would be unconstitutional, and imposes a condition on the meaning the potentially offending words can take to prevent this hypothetical nonconstitutionality. It is difficult fully to understand all the examples of such réserves if a common-law idea of interpretation is clung to. Rarely do the interpretations look quite like the readings given in the House of Lords where a word or phrase is defined. More typically they consist of statements that will have to be true before the measure in the assembly's text will have constitutional validity. A simple example, nearer to the common-law court's version of interpretation, can be found in the Conseil's decision about one aspect of a new revision to the penal code passed by the French parliament in 2003. Amongst many aspects of the code, it reformed the law on prostitutes soliciting for trade, creating a new offence. Though the objectors claimed such a law was a major invasion of personal liberty, the Conseil was content with it as a sensible means to preserve public decency and to counter the trade in human beings. It was concerned merely with a possible injustice from disproportionate sentences:

> It will be possible for the competent court to take account, when pronouncing sentence, of the situation where the accused was acting under threat or constraint. Thus, under this reservation, the criticized disposition in the law is not contrary to the principle of appropriate penalty.[24]

What this amounts to is not so much an "interpretation" or "gloss" on the meaning of any phrase, as an injunction to other bodies, in this case the criminal courts, to act in a particular way.

Other examples seem to be addressed more widely, often to parliament itself. In 1999 the government legislated to create a new "quasi-marriage" institution for France, where existing law has long been felt to overprivilege traditional marriage. This new Pact Civil de Solidarité was, unsurprisingly, heavily challenged by the conservatives in the Senate, but was found entirely in conformity with the constitution except for some "réserves" and the "tightening up" of some sections.[25] The reservations mainly took the form of dictating procedures that would have to be put in place to prevent hypothetical breaches of constitutionality. For example, one challenge was that the registration and centralized collection of certifications

[23] Stone Sweet, *Governing with Judges*, 72 et seq. Stone Sweet translates *réserve d'interprétation* as "binding interpretation"; being unhappy with this but unable to improve it, I leave the phrase in French. Others who criticise the method include Landfried, "Judicial Policy-Making"; and D Manno, *Le Juge Constitutionnel et la Technique des Decisions Interprétatives en France et en Italie* (Paris: Economica; Aix-en-Provence: Presses universitaires d'Aix-Marseilles, 1998). For a more balanced and thorough account, including comparisons to Germany and Italy, see G Drago, *L'Execution des decisions du Conseil constitutionnel: L'effectivité du controle de constitutionalité des lois* (Paris: Economica, 1991).

[24] Schepple, "Constitutional Negotiations."

[25] This is, again, something probably better left untranslated. The actual French is "sous les réserves et compte tenu des précisions ci-dessus énoncées." The case is *Pacte Civil de Solidarité*, 99-419 DC (Conseil constitutionnel).

for such pacts would amount to an invasion of privacy. To prevent this, the Conseil insisted that the procedures for this collection would have to be vetted by the Conseil d'Etat, which in its turn would have to consult other data protection bodies. Similarly a claim that the possibility for each individual to unilaterally end the pact might damage some freedoms was met with the insistence that three months' notice would have to be given in writing not only to a court, but to the other party to the pact.

French commentators have pointed out, in fact, that a large proportion of these réserves are really about parliamentary omissions to notice lacunae in the bills. Sometimes the Conseil allows the bill through anyway, having noted the omissions. More commonly it holds the bill "partially" incompatible with the constitution, leaving parliament to repair the omission in a new version. Such partial annulments are quite distinct from the partial annulment that one might call "for cause," where a clause is held to be fundamentally unconstitutional, not merely possibly so unless remedies against hypothetical cases are implemented. So in a major and hotly contested bill intended to prevent overlarge holdings of newspaper ownership, the Conseil noted that a lacuna existed by which a press conglomerate could, quite legally, circumvent the ceiling of ownership of titles intended by the legislators. As one French commentator puts it:

> The Conseil's interpretation adds nothing to the law. It is a simple invitation, though admittedly a very direct one, to the legislature to bring more coherence to its text, and it shows with precision the way forward.[26]

These réserves are interesting for four reasons. They have been criticized, as noted above, as examples of undue involvement in the policymaking process, or, in the alternative, they can be seen as following directly and inevitably from the restriction to a priori review. They further demonstrate the difficulty of knowing with full confidence just what constitutional law is in France, and they highlight an aspect of constitutional review not seen as clearly elsewhere. The detail of the prescriptions in these reservations might indeed seem an undue interference with the policy process—not one that is necessarily missing in other countries, but certainly some way from merely declaring constitutional values. Is it appropriate to require the creation of a specific authorization from the Conseil d'Etat, and specifically to instruct the latter to consult the Commission nationale de l'informatique et des libertés? Surely it is for the legislator to decide how to deal with a constitutional criticism? This is all the more so because, over and again both the Conseil itself and French commentators justify the use of these reservations precisely on the grounds that they are a means to protect legislative autonomy.[27] The argument is that it is much better to issue a réserve than to strike down some part of the act. As so many of these réserves in fact require parliamentary action anyway, the distinction is less obvious than it might be.

[26]Drago, *Decisions du Conseil constitutionnel*, 165. The case is *Press Case*, 86-210 DC (Conseil constitutionnel).

[27]F Mélin-Soucramanien, *Le Principe d'Égalité dans la Jurisprudence du Conseil Constitutionnel* (Paris: Economica, 1997), 148, and references there.

Many of these constitutional réserves are nearer to an interpretive gloss in the common-law mould, though never quite the same. A good example is the Loi de modernisation sociale, a wide-ranging reform act produced towards the end of the last Socialist government in 2002. Apart from declaring one article of the bill completely incompatible with the constitution, the Conseil issues réserves d'interprétation on ten other articles ranging across the whole of what was somewhat of a scattergun piece pf legislation.[28] One example was very much like a piece of common-law interpretation. Article 101 gave certain rights to employees' committees to call in a mediator when a restructuring was planned by the owners of an enterprise. But it was unclear whether this covered all such restructurings, or only those above a certain level of impact. Considering the "travaux préparatoires," the Conseil issued a réserve restricting this right to situations where at least one hundred jobs would be lost. This is fairly unremarkable, and indeed no great constitutional principle was involved other than that law must be clear. The second example is rather like those discussed earlier. The sections in the new law introducing crimes of harassment, especially in the workplace, were severely criticized by the political Right. The Conseil dismissed claims of lack of legal clarity, amongst others. It did, however, note a danger of disproportionate punishment given that the same actions could found either a general claim of general harassment under the penal code or of harassment in the workplace under the employment code. So it issued one of these réserves aimed at other bodies, in insisting that a potential breach of criminal law proportionality as required by Article 8 of the Declaration of Rights did not "in itself make the establishment of two offences repressing harassment in the two codes contrary to the constitution." This conformity to the constitution was to be dependent on the courts and authorities accepting that the maximum sentence could not be higher than whichever single offence carried the higher penalty. Again, this directive was hardly objectionable in fact, and perhaps better than leaving the National Assembly to work how to avoid disproportionate penalties, but not very obviously an example of deference to parliamentary sovereignty.

My third example from this act demonstrates a very common feature of these réserves, one not often noted by French or English writers, critics or supporters alike. Quite often the réserves deal with a constitutional criticism of a bill by what can best be described as high-sounding vacuity. They recognize a possible constitutional wrong that could come about and announce that the text is compatible with the constitution only if that wrong does not emerge, but with no definition of what future events might constitute such a breach. So Article 159 of the law deals with housing provision for those in difficulty. Some of the ministerial powers to fix rents in the private sector were characterised by the Senate as breaching the rights to private property and to freedom of contract in the 1789 Declaration. The Conseil constitutionnel, after noting various worthy constitutional values having to do with the right to decent housing, and accepting parliament's right to make the better-off support the poorer, did indeed recognize that there was nonetheless

[28] *Loi de modernisation sociale*, 2001-455 DC (2002) (Conseil constitutionnel).

a danger of an undue interference with property rights. It said, therefore, that the article would conform to the constitution under the réserve that the minister did not set rents at a level that would breach the principle of equality of tax burdens.[29] This decision shows the Conseil to be anxious to protect constitutional rights, and achieves absolutely nothing else. It must be remembered that once the act is promulgated, no court may ever again visit it. Thus no actual impact on the future experience of the act is involved by this réserve—no one is going to get judicial review of the minister's rent-fixing habits on the grounds that the Conseil constitutionnel made this *réserve d'interprétation* and the minister is now acting unconstitutionally by breaching it.

Here we have a crucial problem for the Conseil, and one we need to take seriously. It is not that France has a supine court system. Contrary to the historic antipathy to judicial review of legislation, the tradition of French public-law control over administration, via the Napoleonic construction of the Conseil d'Etat is very strong. If the Conseil constitutionnel forced parliament to insert some regulations, some formula, to assess ministerial rent assessment, it would be comparatively easy for an aggrieved property owner to have such an assessment reviewed under the *ultra vires* doctrine. But if the law is deemed to be conformable to the constitution as long as the minister acts "reasonably," which would be an Anglo-Saxon version of this réserve, no one has any recourse, because unconstitutionality in itself is not something that can be argued before the Conseil d'Etat. The question is really about what exactly is implied by saying that a piece of legislation is, in this sense, conditionally constitutional. More than in most systems this makes the characterization of the Conseil's decision equivalent to a different sort of question, that of the enforceability of the Conseil's decisions. Whether constitutional review bodies are in fact obeyed is a vital question everywhere. In France one might go so far as to say that any effective control by decisions of constitutionality becomes one of turning a question of constitutional law into one of administrative law, or of criminal law. For example, in 1997 the parliament passed an act revising immigration law. It was tested before the Conseil, which issued several réserves d'interprétation.[30] One concerned a rule that would allow the executive to take back into detention someone who had been detained and was to be deported, once seven days had passed from the deportee's release. The complainant senators and deputies believed that this could amount to an endless series of detentions, in breach both of the Conseil's own ruling in an earlier decision and the jurisprudence of the Cour de cassation. Here the Conseil constitutionnel wrote in a réserve d'interprétation that restricted to two the maximum number of such detentions that could be based on the same deportation decision. This condition on the constitutionality clearly raises no problem of compliance, because the relevant agencies, the other courts, can be relied upon to operate the clear restriction. Where such compliance cannot be guaranteed, that is, where any nonjudicial branch of the state is concerned, any

[29] In the French, "à un niveau entrainant une rupture caractérisée de l'egalité devant les charges publiques."

[30] *Immigration Issues*, 97-389 DC (Conseil constitutionnel).

réserve has to guarantee, by creating the possibility of an administrative law issue, that they become involved.

It is this problem that explains the apparently undue involvement of the Conseil in the details of policy. Any form of réserve that does not involve a clear instruction to parliament to alter the act in a very specific way would be so much hot air—just like the injunction to the minister to respect the constitutional value of "egalité devant les charges publiques." The only alternative open to the Conseil if it fears that possible future courses of government action could make an admirable act an unconstitutional breach of values is to strike down the clause. Though the Conseil constitutionnel is seen as an enemy of the legislature, the real enemy is the executive, which in France has by no means always been particularly law-abiding. For all the rhetoric, the idea that France is an *État du loi* has been somewhat of an exaggeration. Instead, as Knapp and Wright have said, it has better been characterized as a system of *Étatisation du loi*, the idea of law in the service of the state.[31] Unless one understands this context, within which the Conseil constitutionnel works, it is impossible fairly to judge such apparently arcane matters as the Conseil's use of these réserves d'interprétation. It must be a fine distinction to draw, between annulling, making an airy rhetorical réserve, and writing regulations into a bill. It is not a task that is seen as sympathetically as perhaps it should be.

But seeing why the Conseil has to behave in this way does not make it any easier to create a "coherent" and "deep" set of constitutional doctrines from its frequent use of réserves. It does not help that the wide variety of actual methods covered by the use of réserves is largely ignored. Because the Conseil constitutionnel itself classifies in this one category anything that is neither a decision of conformity nor of partial or complete nonconformity, commentators have lost analytic perspective. I have not cited any of the statistics that tend to show high rates of use of the technique, because they are largely meaningless unless one knows in detail, that is by studying each case, what has actually been done. What is clear is the problem this extensive use gives us in composing an external account of French constitutional doctrine. The problem arises because of the nature of these judgements. The Conseil does not canvass a variety of meanings a clause could imply. It does not explain at any length why a particular "interpretation" is the best to ensure constitutionality—it just chooses one meaning and insists on it as the answer. The result is that we know only something negative—that constitutional values might be offended were some unspecified alternative to a particular meaning to be taken. This is part and parcel of a more general characteristic of the Conseil's jurisprudence: it has not chosen to develop tests of when a breach in an apparent right is nonetheless acceptable. This behaviour is discussed later in the book when the question of constitutional tests is considered, but it is useful to note it here. We know, for example, from the immigration decision, that in this specific case no more than two periods of detention separated by at least seven days, arising from the same immigration decision, will be constitutional. But we know nothing else—

[31] A Knapp and V Wright, *The Government and Politics of France*, 4th ed. (London: Routledge, 2001), 383.

and are therefore unable to develop any insight into the relationship between the right to liberty of the person and the state's duty to ensure civic peace. The whole of the Conseil's jurisprudence is like this, of course, but it is particularly troublesome with this use of a technique that is, after all, a way of saying what *is* constitutional, rather than, where a clause is truck down, what is *not* constitutional.

The final point worth making about the use of these réserves, and again it applies *pari passu* to much of the Conseil's decisions of incompatibility, is how much is a matter of technical and procedural correction. The Fifth Republic has created a fairly complex set of rules for how to legislate, as well as complex boundaries about who can legislate on what. These rules alone would present plenty of opportunities for parliament to fall foul of the Conseil acting simply as a boundary-maintaining agency (as discussed in chapter 1). The problem is more extensive, however. The parliament appears to be very sloppy in its drafting and redrafting processes, leaving the Conseil to issue endless réserves on no substantive points at all. Typical is the case where the 1983 Finance Law set out, in an appendix, plans for an increase in staff for the Ministry of Education, but failed to make financial provision for these employees in the body of the act.[32] The guiding organic law, from 1959, made it quite clear that such "intentions for future action" could not be the basis for revenue expenditure. The Conseil issued a réserve that asserted that the plans could not come in to operation. Organic laws are a crucial aspect of constitutional control over legislative behaviour under the Fifth Republic's constitution. Parliament regularly ignores their requirements, and is as regularly struck down by the Conseil.

In the French case, as much as in considering the Eastern European jurisdictions, it is important to note this concern for the procedural, because procedural values remain at the heart of the political vision the constitution embodies. To take up Knapp and Wright's point, much of what the Conseil constitutionnel is about is precisely the enforcement and creation of a commitment to the rule of law, just as much as in the Eastern European courts, if less dramatically so. There is another way in which one can see that France is, finally, on its way to a true "rule of law"—despite earlier rivalries, the other great "political court" in France, the Conseil d'Etat, is increasingly working with the Conseil constitutionnel to develop general approaches to legal limitations on the state. Indeed the Conseil d'Etat has even continued to develop some of the Conseil constitutionnel's lines of approach after the latter has largely ceased to use them.[33] But equally the Conseil constitutionnel has borrowed some of its methodology from its former rival, particularly in its equality jurisprudence, as is discussed later in the comparative analysis of chapter 7. In fact what has happened over the years is that not only the Conseil d'Etat but even the ordinary civil courts have begun to aspire to some form of constitutional review powers of their own. This gives further insight into the major types of decision the Conseil constitutionnel has made, which collect around two vital points: one is the creation of a value methodology, and the other is the high centrality of one specific value, that of nondiscrimination or equality before the law.

[32] *Finance Law for 1984*, 83-164 DC (Conseil constitutionnel).

[33] Rousseau, *Droit du contentieux*, 108–10, on the *Arrêt Koné* decision of the Conseil d'Etat in 1996.

The Substance of the Decisions

Constitutional Texts

With each of the jurisdiction chapters in this book the story is about a constitutional review body that builds a body of doctrine and values from its interpretation of the constitutional document governing the state, usually doing so slowly, but sometimes very rapidly. Sometimes the problems the courts must address involve making compatible a new constitutional document with an existing constitutional understanding, which is the case in Canada, where a more or less English approach to parliamentary sovereignty was suddenly ended by the imposition onto common law of a binding Charter of Human Rights and Freedoms. Sometimes it has been a matter of resurrecting a long-lost commitment to constitutionality and the rule of law after a repressive interregnum, as in Eastern Europe and perhaps Germany (although it must be said that the longevity and depth of commitment to constitutionality with these jurisdictions often partakes of a golden age myth). Sometimes, South Africa is the purest case, where a court takes upon itself the task of helping to create an entirely new moral order warranted by a constitution that makes a radical break with past values.

What all of these examples have in common is that the identity of the relevant constitutional documents is not questioned. Interpreting the documents, deciding how far they empower courts, can generate controversy even when the documents themselves are agreed on. It is little wonder, then, that in France the situation is so difficult, and it is difficult in two related but separate ways. The legitimacy of constitutional review is problematic, at least to some, as noted above. But equally, as hinted above, the analyst's job of saying just what constitutional doctrine exists, is much harder than elsewhere. Both difficulties share a common cause. The Conseil constitutionnel, before working out what a constitutional document means, and persuading others to accept this interpretation, has first had to decide what documents are to be considered at all, and persuade politicians that this even more difficult step is correct. The distinctiveness of this problem is sometimes hard to grasp. After all, many constitutional review bodies, even the US Supreme Court, root about in legal and legislative history to show that something they want to assert "has always been" part of the politico-legal culture. For example the Czech court, as discussed earlier, has often tried to show that the first Czech republic understood constitutional values the way they want the second republic to do. The Canadian Supreme Court likes, where possible, to refer to pre-Charter decisions. Part of the German constitution actually incorporates Weimar Republic laws, which has aided the German constitutional court in finding historic backing for some of its decisions.

The French situation is categorically different. The Conseil constitutionnel has created the actual constitution, if by constitution we mean that assembly of politically ratified documents which is held to contain rules and values binding the state. The Conseil calls this the *bloc de constitutionnalité*, which I prefer not to translate on the grounds that much-needed mystique is lost if one talks about the "constitutional bloc." The story of the development of constitutional doctrine in France is simultaneously the story of the selection of what goes into this "bloc." This, of course, immediately raises an unanswerable question—have elements been added to the bloc because they allowed the Conseil to decide a particular matter the way it wanted to, or have its decisions depended on the independent realization that the constitutional issue could only be answered by applying a potential item that needed to be incorporated into the bloc? Obviously the answer is likely to be "a bit of both." More importantly, discretion in this area is one-way—you cannot remove an item from the bloc once it has been included. It is my general argument throughout this book that however free a constitutional court may be in one sense to decide a new question according to its political whims, every such decision reduces the degrees of freedom later. In the French case a really radical degree of freedom has been continually narrowed by this process of incorporation.

There is at least one moderately close analogy from elsewhere. Much of the US Supreme court's activity in the first sixty or so years of the twentieth century was about an "incorporation debate." In that case it was about how much of the Bill of Rights, originally only applicable to the federal government, could be brought to bear on the state governments by saying that the post–Civil War Fourteenth Amendment required this. To a large extent decisions of the court thereafter were deeply constrained not so much by the core of the relevant precedents, but by the mere fact that it could not return to a situation where the states were free from the Bill of Rights.[34]

The first major decision by the Conseil constitutionnel (made in 1971, once de Gaulle was dead, and when the Senate and the Assembly disagreed on a crucial issue) was far more important for how it was made than for its substance. For a decision of its importance—many authors have described it as the French *Marbury v Madison*—it is amazingly short, even by French standards. The entire decision, title and all, amounts to only 572 words. The operative part barely needs summary because it merely says:

> Amongst the *Fundamental Principles Recognised by the Laws of the Republic* and solemnly reaffirmed by the Preamble to the Constitution, there is to be found the principle of freedom of association; this principle underlies the general dispositions of the law of July 1st 1901 on contracts of association. (Emphasis added)

The preamble to the Fifth Republic's constitution, itself only two paragraphs long, merely proclaims the French people's "attachment to the rights of man . . . such as are defined by the Declaration of 1789, confirmed and completed by the Preamble of the 1946 Constitution." Only by asserting (1) that the preamble actually binds the state and (2) that therefore anything in the 1946 preamble similarly binds, can one jump to the position the Conseil needed. The 1946 preamble, again "solemnly,"

[34] A very good account, as well as an argument that the court got much of it wrong, is given in AR Amar, *The Bill of Rights* (New Haven: Yale University Press, 1998). An older account of great interest is HJ Abraham and BA Perry, *Freedom and the Court: Civil Rights and Liberties in the United States*, 8th ed. (Lawrence: University of Kansas Press, 2003).

"reaffirms the rights and liberties of man and of the citizen consecrated by the Declaration of Rights of 1789 and the fundamental principle recognized by the laws of the Republic."

What the Conseil did in this decision was to give itself the right to go trawling through the whole corpus of legislation enacted before 1946 to find documentary evidence that a principle it wished to apply existed. In this case the logic of the 1901 statute was held to contradict part of a new law that would require any organized body of citizens, before it could have legal identity, to register with the prefect, as had been required in 1901, and give the prefect the right to refuse registration until a court had decided whether the association's aims were legal. All this despite relatively clear evidence that those who drafted both the 1958 and 1946 constitutions did not intend the preambles to be more than a moral commitment rather than a legally enforceable duty. Even if we disregard this—on the grounds the French sometimes use, which is that by allowing the electorate to validate the constitutions in referendums, the state must be taken to have accepted the legal force of the words—there is some way to go. As a leading French critic of the time asked after the 1971 decision, "Which republics, which laws, what are these fundamental principles?"[35]

Over time the Conseil has given its own answers to these questions: only laws of the Third and Fourth Republics count, and even a single instance of a law contradicting a proposed principle will negate the proposition that it contains a fundamental principle. However, there remains no way that parliament could tell ahead of time that a principle does not lurk somewhere in its own legislative history. Nor can parliamentary opponents of a law who refer it to the Conseil be sure their own arguments will work. It is characteristic of this form of judicial review that the discretion to recognise an underlying principle (or not recognise one) is maximal. The Conseil comes up with unashamedly ad hoc explanations for refusing to see a principle enshrined where others might. In one important case, dealing with nationality, it refused to find as a principle that those born in France of someone herself born in France automatically gained nationality, despite rules to that effect in legislation. Their argument was that such rules had been pragmatic in nature because of fears of population decline, and had not truly represented republican principles or great humanitarian ideas. As an argument it works, but only at the cost of suggesting that all legislation might be seen as similarly pragmatic. One can perfectly well see what the Conseil was getting at, and indeed that might be exactly what the rule about fundamental principle requires as an interpretative device. But it does nothing to reduce the sheer obviousness of the Conseil's discretion.[36]

As an initial reaching for authority, it is hard to imagine a broader trawl net than this initial case. There is a tendency to narrow the application of this approach, and few new fundamental principles have been discovered in recent decades. It is never easy to be quite sure, because of the Conseil's lack of consistency in

[35] J Rivero, "Les principes fondamenteau reconnus par les lois de la République: Une nouvelle catégorie constitutionnelle," 1972 *Revue de droit public* 265–81.

[36] *Nationality Reform Law*, 93-321 DC (Conseil constitutionnel).

its language, but it is probable that no new principle has been asserted by this route since 1989 (though, as suggested above, the Conseil d'Etat may have done such a thing instead). It is, on the other hand, quite easy to find examples where the Conseil has rejected otherwise plausible attempts by the opposition in parliament to show that the majority has offended against such a fundamental principle. So the attempt to show that a recent law on what we might call "continuing professional education" ignored a fundamental principle in a law of 1936 was dismissed on the grounds that it showed no fundamental principle recognised by the 1946 preamble, but only a fundamental principle of employment law as recognised by Article 34 of the constitution, which parliament had every right to amend. This is by no means a rare example of "deference" to the parliament.[37] This tendency, to narrow and specify, to restrict its own possible range, has been continuous, and underlines one crucial fact that has to be taken into account when considering the nature of the Conseil and its jurisprudence—it is young, and has made enormous efforts, quite consciously, to ground its powers more and more firmly in predictable and logically defensible doctrine. Less and less does it make wild leaps to grasp authority, or rely on mere assertion of the existence of some rule or value with no textual backing at all.

Over the next few years after the 1971 decision, the rest of the *bloc de constitutionnalité* was assembled. The constitutional force of the 1789 Declaration was first used fully in 1973 in a case involving possible unequal treatment under tax law, the beginning of the Conseil's deep concern over discrimination discussed more fully in chapter 7.[38] A much more important decision 1975 decision wrapped up all the documents by asserting the constitutional force of all the texts referred to in the preamble to the 1958 constitution. This was the acceptance by the Conseil that nothing in any constitutional text, nor in the "fundamental principles recognised by the laws of the Republic," could be used to invalidate France's first law allowing abortion. This was also one of the cases where the Conseil most clearly defers to parliament, stating categorically that "Article 61 of the Constitution does not give the Constitutional council a general power of judgment and decision identical to that of parliament, but only gives it the authority to pronounce on the conformity with the constitution of laws referred to it."[39]

If the "fundamental principles" allow too obviously for radical discretion, they are nothing compared with the final element of the bloc. The preamble to the fourth constitution in its second paragraph describes its purpose as proclaiming "the following political, economic, and social principles as particularly necessary for our times." It is entirely natural that the Conseil should, therefore, have systematically added these principles to the *bloc de constitutionnalité*. Thus in a series of cases during the Conseil's first active decade, these were picked out and constitutionalized: sex equality for example in 1981, the right to strike in 1979, the freedom to create unions in 1983, asylum rights in 1980, the secular nature of state educa-

[37] *Professional Education*, 2004-494 DC (Conseil constitutionnel).

[38] *Tax Estimation Case*, 73-51 DC (Conseil constitutionnel).

[39] *Abortion*, 74-54 DC (Conseil constitutionnel).

tion in 1977, and many others. In the sex equality case a finance law was challenged on the grounds that it breached the sex equality rule by taxing a married man on his wife's wealth. The Conseil recognised such a rule existed, but found that it was not breached in this instance. Typically of the Conseil, and a typical source of problems in writing about it or trying to construct its jurisprudence, it does not actually say where the rule comes from. It is merely a matter of interpretation by others that the Conseil was relying on the 1945 preamble![40]

No one could object to such a process of piecemeal incorporation of individual rights and values. In this sense it is very much like the slow incorporation of the Bill of Rights in the United States, except that it took the French only a decade and the Americans more than eighty years. The problem arises because, just as the Conseil did not actually tie its 1981 decision to a text, it began to introduce a whole host of constitutional "tests," describing some as principles or rules of constitutional value, some as an "object of constitutional value," some merely as "constitutional demands."[41] None of these were affixed to texts, and French public law academe, even those who supported the Conseil, was unable to construct references for them. The Conseil had, effectively, taken on itself the right to deduce constitutionally necessary rules by analogy to the 1946 preamble with no obvious justification. Again a wide range of desirable things were seen as justified by these amorphous principles and requirements—decent housing and media pluralism, to name only two. Typical perhaps was the constitutionalization of a whole nexus of only partially connected values in one paragraph of one case, while admitting that they needed to be balanced against another and more clearly "text-based" right. In its decision upholding the constitutionality of the Audio-Visual Communications law of 1982 the Conseil held:

> The legislature has to balance, in the context of the current technical state of affairs, the right to freedom of communication which follows from Article 11 of the Declaration of the Rights of Man with objects of constitutional value which are the security of public order, respect for the freedom of others, and the preservation of a pluralist character to expression of socio-cultural matters which these modes of communication, because of their great influence are capable of threatening.[42]

Without denying the huge discretion the Conseil constitutionnel has, or rather, has given itself, by the use of instruments like the fundamental principles, and these latter constitutional objects, we should, perhaps, not attach as much importance to them as do both French academics in general, and all those who oppose the Conseil's power in particular. The objection seems to be that it does not (always) operate from textually identifiable sources. Were the French to live under a traditional "written" constitution, this might be a serious criticism. Using any old statute, or cherry-picking from "principles necessary to this day and age," could be

[40] *Finance Law*, 81–133 DC (Conseil constitutionnel).

[41] The French is "exigence constitutionnelle," which could equally be translated as a "constitutional requirement."

[42] *Audio-Visual Communications*, 82-141 DC (Conseil constitutionnel).

reasonably seen as exceeding a grant of authority from the constitutional document. And of course to those critics, not all French, who believe the preamble to the fifth constitution was never intended to have constitutional force in a legal sense, that might be the case. However, as that battle is long lost, it might be more sensible to learn to live with the result and concentrate on more useful criticisms of the Conseil. But if one does accept the battle is over, that constitutional review has come to stay in France, one has also to accept that it cannot be of a single, determinate document form, the traditional written constitution review. Looked at this way, the PFRLRs, as the French abbreviate the fundamental principles, is the essence of, not an addition to, the constitutional review armoury. The PFRLRs, stressing that constitutional review is a matter of interpreting a whole, and developing, republican constitutional tradition, show an almost common-law-like characteristic of the Conseil's task. It is interesting to note that some French commentators have come to a roughly similar conclusion, equating the Conseil constitutionnel's development of constitutional doctrine to the Conseil d'Etat's development of administrative law.

> It must be admitted that the principles, objectives and exigencies of constitutional value do not find their base in written texts, but are derived or deduced by the Conseil constitutionnel from various sources or by reflection on the necessities of public policy according to the same form of reasoning by which the Conseil d'Etat creates general principles of law.

Given that the French would never admit publicly to having a "common-law approach," this is actually a very strong admission—and the author, Rousseau, admits that it would be disavowed by luminaries of French constitutional law like François Luchaire.[43] To be sure, a clear statement in the 1789 Declaration or one of the more specified rights in the 1946 preamble is a firmer foundation than the result of trawling through republican legislation, which in turn is firmer than the intuition of "une exigence constitutionnelle" as the basis for a decision on constitutional conformity. They are, however, essentially alike in that they are the raw material, rather as are precedents in English common law, for judicial development of rather pragmatic tests of legality—in this case, constitutional legality. The Conseil's decisions are highly pragmatic, and nearly always involve balancing values and texts. As chapter 7 shows, much constitutional review is involved with finding ways to handle not the enforcement, but the limitation, of constitutional rights because of the brute fact that rights cannot be absolute, all law discriminates, and government must go on. The other review bodies covered in this book all have something the French lack—some form of constitutionally prescribed test, linking a statement of core democratic values to the necessary limitation of rights. (The other exception is the United States, which is deliberately included only in chapter

[43] Rousseau *Droit du contentieux constitutionnel*, 111. Luchaire is the great conservative defender of the Conseil as being utterly and purely a traditional legal entity. See F Luchaire and G Conac, *La Constitution de la République française article par article* (Paris: Economica, 1987). He is also the author of the standard multivolume treatise on all the Conseil's decisions, published as *Le Conseil constitutionnel*, 2nd ed., 4 vols. (Paris: Economica, 1997–2002), with a collective coverage of the period 1998–2002.

8.) What the French do is to deduce some of these necessary limitations and balancing weights rather than pretending to find them prewritten into a document. Other countries do the same from time to time. The Australian High Court, having no bill of rights, "imputes"—to use the court's own word—certain necessary rules on freedom of the press from the mere fact that Australia is a competitive party democracy.[44] In the same year the Law Lords in England produced a very similar result, arguing that the logic of democracy required that the common-law right to sue for defamation not be accorded to an elected town council.[45] Both of these decisions, were they generated by the Conseil constitutionnel, would be criticised as showing the discretionary use of some such idea as a constitutional exigency. And it must always be remembered that, because of French judicial style, we only get to see the results of the imputation and deduction, not the reasoning. The Conseil announces that something is or is not constitutionally exigent, but does not share with us the reasoning. Were it to have adopted a different manner, it might, but equally might not, be more convincing to those who currently regard it as a politically motivated loose cannon.

This is why, perhaps, it is itself so loose in its vocabulary. In this sort of task neat doctrine is no particular help and is often a hindrance. One may object to individual decisions; one may oppose entirely the Conseil for not automatically and always deferring to parliament. But it makes relatively little sense to object to how it goes about describing this overall evaluative process. The whole idea of a *bloc de constitutionnalité* is perhaps better seen as a recognition that there exists an inchoate set of values somehow originating in the developed French constitutional and republican tradition, some of which can be more, some less easily, attributed to moments in French history, but all of which it is the duty, now they have been brought into existence, for the Conseil to adumbrate and apply.

The Nationalisation Decision

It is in this light that we can turn to the most infamous of all the Conseil constitutionnel's decisions, that on the nationalisation law of 1982. It is remarkable that the decision is probably more important for doctrine than for substance. It is cited endlessly in French constitutional law texts, not because its finding of constitutional nonconformity produced any startling substantive understanding of, or change in, constitutional reality. (It is hard not to suspect that it is also the least read, as opposed to cited, decision by political scientist critics of French constitutional review.) It is used by French constitutional commentators because of the question it raised about the relationship between the two key documents in the

[44] See J Goldsworthy, "Implications in Law, Language and the Constitution," in G Lindell, ed., *Future Directions in Australian Constitutional Law* (Sidney: Federation Press, 1994). More generally, B Galligan, *A Federal Republic: Australia's Constitutional System of Government*, Reshaping Australian Institutions (Cambridge: Cambridge University Press, 1995). The main case is *Australian Capital Television Pty Ltd v Commonwealth*, 177 CLR 106 (1992).

[45] *Derbyshire CC v Times Newspapers Ltd* , 1 All ER 1011 [1993] (House of Lords). For a further discussion of this issue see Robertson, *Judicial Discretion*, 284–87.

bloc de constitutionnalité, the 1789 Declaration and the 1946 preamble. There is no real doubt that the decision, which did not forbid nationalisation but considerably increased its costs, was at, or over, the limit of legitimate constitutional review. Though it is an exaggeration to liken it to the US cases that so damaged the early New Deal, there are similarities: the first Socialist government elected in postwar France, a major part of that government's programme, and so forth. The main reason the nationalisations decision was so problematic is that it came so early in the history of the Conseil's active phase. If the *Association* decision of 1971 was France's *Marbury v Madison*, the equivalent would have been a major overruling of a federal statute in 1814—and no such thing was attempted by the US Supreme Court for more than a generation after that.

What this meant was that there had been no time for the legitimacy of the Conseil to develop, no time for parties of all political persuasions to realize that it was in their interest to accept constitutional defeats while in government as the price of having a potential ally against the majority when they were out of power. So much is obvious political common sense. There is a more fundamental reason why the case was, from an ideal point of view, premature. The Conseil constitutionnel simply had not had time to develop and fine-tune its doctrine when the nationalisations issue arrived. This was especially problematic because the doctrinal thrust of the decision was to become vital and relatively uncontroversial in other later contexts, because the nationalisation bill was not found to be unconstitutional on any broad ground. Indeed, though the Conseil d'Etat had apparently earlier warned that nationalisation would require a constitutional change, and Mitterrand himself had forecast this while in opposition, the Conseil constitutionnel never attempted to argue that the bill was fundamentally unconstitutional. Could it have? The Socialists certainly feared so, and deployed their own constitutional lawyers to head this response off. (One, Jacques Robert, was later to be appointed to the Conseil by a Socialist president of the Assembly.) It is true that the 1958 constitution itself foresaw industrial nationalisation in Article 34, though all this does is to ensure that any nationalisation should be carried out by parliamentary *loi* and not by decree. To this can be added the clear if limited anticipation of nationalisation in the 1946 preamble, paragraph 9: "Any property or business whose exploitation has or acquires the character of a public service or a de facto monopoly should become the property of the community." Whether or not the wide swathe of banking, for example, nationalized in 1982, could really be brought under this provision is doubtful. But, above all, the Fourth Republic had nationalized a good deal of both industry and commerce, and no one could pretend then that such a policy was not covered by Fundamental Principles of Republican Law. On the other hand this particular argument hardly surfaced. In truth, so little developed was the Conseil's jurisprudence in 1982 that there would have been no insurmountable barrier to claiming fundamental unconstitutionality because of property rights. That the Conseil never tried this line is not cited to its credit by those convinced that it was then, and still is, a conservative political intruder into the legislative domain. Instead the Socialists tended to argue that the Conseil's censure of the bill was mild because it feared a much tougher bill if the first was overruled in a fundamental way.

The document that caused the problem was the 1789 Declaration, but even it can hardly be made to produce a condemnation of nationalisation as such, proprietarian in emphasis though it is. Or at least, the Conseil did not attempt to use it in this way. Instead the Conseil made two arguments. The one most focused on was direct from the 1789 Declaration—in which Article 17 insists that property, being "an inviolable and sacred right," could not be taken away except "on condition of just and prior indemnity." The Conseil ultimately held that the way the compensation formulae in the bill worked did produce injustice under this heading. It is vital to understand that the Conseil did not produce an alternative and preferred method for arriving at a just recompense—it did not substitute its own preferences for the legislators'. Instead, it objected to what it saw as irrational and unjustified application of parliament's own formula. The second complaint about the bill was that it breached the principle of nondiscrimination because of the way it selected enterprises for nationalisation. These two, very similar, attacks, have been characteristic of the way the Conseil has handled a huge number of bills referred to it. The nationalisation decision was the real beginning of a thread of doctrine that, could it only have been established in earlier cases, would have made the decision on nationalisation much less controversial. It was the need to establish the doctrine in such a high-profile case that made the Conseil's decision so risky. Yet what was the alternative? To have allowed the weaknesses of that particular bill through would have made it vastly harder to impose a form of "rational connection" test later. If the government did not have to act carefully and rationally on such an important issue, why make it do so on more trivial ones?

It was necessary first for the Conseil to bring the 1789 Declaration into play vis-à-vis the other documents, because as yet there had been no occasion to rule on the fit of the 1789, 1946 and 1958 constitutions. Though both 1946 and 1789 were independently of "constitutional value," what happened where they both applied? The 1958 preamble described the 1789 rights as being "confirmed and completed" by the 1946 document—does this allow the earlier to overrule the latter, or, as would be more usual in a common-law country, is the last word always supreme? This still remains a live issue in French constitutional law, and we have no need of a final determination here, but the argument of the Conseil is worth noting because of its very pragmatic and political nature.[46] The argument goes like this. Article 2 of the 1789 Declaration asserts that the "ultimate purpose of every political institution is the preservation of the natural and inalienable rights of man. These rights are to liberty, property, security, and resistance to oppression." The Conseil goes on to quote Article 17 as above. It then points out that in 1946 the French people "rejected a draft constitution that would have preceded the provisions on the institutions of the Republic with a new Declaration of the Rights of Man, including, notably, a statement of principles differing from those proclaimed in 1789 by the above mentioned articles 2 and 17." And, "by contrast [in the referendums setting

[46] A former member of the Conseil constitutionnel has argued at great length for the hierarchical superiority of 1789 over 1946: F Goguel, *Cours constitutionnelles européennes et droits fondamentaux* (Paris: Economica, 1982). The leading English expert on the Conseil constitutionnel arguably comes to the same conclusion: Bell, *French Constitutional Law*, 273.

up the 1946 and 1958 constitutions] the French people have approved texts conferring constitutional value on the principles and rights proclaimed in 1789." The Conseil further characterizes the rights in the 1946 constitution, vis-à-vis the 1789 document, as aiming "simply to complete them by the formulation of 'political, economic and social principles as particularly necessary for our times.'" In other words, it is a historical political fact, and not a derivation by the Conseil, that nationalisation must be considered under both of the sets of rights. The vitality of the 1789 right to property is stated, then, with greater force:

> if since 1789 until today, the objectives and the conditions for the exercise of the right of property have undergone an evolution characterized both by a significant extension of its sphere of application to particular new areas and by limitations required in the name of the public interest, the same principles proclaimed by the Declaration of the Rights of Man retain full constitutional value both in so far as they concern the fundamental character of the right to property, whose preservation constitutes one of the purposes of political society, and which is placed on the same level as liberty, security and resistance to oppression, and in so far as they concern the safeguards given to the holders of this right and the prerogatives of public authorities; that the freedom which, in terms of Article 4 of the Declaration, consists in the power to do anything that does not cause harm to another itself cannot be preserved if arbitrary or abusive restrictions are imposed on the freedom of enterprise.[47]

To make absolutely sure of the point, the Conseil goes on to insist that the reference to nationalizing anything with the character of a public service, in the 1946 preamble "has neither the purpose or effect of rendering inapplicable the principles of the Declaration of 1946 recalled above to the operations of nationalizations," and that the reference in Article 34 of the 1958 constitution to "loi" being necessary for nationalisation "does not dispense the legislature from respecting the principles and rules of constitutional value that bind all organs of the State." Given all this, one might not actually expect the Conseil to go on to say, as it immediately does, that it accepts that the reasons for the nationalisations do indeed bring them under the permission of Article 17 of the 1789 Declaration. There follows what was then, and became even more, an important description of the power of the Conseil constitutionnel:

> The legislature's judgment of the necessity of the nationalizations . . . should not be called into question by [the Conseil constitutionnel] in the absence of any manifest error of evaluation, so long as it is not established that the transfers of property and business currently effected would restrict the area

[47] *Nationalizations*, 81-132 DC (Conseil constitutionnel), par. 15. Unless stated otherwise, quotations from this and subsequent cases are based on the translations provided in Bell, *French Constitutional Law*.

of private property and the freedom of enterprise to such an extent as to violate the said provisions of the Declaration.[48]

The first part of this hesitation, the reference to "manifest error," is taken up in chapter 8, which deals comparatively with the question of limitations on rights. The second part is highly reminiscent, though almost certainly not influenced by, the German constitutional court's idea of not breaching the "core" of a right, and is characteristic of ensuing French doctrine. For those opposed to the Conseil constitutionnel's involvement with legislation, the damage is probably done in these first paragraphs, because it is clear that it is not giving a blanket permission to nationalize. Instead it gives due notice that far-reaching breaches of the right to free enterprise, or any arbitrary curtailment of it, may still be found unconstitutional.

But the bill did, in general, pass muster. Why was any of it unconstitutional? Primarily because in two narrowly defined ways, two specific provisions of the bill offended not against property rights per se, but against the constitutional value of nondiscrimination. It really is important to understand how limited, and how technical, was the Conseil's opposition, partly because so much has been made of the nationalisations decision, and partly because it was so typical of the way French constitutional review was to develop. First, Article 13 of the bill listed banks to be nationalized, following a statement of general principles for selection; yet this list omitted three categories—banks with a low capitalization, foreign-owned banks, and "mutualist or co-operative" banks. Partially agreeing with the opposition parliamentarians who had referred the bill, the Conseil constitutionnel objected to the exclusion of this latter group. First it established that the "principle of equality is no less applicable between legal persons as between physical persons, because legal persons being groupings of physical persons, breach of the principle of equality between the former would be equivalent to breach of equality between the latter."[49] The Conseil went on to accept, but to circumscribe, the need for legislation to draw distinctions, in a way the Conseil's jurisprudence has filled out over the years:

> the principle of equality does not prevent a law from establishing non-identical rules with respect to categories of persons who are in different situations, but this can only be the case where the non-identity is justified by a difference in situation and is not incompatible with the purpose of the law.[50]

Having no problem with the first two types of exclusion, the Conseil did object to excluding banks "whose majority share capital belongs directly or indirectly to companies of a mutualist or co-operative character." This positive discrimination

> is justified neither by the specific character of their status, nor by the nature of their activity, nor by potential difficulties in applying the law that

[48] *Nationalizations*, par. 20.

[49] *Nationalizations*, par. 28.

[50] *Nationalizations*, par. 29. The doctrine on equality is well covered by, inter alia, Mélin-Soucramanien, *Le Principe d'Égalité*, especially, in this context, 394–97.

would work against the public interest goals that the legislature intends to pursue.[51]

In a similar way the method of calculating compensation was faulted for arbitrariness, under the general rule from Article 17 of the 1789 Declaration that required "just and prior indemnity." Here the Conseil objected to the fact that the worth of the companies to be nationalized was derived from net accounting position and net profits of companies, excluding their subsidiaries. According to the Conseil constitutionnel this produced unjust differentiation,

> Determined not by a difference in objective economic and financial facts, but by the diversity of the management techniques and methods of presenting accounts followed by the companies, which in itself, should have no bearing on the assessment of compensation.[52]

The Conseil also held, though it appears almost as an afterthought, that the method of accounting would in fact deprive shareholders of compensation for the last pre-nationalisation year, 1981, thus breaching the "just and prior" clause of Article 17. This is all the Conseil did. Of course no one could claim there were no values imposed on French society by this decision. For example, the very argument that legal persons can be equated to real people is not a neutral and necessary legal point—it is a choice, one that had to be made one way or another. More importantly, it is perfectly clear why the socialist majority exempted co-operative banks—they approved of the whole idea of co-operatives, and saw them as ideologically different from ordinary shareholding activities. But the discrimination in their favour is arbitrary *given the justification provided by the act itself.* By itself, it is an unjust discrimination, and one not related to the avowed purpose of the law.

Rather than seeing the decision on nationalisation as a massive and unjustified incursion into legislation, it might be a good deal more plausible to say that the Conseil constitutionnel had no choice if it was ever to develop a jurisprudence reinforcing the idea of the rule of law in France, and if it was to make real the idea that the 1789 Declaration was valid constitutional law. Of course the Conseil could have decided to return to the inactivity of the pre-1971 years. But what it could not do, and refused to do, was to make an exception for a piece of legislation whose authors themselves had thought was probably unconstitutional.[53] By the beginning of 1982 the Conseil had already handed down eighteen important decisions involving the equality principle, covering nearly a quarter of all the cases it had heard since 1971. Over the period 1971 to 1995 fully 40 percent of all the Conseil's decisions would revolve around this principle.[54] In very many of these cases the issue

[51] *Nationalizations*, par. 32.

[52] *Nationalizations*, par. 55.

[53] The politics of the whole issue, including this point about the Socialists' own estimation of constitutionality, is well described in Stone Sweet, *Birth of Judicial Politics*. It is obvious that I share neither his overall theory of the nature of the Conseil, nor his judgement on this particular decision, but I fully accept his political descriptions.

[54] Mélin-Soucramanien, *Le Principe d'Égalité*, table and other useful statistics on this matter, 371–79.

would be the apparent lack of rational justification for a differentiation. It did not help the early years of the Conseil constitutionnel that the nationalisations case happened when it did, but the result was almost predestined.

The decision ought more properly to be seen, as French constitutional lawyers do see it, as a methodological milestone, and a major step in the construction of an antidiscrimination jurisprudence. Members of the Conseil, including Robert, who had briefed the Socialists on the constitutional issue before joining the Conseil, are fond of citing the almost "companion" decision on privatization to demonstrate the propriety of their decision in 1982.[55] The conservative government under the prime minister, Chirac, set out to roll back the state, wishing not only to undo the Socialists' policies of 1982 but also much of the nationalisation of the early Fourth Republic. The Conseil insisted that nothing prevented this as a general policy. Even, they say, if the intention of the 1982 legislators was to create a "public service of credit" by nationalizing the banks, such a policy was not required by the constitution. The 1946 reference to nationalizing monopolies and essential public services authorizes such a policy, but leaves to the legislature the determination of when and if to nationalize anything that could come under the rule.

However, the method of privatization ran a real risk of the state selling off properties below market value, because the bill imposed a timetable specifying when all the listed enterprises must be privatized. The resulting glut on the market, the Conseil foresaw, might well provide undue bargains for purchasers. The Socialist MPs who had referred the bill thought this provision must be unconstitutional because it would enrich some people, not the generality of the population. The Conseil did not disagree that this provision would produce a breach in a general constitutional duty to ensure equality. However, the Conseil added a vital argument of its own. Just as the 1789 document guaranteed to individuals just compensation when they lost property, the state too was entitled to equal protection of this requirement as a property owner. In fact the Conseil did not strike down any part of Chirac's act—it did something subtler. It simply pointed out that any such rushed sale to fit a deadline that involved selling at less than market value would produce these unconstitutional results, and therefore the time limit clause must be interpreted as applying only to sales that could be made at market value. This, and other details, were covered by the issuing of *strictes réserves d'interprétation*. An interesting feature of French constitutional review is also revealed here. The reference to the state's property rights constituted the enunciation of a principle of constitutional law—though it took only twenty-six words in the English translation, and occurs in only one numbered paragraph of the decision.[56] There is no further argument, and the case in which it occurs did not even lead to the striking down of a law. It is this easiness of construction of constitutional principle, commented on earlier, that makes it often very hard to know what the law is, and virtually ensures there will be little serious debate—anywhere else such a casual reference might well be treated as merely *obiter dicta*. Only if one accepts that Lasser's argu-

[55] *Privatizations*, 1986-210 DC (Conseil constitutionnel).

[56] *Privatizations*, par. 58.

ment about the bifurcation of French legal doctrine, discussed earlier, applies also to its constitutional law can anything like a satisfactory development of such vital doctrines be seen in France.[57]

The Press Pluralism Decisions

There are a host of similar, almost casual, enunciations of highly arguable but unargued constitutional rules. One of the most important is another case from that busy French summer of 1986, when the conservative government, lacking control of the presidency, was urgently pushing through legislation to undo or modify its predecessor's work. The previous government in 1984 had passed a law "on the financial transparency and pluralism of press enterprises," which the new government sought to alter in a way that the Socialists who referred the new law thought gave inadequate protection for media pluralism, which the Conseil, in this decision, asserted were "objects of constitutional value."[58] In the second paragraph of the decision the Conseil first admitted that the legislature could always amend or repeal legislation, or adopt new methods, but "the exercise of this power cannot lead to the removal of legal safeguards for requirements having constitutional value." There were basically two complaints about the weakness of the new bill: that it set up less rigorous requirements for financial transparency, and that it allowed too great a degree of concentration of press ownership. The first criticism was rejected by the Conseil, and its brief statement could be taken as an example of deference to parliament:

> even if the provisions of articles 3, 4, 5, and 6 of the law, taken together, do not always permit the public or categories of interested persons to identify immediately those able to exercise control over a specific press publication, their effect is, however, such as to provide essential information, without hiding the fact that the legal persons holding shares in a publishing business and exercising an influence over it can themselves be dependent on individuals or groups external to that publishing business; that thus, the judgment made by the legislature is not vitiated by any manifest error.[59]

Merely being less rigorous than the predecessor legislative rules "does not in itself constitute a ground of unconstitutionality." This is obviously a substantive judgement, but perhaps not one very different from the ones all constitutional courts make—it is as though the right to information had been infringed but not, using the German idea, to its core. What did cause the Conseil to feel that the constitutional objective of pluralism was being weakened in its protection were the details of ownership regulation, because they permitted indirect ownership of more than the otherwise permitted threshold of 30 percent of a particular newspaper market. This limitation did not prevent, in the Conseil's words, "a human person or a group

[57] Lasser, *Judicial Deliberations*. In fairness it must be stressed that Lasser himself does not make this extension.

[58] *Press Case*, 86-210 DC (Conseil constitutionnel), par. 1.

[59] *Press Case*, par. 18.

from using procedures, perfectly legal in company law, to make themselves effectively and fully masters of several existing daily newspapers" without breaching the threshold. Consequently the legislation "has the effect of depriving a principle of constitutional value of legal protection," and the relevant article had to be struck down.

Can we find a clear distinction between the Conseil's permissive attitude on financial transparency and its trenchant line on pluralism? Both involve judgements on the impact of the statutory techniques, and in a rather similar way. On the one hand, the new financial reporting rules will not quite provide as much transparency; on the other, the new ownership rules will not quite protect against excess circulation control. We cannot say that the Conseil should have determined either issue in a different way. I wish merely to point out the sort of detailed investigation of an essentially counter-factual point—"what will happen if . . ."—that the Conseil involves itself in. As it happens, this decision is perhaps slightly unusual in the terseness with which the Conseil announced the doctrine that legislation could not reduce constitutional protection. It went to greater length in justifying the actual value of media pluralism in terms of fundamental rights that the Conseil grounds firmly in the 1789 Declaration, although its words are not obviously closely binding on ownership of publications:

> Free Communication of ideas and opinions is one of the most precious of the rights of man. Consequently, every citizen may speak, write and print freely; yet he may have to answer for the abuse of that liberty in the cases determined by law.

The Conseil's argument, hardly one of its clearest, is that

> in reality the objective to be realized is that the readers, who figure among the essential addressees of the freedom proclaimed by Article 11 . . . should be able to exercise free choice without either private interests or public authorities substituting their own decisions, and without it being possible to make them the subject matter of a market.[60]

Many courts have had to extend the meaning of rather narrow free speech clauses like Article 11 so as to give effective protection for media pluralism, and many examples from several jurisdictions come later in this book. It is unique to the French, however, to have shaped a doctrine of the ratchet effect of a constitutional protection, yet this interesting and powerful theory is never justified or explicated. The Hungarian court, which uniquely has the power to order legislation to fill a constitutional oversight, might well take a step like this (though it would presumably seek to justify it). The Conseil constitutionnel does not pretend to be authorized to insist on legislation to protect something it regards as a constitutionally important phenomenon, yet felt no compunction in granting itself the power to ensure that, once parliament has acted, it cannot derogate. I do not in general consider powerful the claims made that French legislators suffer something like a

[60] *Press Case*, par. 20.

"chilling effect" or an "auto limitation" because of their fears of what the Conseil may do.[61] The point was made in chapter 1, and again when talking of Germany, that this can equally be seen as desirable concern by parliament to obey the constitution for its own sake. It would certainly make some sense, however, to see the Conseil as possibly rather cautious about protecting hitherto unacknowledged constitutional values if it truly believes it is embarking on a one-way street.

It is a good example of how confusing the Conseil's jurisprudence can be that Stone Sweet insists that the Conseil *refused* to use the ratchet effect doctrine in this case, where I see it as not only having been used, but having been given its fullest and clearest formulation.[62] It is true that it was foreshadowed in weaker form in the first press pluralism case in 1984, but then it was presented as part of a general statement of the legislature's duties towards fundamental rights:

> Where it is a question of a fundamental liberty, all the more precious because its exercise is one of the essential guarantees for respect of other rights and liberties and of national sovereignty, the law can only regulate its exercise with a view to making it more effective or to make it compatible with rules or principles of constitutional value.[63]

The Badinter Presidency

By the time the second press case decisions was made, in the summer of 1986, the Conseil had begun a new stage in its development. In March 1986 Robert Badinter was appointed to its presidency by President Mitterrand, who feared that his party would lose the legislative elections and wanted allies wherever possible in power. Badinter was himself a Socialist, a former minister of justice, but above all a lifelong campaigner for human rights. A quotation from him heads the first chapter, which I repeat here as the best summary of Badinter's sense of constitutional mission:

> Le Conseil constitutionnel est une jurisdiction, mais il ne sait pas; mon rôle est de lui faire prendre conscience de sa nature.

He sets himself the task of helping the Conseil improve its legitimacy by being much more clearly a constitutional *court*, and to some extent he succeeded, inasmuch as its reasoning became slightly more explicit, more text based, more intent on canvassing arguments and showing that it was not a political beast. He failed in several of his more concrete aims that would have helped this goal considerably. He (and his personal friend Mitterrand) were unable to get the Conseil the power to hear complaints directly from litigants after laws had been promulgated. (This power was granted only in 2008, as part of a constitutional reform project initiated by President Sarkozy, as mentioned earlier.) He also failed to persuade his colleagues to allow minority and majority opinions. This latter policy might have

61 Stone Sweet, *Governing with Judges*, 75–79.
62 Stone Sweet, *Birth of Judicial Politics*, 1886–88.
63 *Press Pluralism I*, 1984-181 DC (Conseil constitutionnel).

gone a long way to making constitutional argument more persuasive, but it was just too great a breach in the French legal tradition (and indeed, European legal tradition in general).[64] It is notable that a period of decisions that could not by any stretch be regarded as conservative followed shortly after his appointment. It might be thought that personnel matters a good deal; the Conseil became steadily less dominated by councillors appointed by right-wing politicians, until in Badinter's last three years there was actually a six-to-three majority of left-wing appointments. This is almost certainly an oversimplification, though in truth we know almost nothing about the internal dynamics of the Conseil. Badinter's own reign was very much a development of trends originated under Georges Vedel, hardly a figure otherwise of the Left, yet the man who announced the ultimate French heresy, that parliament did not directly express the general will, but only did so when sitting as a constituent assembly.[65] Furthermore Badinter's main preoccupation was consistency across judgements and a slow development of doctrine, both of which would militate against using a political majority to press left-wing, and hold up right-wing, legislation. In many ways the Conseil has sought to achieve this end, and the efforts continued after Badinter's term of office. There have been far fewer sudden announcements of doctrine, and to some extent the Conseil has concentrated on more traditional human rights issues and the ever-present need to spell out fully the meaning of democracy.[66]

It is impossible in the context of a chapter like this to give a survey of French constitutional review, but enough has been said to indicate its basic nature. It is a great drawback that the "big cases" always discussed are from a very limited period of time when French politics was in one of its most intense and conflictual moods. Between 1980 and 1986 France experienced is first ever Socialist president, the first postwar Socialist government, the first period of "cohabitation" between a president and prime minister of opposite political tendencies—and a major economic crisis. This was when the Conseil constitutionnel was in its infancy as a real review body. It had enemies everywhere, not least in the Conseil d'Etat and the ordinary courts. But that was a quarter of a century ago, and it is ludicrous to assess the Conseil on the basis of such a period. It is impossible in anything less

[64] A pro-Badinter account of his period as president of the Conseil is given in Rousseau, *Sur le Conseil constitutionnel.* The quotation above comes from her book, p. 19, and an often engaging personal account of working with him can be found in Robert, *Garde de la République.*

[65] Although no single author is ever given to a Conseil decision, it is widely accepted that Vedel insisted on this formula in a case, in which parliament's amendment procedures were upheld against the objection of the minority who had tried to claim a breach in fundamental parliamentary privilege. As the decision involved a new version of an act that had to be hurried through to take account of the Conseil's own censuring on the previous version, it was in the interest both of the Conseil and of the executive to drive home this point. Vedel's actual words were that the procedure "responded to the requirements of constitutional control, one of whose goals is to allow laws once voted, which only express the General Will in respect of the constitution to be amended without delay for this purpose." *Law on New Caledonia,* 85-197 DC (Conseil constitutionnel), par. 25.

[66] The Conseil has also tried to make its decisions less opaque to the public. An interesting example is that since the late 1990s the council's website has provided not only the texts of its decisions, but the reasoning of those who referred the law and the governments response. Since early in 2004 yet further documentation has been made available.

than a full book to correct the impression left by those first few years. All that can be done here is to give two examples of the Conseil and its political context. First let us consider one of the two situations where the constitution has been amended to avoid decisions of the Conseil. Second, let us look at a more or less typical year in the recent past of the Conseil to show its actual daily life.

The issue of sex quotas for elected office, as already mentioned, ran through French politics from early in the first Socialist government until the end of the twentieth century. If that conflict shows the seriousness of the issue to the Left in France, it equally shows the solidity and continuity of jurisprudence of the Conseil constitutionnel.[67]

Consistency and Constitutional Amendment

Three decisions are annotated together as "quotas par Sexe" under entry 33b in Favoreu and Philip's standard *Grandes decisions du Conseil constitutionnel*, along with a note explaining their "a posteriori insertion," in part justified because Robert Badinter himself thought the initial decision one of the most important ever. In November 1982 conservative deputies referred to the Conseil a law on municipal elections that would have imposed on all political parties fighting an election based on a list system of proportional representation a duty to have not more than 75 percent of their candidates from one sex. Ironically the genesis of this law was one drafted by the previous conservative government's minister for the family and women, Monique Pelletier, who much later become a member of the Conseil constitutionnel. Georges Vedel, later to be the much admired "doyen" of the Conseil but not appointed at this time, publicly commented that the plan would be constitutional in a newspaper article of 1979. The conservatives' version ran out of parliamentary time before the Senate could deal with it, but it had passed the Assembly. In fact the Socialist government of Gaston Deferre had not intended to impose sex quotas—they were written into the law by a back bench amendment, and when the opposition referred the act for other reasons to the Conseil, it was careful not to raise the issue of the constitutionality of that amendment.[68] Instead the Conseil exercised its own right to take up the matter, for it has never regarded itself as bound to decide only on the terms of complaints actually made.

The Conseil ruled that any form of quota that differentiated between candidates on any grounds except the traditional ones like age was in breach both of Article 3 of the 1958 constitution and of Article 6 of the 1789 Declaration. Article 3 actu-

[67] The first constitutional revision was very different, showing the fickleness of a French government *of the Right* when confronted with the sort of human rights decision that any constitutional review body anywhere might make. This was the overturning of a decision protecting asylum seekers' rights in 1993, *Asylum Rights*, 93-325 DC (Conseil constitutionnel). It was particularly odd because the Conseil d'Etat, consulted by the government, gave its opinion that no constitutional change was necessary and a simple ordinary law could have achieved the government's aim while abiding by the Conseil constitutionnel's ruling.

[68] These details are taken from the "Observations" in Favoreu and Philip, *Décisions du Conseil constitutionnel*, 554–60.

ally talks only of voters, and not much was made of it. Article 6 does indeed state that "all citizens, being equal [in the eyes of the law] are equally eligible for all public dignities, positions and employment according to their abilities, and without distinction other than that of their virtues and talents." From this the Conseil asserted,

> It follows from comparison of these texts that the status of citizen itself gives rise to the right to vote and to be eligible on identical terms to all who are not excluded by reason of age, incapacity, or nationality, or for any reason designed to protect the freedom of the voter or the independence of the person elected; that these principles of constitutional value oppose any division of voters or eligible candidates into categories; that this applies to all political elections, especially for the election of municipal councilors.[69]

Although the Conseil, naturally, does not explain any further, academic commentary suggests a very French reason for the firmness with which the Conseil, then and on all future occasions until the constitution was amended, stuck to the idea of the homogeneity of the electorate and the resulting political class. The idea behind this position, according to highly respected commentators, goes to the heart of the French republican tradition, depending on a very Rousseauesque conception of the indivisibility of the general will as ensured by the interchangeability of each voter. One commentator congratulated the Conseil constitutionnel for having reminded the French of this principle of which the politicians were "ignorant or forgetful" but which had been "the basis of constitutional law since the Revolution," even though the Conseil would risk being regarded as antifeminist. The principle in question is that of finding a general will based "not on differences but on that which is common." This writer, typical of those commenting on constitutional law at the time, stated,

> The decision of the Constitutional council is of major doctrinal importance. It is, in effect, the renewed consecration of one of the fundamental rules of constitutional law. An abstract concept tied to the very existence of the body politics, the citizen is the elementary unit, whose interchangeability guarantees, through the perfect homogeneity of this body, the indivisibility of the sovereignty. . . . this aspect must not be dismembered by any differentiation whatsoever by category, the very existence of which would affect the essential nature of the concept and that which it is designed to represent and guarantee.[70]

It has, ever since the Revolution, been a peculiarly French conception that there is some form of "public space," *la place publique*, within which differentiation and distinction cannot be allowed, and the Conseil's decision is seen as resting on, and reminding of, this core idea. The idea, which probably goes back at least to Montesquieu, is still very powerful amongst intellectuals of all political persuasions. It

[69] *Quotas par sexe I*, par. 7.

[70] Léo Hamon, quoted in Favoreu and Philip, *Décisions du Conseil constitutionnel*, 555.

explains, for example, why no group of legislators referred the 2004 law forbidding religious clothes in school to the Conseil constitutionnel. Nor was the decision in 1982 anything like as hotly opposed by the Socialist as is sometimes suggested—the government had not wanted the amendment, and apparently let the Conseil know it did not much care about the decision on this aspect of the bill.[71] I mention this theoretical justification for only one reason—precisely because the Conseil constitutionnel does not! Without an insight into French political culture it is impossible to understand how a decision of the Conseil may reverberate, precisely because it is left to others outside the Conseil itself to make the arguments.

The Conseil certainly did stick to its decision. In January 1999, sixteen years later, a Conseil on which not one of those who made the original decision sat faced a very similar bill.[72] By then the sex equality argument had become stronger, and the new bill would have imposed parity between the sexes in list elections. The Conseil dealt with it very simply—it was "une chose jugée" (the English or Americans would have used Latin and said *res judicata*), a matter already decided. It then quoted, word for word, the core part of the decision as given above. The entire section of the decision dealing with this crucial issue runs to 218 words. This is hardly the work of a politically fluctuating body, or of one that is counter-majoritarian in any partisan way. The trouble, arguably the only trouble, is the refusal to explain itself. It may be, however, that there is a functionality to this terseness. It is an important doctrine in, inter alia, UK law that a precedent is a precedent only for the close details of the case it is drawn from. Despite this doctrine, there is an endless tendency, often quite awkward for the development of the law, to stretch precedents and principles, and indeed judicial obiter, very widely. In constitutional law this is also common in the United States and elsewhere. It cannot as easily happen in France, because in many ways every decision of the Conseil on the constitutionality of a part of an act is precisely and only that—it is a highly specific judgement on one limited piece of legislation, and has no real implications for any other issue, however logically or analogically close. In the French case this showed in the refusal of the Conseil—and its commentators, to treat the *Quotas par sexe* decisions as having any import for the general questions of positive discrimination and so forth. Electoral laws had a very special place in the republican tradition; they required the application of this "obvious" principle, and that was all. Elsewhere the decision would have continually played a part in all subsequent gender equality cases, possibly hampering future courts who would not wish to cast doubt on the original decision but would have wished to find otherwise in analogous cases. That at least cannot happen in France.[73]

Other decisions had occurred touching more directly on electoral uniformity, and all were decided in keeping with this basic decision. In 1999, however, the French political class had become more attached to the equality goal for them-

[71] See Bell, *French Constitutional Law*, 349.

[72] *Quotas par sexe II*, 98-407 DC (1999) (Conseil constitutionnel), pars. 7–9.

[73] See Mélin-Soucramanien, *Le Principe d'Égalité*. Interestingly, Favoreu confesses, in his discussion of the *Quotas par sexe* cases, to having thought the decision did have wider implications for positive discrimination but having "belatedly" seen the light after Mélin-Soucramanien's empirical work.

selves, and called a constitutional convention to amend the constitution to allow such policies. All the revision of July 1999 actually did was to add one sentence to Article 3 of the 1958 constitution. This now concludes with "Statutes shall promote equal access by women and men to elective offices and positions." Another sentence was added to Article 4, on political parties, which now concludes with "They shall contribute to the implementation of the principle set out in the last paragraph of Article 3 as provided by statute."[74] Almost immediately a bill went through parliament providing for, inter alia, more or less equal numbers of male and female candidates in any election where the mechanisms made this equality possible—essentially list-type proportional representation. To put teeth into it, the bill also provided that parties that failed to satisfy this requirement should have their state aid to election expenses cut by a proportional amount.

Inevitably the Right referred the bill to the Conseil constitutionnel, on May 30, 2000. Of course the Conseil upheld the bill, though this result need not have happened had the Conseil really been intent on enforcing its view on the French state, because the amendment was rather weak. The argument, which the Conseil rejected in quite strong language, was that all the new wording did was to set "objectives" as opposed to actually imposing norms, and that mere objectives could not trump the pre-existing clear constitutional principles (buttressed again by the argument that the question of quotas was *une chose jugée*). Or, which comes to much the same thing, "objectives" could not justify penalties imposed by law. The Conseil went much further than it needed to in rejecting the objections to the bill, saying outright that there were no limits to how "the constituent power" could alter constitutional principles, except for certain structural aspects of the constitution. (This latter was to cover, for example, the fact that Article 89, on constitutional amendment, specifically says that "the Republican form of Government shall not be the object of an amendment.") The argument here was probably addressed to some parts of the constitutional law establishment that had recently been playing with a concept the French call *supra-constitutionnalité*, the idea that there are principles almost of natural law that the Conseil could impose regardless of constitutional wording.[75] As the Conseil said, the whole idea was to remove those constitutional objections that it had itself announced in the past, so the question of *chose jugée* could not be raised. Furthermore, considering, as the Conseil often does, the travaux préparatoires for the law, it was obvious that the constituent power had intended to authorize the legislature to do anything that might help bring about equal access to elected office. It could therefore pass laws whether indicative or directive, it being always the legislature's duty to "ensure compatibility between the new constitutional dispositions and the other rules and principles of constitutional value that the constituent power had not intended to

[74] As translated by the Conseil constitutionnel and published on its website at www.conseil-constitutionnel.fr.

[75] This is commented on, inter alia, in Rousseau, *Droit du contentieux constitutionnel*; and Robert, *Garde de la République*. The Conseil had first made it utterly clear that it would not entertain the idea in its decision on the Maastricht Treaty, *EU Treaty*, 92-312 DC (Conseil constitutionnel).

derogate from."[76] As a footnote it is worth noting that the Conseil did find part of the bill unconstitutional, the clause that detailed how the money withdrawn from offending parties should be reallocated. It was purely procedural; an ordinary law as opposed to a special financial bill could not do what it purported to do.

A Typical Year at the Conseil Constitutionnel

It is this frequent carelessness of the French parliament that often gives the impression that the Conseil constitutionnel is overactive. The year of that decision, 2000, was a fairly typical year for the Conseil constitutionnel, and this chapter finishes by surveying it overall.

There was a conservative president, a Socialist government, and the majority of the members of the Conseil (including the president). had been appointed by conservative officeholders.[77] If there was to be any marked tendency for the Conseil to try to impose its own policy preferences on government legislation, this year should have shown it. There is no such pattern. Sixteen laws were considered, of which four only were declared entirely compatible with the constitution. All the remaining twelve were held to be partially nonconforming. This indeed seems prima facie evidence of intrusive policy intervention, until the details are considered. First it should be noted that three of the four completely constitutional laws were of a special nature wherein intervention by the Conseil might be seen more readily as a serious policy incursion—two were "organic laws" and one a "Lois de Pays," that is, a law emanating from a dependent territory, in this case New Caledonia. Yet the Conseil found nothing problematic about any of them. What follows, in tabular form, is an outline description of the laws that did run into trouble.

Details of Legislation found partially unconstitutional for the year 2000.
Points marked (P) and (D) are procedural or antidiscrimination arguments;
(S) indicates a "structural" issue.

A. January 13, 2000, Decision no. 99-423 DC

Loi relative à la réduction négociée du temps de travail

(P) There was a failure to specify with adequate precision what was required by certain clauses, and to specify the legal consequences of failure to conform.

(D) There was an unjustified discrimination in overtime rates for different categories of workers even though there was no relevant difference and it was beyond the individual's control.

The legislation amounted in parts to an excessive restriction on freedom of contract as protected by both the Declaration of the Rights of Man of 1789 and the preamble to the Fourth Republic constitution.

B. March 30, 2000, Decision no. 2000-426 DC

[76] *Quotas par Sexe III*, 2000-429 DC (Conseil constitutionnel), paras. 7 and 8.

[77] Knapp and Wright, *Government and Politics*, 407.

Loi relative à la limitation du cumul des mandats électoraux et des fonctions et à leurs conditions d'exercice

(D) There was no justification for legislating an incompatibility between certain local government executive roles and election to office in local assemblies.

Certain other incompatibilities could not constitutionally be imposed except by an organic law.

(D) There was an unjustified discrimination in voting age for EU elections between French citizens and citizens of other member states.

C. May 4, 2000, Decision no. 2000-428 DC

Loi organisant une consultation de la population de Mayotte

(S) The Conseil announced a réserve d'interpretation to make clear that consultations with the population could only, constitutionally, be of an advisory nature.

(P) The legislation breached Article 39 of the constitution by imposing a future obligation on the government in a procedurally forbidden manner.

D. May 30, 2000, Decision no. 2000-429 DC

Loi tendant à favoriser l'égal accès des femmes et des hommes aux mandats électoraux et fonctions électives

(P) Discussed above—essentially only a minor procedural problem.

E. July 6, 2000, Decision no. 2000-431 DC

Loi relative à l'élection des sénateurs

(S) Imposed alterations to new electoral codes for the Senate to ensure compliance with Articles 3 and 24 of the constitution to ensure equality of the ballot.

F. July 20, 2000, Decision no. 2000-434 DC

Loi relative à la chasse

(P) Irregularities in parliamentary procedure.

(P) Clash with Article 34 detailing the nature of finance laws.

Disproportionate invasion of property rights guaranteed by Declaration of the Rights of Man.

G. July 27, 2000, Decision no. 2000-433 DC

Loi modifiant la loi n° 86-1067 du 30 septembre 1986 relative à la liberté de communication

(S) Problem involving doctrines of separation of powers and "due process" because of an automatic penalty that could be imposed by an executive body.

(P) "Negative incompetence"—lack of precision in a statutory duty and on the nature of the ensuing penalty.

H. December 7, 2000, Decision no. 2000-435 DC

Loi d'orientation pour l'outre-mer

Incompatibilities found:

(D) Unjustified discrimination against some categories of recipients.

(P) Breach of regulations on the nature of finance acts.

(P) Unclarity of restrictions on freedom of enterprise, involving a clash with Article 34 of the constitution.

(P) Unconstitutional injunctions on the government (as in Decision C).

(P) Irregularity of amendment procedures in parliament.

Three réserves d'interpretation were announced:

(S) Regional government officers in overseas departments were the only agents of the Republic who could be dismissed.

(S) The Republic cannot be bound by any international agreements made by overseas departments.

(S) Consultation with population of overseas department on institutional change must be recognised as not binding (as in Decision C).

I. December 7, 2000, Decision no. 2000-436 DC

Loi relative à la solidarité et au renouvellement urbains

Aspects of the legislation amounted to disproportionate interference with property and enterprise rights in Article 4 of the Declaration of the Rights of Man, because they affected contracts already completed.

Clash with Article 72 of the constitution because of the unfairness of certain sanctions against communes that were late in complying with the law through no fault of their own.

(P) Irregular amendment procedures in parliament.

J. December 19, 2000, Decision no. 2000-437 DC

Loi de financement de la sécurité sociale pour 2001

(D) One article imposed unjustified inequalities in taxation.

(P) Six articles were of a nature that cannot constitutionally be legislated in this type of statute.

K. December 28, 2000, Decision no. 2000-441 DC

Loi de finances rectificative pour 2000

(P) One article required authorisation by a special law on social services financing.

(D) One imposed an unjustified inequality in tax burdens.

One imposed a tax burden for unjustified reasons.

(D) Unjustified discrimination in favour of Corsica compared with other regions.

L. December 28, 2000, Decision no. 2000-442 DC

Loi de finances pour 2001

(P) Procedural problems with three articles that cannot be legislated in this type of finance act.

Of the decisions that year, the twelve where the Conseil constitutionnel intervened produced thirty-three "points" where the Conseil interfered with the legislation—again a number that, in abstract, might be thought high, even excessive. But again, examining the details shows a rather different picture. To start with, at least fourteen of the points involve sheer procedural irregularities—parliamentary incompetence of the sort that courts anywhere would automatically pick up. It is in part because of the French tradition of banning courts from querying parliamentary law that such sloppiness is rife, but it also speaks to the essentially weak grasp of the idea of the rule of law in France's political class.

A further seven points involve discrimination or equality arguments, which no one can doubt have been a central concern in French constitutional review (as almost everywhere, and discussed at length in chapter 7). The remaining twelve points are perhaps where we might find the Conseil constitutionnel imposing its values on French society. Yet do we? Six of the points are marked with an "S" to indicate that they were largely defences of structural matters—the role of consultations in external relations, separation-of-powers problems, maintenance of democratic norms in electoral procedures, and so forth. These are all the core business of constitutional courts in any democracy. In some cases reference to the Conseil is mandatory. This leaves only a few points that are problematic. There are three: (A) Loi relative à la réduction négociée du temps de travail, where the Conseil found the legislation amounted in parts to an excessive restriction on freedom of contract as protected by both the Declaration of the Rights of Man of 1789 and the preamble to the Fourth Republic constitution; (F) Loi relative à la chasse, where disproportionate invasion of property rights guaranteed by the Declaration of the Rights of Man was found; (I) Loi relative à la solidarité et au renouvellement urbains, where it was decided that aspects of the legislation amounted to disproportionate interference with property and enterprise rights in Article 4 of the Declaration of the Rights of Man, because they affected contracts already completed. In other words the Conseil constitutionnel insists that France's constitutional heritage includes a strong entrepreneurial and proprietarian element, one about which left-wing governments are prone to be casual. On top of this, the Conseil is involved, as are all such bodies, in preventing unjustified discrimination, has to police boundary problems, and, rather more than most, has to police the state's haphazard approach to procedural regularity. This, all in all, sounds like a fairly normal constitutional review body. Yes private property is more enshrined, or more obviously so, than in some countries. One could sum it up thus: Given the decision on hunting rights, the Conseil constitutionnel would probably have found the law forbidding fox hunting finally passed by the British Labour government in 2005 unconstitutional. And that might be the most one could say in attacking the Conseil as a body undemocratically interfering with the public will.

CHAPTER FIVE

Canada: Imposing Rights on the Common Law

The Pre-Charter Constitution and the Transformation

Canada is important for this book. Even were it not a subject of interest in its own right, it would have to be covered. This is because Canada is the best example we have of importing a whole new constitutional approach to a working and stable political system. Though the actual text of the Canadian Charter of Rights and Freedoms owes little to any other model, the process of establishing it, working out its details, and applying its rules has been one long exercise of legal transportation. Legal transplantation, though controversial, has been common in the jurisdictions covered here, and is bound to become even more important as the worldwide spread of court power furthers the development of an international constitutional legal approach.[1] This process has been commented on in various parts of the book—Canada is a test bed.[2] There was constitutional law in Canada before 1982, even a Bill of Rights. But so completely did the new constitution and Charter transform Canadian constitutional thinking some writers hardly acknowledge the fact. This is not to say that everyone welcomed the Charter, or that even now it is universally popular. Critics range from those who think it is far too invasive on democratic politics to those who think it is not only useless but dangerously so. This latter critique, from the Left, complains that the Charter is nothing more than

[1]A Watson, *Legal Transplants: An Approach to Comparative Law* (Athens: University of Georgia Press, 1993). For Eastern Europe see G Ajani, "By Chance and Prestige: Legal Transplants in Russia and Eastern Europe," 1995 43 *American Journal of Comparative Law* 1, 93–117.

[2]See, for example, B Ackerman, "The Rise of World Constitutionalism," 1997 83 *Virginia Law Review* 4, 771–97. Other useful references can be found in Yoo, "Peeking Abroad?"

another weapon of class war, and dangerous because it diverts attention from real class conflict.[3] Very specifically it shows the strains in going from the UK style of parliamentary supremacy to a doctrine and reality of constitutional supremacy. The very fact that Canada did have a history of constitutional law, and a Supreme Court with judicial review powers, makes it all the better a test case.

To give a flavour of the sort of cases that now occupy the Supreme Court of Canada under the Charter, one can do no better than to consider a case from 2005, *Chaoulli v Quebec*. The case was decided on a seven-to-two split with a coruscating joint dissent and has already been attacked as an extreme invasion of the legislative domain by a court.[4] The Supreme Court struck down a Quebec statute that made it illegal either to buy or to offer private health insurance.[5] This is a bulwark, also present in other Canadian provinces, to ensure the state health system does not lose resources to the private sector. Both the court of first instance and the Quebec Appeal Court had upheld the statute, the former after very lengthy and detailed empirical examination of expert witnesses.[6] The argument of the claimants was very simple. The Quebec health system was overloaded, and involved lengthy waiting lists for many medical procedures. Patients were therefore dying or suffering prolonged and excessive reduction in their quality of life, some of whom could have had private medical treatment had they been allowed to buy private medical insurance.[7] The statute therefore abridged the citizen's right under the Charter of Rights and Freedoms. Article 7 of the Charter provides that "everyone has the right to life, liberty and security of the person and the right not to be deprived thereof except in accordance with the principles of fundamental justice."[8] The leading opinion, by Justice Deschamps, describes how he saw the issue:

> when my colleagues ask whether Quebec has the power under the Constitution to discourage the establishment of a parallel health care system, I can only agree with them that it does. But that is not the issue in the appeal. *The appellants do not contend that they have a constitutional right to private insurance. Rather, they contend that the waiting times violate their rights to life and security. It is the measure chosen by the government that is in issue, not Quebeckers' need for a public health care system.*[9]

What sort of a right is involved here? The right to life can be a simple negative right against the state—when police get too trigger happy in the street, perhaps. It

[3] D Herman, "The Good, the Bad, and the Smugly: Perspectives on the Canadian Charter of Rights and Freedoms," 1994 14 *Oxford Journal of Legal Studies* 4, 589–604. The suspicion that elites shelter their power behind apparently liberal constitutional changes is widespread. See R Hirschl, *Towards Juristocracy: The Origins and Consequences of the New Constitutionalism* (Cambridge: Harvard University Press, 2004).

[4] *Chaoulli v Quebec (Attorney General)*, 2005 SCC 35 (Canadian Supreme Court). For commentary see "Recent Cases—Chaoulli v Quebec (Attorney General)," 2005 119 *Harvard Law Review* 2, 677–84.

[5] *Chaoulli v Quebec (Attorney General)*.

[6] *Chaoulli v Quebec (Attorney General)*.

[7] *Chaoulli v Quebec (Attorney General)*.

[8] Canadian Charter of Rights and Freedoms.

[9] *Chaoulli v Quebec (Attorney General)*, par. 14; emphasis added.

can be held to forbid capital punishment, as the Hungarian Constitutional Court hurried to find in 1990 and the South African court found in 1994.[10] It can be used to ban abortion, given certain assumptions about the legal status of the foetus. In *Chaoulli* it is hard to see the right quite in these simple negative turns.[11] Quebec is being forbidden to do something—restrict insurance—because this policy, in interaction with another policy—the funding level for the public health service—increases the risk to life beyond some nominal level.[12] Justice Deschamps is clear about this: "the waiting times violate their rights to life and security."[13] This only makes sense against a measure, however little specified, of a minimal health entitlement, because clearly the right to life cannot be breached by absolutely any wait. As two of the concurring justices put it, "By imposing exclusivity and then failing to provide public health care of a reasonable standard within a reasonable time, the government creates circumstances that trigger the application of [Article] 7 of the Charter."[14] The dissenters in a sense agree:

> What, then, are constitutionally required "reasonable health services?" What is treatment "within a reasonable time?" What are the benchmarks? How short a waiting list is short enough? How many MRIs does the Constitution require? The majority does not tell us. The majority lays down no manageable constitutional standard. The public cannot know, nor can judges or governments know, how much health care is "reasonable" enough to satisfy . . . [Charter rights]. . . . It is to be hoped that we will know it when we see it.[15]

Chaoulli is not typical of modern Canadian constitutional jurisprudence, but nor is it a "one-off." The Charter has thrown the courts into the policy process in a way that could never have been imagined, or tolerated, by the nineteenth-century politicians who drafted the British North America Act.

Canada as a united political entity came into being when the several different political systems of North America north of the United States voluntarily united into a federation in 1867. This had to be done by UK legislation and with the permission and guidance of the Foreign Office, because none of the existing Canadian political entities had complete freedom and independence, but the initiative was still genuinely Canadian. Indeed, several of what were later to become provinces declined originally to join. The document that served as Canada's new constitution until 1982 was an act of the UK parliament, the British North America Act of 1867. This retained the English Privy Council as the ultimate court of appeal, which role it retained, though later with Canada's consent, until the middle of the twentieth century. The overt intention of the 1867 act was to create a political system as much as possible like that of the United Kingdom, with a doctrine of parliamentary sov-

[10] *Decision of 31st October 1990 on Capital Punishment*, 23/1990 AB (Hungarian Constitutional Court); *S v Makwanyane and Another*, CCT 3/94 (South African Constitutional Court).

[11] *Chaoulli v Quebec (Attorney General).*

[12] *Chaoulli v Quebec (Attorney General).*

[13] *Chaoulli v Quebec (Attorney General).*

[14] *Chaoulli v Quebec (Attorney General)*, par. 105.

[15] *Chaoulli v Quebec (Attorney General)*, Binnie and LeBel, par. 163.

ereignty, or indeed supremacy. However, the most important guiding principle in the unification negotiations had been federalism. As federal systems inevitably require something like a constitutional court to police the borders of functional responsibilities, both Canadian courts and the Privy Council were involved in judicial review of legislation from the beginning of the federation. This aspect was more important, and made the courts more powerful, than might otherwise have been the case, because Canada's chosen form of federation was less clear-cut than some, with a good deal of overlapping responsibilities between the central and provincial governments. Much of the doctrine and some of the issues arising from this original plan continue to be vital in modern Canadian constitutional review.

One recent example was the need to have the Supreme Court clarify the constitutional possibility of the federal parliament passing a "same sex" marriage law. The right to legislate on marriage generally was a federal matter, under Section 91(26) of the Constitution Act of 1867, the former British North America Act. But the provinces retained the right to legislate on "civil rights" under Section 92(13) and on "solemnization of marriage" under Section 92(12) of the same act. As several of the provinces were politically more conservative on such issues than the majority in the federal parliament, a political clash on a human rights issue became in part a matter of constitutional law, not under the human rights provisions of the 1982 Charter, but under the still authoritative original constitution.[16] The Reference re: Same-Sex marriage was also litigated under the 1982 constitution.

For much of the period before 1982 the only way rights issues could be brought before a court was to challenge legislation not on its substance but on the grounds that whichever legislature was concerned was the wrong one. The Privy Council originally, and the Supreme Court later, were deferential to parliamentary sovereignty as long as it was the right parliament. The famous doctrinal phrase was that "the *wisdom* as opposed to the *vires* of an impugned statute was strictly a policy matter for the elected representatives of the people and not for the courts."[17] This did not make either of these courts incapable of political bias, but the biases tended to relate to one issue—a preference for central power versus a Canadian version of the US notion of "states' rights." The framers of the 1867 constitution act had enshrined solutions to the two most powerfully divisive issues of nineteenth-century Canada, language and religion, especially in their educational aspects, as clauses in the constitution itself rather than as in some Bill of Rights appendix. This further diminished any fears of courts being too powerful, because they could more readily be seen as simply applying a black-letter view of the constitution. Though there have been some changes, religion and language rights remain to this day both powerfully divisive, and predominantly covered by the original constitutional settlement, not the 1982 Charter.

This attitude of deference to parliaments was so strongly imbued in the judiciary that an earlier Canadian attempt to provide constitutional backing for civil rights largely failed. This was the 1960 Bill of Rights, which was simply an ordi-

[16] *Reference re Same-Sex Marriage*, 3 SCR 698 (2004) (Canadian Supreme Court).
[17] B Wilson, "Constitutional Advocacy," 1992 24 *Ottawa Law Review* 265–75, 266.

nary, not entrenched, federal parliamentary statute. It has often been criticised as a powerless document both because of its nonentrenched status and because it contained a "notwithstanding" clause that allowed parliament to legislate contrary to its terms by just saying that the Bill of Rights should not apply. In practise the government made almost no use of this power, nor was its nonentrenched status important. What really restricted it was a timidity on the part of the judges, recognised by the post-1982 Supreme Court, a stance it has always claimed to be anxious not to repeat. As the Bill of Rights applied only to federal legislation, its impact was bound in any case to be limited, and much of the activity of the post-1982 court has involved challenges to provincial legislation. (This is also true of much of the more activist work of the US Supreme Court, which is far more likely to strike down a state statute than a federal statute.) One can easily see this pre-1982 timidity in the fate of those who tried to argue that the original federal constitution did in fact have an "implied" bill of rights, in much the same way that the Australian High Court has "imputed" certain political rights like freedom of speech from the structure of the constitution.[18] As late as 1978 the Supreme Court flatly rejected the idea that fundamental freedoms could be derived from the preamble to the constitution.[19] The idea that inherited judicial timidity made constitutional protection of rights empty before 1982 is borne out by the way arguments very similar to those that failed in the 1960s and 1970s were actually used by the court itself in the 1990s, something we shall come to shortly Exactly how and why this timidity disappeared is hard to explain. Most probably it was a consequence of a shift in judicial self-definition of the job.

The political history of the changes that brought a new constitution to Canada in 1982 are too complex to relate here, and do not much affect the way it has operated. To a large extent it was the ambition of one man, the prime minister for much of the 1970s and early 1980s, Pierre Trudeau.[20] Such a development had to be negotiated with the provinces, and the negotiations, especially with Quebec, which feared an entrenched bill of rights, were not easy. There was no intention to change any part of the existing constitution, though it was strongly felt that it ought at long last actually to be the Canadians' own property and not exist in the limbo of a British parliamentary act. Even this was not uncontroversial, because "patriating" the constitution necessarily involved giving Canadians the right to amend it, and there were those as fearful of possible amendments as of an entrenched bill of rights. Losing patience with endless rounds of negotiations with the provinces, the federal government attempted to go it alone, and simply ask London to patriate the version Ottawa wanted.[21]

[18] See JL Pierce, *Inside the Mason Court Revolution: The High Court of Australia Transformed* (Durham, N.C.: Carolina Academic Press, 2006).

[19] *Canada (A.G.) v City of Montreal*, 2 SCR 770 (1978) (Canadian Supreme Court).

[20] An account of repatriation focussing on Trudeau's role is given in G Laforest, *Trudeau and the End of a Canadian Dream* (Montreal: McGill-Queen's Press, 1995).

[21] Probably the most authoritative account of the politics of repatriation is E McWhinney, *Canada and the Constitution, 1979–82: Patriation and the Charter of Rights* (Toronto: University of Toronto Press, 1982).

At this point the Supreme Court became involved, and demonstrated for the first time that it was likely to develop a rich conception of just what the Canadian constitution was. It is an unusual feature in the common-law world that the Canadian Supreme Court is not limited to hearing actual cases. Both the federal and provincial governments can refer abstract questions to the court in a way not unlike, though much more restricted than, the abstract review processes in some continental European systems. The provinces duly referred to the court the question of whether the Ottawa government could arrange a constitutional change by itself. The court's answer was that there was no "legal" barrier, but that the constitution consisted of more than the British North America Act and constitutional law—it contained also political conventions that could not legitimately be ignored. The result was a further round of negotiations that both changed aspects of the Charter of Rights and Freedoms and modified—in very complicated way—the plans for future constitutional amendments. Finally, to assuage Quebec's fears, the new constitution contained a very powerful "opt out" clause by which a province could prevent the Charter or parts of it from applying within its territory. Any use of this proviso can only last for five years, and becomes invalid unless renewed by the provincial legislature. Quebec took immediate advantage of this, with the result that parts of the new constitution did not take effect in French Canada until the late 1980s. By the end of 1982, however, Canada had patriated a constitution that, with the exception of the Charter of Rights and Freedoms, was largely the one it had lived under since 1867, with all of the complex constitutional law of federalism still in place.

Within a very short time the judges on the Supreme Court, though they had all been on the court before repatriation, threw off the shackles of deference to parliaments. Or did they? The answer to that question seems to depend almost entirely on which side of a split in the Canadian academic community, and to a lesser extent in the Canadian polity, one sides with. There are those deeply disappointed with the court because it has not been "active" enough, and those who see it as regularly and illegitimately usurping the democratic privileges of the legislatures. Not surprisingly people take both sides at different times, because the court is bound to be active in the wrong areas at times for those who want it active, and passive in the wrong areas for those who generally want it passive. What is abundantly clear is that many had exaggerated hopes for what the court could do. Who is right is beyond the remit of this book; the argument is essentially one between the Left and Right in Canadian society. At times, however, it will be necessary to draw on the literature the controversy has evoked. As throughout this book, my preference is to let the cases speak—to study what the court has done, not what it has failed to do. The plan of this book involves crucially important "theme" chapters based on comparison of the different ways issues have been treated by courts in different countries. As a consequence of this structure, there are important areas of Canadian jurisprudence that are treated only with the lightest of touches in this chapter because they are discussed at length later. This is unavoidable because no sense can be made of how the Canadian judges have developed the constitution without some reference to some of these matters at this point.

The Defining Decisions

Defining Its Role

The Supreme Court was from the beginning intensely conscious of the need to carve out a new and much more active role, and correspondingly aware how vital its first few decisions would be. The first court faced three partially related tasks. It had to defend the very legitimacy of constitutional review; it had to develop a methodology for Charter interpretation; it had to teach itself to think afresh about the very nature of judicial interpretation in this new legal-constitutional era. The issues are interrelated for obvious reasons—an inadequate new methodology, or an ill-fitting approach to interpretation, could only feed those hostile to the new judicial powers. Not that the court could hope to overcome entirely this hostility. Courts take sides; they have to because the very logic of judicial pronouncement is dichotomous. An appeal is or is not upheld, and there are always losers. Policy in the hands of politicians may not be zero sum, and compromises that leave everyone feeling happy may be possible, but courts do not, in general, deal in compromise. The expectations riding on this court were so high, and so mutually conflicting, that perhaps everyone would be dissatisfied. Where, as in the United States or Australia, a constitutional court comes on line at the same time as the other constitutional actors, it can hope for a collective legitimacy, such that even those opposed to its decisions accept its role. In South Africa, of course, the court preceded the final constitution, possibly actually granting the other actors legitimacy. But in Canada the Supreme Court faced—still faces—the fact that Canada was, in most ways, doing perfectly well without the Charter, and with a much less salient form of judicial review. In such a situation it was very much harder for other political actors to distinguish between approval of the court's actual decisions and approval of its institutional role.

The other related tasks were crucial and difficult. The Charter does not speak for itself—it has a peculiar structure, one that required considerable fleshing out by the court in developing a methodology for Charter adjudication. Finally, there was what amounted to a personnel problem. The Kelsen courts in Europe were designed in part because of a feeling that the ordinary judiciary would be neither temperamentally nor technically capable of constitutional adjudication. The Kelsen courts in Eastern Europe were designed for the further reason that the existing judiciary was deeply tainted by association with the previous regimes. Those who were already sitting on the Canadian Supreme Court were not tainted, and no one could doubt their eminence as common-law judges. But they were common-law judges, and came from a time of deeply felt judicial deference to the legislature. Could they both summon the courage, and learn the new tricks required, to make the Charter work?

Even if it had wished to dodge the question of its own legitimacy, the court had no option but to develop a strong theory of democracy, which would deal, inter alia, with the role of judicial review. This is discussed in the next section. But in fact the court faced the issue squarely and early. In a reference from British Columbia, the constitutional validity of part of its Motor Vehicle Act had to be decided in the second year of the Charter, there having been only a handful of nontrivial previous Charter cases, all important as initial statements.[22] The reference concerned one of the most important but also one of the least clear parts of the Charter, which will concern us throughout this chapter. This is Section 7, which guarantees that "Everyone has the right to life, liberty and security of the person and the right not to be deprived thereof except in accordance with the principles of fundamental justice." The British Columbia act provided a mandatory prison sentence for anyone driving without a valid license, whether or not the person knew the license was invalid or suspended. It was, in lawyers' language, a "strict liability" offence. The problem for the court was whether such a policy, imprisoning those who may have had no traditional criminal intent, no *mens rea*, deprived them of liberty in a way that did not accord with "the principles of fundamental justice," when these principles were not otherwise defined in the Charter.

Reference re B.C. could almost have been set up as a hurdle by someone wanting to trip the Supreme Court, because what it decided is insignificant compared with how it decided. There was no politically neutral way of dealing with the issue; technical decisions on how to answer the case would inevitably act as branch points channelling future constitutional jurisprudence, a situation political scientists call "path dependency." The fact that the case directly raised the legitimacy of judicial review and its techniques was mentioned at the beginning of the main judgement:

> The issue in this case raises fundamental questions of constitutional theory, including the nature and the very legitimacy of constitutional adjudication under the *Charter* as well as the appropriateness of various techniques of constitutional interpretation.[23] (Lamar J.)

Lamar cites the court below as having asserted that the Constitution Act 1982 had added a new dimension to constitutional review by empowering courts to measure "the content of legislation" against the constitutional requirements of the Charter. Though he tries to suggest not all that much is new, he does this by stressing that content has always been fair game, and tries to suggest the court will still abide by the rules it was used to in pre-Charter days, citing a leading case from 1977, where the now chief justice had argued:

> The Courts will not question the wisdom of enactments . . . but it is the high duty of this Court to insure that the Legislatures do not transgress the limits of their constitutional mandate and engage in the illegal exercise of power.[24]

The precise problem, which Lamar notes, is that there was a common view that anything but the narrowest interpretation of Charter language would constitute

[22] *Re B.C. Motor Vehicle Act*, 2 SCR 486 (1985) (Canadian Supreme Court).

[23] *Re B.C. Motor Vehicle Act*, Lamar writing for six judges, par. 10.

[24] *Amax Potash Ltd. v Government of Saskatchewan*, 2 SCR 576 (1977) (Canadian Supreme Court), 590.

the impermissible crossing of the boundary and make the court appear to "question the wisdom of policy." Lamar's own words best describe the quandary and his robust counterargument.

> This is an argument which was heard countless times prior to the entrenchment of the *Charter* but which has in truth, for better or for worse, been settled by the very coming into force of the *Constitution Act, 1982*. It ought not to be forgotten that the historic decision to entrench the *Charter* in our Constitution was taken not by the courts but by the elected representatives of the people of Canada. It was those representatives who extended the scope of constitutional adjudication and entrusted the courts with this new and onerous responsibility. *Adjudication under the Charter must be approached free of any lingering doubts as to its legitimacy.*[25] (Emphasis in last sentence added).

The last sentence has been quoted time and again by the court to justify its actions. Here, though, the danger is even greater, because a narrow versus rich reading of "principles of fundamental justice" was taken by many to equate to a distinction between merely procedural as opposed to substantive conceptions of justice. And this, deliberately, evoked the huge conflict in American constitutional law over procedural versus substantive due process. Substantive due process had been the intellectual justification for the enforcement of laisser-faire economic theory by the Supreme Court in the late nineteenth and early twentieth centuries.[26] This famously culminated in the clash between Roosevelt's New Deal and the Supreme Court in the 1930s. As critics could characterise anything but a narrow and technical reading of Section 7 as tantamount to the most notorious example of judicial policymaking in recent history, the Canadian Supreme Court was forced to make a major choice. It also had to try to deny the implications were anything like that.[27]

Dealing with this point also forced the court to make a second methodological decision, because supporters of the British Columbia position urged that the proper way to decide what the Charter meant was to look at the very recent proceedings of the parliamentary committee on constitutional reform. In truth the relevant legislative proceedings were rather clearer than most, and would much more have supported a narrow (procedural) reading than a richer one. But reference to constitutional conventions and the like has sometimes tended to be a weapon of judicial conservatives, even if they are not necessarily as extreme as American "original intent" theorists. The court therefore had to insist on two points. First, it argued that the procedural/substantive dichotomy was inapplicable to constitu-

[25] *Re B.C. Motor Vehicle Act*, par. 16.

[26] Though of course there are those who argue powerfully that *Lochner* was never like that at all. See JM Balkin, "'Wrong the Day It Was Decided': *Lochner* and Constitutional Historicism," 2005 85 *Boston University Law Review* 677–726.

[27] For an excellent account of how fear of a *Lochner*-like situation had bedevilled the negotiations leading up to the Charter, see S Choudhry, "The *Lochner* Era and Comparative Constitutionalism," 2004 2 *International Journal of Constitutional Law* 1, 1–55. In his broad comparative study, Koopmans comments interestingly on these early decisions. T Koopmans, *Courts and Political Institutions: A Comparative View* (Cambridge: Cambridge University Press, 2003).

tional law, and was an unnecessary and dangerous importation from American law useful there only because of major structural differences in the two constitutions. Second, it insisted that the legislative record should never be given much importance when interpreting the Charter, both because it is difficult to interpret and because it would "freeze" the meaning of what should be a document capable of development and growth. Fundamental justice is then defined by Lamar and the other five justices he writes for as involving a reference to core principles of Canadian legal thought, against which it could never be justified to imprison someone for a strict liability offence. This is done by a careful examination of the way Section 7 and other sections interrelate. All this effort to avoid the appearance of making policy choices was somewhat damaged by the seventh justice, Bertha Wilson, later to be chief justice and with little doubt the most radical person to have yet sat on the court. She certainly agreed with the majority on the result, but got there by a much more direct route that rather too clearly demonstrated how much was a matter of judicial ideology. She considered theories of punishment, decided what the rules for selecting punishments should be, and finished with characteristically strong language. The constitutionality of the legislation depended on

> whether attaching a mandatory term of imprisonment to an absolute liability offence such as this violates the principles of fundamental justice. I believe that it does. I think the conscience of the court would be shocked and the administration of justice brought into disrepute by such an unreasonable and extravagant penalty. It is totally disproportionate to the offence and quite incompatible with the objective of a penal system referred to in [the criminological research she has cited].[28]

Whatever the impact of the different positions, this early case established clearly that the court had no doubt about its own legitimacy, and that it was intent on avoiding reliance on any technique that might restrict its freedom to innovate.

Interpreting a Constitution

Shortly before the *B.C.* reference the Supreme Court had begun the task of developing an appropriate approach to interpreting the Charter in *Hunter v Southam*, which along with *B.C.* and two other cases form the cornerstone of its method to this day.[29] *Hunter* involved a challenge to a warrantless search by government officers of a newspaper office, apparently justified under a piece of federal legislation. This was alleged to breach Section 8 of the Charter, which, echoing a similar provision in the US Bill of Rights, lays down simply that "Everyone has the right to be secure against unreasonable search or seizure." Here a single word required interpreting, "unreasonable," and the Charter says no more about it. The question for the court was what standard, or indeed what sort of standards, it should reach for. The court was very clear about one thing: interpreting a constitution is not the

[28] *Re B.C. Motor Vehicle Act*, par. 128.
[29] *Hunter v Southam Inc.*, 2 SCR145 (1984) (Canadian Supreme Court).

same as the normal common-law judge's duty of interpreting statutes, or indeed any other normal legal document, because it approvingly cited a major US legal thinker who insisted to US courts that they should not "read the provisions of the Constitution like a last will and testament lest it become one." This comparison with a will has become an important part of the court's justification of its methods. The court fell back on a much older ruling on Canadian constitutional adjudication, from the days when the English Privy Council was the final Canadian court, citing Viscount Sankey from the 1930s to the effect that a constitution was like "a living tree." "The British North America Act planted in Canada a living tree capable of growth and expansion within its natural limits. . . . Their Lordships do not conceive it to be the duty of this Board . . . to cut down the provisions of the Act by a narrow and technical construction, but rather to give it a large and liberal interpretation."[30] The "living tree" analogy is cited endlessly in modern cases to justify a nonliteral interpretation. It would have worked perfectly to disallow the recourse to the Parliamentary record attempted in *B.C.* The judges also cited, and it is an interesting reflection on the extent to which the common law internationally agrees about constitutional jurisprudence, a rare reference from a modern English case. The Privy Council until recently remained the court of last resort for various Caribbean commonwealth states. This presented a few UK judges, long before the 1998 Human Rights Act, with the job of interpreting written constitutions, which they undertook quite conscious that such work was different from their normal role. Thus Lord Wilberforce's famous dictum, already quoted in chapter 1, on the matter also appears in *Hunter v Southam*, where he notes that a constitution, unlike other legal documents, is

> sui generis, calling for principles of interpretation of its own, suitable to its character, [and requires] . . . a generous interpretation avoiding what has been called "the austerity of tabulated legalism," suitable to give individuals the full measure of the fundamental rights and freedoms referred to.[31]

All this is important, but largely negative—it tells a judge very little about how to approach the problem, but *Hunter* does give some aid. In particular the case stresses the "purposive" nature of constitutional interpretation, and the fact that it must produce answers that will serve in the uncertain future rather than merely being a solution to the case in front of the court. Much stress is placed on the expected longevity and difficulty of amending a constitution compared with the ease of repealing a particular legislative act. The single judgement in this case was written by Dickson, who shortly thereafter became chief justice, and ranges widely over both English and America common-law cases on search powers. The main stress, though, is that it is crucial to decide what "reasonable" must be taken to mean to validate the important right of being free from unreasonable searches—the interpretative duty is to ensure the right, not to limit it. Especially, Dickson

[30] Both quotations from *Hunter v Southam Inc.*, 156.
[31] *Minister of Home Affairs v Fisher*, AC 319 [1980] (Privy Council).

says, the court must not "consider simply [the act's] rationality in furthering some valid government objective."

In this way the court drew a sharp distinction with much Anglo-Canadian administrative law—constitutions really are different from statutes. The final blow against seeing constitutions as just big acts of parliament was contained at the end. The government council urged the court, if it was not to uphold the statute intact, also not to hold it invalid. Instead, it urged, the court should "read in" terms that would make it legitimate. *Hunter v Southam* was the first time a federal statute was to be struck down by the court under the Charter, and a reading down would avoid this result. To do so, however, would have been to blunt the force of Charter overview, to give the impression that the Supreme Court would in general help the government out. Dickson ended by saying:

> While the courts are guardians of the Constitution and of individuals' rights under it, it is the legislature's responsibility to enact legislation that embodies appropriate safeguards to comply with the Constitution's requirements. It should not fall to the courts to fill in the details that will render legislative lacunae constitutional. Without appropriate safeguards legislation authorizing search and seizure is inconsistent with s. 8 of the *Charter*. As I have said, any law inconsistent with the provisions of the Constitution is . . . of no force or effect. I would hold subss. 10(1) and 10(3) of the *Combines Investigation Act* to be inconsistent with the *Charter* and of no force and effect.[32]

In the comparative focus of this book the last argument marks quite clearly how different common-law constitutional adjudication is from the spirit within which continental European Kelsen courts work. Nothing more alien to the spirit of French *réserves d'interpretation* or German equivalent techniques can easily be imagined.

The third of the setting-up cases is discussed later in the book, when issues of religion and constitutionalism are dealt with, and can be covered quickly here for present purposes. *R v Big M Drug Mart Ltd* was perhaps the most important and even surprising of the early cases in terms of its substance. It struck down a long-established act, the Lord's Day Act, that, amongst other things, largely prohibited trading on a Sunday.[33] It followed shortly after *Hunter v Southam* and largely reflects the ideas about interpretation contained there. In fact the statement in *Big M* is probably clearer than in the preceding case, and worth quoting at length. It is again by Dickson, who was to write many of the most important Supreme Court rulings over the next few years, especially when he became chief justice.

> [*Hunter v Southam* decided that] that the proper approach to the definition of the rights and freedoms guaranteed by the *Charter* was a purposive one. The meaning of a right or freedom guaranteed by the *Charter* was to be ascertained by an analysis of the *purpose* of such a guarantee; it was to be understood, in other words, in the light of the interests it was meant to protect. In my view

[32] *Hunter v Southam Inc.*, 169.

[33] *R v Big M Drug Mart Ltd*, 1 SCR 295 (1985) (Canadian Supreme Court).

> this analysis is to be undertaken, and the purpose of the right or freedom in question is to be sought by reference to the character and the larger objects of the *Charter* itself, to the language chosen to articulate the specific right or freedom, to the historical origins of the concepts enshrined, and where applicable, to the meaning and purpose of the other specific rights and freedoms with which it is associated within the text of the *Charter*. The interpretation should be, as the judgment in *Southam* emphasizes, a generous rather than a legalistic one, aimed at fulfilling the purpose of the guarantee and securing for individuals the full benefit of the *Charter*'s protection.[34]

What *Big M* added was crucial—to clear away any attempt to argue that previous interpretations and meanings must be imported into Charter jurisprudence. The Lord's Day Act had been litigated before, specifically under the Charter's predecessor, the nonentrenched 1960 Bill of Rights.[35] The definitions of religious freedom then given had been restrictive, indeed conservative, and had the court accepted them it would have severely limited the Section 2 guarantee of "freedom of conscience and religion." Yet it was not obvious that all past decisions on an act, especially ones under a form of a bill of rights, had ceased to be binding once the Charter was in place. If not binding, they might at least be persuasive—and the Supreme Court has always been happy to ransack legal history for help. Why not take their own rulings from the past? In the court below it had been argued very powerfully that the Charter refers, when it talks of rights and freedoms, to those existing in Canada at the time of its coming into force. In particular

> It is to be noted at the outset that the *Canadian Bill of Rights* is not concerned with "human rights and fundamental freedoms" in an abstract sense, but rather with such "rights and freedoms" as they existed in Canada immediately before the statute was enacted. . . . It is therefore the "religious freedom" then existing in this country that is safe-guarded by the provisions of s. 2.[36]

This whole approach is flatly denounced: "the *Charter* is intended to set a standard upon which *present as well as future* legislation is to be tested." Dickson goes on to say:

> It is not necessary to reopen the issue of the meaning of freedom of religion under the *Canadian Bill of Rights*, because whatever the situation under that document, it is certain that the *Canadian Charter of Rights and Freedoms* does not simply "recognize and declare" existing rights as they were circumscribed by legislation current at the time of the *Charter's* entrenchment. The language of the *Charter* is imperative. It avoids any reference to existing or continuing rights but rather proclaims in the ringing terms of s. 2 that: "Ev-

[34] *R v Big M Drug Mart Ltd*, 344.

[35] A useful analysis of this earlier human rights initiative is given in EA Driedger, "The Meaning and Effect of the Canadian Bill of Rights: A Draftsman's Viewpoint," 1977 9 *Ottawa Law Review* 303–20.

[36] Quoted in *R v Big M Drug Mart Ltd*, 343.

> eryone has the following fundamental freedoms: (*a*) Freedom of conscience and religion.[37]

With these cases, then, a new era was consciously created. The Charter was supreme; rights came first and were not to be overcome when the government had a rational and valid aim. The Charter was to be interpreted with a special set of future-oriented, "purposive" techniques, and it was never to be interpreted in a way that would "freeze it." These principles were certainly admirable, necessary, but also tremendously vague. The real problem for Canadian constitutional jurisprudence is that they have not become a great deal more specific in the twenty-plus years since they were first evoked. Nor has the commitment not to be "literalist," for example, invariably been obeyed.

Limits to Rights: *Oakes*

The final two setting-up cases were much more specific. One dealt with a novel structural question without a solution, on which constitutional litigation could have made no progress. The other saw the court quite intentionally restricting its own powers in a way that has been deeply criticised but that clearly demonstrates the consequence of giving constitutional review to a common-law court.

Probably the most important single case in the history of the Charter, because of its structural aspect, is *R v Oakes*.[38] Though it was not decided until the third year of Charter applicability, the timing was just happenstance. All the earlier cases might have raised the question *Oakes* dealt with, and there have been very few rights cases since that have not relied on it. (A detailed and critical treatment of *Oakes* is found in chapter 8, on the limitation of rights.) The *Oakes* test means that the court first decides whether the plaintiff has made out a case that legislation breaches the constitution. If it is seen to be *prima facie* unconstitutional, the second stage of the test applies the Charter's exception, set out in Section 1.

Oakes is important here because it is a prime demonstration of the inevitability of judicial power flowing from the very fact of having a written constitution. The Canadian constitution, like the South African constitution it influenced, faces up more openly than some to the brute fact that no political system can treat any right as an absolute, and cannot avoid potential conflicts between separate rights. Because of this the Charter starts with a guarantee, but a limited one:

> The *Canadian Charter of Rights and Freedoms* guarantees the rights and freedoms set out in it subject only to such reasonable limits prescribed by law as can be demonstrably justified in a free and democratic society.

Some of the individual rights also contain their own limitation clauses, as with Section 7's guarantee of "life, liberty and security of the person" that can be taken away, but only "in accordance with the principles of fundamental justice." But even these rights are subject to the Section 1 limitation as well. (Judicial glosses on Sec-

[37] *R v Big M Drug Mart Ltd*, 344.
[38] *R v Oakes*, 1 SCR 103 (1986) (Canadian Supreme Court).

tion 7 continue to be confusing, showing how little resolution the Charter has achieved in over twenty years. As far as Section 7 goes, the judges are not even agreed as to how many rights it protects.) The early decisions on how to use this combination of specifically protected rights and Section 1, which culminated in the rule announced in *Oakes*, were crucial, but none of them inescapably obvious. Take one question—is the identification of a right, the decision as to whether it has been breached, and the decision as to whether the breach is authorised by Section 1 all one intellectual process? Is it in fact part of the true definition of a right, let us say the right to freedom of religion, that an exercise of that right which could legitimately be curtailed as not compatible with "a free and democratic society" is not a right at all? There is no obviously correct answer to that question. On the one hand there is something odd about saying that part of the definition of any right is whether it could legitimately be curtailed—that might leave very few rights indeed. On the other hand no one can really be thought to have a right seriously to impede the public welfare. The argument is not at all an abstract word game, as will become apparent shortly. But it is most definitely a problem that had to be answered by the court if the Charter was to work. No other institution in Canadian society could have answered this unavoidable question. It is a fine example of the claim made in this book—constitutional courts are both necessary and not really "courts." As it turns out, a major criticism by some of the court, including some justices against other justices, is that the rule in *Oakes* is far from being always adhered to.

The rule in *Oakes* is, at least on the surface, clear-cut and intellectually elegant. As a first move the court insisted, in answer to the sort of question posed above, that the Charter requires a two-stage process. First the action or behaviour the citizen wishes to privilege must be shown to be an example of one of the specific rights, and it must be shown that it has in fact been curtailed. As an example, in a recent freedom-of-speech case, *Little Sisters Book and Art Emporium v Canada*, it had to be shown that freedom of speech includes the right to import pornographic material from the United States, and that the way the Customs Service was operating its policies did prevent some such imports.[39] Only after this stage does the question arise whether the right, now acknowledged to exist and to have been denied, was legitimately denied under Section 1. In *Little Sisters* the need to protect Canada from being deluged with gay pornography was found to be enough to satisfy Section 1.[40]

The *Oakes* test goes on to spell out how a court is to decide whether in the case in point the right can be legitimately curtailed because the limitation is reasonable, prescribed by law, and "can be demonstrably justified in a free and democratic society." *Oakes* was about whether someone convicted of possessing drugs could be automatically convicted of intending to traffic in them unless he was able to

[39] *Little Sisters Book and Art Emporium v Canada (Minister of Justice)*, 2 SCR 1120 (2000) (Canadian Supreme Court).

[40] The more general ruling supporting the constitutionality of obscenity laws is *R v Butler*, 1 SCR 452 (1992) (Canadian Supreme Court), later rejected by the South African Court and discussed in chapter 6.

prove otherwise, thus reversing the normal burden of proof in criminal law, which requires the prosecution to prove all elements in the definition of the crime. This right to be presumed innocent is specifically guaranteed under Charter Section 11(d): "to be presumed innocent until proven guilty according to law in a fair and public hearing by an independent and impartial tribunal." There had been a similar right in the Canadian Bill of Rights, under which the jurisprudence had been very pro-prosecution on the issue, again requiring the court to dismiss its own past rulings. Once that was done, there was little difficulty in showing that the accused really did have a right, and convicting him without the prosecution having to prove intent to traffic really was a breach of this right. But could the government get away under Section 1? It was, as the court saw it, a pure example of the "purposive" approach it had advocated in the cases already discussed. The purpose here was to ensure that Canada be a democratic society, requiring the court essentially to create some political theory, to flesh out the single adjective "democratic." The Canadian Supreme Court has often had to do this, and has developed a rich conception of democracy. At this point it is enough to quote Dickson, by now chief justice, in this case:

> Canadian society is to be free and democratic. The Court must be guided by the values and principles essential to a free and democratic society which I believe embody, to name but a few, respect for the inherent dignity of the human person, commitment to social justice and equality, accommodation of a wide variety of beliefs, respect for cultural and group identity, and faith in social and political institutions which enhance the participation of individuals and groups in society.[41]

The Section 1 analysis is always presented in two parts—is the aim of the impugned legislation the solution of a problem sufficiently serious that a society like the one just described would accept a limitation on a listed right? "It is necessary, at a minimum, that an objective relate to concerns that are pressing and substantial in a free and democratic society before it can be characterized as sufficiently important." On the whole this part of the test has proven to be largely rhetorical, because the government does not frequently act so far from democratic legitimacy as to fail it. The working parts of the test came next, where the court operationalized the phrase "reasonable and demonstrably justified." Dickson described this as a "form of proportionality test," but the label is misleading because proportionality in any usual sense is only one part of the three-pronged "subtest" here: (1) the legislation must be carefully designed, not arbitrary or unfair—it must be "rationally connected to the objective" (this is largely borrowed from US constitutional jurisprudence); (2) the legislation must have the minimum impact possible on the rights in question (often called the "minimum impairment" test); and (3) (finally we do get to proportionality) the effects of the legislation must not be so great as to outweigh any possible social value that is being sought. As Dickson put it:

[41] *R v Oakes*, 138.

> Even if an objective is of sufficient importance, and the first two elements of the proportionality test are satisfied, it is still possible that, because of the severity of the deleterious effects of a measure on individuals or groups, the measure will not be justified by the purposes it is intended to serve. *The more severe the deleterious effects of a measure, the more important the objective must be if the measure is to be reasonable and demonstrably justified in a free and democratic society.*[42] (Emphasis added)

As the italicised part of the quotation shows, these various tests or subtests or prongs do interact. Nonetheless, the whole test is a logical and detailed scheme to operationalize a well-intentioned constitutional goal both to have rights and to limit them where really necessary. Of course it depends entirely on the judges on the court at any one time just how difficult a job the government of the day will have. There is a very practical consequence of the *Oakes* test, again not in any way required by the Charter itself. *Oakes* was about burdens of proof in two different ways: substantively it dealt with a burden-of-proof rule in criminal law, but as a generalised test for constitutional legitimacy it had itself to impose a burden-of-proof rule. During the first part of the analysis, when the court is trying to decide whether or not a specific right covers the citizen's actions, it is up to the citizen to convince the court. The person claiming a right has the burden of proof that the Charter does protect him or her in the way alleged. But if he or she does manage to persuade the court of this protection, and a Section 1 analysis is carried out, this burden shifts. If the court is satisfied that a right is breached, the actor, normally the government, who wishes to breach the right has to prove that the legislation passed all the elements of the Section 1 analysis. Though an alternative scheme can be imagined, the two versions of burden of proof are more or less necessary. If a citizen only had to claim a right without having to justify it, cries of "It's my right" might well paralyze government policy, especially because proving the negative, that a right does not exist, would usually be extraordinarily difficult. But once a court is satisfied that a right has been trampled on, the citizen would be in an impossible situation demonstrating that there was no need for this curtailment. His problem would not only be logical, but largely evidential. The government can in principle be expected to be able to show that there was no less impeding solution, or that proportionality was followed, but a private citizen could hardly have the information with which to do so. This is why the tendency at times for judges to conflate both parts of the overall analysis and import Section 1 considerations into an analysis of whether a right exists is so severely criticised—it is a way of supporting the government against the citizen. It may well say something about the lack of complete acceptance of Charter values amongst the Canadian higher judiciary that it does sometimes commit this sin. South Africa has an almost identical limitations analysis, yet it is very rare for a judge to be criticised for conflating the two elements.[43]

[42] *R v Oakes*, 140.

[43] A powerful attack on the court for this conflating of its own test, as well as an excellent analysis of the test, is given in D Beatty, "The Canadian Charter of Rights: Lessons and Laments," 1997 60 *Modern Law Review* 4, 481–98.

Limits to Rights: *Dolphin Deliveries*

In one way or another all of the rules, aims, and tests in the four cases so far covered would have been necessary if the Charter was to work at all. The last important "setting up" case is very different, because it not only could have been decided in a radically different way, but the Charter would have been more, not less, powerful a tool had that been done. At this point, it must simply be noted as an example of how early decisions determine the future course of a new court's work. At several points in the book, and notably when talking about Germany, a key question has been whether a constitution solely regulates the relations between the state and the individual, or whether it has an effect on the legal relations between individuals. It was the German constitutional court's early decision in *Lüth* to give the constitution a form of horizontal effect that has helped make the constitution so formative of German life.[44] But the German court is the prime example of a Kelsen court, quite deliberately not staffed by career judges. In the same year that the Canadian court laid down its powerful rule in *Oakes*, and during this initial phase when it was generally concerned to shore up and legitimize an active role as exponent of the Charter, it made a directly opposite decision to the German court that firmly ruled out any Charter effect between citizens.

The case, always known as *Dolphin Delivery*, involved industrial relations in which an employer managed to get a court injunction preventing a trade union from engaging in secondary picketing of a third-party firm, under the ordinary industrial relations laws in force at the time.[45] The union in question was involved in a dispute with a firm called Purolator, which had locked out the union members. Dolphin Deliveries was an ally of Purolator that the union wished to target by secondary picketing. For technical reasons the actual statutes covering such activity did not apply and common law ruled the case. Dolphin Deliveries managed to get a court to grant it an injunction under common law forbidding the picketing. The union appealed on the constitutional grounds that such a ban breached its right to freedom of expression under the Charter. Whether or not picketing should be seen as a form of protected expression may be arguable, and whether secondary picketing may ever have constitutional protection equally so. Indeed the courts are still not clear on those questions. But answers, even anti-union answers, to those questions would not have brought the court under so much criticism as what they did do.[46] Simply put, the court refused to recognize that the Charter had any effect at all on relations between individuals, and restricted itself to a classical liberal argument that constitutions were there only to rein in the state. There is very little argument in *Dolphin*, certainly not the subtle political theory of which the court has often shown itself capable. Instead the court just asserts that any move

[44] *Lüth*, 7 BVerfGE 198 (1958) (German Federal Constitutional Court).

[45] *Retail, Wholesale and Department Store Union v Dolphin Delivery Ltd*, 2 SCR 573 (1986) (Canadian Supreme Court).

[46] David Beatty claims *Dolphin* to have been the most criticised case in the first ten years of the court's history. D Beatty, "A Conservative's Court: The Politicization of Law," 1991 41 *University of Toronto Law Journal* 147–67.

to allow one private individual to sue another for breach of a Charter right would open up the whole civil law to invasion by the constitution. It might very well do so, but some argument has to be made why this would be a bad thing, and the court simply makes no such argument. It was for the Canadian Supreme Court, entirely populated by people who had made their name as attorneys in private law practise before the Charter, just axiomatic that the constitution should be kept out of private individual relationships, even when the individuals in question were as powerful as major commercial actors. There was some acceptance that the Canadian courts should have an eye on the Charter when developing the common law, but the Supreme Court was adamant that the Charter penetrated no further than that. Only if government is involved or has passed a law in statute or other form can the Charter be invoked.

> I should make it clear, however, that this is a distinct issue from the question whether the judiciary ought to apply and develop the principles of the common law in a manner consistent with the fundamental values enshrined in the Constitution. The answer to this question must be in the affirmative. In this sense, then, the *Charter* is far from irrelevant to private litigants whose disputes fall to be decided at common law. But this is different from the proposition that one private party owes a constitutional duty to another, which proposition underlies the purported assertion of *Charter* causes of action or *Charter* defences between individuals.[47]

The problem with this ruling is that the government may well be forbidden to pass a law that has the same effect as an existing, or newly developed, common-law rule, but that rule would be immune. The apparent acceptance of the Charter being used to develop the common law may be fatally flawed. A court may do that, but a court that refused to develop a common-law rule in light of the Charter, or created a new one contrary to Charter values, could not be appealed against on that point—for the Supreme Court to entertain such an appeal would be a breach of the *Dolphin* rule itself. It is true that in some circles the Canadian court does not have an enviable reputation on industrial relations law, but the motivation for the decision in *Dolphin* seems to be very different. It was a failure of judges from a certain background fully to engage in the possibilities of constitutionalism in society.[48]

The comparison with South Africa is fairly clear. The South African court also initially shied away from developing the horizontal effect of its new constitution, citing *Dolphin* in the leading opinion.[49] In both cases it seems likely that the professional "formation" of judges used to a common-law approach had an impact missing in Germany where a different type of judge sat on the constitutional court. But while the South Africans have tempered this stance somewhat, *Dolphin* re-

[47] *Dolphin Delivery*, 603.

[48] D Pothier, "Twenty Years of Labour Law and the Charter," 2002 40 *Osgood Hall Law Journal* 370–400.

[49] The South African case is *Du Plessis and Others v De Klerk and Another*, CCT 8/95 (South African Constitutional Court).

mains more or less unmodified. For better or worse, these cases demonstrate the steps that any court would have to make when presiding over the insertion of an entrenched rights document into a parliamentary sovereignty political system. Very probably any such court would also have to do what we now come to—the writing of a theory of democracy compatible with judicial review.

The Definition of Democracy

There are three levels at which the Canadian Supreme Court has had to tackle the meaning of democracy. Most frequently the need arises when considering one of the specified rights under the Charter. A Section 1 analysis, as we have seen, requires the court to apply the idea of something being demonstrably justified "in a free and democratic society." Other parts of the Charter have called for similar interpretation. Above all, Section 15, which guarantees equality before the law and nondiscrimination, has caused much sophisticated social theorising, through which discrimination has been held to be an affront to dignity, and dignity to be implied by democracy.[50] The second level of analysis has occurred in cases dealing very directly with one component of democracy, the right to vote. Finally there have been powerful explications of democracy where the court has had to deal, as a result of references, with major structural analyses of the Canadian political system. The first type of analysis is discussed mainly in a later chapter that gives a general comparative study of the nature of limitations on rights. We can move directly to the second type of cases, directly on voting rights. Though there are several such cases, two will suffice to bring out the problems the court has faced.

Fairly early in the post-Charter history, in 1991, the Saskatchewan Court of Appeal was asked on a reference whether the new electoral boundaries imposed by an electoral commission, itself bound by statutory restrictions, deprived citizens of an equal vote in ways that breached Section 3 of the Charter. Section 3 simply states that "Every citizen of Canada has the right to vote in an election of members of the House of Commons or of a legislative assembly and to be qualified for membership therein." The provincial court held that the right to vote was breached, and the province appealed to the Supreme Court, which by a five-to-three margin upheld the appeal, deeming the boundaries to be perfectly compatible with the Section 3 right.

The problem arose because the provincial legislature had passed an act that restricted the freedom of the Boundary Commission, forcing it to produce a boundary map in 1989 significantly less "fair" than the one it had produced as early as 1981. Fairness here refers to the size of the constituencies—the aim was to provide constituencies that did not vary by more than 15 percent from a target derived by dividing the electorate by the number of constituencies. In 1981 no constituency exceeded this 15 percent margin, but under the restrictions imposed in 1989 several urban seats were above this margin, leading to urban underrepresentation. The restrictions in 1989 were that a specific quota of urban and rural seats was

[50] *R v Oakes.*

insisted on, and all urban seats had to be drawn respecting existing municipal boundaries. That this was a political matter in Saskatchewan is obvious—rural overrepresentation has been clung to by conservative politicians worldwide since suffrage began, and the Canadian court is by no means the first to have to deal with the issue. But could it be dealt with in a nonpolitical way? The majority would claim to have done so, largely by finding good reasons to defer to the provincial legislature, while the minority tried to evade the charge of political bias by trying to make equality of representation part of the very definition of voting. Neither position is very convincing, and the majority opinion itself spells out the theoretical gulf between them:

> The question for resolution on this appeal can be summed up in one sentence: to what extent, if at all, does the right to vote enshrined in the Charter permit deviation from the "one person–one vote" rule? The answer to this question turns on what one sees as the purpose of s. 3. Those who start from the premise that the purpose of the section is to guarantee equality of voting power support the view that only minimal deviation from that ideal is possible. Those who start from the premise that the purpose of s. 3 is to guarantee effective representation see the right to vote as comprising many factors, of which equality is but one.[51]

This distinction between a justification based on "one person, one vote" and another based on the idea of "effective representation" allowed the majority to ransack Canadian electoral history to demonstrate that numerical equality has never been seen as the only, or even a deciding, factor. This relied on a distinctly nineteenth-century view expressed by the prime minister of 1872, saying that "other considerations were also held to have weight; so that different interests, classes and localities should be fairly represented."[52] Once it can be established that Canadian history is one where numerical equality is not the only factor, the argument then proceeds by relying on the court's duty to give the Charter a purposive interpretation. The purpose was, in the eyes of the majority, simply to enshrine the existing electoral theory, an argument buttressed by the absence of any suggestion in the parliamentary proceedings on the Charter that Canadian tradition was to be changed. As the actual results of the 1989 redistricting did not produce what the court saw as serious breaches in numerical equality, the Section 3 right had not been breached.

The minority approach, however, does not have to deny that other factors may be legitimate, if these other factors are taken not to be part of the definition of the right, but to be good reasons for *restricting* the right. In other words a pure equal-vote definition of the right to vote in Section 3 still allows consideration of other matters, because any right can be curtailed subject to Section 1. By taking this route the minority produced an answer that might be thought to trump any refined "democracy as effective representation" justification. What happens in the minority argument is that the fact of serious numerical disparity is subject to the

[51] *Reference re Provincial Electoral Boundaries (Sask.)*, 2 SCR 158 (1991) (Canadian Supreme Court), 182.
[52] Quoted in *Provincial Electoral Boundaries (Sask.)*, 184.

twin tests of Section 1—is the aim of the restriction legitimate, and is the method proportional? Here the fact that a much more proportional system had been in effect, and presumably also generated "effective representation," and could have continued were the legislature not to have shackled the boundary commission, becomes decisive:

> The province has failed to justify the need to shackle the Commission with the mandatory rural-urban allocation and the confinement of urban boundaries to municipal limits. The effect of these mandatory conditions was to force the Commission to recommend a distribution which departs from the higher degree of equality achieved in 1981. In the absence of a reasonable explanation as to why this was necessary, the distribution in question is suspect and there is no basis upon which to conclude that the legislature's objective in imposing the mandatory conditions was pressing and substantial.[53]

The case is most useful in demonstrating two aspects of Canadian judicial methodology. The first, briefly touched on earlier, is the tendency of some on the court, while paying lip service to the test defined in *Oakes*, to drop it when it suits them. The majority and minority differences here largely depend on whether one reads justifications in at the first stage and shows that no right has been breached, or leaves them to the second stage, accepting that a breach has occurred and then testing it. Almost invariably the former, anti-*Oakes* strategy will serve the interests of the government better than the latter. Justifications have to be tested against the proportionality limb of the *Oakes* test if used as they ought to be used, in a second-stage test. But the same arguments in justification need not be subject to any test when used to define what the right is in the first place. The second point is the way that pre-Charter history, and not only legal history, is wielded to define theoretical terms and limit political arguments. This we shall see much more of. The majority opinion hinges in the end on a question that is completely unavoidable if a new aspect is to be grafted on to an existing constitution—how much must it be interpreted as continuing the pre-exiting institutions? The court early on refused to accept a broad theory that the Charter only protected rights as they were understood before it came into force. How far does this rejection run? Must the Charter only overcome the past when there is no other way of making sense of it? Or can one take the Charter as an intentional rupture? Given the natural instinct of common-law judges, honed on precedent, to make only minimal necessary alterations to commonly understood legal rules, the instinct to minimise the Charter's impact, especially where so doing accords with deference to elected bodies, must be very strong. The whole question of a "rupture" with the past is implicit if a major constitutional change occurs in all these jurisdictions, as has been shown in several chapters. (A further discussion can be found in chapter 7.) In fact the clash between relying on long-established custom versus a court's duty to modernise is an age-old problem in the common law. A version underlay the conflict over homosexual rights in *Lawrence*, the very first case cited in the book.

[53] *Provincial Electoral Boundaries (Sask.)*, 173.

The other voting rights case in which the nature of democracy had to be reviewed was unusual in several respects. It was a challenge to the federal law that denied prison inmates the right to vote. Such a disqualification is very common internationally, and the victory for the plaintiff shows Canada at the forefront of liberal rights and bears considerable importance in a comparative respect. The case we are concerned with comes from 2002, but the second unusual feature is that it was actually the second time the same plaintiff had brought the complaint to the courts, having already won the issue in 1993.[54] In this first case there was, very unusually, no discussion on the Supreme Court. A unanimous court dismissed the government's appeal four times. The government had admitted that Section 51(e) of the Canada Elections Act, 1985, which contained the ban, was a breach of the Charter Section 3 right to vote. Though the government tried to justify it under Section 1, the Supreme Court stated baldly that the clause failed the proportionality test under the Charter and was too broadly drafted. The law contained a more moderate clause that was not tested in 1993, by which only convicts with sentences over two years were disqualified from voting. In 2002 Sauvé went back to court protesting against even this more restricted ban, and won again, though this time only by a majority of five to four.[55] Only four of the judges in the second case had also heard Sauvé's first challenge to the legislation, and these two split fifty-fifty the second time. Another member of the 2002 court, Arbour, had been in favour of Sauvé when she heard his original case as a member of the lower court whose decision was overturned in his favour by the Supreme Court.

It is a pity that the Supreme Court in 1993 did not publish a full reasoned opinion, because it would help us to know more about why two judges who believed the first ban unacceptable were persuaded by the second. There is somewhat of a giveaway on one aspect that reiterates the issue of whether to define rights restrictively or define them widely and test them under Section 1. Gonthier, who wrote the minority opinion in *Sauvé II*, had been on the unanimous court for *Sauvé I*, In both cases the Crown had conceded that the electoral law was a breach of the Charter voting right, and argued merely that it could be saved as reasonable under Section 1. Gonthier went out of his way to say that he did not regard the new legislation as a breach, and he wished the Crown had not conceded this. Given that he apparently had not objected to the Crown's submission in *Sauvé I*, he must have believed that the very definition of the right depends on the justifications for curtailing it, again a breach of the *Oakes* rule. The minority opinion in fact challenges the entire approach fundamentally, in ways that go far beyond the issue in the case itself, and which demonstrate a very decided degree of deference to legislative power. Gonthier argued that the conflict over the legitimacy of disenfranchisement for convicts was a matter of "social and political philosophy." As such it was so different from the usual constitutional law arguments over policy that it could not be tested in the usual way. Consequently the courts should defer to parliamentary choice in matters like this, and not subject them to any part of the Section 1

[54] *Sauvé v Canada (Attorney General)*, 2 SCR 438 (1993) (Canadian Supreme Court).
[55] *Sauvé v Canada (Chief Electoral Officer)*, 3 SCR 519 (2002) (Canadian Supreme Court).

test. That meant, effectively, that the disenfranchising act was not even a breach of Section 3, hence his unhappiness at the Crown's acceptance of the point. For Gonthier, if the court upheld Sauvé it would be doing nothing but choosing one over another social philosophy, something it is clearly not entitled to do—at least if one accepts a very traditional view of constitutional adjudication. The majority rejected this as a false antithesis:

> The right to vote is fundamental to our democracy and the rule of law and cannot be lightly set aside. Limits on it require not deference, but careful examination. This is not a matter of substituting the Court's philosophical preference for that of the legislature, but of ensuring that the legislature's proffered justification is supported by logic and common sense.[56]

Furthermore the approach Gonthier suggests, "Insulating a rights restriction from scrutiny by labeling it a matter of social philosophy," effectively reverses the *Oakes* test in its burden of proof. "It removes the infringement from our radar screen, instead of enabling us to zero in on it to decide whether it is demonstrably justified as required by the *Charter*." The majority is forced into a very strong statement of the role of a court in a constitutional democracy in order to avoid the almost populist force of Gonthier's reasoning, insisting that deference to the legislature is not appropriate where fundamental rights are concerned.

> This case is not merely a competition between competing social philosophies. It represents a conflict between the right of citizens to vote—one of the most fundamental rights guaranteed by the *Charter*—and Parliament's denial of that right. Public debate on an issue does not transform it into a matter of "social philosophy," shielding it from full judicial scrutiny. It is for the courts, unaffected by the shifting winds of public opinion and electoral interests, to safeguard the right to vote guaranteed by s. 3 of the *Charter*.[57]

The majority does, rather grudgingly, agree that some sort of argument can be made for the aim of the legislation. Making a symbolic stand on criminality and citizenship can qualify as an acceptable goal, but the majority opinion nonetheless opposes it as neither sufficiently narrowly conceived nor rationally connected to an acceptable goal. Again, no other institution in Canadian society could have answered this unavoidable question. In so doing the court produces a very powerful view of the relationship between the court and the fundamentals of democracy, all of it read into a Charter that is actually silent on the question. "The *Charter* charges courts with upholding and maintaining an inclusive, participatory democratic framework within which citizens can explore and pursue different conceptions of the good." Holding up the court as the real champion of democracy the opinion goes on to say that "it is precisely when legislative choices threaten to undermine the foundations of the participatory democracy guaranteed by the *Charter* that

[56] *Sauvé v Canada (Chief Electoral Officer)*, par. 10.
[57] *Sauvé v Canada (Chief Electoral Officer)*, par. 13.

courts must be vigilant in fulfilling their constitutional duty to protect the integrity of this system."[58] This is indeed a powerful argument against those who regard judicial interference with policy as inherently undemocratic, and is echoed further in the final category of cases to be discussed in this section.

There is one other important part of Gonthier's claim for deference that needs to be mentioned, if only because it is a rather rare example of the Canadian court taking notice of academic debate on the whole question of its legitimacy. Supporters of the court have developed an approach to justify it against arguments that judicial review is undemocratic—a theory of court/legislative dialogue. It is best set out in the Canadian context by Peter Hogg, one of the leading pro-court academic commentators, in an article from 1997.[59] The argument is that in practice the Supreme Court's decisions very seldom result in the complete overturn of legislation. At most the court will strike down some aspect of a law, giving rather precise reasons. The federal or provincial parliament then usually rewrites the legislation to get around these criticisms, and the court accepts this second version. This obviously has similarities to the French parliament's reaction to rulings of the Conseil constitutionnel, and probably to German constitutional politics. Indeed one analyst has suggested it is more widely typical of East European jurisdiction, especially in Hungary.[60]

Whether it is descriptively accurate or not in the Canadian context, and whether it is an adequate defence against the charge that judicial review is unconstitutional, it was surely not meant as an actual prescription for how the court should view its activity. Yet this was precisely what Gonthier, who acknowledged Hogg's essay, advocated. The very fact that in *Sauvé I* the court had struck down the broad disqualification clause meant it should show extra deference to the second, more narrowly drawn version litigated in *Sauvé II*. As the majority opinion said, "The healthy and important promotion of a dialogue between the legislature and the courts should not be debased to a rule of 'if at first you don't succeed, try, try again.'" Gonthier himself clearly recognizes that there is something odd about dialogue as an account of the court's role, because his final definition of it is indistinguishable from the majority view of what it is doing:

> Importantly, the dialogue metaphor *does not signal a lowering of the s. 1 justification standard*. It simply suggests that when, after a full and rigorous s. 1 analysis, Parliament has satisfied the court that it has established a reasonable limit to a right that is demonstrably justified in a free and democratic society, the dialogue ends; the court lets Parliament have the last word and does not substitute Parliament's reasonable choices with its own.[61]

[58] *Sauvé v Canada (Chief Electoral Officer)*, par. 15.

[59] P Hogg and AA Bushell, "The Charter Dialogue between Courts and Legislatures (or Perhaps the Charter of Rights Isn't Such a Bad Thing After All)," 1997 35 *Osgood Hall Law Journal* 75. A powerful critique is given in LB Tremblay, "The Legitimacy of Judicial Review: The Limits of Dialogue between Courts and Legislatures," 2005 3 *International Journal of Constitutional Law* 4, 617–48.

[60] See Schepple, "Constitutional Negotiations."

[61] *Sauvé v Canada (Chief Electoral Officer)*, par. 104.

Gonthier is nonetheless fundamentally right about the case involving a clash of rival philosophies that cannot be tested in any normal way. Perhaps this is best demonstrated by the disagreement between the majority and the minority on one specific part of the argument. In keeping with the tendency to equate democracy in part with a respect for human dignity, the majority objects to disenfranchisement as an insult to this dignity. Gonthier does not regard the dignity argument as irrelevant—to him, removing the prisoner's vote is in accordance with dignity, because it accepts that prisoners are free actors who deserve the punishment. Dignity is the most difficult of constitutional-legal concepts, and a constitutional review body that is forced to rely on the idea is by that very fact demonstrating the special nature of the function it performs in the polity.[62]

These two decisions were given by a split court. The Canadian Supreme Court has a very high rate of divided opinions. When it has had to deal with its most abstract, but also most politically contentious, issues, it has naturally tried for a consensus, and the result at times, for example in a famous reference decision on whether Quebec has the right to secede, has been seen by some as a form of high-minded evasion. These opinions inevitably are as important for the court as for those who refer the questions, because the court's own legitimacy is dependent on its answer. There is another important difference of relevance to us. So much of the modern writing on the Canadian court is focused on the Charter that one can be forgiven for thinking that it embraces the whole of Canadian constitutional law. Yet the big structural questions hardly touch on Charter jurisprudence because they are not really about individual rights. It may well be that the post-Charter court is bolder about judicial review, but it is not usually dealing with issues, or using material, that could not have happened before 1982. In trying to understand the nature of judicial review in Canada we need to deal with the whole range of constitutional politics. That the court may be more consensual because more at home dealing with the material the pre-Charter courts handled is hardly surprising, but is germane to the enquiry in this chapter. Some of these structural questions have, naturally. incidentally involved the Charter. One such case involved the question whether it was a breach of the separation of powers, and of the rule of law, for provincial governments directly to cut judicial salaries.[63] Even though this was one of the grand constitutional questions, the court did not manage complete unanimity, one judge still urging deference to the legislature. The division of opinion, though, came about because the argument was in part based on the Charter right of litigants to an unbiased bench as part of a fair trial. Hopeful criminal defendants seized on the theoretical argument that a bench whose salaries were directly determined by the provincial government could not be seen as unbiased. Had the whole case been set in abstract, noncharter, terms of separation of powers, the dissenting judge might well not have dissented. There seems for some to be a wide gap be-

[62]One powerful criticism of the use of dignity in public law is D Feldman, "Human Dignity as a Legal Value—Part I," 1999 *Public Law* 682–702. But see also O Schachter, "Human Dignity as a Normative Concept," 1983 77 *American Journal of International Law* 4, 848–54.

[63]*Reference re Remuneration of Judges of the Provincial Court of Prince Edward Island*, 3 SCR 3 (1997) (Canadian Supreme Court).

tween agreeing to theoretical statements, and actually opposing the government in its dealing with individuals, especially where the criminal law applies.

The Quebec reference is the court's keynote statement on democracy and the shape of the Canadian polity.[64] Known as the *Reference re Secession of Quebec*, it was an attempt to answer two politically loaded questions addressed to it by the governor in council. The main question was “Under the Constitution of Canada, can the National Assembly, legislature or government of Quebec effect the secession of Quebec from Canada unilaterally?” The constitution never mentions secession; the court first had to translate the question into one it believed it was entitled to handle, and then derive a fundamental theory of Canadian constitutional legitimacy.

The translation was needed because several arguments addressed to the court challenged its very right to hear the case, on the grounds that it was not “justiciable,” or that it amounted to what the US Supreme Court calls a “political question,” beyond the bounds of judicial review. The court's defence was that the questions did not “ask the Court to usurp any democratic decision that the people of Quebec may be called upon to make.” The questions, said the court, were “strictly limited to aspects of the legal framework in which that democratic decision is to be taken.” The more strictly the court limited this, of course, the less useful, but the safer for the court, were the answers. The way the arguments for Quebec were cast was that if the citizens of a province, by a clear majority, wished secession, than the democratic nature of the Canadian state must recognize the right to secede. The court had to find a definition of Canadian politics that both recognized democracy but did not lead to this conclusion. It achieved this aim, in the court's own eyes anyway, by both construing democracy away from mere majoritarian preferences, and making democracy only one of four equal standing principles of legitimacy. In the court's earlier response to the reference on patriating the constitution, it had insisted that the actual texts were only part of a broader constitution, and fundamental principles existed that were at most only marginally referenced in the documents. There are four such architectonic principles: federalism, democracy, constitutionalism and the rule of law, and respect for minorities. These are derived not only from 130 years of written constitutional history but, rather grandly, from “an historical lineage stretching back through the ages.” As part of judicial technique, the court saw the underlying principles as incorporated by the preamble to the 1867 constitution, and quoted an earlier judgement discussed above. “In the *Provincial Judges Reference* . . . we determined that the preamble “invites the courts to turn those principles into the premises of a constitutional argument that cul-

[64] A very interesting analysis of this case, which shows how different was the style of the opinion from most, is given in P Horowitz, “Law's Expression: The Promise and Perils of Judicial Opinion Writing in Canadian Constitutional Law,” 2000 38 *Osgoode Hall Law Journal* 1, 101–42, especially 138–40. A full analysis of the constitutional law is given in P Bienvenu, “Secession by Constitutional Means: Decision of the Supreme Court of Canada in the Quebec Secession Reference,” 1999 21 *Hamline Journal of Public Law and Policy* 1–65. A more developed discussion of the politics involved is given very well in an article written before the case came to the court: PJ Monahan, “The Law and Politics of Quebec Secession,” 1995 33 *Osgoode Hall Law Journal* 1, 33–67.

minates in the filling of gaps in the express terms of the constitutional text."[65] One cannot but be struck by the similarity of this logic to much of the argument used by the Conseil constitutionnel to justify the derivation of the *bloc de constitutionnalité*. One crucial point is that "These defining principles function in symbiosis. No single principle can be defined in isolation from the others, nor does any one principle trump or exclude the operation of any other."[66] The court has also always refused to rank charter rights. Its entire approach to constitutional interpretation can best be described as holistic—in this opinion indeed the court refers to the constitution's "internal architecture."

So how do these principles answer the question of the legality of unilateral secession? Or to put it in more realistic terms, how does the court get round the apparent will of Quebec's sovereign people? What was inevitable was that democracy should not be defined just as majority rule; otherwise it would be hard to maintain that democracy was not at odds with the other aspects of constitutionalism identified by the court. The court canvassed various meanings of democracy, and insisted on its vital role in the Canadian constitution, but warned strongly that "It would be a grave mistake to equate legitimacy with the 'sovereign will' or majority rule alone, to the exclusion of other constitutional values."[67] To summarize a lengthy and somewhat repetitive judgement: democracy actually requires the rule of law; federalism requires equality of esteem between majorities at different levels; democracy embraces (from the statement in *Oakes*) respect for minorities, and thus a unilateral secession must be illegal, and not merely politically or morally wrong. The court, however, went further, unwilling to leave Quebec with no gain at all from the reference. Rather, as it found the original patriation claim by the federal government acting alone to be legally acceptable but in breach of conventions, the court finds obligations for both sides here. The obligation, stemming from the intersection of all four unwritten principles, is to good-faith negotiations on both sides. It must be understood that the court is not just giving good political advice here—it claims that there is a *legal* obligation on the political authorities outside Quebec to respect the Quebec popular will by entering into such negotiations, to attempt to respond to Quebec's concerns. At the same time there is a *legal* obligation on Quebec not to commit to secession before good-faith negotiations. The Constitution Act of 1982 confers a right

> to initiate constitutional change on each participant in Confederation. In our view, the existence of this right imposes a corresponding duty on the participants in Confederation to engage in constitutional discussions in order to acknowledge and address democratic expressions of a desire for change in other provinces. This duty is inherent in the democratic principle which is a fundamental predicate of our system of governance.[68]

[65] *Reference re Secession of Quebec*, 2 SCR 217 (1998) (Canadian Supreme Court), par. 53. The opinion referred to is *Reference re Remuneration of Judges of the Provincial Court of Prince Edward Island*.

[66] *Secession of Quebec*, par. 49.

[67] *Secession of Quebec*, par. 67.

[68] *Secession of Quebec*, par. 69.

The court was fully aware of the problem in democratic theory it was setting here. The reconciliation of rights and obligations would be a problem for

> the representatives of two legitimate majorities, namely, the clear majority of the population of Quebec, and the clear majority of Canada as a whole, whatever that may be. There can be no suggestion that either of these majorities "trumps" the other. A political majority that does not act in accordance with the underlying constitutional principles we have identified puts at risk the legitimacy of the exercise of its rights.[69]

Nor is the court unaware of how little it will do in the future if the politics proceeds to these negotiations. The judges several times refer to their necessary limitations, seeing their role as "limited to the identification of the relevant aspects of the Constitution in their broadest sense." They entirely accept that they have "no supervisory role over the political aspects of constitutional negotiations." But the core statement of legality is clear:

> The non-justiciability of political issues that lack a legal component does not deprive the surrounding constitutional framework of its binding status, nor does this mean that constitutional obligations could be breached without incurring serious legal repercussions. Where there are legal rights there are remedies, but . . . the appropriate recourse in some circumstances lies through the workings of the political process rather than the courts.[70]

This must be one of the strongest statements of the importance of a constitutional system and of the idea of constitutional legality. But it has to be admitted that it actually is unclear in what sense a binding status continues when the issues are nonjusticiable. The whole opinion is rich with insights into democracy as a constitutional status, and is likely to be mined for references in future opinions, just as the court of 1998 did itself cite almost every major opinion it had previously issued on the topic. It remains a highly creative judgement, one that manages to use the cloak of legality to cover sage advice to both sides, and of course therefore to limit them. The court actually went so far as to point out how badly it would play on the international scene if either side ignored the obligation to good-faith negotiations. Above all it is a judgement that serves to legitimize the court itself further, and to ensure its role in Canadian political life.

The Court's Record (and the Critics' Reaction)

It was never going to be easy to graft fully fledged judicial review onto a parliamentary sovereignty system, but one can hardly avoid sympathizing with the court, so grudging has been its press in legal academic circles. The main criticism, though, is one the court may have invited by its own uncertainty. Some were bound to

[69] *Secession of Quebec*, par. 93.
[70] *Secession of Quebec*, par. 102.

be disappointed. The left-wing critics, centred round David Beatty, seem to have had an expectation of the Canadian court even more improbable than the French Left's view of how the Conseil constitutionnel should work. Despite saying in an important article that he did "not intend the descriptive part of the essay to be controversial in any way," Beatty asserts forcefully,

> Legally, we find ourselves ruled by a Court controlled by people who have favoured a set of doctrines and modes of analysis that are in conflict with the most basic principles and values underlying the Charter, and that provide much less protection for our rights and freedoms than the Charter is able to guarantee.[71]

But would many agree with his judgement that accepting an electoral finance law cast in more or less standard international terms systematically "discriminates against minor and embryonic political movements"? How many would see a law controlling prostitutes' soliciting as "restricting the freedom of poor and disadvantaged women"? More to the point, Beatty's explanation for why the court swung so rapidly to the right (as he sees it) has been convincingly discredited. Beatty focuses on a major replacement of personnel on the court that happened in its early years. Because the five new justices were all appointed by a Conservative prime minister, and replaced judges appointed by a Liberal, there was for him no mystery. However, statistical analysis a few years later showed that the voting profile of these new judges was in no way different from others appointed by Liberals.[72] Certainly there have been cases that gave the Charter a weaker impact than some might have liked. *Dolphin*, where the court refused horizontal effect, is one such, but it is a decision more plausibly explained in terms of common-law judicial socialization than conservatism. Many of the failures of the court to live up to radical hopes probably stem from much the same aspect as the one that cost them the decision they would have preferred in *Dolphin*. This is the simple fact that Canada has for a long time had a Europe-like body of welfare state style legislation, often in complex codes. Judges have been unwilling to recognize a full constitutional right to strike largely because they have not wanted to disturb a fairly effective and long-established but complicated labour relations code, as in their decision not to overturn a part of the code that excepted rural workers, often criticized by the Left.[73] Even in *Dolphin* a part of the court's justification for refusing horizontal effect was the fear of disturbing well-established and effective human rights codes in the several provinces. Had there been less state support in these areas, the court might well have been bolder.

There is a clue to the real problem the court has had in another attack that Beatty mentions, though he does not pretend that it is as uncontroversial as his assessment of the court's record. Beatty's prime concern in the article referred to here

[71] Beatty, "A Conservative's Court," 151.

[72] JB Kelly, "The Charter of Rights and Freedoms and the Rebalancing of Liberal Constitutionalism in Canada, 1982–1997," 1999 37 *Osgoode Hall Law Journal* 625–79.

[73] *Dunmore v Ontario (Attorney General)*, 3 SCR 1016 (2001) (Canadian Supreme Court).

is that Canadian judges are appointed in an undemocratic manner. This matters for him because, for example,

> Even though the vote of each of Mulroney's appointees would be crucial to how the Court might rule on a future abortion law, for example, the public had no input in determining whether any of these appointments should be given to someone who would take the liberal or the conservative approach.

This is a left-wing version of a more commonly conservative complaint—the impropriety of unelected judges making policy.[74] Beatty ignores the fact that the court actually did strike down the restrictions on abortion in the criminal code, just as public opinion wished.[75] (Of the two dissenters, only one was a Conservative appointee.) Whereas the Left thinks it undemocratic that judges are not selected by the people, most object to the court on the grounds that it does not defer to elected politicians—an indirect version of the same claim for how a judicial review court ought to behave. The proponents of this more predictable complaint have sometimes been called the "Canadian interpretivists."[76] This, an evocation of the most conservative style in American constitutional jurisprudence, is to indicate a preference for narrow readings of the Charter, where the court may do no more than update the application of terms set by the original intent of the drafters. Where the "core meaning" of a right is extended, the court goes too far. "When the judiciary refuses to be guided by original intent in its interpretation of the constitution, it exercises an extra-constitutional and arbitrary form of power."[77] What is interesting is not that there should be such an attack—there cannot be a single country where a court is empowered to strike down legislation where the claim is not echoed. Courts everywhere are attacked by those whose values are infrequently the winners in constitutional litigation, and Canada is inevitably a special case simply because it did manage to function for so long without the Charter. So there are powerful and broad arguments made to the effect that Canadian political culture is in danger from developing a US-style "rights mentality." Such an attack is made by Bogart in *Courts and Country*, bemoaning the potential challenge to the author's sense of Canadian identity that may come about from strong judicial rights activism.[78] Unusually for a distinguished lawyer, part of Bogart's concern is that too much is expected from law, though it is clear that he would be even less happy were the Supreme Court's rulings to become more effective.

[74] Beatty, "A Conservative's Court," 151.

[75] In *R. v Morgentaler*, 1 SCR 30 (1988) (Canadian Supreme Court).

[76] The phrase seems to have been used for the first time in JB Kelly and M Murphy, "Confronting Judicial Supremacy: A Defence of Judicial Activism and the Supreme Court of Canada's Legal Rights Jurisprudence," 2001 16 *Canadian Journal of Law and Society* 3–28. They provide a useful list of the main proponents of this position. The article is a useful balance to the general "counter-majoritarian" argument on judicial review.

[77] This is the description of the interpretivists' position used in Kelly and Murphy, "Confronting Judicial Supremacy," 4.

[78] WA Bogart, *Courts and Country: The Limits of Litigation and Social and Political Life of Canada* (Toronto: Oxford University Press, 1994).

While criticism, either of the limited, almost technical interpretivist critique or in the broader style of Bogart or Beatty, is to be expected, it is the missing opposition to them that is problematic. Few actually believe the court to be activist, and they approve of this. Those who do criticize the attacks on the court do not do so because they accept the need, even the desirability, of a constitutional court striking down legislation. Instead they try to claim it does not actually do so very often. For example, Kelly, both in the article cited above and in earlier work, stresses that any initial appearance of willingness to strike down has been replaced with due deference to the legislature.[79] Others give the game away in the very titles of their works, most notably Hogg and Bushell, whose article on the dialogue theory is subtitled "Or Perhaps the *Charter of Rights* Isn't Such a Bad Thing After All." That article tries to insist that the court very seldom actually prevents the legislature from doing what it wants. Why anyone ever thought that a fully armed judicial review court would not, perhaps frequently, strike down legislation is a mystery. But the fact that the court's supporters try to defend it by playing down this part of its role is indicative of how little committed some Canadian circles are to the very fact of replacing parliamentary sovereignty with constitutional sovereignty. Even Beatty, though he objects to some of what the court has *not* done, shows no faith in a generalized activism.

Blocs and Dissent in the Court

There seems, amongst many commentators, to be a general concern about the mere fact that judges make value decisions, and are not always in agreement on these values, as though Canadians had really believed in a formalist, slot machine jurisprudence until 1982. So there is great concern about the lack of unanimity in constitutional cases. An early article, for example, sees it as striking that there were two dissents in the abortion case, and that the court was split four to two on whether the right to strike was implied by the Charter's freedom of association right. The author of this article summarizes his concern thus:

> Perhaps we need to reflect on the implications of the fact that Canada's top jurists can hear the same arguments and read much the same material relating to a particular Charter claim and yet come to opposite conclusions about that claim. One might pause to wonder what this means for the supposed "inalienability" of the rights enshrined in the Charter.[80]

Others also worry about what they see as a high dissent rate, causing one of the Supreme Court justices even to defend the right of dissent, something no one would worry about in most countries.[81]

[79] Kelly, "Charter of Rights and Freedoms."

[80] AD Heard, "The Charter in the Supreme Court of Canada: The Importance of Which Judges Hear an Appeal," 1991 24 *Canadian Journal of Political Science / Revue canadienne de science politique* 2, 289–307, at 294.

[81] C L'Heureux-Dubé, "The Dissenting Opinion: Voice of the Future?" 2000 38 *Osgoode Hall Law Journal* 495–518.

It is commonly asserted that the court started unanimously but rapidly came to be full of disagreement, and that its dissent rate in constitutional cases, roughly 30 percent over this period, shows a good deal of ideological conflict. Much effort has gone into finding the relevant ideological blocs and spelling out the underlying dimensions of judicial conflict. Individual judicial votes have been carefully canvassed to elucidate this pattern, and in particular the rate by which they vote against the government. In the end, however, very little has been found. A clue to this result might be something virtually never mentioned—the 30 percent dissent rate in constitutional cases is almost exactly the same as the dissent rate in *non*-constitutional cases. This identity of decision behaviour between constitutional and ordinary law is a repeated finding. In 2000 for example there was a 31 percent dissent rate in both areas; in 2001 the court was much more unanimous, with a dissent rate of only 21 percent—indistinguishable between constitutional and other law. There really are no patterns, just what political scientists call "trendless fluctuation," except that constitutional law is no different from any other area of the court's activity.[82]

The truth is simply that the Canadian Supreme Court does not have a strong and coherent judicial ideology, on any issues. The rate of dissent is high, compared with the German or even the South African court, but is nothing like that of the US Supreme Court. But the Canadian Supreme Court differs from its more southerly neighbor in one major way—it does not have two opposing and long-term ideological blocs based on the politics of the appointing president, and highly predictable in the long run of decisions. Efforts to find such blocs have failed—judges vary, of course, but the variance, for example on preparedness to vote against the government, is tiny. Only a few percentage points separate the justices most and least likely to do so, just as the tendency to dissent, with one or two clear exceptions, varies hardly at all.[83] What happens is that judges equally likely to oppose the government just do so on different cases, in no way that is easily attributed to general ideological leaning.

Almost inevitably the early cases were more consensual because they were, in all but name, methodological cases where the court struggled to work out how, in general, to go about its business. The court in its early days can be criticized for the way it went about this process, in particular because of the elaborate legal tests it set up, notably in *Oakes* but in several other early cases, tests that have proved cumbersome. This alone may have produced later dissensus because of the need to force facts and values into such tests to extract what the judges think is a just result. Such an argument has been forcibly made by Paul Horowitz, who interestingly compares the much less technical style of opinion in the Quebec referendum reference to that normally used.[84] And the *Oakes* test, because it is so complex, has

[82] The statistics are my own calculations from the court records.

[83] The best account is given in Kelly, "Charter of Rights and Freedoms." The article also summarises earlier research, and is partially brought further up to date in Kelly and Murphy, "Confronting Judicial Supremacy." See also P McCormick, "Blocs, Swarms, and Outliers: Conceptualizing Disagreement on the Modern Supreme Court of Canada," 2004 42 *Osgoode Hall Law Journal* 100–138.

[84] Horowitz, "Law's Expression."

often been used rather casually, opening the court to further attacks for apparently playing fast and loose with its own methodology. The very structure of the Charter itself may lead to dissensus, because in many cases there are two points at which judges can disagree—has a right been infringed, and if so, is the infringement justifiable? It was, of course, this structure that made the court produce the tests in cases like *Oakes*, and later we consider at length how courts in different countries have handled their limitation clauses. The Canadian court may have made life harder for itself, but there is not even a consistent "bloc" analysis to be drawn on judges who are more or less faithful to *Oakes*.

The defenders of the court tend to argue that even if it was earlier very deferential to the state, it has become much more so. They claim that the court has deliberately changed its docket so that it is more likely to hear cases against executive action, and not cases that involve the constitutionality of legislation—to act more as an administrative law court than a constitutional review body. There is absolutely no evidence available about why the court grants leave to appeal in some rather than other cases. An equally plausible explanation is that the federal and provincial governments of Canada are in fact constitution-respecting entities who have themselves learned how to craft legislation that is constitutionally compliant. There is at least some evidence to support this, if only because we know that government at all levels has changed its policymaking processes to incorporate constitution checking at an early stage. Civil servants at both the federal level and some of the provinces certainly claimed as early as 1992 to be imbued with Charter values, and to have guided this process.[85] An even more plausible explanation is simply that it is early yet, and less than twenty-five years does not allow real trends to appear.

The rate of dissent and the rate of antigovernment decisions has not declined in the last few years, but much of the more obvious targets may have been dealt with early. There is a particular reason why this might be so. A large part of the early litigation was about the equality guarantee in Section 15. This promises that

> Every individual is equal before and under the law and has the right to the equal protection and equal benefit of the law without discrimination and, *in particular, without discrimination based on race, national or ethnic origin, colour, religion, sex, age or mental or physical disability.* (Emphasis added)

The italicized part of the section had to be dealt with by the court immediately, which it did by asserting that any "analogous" group, for example homosexuals, might be entitled to protection from discrimination. The details of this analysis are covered later in the book. Having set up such an interpretation, the court indulged in some years of putting claimants into "analogous" groups, as well as in spelling out exactly what constitutes discrimination, as opposed to legitimately differential treatment. A typical case, known to have had a major impact in the thinking of policymakers, was *Schachter v Canada* in 1992.[86] Here a father of a newborn

[85] PJ Monahan and M Finkelstein, "The Charter of Rights and Public Policy in Canada," 1992 30 *Osgood Hall Law Journal* 501–46.

[86] *Schachter v Canada*, 2 SCR 679 (1992) (Canadian Supreme Court).

child claimed welfare payment for staying home during its first few weeks of life, because a statute specifically granted such an entitlement to a couple who adopted a newborn. New parents are not covered in the first part of Section 15, but the government itself agreed that the policy was discriminatory, and did not even offer a Section 1 justification. *Schachter* is difficult for those who would claim the court was overnegative towards legislative discretion. The opinions in the case actually lambaste the government for giving in too easily, thereby depriving the Supreme Court of argument through which it could decide for itself whether or not discrimination had occurred. Reading the opinions with any care strongly suggests that the court would either have refused to treat the two categories of parents as comparable, or accepted a Section 1 justification for differentiating between them. By the time the case came before the court, the government had amended the law, giving both categories of parents aid, but for a shorter time than the adopters had enjoyed under the previous version. The only reason the case came up for decision was to rule on the legitimacy of the particular technique of resolving such cases. Should the offending part of the statute be struck down? Should all of it be struck down? Should it be made compatible with the constitution by judicially adding words—that is, by adding in "natural parents"? Should part or all of the statute be ruled null and void, but with this ruling postponed to give parliament time to amend the law? The main opinion on the case is an enormously elaborate working out of what sort of remedy would be applicable under what conditions, with the interests of governmental policymaking and the interests of current and potential beneficiaries to this sort of legislation all carefully balanced. It is not possible to describe *Schachter* as either full of, or deficient in, deference to the legislature.

As cases like this multiplied, and a host of possible discriminations were analyzed, there were inevitably many occasions when details of legislation were struck down. They nearly all referred to legislative schemes that predated the Charter, and were not necessarily fought hard by the government. What seems to have been the case is that Canada has, in many ways, adjusted to the Charter, inevitably reducing the conflict between government and court, if indeed there ever was much heat in that conflict. This does not mean that a new generation on the court may not decide to renew a push to extend Charter values, and there are some suggestions that this may happen in the area of positive rights, though the cases in this area (discussed in a later chapter) send conflicting signals at this stage.

The importance of the equality jurisprudence may explain, in a rather different way, the sense of ideological conflict on the court.[87] There may be, or have been, one bloc on the court—some of those in the "interpretivist" movement seems to think so, and on this point, those opposed to them rather agree. Much has been made of the idea that there now exists in Canada something called the "court party," a label invented by one of the conservative critics of the court. A sense of his position can be gained by the quotation he chose to begin the article in which he launched the

[87] A recent monograph on the court by a leading exponent of American-style political science analysis of courts is DA Songer, *The Transformation of The Supreme Court of Canada: An Empirical Examination* (Toronto: University of Toronto Press, 2008). The book casts some light on the ideological conflict in the court since 1982, in a highly nuanced way.

idea.[88] "If you had told the people what the *Charter* was going to mean in 1982—with respect to things like abortion and the Lord's Prayer—you never would have gotten it." This was from an elected conservative politician and former premier of Ontario, David Peterson. To Morton and many who have followed his analysis, the court party is an alliance of interest groups, mainly of the sort political scientists call "new social movements" intent on getting Charter-based recognition for the rights of those others have described as "marginalized" in Canadian history. A leader of one of these groups is quoted by Morton, though not with sympathy:

> The *Charter*'s appeal to our non-territorial identities—shared characteristics such as gender, ethnicity and disability—is finding concrete expression in an emerging new power structure in society. . . . This power structure involves new networks and coalitions among women, the disabled, aboriginal groups, social reform activists, church groups, environmentalists, ethno-cultural organizations, just to name a few. All these new groups have mobilized a broad range of interests that draw their inspiration from the *Charter* and the *Constitution*.

Several analysts have operationalized the concept of the court party by coding cases that refer to the values this broad movement supports, and measuring the tendency of Supreme Court justices to vote in support of the movement. It turns out that justices who tend regularly to vote for Charter-based claims on this "court party" index do not necessarily support putative Charter rights in other cases. Because the Supreme Court has in fact not granted a high proportion of court party claims, Morton notwithstanding, such justices also dissent more than others. (The court only found for an equality claimant in 20 percent of such cases, compared with over 30 percent for "legal" rights.) The "bloc," if there is or was one, is simply identified. They are the female justices: Bertha Wilson (1982—92), Beverley McLachlin, appointed in 1989, later chief justice, Claire L'Heureux-Dubé, appointed in 1987, and Louise Arbour appointed in 1999. It is improbable that these justices do see themselves as a bloc, if only because their voting is much less similar in other Charter areas. but it cannot be an accident that they are all women and all leaders in pro-Charter jurisprudence *on this specific dimension*. But then it says something about Canadian politics and law that the Supreme Court has had so many distinguished women on it. The best summary is that the court, like any court, has judges with particular drives and interests, but no structured patterning.

Echoes of the Common Law

This is probably true of the whole set of issues that have so concerned the court's critics—it has neither been particularly deferential nor conflicted, especially with governments. It has been finding its way slowly from a common-law background,

[88] FL Morton, "The Charter Revolution and the Court Party," 1992 30 *Osgood Hall Law Journal* 628–52.

and with all that entails. As L'Heureux-Dubé says of common-law judges, when justifying dissents:

> From the first days of their legal education, common-law lawyers are instilled with a narrative and an adversarial culture in which the justification of one's reasoning is given pride of place. For this reason, common-law lawyers tend to view the drafting of opinions which seek to justify the choice of one of several competing solutions as indispensable to the legal system. . . . Theirs is a vision of the law and of the role of judicial decisions that readily admits of the possibility of a number of divergent opinions on any given issue.[89]

The vital importance of common law in the working out of the Charter cannot be too strongly emphasized; it also means that the coding of cases as pro or anti legislative authority may be largely meaningless. Consider the following case, *R v Pan*, from 2001.[90] It involved a claim by Pan that his fundamental freedoms had been abridged contrary to Section 7 of the Charter. Section 649 of the criminal code was said to abrogate his fundamental freedoms. The court dismissed his appeal. What he wanted was for the age-old rule on jury secrecy enshrined in Section 649, to be declared unconstitutional. He wanted to adduce in his trial evidence about jury discussions in his earlier trial that had been declared a mistrial. It would be hard at the best of times to see an attack on jury secrecy as a development of human rights, but the obvious external coding of the case would indeed be that a Charter claim was overturned to defend a parliamentary statute. Unfortunately even such a reading would not complete the misdescription. The main reason the court upheld Section 649 was precisely that it did legislate the old common-law rule—the court is far more likely to refer to the common law to interpret the Charter than to change a common-law rule because it breaches a Charter right. The decision of the united court was given, incidentally, by the most recent female appointee, Louise Arbor, whose reputation for radical pro-Charter thinking is already well established.

A final aspect of the common-law inheritance may be important. Common lawyers do not like overturning precedent, but they are adept at "distinguishing" precedents. Inevitably the court has taken some wrong turnings in its decades, but they are all too recent for a court willingly to overturn. The twisting and turning involved in escaping from these wrong turnings without acknowledging that they were mistakes increases the image of a court much torn and very uncertain. This behaviour has been evident with the *Oakes* test for some time. There are regular further examples occurring as the court moves on. A prime example is on a humanitarian issue that has concerned several European countries. As long as the United States retains the death penalty, long an unthinkable punishment in the rest of liberal democracy, countries like Canada and those of Western Europe that have extradition treaties with the United States have a problem. The practice has grown up, and is indeed now required in Europe by the European Court of Human

[89] L'Heureux-Dubé, "The Dissenting Opinion," 502.

[90] *R. v Pan*, 2 SCR 344 (2001) (Canadian Supreme Court).

Rights, of extraditing on capital offences only when guaranteed the death sentence will not be carried out. Yet when the Canadian minister of justice in 1991 ordered the extradition of someone facing the death penalty in California and refused to ask for this guarantee, the Supreme Court, by four to three, upheld his decision, ruling that it was not in breach of any Charter rights.[91] (Justice L'Heureux-Dubé of "court party" fame was in the majority.) The decision was denounced and has long been seen as one of the court's less worthy actions. The issue never completely went away, and in 2001 the court heard a similar appeal in *United States v Burns*.[92] This time the decision was a united one, and it was to hold that the extradition would be unconstitutional. But the two previous Supreme Court cases both decided in 1991, *Ng* and *Kindler*, were not overruled.[93] They were, in the language of the head note to *Burns*, "explained." That is, reasons were found to decide the new case directly opposite to the earlier ones, and still maintain the 1991 cases were good law. The early cases had insisted that the minister must "balance" a set of concerns to ensure fundamental justice, but that the default position would be for extradition, with the guarantee only being demanded in exceptional cases. Now the presumption is the other way around—only exceptional cases could dispense with the guarantee. The court's own conclusion serves best to state this shift:

> The outcome of this appeal turns on an appreciation of the principles of fundamental justice, which in turn are derived from the basic tenets of our legal system. These basic tenets have not changed since 1991 when *Kindler* and *Ng* were decided, but their application in particular cases (the "balancing process") must take note of factual developments in Canada and in relevant foreign jurisdictions. When principles of fundamental justice as established and understood in Canada are applied to these factual developments, many of which are of far-reaching importance in death penalty cases, a balance which tilted in favour of extradition without assurances in *Kindler* and *Ng* now tilts against the constitutionality of such an outcome.[94]

Burns was heard by a Supreme Court panel of eight justices and was unanimous, even though three of them had been in the majority in the 1991 cases. None of the arguments were really new in 2001, none of the facts of death penalties or of international public opinion had actually changed. This is the common-law mind at work—incremental development and the presentation of an apparently seamless web of precedents. Whether it is the best way to transform a parliamentary supremacy system into a constitutional system is perhaps not obvious. But there will be more occasions when early decisions, some of them really bedrock like *Dolphin Deliveries*, will come up for reconsideration, and Canadian constitutional law is likely to get even less predictable and even more tangled as long as common-law precedential thinking dominates.

[91] *Reference re Ng Extradition (Can.)*, 2 SCR 858 (1991) (Canadian Supreme Court).

[92] *United States v Burns*, 1 SCR 283 (2001) (Canadian Supreme Court).

[93] *Kindler v Canada (Minister of Justice)*, 2 SCR 779 (1991) (Canadian Supreme Court).

[94] *United States v Burns*, par. 144.

What Canada has already done for everyone's understanding of constitutional review is clear. It has begun to sketch a justification for constitutional review in liberal democracy. The arguments in the major reference cases, for example, and elsewhere, have been powerful statements that democracy is a multifaceted concept, some parts of which require something very much like a court, and an approach very much like a legal one. This argument will be picked up again in the final chapter.

CHAPTER SIX

South Africa: Defining a New Society

No one gives us rights. We win them in struggle. They exist in our hearts before they exist on paper. Yet intellectual struggle is one of the most important areas of the battle for rights. It is through concepts that we link our dreams to the acts of daily life.

—Albie Sachs, later a member of the South African Constitutional Court, *Protecting Human Rights in a New South Africa*[1]

Structural Rulings

In the few years since its first decision in 1995, the South African Constitutional Court has made history in so many ways that it might be hard to know where to start.[2] Or for a lawyer it might be hard. But for a political scientist there is no choice. One decision stands out as unique in the history of judicial review anywhere, demonstrating beyond any question an act of political choice—and a technically very difficult political choice—but a decision ironically, that was forced on the court by politicians. This is the case usually known as the *First Certification Decision* from 1996, when it fell to the Constitutional Court to say whether the constitution proposed by the constitutional assembly was actually constitutional or not. The reflexivity of constitutional review discussed in chapter 1 has never been so stark.[3] Albie Sachs, onetime African National Congress activist and member of the original ANC delegation to the Multi-Party Negotiating, later to be a member of the court that gave that decision, describes the difficulties.[4] His description of the

[1]Quoted in MA Burnham, "Cultivating a Seedling Charter: South Africa's Court Grows Its Constitution," 1997 3 *Michigan Journal of Race and Law* 3.

[2]The first-ever decision was *S v Zuma*, CCT 5/94 (South African Constitutional Court).

[3]*Certification of the Constitution of the Republic of South Africa*, CCT 23/96 (South African Constitutional Court).

[4]A good introduction to the constitution-building process is J Sarkin, "The Drafting of South Africa's Final Constitution from a Human-Rights Perspective," 1999 47 *American Journal of Comparative Law* 1, 67–87. An exhaustive account of negotiations on each section of the interim constitution is R Spitz, *The Politics of Transition: A Hidden History of South Africa's Negotiated Settlement* (Oxford: Hart, 2000).

process makes it clear the court had to engage in, not only political, but political-science, theorising of the highest order.

> This principle said that the new constitutional text should not substantially reduce the powers the provinces had under the Interim Constitution. How do you weigh powers? They are not expressed in pounds or kilograms. You are dealing with clusters of competencies. You are dealing with institutions. You are dealing with the Civil Service. You are dealing with finance. All of these things impact upon powers. We had to examine every aspect of the relationship between provincial government and the national government to see if, at the end of the day, the powers were substantially less than they were in terms of the Interim Constitution.[5]

The principles Sachs is referring to were the thirty-four constitutional principles that negotiators in the transition process of 1993–1994 had agreed should be respected when the national assembly elected in the first-ever democratic election in 1994, acting as a Constitutional Assembly, drew up the final constitution to replace the interim constitution under which the election had been held. A deal had been cut in negotiations between the government and National Party on the one hand and the ANC and other parties on the other in order to make the move to democracy possible. The ANC held that no constitution drafted by an unelected group of politicians could really be said to command national and interracial legitimacy, and that the country's constitution must, therefore, be written after the first democratic election. The government/NP side could not accept that its interests should be entirely at the mercy of this inevitably ANC dominated constitutional convention. The deal was that an interim constitution would be drafted by the negotiators, along with a set of constitutional principles that the subsequently drafted final constitution would have to abide by. As the interim constitution would have a constitutional court written in, something everyone agreed to, this body could be the referee as to whether the final document did abide by the constitutional principles.[6]

Even the more typical questions the court found itself having to answer were harder than normal constitutional review, because inevitably the "principles" were looser, more aspirational than would be formal constitutional text. Naturally this led to problems with alternative readings of the new constitutional text, where one reading could be incompatible with the principles, another acceptable. The court was acutely aware of future dangers in this ambiguity, and insisted on its glosses having definitional effect in the future. Where they choose a construction that makes the constitution compatible with the constitutional principles, the approach

[5] A Sachs, "The Creation of South Africa's Constitution," 1997 41 *New York Law School Law Review* 669.

[6] It is unclear to what extent the ANC side would have supported a constitutional court but for this political need. There is good reason to believe that it would have preferred the interim constitution to have much less of a worked-out bill of rights for the new court to impose than it finally had to agree to. See Sarkin, "South Africa's Final Constitution." See also Chanock, "Post-Calvinist Catechism."

> has one important consequence. Certification based on a particular interpretation carries with it the implication that if the alternative construction were correct the certification by the Court . . . might have been withheld. In the result, a future court should approach the meaning of the relevant provision of the NT on the basis that the meaning assigned to it by the Constitutional Court in the certification process is its correct interpretation and should not be departed from save in the most compelling circumstances.[7]

How much this will affect the work of the Constitutional Court in the future is yet to be seen. But it necessarily restricts the interpretative freedom of future courts more than has been historically usual. In other cases the constituent assembly has produced a text that remains open to any plausible future interpretations. There was a further problem of finality—the court itself could not go back to the constitutional principles (CPs) in the future:

> Once this Court has certified a text . . . that is the end of the matter and compliance or non-compliance thereof with the CPs can never be raised again in any court of law, including this Court. That casts an increased burden on us in deciding on certification. Should we subsequently decide that we erred in certifying we would be powerless to correct the mistake, however manifest.

All of this argued for considerable deference to the constituent assembly, which the court willingly gave where it could. "This Court has no power, no mandate and no right to express any view on the political choices made by the CA in drafting the NT. . . . the wisdom or otherwise of any provision of the NT is not this Court's business." Of course constitutional courts are always saying things like that, but in this case it was meant—the court was only too aware of the precariousness of its own, and the whole constitution's, legitimacy.

For much of the new document, especially the bill of rights section, there was little difficulty anyway. The interim constitution had a special role here, because the relevant CP specifically called on the constituent assembly to give "due consideration to inter alia the fundamental rights contained in Chapter 3." Otherwise it was almost an empirical process—as the CP required the new bill of rights to contain all "universally" found "fundamental rights, freedoms and civil liberties," all the court did was to check that adequate protection was given to any candidate for such universality. The court insisted that this was a minimum test, and that the CA could add anything else it wished, which has turned out to be especially important in the area of positive rights. Furthermore, the court resolutely refused to allow arguments based on differences between the interim constitution and the new constitution. So, for example, when the new constitution dropped some of the language in the exceptions clause, allowing rights be overturned more easily, the court made it clear that the assembly was entitled to its own view of how, and how far, rights should be protected. It was not bound by the results of earlier negotiations from a context where the balance of political forces was different, provided only that the part of those negotiations intended to have future effect, the CPs, were

[7] *Certification of the Constitution of the Republic of South Africa*, par. 43.

honoured. In the end there was relatively little to deal with in this area. The assembly seems to have taken a good deal of notice of court decisions interpreting the interim constitution. As the court noted in accepting a weaker rights protection under the limitations clause than the interim constitution might have given:

> The content this Court gave to the limitations clause in [the interim constitution] in *S v Makwanyane and Another* conformed to that interpretation. Indeed [the new clause] is substantially a repetition of what was said in that judgment.

The difficulties were nearly all in the huge task of structural analysis forced on the court by the CPs on national versus provincial power, the really political matters. What Chapter 1 described as structural, or boundary, problems always occupy constitutional review bodes, particularly in the early years of a new system. They continue to occupy a major part of the caseload of the South African Constitutional Court, as we shall see. But there is a huge difference between interpreting a fixed constitution to decide whether some putative exercise of power was *intra vires* the grant of authority in that constitution, and deciding whether a constitutional design satisfies a vague political remit. Constitutional Principle XVIII states bluntly that "The powers and functions of the provinces defined in the Constitution . . . shall not be substantially less than or substantially inferior to those provided for in this [i.e., the interim] constitution." Add the word *discuss* after that, and one has a political science finals question, rather than anything that looks like the usual material of constitutional review. The greatest analytic problem the court faced was that the interim constitution had provided for a senate with ten representatives from each province, selected by the parties in the provincial legislature. This was replaced in the new constitution by a "Council of the Provinces," still with ten members from each province, but now roughly modelled on the German Bundesrat with the delegations appointed by the provincial governments. The provinces were new creations anyway, replacing the hated homelands and other bits and pieces of apartheid political structure. Although only two years separated the interim and new constitutions, this had been long enough for these new provinces to become political entities aware of, and eager to preserve, their own interests. The result was contradictory arguments addressed to the court by counsel for the Constitutional Assembly against a series of counsel for different provinces. It is quite impossible even to summarise the argument of the court on this issue, at least in part because it is unclear just how it came to its decision. Nor does it greatly matter—the fact that the court did take on the task, found against the CA, and forced changes to be made before finally certifying the constitution, is all that really matters. But some clues to the overall approach of the South African court can be gained from its judgement on the matter.

In carrying out this piece of political science, the court made certain assumptions that are not obviously necessary, and certainly were not forced on it by the legal material. To start with, it drew a distinction between "the power and the capacity of provinces collectively to resist the will of the national government and the power of an individual province to do so," and further insisted that the court had to look not only at the changes in individual powers of the provinces, but also at "the structural and other changes in the NT that bear upon their collective power."[8] The biggest of these "structural" matters is the replacement of the Senate with the National Council of Provinces (NCOP). The court regarded it as very important because political parties dominated the Senate, it being a contingent matter whether or not the power balance in the Senate would reflect that in the House, depending inter alia, on the timings of elections and so on. In the eyes of the court the new constitutional arrangements probably made the NCOP a more suitable structure for representing provincial interests:

> The method of nomination of senators does, however, detract from the weight to be given to the Senate as a source of collective provincial power. As an institution it is more a House in which party political interests are represented than a House in which provincial interests are represented, and this has to be taken into account in evaluating the effect of the changes introduced by the NT in so far as they are relevant to the issue of collective provincial power.

The court went on to say that the sheer uncertainty about how the new institutions would work made it impossible to take a firm view. Yet what it was uncertain about is whether or not the NCOP would enhance provincial power, which was equally forbidden by the CP. This, though, was only a background factor, because the court still had to go through the lists of provincial and national competences, questions of reserved powers, and the fact that other clauses of the new constitution gave the national government, under certain conditions, override powers even in areas of pure provincial authority. Using more familiar language, the court refers to this latter power as a presumption, possibly a rebuttable presumption, in favour of national authority. On balance the court decided that provincial power had been, at least marginally, reduced. But the CP called for it to establish whether there had been a "substantial" diminution (or increase) in provincial power. Answering this question, the court said, "might involve some element of subjective judgement, *but it is ultimately an objective exercise* which must be performed by our having regard to all relevant factors."[9] There followed a very detailed examination of each provincial power and each challenge by the provinces to the new constitution. It is of particular importance to the future of this constitution and its court that on several important aspects, the court's ability to give the new constitutional text a clean bill depended on the court's own interpretation of the meaning of various clauses. Thus the constitution came into force already "annotated," as it were, as noted above. Nor are these trivial points. To take one example, the NCOP would have no right to control a "money bill," yet the provinces' foes have rights to an "equitable share" in the tax yield. Only because the court said outright that such bills are not money bills can this particular aspect of the constitution pass muster. But the force of this decision will very much depend on future courts taking the

[8] *Certification of the Constitution of the Republic of South Africa*, pars. 317–18.

[9] *Certification of the Constitution of the Republic of South Africa*, pars. 317 and 341; emphasis added.

same view of their own limitation of interpretation.[10] Other constitutional courts have never had a force of precedent quite so strongly imposed on them by their predecessors.

The actual decision the court had to make represents the circularity and reference problems of constitutional review at its highest. As the judges point out, the answer to the broad question of CP XVIII (2) actually depends, counter-factually, on whether specific criticisms they make of individual powers and arrangements are satisfactorily dealt with in the revisions. But, the court said, even if two peculiarly important and muddy areas were clarified in the right way, it is impossible to certify that CP XVIII (2) would be satisfied by the new constitution. There are four areas of clear reduction in provincial power—provincial police powers, tertiary education, the design of local government, and powers over "traditional leadership." The court then makes a rather curious assumption—these four power reductions, they say, are not in themselves enough to constitute substantial reduction in provincial power, but they are if combined with the changes in the override powers of national government. In the interim constitution the national government could only impose norms where they are required for the "effective performance" of policy in question. In the court's eyes this was a weaker override clause than the one newly proposed, which was that an override be "in the interests of the country as a whole." The resulting weighting is just bluntly stated, with no further explanation:

> If the curtailment of powers and the override provisions referred to in the preceding two paragraphs are taken together, their combined weight in the context of the NT as a whole is sufficient to be considered substantial. It therefore follows that the NT does not satisfy CP XVIII.2.[11]

The French Conseil constitutionnel could not have been terser, though there may have been no alternative approach. The first draft of the new constitution was thus rejected on this and fourteen other parts of the CPs, though the court did say, to cheer up the politicians, that the rejections "should present no significant obstacle to the formulation of a text which complies fully with those requirements."

The Constitutional Assembly moved rapidly, and sent a revised document, the amended text (AT) back by early October, allowing the court to hold new hearings and give its final judgement in December 1996. It is common for political scientists to see the interaction between legislatures and constitutional review bodies as a form of bargaining, and the analogy holds well here.[12] The CA made relatively few

[10] *Certification of the Constitution of the Republic of South Africa*, par. 421: "It is therefore our considered view that bills determining a province's equitable share are not money bills and are subject to the procedure set out in NT 76(1)."

[11] *Certification of the Constitution of the Republic of South Africa*, par. 481.

[12] For example, Schepple, "Constitutional Negotiations." A more theoretical approach to a similar sort of issue is well demonstrated in N Schofield, "Constitutions, Voting and Democracy: A Review," 2001 18 *Social Choice and Welfare* 3, 571–600. The bargaining analogy is often used with reference to the French Conseil constitutionnel, though not necessarily very successfully. A typical example would be G Vanberg, "Legislative-Judicial Relations: A Game-Theoretic Approach to Constitutional Review," 2001 45 *American Journal of Political Science* 2, 346–61.

changes, the minimum necessary to satisfy the court, but they sufficed. Just as it had been the area of national versus provincial relationships that had caused the court most trouble the first time, this was the area where the Constitutional Assembly was least willing to compromise. All the other concerns raised in the first judgement, plus those arising freshly from complainants, took up less space in the second judgement than this single issue. Indeed the rest of the issues might have been dealt with more rapidly, but the court clearly felt it had to mark its approval of the new document very firmly. Typical is its treatment of a complaint from the province of Kwa-Zulu Natal that CP II had not been complied with. The CP required of the final constitution that

> Collective rights of self-determination in forming, joining and maintaining organs of civil society, including linguistic, cultural and religious associations, shall, on the basis of non-discrimination and free association, be recognised and protected.

Counsel for the province claimed that the wording of the relevant part of the AT, Section 31, was inadequate. What he was really getting at was rather different from the verbal differences he complained of, because the new text provided a perfectly adequate coverage for the CP II rights, given a particular interpretation of what CP II was all about. The new protection stated:

> (1) Persons belonging to a cultural, religious or linguistic community may not be denied the right, with other members of that community—
> (a) to enjoy their culture, practise their religion and use their language; and
> (b) to form, join and maintain cultural, religious and linguistic associations and other organs of civil society.
> (2) The rights in subsection (1) may not be exercised in a manner inconsistent with any provision of the Bill of Rights.

All the KZA could directly complain of was the restriction to cultural, religious and linguistic associations. The court, however, astutely went out of its way to deal with the subtext, which was the hope for a constitutional protection of some degree of potential autonomy. "In this context 'self-determination' does not embody any notion of political independence or separateness."[13] Instead of dismissing the complaint summarily, the court went on to give a resounding imprimatur to the political values defined and protected by the constitution:

> The AT is based on founding values which include human dignity, the achievement of equality, the recognition and advancement of human rights and freedoms, the supremacy of the Constitution and the rule of law. It makes provision for a multi-party system of democratic government, with provision for three levels of government, to ensure accountability, responsiveness

[13] *Certification of the Amended Text of the Constitution of the Republic of South Africa* CCT 37/96 (South African Constitutional Court), par. 24.

> and openness. This provides a protective framework for civil society, which is enhanced by institutional structures such as the Public Protector, the Human Rights Commission, the Commission for the Promotion and Protection of Rights of Cultural, Religious and Linguistic Communities, and the Commission for Gender Equality, and ultimately by AT ch 2 which contains a justiciable Bill of Rights. The Bill of Rights is described as a "cornerstone of democracy," and the state is required to respect, protect, promote and fulfil these rights, which are enforceable by an independent judiciary.[14]

This is not to say that the court pulled its punches. The lengthy section on provincial powers is replete with acknowledgement of how minimal the changes were that the CA had been prepared to make in allowing provincial power. If its original condemnation had been marginal, a matter of weighting various factors with the result that the first text just failed, the new one equally only just passes. In three of the four specific power areas that had been regarded as showing diminution of provincial power, the court ruled that their position had not been improved in the new text. What tipped the balance, as it had the other way around the first time, was the more legal question of the presumption in favour of national legislation when it clashed with provincial legislation. Here the CA, presumably intentionally, gave the court an authority it could hardly resist. Instead of writing in a presumption in favour of the national government, the new text just provides that

> When there is a dispute concerning whether national legislation is necessary for a purpose set out in subsection (2)(c) and that dispute comes before a court for resolution, the court must have due regard to the approval or the rejection of the legislation by the National Council of Provinces.

The overall judgement is hardly enthusiastic: "In the result, the powers and functions of the provinces in terms of the AT are still less than or inferior to those accorded to the provinces in terms of the IC, but not substantially so."[15] But that was enough. South Africa had a new constitution, and one on which the imprimatur of its Constitutional Court was very significant, both in practical ways and, above all, in the joint legitimacy it gave to the constitution and the court. It is doubtful if the court could have continued, as it has, with a series of brave judgements that have not always been to the liking of either the government of the public had it not had this very special introductory role. This whole episode in South African constitutional history deserves very through study, not least from the viewpoint of the bargaining approach to court/legislative relations, but no such enterprise can be attempted here. I have spent so long on it not only because it is so important an episode in its own right, but to give a flavour of the court's approach—a subtle and cautious mix of legalism and political realism.

[14] *Certification of the Amended Text of the Constitution of the Republic of South Africa*, par. 25.
[15] *Certification of the Amended Text of the Constitution of the Republic of South Africa*, par. 204.

Structural Concerns Postcertification

The certification period did not end the court's involvement with structural matters. It is useful here to look briefly at actual litigation on the institutional nature of democracy. These cases further develop the court's approach, as well as establishing its credentials as a body fully aware of the need for due deference to political authority where that is constitutionally possible. One strong objection to the new constitution during the first hearing related to a stipulation imposed by the interim constitution was that the electoral system should contain an "antidefection clause" whereby anyone elected on a party list who sought to change party allegiance subsequently should lose his or her seat.[16] The new version retained this stipulation, producing a powerful argument from opponents that such a restriction was undemocratic. The arguments on both sides and by the court are too rich to go into here, but a flavour can be given by the court's own summary:

> The objectors contend that the anti-defection clause creates an imperative form of representation which cannot be reconciled with the CPs. They place particular reliance on CPs I, II, IV, VI, VIII and XVII, submitting that legislators are subjected to the authority of their parties in a manner inimical to accountable, responsive, open, representative and democratic government; that universally accepted rights and freedoms, such as freedom of expression, freedom of association, the freedom to make political choices and the right to stand for public office and, if elected, to hold office, are undermined; and that the anti-defection clause militates against the principles of "representative government," "appropriate checks and balances to ensure accountability, responsiveness and openness" and "democratic representation." The enactment of this anti-defection clause is justified by counsel for the CA on the grounds that it is desirable to secure a more stable government and to avoid corruption in legislatures.

The court rejected these objections with a mixture of empirical reference (e.g., such systems exist elsewhere in perfectly respectable democracies) and fundamental democratic theory. The court was not merely deferring to the CA: it made its own quite fundamental choice in support of the antidefection clause.

> Under a list system of proportional representation, it is parties that the electorate votes for, and parties which must be accountable to the electorate. A party which abandons its manifesto in a way not accepted by the electorate would probably lose at the next election. In such a system an anti-defection clause is not inappropriate to ensure that the will of the electorate is honoured. An individual member remains free to follow the dictates of personal conscience. This is not inconsistent with democracy.[17]

[16] The argument of the court on this issue is given in pars. 180–88 of *Certification of the Constitution of the Republic of South Africa*.

[17] *Certification of the Constitution of the Republic of South Africa*, par. 186.

So far so good, because the strong majority in the assembly and the court agreed, and the dissent was easily pushed aside. However, the actual development of politics in the new democratic South Africa changed the minds of the ruling political forces, especially the ANC. The ANC began to attract elected politicians from other parties, both at the national, and perhaps more frequently the provincial level. In 2002 four acts were passed amending the constitution to allow a limited right of floor crossing. They were appealed on the grounds that they could not be legitimate constitutional amendments, both for procedural reasons, and because they were so fundamental as constitutional changes that the amendment processes used were illicit. It was claimed that the amendments undermined the basic structure of the constitution, were inconsistent with the founding values that are set in Section 1 of the constitution, and were inconsistent with voters' rights under the Bill of Rights.

The court had to be very careful in its judgement, because it needed both to uphold the vital importance of constitutional stability and, as part of actually doing that, in fact invalidate the key act. But it had to do so in a way that would not encourage political forces in the new democracy to think that the court was always likely to reject constitutional amendments, nor that it would defy the legislature except when absolutely necessary. The court started with a firm reminder about its own impotence in the face of legitimate action by the national assembly, when acting either as a primary legislator or constitutional amendment body.

> This case is not about the merits or demerits of the provisions of the disputed legislation. That is a political question and is of no concern to this Court. What has to be decided is not whether the disputed provisions are appropriate or inappropriate, but whether they are constitutional or unconstitutional. It ought not to have been necessary to say this for that is true of all cases that come before this Court. We do so only because of some of the submissions made to us in argument, and the tenor of the public debate concerning the case which has taken place both before and since the hearing of the matter.[18]

A measure of how easy some forces thought it might be to get the court to overturn a constitutional amendment was given by the way counsel for the complainants jumped on an *obiter* from a previous case on constitutional amendment at the provincial level. The court had said then that it could imagine some such situation:

> It may perhaps be that a purported amendment to the Constitution, following the formal procedures prescribed by the Constitution, but radically and fundamentally restructuring and reorganising the fundamental premises of the Constitution, might not qualify as an "amendment" at all.[19]

[18] *United Democratic Movement v The President of the Republic of South Africa* CCT 23/02 (South African Constitutional Court), par. 11.

[19] *Premier of Kwazulu-Natal v President of the Republic of South Africa*, CCT 36/95 (South African Constitutional Court), par. 47.

In fact the court in that case had made it clear it was thinking about an amendment so extreme that it actually abolished democracy—they were actually following the argument in a leading Indian High Court case. (The use of foreign jurisprudence is a very important power the South African court has been granted, and which it uses very frequently.) The removal of the antidefection clause could hardly be claimed to be an attack on democracy of that order. But other arguments caused the court more trouble, largely because of the strong support it had itself given to the rule. Indeed it was forced to consider its earlier arguments and put a completely new gloss on them. The judgement reads, once again, like a complex piece of democratic theory written by a political scientist with a specialism in electoral systems. The court drew what comfort it could from the silence of other constitutional courts on the issue, while hardly attempting to hide its own distaste for the constitutional provision. The whole passage shows deference to the legislature at its fullest:

> We were referred in argument to a number of democratic countries with proportional representation systems in which defection is not allowed. No case was cited to us, however, in which a court in any country has ever held that, absent a constitutional or legislative requirement to that effect, a member of a legislature is obliged to resign if he or she changes party allegiance during the life of a legislature. In our view such a requirement, though possibly desirable, is not an essential component of multi-party democracy, and cannot be implied as a necessary adjunct to a proportional representation system. Where the law prohibits defection, that is a lawful prohibition, which must be enforced by the courts. But where it does not do so, courts cannot prohibit such conduct where the legislature has chosen not to do so.[20]

Despite its earlier advocacy of the antidefection ban, the court was clear that its duty was now to permit the amendment—if it could be accepted procedurally. The court dismissed summarily another challenge with words that might token a political naïveté, except that the court, both here and elsewhere, gives plenty of evidence that it has no such weakness. The challenge was a fundamental one—to the very idea of the rule of law.

> Our Constitution requires legislation to be rationally related to a legitimate government purpose. If not, it is inconsistent with the rule of law and invalid The appellants contend that the purpose of the disputed legislation is to enable the ANC and the NNP to take advantage of the breaking up of the DA. *This argument equates purpose with motive. Courts are not, however, concerned with the motives of the members of the legislature who vote in favour of particular legislation*, nor with the consequences of legislation unless it infringes rights protected by the Constitution, or is otherwise inconsistent with the Constitution.[21]

[20] *United Democratic Movement*, par. 35.
[21] *United Democratic Movement*, pars. 55–56.

It is very improbable that motives must, or even can, always be ignored, and in fact in this case parliamentary motives were actually discussed by the court. Nonetheless they were surely right to stress that doing the right thing for the wrong reason was constitutionally acceptable. As it happens the court found that there were procedural irregularities in the amendment process for the Membership Act, which referred to the national assembly. To reach this conclusion, the court delved deep into political history. The antidefection clause had obviously been politically controversial from the beginning. As a result the new constitution had made provision for it to be removed by an easy procedure, as long as this was done "within a reasonable period after the new constitution took effect." The Constitutional Court itself suggested that this unusual procedure was followed because "the anti-defection issue was one that the Constitutional Assembly could not resolve and decided to deal with on the basis of a transitional provision, leaving the principal issue to be determined at a later date.[22] Barely had the first assembly been elected under the new constitution than it set up a committee to advise on whether there should be an amendment removing the floor-crossing ban. This committee reported a year later, in June 1998, strongly recommending the ban be kept, and the issue was dropped. It returned to the political agenda only after a breakup of the Democratic Alliance in 2002 that led to some elected representatives wishing to transfer to the ANC. The assembly hastily wrote four acts, using the special procedure that the constitution had allowed for the Membership Act. This is where the Constitutional Court took its stand. It refused flatly to agree that "within a reasonable time" could cover not bothering to take action for four years. There is no political naïveté in a court that openly states:

> It seems clear to us that if Parliament had wished to modify the anti-defection provisions it could reasonably have done so at the time the ad-hoc committee reported and recommended against any change. Allowing for the time required for drafting of legislation and for public debate, the legislation could reasonably have been passed during 1999. *The fact that it was only passed some three years later was due to the change in the political climate, rather than to constraints of time.*[23]

Nor was the court going to give the assembly leeway because of its generally difficult task:

> Although regard must be had to the difficulties confronting a young Parliament faced with the need to transform many of the laws of the country and bring them into line with the political changes which have taken place since 1994, *there is nothing to suggest that this was the reason for the delay in amending Item 23A*. Having regard to all the circumstances, we are unable to conclude that an amendment passed more than five years after the Con-

[22] *United Democratic Movement*, par. 95.

[23] *United Democratic Movement*, par. 103; emphasis added.

stitution came into force, to change a provision which had only another two years to run, was passed within a reasonable period.[24]

Deference and Procedural Propriety

This is a strong but focussed court. However strongly it will oppose the government in the protection of substantive rights, it is much less prepared to uphold challenges to the structural workings of South African politics. Though the justices will most certainly enforce the letter of the constitution in procedural matters, in few if any of the cases that have raised structural questions—especially about separation of powers and centre/local relations—have complainants succeeded. Like everything in a new political system, this position may evolve with the court's growing experience, though the care to avoid even seeming to breach the separation of powers is likely to remain. In a recent pair of linked cases the Constitutional Court has overturned legislation on procedural grounds, in a way that goes right to the heart of how the legislature can go about its business. The judgements were complex and sophisticated exercises in thinking out the necessary meanings of the separation of powers and the legitimacy of a constitutional court involving itself in parliamentary procedure. In particular they touch on a doctrine otherwise found only in Hungary, of the "constitutional omission." This is the situation where rather than the legislature trying to pass something that is invalid because unconstitutional, it rather fails to do something the constitution seems to require. If future cases pick up on this, South African constitutional law will be all the richer.

Both cases involved challenges to the validity of laws that, it was claimed, were passed without the National Council of Provinces giving full weight to its obligation to facilitate public involvement in its legislative processes. In one the complaint was about complete failure of a province to hold public meetings or solicit the public's views before consenting to a border change that moved an entire community into the next-door province.[25] The other case involved challenges to four health policy laws that were similarly seen as having been passed without adequate public involvement even though two of them, one regulating "Traditional Health Providers," one detailing abortion procedures, were highly controversial. No one suggested that any part of the Bill of Rights was breached. No suggestion was made that for any other reason Parliament could not legislate in these areas. Yet the court did find that the constitution valued participatory democracy so highly that laws like these would still be invalid if the way parliament proceeded breached the constitutional requirement for public participation in the legislative processes of the NCOP and the provincial legislatures. The judgements in both cases are extraordinarily complicated, and involve sweeping coverage of both international law and

[24] *United Democratic Movement*, par. 105; emphasis added.

[25] *Matatiele Municipality v President of the Republic of South Africa*, CCT 73/05 (South African Constitutional Court).

the constitutional law of several countries. At all stages the court was careful to limit its incursion, and continually reminded itself and the public that it must not transgress the separation of powers. Nonetheless the value of participation is seen as so crucial to the whole constitutional enterprise that the court felt itself forced make a ruling of invalidity. As is often the case in its most far-reaching decisions, the court appealed to the history of the struggle for democracy in South Africa to justify its position. Initially the argument is almost textual:

> Our Constitution was inspired by a particular vision of a non-racial and democratic society in which government is based on the will of the people. Indeed, one of the goals that we have fashioned for ourselves in the Preamble of the Constitution is the establishment of "a society based on democratic values, social justice and fundamental human rights. The very first provision of our Constitution, which establishes the founding values of our constitutional democracy, includes as part of those values a multi-party system of democratic government, to ensure accountability, responsiveness and openness."[26]

But a much more impassioned grounding followed:

> The nature of our democracy must be understood in the context of our history. As has been observed, during the struggle against apartheid, a system that denied the majority of the people a say in the making of the laws which governed them, the people developed the concept of the people's power as an alternative to the undemocratic system of apartheid. This concept ensured that the people took part in community structures that were set up to fight the system of apartheid. But as has been observed, the significance of these "organs of the people's power" went beyond their intended purpose: "They were also seen as crucial in laying the foundation for the future participatory democracy that [the people] were fighting for and that we are operating under. This emphasis on democratic participation that was born in the struggle against injustices is strongly reflected in our new democratic Constitution and the entrenchment of public participation in Parliament and the legislatures."[27]

A measure of how determined the court is to keep within its powers, even when it does directly interfere with the practices of other branches, is given in this case. The court argued that it ought never intervene in the process of passing a bill—not until the bill was actually passed and signed by the president would it rule. To do otherwise would be an impermissible involvement in parliamentary activity. One of the four health acts objected to had in fact been only a bill, as yet unsigned by the president, at the time a pressure group, Doctors for Life International, instituted litigation. Even though the legislation in question, regulations on infertility

[26] *Doctors for Life International v The Speaker of the National Assembly*, CCT 12/05 (South African Constitutional Court), par. 61.

[27] *Doctors for Life International*, par. 62.

treatment, had been fully promulgated before the court made its decision, it still ruled that it could not be challenged in this case. Such a consideration for the niceties may salve the court's conscience, but is hardly likely to cheer up the National Council of Provinces, which from now on will be required to carry out much more extensive public consultation on any legislation that the court may later decide was highly controversial. The legislature may even notice, as argued by Yacoob, dissenting in both cases, that the plaintiff had not even asked for the legislation to be struck down, simply for a declaration that the NCOP ought to have consulted more widely.

There is no question the court knew what it was doing—supporting the argument that it was the only court in South Africa entitled to make such a ruling, Ngcobo, the author of the majority opinion in *Doctors for Life*, says of an earlier case touching on much the same issues:

> The basic reasoning of the Supreme Court of Appeal was that the question whether Parliament has fulfilled its obligation to facilitate public involvement is "pre-eminently a crucial political question." . . . I agree with this reasoning and conclusion.[28]

The court does not regard "crucial political questions" as something to dodge (the "political question" doctrine in North America has always been used in this way; finding a political question is the way for a court to refuse to get involved). In South Africa labelling something a "political question" is just to say that it can only be handled by the Constitutional Court. All one can safely say at this point is that the court will not easily transgress against parliamentary autonomy, but that it certainly can reach out if convinced of the pressing urgency of the values involved.

Socioeconomic Rights

Those who know only a little about South African jurisprudence will naturally expect a serious discussion of socioeconomic, or "positive," rights. These are, of course vitally important. Socioeconomic rights, if they are problematic at all, are so because they seem to raise structural questions about the relationship and the balance of power between courts and the executive. This was in fact one of the challenges raised to the new constitutional text in the certification hearings. Sections 26–29 of the text guarantee various socioeconomic rights, specifically to housing, health care, sufficient food and water, social security, and basic education. The main objection, as characterised by the court, was that these were incompatible with the separation of powers

> because the judiciary would have to encroach upon the proper terrain of the legislature and executive. In particular the objectors argued it would re-

[28] *Doctors for Life International*, 21.

> sult in the courts dictating to the government how the budget should be allocated.[29]

The court dismissed the objection summarily, making the obvious point that many more normal rights-enforcing decisions have budgetary implications, as, for example, extending welfare rights to a broader category of recipients, or even granting legal aid. As such the court is partially right to argue that

> In our view it cannot be said that by including socio-economic rights within a bill of rights, a task is conferred upon the courts so different from that ordinarily conferred upon them by a bill of rights that it results in a breach of the separation of powers.

There is an important difference that the court tries to glide over. Where a question of extending the scope of a welfare scheme arises, it is a matter of interpreting a statute. The government is left with the choice of making it more inclusive after a court order, or changing it radically to maintain a budget line—as happened on more than one occasion when the Canadian Supreme Court began to find welfare rules unconstitutionally discriminatory. The sort of socioeconomic rights that raise balance-of-power problems are those arising directly from the constitution, not those whose application is governed by equality rights within the constitution. When forced to address this point more closely by a second objection, the court was less convincing. It treated the issue as one of the "justiciability" of socioeconomic rights, and argued:

> Nevertheless, we are of the view that these rights are, *at least to some extent, justiciable*. As we have stated in the previous paragraph, many of the civil and political rights entrenched in the NT will give rise to similar budgetary implications without compromising their justiciability. The fact that socio-economic rights will almost inevitably give rise to such implications does not seem to us to be a bar to their justiciability. *At the very minimum, socio-economic rights can be negatively protected from improper invasion.*[30]

To assess the way in which socioeconomic rights are fully entrenched in the working understanding of the constitution created by the court, one also has to see the way the rights themselves are constructed in the text. As examples we can take the rights to housing and health, sections 26 and 27 of the constitution.

> S26 Housing
>
> 1. Everyone has the right to have access to adequate housing.
> 2. The state must take reasonable legislative and other measures, within its available resources, to achieve the progressive realisation of this right.
> 3. No one may be evicted from their home, or have their home demolished, without an order of court made after considering all the relevant circumstances. No legislation may permit arbitrary evictions.

[29] *Certification of the Constitution of the Republic of South Africa*, par. 77.

[30] *Certification of the Constitution of the Republic of South Africa*, par. 78; emphasis added.

S27 Health care, food, water and social security

1. Everyone has the right to have access to
   a. health care services, including reproductive health care;
   b. sufficient food and water; and
   c. social security, including, if they are unable to support themselves and their dependents, appropriate social assistance.
2. The state must take reasonable legislative and other measures, within its available resources, to achieve the progressive realisation of each of these rights.
3. No one may be refused emergency medical treatment.

Though the initial statement of the rights in the first subsections is strong, the language is immediately weakened by the formulation of the right as being "to have access to." The real weakening, which must hold back even a court as determined as the South African court, is the second clause of each section—"reasonable . . . effort," "within its available resources," "progressive realisation of . . ." The position is not impossible for a court determined to uphold socioeconomic rights: it is clearly possible to hold that state action does not live up to "reasonable legislative and other measures," even "within its available resources." And even though "access to . . . health care services" is not quite the same as an absolute right to some drug or treatment, it is not negligible. But short of bad faith by the government, any major awarding of medical or housing rights in excess of whatever the government does make available would be very hard to defend as within ordinary separation-of-powers lines.

The actual decisions of the court in this area have indeed not come anywhere close to such an invasion of other branches' autonomy. There are, in the end, only two major decisions so far that can really be described as upholding socioeconomic rights against the state. These are *Grootboom* in 2000 and *Treatment Action Campaign* in 2002, the first a housing case, the latter a right-to-health case. Some time before either of the famous cases, however, and in its own way just as important, was one in which relief was denied, *Soobramoney v Minister of Health (Kwazulu-Natal)*, decided in 1997.[31] In the light of likely reactions to *Chaoulli* in Canada, discussed earlier and of the dissent in that case, *Soobramoney* is especially important. In this case, a chronic renal failure patient was refused dialysis in hospital because scarce resources were targeted on patients who could be cured, or who were fit enough to receive a transplant.[32] Soobramoney fell into neither category, and had run out of money to continue dialysis in private clinics.[33] He argued that the right-to-life clause in the South African constitution required the health service to admit him, and that the state should make more funds available so that

[31] *Soobramoney v Minister of Health (Kwazulu-Natal)*, CCT 32/97 (South African Constitutional Court). This case, as well as others of interest to us here, is discussed in BG Ramcharan, *Judicial Protection of Economic, Social and Cultural Rights: Cases and Materials*, Raoul Wallenberg Institute Human Rights Library (Leiden: Martinus Nijhoff, 2005).

[32] *Soobramoney v Minister of Health.*

[33] *Soobramoney v Minister of Health.*

others better placed to benefit would not be denied treatment.[34] The claim was based not just on a general extension of the basic right-to-life clause, but on the very specific language that the South African constitution uses to provide "positive" rights, in particular Section 27.

The court had no difficulty in refusing Soobramoney's claim, largely because of its reading of subsection (2). At this stage in its history, the court decided the state would not be required to provide resources.

> If all the persons in South Africa who suffer from chronic renal failure were to be provided with dialysis treatment—and many of them, as the appellant does, would require treatment three times a week—the cost of doing so would make substantial inroads into the health budget. And if this principle were to be applied to all patients claiming access to expensive medical treatment or expensive drugs, the health budget would have to be dramatically increased to the prejudice of other needs which the state has to meet.[35]

This conclusion is combined with quite traditional self-warnings about courts getting into areas they should evade, and a useful awareness that the problems would not be absent even in a richer country. As Sachs says, "however the right to life may come to be defined in South Africa, there is in reality no meaningful way in which it can constitutionally be extended to encompass the right indefinitely to evade death."[36] What is important, though, is that the judgements contain no words that could be taken to preclude the general idea that the court might order government action where conditions made it possible. From a comparative perspective, *Soobramoney* ought to be seen as showing that no one need fear courts being economically illiterate and spendthrift with national resources. Much of the argument from the separation of powers is shown to be irrelevant, as it is in other South African Constitutional Court cases on positive rights when they are granted. It also shows that it is possible to deny specific positive demands for rights without denying their overall legitimacy.

Vital, and indeed brave, though both these decisions were, they do not accord very closely with the idea of court-imposed socioeconomic rights that frighten theorists committed to a liberal negative rights constitutionalism. They are, for example, a good deal less intrusive on government budgetary autonomy than some of the cases decided in Eastern Europe since 1990. They are considerably less intrusive in well-established health schemes than the recent Canadian decision, discussed in the previous chapter.[37] First, *Grootboom* recognised a restricted right to housing in the special context of squatters who had been evicted from their shantytown by a private landowner. By the time the Constitutional Court's order was issued, emergency housing of a sort had been provided. What was at stake essentially was whether or not the provisions in the existing housing relief plan were adequate. They were found not to be, and a declaratory order was made forcing the

[34] *Soobramoney v Minister of Health.*

[35] *Soobramoney v Minister of Health*, par. 28.

[36] *Soobramoney v Minister of Health*, par. 57.

[37] *Chaoulli v Quebec (Attorney General)*, 2005 SCC 35 (Canadian Supreme Court).

relevant local authority to devise better plans that would fulfil the constitutional obligations. The order is prefaced by this statement by the court:

> I am conscious that it is an extremely difficult task for the state to meet these obligations in the conditions that prevail in our country. This is recognised by the Constitution which expressly provides that the state is not obliged to go beyond available resources or to realise these rights immediately. I stress however, that despite all these qualifications, these are rights, and the Constitution obliges the state to give effect to them. This is an obligation that courts can, and in appropriate circumstances, must enforce.[38]

What the decision orders is basically that the local authority get on properly with a job it had failed to do right or with sufficient haste the first time, especially as concerns those in emergency need of housing.

> Neither section 26 nor section 28 entitles the respondents to claim shelter or housing immediately upon demand. The High Court order ought therefore not to have been made. However, section 26 does oblige the state to devise and implement a coherent, co-ordinated programme designed to meet its section 26 obligations. The programme that has been adopted and was in force in the Cape Metro at the time that this application was brought, fell short of the obligations imposed upon the state by section 26(2) in that it failed to provide for any form of relief to those desperately in need of access to housing. In the light of the conclusions I have reached, it is necessary and appropriate to make a declaratory order. The order requires the state to act to meet the obligation imposed upon it by section 26(2) of the Constitution. This includes the obligation to devise, fund, implement and supervise measures to provide relief to those in desperate need.[39]

What a decision would look like in the absence of the government making some attempt, however inadequate, to provide for the rights in sections 26–29 we have no idea, of course.[40] It is perhaps fortunate that no major case has come up on the Section 28 rights to education, where the continued reliance on school fees might force the court into a more direct attack on government budgetary priorities.[41] The critics of *Grootboom*, and there indeed were some, focus on what they see as a glaring weakness—the refusal to spell out any "minimum core" standards for socio-economic rights.[42] Various international bodies have issued minimum core defini-

[38] *Grootboom and Others v Government of the Republic of South Africa and Others*, CCT 11/00 (South African Constitutional Court), par. 94.

[39] *Grootboom*, par. 95.

[40] Some further progress has been made on housing rights, including an important case that also involved a link to the very basic idea of the "rule of law": *President of the Republic of South Africa v Modderklip Boerdery (PTY) Ltd.*, CCT 20/04 (South African Constitutional Court).

[41] E Berger, "The Right to Education under the South African Constitution," 2003 103 *Columbia Law Review* 3, 614–61.

[42] See, for example, D Bilchitz, "Towards a Reasonable Approach to the Minimum Core: Laying the Foundations for Future Socio-Economic Rights Jurisprudence," 2003 19 *South African Journal on Human Rights* 1–26; and M Wesson, "*Grootboom* and Beyond: Re-assessing the Socio-economic Juris-

tions over the years, and South African rights activists were eager to have the court embrace them. The court gave no principled argument against so doing, stressing instead the empirical and theoretical difficulties, and its own lack of information. It identified instead a form of reasonableness test, and showed that minimum core arguments, even if possible, would only be in aid of reasonableness analysis.

> There may be cases where it may be possible and appropriate to have regard to the content of a minimum core obligation to determine whether the measures taken by the state are reasonable. However, even if it were appropriate to do so, it could not be done unless sufficient information is placed before a court to enable it to determine the minimum core in any given context. In this case, we do not have sufficient information to determine what would comprise the minimum core obligation in the context of our Constitution.[43]

The *Treatment Action Campaign* case is, on its facts, even further removed from anything that could be characterised as an invasive court imposing socioeconomic rights (such cases do exist, from other jurisdictions, and they are discussed later in the book). The point is that the South African court has never been seriously asked, and if asked would clearly decline, to undertake any such great invasion of executive/legislative territory. TAC was a pressure group seeking to force the South African government to change its very restrictive policy towards the provision of a specific drug to a specific type of patient. Nevirapine is a drug shown to be extremely effective in preventing HIV-positive mothers transferring the condition to their newly born children. The South African government, with its extraordinary attitude to HIV/AIDS, would only allow the drug to be prescribed in a few test centres, even though its makers were prepared to provide it free to all hospitals and medical centres in the country. The government insisted that its regional test centres would in the long run provide the data on which to base an effective anti-AIDS programme. In the meantime, hundreds of children were inheriting the disease, when this could easily and cheaply be prevented. After a lengthy campaign TAC got its case to the Constitutional Court, arguing that this restrictive policy was in breach of the Section 27 health rights cited above.[44] Once again the court faced and rejected a minimum core argument, and relied heavily throughout on its own arguments in *Grootboom*. The textual basis for a minimum core argument is in fact quite strong—it suggests that the structure of sections like Section 27 on health implies two rights, not one. Section 27(1): "Everyone has the right to have access to—(a) health care services, including reproductive health care implies." This would be an absolute right to minimum provision. Section 27(2): "The state

prudence of the South African Constitutional Court," 2004 20 *South African Journal on Human Rights* 2, 284–308.

[43] *Grootboom*, par. 33.

[44] For a general account of the Treatment Action Campaign story see S Friedman and S Mottiar, "A Rewarding Engagement? The Treatment Action Campaign and the Politics of HIV/AIDS," 2005 33 *Politics & Society* 4, 511–65. The case is analysed in several places. A good start is D Bilchitz, "South Africa: Right to Health and Access to HIV/AIDS Drug Treatment," 2003 1 *International Journal of Constitutional Law* 3, 524–33.

must take reasonable legislative and other measures, within its available resources, to achieve the progressive realisation of each of these rights." This would be a second right to have the state act reasonably at a greater level of provision. The court has not much let itself be troubled with "intention of the framers" arguments, but as it has never totally rejected minimum core approaches for the future, there must be some chance that a future court might live up to what is as yet a somewhat undeserved reputation for activism on socioeconomic rights.

The court entertained no doubt, however, that socioeconomic rights were justiciable:

> The question in the present case, therefore, is not whether socio-economic rights are justiciable. Clearly they are. The question is whether the applicants have shown that the measures adopted by the government to provide access to health care services for HIV-positive mothers and their newborn babies fall short of its obligations under the Constitution.[45]

But the ruling is supported along the lines of *Grootboom's* reasonableness approach. Borrowing from *Grootboom*, the court announced that a such a policy "must be balanced and flexible and make appropriate provision for attention to . . . crises and to short, medium and long term needs. A programme that excludes a significant segment of society cannot be said to be reasonable." More generally:

> [To] be reasonable, measures cannot leave out of account the degree and extent of the denial of the right they endeavour to realise. Those whose needs are the most urgent and whose ability to enjoy all rights therefore is most in peril, must not be ignored by the measures aimed at achieving realisation of the right.[46]

Both of these cases, then, revolved around a court assessment of how adequate an ongoing programme was. They show that the court will take very seriously its duty to impose the duty the constitution itself imposes on the state—not that it will use the constitution to construct its own vision of those duties. As some critics occasionally voice doubt about the effectiveness of the court's rulings, it is worth quoting its order here in full:

> The Government is ordered without delay to:
>
> [3.] a) Remove the restrictions that prevent nevirapine from being made available for the purpose of reducing the risk of mother-to-child transmission of HIV at public hospitals and clinics that are not research and training sites.
>
> b) Permit and facilitate the use of nevirapine for the purpose of reducing the risk of mother-to-child transmission of HIV and to make it available for this purpose at hospitals and clinics when in the judgement of the attending medical practitioner acting in consultation with the medical superintendent of the facility concerned this is

[45] *Treatment Action Campaign*, par. 25.

[46] *Treatment Action Campaign*, par. 68.

medically indicated, which shall if necessary include that the mother concerned has been appropriately tested and counselled.

c) Make provision if necessary for counsellors based at public hospitals and clinics other than the research and training sites to be trained for the counselling necessary for the use of nevirapine to reduce the risk of mother-to-child transmission of HIV.

d) Take reasonable measures to extend the testing and counselling facilities at hospitals and clinics throughout the public health sector to facilitate and expedite the use of nevirapine for the purpose of reducing the risk of mother-to-child transmission of HIV.

4. The orders made in paragraph 3 do not preclude government from adapting its policy in a manner consistent with the Constitution if equally appropriate or better methods become available to it for the prevention of mother-to-child transmission of HIV.

The ruling in the final paragraph also shows how careful the court is not to shackle the government in its good-faith policymaking. In a sense the decision is much nearer to administrative law in its approach to socioeconomic rights than it is to the court's creative action on other sorts of rights. The court has taken seriously its role to help transform South African culture. The government is already, if at times incompetently, transforming the socioeconomic basis of poverty and neglect. However, it is a broader transformation that the court seeks, discussed later. At this stage we need to turn to another question to which the South African court may, though in a faltering way, be giving a radical answer.

The Reach and Depth of the Constitution

More than with older, more traditional constitutions, the South African court has had to deal with the question of exactly who the constitution speaks to and protects, and from whom. In legal language, this is partly the question of whether the constitution has "horizontal effect." Does it apply the norms of the constitution to conflicts between private actors, or only to the relationship between the state and the individual? Should the constitution be seen as intended to spread its values throughout South African social and economic relationships? We have seen this issue arise early under the Canadian Charter, in *Dolphin*. It also arose early in the history of the new South African constitution. The case, still controvertial and commented on, is *Du Plessis v De Klerk*, arising in 1995 under the interim constitution.[47] The case arose out of a defamation action instituted before the constitution

[47] *Du Plessis and Others v De Klerk and Another*, CCT 8/95 (South African Constitutional Court). A sample of the journal literature on the case and its implications would include S Woolman and D David, "'The Last Laugh': *Du Plessis v De Klerk*, Classical Liberalism, Creole Liberalism and the Application of Fundamental Rights under the Interim and Final Constitution," 1996 12 *South African Journal on Human Rights* 361–404; and C Sprigman and M Osborne, "Du Plessis is *Not* Dead: South Africa's 1996 Constitution and the Application of the Bill of Rights to Private Disputes," 1999 15 *South African Journal on Human Rights* 25–51.

came into force by De Klerk's company Wonder Air, after it had been identified in the *Pretoria News* as being implicated in the unlawful supply of arms by UNITA in the Angolan civil war. After the constitution came into force, the defendant tried to argue that the alleged defamation was not unlawful because it was protected by the right to freedom of speech and expression in terms of Section 15 of the constitution. The main issue referred by the lower court was whether Chapter 3 of the constitution was applicable to legal relationships between private parties.

It might seem odd to analyse *Du Plessis*, given that the court decided not to apply a horizontal effect. It is precisely because in it one can see the tension between this decision and the general thrust of modern South African jurisprudence that it helps us to evaluate the court's work, and its progress. From the earliest days of South Africa's postapartheid constitutional discourse, one finds, repeatedly and proudly, claims that the constitution is indeed meant to be a value-pervading instrument. In this early case, this approach seemed to be rejected, through a fear of horizontal effect.[48] The majority's argument in *Du Plessis*, like the Canadian argument in *Dolphin*, is purely pragmatic, focussed largely around the idea that imposing constitutional values on the common law is too big a task, an inappropriate task, for the Constitutional Court. At the same time, the dissent by Kriegler is the most powerful of all cries that under a new constitution, this is a task that absolutely must be carried out. For the majority, the problem of horizontal effect was just too great. The main opinion by Kentridge is full of such anxieties, amounting almost to a confession of inadequacy on the part of the Constitutional Court. The argument is essentially that constitutional review is difficult, and the judges should defer to parliament even where, because it was common law, there was no parliamentary intent to defer to!

The majority's preference is that constitutional values should permeate via the routine common-law interpretative work of the ordinary courts. However, this position, perhaps the commonest internationally, is subject to a fatal logical flaw. What if the ordinary courts do not perform this role? What happens where a litigant pleads that the existing law be modified in the light of the constitution and the court refuses? Either this refusal gives a right of appeal to the constitutional court, or the constitutional values have no operationalization within the system. There is no way out for the "top" court. If it truly believes in a mission to transform society, it cannot logically deny a form of direct horizontal effect, cannot permanently evade taking cases. In fact even those who support the decision in *Du Plessis* have had to read a long stop protection by the Constitutional Court into the majority opinion, somewhat unconvincingly.[49] Whatever they may say, only a judge committed to a traditional limited constitutionalism can take the position the majority

[48] The SACC has moved on from this early position in *N K v Minister of Safety and Security*, CCT 52/04 (South African Constitutional Court). The argument was a development of ideas found five years earlier in *Carmichele v The Minister of Safety and Security*, CCT 48/00 (South African Constitutional Court), so it can be seen that the restrictive approach discussed in this section was not long lasting.

[49] Sprigman and Osborne, "Du Plessis." The decision was generally criticized by South African commentators for failing to live up to the promises of the constitution, though there is misgiving as to whether the situation will change under the final constitution.

took on this case. But it was not only those whose commitment to the all-pervasive idea of a constitution might in any case have been weak who rejected horizontality. The oddity of the decision is perhaps best shown by the fact that the court's most radical member, Justice Sachs, stated:

> I have no doubt that given the circumstances in which our Constitution came into being, the principles of freedom and equality which it proclaims are intended to be all-pervasive and transformatory in character. We are not dealing with a Constitution whose only or main function is to consolidate and entrench existing common law principles against future legislative invasion. Whatever function constitutions may serve in other countries, in ours it cannot properly be understood as acting simply as a limitation on governmental powers and action. Given the divisions and injustices referred to in the postscript, it would be strange indeed if the massive inequalities in our society were somehow relegated to the realm of private law, in respect of which government could only intrude if it did not interfere with the vested individual property and privacy rights of the presently privileged classes. That, to my mind, is not the issue. I accept that there is no sector where law dwells, that is not reached by the principles and values of the Constitution.[50]

It is remarkable to find that his opinion, which could be the paradigm of active interpretation, continues as though simply an addendum to the defence from technical inadequacy: "The judicial function simply does not lend itself to the kinds of factual enquiries . . . which appropriate decision-making on social, economic, and political questions requires."[51] This argument, for what it is worth, is at least as applicable to the enforcement of positive or socioeconomic rights, about which Sachs is deeply enthusiastic. Given such reluctance even from a judge like Sachs, it is hardly surprising that the one dissenter, Kriegler, starts his opinion by castigating them:

> The second point concerns a pervading misconception held by some and, I suspect, an egregious caricature propagated by others. That is that so-called direct horizontality will result in an Orwellian society in which the all-powerful state will control all private relationships. . . . That is nonsense. What is more, it is malicious nonsense preying on the fears of privileged whites, cosseted in the past by *laissez faire* capitalism thriving in an environment where the black underclass had limited opportunity to share in the bounty. I use strong language designedly. The caricature is pernicious, it is calculated to inflame public sentiments and to cloud people's perceptions of our fledgling constitutional democracy. "Direct horizontality" is a bogeyman.[52]

Kriegler makes a strong case for not just the desirability of direct horizontal effect, but its necessity:

[50] *Du Plessis*, par. 177.
[51] *Du Plessis*, par. 180.
[52] *Du Plessis*, pars. 120–22.

> The way I read the Preamble and the Postscript, the framers unequivocally proclaimed much more sweeping aims than those. . . . Apparently accepted by some of my colleagues. Our past is not merely one of repressive use of state power. It is one of persistent, institutionalized subjugation and exploitation of a voiceless and largely defenceless majority by a determined and privileged minority.[53]

His conclusion is very simple, and in many ways more strict constructionist than the otherwise more conservative majority:

> My reading of Chapter 3 gives to the Constitution a simple integrity. It says what it means and means what it says. There is no room for the subtleties and nice distinctions so dear to the hearts of mediaeval theologians and modern constitutional lawyers. The Constitution promises an "open and democratic society based on freedom and equality," a radical break with the "untold suffering and injustice" of the past. It then lists and judicially safeguards the fundamental rights and freedoms necessary to render those benefits attainable by all. No one familiar with the stark reality of South Africa and the power relationships in its society can believe that protection of the individual only against the state can possibly bring those benefits. The fine line drawn by the Canadian Supreme Court in the *Dolphin Delivery*[54] case and by the US Supreme Court in *Shelley v Kraemer*[55] between private relationships involving organs of state and those which do not, have no place in our constitutional jurisprudence. . . . We do not operate under a constitution in which the avowed purpose of the drafters was to place limitations on governmental control. Our Constitution aims at establishing freedom and equality in a grossly disparate society. And I am grateful to the drafters of our Constitution for having spared us the jurisprudential gymnastics forced on some courts abroad. They were good enough to say what they mean. The Constitution applies to all three of the pillars of state and Chapter 3 applies to everything they do.[56]

A question for readers of this book is whether they wish to continue to see Western constitutions as designed solely as though "the avowed purpose of the drafters was to place limitations on governmental control," or even whether that option is any longer available. It is worth remarking that between the interim and final constitutions, the South African Constituent Power seems to have had a view: the language in Section 8(2) of the final constitution all but strikes out the arguments used by Kentridge in *Du Plessis*.[57] It must of course be noted that the South

[53] *Du Plessis*, par. 125.

[54] *Retail, Wholesale and Department Store Union v Dolphin Delivery Ltd*, 2 SCR 573 (1986) (Canadian Supreme Court).

[55] *Shelley v Kraemer*, 334 US 1 (1948) (US Supreme Court) The United States has no real doctrine of horizontal effect, though a weak version exists under the label of "state action," for which *Shelley* is the foundational case.

[56] *Du Plessis*, par. 147.

[57] Woolman and Davis, "The Last Laugh."

African constitution is, to use a more American phrase, more aspirational than any other, or more clearly so anyway.

But if this was the beginning, the court has shown many signs of becoming braver in the reach it gives to the constitution. A very good example of how to read existing legal doctrine through constitutional eyes is a more recent case where three policemen while on duty gave a lift to a woman stranded in a city and then raped her.[58] A standard common-law problem of vicarious liability was transformed into a constitutional issue when the Constitutional Court overturned the courts below.[59] The lower courts had insisted on applying a test by which the huge deviation between what the policemen did and what their employer could intend them to do made the latter not vicariously liable. This is a very clear indicator that at least some modern constitutions are value-imposing public decisions and not road maps. Here, O'Regan, for the court, early equates the South African constitution to the German constitution. She cites approvingly a German statement that the Basic Law embodies "an objective value system which, as a fundamental constitutional value for all areas of the law, acts as a guiding principle and stimulus for the Legislature, Executive and Judiciary." O'Regan insists that "Our Constitution is not merely a formal document regulating public power. Like the German Constitution, it also embodies an objective, normative value system."[60] The full extent of this radiation of constitutional values is considerable. It extends to a duty to "be alert to the normative framework of the Constitution not only when some startling new development of the common law is in issue, but in all cases where the incremental development of the rule is in issue."[61] In the present case the constitutional right to safety combined with the police force's duty to ensure this right, making the police authority liable vicariously. Not only did the policemen rely on their positions to trick the woman into trusting them, but they committed a further sin of "constitutional omission" because their duty was precisely to protect her.[62] The idea of the radiating effect of the constitutional values is often tied up with a major aspect of the court's thinking, the centrality of the idea of human dignity.

The Role of Human Dignity

Human dignity is the prime value in the constitution and serves as the touchstone to assess the presence of a justiciable right rather than any technical distinction be-

[58] *N K v Minister of Safety and Security.*

[59] CJ Roederer, "The Constitutionally Inspired Approach to Vicarious Liability in Cases of Intentional Wrongful Acts by the Police: One Small Step in Restoring the Public's Trust in the South African Police Services," 2005 21 *South African Journal on Human Rights* 4.

[60] *N K v Minister of Safety and Security*, par. 15.

[61] *N K v Minister of Safety and Security*, par. 17. Section 39 (2) of the South African constitution reads: "When interpreting any legislation, and when developing the common law or customary law, every court, tribunal or forum must promote the spirit, purport and objects of the Bill of Rights."

[62] The duty of a court to act where legislation is inadequate and leads to a constitutional omission is also found explicitly in the Hungarian constitution, though there it does not apply to acts of individuals. See Sólyom and Brunner, *Constitutional Judiciary*.

tween positive and negative.[63] Rather than seeing rights as isolated claims, the court has stressed that rights are interrelated, and all follow from "the founding values of human dignity, equality and freedom." This is not a mere philosophical reflection; "the proposition that rights are inter-related and are all equally important, has immense human and practical significance in a society founded on these values."[64] This quotation is from a case in which the court invalidated a policy of denying noncitizen permanent residents full welfare rights. Though the case in part depended on a discrimination argument, much of the court's ruling was openly one of enforcing a positive right to minimum welfare. Mokgoro, quoted here, also relies on a completely different case relating to the right of spouses to settle in South Africa, to make the point about the fundamental basis in human dignity:

> In this case we are concerned with these intersecting rights which reinforce one another at the point of intersection. The rights to life and dignity, which are intertwined in our Constitution, are implicated in the claims made by the applicants. This Court in *Dawood* said: "Human dignity . . . informs constitutional adjudication and interpretation at a range of levels. It is a value that informs the interpretation of many, possibly all, other rights. . . . Section 10, however, makes it plain that dignity is not only a *value* fundamental to our Constitution, it is a justiciable and enforceable *right* that must be respected and protected."[65]

A right to dignity is not a right in any normal way that a thinly read constitution could embrace, but perhaps the whole point of thick readings is that the very distinction between a right and a value disappears. Dignity is not, of course, the only fundamental value that underlies these interlinked rights, and indeed *Khosa*, because of its element of discrimination, also focuses sharply on equality, given equal status to dignity in the judgement. But dignity is crucial because were there not a basic positive right to welfare, the state might have succeeded in its pragmatic argument for giving welfare resources only to citizens, as an economic necessity. As such it might have satisfied the court that the discrimination claim was acceptable under the limitation clause in the constitution.[66]

The South African Constitutional Court takes further the idea of an interlinkage between rights by seeing positive rights as having aspects of negative rights, and in particular the court does so when dealing with issues connected to the tra-

[63] An extensive debate has ensued in South Africa about the centrality of dignity as a driving force in what is now being called "transformative jurisprudence." Not all commentators are entirely happy with its centrality, fearing it may take away from the straightforward importance of equality. See, e.g., S Cowan, "Can 'Dignity' Guide South Africa's Equality Jurisprudence?" 2001 17 *South African Journal on Human Rights* 34–58; A Fagan, "Dignity and Unfair Discrimination: A Value Misplaced and a Right Misunderstood," 1998 14 *South African Journal on Human Rights* 220–47.

[64] *Khosa and Others v Minister of Social Development and Others*, CCT 12/03 (South African Constitutional Court), par. 40, again relying partially on *Grootboom*.

[65] *Khosa*.

[66] For a very interesting discussion of the way the court relies on dignity conceptions in its work, though it focuses on rather different cases, see J Barrett, "Dignatio and the Human Body," 2005 21 *South African Journal on Human Rights* 4, 168–206.

ditional horizontal/vertical discussion. In fact the idea that a positive right would be justiciable in this way goes back to the initial statement in the hearing on certification of the constitution: "at the very minimum, socio-economic rights can be negatively protected from improper invasion."[67] An example of this combination of approaches is the *Rail Commuters* case, where plaintiffs sought a declaration that a commuter railway company operating services with a heavy rate of violent crime was in breach of a constitutional duty to protect life.[68] The claim was that the ordinary statutes that applied must be interpreted in the light of this constitutional value. Their argument, rejected in the ordinary courts, was that the statutory requirement that the rail services be operated "in the public interest" be read alongside the constitutional injunction that "The state must respect, protect, promote and fulfill the rights in the Bill of Rights," and in particular sections 11 and 12 of the constitution, which promise that "every one has the right to life" and "everyone has the right to freedom and security of the person, which includes the right . . . to be free from all forms of violence from either public or private sources." O'Regan, for the court, had no difficulty in holding that the statute in question must be interpreted to "promote the spirit, purport and objects of the Bills of Rights."[69] She comments:

> The rights contained in the Bill of Rights ordinarily impose, in the first instance, an obligation that requires those bound not to act in a manner which would infringe or restrict the right. . . . The obligation is in a sense a negative one, as it requires that nothing be done to infringe the rights. However, in some circumstances, the correlative obligations imposed by the rights in the Bill of Rights will require positive steps to be taken to fulfill the rights.[70]

The inevitable argument about budgetary implications was raised—but, as O'Regan says:

> an organ of state will not be held to have reasonably performed a duty simply on the basis of a bald assertion of resource constraints.[71]

The basic argument in *Rail Commuters* had been made earlier; for example, that the Prevention of Family Violence Act of 1993 "has to be understood as obliging the State directly to protect the right of everyone to be free from private or domestic violence."[72] Much followed from the first important case where the obligation of the courts to develop the common law in the light of the constitution was firmly established. Part of the reason that this case, *Carmichele v The Minister of Safety and Security*, was needed was to bring the jurisprudence on the development of the common law into line with the much firmer stand taken by the final consti-

[67] *Certification of the Constitution of the Republic of South Africa*, par. 78.
[68] *Rail Commuters Action Group v Metrorail*, CCT 56/03 (South African Constitutional Court).
[69] *Rail Commuters Action Group v Metrorail*, par. 52.
[70] *Rail Commuters Action Group v Metrorail*, par. 69.
[71] *Rail Commuters Action Group v Metrorail*, par. 88.
[72] *S v Baloyi (Minister of Justice and Another Intervening)*, CCT 29/99 (South African Constitutional Court), par. 11.

tution after the weakness of the court's decision in *Du Plessis* discussed earlier.[73] From *Carmichele* in 2000 onwards, a stream of cases has pushed further this basic approach—that nothing should stand in the way of the instantiation of constitutional values in the working of the law.

Carmichele itself concerned the responsibility of the police to have prevented a rape when they were well advised of its possibility.[74] The court talked of the need to engage in a proportionality exercise balancing community and individual interest, but stressed that "that exercise must now be carried out in accordance with the "spirit, purport and objects of the Bill of Rights," and the relevant factors must be "weighed in the context of a constitutional state founded on dignity, equality and freedom and in which government has positive duties to promote and uphold such values."[75] In the case the court deliberately contrasts its perception of this duty to develop the common law with the Canadian situation and distances itself from American doctrines while expressly supporting the ECHR position in *Osman*.[76] The extent to which the new constitutionally enshrined values are to trump other considerations is given in an extremely interesting suggestion that has much relevance to my main theme here: "under section 39(2) of the Constitution concepts such as 'the wishes . . . and the perceptions . . . of the people' and 'society's notions of what justice demands' might well have to be replaced, or supplemented and enriched by the appropriate norms of the objective value system embodied in the Constitution."[77]

Other cases include giving extra protection for debtors having their house taken by lenders in the procedure of the magistrates' courts,[78] the development of *Grootboom* in an ever extending list of housing protection cases for those who have been forced to occupy land for shantytowns,[79] and even a case where an old law allowing trespassing cattle to be impounded was found constitutionally wanting because of its threat to the livelihood of the very poor.[80] *Modderklip*, mentioned earlier, saw the Constitutional Court dodge the direct issue of horizontal application, though that claim had been accepted in the court below. The case is particularly interesting because it shows the court's continual effort to craft new techniques to deal with the implications of reading the constitution thickly. The Constitutional Court provided what it described as "constitutional damages" by a route alternative to horizontal applicability, suggesting again that the characterisation of rights in such a way is simply not helpful. Land had been occupied by squatters that Modderklip had offered to sell to the local authority. It refused, but both the squatters and the police also refused to enforce the eviction order Modderklip had gained from a court. The Constitutional Court took the interesting line that the rule of law itself

[73] *Carmichele v The Minister of Safety and Security.*

[74] *Carmichele v The Minister of Safety and Security.*

[75] *Carmichele v The Minister of Safety and Security*, par. 43.

[76] *Osman v UK*, 5 BHRC 293 (1998) (European Court of Human Rights).

[77] *Carmichele v The Minister of Safety and Security*, par. 56.

[78] *Zondi v Member of the Executive Council for Traditional and Local Government Affairs*, CCT 73/03 (South African Constitutional Court).

[79] See, e.g., *President of the Republic of South Africa v Modderklip Boerdery (PTY) Ltd.*, CCT 20/04 (South African Constitutional Court).

[80] *Zondi.*

was a value the plaintiff was entitled to have enforced. But, the court argued, eviction was now impossible because the huge number of squatters who had taken advantage of the state's inaction. Consequently the award of damages, which could be replaced by the authority simply buying the land, would satisfy both the land need of the squatters and Modderklip's constitutional entitlement. Whether or not there is a horizontal effect did not need to be decided because

> Section 11 of the Constitution refers to the "supremacy of the constitution and the rule of law" as some of the values that are foundational to our constitutional order. The first aspect that flows from the rule of law is the obligation of the state to provide the necessary mechanisms for citizens to resolve disputes that arise between them.[81]

Though it might in some sense be more satisfactory to have had an outright ruling that Modderklip had an enforceable horizontal constitutional right against the squatters, finding instead a positive right to have the rule of law enforced is yet another example of the drive the court has to find any way that will work to thickly interpret the constitution to ensure the sway of its core values over the society. This right is a true positive right because

> The obligation on the state goes further than the mere provision of the mechanisms and institutions referred to above. It is also obliged to take reasonable steps, where possible, to ensure that large-scale disruptions in the social fabric do not occur in the wake of the execution of court orders, thus undermining the rule of law.[82]

One might sum up South African jurisprudence as amounting to a determination to make all aspects, and all the machinery, of law combine to establish the core values through an understanding that precise differences between types of rights, which are themselves all intermixed, are irrelevant. The values both are themselves rights and underpin any specified rights. Though the court still uses the terminology of socioeconomic or positive rights, little or nothing seems to depend on it.

Transformation and Equality

Throughout almost any opinion of the court runs a repetitive theme—the job of the court is to apply a new type of constitution in a new way. One of the clearest statements, still frequently cited, was in the crucial early case that controversially abolished the death penalty.[83]

[81] *Modderklip*, par. 39.

[82] *Modderklip*, par. 43.

[83] The decision was extremely unpopular, leading to attempts in parliament to hold a national referendum to restore the death penalty. See P Maduna, "The Death Penalty and Human Rights," 1996 12 *South African Journal on Human Rights* 193–217. It remains so, and the court's decision to hold unconstitutional the deportation of someone to the United States without the government getting a guarantee against execution has revived the feelings. See, generally, M Du Plessis, "Between Apology

In some countries, the constitution only formalises, in a legal instrument, a historical consensus of values and aspirations evolved incrementally from a stable and unbroken past to accommodate the needs of the future. The South African constitution is different: it retains from the past only what is defensible and represents a decisive break from, and a ringing rejection of, that part of the past which is disgracefully racist, authoritarian, insular, and repressive, and a vigorous identification of and commitment to a democratic, universalistic, caring, and aspirationally egalitarian ethos expressly articulated in the constitution. The contrast between the past that it repudiates and the future to which it seeks to commit the nation is stark and dramatic.[84]

There are many other cases containing such statements. Justice Albie Sachs, always a good bet for ringing language, said in another early case, discussed later:

> I have no doubt that given the circumstances in which our Constitution came into being, the principles of freedom and equality which it proclaims are intended to be all-pervasive and transformatory in character. We are not dealing with a Constitution whose only or main function is to consolidate and entrench existing common law principles against future legislative invasion. Whatever function constitutions may serve in other countries, in ours it cannot properly be understood as acting simply as a limitation on governmental powers and action.[85]

Kriegler, in his truly radical dissent in the same case, makes a claim for the uniqueness of the South African constitution that is worth reading at length:

> It is therefore no spirit of isolationism which leads me to say that our Constitution is unique in its origins, concepts and aspirations. Nor am I a chauvinist when I describe the negotiation process which gave birth to that Constitution as unique; so, too, the leap from minority rule to representative democracy founded on universal adult suffrage; the Damascene about-turn from executive directed parliamentary supremacy to justiciable constitutionalism and a specialist constitutional court, the ingathering of discarded fragments of the country and the creation of new provinces; and the entrenchment of a true separation and devolution of powers. Nowhere in the world that I am aware of have enemies agreed on a transitional coalition and a controlled two-stage process of constitution building. Therefore, although it is always instructive to see how other countries have arranged their constitutional affairs . . . when I do conduct comparative study, I do so with great caution. The survey is conducted from the point of vantage afforded by the South African Constitution, constructed on unique foundations, built according to a unique design and intended for unique purposes.[86]

---

and Utopia—the Constitutional Court and Public Opinion," 2002 18 *South African Journal on Human Rights* 1–40.

[84] Mahomed in *S v Makwanyane and Another*, CCT 3/94 (South African Constitutional Court).

[85] *Du Plessis*, par. 117.

[86] *Du Plessis*, par. 127.

Not only the reported cases, but extracurial judicial discussion makes clear how strong is this sense that the South African court is doing something new. A powerful example is a lecture given by a member of the Constitutional Court, and now deputy chief justice of the Republic of South Africa, Dikgang Moseneke. He calls for a "creative jurisprudence of equality" to make social justice "a premier foundational value," and argues that "implicit in this proposition is that the constitution enjoins the judiciary to uphold and advance its transformative design."[87] Moseneke is under no illusion that the court's task is easy or uncontroversial: "the meaning of transformation in juridical terms is as highly contested as it is difficult to formulate."[88] It is relevant that Moseneke, though already a judge, was not on the Constitutional Court at the time he gave this lecture, and overtly refers to his struggle not to give a catalogue of their decisions he disagrees with. He readily acknowledges that others too see this as a problem, citing Sachs in a nondiscrimination case where a rich white man argued he was discriminated against. "Just as the transformation of our harsh reality is by its very nature difficult to accomplish, so it is hard to develop a corresponding and appropriate jurisprudence of transition."[89] Sachs was in a minority, not wishing to agree that the man had been discriminated against. (The case is discussed in detail later in the book.) The core idea of the lecture, and of most of the literature that faces up to the idea of transformative jurisprudence, is articulated in a lengthy but vital passage:

> Liberal legalism balks at the idea of transformative adjudication. The primary objection is that such jurisprudence invites judges to accomplish political objectives. The judicial mindset seeks a distinct differentiation between the legislative and the judicial function. On this approach, the judicial function primarily is directed at providing legal interpretation of texts of rules of law as distinct from imposing subjective intellectual, ethical or other preferred views. In liberal jurisprudence, a value driven adjudicative style which permits extra legal considerations is to be avoided. . . . Judicial interpretation under the Constitution has placed different imperatives upon the adjudicator. Austere legalism more suited to interpretation of statutes is not commendable to constitutional interpretation. The intention of the drafter is of little avail in constitutional interpretation. As intimated earlier, the salutary approach to constitutional interpretation is one which provides the most adequate response to the countermajoritarian dilemma by giving effect to the underlying values of the Constitution. It seems to me that our constitutional design of conferring vast powers of judicial review to the courts becomes optimal only if the courts are true to the constitutional mandate. It is argued that, in their work, courts should search for substantive justice, which is to

[87] D Moseneke, "The Fourth Bram Fischer Memorial Lecture: Transformative Adjudication," 2002 18 *South African Journal on Human Rights* 309–19, 314.

[88] Moseneke, "Bram Fischer Memorial Lecture," 315. It is relevant that Moseneke, though a judge, was not on the constitutional court at the time he gave this lecture, and overtly refers to his struggle not to give a catalogue of its decisions he disagrees with.

[89] *City of Pretoria v Walker*, CCT 8/97 (South African Constitutional Court), par. 101.

> be inferred from the foundational values of the Constitution. After all, that is the injunction of the Constitution transformation.[90]

Effectively Moseneke is saying not just that the court *may* be more judicially active than some would prefer, but that it is only legitimate if it is active in making policy choices and imposing values. He adopts precisely the model of constitutions argued for throughout this book. "The constitution is a repository of 'the values which bind its people.'"[91] What these values are we can leave for analysis shortly—it is the core idea of a necessarily value infused adjudication that is crucial at this point. Moseneke seems primarily to be thinking of questions relating to the scope of judicial review, certainly given some of the case references he makes. Thus, the legitimacy of court-enforced "positive" or socioeconomic rights, and of the constitution bearing on relations between nonstate actors, is crucial to his sense of transformatory adjudication. Certainly these issues have produced many of the firmer judicial commitments to such a form of judicial review. Thus the Kriegler citation, from *Du Plessis*, was occasioned by Kriegler's attempt to argue for an extensive "horizontal effect" for constitutional rights. Although both these areas are vital for understanding the nature of South Africa's constitutional jurisprudence, it is more useful to discuss them later, primarily in a comparative context. Little more will be said about them here. The demands of transitional jurisprudence in its supporters' view are that no actor, and no type of right, be excluded from constitutional purview. As Moseneke says, "the ubiquitous sway of the constitution extends to the common law," citing Chaskalson, long the presiding judge of the court: "There is only one system of law. It is shaped by the constitution which is the supreme law, and all law, which includes the common law, derives its force from the constitution and is subject to constitutional control." The common law "must be developed to fulfil the purposes of the constitution."[92]

If judges are to be so important in the working out of the transformation, they must themselves be committed to the new values, as well as to the judicial methodology Moseneke and others regard as necessary. This leads to an unusually open concern for the legal culture within which the courts act. Moseneke makes this point trenchantly:

> The new legal order liberates the judicial function from the confines of the common law, customary law, statutory law or any other law to the extent of its inconsistency with the Constitution. This is an epoch making opportunity which only a few, in my view, of the High Court judges have cared to embrace or grasp. A substantive, deliberate and speedy plan to achieve an appropriate shift of legal culture at the High Courts and Magistrates' Courts is necessary. After all, it is the Constitution that confers substantial review powers on the judiciary. However, without an appropriate legal culture

[90] Moseneke, "Bram Fischer Memorial Lecture," 316.

[91] Moseneke, "Bram Fischer Memorial Lecture," 315.

[92] *Pharmaceutical Manufacturers of South Africa: In re Ex Parte President of the RSA*, CCT 31/99 (South African Constitutional Court), par. 44.

> change the judiciary may become an instrument of social retrogression. In time the judiciary will lose its constitutionally derived legitimacy.[93]

We shall consider this important issue of legal culture shortly. It is necessary first to look more closely at the idea of transformation. However important problems of the scope of judicial rights enforcement may be, they do not go to the heart of both the nature and the problem of transformative jurisprudence. What is to be transformed, and according to what values, by what judicial methodologies? It is far too easy to take the most important brute fact of South Africa—that it was once an apartheid regime and is now governed by a (black) majority—as the whole of the transformation. Were this the case, much of the caseload of the Constitutional Court would disappear, and certainly many of its most controversial and intellectually adventurous decisions. The truth is that the values seen by the judiciary as enshrined in the constitution, the value code towards which South African society is to be transformed with judicial help, are even more wide ranging than the overturning of a history of racial oppression. The constitution is unambiguous in its wide-ranging commitment to equality, and in the court's eyes, this has meant gender and sexual-preference equality every bit as much as it has involved racial equality. And there lies the problem, because the transformation dreamed of, while it may accord with the values of South Africa's intellectual elite, black and white, does not sit easily with entrenched attitudes in the mass public. Nor do other values, second nature to such an elite, necessarily accord with the several cultures of the new South Africa. After all, the very first statement cited here in support of the idea of transformation by judges, from the court's first really major case, was the hotly contested death penalty case. Black or poor, white or rich, the death penalty was no more unpopular with mass opinion in South Africa than, probably, anywhere else in liberal democracy, and certainly as popular as in the United States.[94] When Mahomed in that case talked about "a ringing rejection of that part of the past which is disgracefully racist, authoritarian, insular, and repressive," he was facing the fact that repressive and authoritarian attitudes are not restricted to white racists.

Of course the South African constitution requires the transformation of its society, and the judges' job in that transformation is far bigger than in most constitutional review systems. Constitutions do not typically present themselves as calling for great change. The Canadian Charter of Rights and Freedoms was so clearly presented as just a matter of giving rights a firmer basis that it took a series of cases for the Canadian Supreme Court to establish that rights protection could go further than those rights accepted by Canadian courts before they had a enforceable Charter. The US Bill of Rights itself was thought to do no more than establish existing common-law rights safely in the new system. France's Conseil constitutionnel in its *bloc de constitutionnalité* has worked hard to give its decisions the force of a

[93] Moseneke, "Bram Fischer Memorial Lecture," 318.

[94] JL Gibson and GA Caldeira, "Defenders of Democracy? Legitimacy, Popular Acceptance, and the South African Constitutional Court," 2003 65 *Journal of Politics* 1, 1–30. This article shows how risky the death penalty decision must have seemed at the time for the court's legitimacy.

history reaching back to 1789. East European constitutional courts have variously referred to pre-Soviet constitutional values or to the need to preserve most of the Communist-era law as good law. The German court often leans heavily on Weimar jurisprudence. Yet the very fact of entrenching a statement of rights forces a court to make its society live up to values much more easily assented to in abstract than in concrete situations. What is different about the South African court is both the huge range of changes deemed necessary, and a certain sense of urgency—that, and an openness about what it is doing, a willing transparency about its actions. There is an old story told about the relationship between Britain's radical legal reformer and head of the Appeal Court in the 1960s, Lord Denning. The then senior Law Lord is reputed to have said that what he objected to about Denning was not that he went about changing the law—"we all do that"—but that he "goes about admitting he's doing it." Lord Denning would have been at home on this court. This is not in any way to trivialise the work of the South African court—rather the point here is that studying an overtly transformative jurisprudence is not only of value in its own right, but as a lens through which to see much of what goes on, in a muted way, elsewhere. As chapter 1 made clear, the whole of this book is concerned, in one way or another, with the transformative function of constitutional jurisprudence.

Consider the question of same-sex marriages. This is an issue the Canadian courts have had to deal with over roughly the same time frame that it has concerned the South African courts. After several gender-identity cases in which the court has pecked at the fringes of this hugely symbolic issue, it finally grasped the bullet and ruled, in 2005 that marriage, full marriage and not some form of "civil partnership," could not be denied to any couple who wished it. The arguments, by the litigants on both sides and by the court, are uncannily similar in the two countries. The South African case, *Ministry of Home Affairs v Fourie* in 2005, could be replaced in this analysis with *Halpern v Canada (Attorney General)*, in 2003 with only slight differences in rhetoric.[95] The rhetoric matters, however, in displaying the sense of outrage against the past, and the strong sense that modern South Africa must end all forms of institutionalised discrimination, even if no practical consequences follow from the discrimination. Attacking the idea that enough had already been done to remove practical discrimination against gays, Sachs wrote that

> Finally, our Constitution represents a radical rupture with a past based on intolerance and exclusion, and the movement forward to the acceptance of

[95] *Ministry of Home Affairs v Fourie*, CCT 60/04 (South African Constitutional Court); *Halpern v Canada (Attorney General)* (2003), 65 O.R. (3d) 161 (Ontario Court of Appeal). The cases dealing with the issue substantively are all from provincial courts where the decisions, in favour of same-sex marriages, were not appealed. The Canadian Supreme Court has dealt with the issue only as part of a reference from the federal government asking if the proposed federal act backing these decisions would be constitutional. In this context the Supreme Court had to deal with it only in terms of procedure and separation-of-powers doctrines, though it left no doubt that it agreed with the provincial courts; *Reference re Same-Sex Marriage*, 3 SCR 698 (2004) (Canadian Supreme Court).

> the need to develop a society based on equality and respect by all for all. Small gestures in favour of equality, however meaningful, are not enough.[96]

It is quite hard to characterise the special flavour of South African constitutional argument, a problem the radical critics dissatisfied with the court themselves find. In part it is that the court is concerned not just with the plaintiffs, and removing their suffering, but with the overall society. The cases are vehicles for overall social remodelling, rather than merely problems to be solved:

> In each case, space has been found for members of communities to depart from a majoritarian norm. The point was made in *Christian Education* that these provisions collectively and separately acknowledge the rich tapestry constituted by civil society, indicating in particular that language, culture and religion constitute a strong weave in the overall pattern. For present purposes it needs to be added that acknowledgement of the diversity that flows from different forms of sexual orientation will provide an extra and distinctive thread to the national tapestry. *The strength of the nation envisaged by the Constitution comes from its capacity to embrace all its members with dignity and respect.*[97]

And:

> *Accordingly, what is at stake is not simply a question of removing an injustice experienced by a particular section of the community. At issue is a need to affirm the very character of our society as one based on tolerance and mutual respect.* The test of tolerance is not how one finds space for people with whom, and practices with which, one feels comfortable, but how one accommodates the expression of what is discomfiting.[98]

Albie Sachs, who wrote this, here and elsewhere has written with passion about the need for religious freedom and respect for religion as well as, often, on behalf of gays. He is himself a heterosexual atheist, as probably are his colleagues, all of whom share these views, if only seldom his rhetorical skills.

Another Look at Dignity

Equally important, and equally hard to grasp as an aspect of South African constitutional argument, is the stress the court places on what South African critics call substantive rather than formal equality (a concept found also in Canadian Supreme Court argument). It appears to mean an attempt to understand the full lived experience of those discriminated against. Two of the leading critiques by those who believe that the court strays from its duty define the approach, which they approve of, thus:

[96] *Fourie*, par. 59.
[97] *Fourie*, par. 61.
[98] *Fourie*, par. 38; emphasis added.

> In interpreting and applying substantive equality in its judgments, the Court has rejected a jurisprudence of comparison between abstract individuals in favour of a jurisprudence of context which seeks to understand the impact of an alleged rights violation in the actual circumstances of social life. It has also addressed the question of disadvantage. This connotes an important jurisprudential shift from pure legal liberalism to an accommodation of a more critical framework. In this sense, it can be argued that the Constitutional Court is engaging the boundaries of constitutional jurisprudence in its endeavour to develop an appropriate transformative jurisprudence for South Africa.[99]

It is hard to do more than convey the flavour here. The following passages may help:

> The exclusion of same-sex couples from the benefits and responsibilities of marriage, accordingly, is not a small and tangential inconvenience resulting from a few surviving relics of societal prejudice destined to evaporate like the morning dew. It represents a harsh if oblique statement by the law that same-sex couples are outsiders, and that their need for affirmation and protection of their intimate relations as human beings is somehow less than that of heterosexual couples. It reinforces the wounding notion that they are to be treated as biological oddities, as failed or lapsed human beings who do not fit into normal society, and, as such, do not qualify for the full moral concern and respect that our Constitution seeks to secure for everyone. It signifies that their capacity for love, commitment and accepting responsibility is by definition less worthy of regard than that of heterosexual couples. It should be noted that the intangible damage to same-sex couples is as severe as the material deprivation. To begin with, they are not entitled to celebrate their commitment to each other in a joyous public event recognised by the law. They are obliged to live in a state of legal blankness in which their unions remain unmarked by the showering of presents and the commemoration of anniversaries so celebrated in our culture.[100]

Or:

> It is as if they did not exist as far as the law is concerned. They are implicitly defined out of contemplation as subjects of the law. . . . [The constitution] cannot be read as merely protecting same-sex couples from punishment or stigmatisation. . . . [The rights] also go beyond simply preserving a private space in which gay and lesbian couples may live together without interference from the state. Indeed, what the applicants in this matter seek is not the

[99] C Albertyn and B Goldblatt, "Facing the Challenge of Transformation: Difficulties in the Development of an Indigenous Jurisprudence of Equality," 1998 14 *South African Journal on Human Rights* 248–76, 255.

[100] *Fourie*, par. 72.

right to be left alone, but the right to be acknowledged as equals and to be embraced with dignity by the law.[101]

Not that this stress on substantive equality and understanding the situation is entirely a matter of Weberian *Verstehen.* Sachs carefully lists a host of pragmatic disadvantages of not being a married couple. As he says, the words "'I do' bring the most intense private and voluntary commitment into the most public, law-governed and state-regulated domain." His list includes the reciprocal duty of support; the right of both parties to occupy the joint matrimonial home; rights under insolvency law; rules relating to evidence by spouses against each other. More generally, "Marriage stabilises relationships by protecting the vulnerable partner and introducing equity and security into the relationship" and is a major source of socioeconomic benefits such as the right to inheritance, medical insurance coverage, adoption, access to wrongful death claims, spousal benefits, bereavement leave, tax advantages and post-divorce rights. It is this sort of effort to see deeply into the consequences of discrimination under the law that best characterises South African constitutional jurisprudence.

If part of transformative jurisprudence refers to scope, and part to enforcing core values like that of the right to life, most of the controversy actually comes from the explication and enforcement of this one value: equality. The constitution is seen by everyone as determinably and centrally egalitarian. South Africa is to become a completely egalitarian society—completely in the sense of equal before the law, not necessarily in terms of equality of outcome. It is for this reason that issues like gender equality and equality regardless of sexual identity have been so important in the Constitutional Court's jurisprudence. But this process has been bedevilled by a curious conflict that has emerged over another key word in the constitution—*dignity*. What role does dignity play in the spelling out of core constitutional values? It can be seen at work in *Fourie*, but is often even more important in other arguments.

South Africa is hardly the first country during the renaissance of constitutionalism to rely heavily on the concept of dignity. As we have already seen, it is vital in modern German constitutional thought, and German thinking has much influenced the South Africans, as it has Eastern Europe, where the Hungarian court at least has made rich use of the idea of dignity. In fact the country whose use of the idea most closely parallels South Africa is Canada, whose cases are very frequently cited in the South African court. The idea has even been used by the French Conseil constitutionnel, to the irritation of one of the few English lawyers to discuss the idea, almost inevitably disparagingly.[102] In 1993 the Conseil grounded a ruling that the ideal of protecting human dignity includes a positive duty to take social action to provide conditions in which dignity can flourish—this in a case involving legislative measures to provide decent emergency housing for the homeless. The South African use of the value and right of dignity is discussed comparatively later in the book. A brief account will therefore suffice here. It is important to see

[101] *Fourie*, par. 77.

[102] Feldman, "Human Dignity."

that the South African constitution does treat dignity in this dual way—it is both a prime value that should guide all constitutional adjudication, and a specific right in its own. This is best brought out in an article by Cowan that seeks to moderate the initial concern some had with what they thought as the court's undue reliance on the idea.[103] So important had the criticism seemed at the time, though, that the Constitutional Court had felt the need to defend itself, in a concurring opinion by Sachs, in the first gay equality case.[104] Several major lectures by members of the court have stressed the centrality of dignity to their thinking.

The typical use of "dignity" is in assessing whether some unequal treatment under the law amounts to unconstitutional discrimination. Equality is itself both a right and an interpretive value, but the court has found it easier to use dignity as a yardstick: unequal treatment is discrimination when the treatment is likely to cause a group or individual to be treated as less worthy than others, or seen as less fully valued in society. As some of the argument in the literature has it, equality is a comparative concept, and needs a substantive value to apply to. Much the same thought runs through the Canadian nondiscrimination cases. The criticisms have been twofold: one is that dignity is too slippery and undefined a concept, leading to massive degrees of judicial value injection into constitutional argument; the other is that it is too restrictive, and too individualistic, potentially blinding the court to serious inequalities. Often both criticisms are made at the same time.

Perhaps the best way to get some leverage on this debate, and the general tenor of South African jurisprudence, is to look briefly at the cases most often cited in the literature, and by the court itself, where the equality test was first fully developed. (These cases are considered in detail later in chapter 7.) At this stage we need only be concerned with the role of the dignity concept for South Africans. As it happens, two of the three cases in the paradigm serve to make important points apart from those the South Africans critics themselves note. The first case in the process of building the equality doctrine is curious because of its utter simplicity, involving a complaint about a fire control law. As one critic comments:

> There was probably even less of a lifting of any jurisprudential eyebrow when the judges concluded that the differentiation between owners of land inside fire-control areas and others "cannot, by any stretch of the imagination nation, be seen as impairing the dignity of the owner or occupier of land outside the fire control area." The surprise was rather in the effort that had been undertaken to arrive at this seemingly obvious answer.[105]

[103] Cowan, "Dignity." In many ways this was a reply to a series of earlier articles, including, most importantly, C Albertyn and B Goldblatt, "Development of an Indigenous Jurisprudence of Equality," 1998 14 *South African Journal on Human Rights* 248–76; D Davis, "Equality: The Majesty of Legoland Jurisprudence," 1999 116 *South African Law Journal* 398; and Fagan, "Dignity and Unfair Discrimination."

[104] *National Coalition for Gay and Lesbian Equality v Minister of Justice*, CCT 11/98 (South African Constitutional Court).

[105] The case is *Prinsloo v Van Der Linde*, CCT 4/96 (South African Constitutional Court). The comment comes from Davis, "Equality," n. 45.

In a nutshell, the relevant law treated landowners differently in terms of the legal duties to avoid bushfires according to whether or not their property was in or outside certain zones. As this was the first time the interim constitution's Section 8 protection against discrimination had been tested, the court was forced to find a way of distinguishing differentiation, which all statutes need to contain, from discrimination, forbidden by Section 8(2):

> No person shall be unfairly discriminated against, directly or indirectly, and, without derogating from the generality of this provision, on one or more of the following grounds in particular: race, gender, sex, ethnic or social origin, colour, sexual orientation, age, disability, religion, conscience, belief, culture or language.

The phrase "without derogating from the generality of this provision" clearly indicated that other differentiations could be illicit, but it did not specify which ones. The Canadian court has had exactly the same problem, and has developed a concept of "analogous grounds." The South African court, here more perhaps than in any area, has relied heavily on Canada. The idea of equal dignity was largely imported into Canadian Charter jurisprudence for this purpose, and though it does not use exactly the same argument, the South African court acknowledges its debt. From the beginning it was aware that everything it did had to be done under the light of the need for transformation. The opinion in *Prinsloo* argues that ordinary "'differentiation' . . . very rarely constitutes unfair discrimination in respect of persons subject to such regulation, without the addition of a further element," but places this search for the extra ingredient in a more general understanding of the aims of the new constitution: "the new constitutional order constitutes a bridge away from a culture of authority . . . to a culture of justification."[106] Whatever is used to bridge the conceptual gap between differentiation and discrimination must resonate with the political culture of transformation. Thus dignity, already central to the new constitution, is taken to be the essence of nondiscriminatory behaviour.

> Given the history of this country we are of the view that discrimination has acquired a particular pejorative meaning relating to the unequal treatment of people based on attributes and characteristics attaching to them. We are emerging from a period of our history during which the humanity of the majority of the inhabitants of this country was denied. They were treated as not having inherent worth; as objects whose identities could be arbitrarily defined by those in power rather than as persons of infinite worth. In short, they were denied recognition of their inherent dignity. Although one thinks in the first instance of discrimination on the grounds of race and ethnic origin one should never lose sight in any historical evaluation of other forms of discrimination such as that which has taken place on the grounds of sex and gender. In our view unfair discrimination . . . *principally means treating*

[106] *Prinsloo v Van Der Linde*, pars. 25–27.

> *persons differently in a way which impairs their fundamental dignity as human beings, who are inherently equal in dignity.*[107]

The fact that no one could plausibly argue that there was any loss of dignity in being classified as a landowner owing a special duty of care to avoid bushfires helps the court, which needed a completely nondiscriminatory measure for its first case, so that its powerful legal-cultural argument not be lost in a discussion about whether dignity was involved. It clearly was not, allowing the promotion of its definitional status to stand out clearly.

The briefest look at any case where something like a claim for a loss of dignity can plausibly be made shows how very difficult the doctrine actually is to apply, however necessary it may be to link transformative needs to a cultural understanding of inequality in South Africa. Announced on the same day as *Prinsloo*, for example, was an important case where the power of the president to use his clemency powers was challenged. Nelson Mandela had issued an order giving early release from prison to mothers of young children. It was challenged immediately by a male prisoner with a young son, on the grounds that he was being discriminated against on grounds of sex, a clearly specified ground for finding discrimination.[108] It is not easy to make sense out of *President of the Republic of South Africa v Hugo*, except to suggest that it would have been an awful case on which to base the new equality doctrine. Some of the justices agreed that Hugo was being discriminated against, but that this was justified, some that he was not being discriminated against at all. What was crucial was that Mandela had clearly had noble intentions, and that Hugo was male not female. There were five different opinions in this case, only one of which actually held that Hugo had been discriminated against. The only interesting part is the dispute between a supporter of the majority opinion, O'Regan, and the lone dissenter, Kriegler. O'Regan has probably never missed a chance to find a woman discriminated against. Kriegler had one of the sharpest minds on the court, and was generally a radical thinker. For him the discrimination was apparent in the brute fact that the president had relied on a discriminator, gender and child-rearing practices, in a way that furthered the society's stereotyping. For O'Regan such purism is too early in history, and the mere fact that women do shoulder so much of the burden of child rearing made discrimination in their favour acceptable. As Kriegler says himself, "this is not only a hard case but an awkward one for the development of our equality jurisprudence, one in which its application to reality is slippery." What is at stake in the confrontation between O'Regan and Kriegler is a difficult piece of sociological analysis. For Kriegler:

> In my view the notion relied upon by the President, namely that women are to be regarded as the primary care givers of young children, is a root cause of women's inequality in our society. It is both a result and a cause of prejudice;

[107] *Prinsloo v Van Der Linde*, par. 31; emphasis added.

[108] *President of the Republic of South Africa v Hugo*, CCT 11/96 (South African Constitutional Court).

> a societal attitude which relegates women to a subservient, occupationally inferior yet unceasingly onerous role. It is a relic and a feature of the patriarchy which the Constitution so vehemently condemns. . . . [The constitution was] designed to undermine and not to perpetuate patterns of discrimination of this kind. Indeed I find it startling that the appellants could have placed this fact before the Court in order to establish that their conduct does not constitute unfair discrimination. I would have thought that this is precisely the kind of motive that the respondent might have attempted to divine in the appellant's conduct in order to condemn it.[109]

In contrast O'Regan develops a version of the doctrine where the experience of the groups involved counts more than pure legal logic:

> To determine whether the discrimination is unfair it is necessary to recognise that although the long-term goal of our constitutional order is equal treatment, insisting upon equal treatment in circumstances of established inequality may well result in the entrenchment of that inequality.

And she goes on to say:

> In this case, mothers have been afforded an advantage on the basis of a proposition that is generally speaking true. There is no doubt that the goal of equality entrenched in our constitution would be better served if the responsibilities for child rearing were more fairly shared between fathers and mothers. The simple fact of the matter is that at present they are not. Nor are they likely to be more evenly shared in the near future. For the moment, then, and for some time to come, mothers are going to carry greater burdens than fathers in the rearing of children. We cannot ignore this crucial fact in considering the impact of the discrimination in this case. With respect, therefore, I cannot agree with Kriegler J that it is a "profound and troubling" disadvantage for women when the President says that mothers play a special role in nurturing children. The profound disadvantage lies not in the President's statement, but in the social fact of the role played by mothers in child rearing and, more particularly, in the inequality which results from it.

But of course Kriegler was not trying to produce some formalist theory of equality that ignores the sociology of South Africa—he was trying to argue that one cannot build an egalitarian society with inegalitarian and ad hoc arguments. This is not a case where *dignity* appears much. In the majority opinion it appears only twice. First, the aim of the constitution is defined as "the establishment of a society in which all human beings will be accorded equal dignity and respect regardless of their membership of particular groups."[110] The second time is simply to assert, "it cannot be said that the President's action had not fundamentally im-

[109] *Hugo*, par. 73.
[110] *Hugo*, par. 41.

paired their rights of dignity or sense of equal worth."[111] O'Regan at no point refers to the right or value of dignity.

However the third of the trio of cases where the equality jurisprudence was crafted finds O'Regan in a different situation. Like the other two, the case came under the interim constitution, and the problems have become marginally simpler since the final constitution has been in place. In several cases the problems and uncertainties of the court led the constitution makers to firm up rights the court had been weak about. *Harksen v Lane* in 1997 does not, on the face of it, sound like an issue of pressing constitutional importance even if it is nearer to such a case than *Prinsloo* and is deeply focussed on technical bankruptcy law.[112] The law required that, where a bankrupt had a solvent spouse, all the spouse's property had to come under control of a legal officer, the master in bankruptcy, to prevent fraudulent transfer of funds. Before such a spouse could deal with his or her own property in any way, a court order had to be applied for, taking time and forcing the spouse to incur costs. This was challenged by Mrs Harksen, not by any means a poor or underprivileged person, as unconstitutional. There were several putative grounds, but the only workable one was that as no one else, however related to a bankrupt, was covered by this ban, it amounted to discrimination on the basis of marital status. As with *Prinsloo*, the ground for differentiation, here marital status, was not mentioned in the relevant section of the interim constitution.[113]

Dignity has a dual role to play in this sort of case. First, it is relied on to demonstrate that the categorisation in question is one that is inherently discriminatory. Every justice who wrote in this case agrees that referring to marital status does have the potential to lower dignity, and this involves discrimination. It ought to be noted that part of the concern is not just that a distinction has in the past been used in an antidignitarian way, but that it might in future be if enshrined in law. So Goldstone, for the majority, insists, as part of his definition of the nature of discriminatory categorisations, that

> These grounds have the potential, when manipulated, to demean persons in their inherent humanity and dignity. There is often a complex relationship between these grounds. In some cases they relate to immutable biological attributes or characteristics, in some to the associational life of humans, in some to the intellectual, expressive and religious dimensions of humanity and in some cases to a combination of one or more of these features.[114]

Treating solvent spouses and only solvent spouses as warranting this special legal status does "have the potential to demean persons in their inherent humanity and dignity." But even those distinctions that are found to be discriminatory can be justified—and here dignity comes in again. If one can show that the impact of the discrimination is also likely to damage one's dignity, then it will not be justi-

[111] *Hugo*, par. 49.

[112] *Harksen v Lane NO*, CCT 9/97 (South African Constitutional Court).

[113] Most probably as a result of the difficulties in *Harksen*, the final constitution has added marital status to the list.

[114] *Harksen v Lane NO*, par. 32.

fied. Unfortunately for Mrs Lane the majority held that "the inconvenience and burden of having to resist such a claim does not lead to an impairment of fundamental dignity or constitute an impairment of a comparably serious nature." The dignity claim had not moved from potential to actual. (It may well be thought that having dignity crop up more than once in one constitutional test is rather unnecessary, but that is how the test has been constructed, as we shall see later.) O'Regan and Sachs, the other dissenter, cannot therefore rest with proving the potential for marital status to be a dignity-lowering discriminator—they have to show that it really is such, in the context. O'Regan does this largely by fiat—she simply differentially weighs the impact with little background analysis, though commentators have done a better job of showing how a poor black female spouse would be very much more than inconvenienced by the law.

It fell to Sachs, as often, to show why the marital status discrimination really does affect human dignity. The actual facts of the disadvantage matter relatively little:

> In my view . . . the . . . Act represents more than an inconvenience to or burden upon the solvent spouse. It affronts his or her personal dignity as an independent person within the spousal relationship and perpetuates a vision of marriage rendered archaic by the values of the interim Constitution.[115]

He tries to get inside the spirit of the law in question, noting that

> Its underlying premise is that one business mind is at work within the marriage, not two. This stems from and reinforces a stereotypical view of the marriage relationship which, in the light of the new constitutional values, is demeaning to both spouses.[116]

It is this diminishment of human autonomy in the law that causes the affront to dignity:

> Being trapped in a stereotyped and outdated view of marriage inhibits the capacity for self-realisation of the spouses, affects the quality of their relationship with each other as free and equal persons within the union, and encourages society to look at them not as "a couple" made up of two persons with independent personalities and shared lives, but as "a couple" in which each loses his or her individual existence. If this is not a direct invasion of fundamental dignity it is clearly of comparable impact and seriousness.[117]

As often, it will be noted, it is this driving concern the court has for recreating whole social patterns, for the general transformation of society that is crucial. It is indeed a demand for sociological insight:

> The incremental development of equality jurisprudence presaged by *Prinsloo* requires us to examine on a case by case basis the way in which a chal-

[115] *Harksen v Lane NO*, par. 83.
[116] *Harksen v Lane NO*, par. 85.
[117] *Harksen v Lane NO*, par. 89.

> lenged law impacts on persons belonging to a class contemplated by section 8(2). In particular, it is necessary to evaluate in a contextual manner how the legal underpinnings of social life reduce or enhance the self-worth of persons identified as belonging to such groups.[118]

Finally it is worth noting Sachs's sharp sense of why legal trivia may matter very much indeed:

> The intrusion might indeed seem relatively slight. Yet an oppressive hegemony associated with the grounds contemplated by section 8(2) may be constructed not only, or even mainly, by the grand exercise of naked power. It can also be established by the accumulation of a multiplicity of detailed, but interconnected, impositions, each of which, de-contextualised and on its own, might be so minor as to risk escaping immediate attention, especially by those not disadvantaged by them. The path which this Court embarked upon in *Prinsloo v Van der Linde and Another*[9] and *President of the Republic of South Africa and Another v Hugo*,[10] and as confirmed in the judgment of Goldstone J in the present matter, requires it to pay special regard to patterns of advantage and disadvantage experienced in real life which might not be evident on the face of the legislation itself.[119]

Although the majority considered it necessary to do enough sociology to find that Mrs Harkens was discriminated against, only the minority did enough to convince themselves it mattered. The case shows very clearly both that dignity can be a powerful egalitarian doctrine for constitutional review, and also how unstable it will always be. This is indeed the more general problem, closely involved with the whole stress on substantive rather than formal equality.

Substantive Equality

One of the other criticisms made of the court's reliance on dignity is that such an approach leads it away from "substantive equality." In practise this seems to mean that groups who have not suffered historically may be allowed to plead discrimination against policies intended to help the historic sufferers, and that this ought not to be allowed. One case that, it is argued, shows this is the only one I am aware of where race was successfully challenged as the underlying reason for discrimination—but by a white man, not a black. *City of Pretoria v Walker*, from 1997, is discussed at some length in chapter 7, and only the barebones of it will be mentioned here.[120] Walker complained that he was being discriminated against because the city council selectively enforced debts for water supply against him and others in a rich suburb when it made no real effort to collected back payments from poor black areas. At least on the face, it was a clear-cut case of discrimination. It may

[118] *Harksen v Lane NO*, par. 88.
[119] *Harksen v Lane NO*, par. 89.
[120] *City of Pretoria v Walker*.

well have been a justified policy nonetheless, because the council argued it was trying to cope with a long-standing culture of nonpayment in the poor areas, and Walker did, after all, owe the money.

The majority of the court ultimately, if unhappily, found for Walker. The court indicated that it might have been swayed by the policy arguments, except that "the policy was neither rational, nor coherent, nor an official one. As critics have pointed out, the policy 'was carried out in a secret manner, with no information to the public.' "[121] Partly because of this the court ultimately agreed that the policy "affected (the white residents) in a manner which is at least comparably serious to an invasion of their dignity," and insisted "no members of a racial group should be made to feel that they are not deserving of equal concern, respect and consideration."[122]

One of the more trenchant and radical critiques of the court contains a revealing quotation from a Canadian perspective:

> Perhaps this is the ultimate paradox of the *Charter:* whilst feminist organisations are attempting to develop situated and contextual theories of equality which will address women's social and historical subordination, simultaneously innumerable other litigants, including defendants charged with sexual assault offences and right-to-life organisations, are invoking the *Charter* to claim a formal equality which may well erode victories which feminists believe that they have already won.[123]

There is little doubt that a richly described background may often help judges see a case as "really" about issue X rather than a superficially apparent issue Y. In the *Lawrence* case with which this book begins, Justice Scalia claimed that a law forbidding sodomy between people of the same sex did not discriminate between men and women—it equally forbade men to sodomize men and women to sodomize women.[124] The majority of the court thought the Texas statute discriminated between heterosexuals and homosexuals. This is the sort of "surface versus reality" distinction that plagues antidiscrimination arguments in constitutional jurisprudence. But the surface cannot just be safely ignored.

So much, often beneficial but also potentially dangerous, depends on this idea of "substantive" justice—on what sociologists might refer to as the "framing" of the issues. This is obvious to some of the justices themselves. In a recent case, *Volks v Robinson* considered the inheritance rights of survivors under the Maintenance of Surviving Spouses Act 27 of 1990. Sachs in dissent, supporting Robinson, revealingly says:

> I find myself in disagreement with the judgment both as to the approach utilised and to the conclusion reached, and totally so. This is not because I

[121] I am citing the summary given by the critics of the judgement themselves, Albertyn and Goldblatt, "Facing the Challenge," 260.

[122] *City of Pretoria v Walker*, par. 81.

[123] Cited in Albertyn and Goldblatt, "Facing the Challenge," 250.

[124] *Lawrence v Texas*, 539 U.S. 558 (2003) (US Supreme Court).

would challenge the legal logic used, which appears to be impeccable within the framework adopted. It is because *I would locate the issue in a completely different legal landscape.*[125]

He was not alone in dissent; Sachs is cited so frequently in this chapter more because his style is so clear and dramatic than because he is a maverick—his dissent rate is not much higher than any other justice. (In this case the courts below had all thought the decision in *Harksen* required them to find for Robinson. Sachs's reasons were different, but demonstrably therefore not maverick.) The case is a fine example of framing, and of the reach some of those committed to transformation jurisprudence wish the law to have. The issue was not complex. Robinson was the never married, long-term companion of a man who died leaving her something in his will, but not all that the law would have required had she been married to him. Her argument was discrimination on marital status—a formal marriage to him would have granted something. Her actual status was indistinguishable in all important ways from that of a wife. Therefore the act, new though it was, and though intended to deal with injustice arising from inheritance law, was claimed to be unconstitutional in this respect. The majority were robust in their argument. They recognized the weak and often abused position of women in nonmarried partnerships, and pointed out that no law requires maintenance of such women by their male partners. How then could the law of inheritance impose a duty after death that never existed during life? As the majority opinion said, "The Act applies to persons in respect of whom the deceased person (spouse) would have remained legally liable for maintenance, by operation of law, had he or she not died." Even if discrimination exists in the act, the majority opinion insists, in the context it is not unfair:

> it is not unfair to make a distinction between survivors of a marriage on the one hand, and survivors of a heterosexual cohabitation relationship on the other. In the context of the provision for maintenance of the survivor of a marriage by the estate of the deceased, it is entirely appropriate not to impose a duty upon the estate where none arose by operation of law during the lifetime of the deceased. Such an imposition would be incongruous, unfair, irrational and untenable.[126]

The opinion is also much more robust than often on the use of the dignity argument. Here, though, it is not the value of dignity used in a test constructed by the court, but the direct right to dignity under Section 10 of the constitution that was argued.[127] The writer of the opinion bluntly points out,

> I do not agree that the right to dignity has been infringed. Mrs Robinson is not being told that her dignity is worth less than that of someone who is

[125] *Volks v Robinson*, CCT 12/04 (South African Constitutional Court), par. 151; emphasis added.

[126] *Volks v Robinson*, par. 60.

[127] Constitution of the Republic of South Africa, Section 10: "Everyone has inherent dignity and the right to have their dignity respected and protected."

married. She is simply told that there is a fundamental difference between her relationship and a marriage relationship in relation to maintenance.

This is a powerful point because most discussion on the court, and in many other jurisdictions, takes it for granted that if some category of people are treated less well than others, that in itself reduces their dignity—making the argument from dignity often perilously close to a tautology. The majority's decision was clearly a narrow reading, in the sense that they were restricting a benefit by sticking to a legal perspective. But it is a legal perspective, and the strategy for the dissenters—more fully expressed in the joint opinion of Mokgoro and O'Regan—is equally legal. They just apply a completely different branch of the law, the rapidly developing family law rather than the law of inheritance. One could find an analogous example on any day in the high court of any country where more than one legal framework could be brought to bear on facts. But here it is qualitatively different, because Mokgoro and O'Regan apply a more profoundly transformative power to the decisions of their own court. Their argument is essentially that the whole approach the majority follows fails to understand what the constitution is about. They regard the approach as "defeating"

> the important constitutional purpose played by the prohibition on discrimination on the grounds of marital status. For if it does not constitute unfair discrimination to regulate marriage differently from other relationships in which the same legal obligations are not imposed upon the partners to that relationship by the law, *marriage will inevitably remain privileged. We do not consider this would serve the constitutional purpose of section 9(3), and its prohibition of unfair discrimination on the grounds of marital status.*[128]

Nowhere in *Harkens*, which is the basis for the "prohibition of unfair discrimination on the grounds of marital status," is there a courtwide agreement that marriage should retain any privileged status it might have. Yet to deny that it does do so restricts the transforming power of the court's decisions. *Volks* is not about "substantive" equality in the sense of the majority taking a narrow legalistic position and ignoring facts. Indeed the majority opinion discusses at length the situation of poor women dependent on men who will not marry them. It concludes that they will not be helped by the change in the act Robinson wants. On the other hand the minority position does show a particular cast to how the law can be interpreted if wholesale social change is required. Because O'Regan and Mokgoro have a particular idea in mind about just why the majority approach is wrong, which might be described as holistic (or, in a nonpejorative sense, opportunistic). The problem is not really, they say, that cohabiting partners are not afforded equivalent rights to marriage as stipulated in the act. Rather the problem is that

> neither [the act] nor any other legal rule regulates the rights of surviving partners to cohabitation relationships which were socially and functionally

[128] *Volks v Robinson*, par. 118; emphasis added.

similar to marriage, when those relationships are terminated by death and where that surviving partner is in financial need.

Thus, as the act does in practice take care of spouses, it ought to be extended to others simply to remove a legal void. It is the failure to extend a legal tool that is the constitutional failure. The policy position implied here is very radical—the legislature may not solve problems for some groups while ignoring equivalent suffering for other groups. To do so would be discriminatory because it would be accepting some groups as more worthwhile than those not covered, if an equivalent problem will continue to exist for those others. Sachs's formulation may be more evocative: "Judicial dispassion does not exclude judicial compassion; the question of fairness must be rigorously dealt with, but in a people-centred and not a rule-centred way." But the idea of opportunism applies as well—where something comes up that can be used to make wider social changes, it should be used.

Sachs's previous sentence ran, "The enquiry as to what is fair in our new constitutional democracy accordingly does not pass easily through the eye of the needle of black-letter law."[129] Therein lies perhaps the major problem for the future of South African constitutional jurisdiction—will black-letter law, its practitioners and their habits, ultimately strangle transformation in the face of the extreme relativism of framing? The black-letter restrictive approach is always available, and has its attractions even to the generally progressive men and women who get appointed to the Constitutional Court. There are plenty of examples that would not seem out of place in a much more restrictive judicial world. In *Jordan v The State*, for example, the court split six to five, on the question of whether a law criminalising prostitution breached the gender equality requirement.[130] The majority held it did not, because the law was facially nondiscriminatory—it applied to both male and female prostitutes. The minority found that there was discrimination, because the law, by making prostitution the offence, penalised only one of the actors, the prostitute, and not the client. Thus there was, at least, indirect discrimination, because so very many more prostitutes are women than men. This latter argument was dismissed by the majority on the technically true but empirically unrealistic grounds that the men who consorted with prostitutes could be prosecuted for aiding and abetting the act! As long as decisions like this, and arguments like this, can still be made in the courts, it is uncertain that the search will continue for a frame of reference producing "substantive" justice that will allow transformative judgement. One can understand the anxiety of those who wish South Africa to move rapidly in social progress.

Legal Culture

The general area of problems that arise here is most easily summed up as one of legal culture. This is a concept of great importance throughout this book, relevant to all the countries surveyed. John Bell, for example, has used the concept very

[129] *Volks v Robinson*, par. 152.

[130] *Jordan v The State*, CCT 31/01 (South African Constitutional Court).

powerfully in a recent comparative study of European judiciaries, with no sense that it is an adventurous or contentious concept. Even more relevant may be his study *French Legal Cultures*, because the deliberate plural in his title indicates how complex, partial, and fragmented legal ideologies can be.[131] It is most obviously present in discussions of South Africa. *Legal culture* is somewhat of a sociological term of art, meaning at least partially different things to each analyst who uses it, but there is a general common thrust. A leading critic of South African legal culture defines it this way:

> By *legal culture*, I mean professional sensibilities, habits of mind, and intellectual reflexes: What are the characteristic rhetorical strategies deployed by participants in a given legal setting? What is their repertoire of recurring argumentative moves? What counts as a persuasive legal argument? What types of arguments, possibly valid in other discursive contexts (e.g., in political philosophy), are deemed outside the professional discourse of lawyers? What enduring political and ethical commitments influence professional discourse? What understandings of and assumptions about politics, social life and justice? What "inarticulate premises, are culturally and historically ingrained" in the professional discourse and outlook?[132]

The concern many have is that though the few people on the Constitutional Court are fully engaged in the transformation ideal, the majority of judges in the ordinary courts, and perhaps the bulk of professional lawyers, lag a good way behind. As the quotation suggests, it is not necessarily a matter of the legal professional failing to share political values with the transformers, more that their professional socialisation prevents them fully using and understanding novel ways of thinking about and employing legal doctrines. Another critic with similar concerns has gone so far as to liken the difference in approach between those fully committed to this new jurisprudence and those still wedded to old ways of doing law as akin to the difference between fully autonomous minds and those suffering from a process of brainwashing, where the latter are just unable to conceive of the new law's full potential.[133] The worry is not only shared by the more sociologically attuned scholars like Roederer and Klare. It was evoked by Moseneke in the lecture discussed earlier—indeed as a judge, then of the Pretoria High Court and now deputy chief justice of the Constitutional Court, his concern must be taken seriously:

> This is an epoch making opportunity which only a few, in my view, of the High Court judges have cared to embrace or grasp. A substantive, deliberate and speedy plan to achieve an appropriate shift of legal culture at the High

[131] Bell, *Judiciaries within Europe*; Bell, *French Legal Cultures*.

[132] KE Klare, "Legal Culture and Transformative Constitutionalism," 1998 14 *South African Journal on Human Rights* 146–88. A very interesting application of the idea of legal culture written by a constitutional scholar of France is Bell, *French Legal Cultures*.

[133] CJ Roederer, "Post-matrix Legal Reasoning: Horizontality and the Rule of Values in South African Law," 2003 19 *South African Journal on Human Rights* 57–81.

> Courts and Magistrates' Courts is necessary. After all, it is the Constitution that confers substantial review powers on the judiciary. However, without an appropriate legal culture change the judiciary may become an instrument of social retrogression. In time the judiciary will lose its constitutionally derived legitimacy.[134]

Similar warnings about the extent to which the bulk of the South African judiciary is really capable of using the new possibilities, even if it shares the core values, abound in the more "mainstream," even the highly technical, legal literature. It is precisely because it concerns those involved in technical constitutional argument that it matters most. In the end the details matter tremendously—a really effective legal transformation requires the technicians, not just the Albie Sachses and Kate O'Regans of the court, or the consciously "post-modern" legal philosophers in the journals, to embrace new ways of legal thinking. One of the most pressing statements of concern comes from the author of a complex article on such detailed adjudicatory puzzles. The very title of the article "Progressive Indirect Horizontal Application of the Bill of Rights" speaks to its technical respectability. Yet its author ends with the following anxiety.

> Heaven forbid that our legal system become the function of a rivalry between a reactionary common-law judiciary and a progressive Constitutional Court. Heaven of course also forbid that our legal system become the function of co-operation between a reactionary common-law and reactionary constitutional-law judiciary, but let us rather not even think about this possibility for now.[135]

Van de Walk is slightly disingenuous—he is somewhat of a critic of the Constitutional Court as well as of the common-law courts, being one of those who object to the court interpreting away the minimum core approach. He has described it as showing that "artful evasions in the face of burning questions are not beyond the judges of the Constitutional Court," and insisting that "There is certainly no rule or principle of constitutional interpretation that required this move."[136] It is this fear that the legal establishment, including at times the Constitutional Court itself, is involved in "artful evasions" that fuels many people's worries about legal culture. Although much of the discussion is set at a rather unspecific and abstract level, there is a concrete problem of constitutional interpretation and application that focuses anxieties about the width and depth of legal commitment to transformation. In fact it is what Van der Walt's article is about, what C. J. Roederer's "Post-Matrix Legal Reasoning" concentrates on, an issue that has bedevilled the full development of South African constitutional law since the earliest case in

[134] Moseneke, "Bram Fischer Memorial Lecture," 318.

[135] J Van Der Walt, "Progressive Indirect Horizontal Application of the Bill of Rights: Towards a Co-operative Relation between Common-Law and Constitutional Jurisprudence," 2001 17 *South African Journal on Human Rights* 341–63.

[136] Van Der Walt, "Progressive Indirect Horizontal Application," 351 n. 29. As it is one of those articles with much of the argument carried on in the footnotes, it is fair to cite him for this.

which the court disappointed its more radical or optimistic critics. It is the same issue as concerned the Canadian Supreme Court's most criticised early decision in *Dolphin*, the issue of whether or not constitutional rules apply in conflicts between individuals as well as between individuals and the state, usually known as the debate over "horizontal effect." The South African cases on this start with *Du Plessis v De Klerk* in 1995 and have not ended yet. Only a part of the debate is touched on here; it helps explain the whole concern over legal culture, especially in South Africa. A later section of this chapter deals more fully with legal culture, which is visited again in chapter 8. Both countries face the issue because both are examples of a common-law jurisdiction used to a highly positivistic legal culture without real constitutional review, overnight having to meld such a common-law base into a constitutional supremacy polity.

No one sees the Canadian Charter of Rights and Freedoms as having remotely the same transformative goal as the South African constitution, yet the problems are much the same, if in a diluted way. The South African version can be put in a nutshell. If South Africa is to be transformed legally into an egalitarian society based on dignity, what about the mass or ordinary law, the common law, which much more frequently affects ordinary people in their daily lives than the constitution itself does? Van der Walk discusses a judgement he believed fell outside the new legal culture, though correct in its result, and which he thought echoed the mistake made in *Du Plessis*:

> Is there a stratum of social life outside the scope of legal relationships which for this reason does not engage the application of the Bill of Rights? Is it so that there are social relations between private individuals which do not found causes of action and on which the law for this reason, and the 1996 Constitution for that matter . . . have no bearing?[137]

There are actually two types of situations covered here. One is where there is an existing common law covering some conflict between two individuals, but which is thought by one or other of them not to live up to the new constitutional values. The other type of conflict is where there is no existing common law or statutory rule at all, and yet one party to the conflict thinks the other person's actions are similarly in conflict with the values of the new constitution. It is a particular issue in South African jurisprudence because the constitution can clearly be seen not to accept such a situation. Section 8 of the final constitution was drafted specifically because the framers were concerned that court decisions under the interim constitution had not fully developed the idea of constitutional permeation of common law. It was in fact the decision in *Du Plessis* that was seen as requiring the toughening of language in the final constitution. Insisting that the Bill of Rights binds all state actors (including the courts) and applies to all law, Section 8(3) provides that

> When applying a provision of the Bill of Rights to a natural or juristic person in terms of subsection (2), a court . . . in order to give effect to a right in the

[137] Van Der Walt, "Progressive Indirect Horizontal Application," 354.

Bill, must apply, or if necessary develop, the common law to the extent that legislation does not give effect to that right.

There has been an ongoing debate, both in the journals and indeed in the court, about exactly what this requires. The debate at times becomes so rarefied that there is no point in trying to follow it here. At base it is between those who favour a "direct" as opposed to an "indirect" horizontality. A direct horizontality essentially means that a citizen can ask the courts to make a decision based directly on the constitution to uphold his or her rights against another citizen. Indirect horizontality means that the sub-constitutional law must be used, and modified by the ordinary courts if it clashes with the constitution. One might be forgiven for thinking the difference is trivial—many of the professional articles come to this conclusion as well. After all, even if it is up to the ordinary courts to modify the common law in the light of the constitution, when they fail to do so, there must be an appeal to the Constitutional Court on precisely that matter. The difference is not entirely and always a trivial matter, for it may often be the wrong approach to ask for a constitutional judgement when the ordinary law, modified if necessary, will do.

There was one case that demonstrates this well—where someone who stood to gain damages for police brutality under the common law sought *also* to be awarded damages for breach of his right not to be tortured under the constitution. These damages, which came to be called "constitutional damages," were asked for as a mark that the state itself had done wrong, and were not justified, even by the plaintiff, as required to compensate him for actual harm.[138] The Witwatersrand Local Division of the Supreme Court had refused this request, and the Constitutional Court upheld that decision. The decision is said to be evidence that the Constitutional Court favours indirect horizontality, which it may well do. Had it found otherwise, the decision would be cited as evidence of a failure of the ordinary courts fully to engage in the new legal culture. The truth is that the Constitutional Court itself, by these standards, fails to believe in its own culture—this was established at the beginning, when *Du Plessis* failed to impose direct horizontal effect. Much of the confusion has come from the unwillingness of the Constitutional Court to use its powers to supersede common law where the dispute is between citizens, and the state has not formally been a party in the litigation. Yet the same court has at other times been fully prepared to make the constitution influence common law. So, for example, in a case where rail commuters sued both police and the (nationalised) commuter railway for failing to protect travellers from criminal attacks, the Constitutional Court insisted that the statutory duties involved had to be interpreted through the constitutional rights to safety. In so doing it overturned the Supreme Court of Appeal, which had found for the authorities. But *that* court had overturned the original judgement in the High Court that itself recognised the role of the constitution.[139] Constitutional damages have indeed been awarded by the court in supporting the claim by a landowner that the local authority had done

[138] *Fose v Minister of Safety and Security*, CCT 14/96 (South African Constitutional Court).

[139] *Carmichele v The Minister of Safety and Security*.

nothing to protect him against squatters seizing his farmland.[140] In the latter case the courts below had all thought the same thing.

Perhaps the strongest evidence that the Constitutional Court will force ordinary courts to develop the law if they do not so willingly comes from a case where a woman, raped by on-duty police officers, tried to make the state itself liable because of her constitutional rights. The courts below had all held she had no cause of action against the state itself. The Constitutional Court disagreed, even though that was accepted as a correct common-law decision unless one read in a constitutionally imposed alteration. The trouble was that the plaintiff had not in fact made the constitutional argument in the ordinary courts. Nonetheless the constitutional court held the lower courts had a duty to have done so on their own initiative.[141]

There have been several more cases where "ordinary" law has been modified to grant constitutional rights between citizens by the Constitutional Court, sometimes overturning, sometimes supporting, the lower courts. It is in fact a major research problem to estimate how fully the new legal culture has permeated ordinary courts. Of course one could simply look at appeals and count how many times a plaintiff has succeeded in getting a court to give a decision it would not have given without the constitutional change, but this implies tremendous difficulties in asserting counterfactuals. It is not a trivial problem, however, and cannot be ignored. One constitutional court, the Hungarian, has taken serious note of the gap between what legal theory might expect and what actually happens in the courts, and developed the idea of "law in action" against which to measure the necessary steps they should take in promulgating constitutional law. We can, though, ask the following question. Why has the South African Constitutional Court been as cautious as it has in imposing constitutional rights on the common law? And why might there be a problem with the depth and reach of the constitutional legal culture?

One problem is that the South African Constitutional Court has a double problem in ensuring the reach of its jurisprudence. It is a "Kelsen court," set apart from the ordinary hierarchy of courts rather than being the summit of that hierarchy staffed with the same sorts of people. As such it has the problems that are found, for example, throughout Eastern Europe, and possibly even in Germany, of envy and resentment that decisions may be reversed by newcomers outside the professional chain of most judges. It had to be created as such for the same reason the Eastern European constitutional courts were organized on that model—because there was fear on the part of a significant element of the political class that the ordinary courts and ordinary judges would not be fully engaged with the spirit of the constitution. The existing court system was not trusted to be sympathetic to the imperative of transformation. In such an institutional context it behoves the new court to tread warily and seek to build it legitimacy within the legal profession.

That might be enough of a problem, but the court is unique in having such a role inside a common-law culture. Common lawyers, whether in England, South

[140] *Modderklip.*

[141] *Carmichele v The Minister of Safety and Security.*

Africa, Canada, or Australia have a pride in the creative problem-solving power of their centuries-old legal tradition. We saw the problems this has caused for the Canadian Supreme Court in the last chapter. Throughout this domain there is a tendency to believe that the common law can protect rights every bit as well, if not better, than any constitution, which is seen as much more like the imposition of the codified legal systems of the European continent. In the United Kingdom, for example, in the years before and immediately after the Human Rights Act incorporated the European Convention on Human Rights into English law, the House of Lords would go to enormous lengths in their opinions to find common-law rights to support their decisions, and to trumpet the fact that they had no need of the European Convention.[142] Even the continental systems have some such problems—the German equivalent to horizontal effect has often been criticised as unnecessary given the capacities of the German code, and as we have seen, the French Conseil constitutionnel took some time to become legitimate in the eyes of its rival, the Conseil d'Etat. The South African Constitutional Court, for all its members are political radicals, consists entirely of people whose legal training and experience was, until their elevation to it, as practitioners of the South African brand of common law, and they write opinions for lawyers even more thoroughly steeped in its traditions. Even if they did not have to tread carefully not to alienate their fellow lawyers on whose support they are dependent, they would not find it easy themselves always to think outside that box. And yet it is quite crucial that the constitutional values come to permeate the whole of South African legal thinking, else there is a real danger that a failure of this legal culture would

> leave individuals free to perpetuate advantages, privileges and relations, quite immune from the discipline of [the constitution]

because

> in practical terms, the average South African may now be more likely on a day-to-day basis to have her or his human dignity and other fundamental rights threatened by the actions of entities and individuals who are not in any sense organs of state, than by agents clothed with public power.

Both of these quotations come from the majority opinions in *Du Plessis*, where the problem may be said to have started.[143]

[142] See Robertson, *Judicial Discretion.*

[143] *Du Plessis*. The first is from Mahomed, par. 75 and the second from Mokgoro, par. 168.

CHAPTER SEVEN

Tests of Unconstitutionality and Discrimination

Democracy must infringe certain fundamental values in order to maintain others. It is important for judges to know how foreign law treats this question and what techniques it uses. Does it employ a technique of balancing or of categorization? Why is one technique preferred over another? Every legal system grapples with the issue of constitutional limitations on human rights. What are these limitations and what technique was used to reach them?

—Aharon Barak, "Response to *The Judge as Comparatist*"[1]

The Need to Limit Rights

At the heart of constitutional review lies the fact that no rights are absolute, and government must go on, though constitutional texts and the traditions of constitutional law often hide this. The truth is that the underlying reality, what the Hungarians call "the living law," of even the strongest bills of rights might better be translated as something like: "The following list of rights indicate things governments really shouldn't do unless they absolutely have to." If this is true of most rights, it is even more true of the right against discriminatory or unequal treatment. All legislation, all policymaking, is inherently discriminatory. Something is taken from, given to, allowed to, prohibited to, some category of people for the good of other people. Some constitutions acknowledge this trade-off openly, by containing a form of limitations clause. Limitations clauses occupy a middle ground on a spectrum that we can imagine characterising the national differences in how constitutional policing of government policy is characterised. At one end there are systems like that of the United States, where there is no formal acknowledgement of the need to treat rights as less than absolute. Such systems have judicially created "tests" or doctrines that operate by defining and redefining rights so that some government action turns out not actually to breach what the right is "really" about. The other end of the spectrum consists of countries where, in the constitution itself, but more usually by judicial interpretation, rights and poli-

[1] A Barak, "Response to *The Judge as Comparatist*: Comparison in Public Law," 2005 80 *Tulane Law Review* 195–202, 197.

cies are seen as always involving a balancing act by the courts, most probably by the use of a concept like proportionality. In the middle are the limitation clause systems where an attempt is made to spell out the conditions under which a right must make way for legislation. This chapter is an attempt to describe the positions on this spectrum, and to ask whether they can in reality be distinguished, and whether it actually matters where a country lies on it. Are all methods of deciding when a right trumps policy essentially the same? Do the tests really do the intellectual work, that is, do they lead very clearly to particular decisions, or do they only serve to shape the contours of the discussion? Are they quite illusory, nothing more than formulae in which to announce decisions that come from other intellectual processes or from judicial gut feelings?

Tests that make legislation harder to get past a constitutional screening mechanism arguably show a more powerful court than permissive tests suggest. But this is not itself a causal statement—the power of the courts is unlikely to stem just from the tests they use. It may be more accurate to take the power of the tests used as an indicator of court power: only powerful courts can apply rigorous tests to constitutionally dubious legislation. Nonetheless it is unlikely that tests are never more than symptoms. Given the huge importance of the intellectual apparatus a court develops to do its work, the power of tests they devise, or are required to apply by the constitutional text, will itself feed back into doctrine and shape further decisions.[2] Even if one believes that the members of constitutional tribunals, by and large, just exercise their ideological intuitions in coming to decisions, they have to express these decisions in the language of constitutional jurisprudence. In so doing jurists have to be very careful because the really important thing about a constitutional decision is not the result in the instant case. Rather it is the way the decision in the specific case will influence and control the much larger number of future cases that will be dealt with routinely by lower courts. Indeed the constitutional tribunal must at least hope that what it says will prevent politicians and civil servants from even drafting legislation that might cause a future law case. This is where tests are peculiarly important. The initial pronouncement of a test might be more or less a dressing up of intuition. But for future lower-court judges it becomes something they have to apply to justify their decisions; and for legislators and administrators it becomes literally a test, or gauge, through which they have to steer their projects. As evidence of this, we have seen how closely provincial and federal civil servants in Canada studied early discrimination judgements by the Supreme Court.[3]

This chapter primarily examines the standard constitutional tests used in Germany, South Africa, and Canada, with some additional comments on France. Though it could be argued tests do not exist in France, it shows the contrast with systems that rely more directly on pure "proportionality" to do the work. By this

[2] From the viewpoint of normative constitutional theorists this entire field and especially the later sections on "proportionality analysis" are most interestingly and powerfully discussed in R Alexy, *A Theory of Constitutional Rights* (Oxford: Oxford University Press, 2002).

[3] See, for example, the discussion in PJ Monahan and M Finkelstein, "The Charter of Rights and Public Policy in Canada," 1992 30 *Osgood Hall Law Journal* 501–46.

I mean that an idea, "proportionality," which lies within many more rigidly structured tests and which I develop shortly, may in fact be all that is ever really at work. These new systems are most usefully seen in contrast with the United States. What follows is necessarily lengthy because of the need as fully as possible to survey the different approaches to be found to limiting constitutional rights.

The Argument in Brief

The first stage is to identify a difference between the United States and some other liberal democracies. The US Supreme Court has been characterised as having developed "a complex, increasingly code-like sprawl of two-, three-, and four-part tests, each with its limited domain."[4] In contrast, other countries attempt to develop a single principled method to analyze the acceptability of incursions into rights. In the United States the concentration is almost entirely on whether a presumption in favour of judicial deference to the constitution can be overridden.[5] Elsewhere the concentration is often on the applicability of an overriding value, usually either "democracy" or "dignity." In many countries even this approach gives way to an analytically simple idea that all rights limitations must be "balanced" or that such limitation is always allowable, but only ever where it is "proportional." The United States has elements of both balancing and proportionality doctrine, but always constrained by the "tests"; other countries sometimes use intellectual constructs very similar to US-style tests, but only as an aid to the more general analysis. Apart from investigating the different ways these approaches work, we need to keep in mind the core question of whether any of these approaches and distinctions actually make any real difference.

The huge and historically prior constitutional jurisprudence of the US Supreme Court lies like a shadow over all others. For it is in this first of all constitutional review systems that the attempt to automate constitutional decisions, in part to hide the creativity of the process, started and has been perhaps most problematic. American jurisprudence has also the best-known and "clearest" tests, and serves as a vital contrast to the more nuanced attempts of other jurisdictions. Though antidiscrimination legislation is a major context in which tests for limiting rights apply, I also compare tests used for judicial limitation of speech rights. A contrast such as this is necessary precisely because, while no state can avoid discrimination, some at least think that all states should avoid censorship. It is also true that many problems can be seen as either matters of discrimination or as straightforward protection of rights. The very first case mentioned in this book, which was also from America, is *Lawrence v Texas*, on the right to private sexual freedom.[6] But one of the opinions in the case analysed the issues entirely from a nondiscrimination perspective, a choice of strategy explicitly rejected by the majority of justices. The majority did not reject it because they thought it wrong, but because it would

[4] RH Fallon, "Implementing the Constitution," 1997 111 *Harvard Law Review* 54–152, 56.

[5] Roosevelt, *Myth of Judicial Activism*.

[6] *Lawrence v Texas*, 539 U.S. 558 (2003) (US Supreme Court).

not take them as far in changing the law as concentrating directly on the rights claim. Naturally the following country sections do not pretend to be adequate accounts of the actual constitutional law in the jurisdictions in common; they are mere sketches, used to demonstrate models and approaches for theoretical examination. Unfortunately they are necessarily long sketches, in order fully to draw out the complexity of this whole area of constitutional argument, and the numerous problems befalling all courts faced with the issues.

Constitutional Tests in the United States

America versus the World

It must be said at the beginning of this section that American jurisprudence on the subject of constitutional testing is enormous, enormously rich, and often enormously difficult. This applies both to the actual mass of judicial pronouncement and argument, and the even greater mass of the scholarly treatments. One leading article, Richard Fallon's hugely influential 1997 study, identifies no less than eight major groupings of tests.[7] These are forbidden-content tests, suspect-content tests, balancing tests, non-suspect-content tests, effects tests, appropriate-deliberation tests, purpose tests, and aim tests. Each of them is subdivided. In this plethora of methods of testing legislation almost everything that occurs in different guises elsewhere in democratic constitutionalism can probably be found by analogy. Nonetheless they are all roughly the same in structure, and all of them are needed because America lacks the approach used in almost all other liberal democracies. Much of this chapter is involved in spelling out this crucial difference. It goes without saying that this section does not attempt a full portrayal of the American approach. What follows are typical examples of US testing from a tiny number of cases, chosen to raise basic questions. Most American commentators, it is safe to say, find it either difficult or unrewarding to think about constitutional limitations without the mechanism of doctrinal tests. Even a book for laymen, Kermit Roosevelt's recent brilliant account of judicial decisions, *The Myth of Judicial Activism*, is wedded to the common approach.[8] In his own terms Roosevelt argues that all constitutional decisions are really about whether the court should defer to the legislature, and that they must always use tests, and tests of relatively simple logical form, to answer this core question.

Given this reliance on tests, it is ironic that one of the most familiar American judicial statements in the area of testing is actually a refusal to apply any test at all.[9]

[7] Fallon, "Implementing the Constitution." Similar treatments can be found in K Roosevelt, "Constitutional Calcification: How the Law Becomes What the Court Does," 2005 91 *Virginia Law Review* 1649–1710; or MN Berman, "Constitutional Decision Rules," 2004 90 *Virginia Law Review* 1–139.

[8] Roosevelt, *Myth of Judicial Activism*.

[9] There is an enormous literature on how US constitutional review works. A vital article concerned with some of the issues here is RH Fallon, "Individual Rights and the Powers of Government," 1993 27 *Georgia Law Review* 343.

This is Justice Black's repeated refusals to allow any statute to limit First Amendment speech rights by insisting on a literal reading of the amendment. To Black the phrase "congress shall make no law . . . abridging the freedom of speech, or of the press" meant exactly what it says, and enabled him repeatedly to reject any governmental interference with such matters. Black was not invariably opposed to creative interpretation and recognized that in some areas the constitution did not allow of literal interpretation—and then he was amongst the most creative of constitutional judges.[10] The difference between Black and his colleagues was that in the First Amendment case he saw no justification for writing into the founders' language some extra phrase. He was not impressed with the idea that a court could allow such infringement when it detected, for example, "a clear and present danger" to society. Black, of course, had been scarred as a Democratic senator by the court's too eager interpretation of the constitution to thwart the New Deal. He did not sit on the court during and immediately after World War I, when the clear and present danger test was crafted by Oliver Wendell Holmes in considering the constitutionality of the 1917 Espionage Act.[11] This act provided for prison sentences for those who distributed antimilitary leaflets to army volunteers. Agreeing that such activities threatened recruitment in a time of national emergency, the court accepted its constitutionality. The "clear and present danger" test, hardly ever actually used in those words, was meant to indicate that where there was great immediacy of a real threat, the First Amendment rights had to give way. The clear and present danger test was replaced, ultimately, by a more subtle First Amendment jurisprudence and by tests designed according to the overall architecture that most US tests of constitutionality have taken on.[12] Black's approach, which was to identify the few absolutes in the constitution and stick rigidly to them, was possible only because the US constitution does not, on its face, accept any limitation to rights—hence the need to ignore Black's style of argument and craft doctrines like clear and present danger. When some real or perceived danger as severe as an interruption to recruitment during a war comes along, the Supreme Court not only has to invent doctrine, by to justify the very right to have such a doctrine of limitations, putting itself always at the mercy of strict constructionism. It is always easier to argue that one's judicial brethren should not be making a certain type of argument *at all* than to show that their argument is actually wrong, and then to have to provide a better way of dealing with a problem.

This is where US jurisprudence is most different from that of perhaps all other constitutional courts. The drafters of more modern constitutions have not thought in terms of absolute rights. Thus Article 10 of the European Convention on Human Rights, which gives speech rights equivalent to the First Amendment in clause 1, goes on in clause 2 to say

[10] T Yarbrough, *Mr Justice Black and His Critics* (Durham, N.C.: Duke University Press, 1988).

[11] *Schenck v United States*, 249 US 47 (1919) (US Supreme Court).

[12] *Clear and present* was taken up into a general jurisprudence of speech issues connected to hate and violence, and over fifty years became the modern incitement rule in *Brandenburg v Ohio*, 395 US 444 (1969) (US Supreme Court).

> the exercise of these freedoms . . . may be subject to such formalities, conditions, restrictions or penalties as are prescribed by law and are necessary in a democratic society, in the interests of national security, territorial integrity or public safety, for the prevention of disorder or crime, for the protection of health or morals for the protection of the reputation of others, for preventing the disclosure of information received in confidence, or for maintaining the authority and impartiality of the judiciary.

The American constitution does not even include the broader acceptance that rights cannot be completely incapable of limitation contained in Article 1 of the Canadian Charter, which reads:

> The Canadian Charter of Rights and Freedoms guarantees the rights and freedoms set out in it subject *only to such reasonable limits prescribed by law and as can be demonstrably justified in a free and democratic society.* (Emphasis added)

The nearest most modern constitutions come to treating rights as absolute is in a form of words apparently originating in the German constitution, by which, though limitations are accepted, they must never breach the "essential content."[13] This rule is hardly ever used in Germany, and other jurisdictions with it, like Hungary, make little more use. Indeed, though South Africa had it in the interim constitution, it was dropped from the final version, probably because of the difficulty judges had in applying it, from the earliest of their major cases.[14]

The European Convention, as with other modern rights documents, effectively imposes an ordering of rights, because the first few do not have the "subject to such . . ." limitation, but the US constitution recognizes no ranking of importance in its Bill of Rights.[15] Thus the US court has had to struggle to find ways of allowing governments, state as well as federal, to do certain things sometimes that it forbids them to do at other times. It has produced no overall doctrine of when a right can be breached but instead has created a whole set of constitutional tests. There are dozens, perhaps hundreds, of subject-specific tests, just as there hundreds of tests in common law and statutory interpretation to standardise the application of precedent and the reading of legislation. Over the last half century, however, these tests have been polished and standardised so that most adhere to a general

[13] German Basic Law, Article 19, "(1) Insofar as under this Basic Law a basic right may be restricted by or pursuant to a law, . . . (2) In no case may a basic right be infringed upon in its essential content."

[14] See, for example, *S v Makwanyane and Another*, CCT 3/94 (South African Constitutional Court), especially Chaskalson, par. 133, and Ackerman, par. 298.

[15] This is not to say that there is no use of American-style tests elsewhere. It has even been powerfully argued that the ECHR itself ought to use an American-style "strict scrutiny" test. See O Gross and F Ní Aoláin, "From Discretion to Scrutiny: Revising the Application of the Margin of Appreciation Doctrine in the Context of Article 15 of the European Convention on Human Rights," 2001 23 *Human Rights Quarterly* 625–49. Many commentators think the jurisprudence of the German constitutional court in this area amounts to the use of levels-of-scrutiny tests. See S Baer, "Equality: The Jurisprudence of the German Constitutional Court," 1999 5 *Columbia Journal of European Law* 249. This is discussed in detail later.

formula that tends to have the effect, compared with other jurisdictions, of making some rights virtually impregnable but making others much less strongly protected by the constitution. The general form of a constitutional test in the United States, whether for a specific right or for the general right against discrimination, revolves around the idea of the court's duty of scrutiny. Originally developed to handle claims of discrimination, especially racial discrimination, under the Fourteenth Amendment, scrutiny tests come at two, or sometimes three, levels; strict scrutiny, ordinary (or minimum) scrutiny, and, occasionally, an intermediate level of "heightened scrutiny."

The Idea of Scrutiny

The essence of the scrutiny test is a triple analysis—how important is the governmental goal pursued, how important is the threatened constitutional right, and how appropriate/necessary/suitable is the means suggested, especially the classification of citizens involved. Strict scrutiny, the test originally applied to putative racial discrimination, forbids any discrimination based on race categories unless the government can prove that the categorisation is "closely related" to a "compelling government interest," where "closely related" usually means that the legislation involves the least intrusive or least restrictive means to achieve this compelling end. The early history of the test is instructive. It was first hinted at in a case from 1938, the year after the Supreme Court gave up the practise of strictly investigating government economic legislation in favour of outright deference to Congress. In a famous footnote to an otherwise unimportant case, the court indicated that there might be situations where there would be "a narrower scope for the presumption of constitutionality." Three such situations were outlined: where there was a specific prohibition in the Bill of Rights; where legislation threatened the democratic process; and where, as for example with religious or racial minorities, there might be prejudice against "discrete and insular minorities." This latter was a very clearly political problem, because the prejudice might be one that threatens "seriously to curtail the operation of those political processes ordinarily to be relied upon to protect minorities, and which may call for a correspondingly more searching judicial inquiry." In other words deference to Congress can only be overcome when there is reason to think that Congress is not functioning properly.[16] *Carolene Products* was about interstate transport of impure foods. In what is both the best article on this famous footnote, and possibly the most literate article in any law review, Jack Baldwin describes the whole process of discrimination jurisprudence with words that could be the theme for this entire book:

> The goal of *Carolene Products* is to restore them [excluded groups] to their rightful place within the polity through judicial supervision of the results of the democratic process. The role of the judiciary is to exclude legislation

[16] *Carolene Products v United States*, 304 US 144 (1938) (US Supreme Court). Only four of the justices agreed to the footnote, but it has been quoted endlessly since.

> which is the result of impurities in the process, and by this exclusion, include those persons previously excluded, or prevent their future exclusion.[17]

Where discrimination is involved, strict scrutiny will also require an analysis that shows that the classification is neither over- nor underinclusive: it does not affect more people or a wider range of people than necessary, and it does not leave out some who ought to be affected if anyone is to be. This test is used not only to assess discriminatory measures, but any infringement on a "fundamental constitutional right." In effect it is like Black's rights-absolutism, because it is virtually impossible to challenge. Apart from anything else, where a plaintiff can persuade the courts that the test is the relevant one, the burden of proof then falls on the government to show that it does satisfy the "close and compelling aspects," rather than the plaintiff having to show that government action does not do so. In the Supreme Court's own words:

> Requiring a State to demonstrate a compelling interest and show that it has adopted the least restrictive means of achieving that interest is the most demanding test known to constitutional law.[18]

So seldom has any legislation passed the strict scrutiny test that a leading commentator described it, as early as the 1970s, as "strict in theory and fatal in fact."[19] It may be that the court is beginning to loosen its application of strict scrutiny. In 2003 many were surprised when a case involving race-based quotas for entry to law school came up.[20] The court agreed that strict scrutiny was applicable, but went on to find both a compelling interest—providing a heterogeneous student body—and that an admissions system that took race into account could, under special conditions, be sufficiently narrowly tailored. As one commentator said, just before the case was heard:

> No legal doctrine is more familiar to the student of constitutional law than the strict scrutiny test. Its twin requirements of "compelling purpose" and "narrow tailoring" for racially discriminatory laws are the stuff of which multiple-choice questions on bar examinations are made.[21]

[17] JM Balkin, "The Footnote," 1989 83 *Northwestern University Law Review* 1, 275–320, at 283.

[18] *Employment Div., Dept. of Human Resources of Oregon v Smith*, 494 US 872 (1990) (US Supreme Court).

[19] G Gunther, "Foreword: In Search of Evolving Doctrine on a Changing Court: A Model for a Newer Equal Protection," 1972 86 *Harvard Law Review* 1. The test was in fact created on what may be its only example of a government passing it, in the infamous consent of the Supreme Court to the internment of Japanese Americans in World War II, *Korematsu v United States*, 323 US 214 (1944) (US Supreme Court). The "fatal in fact" assertion was made by Justice Marshall in *Fullilove v Klutznick*, 448 US 503 (1980) (US Supreme Court).

[20] *Grutter v Bollinger*, 123 S. Ct. 2325 (2003) (US Supreme Court). For an analysis see M Tushnet, "United States: Supreme Court Rules on Affirmative Action," 2004 2 *International Journal of Constitutional Law* 1, 158–73.

[21] GL Heriot, "Strict Scrutiny, Public Opinion, and Affirmative Action on Campus: Should the Courts Find a Narrowly Tailored Solution to a Compelling Need in a Policy Most Americans Oppose?" 2003 40 *Harvard Journal on Legislation* 217. An analysis of the case after the result is given in RC Post,

Strict scrutiny is indeed strict and tough as a test. There are, however, other signs that strict scrutiny may becoming, if not less strict, at lest less automatically fatal. In 1995, *Adarand Constructors, Inc. v Pena* relied heavily on the question of whether race was ever to be allowed to serve as a legislative discrimination—in this case as a positive discriminator.[22] Though no substantive result was reached, O'Connor's opinion for the court involved four justices associating themselves with the statement that

> It is not true that strict scrutiny is strict in theory, but fatal in fact. Government is not disqualified from acting in response to the unhappy persistence of both the practice and the lingering effects [of past discrimination].

This has been picked up by several commentators. What has not been given as much weight as it might deserve was Justice Scalia's concurring opinion in the case, where he comes close to arguing for dumping the entire framework of levels of scrutiny. I discuss this shortly in the context of some Canadian criticisms of both the US test and the Canadian version. By contrast to the past strictness of suspect category classification, the opposite end of the spectrum, ordinary, or "deferential" scrutiny, may well strike continental Europeans as remarkably soft. The fact that it is sometimes called "deferential scrutiny" gives a flavour of how it operates and why. Essentially under this much weaker test, the government merely has to establish a "rational connection" between a legitimate governmental goal and the mechanism of the statute. It came about from the Supreme Court's retreat from *Lochner*.[23] Even under deferential scrutiny, and even on socioeconomic matters, the court has occasionally struck down legislation on the grounds that the categorisation in the act did not even have a weak rational connection to the purpose. So in a case as early as 1973 the court invalidated part of a federal welfare programme that limited food stamps to households of related persons. The court seems to have been pretty sure that this part of the act, which was an amendment to the original, had the deliberate aim of hitting at hippy communes, and ruled that the related persons limitation was "an irrational classification in violation of the equal protection component of the Fifth Amendment."[24] The majority opinion, by Justice Brennan, went on to describe the classification as "not only 'imprecise'; it is wholly without any rational basis" and irrelevant to the statute's avowed twin purposes of feeding the poor and helping agriculture. Even a case like this and with a test as simple as this, there is room for judicial disagreement. Not able to produce an even easier test, the minority simply disputed the quasi-factual basis, inventing a rational connection—restricting the households to related persons ensured the household was a real one, and not just created for the sole purpose of collecting food stamps.

"The Supreme Court, 2002 Term: Foreword: Fashioning the Legal Constitution: Culture, Courts, and Law," 2003 117 *Harvard Law Review* 4.

[22] *Adarand Constructors, Inc. v Pena*, 513 US 1108 (1995) (US Supreme Court).

[23] *Lochner v New York*, 198 US 45 (1905) (US Supreme Court), is often taken as the epitome of unwarranted judicial interference with government policy.

[24] *US Department of Agriculture v Moreno*, 413 US 528 (1973) (US Supreme Court).

The logic of deference to Congress goes a long way, and legitimately so if the court is to avoid the usual criticisms of invading legislative space. If a defendant government can persuade the court to apply the weak scrutiny standard, it can write legislation that others see as trumping even First Amendment rights. In *Eldred v Ashcroft*, from 2002, Congress extended copyright by an extra twenty years even for works that had just come out of copyright and become other people's property. This decision was attacked on the grounds that it involved an infringement on speech rights, but the Supreme Court was not swayed against Congress by such an invocation of the First Amendment:

> we turn now to whether it is a rational exercise of the legislative authority conferred by the Copyright Clause. *On that point, we defer substantially to Congress.* . . . ("[I]t is Congress that has been assigned the task of defining the scope of the limited monopoly that should be granted to authors . . .")

and

> [This legislation] reflects judgments of a kind Congress typically makes, *judgments we cannot dismiss as outside the Legislature's domain.*[25]

In vain for the minority to argue that the tests are irrelevant, as Justice Stevens urged:

> Consequently, I would review plausible claims that a copyright statute seriously, and unjustifiably, restricts the dissemination of speech somewhat more carefully than reference to this Court's traditional Commerce Clause jurisprudence might suggest. . . . There is no need in this case to characterize that review as a search for "congruence and proportionality," or as some other variation of what this Court has called "intermediate scrutiny. . . ." Rather, it is necessary only to recognize that this statute involves not pure economic regulation, but regulation of expression, and what may count as rational where economic regulation is at issue is not necessarily rational where we focus on expression—in a Nation constitutionally dedicated to the free dissemination of speech, information, learning, and culture. In this sense only, and where line-drawing among constitutional interests is at issue, I would look harder than does the majority at the statute's rationality. . . . Thus, I would find that the statute lacks the constitutionally necessary rational support (1) if the significant benefits that it bestows are private, not public; (2) if it threatens seriously to undermine the expressive values that the Copyright Clause embodies; and (3) if it cannot find justification in any significant Clause-related objective. Where, after examination of the statute, it becomes difficult, if not impossible, even to dispute these characterizations, Congress' choice is clearly wrong.

[25] *Eldred et al v Ashcroft, Attorney General*, 123 S. Ct. 769 (2003) (US Supreme Court); emphases added.

This of course is one of the points of using tests—it allows the majority who can agree on a suitable test just to disregard the sorts of issues of detail that Stevens is bringing up. However, as discussed later especially in the South African context, complete consensus on the test does not prevent detailed disagreement. So much in US constitutional review, therefore, depends on getting agreement on which test to use—once there, the results can flow fairly automatically. The question of the relevant test is all-pervasive. Consider the following. Under its own doctrine, the court has allowed the federal government to impose liabilities on the states for failing to reach some standards of provision for their citizens. This based on the Fourteenth Amendment, which provides for Congress to pass legislation enforcing the amendment's guarantees of due process and equal rights. Under the same court-defined doctrine the federal government has to demonstrate that there is an empirical patterns of rights abuse before states can be so disciplined. In recent years a majority on the court has on one occasion wanted to defend the states against obligations under the Americans with Disabilities Act, while another has wanted to enforce sexual equality legislation. In the former there was a wealth of congressionally developed empirical evidence; in the second there was very little. How was the court to allow federal interference the second time when it had overruled it the first time? Well, the right not to be discriminated against because of a disability is, apparently, a second-order right, depending only on Congress itself, and not in the constitution, whereas freedom from gender-based discrimination has been found to be implicit in the Bill of Rights. Consequently as the second right comes under "heightened scrutiny," the evidential requirement to overturn it is much more demanding than what is needed to overturn the disability right, which comes only under the "rational connection" test. Therefore the ban on Title 1 of the Americans with Disabilities Act need not require the court to ban the family leave provisions in the Family Medical Leave Act (this despite all talk about deference and the need only for minimum scrutiny of much congressional legislation).[26]

A simple demonstration of how much can be achieved if minimum scrutiny suits the court is *Cleburne v Texas* from 1985, where a city managed to get sustained an ordinance forbidding the building of "a group home for the mentally retarded." The state court of appeal had struck it down on the grounds that mental retardation was a "quasi-suspect" classification; therefore, under the "heightened scrutiny" equal protection test the ordinance was "facially invalid" because it did not substantially further an important governmental purpose. The Supreme Court ruled that mental retardation was not a quasi suspect category, with the following bizarre justification:

[26]The disability case is *University of Alabama v Garrett*, 531 U.S. 356 (2001 (US Supreme Court); the family leave case is *Nevada Department of Human Resources v Hibbs*, 123 S. Ct. 1972 (2003) (US Supreme Court). On the latter see GR MacConaill, "*Nevada Department of Human Resources v. Hibbs*: Does Application of Section 5 Represent a Fundamental Change in the Immunity Abrogation Rules of New Federalism, or Have the Burdens Simply Shifted?" 2004 109 *Penn State Law Review* 4, 831.

> Mentally retarded persons, who have a reduced ability to cope with and function in the everyday world, are thus different from other persons, and the States' interest in dealing with and providing for them is plainly a legitimate one. The distinctive legislative response, both national and state, to the plight of those who are mentally retarded demonstrates not only that they have unique problems, but also *that the lawmakers have been addressing their difficulties in a manner that belies a continuing antipathy or prejudice and a corresponding need for more intrusive oversight by the judiciary than is afforded under the normal equal protection standard. Moreover, the legislative response, which could hardly have occurred and survived without public support, negates any claim that the mentally retarded are politically powerless in the sense that they have no ability to attract the attention of the lawmakers.*)[27]

This may be good law—though I doubt it is any such thing—but it is awful political science.

The intellectual (or ideological) problem with tests comes from the prior decisions that have to be made in applying them. First, the plaintiff's claim has to be characterized as genuinely involving a right, and that right has to be, as it were, catalogued. Second, the relevant test has to be chosen. Finally, and equally problematic, the legislative behaviour has to be described in such a way as to lead the interaction of the first two criteria to yield a result. As often as not the judicial disagreement is on this third dimension, characterizing what exactly it is that a piece of legislation does.

Scrutiny and Expressive Rights

In its free speech jurisprudence the US Supreme Court has developed a doctrine in which real attempts by government to censor and prevent particular ideas being expressed require the strictest possible scrutiny and will hardly ever be allowed—approaching Black's literalism in effect if not language. The court has always recognized, however, that the state needs to be able to prevent some type of expression—very noisy loudspeakers, dangerously distracting signs on highways, leafleting that creates major litter problems, and so on. The former, requiring strict scrutiny, is labelled "content-based" to distinguish it from regulations falling into the latter type, which naturally require minimum or perhaps, at the most, intermediate or "heightened" scrutiny.

In *Good News Club v Milford Central School*, from 2001, a school that under New York State legislation allowed its premises to be used for limited public purposes, meetings of the Boy Scouts, and so forth, refused to allow one particular group to hold meetings. This was a group in which children were taught "fam-

[27] *City of Cleburne, Texas v Cleburne Living Center Inc.*, 473 US 432 (US Supreme Court); emphasis added.

ily values" from a religious perspective.[28] The association sued, alleging that this amounted to a "content-based" restriction on free speech, and that neither tests of compelling state interest nor a least restrictive means test could be satisfied. This categorization of the activity was accepted by the majority on the Supreme Court, which agreed with the plaintiff association on the near inevitable consequences of the applicable test. The dissenters found instead that what was going on was a full-blown religious service. In their view the well-established court jurisprudence on not allowing religion in schools inverted the problem—the school district could not constitutionally allow the Good News Club to hold its meetings. Indeed the dissent went so far as to suggest that to do so would amount to be breach of the First Amendment ban on establishing a religion. All that really separated the majority and the dissenters was a different judgement on how crucial and central to the meetings were, for example, the frequent attempts by the group leaders to get the children to "ask Jesus for his help in being good," and so forth. Had there been no test available, the whole focus would have had to be on the credibility of describing the Good News Club activities as essentially religious. The case would have had to be argued fully on the religious rights part of the First Amendment.

Similarly in *Hill et al v Colorado*[29] a state law regulating protest behaviour outside medical facilities was clearly intended to prevent right-to-life groups from harassing women seeking abortions. The case depended on the content-based versus content-neutral characterization of the law.[30] Facially it was indeed content neutral, as no reference was made to what the protesters were saying, and this allowed the majority to apply only minimum scrutiny. Whatever one may think of Justice Scalia's view of jurisprudence, no impartial reader could fail to prefer his detailed description of the act and its genesis, which made it abundantly clear that the Colorado legislature was specifically trying to protect women from having to hear the views of right-to-lifers. Whether this made it content-based or not, which was Scalia's interpretation, much better constitutional law would have emerged from facing up to the actual issues involved, which had much more to do with a putative "right to be left alone," and other privacy rights than with an erudite characterization in terms of an abstract test.[31]

[28] *Good News Club v Milford Central School*, 533 US 98 (2001) (US Supreme Court). For comment see TA Schweitzer, "Supreme Court Rules in Favor of Religious Club's Right to Meet on Public School Premises: Is This Good News for First Amendment Rights?" 2001 18 *Touro Law Review* 127.

[29] *Hill et al v Colorado*, 530 US 703 (2000) (US Supreme Court). A very useful discussion that highlights points I go on to make about Canadian jurisprudence in this area is DL Beschle, "Clearly Canadian? *Hill v. Colorado* and Free Speech Balancing in the United States and Canada," 2001 28 *Hastings Constitutional Law Quarterly* 187.

[30] There had been previous cases with fact bases very similar to *Hill*, notably *Madsen v Women's Health Center, Inc.*, 114 S. Ct. 2516 (1994) (US Supreme Court), which is discussed in JM Atwood, "Constitutional Law—a New Level of Means-End Scrutiny Applied to Content-Neutral Injunctions That Limit Protected Speech," 1995 29 *Suffolk University Law Review* 6, 1189–98.

[31] There are American commentators who do not believe that even strict scrutiny produces stable recognition of the primacy of rights in the speech area. See E Volokh, "Freedom of Speech, Permissible Tailoring and Transcending Strict Scrutiny," 1995 44 *University of Pennsylvania Law Review* 2417–61.

It could be argued that, in the United States anyway, tests have virtually no real controlling effect, because they amount only to shortcut ways of expressing much more fundamental judgements. In the end they mask the action of the court in making fine-tuned moral judgements for the society. That would not mean that tests might not be pernicious, because they also cover up, to the court as well as the public, just what the court really means by some of its doctrines. One crucial idea, that there ought to be a "constitutional exception for religious practice," demonstrates this well. In one of the major cases where the Supreme Court developed doctrine on this a high level of scrutiny was applied to the government's action in refusing a tax exception to religious sect.[32] As nearly always in this area, the government actually won, but only by appearing to pass the test. There was a separate concurrence by Justice Stevens, who flatly contradicted the court in its empirical assessment, showing that the government would have no significant difficulty in granting the exception and might even benefit from it. Stevens agreed that the Amish plaintiff should lose, but objected to the misleading way the court continued to enunciate its doctrine in these cases:

> The clash between appellee's religious obligation and his civic obligation is irreconcilable. He must violate either an Amish belief or a federal statute. According to the Court, the religious duty must prevail unless the Government shows that enforcement of the civic duty "is essential to accomplish an overriding governmental interest." That formulation of the constitutional standard suggests that the Government always bears a heavy burden of justifying the application of neutral general laws to individual conscientious objectors. In my opinion, it is the objector who must shoulder the burden of demonstrating that there is a unique reason for allowing him a special exemption from a valid law of general applicability.

Stevens insisted that "there is virtually no room for a 'constitutionally required exemption' on religious grounds," repeating himself in a vital footnote:

> I believe, however, that a standard that places an almost insurmountable burden on any individual who objects to a valid and neutral law of general applicability on the ground that the law proscribes (or prescribes) conduct that his religion prescribes (or proscribes) better explains most of this Court's holdings than does the standard articulated by the Court today.

It is easy enough to see political reasons for the Supreme Court, in the West's most obviously nonsecular society, finding it convenient to impose constitutionally mandated secularism through tests that appear in fact to privilege religion. But if that is possible, it remains to decide how important this, or any other test, actually is. This point will become clearer with a demonstration of how different tests work in countries where the constitution or the legal culture make rights limita-

---

Others clearly would prefer a return to something more like Black's absolutism: C Osborn, "Constitutional Scrutiny and Speech: Eroding the Bedrock Principles of the First Amendment," 1990 44 *Southwestern Law Journal* 1013–44.

[32] *US v Lee*, 455 US 252 (1982) (US Supreme Court).

tion easier. For, as Beschle has said, contrasting the "balancing" approach to rights limitation with the more absolutist American style, American jurists accomplish their task often through "semantic gymnastics—by redefining the 'absolute rule' to narrow it in largely the same way that balancing itself would."[33]

Constitutional Tests in Canada

Chapter 6 has already described the major thrusts of Canadian constitutional review, but deliberately did not comment much on the actual process of developing precise tests for constitutionality. Though both nondiscrimination and substantive rights testing were combined while talking about the United States, the focus here is more on the way the Canadian Supreme Court has gone about applying the antidiscrimination clauses of the Charter.[34] To a large extent discrimination and substantive rights are handled everywhere with roughly the same logic, in part because they are often intellectually interchangeable. As we have just seen, for example, with religious rights many complaints of infringement on religious freedom are interchangeable with claims that a general law unfairly presses on those of a specific religion, thus producing de facto discrimination.

The Canadian View of American Approaches

The Canadian Supreme Court could hardly be expected entirely to ignore US discussions on testing the legitimacy of legislation that imposes differential burdens on different categories of citizens. So in an early case defining the sorts of differentiations that might involve discrimination, *Andrews v Law Society of British Columbia*, the Canadian court directly quoted the "discreet and insular minorities" language from *Carolene*.[35] It is an early indication of the more thoughtful Canadian analysis that one of the justices who used the allusion, Wilson, actually went on to say:

> I believe also that it is important to note that the range of discrete and insular minorities has changed and will continue to change with changing political and social circumstances. . . . It can be anticipated that the discrete and insular minorities of tomorrow will include groups not recognized as such today.

In fact a crucial difference was outlined by Justice McIntyre, who noted that American judicial thinking had "led to the development of varying standards of scrutiny of alleged violations of the equal protection provision which restrict or

[33] Beschle, "Clearly Canadian?" 189.

[34] A good survey, concentrating on the US/Canadian distinction is JM Pellicciotti, "The Constitutional Guarantee of Equal Protection in Canada and the United States: A Comparative Analysis of the Standards for Determining the Validity of Governmental Action," 1997 5 *Tulsa Journal of Comparative & International Law* 1.

[35] *Andrews v Law Society of British Columbia*, 1 SCR 143 (1989) (Canadian Supreme Court).

limit the equality guarantee within the concept of equal protection itself."[36] McIntyre's argument, like many Canadian judicial criticisms of US constitutional tests, comes from the belief that it is the American lack of anything like the general limitation clause in Section 1 of the Canadian Charter of Rights and Freedoms that forces the US Supreme Court into treating rights as absolute, or at least pretending that it does.[37] In a very important freedom of speech case the Canadian court was pressed to apply something like the US ban on "content-specific" control. Justice La Forest, for the majority, first made the following cautionary point about US jurisprudence in general:

> applying the Charter to the legislation challenged in this appeal reveals important differences between Canadian and American constitutional perspectives. . . . Section 1 has no equivalent in the United States, a fact previously alluded to by this Court in selectively utilizing American constitutional jurisprudence. . . . Of course, American experience should never be rejected simply because the Charter contains a balancing provision, for it is well known that American courts have fashioned compromises between conflicting interests despite what appears to be the absolute guarantee of constitutional rights.[38]

La Forest showed neatly that the Americans themselves cannot really claim to use a simple content / content neutral test:

> I am somewhat sceptical . . . as to whether this view of free speech in the United States is entirely accurate. Rather, in rejecting the extreme position that would provide an absolute guarantee of free speech in the Bill of Rights, the Supreme Court has developed a number of tests and theories by which protected speech can be identified and the legitimacy of government regulation assessed. Often required is a content-based categorization of the expression under examination. As an example, obscenity is not protected because of its content . . . and laws proscribing child pornography have been scrutinized under a less than strict First Amendment standard even where they extend to expression beyond the realm of the obscene. . . . In short, a decision to place expressive activity in a category which either merits reduced protection or falls entirely outside of the First Amendment's ambit at least impliedly involves assessing the content of the activity in light of free speech values.[39]

At the very least these comments from practising constitutional judges suggest that the analysis in the previous section is not hopelessly academic. Others clearly

[36] *Andrews v Law Society of British Columbia*, 177.

[37] Section 1 of the Charter reads: "The *Canadian Charter of Rights and Freedoms* guarantees the rights and freedoms set out in it subject only to such reasonable limits prescribed by law as can be demonstrably justified in a free and democratic society."

[38] *R. v Keegstra*, 3 SCR 697 (1990) (Canadian Supreme Court).

[39] La Forest cites one of the major US academic articles on the whole idea of balancing, TA Aleinikoff, "Constitutional Law in the Age of Balancing," 1987 96 *Yale Law Review* 943.

agree that the tests may really be a cover for a different type of analysis of when a right may legitimately be restricted.

The Canadian Limitation of Expressive Rights

As the American section started with a discussion of freedom of speech, *Keegstra* will serve well to show just what the Canadians do mean by stressing the role of their Section 1 in constitutional testing. There is a practise in the Canadian Supreme Court whereby the justices, at the end of their lengthy and complex reasonings, state the precise constitutional questions addressed to them and give one-word answers. Nothing can more graphically demonstrate how far Canadian freedom of expression jurisprudence differs from that of the United States than for me to replicate these questions and answers from *Keegstra*. For the majority:

1. Is s. 281.2(2) of the Criminal Code of Canada, R.S.C. 1970, c. C-34 (now s. 319(2) of the Criminal Code of Canada, R.S.C., 1985, c. C-46) an infringement of freedom of expression as guaranteed under s. 2(b) of the Canadian Charter of Rights and Freedoms?

   Answer: Yes.
2. If s. 281.2(2) of the Criminal Code of Canada, R.S.C. 1970, c. C-34 (now s. 319(2) of the Criminal Code of Canada, R.S.C., 1985, c. C-46) is an infringement of s. 2(b) of the Canadian Charter of Rights and Freedoms, can it be upheld under s. 1 of the Canadian Charter of Rights and Freedoms as a reasonable limit prescribed by law and demonstrably justified in a free and democratic society?

   Answer: Yes.

And, for good measure:

3. Is s. 281.2(3)(a) of the Criminal Code of Canada, R.S.C. 1970, c. C-34 (now s. 319(3)(a) of the Criminal Code of Canada, R.S.C., 1985, c. C-46) an infringement of the right to be presumed innocent, as guaranteed under s. 11(d) of the Canadian Charter of Rights and Freedoms?

   Answer: Yes.
4. If s. 281.2(3)(a) of the Criminal Code of Canada, R.S.C. 1970, c. C-34 (now s. 319(3)(a) of the Criminal Code of Canada, R.S.C., 1985, c. C-46) is an infringement of s. 11(d) of the Canadian Charter of Rights and Freedoms, can it be upheld under s. 1 of the Canadian Charter of Rights and Freedoms as a reasonable limit prescribed by law and demonstrably justified in a free and democratic society?

   Answer: Yes.

The dissenters said Yes, No, Yes, No. No one denied that the legislation both denied freedom of speech and the right to be presumed innocent. One could not find such a pattern in any American case, though a similar fact-set that produced a split decision on constitutionality like this might well be found.

Keegstra was a high school teacher who proclaimed extreme anti-Semitic doctrine in his classes, and had done so for years. He produced all the old anti-Semitic libels, engaged in Holocaust denial, and, in sum, taught that Jews, "in contrast to the open and honest Christians, were said to be deceptive, secretive and inherently evil." As the majority opinion notes, "Mr. Keegstra expected his students to reproduce his teachings in class and on exams. If they failed to do so, their marks suffered." The relevant section of the legislation under which he was prosecuted stipulates that

> (2) Every one who, by communicating statements, other than in private conversation, willfully promotes hatred against any identifiable group is guilty of . . . an indictable offence. . . .
>
> A defense is provided by (3) No person shall be convicted of an offence under subsection (2) (a) if he establishes that the statements communicated were true.

It is because this defence seems to reverse the normal burden of proof in a criminal trial that the second constitutional question had to be answered. The immediately relevant clauses of the Charter of Rights and Freedoms read:

> 2.Everyone has the following fundamental freedoms:
> (b) freedom of thought, belief, opinion and expression, including freedom of the press and other media of communication
> 11.Any person charged with an offence has the right
> (d) to be presumed innocent until proven guilty according to law in a fair and public hearing by an independent and impartial tribunal

Any interpretation in the context of the Keegstra trial would inevitably be colored also by clauses 15 and 27:

> 15. (1) Every individual is equal before and under the law and has the right to the equal protection and equal benefit of the law without discrimination and, in particular, without discrimination based on race, national and ethnic origin, colour, religion, sex, age or mental or physical disability.
> 27. This Charter shall be interpreted in a manner consistent with the preservation and enhancement of the multicultural heritage of Canadians.

An American court faced with this situation would have to find a way of showing that what Keegstra had said, and what Section 319 of the code criminalizes, does not qualify as free speech within the meaning of Section 2(a) of the Charter. Otherwise, there being no pretence here of "clear and present danger," Section 319 of the Code simply could not stand. The Canadians famously use instead a two-stage test, initially set down in *R v Oakes*, a major case from 1986 shortly after the Charter came into force, described in chapter 6.[40] Under the *Oakes* test the court first decides whether the plaintiff has made out a case that legislation breaches the

[40] *R v Oakes*, 1 SCR 103 (1986) (Canadian Supreme Court).

constitution. If it is seen to be *prima facie* unconstitutional, the second stage of the test applies the Charter's exception, set out in Section 1.

The power of the test in the Section 1 analysis comes partly from the court's gloss on the whole idea of what is meant by a free and democratic society. It comes equally from the fact that the judges do require a demonstrable justification. In fact the Canadian Supreme Court has not been immune to a temptation to try to avoid Section 1 analyses by taking the justification forwards into the Charter and applying it within the initial decision on whether the legislation in question, justifiably or otherwise, actually does breach one of the rights. This is effectively to turn the Charter towards an American-style absolute rights approach—by the same device of allowing necessary incursions into rights by pretending the issue is not covered by the definition of the right. At this stage it is enough to say that the court was invited to do just this in *Keegstra* and refused the easy option. It was argued, for example, that hate speech could not be seen as a form of expression that merited protection by Section 2. The argument was buttressed by the observation that Canada was signatory to various international agreements condemning such propaganda. Nonetheless the court was unanimous that the content of expression, however awful, could not be used to deny that statements intended to convey meaning were, *all of them*, protected—protected, unless Section 1 trumps. Many other cases on speech have been analyzed by the court in this way. The Supreme Court of Canada is not necessarily more protective than many jurisdictions of freedom of speech, but it is clearer about the fact that it lets the government abridge it. How easy it is for the government to get this leeway is a matter of debate.

The ruling case on freedom of speech where obscenity is involved is *R v Butler*, from 1992.[41] The judges were unanimous that a "content" specification would not do, because to ban obscene material for this reason would be tantamount to banning it because it offended against general moral beliefs. Thus the criminal code ban on obscene material was a denial of the guarantee of freedom of expression in Section 2(b) of the Canadian Charter. However, some forms of morality may constitute a valid reason that rescues the law under Section 1. Obscene material, it was claimed, was dangerous to society, and thus could be banned:

> Section 163 of the *Code* is aimed at preventing harm to society, a moral objective that is valid under s. 1 of the *Charter*. The avoidance of harm to society is but one instance of a fundamental conception of morality. In order to warrant an override of *Charter* rights the moral claims must be grounded; they must involve concrete problems such as life, harm and well-being, and not merely differences of opinion or taste. A consensus must also exist among the population on these claims. The avoidance of harm caused to society through attitudinal changes certainly qualifies as a fundamental conception of morality. It is well grounded, since the harm takes the form of violations of the principles of human equality and dignity.[42]

[41] *R. v Butler*, 1 SCR 1 (1992) (Canadian Supreme Court).

[42] *R. v Butler*, 8.

Interestingly the court characterizes the test as being "concerned not with what Canadians would not tolerate being exposed to themselves, but with what they would not tolerate other Canadians being exposed to." Nor does the court hold the government to a high standard of evidence on the scientific assumptions. The court was content to state, "While a direct link between obscenity and harm to society may be difficult to establish, it is reasonable to presume that exposure to images bears a causal relationship to changes in attitudes and beliefs." As noted below, at least one other constitutional court has been unwilling to accept such a standard.

Oakes: The Basis of the Tests

The *Oakes* test, developed by then Chief Justice Dickson, is complex and itself involves several stages. In its first stage, the test requires the *respondent* to demonstrate that the "objective sought to be achieved by the impugned law must relate to concerns which are 'pressing and substantial' in a free and democratic society." It is important to see that there is a real problem with attempts to bypass the Section 1 analysis by smuggling it into the first stage of the whole discussion, because between the two stages the burden of proof switches. While it is up to the complainant to convince the court a right has been abridged, it is up to the state, if the complainant succeeds, to justify this incursion. But even if the state can provide a general justification by showing that the legislation does relate to a "pressing and substantial" issue, and one that remains pressing and substantial even when it is to be applied in a "free and democratic nation," the legislation may still fall.

The definition of a free and democratic society has been left, in Canada, very much to the judges. Dickson made a good stab at encapsulating it when laying down his test, so at the minimum the court has to be satisfied that legislation is compatible with his ideal, in which democratic principles

> embody, to name but a few, respect for the inherent dignity of the human person, commitment to social justice and equality, accommodation of a wide variety of beliefs, respect for cultural and group identity, and faith in social and political institutions which enhance the participation of individuals and groups in society. The underlying values and principles of a free and democratic society are the genesis of the rights and freedoms guaranteed by the *Charter* and the ultimate standard against which a limit on a right or freedom must be shown, despite its effect, to be reasonable and demonstrably justified.[43]

The Canadian court is fully aware of how subjective the Section 1 test must be. As was noted in L'Heureux-Dubé's dissent in *Keegstra*:

> The exercise is one of great difficulty, requiring the judge to make value judgments. In this task logic and precedent are but of limited assistance. What must be determinative in the end is the court's judgment, based on an

[43] *R v Oakes*, 64.

> understanding of the values our society is built on and the interests at stake in the particular case. . . . this judgment cannot be made in the abstract. Rather than speak of values as though they were Platonic ideals, the judge must situate the analysis in the facts of the particular case, weighing the different values represented in that context. Thus it cannot be said that freedom of expression will always prevail over the objective of individual dignity and social harmony, or vice versa.[44]

Proportionality as a Limiting Device

The second limb of Dickson's approach has come to be known as a "proportionality" test, though it differs somewhat from that concept as typically used in continental European constitutional jurisprudence.[45] There are usually three substages to the proportionality test, two of which look much like US constitutional tests. The legislation has to be shown to have a rational connection to the aim, and it has to cause "minimal impairment." Finally, and this is where the test ends up more like its European counterpart, there has to be proportionality between the likely impact of the legislation and the good to be achieved. (A full proper discussion of proportionality is left until the discussion on Germany and France.) All in all there are plenty of ways that a court can find legislation unconstitutional—but each aspect is so open to subjective interpretation that no judge who wants to support the government need worry about having to apply the *Oakes* test. Certainly as originally formulated the test was intended to be rigorous—as Dickson said:

> Having regard to the fact that s. 1 is being invoked for the purpose of justifying a violation of the constitutional rights and freedoms the *Charter* was designed to protect, a very high degree of probability will be, in the words of Lord Denning, "commensurate with the occasion." Where evidence is required in order to prove the constituent elements of a s. 1 inquiry, and this will generally be the case, it should be cogent and persuasive and make clear to the Court the consequences of imposing or not imposing the limit. . . . A court will also need to know what alternative measures for implementing the objective were available to the legislators when they made their decisions.[46]

Perhaps unfortunately, *Oakes* itself was an open-and-shut an example of unconstitutional legislation. It related to Section 4(2) of the Narcotic Control Act, which made possession of any amount of a controlled drug evidence of intent to supply unless the accused himself could prove the opposite. (This reversal of the burden of proof, contrary to Section 11 of the Charter, was also a subsidiary issue in *Keeg-*

[44] L'Hereux-Dubé in *R. v Keegstra*, 845.

[45] American constitutional scholars are fully aware of the possible attractions of Canadian proportionality doctrine, often prompted by *Keegstra*. See VC Jackson, "Ambivalent Resistance and Comparative Constitutionalism: Opening Up the Conversation on 'Proportionality,' Rights and Federalism," 1999 1 *University of Pennsylvania Journal of Constitutional Law* 583–639.

[46] *R v Oakes*, 68.

stra.) The court found no rational connection between this denial of a right and any legitimate end. As a result, Dickson did not spell out the proportionality part of his test in any detail. Yet it is this last part of the test, proportionality properly so called, that calls most obviously for a subjective moral decision by the judge. This is, indeed, what happened in *Keegstra*. No one on the court disputed that Section 319 of the criminal code was in breach of Section 2 of the Charter. But equally, no one disputed that the aim was acceptable in a free and democratic society—quite the opposite, because all of the values involved in Dickson's definition of democracy, and especially human dignity, cried out for protection.

The lone dissentient, L'Heureux-Dubé, had problems with all three of the subsequent part-tests, with the rational connection aspect as well as with the more general proportionality of means and ends. She has always been anxious to stress that it is the effect, not the intention, of legislation that is relevant. Indeed, she has made the point, as she does in *Keegstra*, that "the Charter could easily become diluted if an intention on the part of government to act on behalf of a disadvantaged group sufficed in all cases to establish the necessary rational connection between the legislation and its objective." Obvious though this may be, something very much like that came to be argued in later cases, heroically opposed by this same justice. What determined the dissent in the end was something familiar to all who read constitutional judicial opinions—not a disagreement about values, but about quasi empirical matters. L'Heureux-Dubé was convinced that the offending section would likely rebound and worsen the situation by giving publicity to racists and anti-Semites. She likened it to the way the court had disputed the logic of the state in *Morgentaler*.[47] (This was the abortion decision where the state had tried to claim that the abortion law was aimed at protecting women's health when it actually caused deaths.) L'Heureux-Dubé rejected, as it were, the government's social science, not its values. As a consequence, there could be no rational connection. One can hardly argue that a piece of legislation employs means rationally connected to its aim if the effect is likely to worsen the situation. Hence the importance of concentrating on the effect, not the intention, of legislation when considering rational connection. The whole approach via criminal law fails the "less intrusive measures" part of the test, because there are, according to the judge, other nonpenal and more effective ways of dealing with ethnic prejudice. Finally, because L'Heureux-Dubé thought the code overbroad here—it had already caught innocent people—and because the punishment was disproportionately heavy for some of the offences that might come under it, it failed proportionality.

Proportionality tests inevitably involve this sort of social science second-guessing: perhaps all constitutional tests do. But by their very nature proportionality tests can hardly be carried out under a "deference" rubric. The truth is that though Dickson constructed an apparently complex and multistage test, each limb of the second half of the Section 1 analysis it is really only a paraphrase of the others. Rational connection may stand alone, and may even be given a deference colouring, but the rest amount to saying little more than that the judge must de-

[47] *R. v Morgentaler*, 1 SCR 30 (1988) (Canadian Supreme Court).

cide whether he or she would go about solving the problem this way, taking both empirical predictions and moral balance into account. Is this unavoidable if anything but an "absolute rights" approach is to be attempted? This problem looms larger when we look at the discrimination tests where Section 1 of the Charter is combined with Section 15.

Controlling Discrimination

The Canadian functional equivalent to the Fourteenth Amendment to the US constitution is Section 15 of the Charter:

> Every individual is equal before and under the law and has the right to the equal protection and equal benefit of the law without discrimination and, in particular, without discrimination based on race, national or ethnic origin, colour, religion, sex, age or mental or physical disability.

As with any right, the right against discrimination is subject to the Section 1 limitation because it has to be theoretically possible that a discriminatory law might be "demonstrably justified in a free and democratic society." Part of the dispute amongst the justices since the Charter came into force is indeed about the relevance of Section 1, and at what stage the (judicially developed) rational connection test should be applied. A two-stage approach is enforced by the constitution itself; but, as in the case of a denial of a substantive right, most of the machinery of constitutional testing has been created by the judiciary in interpreting the meaning of the relatively sparse Charter phrases.

It was not until 1989, seven years after the Charter came into force, that Section 15 gained its first serious judicial gloss, in *Andrews v Law Society of British Columbia*,[48] where a unanimous judgement authored by McIntyre set out a constitutional assessment technique that has broadly been followed since.[49] The Canadian court early on refused to take advantage of the possibility of creating horizontal effect. Consequently it is first necessary for a plaintiff to establish that the unequal treatment he or she claims to suffer from can be laid firmly at the government's door. This requirement has been nontrivial, because the Supreme Court has held the line very firmly on it. It has, for example, refused to accept a complaint of unequal treatment because of age from university staff, on the grounds that the universities are self-governing.[50] Once the government has been inculpated, the

[48] *Andrews v Law Society of British Columbia*. Though the Charter generally came into force in 1982, Section 15 did not take effect until three years later, to give government time to adjust. An interesting comparison of *Keegstra* and *Andrews* is found in D Bottos, "*Keegstra* and *Andrews*: A Commentary on Hate Propaganda and the Freedom of Expression," 1989 27 *Alberta Law Review* 13, 461–75.

[49] The early cases are well described, along with a useful US comparison, in Pellicciotti, "Constitutional Guarantee." CD Bavis, "*Vriend v. Alberta, Law v. Canada, Ontario v. M. and H.*: The Latest Steps on the Winding Path to Substantive Equality," 1999 37 *Alberta Law Review* 683, gives a detailed account of later cases where judicial disagreement surfaced.

[50] *McKinney v University of Guelph*, 3 SCR 229, at 229 (1990) (Canadian Supreme Court). For comment see G Campeau, "McKinney et ses Consequences Pour les Groupes Defavorises," 1992 8 *Journal of Law and Social Policy* 3, 229–53.

first important step is to establish that the plaintiff has been treated unequally to his or her disadvantage. In the originating case, Andrews had been denied the right to become a barrister in British Columbia because he was not a Canadian citizen, something the law in the province required. For a plaintiff to win, the alleged disadvantage must offend one of four different versions of due process and equal opportunity—equality before and under the law and equal protection and equal benefit. Whether anything whatsoever has ever followed from this multiplicity of equality guarantees is far from clear, but it is clear that the court has sought to make Section 15 a real protection for substantive equality, and has intentionally rejected an earlier Canadian acceptance of merely formal equality. As McIntyre said in *Andrews*:

> Thus, mere equality of application to similarly situated groups or individuals does not afford a realistic test for a violation of equality rights. For, as has been said, a bad law will not be saved merely because it operates equally upon those to whom it has application.

The more difficult job McIntyre faced was giving some way of distinguishing between different treatment and discriminatory treatment. All laws, to repeat myself, proceed by classifying, and thus create distinctions. Some classifications are unacceptable. Which and why? That, after all, was what the footnote to *Carolene* tried to answer, and it is the primary question that all constitutional review bodies must face. The Charter helps only to a point, providing what the court has called "enumerated grounds": "in particular, without discrimination based on race, national or ethnic origin, colour, religion, sex, age or mental or physical disability." The "in particular" has been accepted without any objection as allowing the courts to find other grounds of unequal treatment to be discriminatory. This move is typical in jurisdictions with a similar listing (the South African Constitutional Court has done the same thing). As citizenship is not enumerated, so *Andrews* could not have proceeded otherwise. McIntyre's general formula has been followed in most cases:

> discrimination may be described as a distinction, whether intentional or not but based on grounds relating to personal characteristics of the individual or group, which has the effect of imposing burdens, obligations, or disadvantages on such individual or group not imposed upon others. . . . Distinctions based on personal characteristics attributed to an individual solely on the basis of association with a group will rarely escape the charge of discrimination, while those based on an individual's merits and capacities will rarely be so classed.

This has tended to be described as an "immutable characteristic" definition—the reason for unequal treatment depends on something the plaintiff can do nothing about. Thus, for example, it was crucial to the gay rights campaign that homosexuality should be accepted as "immutable," not a lifestyle choice.[51] Citizenship, though

[51]This legal move has not always been welcomed by gays, even where it has been used to protect them from persecution. See, as an example, N LaViolette, "The Immutable Refugees: Sexual Orientation in *Canada (A.G.) v. Ward*," 1997 55 *University of Toronto Faculty of Law Review* 1, 1–41.

it can be changed, takes time and is not changeable at the whim of the individual. Ironically it was disagreement on just this point that made McIntyre and another justice ultimately find that Andrews had not been discriminated against unjustifiably. When it came to the Section 1 test, the majority agreed that the act had a laudable aim—to recognize the importance of the legal profession in running Canada, but refused to see distinction on such a semi-immutable characteristic as proportional to the aim. Thus Andrews won his case, but in a way that limited its impact on discretion rules. McIntyre disagreed, because it was legitimate to ensure that lawyers had a real stake in the administration of justice, something he, perhaps oddly, believed followed from citizenship. Because denial of citizenship was not permanent, the act was therefore proportional. Oddly, few commentators have noted that the judge seemed to be having his cake and eating it—either citizenship was analogous to, say, ethnicity or it was not. It makes no sense to argue that Section 1 proportionality is not offended because the criterion by which Mr. Andrews was discriminated against was not really discriminatory. But that foretells the confusion the court has frequently found itself as this apparently simple judicial methodology for dealing with the meaning of Section 15 has developed. *Andrews* gave McIntyre the rare status of having authored a standard judicial test in a case where he was ultimately in dissent.

As it turned out, McIntyre's reasoning under the Section 1 analysis foreshadowed the problem that has haunted Canadian antidiscrimination jurisprudence. Quite often groups on the court have tried to avoid finding that a laudable act using sensible and relevant criteria is unconstitutional. Even the weaker judgement that the act *would be* unconstitutional and *is discriminatory* but is saved by Section 1 is obviously something no court really wants to argue unless forced to. It is, in a sense, the opposite of what McIntyre warned about when setting up the test; he was worried by the thought of a bad law being saved "merely because it operates equally upon those to whom it has application." Here we have the problem of a good law failing because it operates unequally. Another way of saying this is to repeat the theme earlier introduced as crucial—the problem for constitutional courts is to allow legislation to operate by categorization without offending equality. The tendency then has been to bring Section 1 analysis into Section 15 analysis, and make the test of whether a categorization is discriminatory turn on whether it has a rational connection to the intention of the act. Yet unless a court operates with something like the US level-of-scrutiny doctrine, combined as that is with considerable deference to legislatures, this approach cannot be right. Some judges on the Canadian court have tried to work out the problems by explaining—at least to themselves—what exactly it is that is wrong with discrimination. If one is clear about the nature of the evil involved, distinctions among the nondiscriminatory, the discriminatory but justified, and the unjustifiably discriminatory begin to look feasible.

The Equality Trilogy

A split began to emerge only a little after *Andrews*, and by 1995, in a group of cases that has come to be known as the "Equality Triangle," it crystallized into three theories of how to do Section 15 analysis.[52] As a result, shifting coalitions of judges produced notably different results according to the methodology adopted in conceptually similar cases, leading many critics to argue the court had lost its commitment to a broad and generous support of substantive equality. The cases dealt with whether insurance policies differentiating between married couples and common-law partnerships discriminated (yes, and unjustifiably);[53] whether restrictions of benefits to opposite-sex spouses under welfare law discriminated by sexual orientation (yes, but justifiably);[54] whether the tax laws requiring disclosure of child support discriminated by parental status or sex (neither).[55] As unofficial spokesman for one group, Gonthier argued for the group in *Miron* that once a disadvantaging distinction has been shown to exist, the court should ask whether it is based on an enumerated or analogous criterion. But then the values underlying the act, in other words its aim, should be considered. In Gonthier's words:

> This third step thus comprises two aspects: determining the personal characteristic shared by a group and then assessing its relevancy having regard to the functional values underlying the legislation.

Where the distinction drawn does comply with the purposes of the act, it cannot usually be said to be discrimination, though he does admit, perhaps grudgingly, "Of course, the functional values underlying the law may themselves be discriminatory. Such will be the case where the underlying values are *irrelevant to any legitimate legislative purpose*" (emphasis added). This is not so much a highly deferential test as a highly judge-dependent one, because the impact depends entirely on how the judge characterizes the underlying values. In *Miron* Gonthier held that the underlying purpose of the rule was indeed to uphold and protect full marriage over common-law marriage, and the distinction was therefore not irrelevant, and the act not in breach of Section 15. (Gonthier and the three judges who supported him were in a minority.) The bulk of the rest of the court did reject this new approach, largely because they were themselves concerned by the circularity (though the result only came about because Justice Sopinka, who had supported a Gonthier approach in *Egan* on gay rights, joined the *Egan* minority on the question of spousal insurance rights in *Miron*). The main exponent of *Andrews* orthodoxy, McLachlin, said in the majority opinion in *Miron*:

> the reasoning may be seen as circular. Having defined the functional values underlying the legislation in terms of the alleged discriminatory ground, it follows of necessity that the basis of the distinction is relevant to the legislative aim. This illustrates the aridity of relying on the formal test of logical relevance as proof of non-discrimination under s. 15(1). The only way to break out of the logical circle is to examine the actual impact of the distinction on members of the targeted group.

[52] Bavis, "*Vriend v. Alberta.*"
[53] *Miron v Trudel*, 2 SCR 418 (1995) (Canadian Supreme Court).
[54] *Egan v Canada*, 2 SCR 513 (1995) (Canadian Supreme Court).
[55] *Thibaudeau v Canada*, 2 SCR 627 (1995) (Canadian Supreme Court).

The real trouble with the Gonthier approach, of course, is that it depends on the standpoint from which one assesses the plaintiff. Homosexual couples are not discriminated against by the definition of spouse if one considers them, as did Gonthier, as just one of many examples of people who keep house together and who are not married to each other. But a gay couple is unlikely to see their domestic arrangement as more akin to siblings living together than to a married heterosexual couple. Compared to such couples, whom gays will treat as the relevant comparison but the judge did not, they are indeed being singled out. And they are being discriminated against precisely *because* the legislation aims to support heterosexual marriage arrangements. But as Gonthier is unlikely to see this as an example of discrimination "irrelevant to any legitimate legislative purpose," his choosing the viewpoint is determinative.

But there was a third voice, most pronounced in *Egan*, but running not only through all the "Equality Triangle" cases, but many subsequent ones. L'Heureux-Dubé produced there a genuinely radical approach to discrimination analysis that is both based on a more subtle understanding of the nature of the constitution, and more promising of real equality, however unlikely it may be that the court as a whole will ever accept it. She takes seriously McLachlin's stress on the "actual impact," but adds to it a rejection of the main approach from *Andrews* onwards. In a section enticingly headed "Frameworks vs. Rigid Legal Tests" she starts by stating bluntly what might be said of much of the case work from all the countries covered in this chapter:

> Equality and discrimination are notions that are as varied in form as they are complex in substance. Attempts to evaluate them according to legal formulas which incorporate rigid inclusionary and exclusionary criteria are doomed to become increasingly complex and convoluted over time as "hard" cases become the rule rather than the exception. I prefer to steer clear of those rocky shoals, if at all possible, and to adopt a pragmatic and functional approach to s. 15.

Describing *Andrews* as "an extremely good start," L'Heureux-Dubé nonetheless is concerned:

> As cases become more and more difficult, however, I believe that it is becoming increasingly evident that we may have been putting the cart before the horse. Although s. 15 is a general guarantee of "equality without discrimination," we have failed to put "discrimination," itself, at the forefront of our analysis. Instead, we have begun to define ourselves into boxes by making "grounds" a precondition to discrimination. As such, we may be denying s. 15 relief to persons who are victims of legislatively sanctioned discrimination, but who are unable to fit themselves into an established or analogous "ground."

Believing that the tests have distorted fundamental analysis, she insists that the preferable approach would be to "give independent content to the term 'discrimination,' and to develop s. 15 along the lines of that definition." Her way of doing this is to focus on the idea of human dignity and to insist that it has characterized true Charter interpretation ever since the first major case, *Big M Drug Mart Ltd.*[56] L'Heureux-Dubé argues that, more than any other right in the Charter, Section 15 gives effect to this value.[57] Equality itself can only make sense wedded to this idea of equal human dignity.[58] She quotes widely from previous cases where this has been said, but not built on, starting with McIntyre himself in *Andrews*:

> The promotion of equality entails the promotion of a society in which all are secure in the knowledge that they are recognized at law as human beings equally deserving of concern, respect and consideration.

She canvasses others like Wilson in *Guelph*, a case that notoriously failed to protect against discrimination:

> It is, I think, now clearly established that what lies at the heart of [Section 15] is the promise of equality in the sense of freedom from the burdens of stereotype and prejudice in all their subtle and ugly manifestations.

The essence of her understanding of equality is one that takes the experience of the complaining group as core, and is unashamedly subjective (she describes it in places as a "subjective-objective" test). It is best to use her own words, because it is a position easily mischaracterized.

> A person or group of persons has been discriminated against when members of that group have been made to feel, by virtue of the impugned legislative distinction, that they are less capable, or less worthy of recognition or value as human beings or as members of Canadian society, equally deserving of concern, respect, and consideration. These are the core elements of a definition of "discrimination."

Rejecting the idea that courts should judge discrimination by the feelings of the most sensitive of its citizens, but equally contemptuous of standards based on the "reasonable, secular, able-bodied, white male," L'Heureux-Dubé defines her "subjective-objective" standard as "the reasonably held view of one who is possessed of similar characteristics, under similar circumstances, and who is dispassionate and fully apprised of the circumstances." This stress on proceeding by centring on discrimination as the subjective consequence of legislation also requires abandoning the reliance of analogies to the enumerated grounds, and especially on the "immutable characteristics" argument. After all, as she argues, there might have been only two or three, or maybe no, enumerated grounds. Suppose religion had been left out

[56] *R. v Big M Drug Mart Ltd.*, 1 SCR 295 (1985) (Canadian Supreme Court).

[57] There has been surprisingly little in the academic literature written on the concept of dignity in Canadian jurisprudence. One interesting exception is DG Réaume, "Discrimination and Dignity," 2003 63 *Louisiana Law Review* 645–95. Although "dignity" appears quite often in US judicial opinions, it seldom plays an overall organising role as elsewhere, especially in Germany. One recent brave effort to give a dignitarian explanation for a wide range of US constitutional doctrine is MD Goodman, "Human Dignity in Supreme Court Constitutional Jurisprudence," 2005 84 *Nebraska Law Review* 740–94.

[58] However attractive this approach may be, it should be noted that in South Africa, where it has become common ground for the court, some commentators regard it as a dangerous, equality-limiting method. See Cowan, "Dignity"; and Fagan, "Dignity and Unfair Discrimination."

of the list; as it is a matter of fundamental choice, it could not have been brought into discrimination analysis by immutability. As is common amongst the rebels on constitutional courts, she is at least as "realistic" as any academic legal realist about judicial argument:

> the finding of "analogousness" will be driven by the result we want to reach. If we want to conclude that the impugned distinction is discriminatory, then we find the grounds to be analogous. If we want to conclude that a distinction is non-discriminatory, then we simply say that although the ground "may be analogous in some contexts," it is not in this case.

Discrimination analysis, were the court to follow L'Heureux-Dubé, would go like this. First, is there a legislative distinction? Does this result in the denial of one of the four equality rights? Is this because of membership "in an identifiable group"? Finally, is the distinction discriminatory? This last is to be judged from the "subjective-objective perspective." Of course much remains to be spelled out—and is spelled out in her judgement—about how to go about this analysis, but the essence is clear already. The sorts of matters to be considered would include, for example, questions of historical disadvantage, current vulnerability to stereotyping, or marginalization. Even the classic membership in a "discrete and insular minority" is mentioned. Her application to the facts of the case in *Egan* gives as good a picture as any of how her analysis would work:

> Although the claimants cannot be said to suffer any economic prejudice from the distinction since they are each entitled as individuals to a certain minimum income level, it cannot be overlooked that the rights claimants have been directly and completely excluded, as a couple, from any entitlement to a basic shared standard of living for elderly persons cohabiting in a relationship analogous to marriage. This interest is an important facet of full and equal membership in Canadian society. Given the marginalized position of homosexuals in society, the metamessage that flows almost inevitably from excluding same-sex couples from such an important social institution is essentially that society considers such relationships to be less worthy of respect, concern and consideration than relationships involving members of the opposite sex. This fundamental interest is therefore severely and palpably affected by the impugned distinction.

L'Heureux-Dubé's views have been cited extensively. This is not only because her opinion in *Egan* is one of the most penetrating pieces of constitutional interpretation anywhere. Its value here is that it demonstrates very well how rapidly any workable form of balancing test becomes a much more fundamental exercise in applied value judgement. One may reject such judgements, and prefer to stick as closely as Americans have tried to stick to the idea of absolute rights. Or one may openly adopt the idea of constitutional adjudication being the working out of the implications of a democratic vision, which is what this justice has tried to do. But there is probably no middle situation where legal tests can produce answers in a world that, in reality, demands balance between value and efficiency.

One might summarize the Canadian experience by noting first that the detailed tests are all judge-made. In a sense the various judicial pronouncements about how to handle the implications of not having absolute rights amount to nothing but giving each other advice. They are alternative lists of steps to making substantive judgements on democratic needs. It might be expected that the Canadian Charter will facilitate these judgements better than some constitutional documents because it does at least sketch what is meant by democracy, though very lightly. The Canadian tests are fragile, however. It is still not really possible to identify an entrenched and stable methodology, even if the disagreement on substance is limited. In particular the judges do not seem to find it easy to separate the question of whether a right has been breached with the separate question of whether the breach is justified. Furthermore, there is a continuous danger of circularity so that judicial instincts that government action is sensible and justified tend to lead to the finding that the constitution—or democratic ideals—never forbade the action in question anyway. In this sense there is an "Americanization" of the court's processes. If all this is inevitable, as it might be, then the position taken by L'Heureux-Dubé amongst others may be seen as preferable because of its greater honesty. It focuses on what anybody but a judge would think of first of all—has anyone been hurt, and how badly?

In comparison, I now turn to the South African experience, itself heavily influenced by Canada. It might be thought that because the South African constitution more fully spells out the values inherent in egalitarian democracy, and is in places more prescriptive about testing, that its constitutional court will have had an easier task. After all, South Africa is the home to what has come to be known as "transformative jurisprudence."[59] Thereafter I turn to proportionality in its home context of continental European constitutional argument.

Constitutional Tests in South Africa

The Formal Test

South African constitutional review has been heavily influenced by Canada, as was its constitution. But though the constitutional logic may be very similar, the socio-political context is dramatically different; this difference shows itself clearly in the attitudes and language of the judges on the Constitutional Court. These twin facts make South Africa a useful comparator to expand the earlier comments about the Canadian approach to the Charter. As with the Canadian, and indeed all recent constitutions, rights are not seen as absolutes. The South African equivalent of the Canadian Charter's Section 1 is Section 36, which reads:[60]

[59] For a judicial view of this idea, see Moseneke, "Bram Fischer Memorial Lecture."

[60] There is a problem with numbering, because many of the cases discussed here were decided under the interim constitution of 1994. The differences between the versions matter where I indicate, but not otherwise. Which text is being referred to will be specified.

(1) The rights in the Bill of Rights may be limited only in terms of law of general application to the extent that the limitation is reasonable and justifiable in an open and democratic society based on human dignity, equality and freedom, taking into account all relevant factors, including

a. the nature of the right;
b. the importance of the purpose of the limitation;
c. the nature and extent of the limitation;
d. the relation between the limitation and its purpose; and
e. less restrictive means to achieve the purpose.

(2) Except as provided in subsection (1) or in any other provision of the Constitution, no law may limit any right entrenched in the Bill of Rights.

It is obvious that this limitations section is written in a much more technical manner than the Charter's Section 1. As a reminder, the limitation to abridging a right in Canada requires only that the legislation set "such reasonable limits prescribed by law as can be demonstrably justified in a free and democratic society," and does not specify the constitutional tick boxes in subsections 1a to 1e, familiar as they are from judicial argument. (Each of the five could be found easily in almost any US case involving a limitation on a right, even if expressed differently.) Here, and elsewhere in the final constitution there is clear evidence of the redrafting being influenced by how the judges on the Constitutional Court discussed issues in their first years of hearings. The old limitation, set out in Section 33, simply provided that

The rights entrenched in this Chapter may be limited by law of general application, provided that such limitation—

a. shall be permissible only to the extent that it is—
   i. reasonable; and
   ii. justifiable in an open and democratic society based on freedom and equality.

Dignity was added, as was the spelling out of factors needing consideration. Something was removed too. The earlier constitution had borrowed a potentially crucial restriction on legislation where, in 33(1)(b), it had ruled that laws "shall not negate the essential content of the right in question"—this had been commented on negatively by the Constitutional Court, which claimed not to know what it meant. The idea, of course, comes from the German constitution, but is found elsewhere, for example in Hungary and even, in different language, in France. To some extent, the process by which a negotiated interim constitution was replaced with a final constitution—more carefully, and much more democratically, derived—allowed for experimentation. Thus although it might seem that Section 36 is much more prescriptive than Section 33, or than equivalents in other constitutions, it really is mainly a matter of appearances. In reality how the judges go about interpreting the constitution is as much their business in South Africa as elsewhere.[61] Certainly

[61] There are exceptions. The final constitution enforced some considerations the judges had not been happy with in the interim constitution, as discussed in chapter 6.

there has been no major change in the direction of judicial reasoning on limitations between those cases adjudicated under the old and new constitutions.

In practise the Constitutional Court of South Africa has not been very willing to make use of the limitations clause in either version. This is not because it has been very restrictive of government freedom to legislate. The court certainly has struck down legislation and taken other forceful action, as in cases affecting "positive rights."[62] But it has also been flexible, and frequently reminded itself of the special circumstances of a state trying to re-create a society along new value lines. Often where Section 33 or 36 has been taken into account, it is more in way of an insurance policy, after the judges have come to the conclusion that no substantive right has, in fact, been breached. Given this, they will often go on to say, using the famous legal strategy of "the argument in the alternative," that even if such an such a section has been breached, the legislation is saved by the limitations clause.

An example is a case from 2003 involving special court arrangements to try people under the Prevention of Organised Crime Act, 1998. The Constitutional Court overruled a lower court that had found a breach of the constitution, saying that the High Court had not properly interpreted the powers granted in the act. The opinions went on to say, however, that even though their own interpretation might still limit the Section 34 right for a brief period of time, the pressing concerns of the fight against organised crime would save the act under Section 36.[63] In contrast, ten months later in *Shaik* the High Court had found a restriction on the right to silence unconstitutional but saved by Section 36. The Constitutional Court struck down the appeal on the grounds that it was moot, and refused to discuss the Section 36 question on the grounds that the proceedings below had been so inept that "accordingly a proper justification enquiry under Section 36(1) of the Constitution could not and cannot now be conducted." The court was in fact concerned that the statute might *not* be saveable because of overbreadth,[64] but that the case was not a safe one through which to strike down an important statute.

Where the court is sure that a right has been breached, its obligatory glance to see if there is a limitations clause escape tends to be perfunctory and frankly subjective. In such cases there is little or no sense of deference to legislative or executive priority with the South African court. Typical was a case over regulations forbidding people serving in the National Defence Forces from joining trade unions. This was seen as an open-and-shut breach of the constitutional rights both to join unions and to enjoy freedom of expression. The main opinion of the court, written by Justice O'Regan. summarily (and partly inaccurately) noted that the only

[62] For example, *Grootboom and Others v Government of the Republic of South Africa and Others*, CCT 11/00 (South African Constitutional Court), on housing rights, and *Minister of Health and Others v Treatment Action Campaign and Others,* CCT 8/02 (South African Constitutional Court), on rights of HIV-positive pregnant women. A good treatment of these cases in terms of rights limitations is K Iles, "Limiting Socio-economic Rights: Beyond the Internal Limitations Clause," 2004 20 *South African Journal on Human Rights* 3, 448–65. But see also my discussion in earlier chapters.

[63] *National Director of Public Prosecutions v Mohamed NO and Others*, CCT 44/02 (South African Constitutional Court).

[64] *Shaik v Minister of Justice and Constitutional Development and Others*, CCT 34/03 (South African Constitutional Court).

countries that had such a full ban were those where there was no constitutional right to join unions. As other countries with such a right allowed unions, it could not be incompatible with discipline to have unionised soldiers, and therefore there was no chance of a Section 36 defence. The only other judgement, concurring, did not even consider the issue.[65]

South Africa and Restrictions on Expression

Perhaps the most useful example of the inutility of Section 36 is the leading South African case on freedom of speech, *Case v Minister of Safety and Security* in 1995, amongst the very earliest of the court's decisions.[66] As discussion of both Canadian and American constitutional testing began with the speech issue, this case, dealing with pornography, is especially helpful. The case is a delight for any aficionado of constitutional argument; it has two major opinions that the offending legislation is unconstitutional, whose writers, Didcott and Mokgoro, go out of their way to state that they do not agree with each other's reasons. Further, it has two other opinions highlighting special arguments modifying the majority opinion. The majority opinion is not the one containing the order of unconstitutionality with which every one of the justices agrees. This is signed by only its author, Mokgoro. Finally, the court's resident intellectual, Sachs, wrote an opinion concurring with *both* Mokgoro and Didcott. It was early days for the court. What was never at stake was that the legislation, Section 2 of the Indecent or Obscene Photographic Matter Act, 1967, a hangover from deep in the apartheid past, was unacceptable. That the act was never going to pass muster might have been evident by the shotgun nature of the constitutional questions posed to the Constitutional Court by the court below:

> Whether the provisions of section 2(1) of the . . . Act . . . are inconsistent with the provisions of Chapter 3 of the Constitution, in particular the provisions of section 8 (equality), 13 (the right to privacy), 14(1) (the right to freedom of conscience), 15 (freedom of speech, expression and artistic creativity), 24 (administrative justice) and 33(1) (the permissible limitations of the fundamental rights entrenched).

Equally important was the way the minority religious and racist values of the past rankled with the court. Mokgoro characterises this past as one where South Africans had been subjected to a system of censorship that was intended "to impose the Calvinist morality of a small ruling establishment on the entire population." She

[65] *South African National Defence Union v Minister of Defence*, CCT 27/98 (South African Constitutional Court). O'Regan claims that France is one of the countries that ban military unions but do not have the right to join a union. Such a right is clearly written into the preamble to the Fourth Republic constitution, itself incorporated into the Constitution of the Fifth Republic. See Bell, *French Constitutional Law*.

[66] *Case and Another v Minister of Safety and Security and Others; Curtis v Minister of Safety and Security and Others*, CCT 20/95 (South African Constitutional Court).

cites extensively from the report of the committee whose deliberations shaped the drafting of the 1963 precursor act. For example:

> In undesirable illustrations the female figure is presented . . . pre-eminently in scanty or inadequate attire. . . . The position has, in fact, become so serious that any right-minded person will ask what the consequences for Western civilisation and culture in this country are likely to be if action to combat [such illustrations] is not taken without delay.

Or:

> European women are portrayed . . . alluringly in calendars which have been distributed on a considerable scale among the Bantu in recent years. . . . consideration must apparently be given at least to the possibility that illustrations of European women are more attractive to the Bantu than those of Bantu women.

Mokgoro restricts herself entirely to the question of Section 15, the right to freedom of speech, expression, and artistic creativity, and asks immediately whether pornography is indeed material protected by the section. She attributes to an American approach the idea that sexually explicit material is not what the constitution is about, citing US case law widely, but concluding with a comment that fits well with the idea that US jurisprudence belongs some distance from the position one would put South Africa in.

> The United States approach is, at least in part, a reflection of the fact that the American bill of rights does not contain a limitations clause. Where, as in the case of our Constitution, the listing of rights is accompanied *by a clause that provided for the limitation, on a principled and considered basis*, of all enumerated rights, the better approach would seem to be to define the right generously, and to interpose any constitutionally justifiable limitations only at the second stage of the analysis. That, in fact, is the approach that this Court has adopted. (Emphasis added)

She does define the right generously, so that the possession of pornographic material is, in principle, protected. This done, she can turn immediately to the limitations argument, and here comments at length on foreign, mainly Canadian, cases, and especially *R v Butler* from 1992.[67] Indeed she is suspicious that it really hides a much more authoritarian and traditional attitude to sexual matter in speech cases:

> I would note that the *Butler* decision's willingness to posit the harmful effect of certain classes of sexually explicit material, notwithstanding that this effect was not, as the Court conceded "susceptible to exact proof," but based instead upon a "substantial body of opinion," has been criticised as a cover for *de facto* deference to morality-based evaluations. Moreover, just as it is often culturally subordinated groups that in the United States bear the brunt of American obscenity regulation, the manner in which *Butler* has been ap-

[67] *R v Butler*, 1 SCR 452 (1992) (Canadian Supreme Court).

> plied offers a cautionary tale regarding how well-intentioned legislation may be enforced in practice to suppress marginalised discourses that lack a powerful political constituency.

In any case she wants to dodge the whole question of what general considerations might allow the state to tackle the purely pornographic. In part this is deference to the parliamentary realm, and partly a cautious unwillingness to define anything that does not have to be defined at this early stage of the court's jurisprudence:

> It is not for this Court to propose a definition that could live with that right. That would usurp the role of the legislature. Rather, it is our task here to consider, mindful of the Constitution's directive that, if it is possible to save legislation by restrictive interpretation we should do so, whether the existing law comports with the right of free expression embodied in the Constitution.

The rest of the decision is very quick, despite the extensive coverage of limitation arguments in other jurisdictions.[68] Mokgoro rules that the character of the statute makes it overbroad, thus answering all Section 33 limitation questions very simply:

> the Attorney-General conceded that the Act amounted to a "loaded shot gun" with which the government that promoted the Act intended to "hit everything." Indeed, no one before the Court appeared to be willing to defend the statute in its present form.

And, therefore:

> The consensus fostered by these concessions affords this Court the opportunity to adjudicate this matter on the basis of overbreadth analysis, without reaching the issues of (a) whether the Legislature may, consistent with the new Constitution, regulate sexually explicit material at all; and, (b) if so, what form of definition of proscribed sexually explicit material will pass constitutional muster. As to the first issue, I propose to simply assume, for purposes of this matter, an answer in the affirmative. As to the second, for purposes of overbreadth analysis I need not attempt to formulate a constitutionally permissible definition.

It was this narrowness of Mokgoro's reasoning, the fact that it left room for at least the possibility of the state banning pornography, that seems to have made Didcott write, and the whole of the rest of the court support, an alternative explanation of why the act is unconstitutional. Unlike Mokgoro, they were not content to leave so much unanswered.

[68] Mokgoro specifically points out that in *Butler* the legislation survived only because the rule was justifiable under the limitations clause, because, inter alia, the code did not prohibit serious work of scientific, artistic or literary merit, nor did it affect the private possession or viewing of explicit materials. Her interpretation of the South African legislation meant it might do such things.

Didcott, as was often the case with his judgements, had a largely strategic reason for bringing the case under the privacy clause. The actual offence charged in this case was merely possession of pornographic material. To get it under Section 15, Mokgoro had had to argue that X's right to receive information and the like was a necessary component of the right to express. Didcott does not so much doubt this as not wish to decide any matters that do not need to be decided. Though he often took this course further than his colleagues, it was a natural policy stance of a brand-new court with a brand-new constitution—it had only come into effect a year earlier—to decide everything on the narrowest of points. Section 13, the right to privacy, could be decided much more simply, requiring no argumentative steps before the limitations analysis, thus maintaining the court's freedom to manoeuvre for the future. Didcott argues very simply that

> What erotic material I may choose to keep within the privacy of my home, and only for my personal use there, is nobody's business but mine. It is certainly not the business of society or the state. Any ban imposed on my possession of such material for that solitary purpose invades the personal privacy which section 13 of the interim Constitution guarantees that I shall enjoy. Here the invasion is aggravated by the preposterous definition of "indecent or obscene photographic matter" which section 1 of the statute contains. So widely has it been framed that it covers, for instance, reproductions of not a few famous works of art, ancient and modern, that are publicly displayed and can readily be viewed in major galleries of the world. That section 2(1) clashes with section 13 seems to be indisputable.

As the last sentences show, Didcott too relies purely on the overbreadth argument to dispose of the limitations argument. Didcott and those who agreed with him may have thought of this approach as minimising assumptions for the future. Mokgoro, though, may well be right in pointing out that by giving such a broad definition of privacy, it simply stores up a different set of potential problems. In truth, there is probably no such thing as a neutral or minimising argument in constitutional review, despite the common and widely held belief to the contrary. All approaches here have in common the idea that the court can pick and choose what part of Section 33 or 36 it finds most convenient. Both Didcott's and Mokgoro's opinions dismiss without reasoning plausible arguments to do with more substantive rational connections under the limitations clauses—the Canadian social harm argument being just one. Indeed Didcott sketches, only to ignore, an argument for invading privacy: if consumers fear prosecution merely for possession, the economic incentive to make pornography diminishes. Two other justices felt it necessary to issue short concurrences with Didcott just to restrict the sweeping nature of his apparent defence of privacy under all conditions.

If all the other judges got themselves in something of a tangle in trying to find the narrowest possible grounds for ruling the act unconstitutional, Sachs took the opposite tack, insisting that Mokgoro's and Didcott's arguments were complementary to each other, and adopted both of them, thus showing, perhaps, the artificiality of "high precision" testing:

> The invasion of privacy can be regarded as reducing any possible justification for the violation of the right to free expression. At the same time, the infringement of privacy becomes harder to countenance when it targets communicative matter, which may vary from . . . D. H. Lawrence . . . to the egregious degradation of the videos seized in the present case. Such material covers a range significantly different from, say, stolen goods, drugs or arms, the intrinsic harmfulness of which are universally recognized. Indeed, it seems strange that what one can do in one's bedroom one cannot look at in one's bedroom. The definitional overbreadth and operational heavy-handedness are common to invasions both of free expression and of privacy. I do not feel it necessary or even advantageous to confine my decision to the infringement either of expression or of privacy, since there is so much overlap between them.

South Africa's Equality Trilogy

Dodging issues seldom works. Ironically it might help were the South African Constitutional Court less consensual, making for clearer lines of constitutional argument. This is a particular problem with its equality jurisprudence, where there is a tendency to agree on methodology at all costs, even when serious substantive disagreements still arise that have to be dealt with inside an agreed method. South Africa has not experienced the Canadian problem of tests being reconsidered by groups on the court within years of being apparently consensually established. This is probably because no one can doubt the fierce commitment of South African constitutional judges to wide-ranging substantive equality, nor the huge difficulties they perceive in transforming their society into an egalitarian world.[69] Substantive disagreement combined with methodological unity appeared in the defining cases themselves.

There are three cases usually treated as the foundations of South African equality thinking under the nondiscrimination sections of the two constitutions: *Harksen v Lane, President of the Republic of South Africa v Hugo*, and *Prinsloo v Van Der Linde*.[70] Not only do textbooks rely on them, especially on *Harksen*, but the judges themselves cite all three as their own version of the Canadian "Equality Triangle." The proceedings in all three started in 1995, and they were thus handled under the interim constitution. Section 8 of the interim constitution governed discrimination and equality issues, and stated:

[69] This is well documented, along with some of its problems, in DM Davis, "The Shaping of a New Democracy within the Context of Tradition: Equality and the Respect for Diversity," in VC Jackson and M Tushnet, eds., *Defining the Field of Comparative Constitutional Law* (London: Praeger, 2002).

[70] *Harksen v Lane NO*, CCT 9/97 (South African Constitutional Court); *President of the Republic of South Africa v Hugo*, CCT 11/96 (South African Constitutional Court); *Prinsloo v Van Der Linde*, CCT 4/96 (South African Constitutional Court). For extensive analysis of these cases that also takes account of similarities with other jurisdictions, see Z Motala and C Ramaphosa, *Constitutional Law: Analysis and Cases* (Oxford: Oxford University Press, 2002).

> (1) Every person shall have the right to equality before the law and to equal protection of the law.
> (2) No person shall be unfairly discriminated against, directly or indirectly, and, without derogating from the generality of this provision, on one or more of the following grounds in particular: race, gender, sex, ethnic or social origin, colour, sexual orientation, age, disability, religion, conscience, belief, culture or language. . . .
> (4) Prima facie proof of discrimination on any of the grounds specified in subsection (2) shall be presumed to be sufficient proof of unfair discrimination as contemplated in that subsection, until the contrary is established.[71]

The structure is very similar to the Canadian model, including the distinction between specified and—as the South Africans have also termed them—analogous grounds, with the former constituting presumptively unfair discrimination. The formal difference is that most of what the South African constitution contains explicitly was left to judicial development in Canada. The real differences are twofold. First, although the Section 33/36 limitation clauses still provide one last chance for government action to be found nondiscriminatory, it has hardly ever had that effect—nearly all the analytic work is done within Section 8/9 essentially by incorporating rational connection and like arguments into that part of the analysis. Second, the Canadian influence that has most clearly come across is L'Heureux-Dubé's approach—she is often quoted directly—with concentration always on the effect of the actual law proposed. This is explicable not only because of the power of her thinking, but because the South African court, as shown in chapter 6, is predisposed to such an approach in general.

It should not be thought that the South African court makes the same mistake that some Canadian judges are accused of making—running together limitations clause analysis with the question of whether there is discrimination. Though dissenters may accuse the majority of doing so from time to time, the distinction is clear in all their minds. So in the first of the trio of cases, *Hugo*, the lone dissenter was Kriegler, who wanted to find that discrimination had occurred. He suggests that the majority has made this limitations/discrimination analysis mistake:

> Third, in invoking factors such as public reactions to the release of many prisoners and administrative efficiency, the majority applies a section 33(1) analysis at the point of looking for a rebuttal of unfairness.

Whether Kriegler was correct or not, no one from the majority suggested that it would have been acceptable for it to do what it was accused of. The fact is, as suggested earlier, that limitations analysis has little work to do in South African equality jurisprudence because the court is so very unlikely to find what Kriegler calls "justification, possibly notwithstanding unfairness." (Ironically one of those who concurred in the result but not in the reasoning in this case *did* use Section 33, having found discrimination existed, but the situation was highly unusual.)

[71] The analogous Section 9 in the final constitution is very similar. Pregnancy and birth are added as specific grounds.

Hugo was almost the paradigm of a "hard case." The president had used his prerogative powers to grant an amnesty to women prisoners with children under the age of twelve for the most sincere of humanitarian reasons. But this was a prima facie case of discrimination, because it was based on a specified ground, gender, from Section 8(2), which Section 8(4) makes presumptively unfair. For every conceivable reason, political, moral, and jurisprudential, the court had to find that the president's use of his prerogative was acceptable. This meant it had to find that he could overcome the presumption that the structure of the test imposed, in this case a test prescribed by the constitution itself, not previous judicial argument. The aim—the welfare of children—was laudable. The method, to free mothers only, blunt though it may be, was the only politically possible one because men prisoners outnumbered women by fifty to one. (And this, of course, was what Kriegler objected to finding in the discrimination analysis.) The real key was the finding that male prisoners were not unfairly treated because (*a*) they had no right to release and were not losing something, merely failing to get a special advantage and (*b*):

> The Presidential Act may have denied them an opportunity it afforded women, *but it cannot be said that it fundamentally impaired their rights of dignity or sense of equal worth.* (Emphasis added)

The disagreements in *Hugo* show just how hard it is to create workable tests. The South African court is genuinely very highly consensual on both method and value, and it still runs into these problems. The main problem was this. A major part of the justification for releasing mothers and not fathers was the acceptance of a generalisation that women played a much more important part in child rearing than men in South African society. This served to show the discrimination was not unfounded, and was not unfair. But the court is committed to the idea that a major premise of the constitution is that stereotypical thinking is the real evil of discrimination. Could one allow a stereotype as an argument that the distinction drawn was not discrimination? The majority is not unaware of the problem:

> The fact, therefore, that the generalisation upon which the appellants rely is true, does not answer the question of whether the discrimination concerned is fair. Indeed, it will often be unfair for discrimination to be based on that particular generalisation. Women's responsibilities in the home for housekeeping and child rearing have historically been given as reasons for excluding them from other spheres of life.

In this particular case, however, the majority deems it acceptable to rely on this generalisation. Mokgoro agrees with Kriegler in disputing this acceptance. Quite to the contrary:

> In my view, denying men the opportunity to be released from prison in order to resume rearing their children, entirely on the basis of stereotypical assumptions concerning men's aptitude at child rearing, is an infringement upon their equality and dignity.

Dignity, which is important to some Canadian justices, is vital in South African jurisprudence, as shown in earlier chapters. Mokgoro, however, finds the empirical difficulties of also releasing men to be a sufficient factor to save the president's actions under Section 33. It has to be wondered whether on any less sensitive case she would have reached that latter conclusion. One practical difficulty for the court in this case was that it did not oppose the clearly privileged to clearly underprivileged people. The most complex argument is the one that tries to make some sense out of the need to use a suspect category to combat inequality itself. The judges in the case make several references to this similarity with US jurisprudence. Consider, for example, O'Regan, trying to draw attention back, rather like L'Heureux-Dubé, to the fundamental question of unfairness. She criticises Kriegler:

> In my view, his approach is too restrictive. Even where discrimination in a particular case arises from reliance upon a stereotype or generalisation, the focus of the section 8(2) determination must remain whether the impact of the discrimination was unfair.

Whether it is pure pragmatism or not, O'Regan here and elsewhere distinguishes between the long-term goal of creating equality and the brute fact that insisting upon equal treatment in circumstances of established inequality may well result in the entrenchment of that inequality. One must always look at the groups in question and at the effects of the discrimination. She often takes a robust approach to such considerations:

> The more vulnerable the group adversely affected by the discrimination, the more likely the discrimination will be held to be unfair. Similarly, the more invasive the nature of the discrimination upon the interests of the individuals affected by the discrimination, the more likely it will be held to be unfair.

Can O'Regan's approach can be generalised into a method of applying the commonly agreed upon methodology of discrimination analysis? As Ackerman, Sachs, and O'Regan say ruefully elsewhere: "While our country, unfortunately, has great experience in constitutionalizing inequality, it is a newcomer when it comes to ensuring constitutional respect for equality."[72]

By the third of the equality triangle, the approaches and tests had become fairly well established. If *Hugo* was unusual because of the bleak underprivileged status of both sides to the dispute, *Harksen* featured a protagonist hard to find sympathy for—even more so given that what was at stake was discrimination in property rights. A wife was fighting a law that pools a solvent spouse's property with an insolvent one during bankruptcy proceedings until it can be firmly established that the solvency is not simply shielding actual assets that should go to creditors. In itself, this is not the stuff on which constitutional angst is based. But of course courts

[72]This comes from the majority ruling in *Prinsloo*, which gives extensive reasons for thinking that discrimination jurisprudence from other countries can be of very little help. The comment is often quoted in subsequent cases.

cannot choose the arena for protecting rights.[73] *Harksen* is important because the majority opinion deliberately set out to crystallise the court's equality jurisprudence, despite paying due deference to previous warnings in *Prinsloo* that it

> should be astute not to lay down sweeping interpretations at this stage but should allow equality doctrine to develop slowly and, hopefully, surely. This is clearly an area where issues should be dealt with incrementally and on a case by case basis with special emphasis on the actual context in which each problem arises.

At the risk of overrepetition it is probably worth summarising this judicial statement of proper procedure.

> Section 8(1)
>
> Does the rule differentiate between people or categories of people?
>
> If so, is there a rational connection between the differentiation in question and a legitimate governmental purpose?
>
> If so, there is no breach of Section 8(1). *But*:
>
> Section 8(2)
>
> Despite such rationality, does the differentiation nonetheless amount to unfair discrimination? This requires a two stage analysis:
>
> 1. Does the differentiation amount to "discrimination" and, if it does,
> 2. Is this "unfair discrimination"?
>
> If the differentiation is on a listed ground, the answers are automatically "Yes" and "Yes."
>
> If not, is it discrimination on an unspecified ground? The answer will be Yes where it is "based on attributes or characteristics which have the potential to impair the fundamental dignity of persons as human beings, or to affect them adversely in a comparably serious manner."

Finally, where the test has gone all the way to the previous paragraph and the answer is still Yes, was this discrimination "unfair"? At this point, to continue in a formulaic manner is unproductive. By this stage there is simply too much to consider, too many sociological and jurisprudential factors that might be relevant. The author of the opinion, while noting that the constitution is trying to protect human dignity, quotes L'Heureux-Dubé in *Egan*: "Dignity [is] a notoriously elusive concept. . . . it is clear that [it] cannot, by itself, bear the weight of s.15's task on its shoulders. It needs precision and elaboration." As L'Heureux-Dubé would approve, this statement of the test stresses the primacy of "the experience of the 'victim' of discrimination." Ultimately it is the impact of the discrimination that determines whether the discrimination is unfair. This is admirable. But is it a test? Various factors are suggested as worth considering, though it is also stressed that

[73] However, justices do look for cases where moral lines are clear when they wish to make major legal statements. Sachs has commented that he regrets no major religious rights case has occurred where the protagonist was more sympathetic.

they are not conclusive or final. They are the usual ones: What is the "position of the complainants in society"? Are they "historical victims"? What is the nature and purpose of the power in question? *Hugo* is cited to show that the absence of unfairness there lay partly in fact that the president's aim was to protect women with children who were both vulnerable and the victims of past discrimination.

One might think that an intellectual slippage has occurred here, because the focus seems to have shifted from the group who is complaining to the group who is to benefit. (Equally, there are shades of double counting because the Section 33 analysis is still to come, with a "weighing of the purpose and effect of the provision in question.") But the truth is that none of these lists or tabulations can get very far from being an impressionistic listing of the sorts of considerations a sensible and decent judge will think about when forming the intuitive judgement about unfairness. This is precisely why the South African courts are so often split on the result of assessing the implications of an agreed methodology. It is also worth noting how much more complex the judicial version of the analysis is than the already rather prescriptive language of Section 8.

The actual results in *Harksen* follow this typical pattern. At issue is whether a statute that differentiates between a bankrupt's spouse and others who may have had similar dealings with him is discriminatory. The majority holds that there is a rational justification for this differentiation, and that the purpose of the act, to prevent bankrupts from concealing assets, is helped by the provision. So the question now becomes one of whether this is discrimination, marital status not being a specified ground. Again the majority have no problem finding that it is discrimination, because other people, including a bankrupt's children, may have a similarly close relationship but are not covered. Stating that "The differentiation does arise from their attributes or characteristics as solvent spouses, namely their usual close relationship with the insolvent spouse and the fact that they usually live together in a common household," the court goes on somewhat gnomically to insist that "These attributes have the potential to demean persons in their inherent humanity and dignity." But is the discrimination unfair? Applying the considerations described above, we find that spouses are not a "vulnerable . . . group adversely affected by . . . discrimination." The majority argues that "the purpose of the [act] is to protect the public interest by protecting creditors and this does not offend the values of section 8." Finally the effect on the discriminated group is described as merely inconvenience:

> Looked at from the perspective of solvent spouses, it is the kind of inconvenience and burden that any citizen may face when resort to litigation becomes necessary. . . . Again, the inconvenience and burden of having to resist such a claim does not lead to an impairment of fundamental dignity or constitute an impairment of a comparably serious nature.

So all is well, and Section 33 need not come into it. Why then was the court split five to four with O'Regan and Sachs writing powerful dissents? The judges did not disagree on any aspect of the test as a method. As far as O'Regan is concerned the disagreement is truly narrow: she simply asserts that there is a damage to the interests of solvent spouses that is "substantial and sufficient to constitute unfair discrimination." She does not, for example, accept that past social patterns and expectations make discrimination on the basis of marital status tantamount to gender discrimination, as counsel had tried to argue. That a constitutional decision might depend on something as narrow as this disagreement is genuinely odd.

Sachs, however, explains rather more fully what might be wrong about the discrimination. Attacking the majority's characterisation of the impact as "mere inconvenience," he argues in a way that more fully shows how the values of Section 8 become involved:

> In my view, section 21 . . . represents more than an inconvenience to or burden upon the solvent spouse. It affronts his or her personal dignity as an independent person within the spousal relationship and perpetuates a vision of marriage rendered archaic by the values of the interim Constitution.

Sachs's position rests on two different sociological or historical arguments. The first goes to human dignity. Describing the traditional concept of marriage as almost denying the independent existence of the partners, he suggests that the image of marriage in the act as its underlying premise is "that one business mind is at work within the marriage, not two." This offends against the constitution's values because it "stems from and reinforces a stereotypical view of the marriage relationship which, in the light of the new constitutional values, is demeaning to both spouses." All this does, perhaps, is to make O'Regan's points more colourfully. It is his second attack that shows how imaginative a fully fledged commitment to producing equality through antidiscrimination jurisprudence needs to be. But Sachs's discussion reveals how problematic it is that a case can depend on the estimate of whether a complainant has suffered substantially or not. I quote Sachs at length here:

> Nor is the degree of inconvenience the critical factor. Rather, what is most relevant to the question of unfairness is the assumption which puts together what constitutional respect for human dignity and privacy requires be kept asunder. This is one of those areas where to homogenise is not to equalise, but to reinforce social patterns that deny the achievement of equality as promised by the Preamble and section 8. The intrusion might indeed seem relatively slight. Yet an oppressive hegemony associated with the grounds contemplated by section 8(2) may be constructed not only, or even mainly, by the grand exercise of naked power. It can also be established by the accumulation of a multiplicity of detailed, but interconnected, impositions, each of which, de-contextualised and on its own, might be so minor as to risk escaping immediate attention, especially by those not disadvantaged by them.

Enough has been said to show the fundamental difference between South Africa and both Canada and the United States in its application of constitutional tests. South African judges disagree, when they disagree, about characterising impact, not about the logic of tests. The North Americans may indeed also do so, but the overt disagreement is about testing methodology, as though one only has to get that right to take away the problems. For this reason alone it might seem that Canada belongs nearer to the United States on the spectrum that may underlie court attitudes to rights limitations. The opposite end of the spectrum, as argued later, is taken by Germany and France.

Indirect Discrimination

One final case from South Africa needs to be considered. It is the nearest to an important methodological difference that has yet arisen, and it may foretell future problems of a different order than the previous disagreements on detailed weightings. Decided a year after the equality trilogy, *City of Pretoria v Walker* centred round the less-examined problem of indirect discrimination.[74]

The postapartheid council of Pretoria had to govern and manage a new urban conglomerate that had added two poor and black towns to the old white and rich city. One of the most serious problems was providing water supply, and charging for it in a way that actually led to the city being paid. The old city continued to be treated as it had been, with water supply charged on the basis of monitored usage. The new black areas, where the monitoring equipment was not in place, was covered by a flat-rate tariff that worked out cheaper than the typical rates charged to the old city inhabitants. A white pressure group organized a payment strike and claimed to be discriminated against because of this differential charge level. It also complained against a city policy by which payment arrears for those with metered water led to court orders and legal action to enforce payment, while negotiations were the method used for the new black areas. It was only this second issue the court accepted might raise a valid issue. But on it, the majority of the court did find indirect discrimination on the basis that the areas, though defined geographically, were essentially racially homogenous and thus to prosecute inhabitants of old Pretoria but not of the new towns was to apply a racially based and therefore discriminatory policy. Racial discrimination being a listed ground, the city was unable to justify its policy, and the Section 33 analysis also failed to acquit them. Left at that stage, the case would have been a good example of how evenhanded the new constitution is, with the majority opinion even going so far to say of the white complainant that

> The respondent does however belong to a racial minority which could, in a political sense, be regarded as vulnerable. It is precisely individuals who are members of such minorities who are vulnerable to discriminatory treatment and who, in a very special sense, must look to the Bill of Rights for protection. When that happens a Court has a clear duty to come to the assistance of the person affected. Courts should however always be astute to distinguish between genuine attempts to promote and protect equality on the one hand and actions calculated to protect pockets of privilege at a price which amounts to the perpetuation of inequality and disadvantage to others on the other.

[74] *City of Pretoria v Walker*, CCT 8/97 (South African Constitutional Court).

One uncharacteristic aspect of this case is that the majority opinion took some effort to dispute the arguments of the dissenter, Justice Sachs. Usually, as with the English House of Lords, opinion writers just ignore counterarguments in other opinions.[75] It was necessary to do otherwise here because what Sachs had to say might, if accepted, make a considerable mess of South African equality jurisprudence. Sachs started by acknowledging that

> Just as the transformation of our harsh social reality is by its very nature difficult to accomplish, so is it hard to develop a corresponding and appropriate jurisprudence of transition.

He went on to describe his own reaction to the case; "I find it jurisprudentially incongruous to regard the complainant as a victim of unfair discrimination." His reason for finding that there was no indirect discrimination is crucial, and challenging to the orthodoxy of the tests. Indeed his argument essentially destroys the usual basis common to most jurisdictions for indirect discrimination analysis: "Nor, in my view, was there indirect discrimination on the grounds of race simply because whites lived in one area and blacks in another." He claims that "the policy of selective enforcement was based on the identification of objectively determinable characteristics of different geographical areas, and not on race."

It is not just that Sachs is making a different guess abut the underlying motives of Pretoria's civil servants; it was accepted by all on the court that intention has no relevance. Rather he is proposing a completely new test of when indirect discrimination may be found. Indirect discrimination in most jurisdictions works by showing that what Americans might call a "facially neutral" discriminatory characteristic that happens to be highly correlated to a protected characteristic can amount to unconstitutional discrimination. Without such a logic, there can be no restriction on indirect discrimination. Sachs's concern is that the huge amount of social reconstruction needed cannot be safely undertaken if indirect discrimination is easy to establish—essentially because there will be many policies that could be seen in that light. His opposition goes to the entire purpose of Section 8, and its replacement, Section 9.

> Looked at in its historical setting, the text makes it clear that equality is not to be regarded as being based on a neutral and given state of affairs from which all departures must be justified. Rather, equality is envisaged as something to be achieved through the dismantling of structures and practices which unfairly obstruct or unduly attenuate its enjoyment. In this framework, the presumption of unfairness as provided for by section 8(4) makes perfectly good sense when there is either overt or direct differentiation on one of the specified grounds such as race or sex, or where patterns of disadvantage based on such grounds are being reinforced without express reference but as a matter of reality. *On the other hand, the presumption makes no sense at all when invoked to shield continuing advantage gained as a result of past discrimination from the side-*

[75] See, on this point, Robertson *Judicial Discretion.*

> *winds of remedial social programmes designed to reduce the effect of such structured advantage.* (Emphasis added)

He was, as he admits openly, making a policy argument, and one that in a sense suggests an extreme form of judicial deference in cases of indirect discrimination.

> In our still fragmented and divided country, with its legacy of racial discrimination and its deeply entrenched culture of patriarchy, and with its practices and institutions based on homophobia or on a lack of attention to the most elementary rights of disabled people, almost every piece of legislation, and virtually every kind of governmental action, will impact differentially on the groups specified in section 8(2) of the Constitution. There are strong policy and practical reasons for holding that something more than differential impact is required before indirect discrimination under section 8 can be inferred.

This remains a minority view, but the final constitution does not solve it because the language is not relevantly different from that of the interim constitution. As yet there have not been cases that the court has been unable to handle by finding that discrimination, if it occurred, was justifiable. But there must be a strong argument, if only from intellectual honesty, for taking Sachs's approach seriously in the context of transformative jurisprudence. Yet this does not restrict the scope of the problem much, because all constitutions have an ongoing transformative role where values and expectations develop.

These three case studies show how very hard it is to formalize any approach to constitutional limitations on the right to equality, or more generally, to any constitutional right. Or, alternatively, that formalizing an approach does not serve to make decisions any easier, or to remove them from the realm of individual judicial ideological preference. I turn to continental European jurisdictions, more experienced with the core idea of proportionality to see how they fare.

Constitutional Tests in Germany

Germany's Basic Approach

Even using this subheading, to maintain comparability with the other sections, produces some unease in discussion of Germany. To be sure, the core question is still there—how does the German constitutional court decide whether or not a right in the Basic Law may be overridden? But as chapter 2 indicated, it is hard to phrase the issues in the same language as with the previous three countries. To start with, a good deal of the German caseload does not, strictly speaking, involve striking down legislation. Instead, it deals with complaints that the administration, the government, or a lower court has failed to respect the constitution. More fundamentally the Germans do not as easily conceive of the situation as an isolated or isolatable right being contravened for policy reasons by government action. At a purely formal level the situation is the same in Germany as in the United States,

Canada, or South Africa. There is a bill of rights binding, amongst other powers, the federal parliament. There is, unlike the United States, the equivalent to a limitations clause. Article 19 serves this purpose, though the language is rather different from the Canadian Section 1 or South Africa's Section 33.

> Article 19 [Restriction of basic rights]
>
> (1) Insofar as, under this Basic Law, a basic right may be restricted by or pursuant to a law, such law must apply generally and not merely to a single case. In addition, the law must specify the basic right affected and the Article in which it appears.
>
> (2) In no case may the essence of a basic right be affected.

Oddly, for a court least as committed to human rights as any other, very little use has been made of this direct textual grant of power in assessing the constitutionality of laws and actions. One can perhaps see why. On the face of it anyway, Article 19(1) seems fitted for the very rare occasion—perhaps a national emergency, where the government seeks intentionally and with clarity of purpose, to restrict a right. In fact governments are much more likely to be indifferent to a right, and to defend themselves with the claim that the legislation does not, really, infringe a right properly understood. As such, government action everywhere probably fits the US Supreme Court's approach. Nor does the restriction not to damage "the essence of a basis right" work very well in other contexts. It is possible that German constitutional justices have found it as opaque as the South Africans when an equivalent was put into the provisional constitution, a point commented on earlier, and revisited in the concluding chapter of this book. It is even more likely, though, that Article 19 appears underused because of another feature of the German constitution, one it shares with other European documents like the European Convention on Human Rights. Many of the other articles of the constitution contain their own internal limitations clauses. Article 2 shows two versions of these limiting clauses:

> Rights of liberty (1). Everyone has the right to the free development of his personality insofar as he does not violate the rights of others or offend against the constitutional order or the moral code. (2). Everyone has the right to life and to inviolability of his person. The freedom of the individual is inviolable. These rights may only be encroached upon pursuant to a law.

Article 2(1) protects free development of personality subject to relatively precise restrictions, not to "violate the rights of others or offend against the constitutional order or the moral code." Article 2(2) simply says, *ceteris paribus*, that individual freedom "rights may only be encroached upon pursuant to a law," though this means more than it might in some countries, because no mere regulation, administrative order, or local by-law would count as "a law," which invariably means a full parliamentary statute. My process here, looking only at general limitation rules, therefore underestimates the extent to which Germany provides possibilities for restricting the reach of rights. Furthermore, Article 19 is referred to relatively rarely precisely because of the judge-made "proportionality" limitation, which comes into play before the ultimate limit set by Article 19 is reached.

The German constitution does provide, in the next article after the general limitation of Article 19, the usual brief self-description of the state, familiar in type from the Canadian Charter and South African constitution. It is both shorter and significantly different from the other examples. Germany is defined as a "a democratic and social federal state." The word *social* has turned out to be a useful guiding principle for certain types of cases, but the most important gloss on *democratic* comes from the court's own extrapolation from other clauses in the constitution. This is the idea of Germany as a "militant democracy," by which is meant that the state will not allow its own liberal nature to be used to overthrow it.[76] As such, it is a strong limitation on certain rights both to expression and political organisation, originating in the first case to ban a political party.[77]

To a large extent the language in which rights are expressed does the work of limitations clauses because most of them are not set in absolutist terms. Not only that, but the details of the limitations are often spelled out. The second most important right in the court's jurisprudence, the right to personal freedom guaranteed in Article 2, sets out that "Every person shall have the right to free development of his personality," but only so long as "he does not violate the rights of others or offend against the constitutional order or the moral law." Despite the slightly archaic sound of a ban on violating "the moral law," one might argue that such a limitation is implicit in any freedom clause, but it is crucial that the Basic Law does not rely on implication. Article 5, on rights of freedom of expression, is more detailed in what it grants than many; it covers the right to "express and disseminate his opinions in speech, writing, and pictures," it guarantees specifically not only press freedom but also "freedom of reporting by means of broadcasts and films," and says bluntly, "There shall be no censorship." However, anyone who took that last phrase to be exceptionally strong may be brought aback by Article 2(2):

> These rights shall find their limits in the provisions of general laws, in provisions for the protection of young persons, and in the right to personal honour.
>
> And indeed honour has been found commonly to restrict article 2 rights.

Article 7 grants a variety of rights to freedom of choice in education, including, unusually, specifying that there is a right to establish private schools, though they require approval from the Länder. Approval cannot be given, however, unless "segregation of pupils according to the means of their parents will not be encouraged thereby."

[76] An interesting discussion, in the context of this chapter, is RJ Krotoszynski Jr., "A Comparative Perspective on the First Amendment: Free Speech, Militant Democracy, and the Primacy of Dignity as a Preferred Constitutional Value in Germany," 2004 78 *Tulane Law Review* 1549. An account of the application of the doctrine in constitutional adjudication is G Brinkmann, "Militant Democracy and Radicals in the West German Civil Service," 1983 46 *Modern Law Review* 584–600.

[77] *The Communist Party Case*, 5 BVerfGE 85 (1956) (German Federal Constitutional Court).

It might seem that the constitutional court's job has not been to find ways to allow necessary legislation but to preserve rights against their own limiting clauses. If that is so, it has certainly been successful, though there are areas, especially with expressive rights, where some liberals regard the limitations as excessive, particularly when compared to those in the United States. We get clues to why this is so, as well as to how it has come about, by looking at the text of another right, the right to property. Though the right is strongly asserted, it is nonetheless cast in an unusual way. Article 14 starts in a straightforward way: "(1) Property and the right of inheritance shall be guaranteed. Their content and limits shall be defined by the laws." It immediately qualifies this: "(2) Property entails obligations. Its use shall also serve the public good." Thus the "social" state comes alive in the Basic Law's own rights section. Much more detail about these possible limitations follows:

> (3) Expropriation shall only be permissible for the public good. It may only be ordered by or pursuant to a law that determines the nature and extent of compensation. Such compensation shall be determined by establishing an equitable balance between the public interest and the interests of those affected. In case of dispute respecting the amount of compensation, recourse may be had to the ordinary courts.

It is this balancing of interests and of values that runs through the whole of German constitutional adjudication, whether or not the text of a right in the Basic Law explicitly requires it.

It is impossible to understand the German approach to constitutional testing unless one grasps, as chapter 2 attempts to explain, the whole idea of the constitution as an integrated set of values. (Though it is sometimes loosely claimed that the Germans have a hierarchically ordered set of values, this is true only in the sense that Article 1, the right to dignity is supreme, and indeed cannot be amended.) There are many who do not accept this, or at least do not accept the sorts of decisions the court gives because of it. The German constitutional court does not like giving absolute answers to what it probably thinks are oversimplified questions, and this reluctance offends those who win, as often as those who lose, because they do not win "clearly enough." In chapter 2 the much maligned *Co-determination* case was discussed.[78] One might almost think, reading some of the criticisms, that the court had struck down the law. In fact it accepted it, but left open whether a more full-blooded version of the reform in question would be constitutional. Similarly, deeply committed Europeanists objected to the decision in the *Maastricht* case.[79] Here the complaint was that the court insisted that though the treaty was acceptable, there were limits to how much sovereignty the constitution would

[78] *Co-determination Case*, 50 BVerfGE 290 (1979) (German Federal Constitutional Court). A useful comment is Streeter, "Co-determination in West Germany." Stone Sweet is probably the most severe critic of the decision, in various publications, notably in *Governing with Judges*.

[79] *Maastricht Case*, 89 BVerfGE 155 (1993) (German Federal Constitutional Court). See A Rainer, "The Treaty on European Union and German Constitutional Law: The German Constitutional Court's Decision of October 12, 1993, on the Treaty of Maastricht," 1994 9 *Tulane European and Civil Law Forum* 91–145.

allow Germany to give up. The court is not prepared to give open-ended and absolute judgements. It will not authorise ahead of time policies similar to but more extensive than the legislation it is dealing with, because it does not accept that any value is an absolute.

Limiting Free Speech

It is in decisions on freedom of speech that this refusal to give broad answers shows itself most clearly. There are no great cases in which serious legislative attempts to curtail freedom of speech have been struck down by the German constitutional court, though this does not mean, as we shall see later, that the value has never been upheld. In fact to study the FCC's work on freedom of speech, as I do here largely through its use of Article 5, gives a potentially misleading impression. Article 5 bans restrictions on speech except as contained in "General Laws," interpreted to mean laws that have as their purpose the protection of some other legal good, but that may incidentally affect speech rights. As the government seldom intentionally attacks freedom of speech in itself, the real problem for the court is thrown back onto a proportionality analysis *within* Article 5's coverage. One area I have sadly not been able to cover properly in this book, jurisprudence on freedom of broadcasting, particularly shows the FCC as just as supportive of expression rights as any other constitutional court.

One case that upheld a statute serves to show the court's approach as well as the way the nature of the German constitutional text plays into this stance. Germany has a Youth Protection Act giving the state very broad powers to carry out its remit. Part of the act authorises the setting up of a board empowered to ban the sales of material, including sound recordings, that threaten the moral development of the young. This board of "experts" has been quite active over the years. It was, for example, under this act that Germany banned the distribution of neo-Nazi rock music in the early 1990s as part of the effort to suppress far-right extremism.[80] The constitutionality of the act was tested early in its life, especially in the *Heinrich* case in 1960.[81] It was upheld in *Heinrich*, but at other times, for example in the *Nudist Magazine* case, an application of the act has been held unconstitutional.[82] As noted before, German constitutional law is as much about the application of laws as about their innate constitutionality. Heinrich's appeal had been against a ban on advertising catalogues that were themselves banned under the act. In the second case a general interest magazine promoting nudity also came under a ban. What the court did was to vindicate the general terms of the Youth Protection Act as it applied against an Article 5. It was rather simple to grant that "the legislature may thus adopt measures designed to prevent children from gaining access to such materials," because Article 5 itself expressly says that freedom of speech may be

[80] DA Jacobs, "The Ban of Neo-Nazi Music: Germany Takes On the Neo-Nazis," 1993 34 *Harvard International Law Journal* 563. See also, and more generally for this section, Krotoszynski, "Comparative Perspective."

[81] *Heinrich Case*, 11 BVerfGE 234 (German Federal Constitutional Court).

[82] *Nudist Magazine Case*, 30 BVerfGE 336 (German Federal Constitutional Court).

limited by "provisions for the protection of young persons." What was needed, and this was spelled out more fully in the *Nudist Magazine* case, was careful balancing between the constitutional values in question, and careful tailoring of legislation by the parliament. The difference, then, in the *Nudist Magazine* case involved not different categorisation, but the sheer facts of the case.

This is typical of German constitutional adjudication, and leaves the idea of tests somewhat out of focus. Beatty argues, in an article on religious freedom under constitutions, that this German approach is shared by individual judges in other countries, though is nowhere else dominant. His analysis and mine are certainly compatible, and it is convenient to adopt his terminology here.[83] Beatty describes the Anglo-American approach as being entirely concerned with interpreting constitutional texts, relying on historical experience and precedent to eke out meaning. This he compares with what he calls the more "pragmatic" approach of, inter alia, the German court. Although the starting point for these courts still has to be the constitutional text, the real focus is on the factual details, and the precise terms of the law in question. The actual process of constitutional interpretation, according to Beatty, is not expected to find "a definition or rule that categorically settles the outcome of a case." Instead it "only identifies principles and criteria courts can use to evaluate the validity of the law and the rights and other interests it affects." Such an approach may be better suited to a Kelsen court than to supreme courts that are also charged with constitutional interpretation. This approach of adducing principles above all requires proportionality between means and ends and empirical effect, and it has to "insist on a measure of proportionality between all three." Beatty is primarily concerned with religious liberty rights in this article, but what he says of the German court's orientation in that area applies much more broadly:

> the German Court has said the state must strive to "reach an optimization of the conflicting interests" that are affected by the relevant law and avoid policies that are "excessive." . . . where it perceives that there is a conflict of competing rights at stake, the Court relies on a "principle of practical concordance" according to which, "no one of the conflicting legal positions [is to] be preferred and maximally asserted, but all [are to be] given as protective as possible an arrangement."

Testing Rights and the Value of Governance

Chapter 2 expounds a general interpretation similar to Beatty's. The easiest way to grasp the court's overall attitude to testing constitutionality is to realise that there is, in one way, always a clash between values. Even where on the surface the question is whether or not a sole, identified, basic right can trump a statute, there is a value clash. The "missing" value is the value of governance. This shows

[83] D Beatty, "The Forms and Limits of Constitutional Interpretation," 2001 49 *American Journal of Comparative Law* 79. (I part company with him on his analysis of the South African cases.)

at its clearest in a case mentioned in chapter 2, *Glycol*, though German academics have interpreted what went on in that case somewhat differently.[84] The question in the case was whether the government was entitled to issue health warnings about contaminated wine. In general it was a question about the wine distributors' rights to protection of their property rights (and the right not to be defamed in the companion case concerning members of certain religious sects). The situation was complicated by the fact that the government appeared to have acted without statutory backing. To the dismay of many commentators the court found that there was an overarching right (or duty) to govern, which provided the countervailing value to those claimed by the affected parties. This is a rather specific example of a general assumption, so deep that few even notice it. In a way, this assumption replaces the limitations clause, or at least makes such a clause redundant. The assumption is basically that government, whether executive or legislature, has the right to act in the public interest. Constitutions in many common-law countries, particularly but not only the United States, came into being to protect the reverse assumption. To some extent, most constitutions with rights attached are Lockean, committed to the position that governments ought not to act unless it is absolutely necessary to protect constitutionally specified ends.[85]

The state in continental Europe, on the other hand, often has a primacy. The constitutional question will be whether or not it can be limited for particular reasons in specified contexts. How this works out depends hugely on the immediate and more distant paths to constitutionalism. France and Germany have different attitudes historically both to the state and to the legitimacy of judicial interference, while the Eastern European societies share similar immediate pasts all of which condition the approaches in detail. But these path dependencies should not blind us to their similarities. What they all have in common is a jurisprudence that inverts the liberal priority of questioning. Not, "Can this right be limited?" but "Can this action be limited by this right?"[86] In such a situation, testing is bound to be the finely tuned balancing of proportionality. This emphatically does not mean that constitutional protection of rights values will be weaker. No Western liberal democracy, to take one example, has a court that would dare to strike down the government's budget because it failed to provide protection for crucial human rights. Yet both Poland and Hungary have done just that, as discussed elsewhere in this book. What it does mean is perhaps best characterised as a matter of the government having rights as well.

All cases are cases of conflict between rights, to be sorted out intelligently according to a much more traditional principle, the principle of the "rule of law." It

[84] *The Glycol Case*, 1 BvR 558, 1428/91 (2002) (German Federal Constitutional Court). For a discussion see Rogers and Vanberg, "Judicial Advisory Opinions."

[85] This is a point often made specifically in the South African court when it contrasts the South African constitution with typically liberal ones. But even South Africa lacks anything like the German conception of the power to act.

[86] The pro-state stance is not restricted to civil-law countries. It is clearly part of the judicial orientation in the United Kingdom, and not just because there is no constitutional review. Judicial attitudes towards the state in the exercise of judicial review of administration often take this stance.

was that aspect of the rule of law which protects "legitimate expectations," and the value of "legal certainty" that led the Hungarian court to strike down part of the budget, not a specified right to, for example, property.[87] This point was dealt with at length in chapter 3. This is very much the case with the German approach to constitutional testing. In one version or another the idea that "proportionality" of legislative means to ends, and of the value of the good to be achieved compared with the suffering caused in achieving it, is at the heart of the German constitutional court's rulings. No jurisdiction has a monopoly on any constitutional term. Proportionality can occur as a technique or value outside the code law world, as we have seen in Canada. It does indeed get discussed in unlikely contexts, for instance in Australian constitutional law, even though Australia has no bill of rights.[88] It is increasingly talked of in UK administrative law, though often in a rather dismissive manner. One quick search found 183 American law journal articles with the word *Proportionality* in the title, but in America proportionality analysis has a much more restricted and technical application.[89] There are traces of proportionality doctrine even the United States, of course. Justice Kennedy has adopted "proportionality" language when assessing the legitimacy of congressional displacement, through Section 5 of the Fourteenth Amendment, of state autonomy.[90] Elsewhere some suggestions have occurred, noticeably in Thurgood Marshall's dissent in *San Antonio v Rodriguez* (1973), where he came close to urging the abolition of tests and the outright use of proportionality.[91]

Despite all of this, the intellectual home of proportionality when talking of rights limitation is continental Europe, and especially Germany. It can come as a surprise, therefore, to discover that the word does not appear in the Basic Law.[92] Why then is Germany the home of proportionality? The answer is that the Basic Law does commit Germany to being a *Rechtsstaat*, and Germany has a long tradition, dating at least to the late eighteenth century, of the rule of law implying proportionality in administrative law.[93] (It must be remembered that "rule of law" is a deeply inadequate rendering into English of the connotation in continental European languages of *Rechtsstaat*. It is a much richer and substantive concept, again a point made at length in earlier chapters. Amongst other differences, conti-

[87] An interesting discussion of the difficulty of applying the idea of the "rule of law" in the United States is given in Fallon, "The Rule of Law." If the idea is as inchoate as he thinks even in a common-law country, it is not surprising that its translation into *Rechtsstaat* should be problematic. An empirical investigation into popular attitudes to the rule of law is given in JL Gibson and GA Caldeira, "The Legal Cultures of Europe," 1996 30 *Law and Society Review* 1, 55–86.

[88] BF Fitzgerald, "Proportionality and Australian Constitutionalism," 1993 12 *University of Tasmania Law Review* 265–322.

[89] Justice Kennedy has adopted "proportionality" language when assessing the legitimacy of congressional displacement, through Section 5 of the Fourteenth Amendment, of state autonomy. I am grateful to one of the reviewers of my book for pointing this out to me. The words here are from him.

[90] I am grateful to one of the publisher's reviewers of this book for this and the following point.

[91] *San Antonio School District v Rodriguez*, 411 US 1 (1973) (US Supreme Court).

[92] However, it does appear in some of the Länder constitutions.

[93] Currie, *Constitution of Germany*, 307–10.

nental legal thinkers have always thought that proportionality was actually part of the idea of the rule of law.)[94]

Herein lies another clue to understanding continental European constitutional testing, which is that it helps to imagine constitutional adjudication as a grander version of administrative law, where the constitution applies to the whole state, much as statutory authority applies to administrative action. At times the process of constitutional testing can look almost as mechanical and rule bound as in other jurisdictions. The German court for example, always checks that there is a proper statutory basis for action that might threaten a basic right—this is what was at stake in the *Glycol case*. This is because the statutory basis is so clearly important to an idea of the rule of law derived from a healthy administrative law tradition, something France has every bit as much of as has Germany. Nudist magazines were acceptable because banning them was overreaction given the rights of parents to encourage their children into such a healthy (and traditionally popular) German habit. It was not disproportionate to prevent Herr Heinrich from distributing seedy catalogues to the young. In both cases the validity of a statute depended on balancing rights proportionately, where the constitution relatively unambiguously legitimates conflicting rights. A typical German judicial dictum is that "No one of the conflicting legal positions [is to] be preferred and maximally asserted, but all [are to be] given as protective as possible an arrangement."

Development of the Proportionality Test

The proportionality test was most clearly first stated in a case that also used the formal limitation clause, Article 19(2), "In no case may the essence of a basic right be affected." A statute would have allowed involuntary committal to a mental hospital for what the law itself described as "improvement." The court held:

> It is not amongst the tasks of the state to "improve" its citizens. The state therefore has no right to deprive them of freedom simply to improve them, when they pose no danger to themselves or to others . . . since [this purpose] cannot constitute a sufficient ground for the deprivation of personal liberty, [the statute] encroaches upon the essential content of the basic right.[95]

At the same time the court also held that such a committal would offend "the principle of proportionality that is rooted in the rule of law." Fully unpacked, the proportionality "principle" can be made to look very much like the complex testing rules of other courts. All the ingredients are there. Was the least intrusive means

[94] Sadurski, Czarnota, and Krygier, *Spreading Democracy*, contains extended discussions of the concept as applied in some European jurisdictions. An excellent formal statement of the meanings of the concept is given in RS Summers, "Principles of the Rule of Law," 1999 74 *Notre Dame Law Review* 1691–1711. A critical consideration of the need for greater thought about the concept is given in G Pearson and M Salter, "Getting Public Law Back into a Critical Condition: The Rule of Law as a Source for Immanent Critique," 1999 8 *Social Legal Studies* 4, 483–508.

[95] Quotation taken from Currie, *Constitution of Germany*, 307; *Committal Case*, 22 BVerfGE 180 (German Federal Constitutional Court).

used? Is there a rational connection? The court may even apply different intensities of scrutiny in different areas. But these are all handled flexibly, and only as a way of getting at the core evaluation of the relative value of means, ends, and impositions. Proportionality is an ever-present consideration, though, occurring in judicial reasoning almost whenever a right is considered for restriction. Germany, almost alone in the European Union, has to failed to ratify the European Directive that set up a Europe-wide arrest warrant. This is so because the Federal Constitutional Court struck down Germany's enabling legislation as a breach of Article 16(2) of the Basic Law, which protects against extradition. Article 16 does not contain an absolute ban, but the court held that features of the European Arrest Warrant disproportionately infringed the liberty right; German citizens might too easily be surrendered when there was a good basis for them to be tried at home, and so on.[96] The proportionality principle cuts both ways, though. With very few exceptions, any right may be infringed, given a suitable proportionality between means, ends, and the value of outcomes. Where the court really wants to protect a right as approaching absolute status, to avoid the argument that proposed legislation actually is a proportionate response, it has to invoke human dignity. In a specific legal sense the right to life is inferior to the right to human dignity in this form of analysis.

> Any violation of human dignity immediately calls for the unconstitutionality of the statute or the administrative action. In contrast to the fundamental rights provisions in the Basic Law, the dignity clause does not allow for a legal limitation. The difference may be shown by contrasting dignity (Art. 1 (1) sentence 1 Basic Law) with the fundamental right to life (Art. 2 (2) Basic Law). The right to life, according to Article 2 (2) sentence 3 of the Basic Law, entails a limitation: Statutes may infringe the right to life if they can be legally justified under the proportionality principle. . . . The dignity clause, however, does not contain any limitation clause. In contrast to all other fundamental rights provisions in the German constitution it leads to an all or nothing approach and gives unlimited, absolute protection.[97]

The force of this comment becomes clear when one considers the issue it was written about—it was the court's striking down of post-9/11 legislation that would empower the federal government to shoot down a hijacked aircraft that terrorists were going to use as in the attack on the Twin Towers. There were various grounds for this decision, but the only way to make it an absolute ban was to tie in the dignity clause. Shooting down the plane, and thus killing innocent passengers might be seen as proportional. But denying their dignity by treating them as means to an end could never be legitimate. Interestingly the author of the article quoted considers that invoking the dignity clause is the equivalent of using "strict scrutiny."

[96] S Mölders, "Case Note—the European Arrest Warrant in the German Federal Constitutional Court," 2006 7 *German Law Journal* 11. An interesting consideration of proportionality and EU/state relations seen through German and Italian cases is given in M Poto, "The Principle of Proportionality in Comparative Perspective—Part II/II," 8 *German Law Journal* 9.

[97] Lepsius, "Human Dignity."

Equality and Nondiscrimination

When it comes to examples of equality jurisprudence we find a similar difficulty in making the German experience and that of the other courts covered here fit together. The first thing to note is that the Basic Law does not actually have an antidiscrimination clause as such. Instead it has a potentially much more full-blooded general equality clause, with a form of antidiscrimination clause as one subsection;

> Article 3 [Equality before the law]
> (1) All persons shall be equal before the law.
> (2) Men and women shall have equal rights. The state shall promote the actual implementation of equal rights for women and men and take steps to eliminate disadvantages that now exist.
> (3) No person shall be favoured or disfavoured because of sex, parentage, race, language, homeland and origin, faith, or religious or political opinions. No person shall be disfavoured because of disability.

As is common in the German constitution, aspects of the right to equality are also buttressed in other places. So Article 33(2) insists that "Every German shall be equally eligible for any public office according to his aptitude, qualifications, and professional achievements." Article 33(3) gives further protection to religion, especially in the context of civil service employment, by establishing that

> Neither the enjoyment of civil and political rights, nor eligibility for public office, nor rights acquired in the public service shall be dependent upon religious affiliation. No one may be disadvantaged by reason of adherence or nonadherence to a particular religious denomination or philosophical creed.

The Germans have not really had to agonise about the legitimacy of differentiation in general, or consider the distinction between differentiations that amount to discrimination and others, or the question of whether some discrimination is unfair, and so on. Nor is there much discussion of why discrimination is bad. Notably, in a constitution otherwise replete with the value of dignity, the word is not much referred to in the constitutional text concerning specific rights. Dignity is brought into Canadian, South African, even American discussion because those countries are concerning themselves with nondiscrimination in ways that do not just fall naturally under the idea of equality, and therefore need justification. This again comes from the essential simplicity of the German constitutional situation. Equality, in some sense or other, cannot be doubted as a value in modern society, particularly one self-described as a "social state." Equality is very clearly enshrined by Article 3. At the same time, a society with the conception of the state sketched above is not likely to bother debating the obvious fact that all law requires discrimination. Where particular political worries or goals pressed hardest at the time of drafting the constitution, they are mentioned specifically. Thus there is the commitment to substantive gender equality in Article 3(2), and the double protection against religious discrimination provided by 3(3) and 33(3). But there is no overarching consideration of unjustified discrimination as something that might be practised and mar the society, in contrast, for example, to the analysis actually embedded in the South African constitutional text, or the Canadian judge-made rules. Simple as the overall situation may be, the actual rulings of the court are so numerous, diverse, and possibly contradictory that it is difficult even to survey them here. Susanne Baer, in a valuable discussion of gender equality, starts her article by noting that

> Almost every German analysis of the subject opens with two observations: first, the right to equality is the most frequently cited right in the jurisprudence of the German Constitutional Court and, second, the equality doctrine is the area of constitutional law containing the greatest number of conundrums.[98]

Very basically the court has concentrated on a flexibly interpreted arbitrariness rule for its equality doctrine, which is largely based on what is often called the "General Equality Rule," coming from 3(1).[99] To be sure, it has accepted that the specified grounds in 3(2) play a special role, but they tend to be interpreted very narrowly, and it is not clear that much greater protection is provided to those who can bring themselves under a specified ground than others enjoy from general equality. As an example, facial discrimination on a specified ground need not be fatal to legislation, if legislative intent is nondiscriminatory. Other jurisdictions have been very wary of taking notice of intent, as noted in the South African section above. Thus disproportionately generous funding of religious schools was upheld in 1987 because the aim was not to privilege a religion in itself, and there was ample constitutional backing for state support to religious education, amounting, under one interpretation, even to an obligation to support it.[100]

Arbitrariness needs to be truly arbitrary to worry the German court. There has to be no intelligible reason for a distinction, to the extent that it has to be one that offends against basic conceptions of justice. The court has in fact developed its equality jurisprudence along proportionality grounds, just as it has its basic constitutional testing. Thus situations where basic rights are affected disproportionately between classes or groups are likely to be handled by considering the proportionality between the classification and the importance of the right.[101] Because the court's equality jurisprudence is so lacking in categorical absolutes, and so much concerned with what Beatty would see as pragmatism, its decisions have changed as the society's general understanding of social reality has changed. It is probably this that leads to the commentators' *cri de coeur* noted by Baer.

[98] Baer, "Equality."

[99] M Sachs, "The Equality Rule before the German Federal Constitutional Court," 1998 *St Louis-Warsaw Transatlantic Law Journal* 139.

[100] *Religious Schools Funding Case*, 75 BVerfGE 40 (German Federal Constitutional Court).

[101] However, Sachs, "Equality Rule," regards this as confusing two separate trains of thought in the court; it is widely agreed amongst other commentators.

It is not that the court keeps changing its mind about how to analyse the situation, as with the Canadians and perhaps the Americans. Rather it is that cases will not fit into a neat set of classifications without these rule-like analyses themselves. The change in the court's perceptions of rational connection are a good example. In 1963 the court upheld a law that made it harder for a widower than a widow to get a survivor's pension on the grounds that the idea of the pension was to make up for income drop after a spousal death, and women did not contribute in the same way to the household income as men. The decision, and others like it into the late seventies, was overtly based on a sociology of the family in which women did not work outside the home. But in 1979 the court overturned a statute that allowed women but not men an extra day of paid holiday per year to deal with "household responsibilities." The opinion expressly described the legislation as based on "the 'conventional conception' that it was the duty of the woman to take care of household responsibilities."[102]

Another reason for the difficulty in categorising German equality decisions also arises from this pragmatic, effects-oriented, and proportionality-imbued approach. Baer's article is largely addressed to the question of how the court "frames" the inequality, or, in technical continental European legal language, what is the *tertium comparationis.* She discusses a case where a female blue-collar worker complained about a statute that provided her a much shorter notice before sacking than a white-collar worker would have been entitled to.

> [If] we construct her case to focus on the difference in treatment of white-collar and blue-collar employees, the issue in the case is the general right to equality. However, if we construct her case around the right to work and survival, the issue would be human dignity and personal freedom or the welfare principle guaranteed in German constitutional law. If we see her case in the setting of a gender segregated workplace where women are generally blue-collar employees and are consequently hurt the most by job losses during recessions, we would see it as a case of gender discrimination. Since the Tertium Comparationis determines the standard of review in standard comparison doctrine, our choice of Tertium Comparationis will shape the outcome of the case.[103]

In many ways this is comparable to the "framing" arguments made about decisions of the South African Constitutional Court by those concerned to further "substantive equality." Indeed Baer also notes, "In German constitutional law, it is often said that dignity is the Tertium Comparationis." She goes on to say that this, if taken seriously, would mean that absolutely every discrimination would be subject to challenge. It would require "courts to compare individuals as individuals to individuals." This may in part explain its notable rarity as a major part of the court's discussions in this area. Furthermore, the court has quite deliberately set

[102] M Battacharyya, "From Nondifferentiation to Factual Equality: Gender Equality Jurisprudence under the German Basic Law," 1996 21 *Brooklyn Journal of International Law* 915.

[103] Baer, "Equality."

up different standards for different functional areas, meaning that there cannot be a single well-articulated logical test for discrimination. In the case where it was introduced, the proportionality test for equality under Article 3(1) was summed up by the court as follows:

> there must be differences of such type and weight between them that they can justify unequal treatment. Unequal treatment and justification must be adequately related to each other.[104]

Such a test will almost automatically lead to different applications in different functional areas, if only because the rights in question will appear differentially. For example, one of the areas where a specific test has been worked out is for welfare entitlement. As welfare entitlement itself has a relatively shaky grounding in the Basic Law, as discussed in chapter 2, it is not surprising that proportionality produces a rather deferential approach. Where gender discrimination is concerned, the court has become a good deal tougher over the years, as is shown by the *Night Workers* case also discussed in that chapter.[105]

Inevitably many of the German decisions are very similar to those we have looked at from rule-bound jurisdictions; so is the detailed reasoning. Distinctions based on the specified grounds of Article 3(2) do indeed receive "stricter scrutiny" than others. Not only that, but, as though they had been reading the North American reports, this scrutiny can be weakened where the differences are not immutable but based on "lifestyle choice." It is hardly surprising that people in similar jobs—members of constitutional adjudication bodies—dealing with similar issues and committed to the very broad Western consensus about decency in society should come up with detailed analyses that are similar and produce similar results. This is even more to be expected if a major thesis of this book is correct, that nondiscrimination is the core value of modern constitutionalism. It must be said that in Germany as much as in Canada, the idea of a "proportionality test" is very broad, often containing all the different steps, like rational connection, that other courts go through without using the word. What I mean primarily by proportionality here is what many characterise under the label of "proportionality in the narrower sense" as a final or sometimes "third" step. Baer says of this that

> What might be most important is that this step of the equality test serves as a safety net regarding all aspects which have not yet surfaced in earlier parts of the test.

However, my understanding of the force and use of the idea of proportionality is very different: it is not a sweeping up of unconsidered trifles, but the very heart of the activity, the core decision about whether, all things being said, a particular distinction is justified in terms of its good effect minus its bad effects. In this sense Germany relies on proportionality more thoroughly than do other jurisdictions. The difference between Germany and the other countries remains: no effort is

[104] Quotation taken and amended from Baer, "Equality."

[105] *Night Work Decision*, 85 BVerfGE 191 (1992) (German Federal Constitutional Court).

made to produce systematic single sets of rules to govern government action in equality cases any more than in other rights limitation cases. Piecemeal adjudication of means and effect is all and everything. Baer quotes a leading German scholar, Bernhard Schlink, as categorising the proportionality test as one where "the Court applies a necessarily decisionistic interpersonal benefit comparison," saying afterwards that "this may simply be politics." The difference, of course, is that politics, being the clash of interests, may well discriminate against the weak; the court may be making the decision the government *ought to have made*, but this may also be to say no more than that the government ought to obey the rule of law. That is why we have courts in general—to make sure that the rule of law does prevail. The rule of law is a gestalt, not a set of specific tests.

Constitutional Tests in France

Proportionality in Other Words

So different is French judicial review, as argued extensively in chapter 4, that it will be looked at very briefly here. It could be said that France, in its inevitably terser way, is much like Germany (terser because of judicial styles, as discussed elsewhere). Certainly a version of proportionality has been its standard argument for invalidating laws submitted to the Conseil constitutionnel since, or perhaps slightly before, the great nationalisations decision of 1982.[106] The reason one must hesitate is that French commentators do not require the actual words of the Conseil's "tests" before claiming a case was based on one of them. What has come to be known as the test of *proportionnalité* used to go, occasionally still goes, under a different label, and even that has not been insisted on completely. Dominique Rousseau, for example, argues that this equivalent term first appeared "implicitly" in 1981 in one of the first major decisions when substantive legislation was rejected, the *Sécurité et Liberté* case.[107] Here what was "implicit" is the older version of the test, where the Conseil requires parliament have committed "un erreur manifeste." In 1981 an implicit equivalent arises, interestingly and for us usefully, where the Conseil is explaining the *limits* to its authority. The Conseil notes that the senators and deputies who referred the law claimed that the Conseil had the power to censure aspects of the law that "to their eyes" (i.e., the referrers) breached Article 8 of the Rights of Man. The Conseil replied that

> Article 61 of the Constitution does not give the Conseil constitutionnel a general power of assessment and decision identical to parliament's, but only gives it the authority to pronounce on the compatibility of laws referred to it

[106] French academics have not written a great deal about the idea of "tests," perhaps because the concept itself does not fit well with the general rhetoric of law. A vital exception is Rousseau, *Droit du contentieux constitutionnel.* The relevant section, 46 et seq, is actually titled "Le Test de proportionnalité," a phrase I have not found in any comparable French work.

[107] *Sécurité et Liberté*, 81-127 DC (Conseil constitutionnel).

> with the constitution. Therefore, in carrying out this task, the Conseil may not substitute its own judgement for the legislator's regarding the necessity of the penalties it attaches to crimes it defines as long as no part [of the relevant section of the law] is *manifestly contrary to the principle* contained in Article 8 of the Declaration of 1789. (Emphasis added; my translation)

The italicised words are held to be the equivalent of the "manifest error" "test" that surfaced properly in 1982. Again explaining its limitations, the Conseil stated that it could not challenge parliament's assessment that nationalisation was necessary "in the absence of manifest error." Upholding the general principle of nationalisation, it went on to say that "it has not been established that the transfer of property and enterprises operates as a restraint on private property and freedom of enterprise to the point of misreading the dispositions of Article 17 of the Declaration of 1789."[108] The Conseil went on, of course, to find other problems with the law. The proportionality principle in French constitutional adjudication, as in German, actually serves three logically different purposes. It is used to see if parliament has struck the right balance between two competing constitutional requirements. Where only one constitutional principle is involved, proportionality checks, second, that the extent of the impact on the value in question is not excessive. Third, it is used in equality cases. The language used has changed somewhat. It is much less common now to talk of "manifest error," but instead to talk about a law as "manifestly disproportionate" or "an excessive infringement" on a right or principle. This is explained by most commentators as an attempt to sound less offensive to parliamentarians, though the alternative phrases, at least in English, sound not much less hurtful. The general thrust is given well in the phrase used by the Conseil in accepting as constitutional a law modifying the rules for privatization as set up by the 1986 Privatisation Law. The Conseil noted that the property restrictions were only temporary and could only be imposed by a minister, who had to give reasons in public for his or her actions, which had to involve the national interest. Therefore it ruled:

> given that the law without destroying the right to property [only] limits certain modes of exercising that right, it does not impose such an infringement as to constitute a complete negation of the meaning and import of that right.[109]

The "negation of the meaning and import" does of course sound very much like the German and Hungarian "essential content" rule. This test has been one that governments usually pass, though there have been some strikings down of acts for disproportionate legislation, and over a wide range of constitutional principles. As an example, in 1993 the Conseil struck down part of an anticorruption law that

[108] My translation. I can find no better translation of *liberté d'entreprendre*, but it is a freedom not easily equated with anything in an English-language constitution.

[109] *Privatization Modification Law*, 89-254 DC (Conseil constitutionnel). My translation. The key word in the French is *dénaturé*. This could well be translated to equate to the German ban on attacking the "essential content" of a right.

gave the police extreme powers to seize papers and documents as "an excessive infringement of the right to privacy." In the same year it struck down aspects of nationality and immigration laws as having "disproportionate sanctions" and involving "an excessive restriction on individual freedom."[110]

The German section noted the relationship between constitutional adjudication and the existence of a strong history of administrative control over the executive. In that context it is worth noting that the origin of the proportionality test in French public law is not the Conseil constitutionnel, but the Conseil d'Etat, which is generally agreed to have introduced the doctrine in 1971.[111] The Conseil constitutionnel has certainly adopted that body's description of what goes on in such a test. It directly referred to a "cost-benefit analysis" as an appropriate measure of legality. It should also be noted, as might be guessed from the discussion in chapter 4, that the Conseil has not only used proportionality to annul or accept a law, but also used it extensively in justifying the application of a "réserve d'interprétation," as for example in its reading down the section on penalties in a law aimed at increasing the transparency of financial markets.[112]

Proportionality and Discrimination

There has been extensive use of proportionality in France's constitutional adjudication over equality. However, a warning is necessary, already addressed at greater length in chapter 4. Because of the unusual role of academic commentators in French law, the previous sentence has to be taken more to mean that French experts regard proportionality as an important test than that the Conseil itself overtly uses it. There is nonetheless a strong argument that can be made linking these two so that use of a concept by the academics may well imply its vitality for the judges as well.[113] French constitutional jurisprudence on equality has been covered already in chapter 4, though there the focus is on substance rather than procedure. Consequently it suffices here merely to restate one point. The French *bloc de constitutionnalité*, as opposed to any specific constitutional doctrine, has both a general equality principle and, scattered here and there, what amounts to a list of proscribed criteria. Far more work has been done by the Conseil with the general doctrine than with special characteristics, and the government has seldom lost on the latter. Mirroring in its own legal terminology a common theme abroad, the Conseil has tended to produce two general sorts of restrictions on what we might think of as discrimination. They are expressed in terms of when the "principle of equality" will not be an obstacle to a law, and the impression given is that the prin-

[110] *Nationality Reform Law*, 93-321 DC (Conseil constitutionnel), *Identity Control Law*, 93-323 DC (Conseil constitutionnel).

[111] On this point, but also more generally for this section, X Philippe, *Le contrôle de proportionnalité dans les jurisprudences constitutionnelle et administrative françaises*, Science et droit administratifs (Paris: Economica and Presses universitaires d'Aix-Marseilles, 1990).

[112] *Financial Markets Law*, 89-260 DC (Conseil constitutionnel).

[113] Lasser, *Judicial Deliberations*. Lasser argues convincingly for the importance, as part of doctrine itself, of academic analyses of cases in the French context.

ciple is terribly important, but that almost anything that brings the law within either of these gateways will suspend further consideration. The two restrictions are labelled (my translation) "differences of situation" and "general interest reasons." The Conseil has said, *re* the first, "the principle of equality does not present an obstacle to a law establishing different rules for those in different situations," and of the second, "the principle of equality does not oppose legislative derogations from equality for reasons of the public interest."

The first rule is conditioned by a slightly curious statement that these situational differences will "usually" only justify different treatment if the difference in the rules "is not incompatible with the purpose of the law." Whatever this may mean in detail, it is fairly obviously a broad grant to make distinctions that will be judged in terms of their fit to the legislative aim. The second exception is limited in a more familiar way: there has to be a rational connection between the inequality introduced and the general interests that are to be protected, which must be specified. Because of the nature of French constitutional adjudication, it is impossible to go much further than this with any authority. Academics spend a great deal of time trying to find inductive generalisations of underlying rules the Conseil follows, but the Conseil itself never says more than that such and such a differential treatment is or is not proportional either to the different situations or the legislative aim. Whether it talks of manifest error, manifestly disproportionate impact, excessive infringement, or whatever, the Conseil constitutionnel never goes beyond simply asserting that the law does or does not exhibit the specific quality. There are no complex subrules, no hierarchically organised tests, no list of things to be looked for, and no lengthy disquisitions on dignity, the meaning of democracy, or the nature of French society. This would be out of keeping with French legal tradition, as described in chapter 4. But it does make it hard to present the French system as anything but a set of instant intuitive judgements.

Against this view French constitutional lawyers struggle to build systems of explanation.[114] There is no way of proving that they are what really goes on in the Conseil's deliberations. One example of the ambiguity in the situation is salutary. When dealing with equality issues the Conseil can either rely on general and unspecific mentions of the "principle of equality," or make specific references to particular clauses in specified texts in the overall *bloc de constitutionnalité*. Of the 294 allegations of unconstitutional inequality in legislation referred to the Conseil between 1973 and 1995, 211 relied on unspecified general references to a principle of inequality, and only 83 were based on identifiable constitutional texts.[115] (Over half of these were to the 1789 Declaration.) In that sense, the Conseil would seem to be fairly free-floating. But it is also true that where the Conseil did rely on the general principle, it found against the government only 13 percent of the time. Where it could find a specific constitutional text to apply, it annulled 35 percent of

[114] See, for example, L Favoreu, "The Principle of Equality in the Jurisprudence of the Conseil Constitutionnel," 1992 21 *Capital University Law Review* 165–97.

[115] This is much greater than the actual number of laws referred involving equality. Where several parts of a law are claimed to be discriminatory, each part is counted. There were 124 constitutional decisions on the issue.

the laws referred to it.[116] Does this mean that the Conseil does rely on rules more than it seems? One argument that finds favour with some French commentators is that the Conseil is actually always much more rule-bound than it seems, but it simply does not say so. One author refers to an "editorial economy" that leads the counsel to avoid spelling out the specific text in each case. Another says that when the Conseil just invokes a "principle of equality" it "does not mean to disown the texts that are its source. But *brievitatis causa*, it standardises the whole idea in the most general way." The trouble is that we have no way of knowing how "controlled" the Conseil's decisions are.

Summing Up

This chapter has run together two concerns that are normally treated separately: the general issue of the limitations of constitutional rights, and the more specific question of constitutional constraints on legislative discrimination. They fit perfectly well together for my purposes. Either one can see discrimination jurisprudence as a special case of limitation of a general right to equality, or see many discrimination cases as attempting, by showing discrimination, to uphold a general right. In either reading, we can see the sampled countries as occupying a position on a spectrum that has the United States at one end and France at the other. Germany would be nearer to France than other countries, and both South Africa and Canada nearer to the United States than to the French/German grouping. Exactly what order we should impose on Canada versus South Africa is harder to know. What is this spectrum about? The United States attempts to stick to a number of clear-cut rules from which its courts are unwilling to grant the executive exemptions, but otherwise leave it free. France decides almost everything on a pragmatic first-principles basis with neither rules nor exceptions. In the middle we have the attempt to set relatively clear rules with the understanding that any rule may be broken if the offending legislative action itself can be brought under a meta rule. When it comes to the more detailed and specific question of permitting limitations on the duty of the state not to discriminate, this central position becomes much more complex.

The middle position is characterised by an attempt to solve the problem by having relatively clear constitutional rules, which may not be broken by the state unless the state can bring its legislation under a second set of rules specifically justifying such action. In a way it is another version of Hart's primary and secondary rule distinction.[117] The Canadian and South African positions are so close that it would make more sense to describe them as covering together a range of possible stances, and to locate individual judges from each country, rather than the whole courts, on our hypothetical spectrum, fitting some towards the American, some towards the French, pole, inside this central ground. It is an interesting thought experi-

[116] Mélin-Soucramanien, *Le Principe e'Égalité*.

[117] HLA Hart, *The Concept of Law* (Oxford: Clarendon Press, 1972).

ment to imagine South Africa's Sachs and Canada's L'Heureux-Dubé on the same bench.[118] This appears, of course, as institutional incoherence. With Canada above all the inability of the court to agree about how to use the tests cannot have helped the legitimacy of its antidiscrimination jurisprudence. Nor perhaps has the tendency of the South African court to disagree so much on the results while agreeing on the tests made the latter very convincing. Whether there is a general rule here is uncertain. Courts that do not allow dissents and concurrences, for example Germany before 1971, France still, may be able to issue firmer rules. But these rules are likely to be much less clear, because they imply a hard-bargained internal process to arrive at any publishable result. Furthermore a flourishing democracy rather entails public disagreement even if it has costs. The European Court of Human Rights would probably have less legitimacy and effect were it to insist on single opinions, and the ECJ might have more if it allowed dissent.

Canada and South Africa share much of the weaponry of judicial review. First, there is the use of one or two primary values that must be preserved even if the state is to be allowed an incursion into a rights-protected area. Democracy and dignity occupy the heights in this debate, either by specific command of the constitution or by judicial glossing. The former is usually less helpful, though judicial attempts to fill out the concept can in themselves be useful contributions to a national debate. I have in mind something like the spelling out of similar concepts in the Eastern European jurisdictions. Democracy as a concept can have an analytic cutting edge with issues most obviously logically related, such as freedom of speech. Dignity has come into its own above all in antidiscrimination jurisprudence, though perhaps not always usefully. Nonetheless, it provides some sort of general test of when a rational distinction in legislation with a legitimate aim may still not be an acceptable basis for differential treatment. The other commonality to these jurisdictions, and again something used in such a way as to make some judges of one country nearer to others from another than to their own colleagues, is the idea of a "two step" analysis. One might really think of the two-step process as a summary of the entire business of constitutional testing: forcing the arguments to concentrate on first identifying a constitutional right and then deciding whether or not it has actually been intruded on, before talking about the justification process.

It might be argued that the German process can also be described this way. The vital difference is that in South Africa and Canada the courts are required to use this form of analysis, whereas in Germany the judges have found it often convenient so to do. Where it is merely judicially convenient, it is also close to tautology. What marks the two-stage process, when constitutionally required, is precisely the way it distinguishes the centre from both ends. On the one hand it refuses the coalescence of the United States, where argument often seems to imply that if a state

[118] A very good survey of her jurisprudence is found in M Liu, "A Prophet with Honour: An Examination of the Gender Equality Jurisprudence of Madam Justice Claire L'Heureux-Dubé of the Supreme Court of Canada," 2000 25 *Queen's Law Journal* 417–78. One of the clearer of her own statements is C L'Heureux-Dubé, "Realizing Equality in the Twentieth Century: The Role of the Supreme Court of Canada in Comparative Perspective," 2003 1 *International Journal of Constitutional Law* 1, 35–57.

action is justified, then there is no right that has been abridged. On the other it distinguishes from the French end by insisting that there are rules that are broken, perhaps legitimately, and not merely values or principles that are balanced. There is real value in saying that yes there is a right here, and yes the government is planning to breach it. If nothing else, it clarifies the governmental action and sharpens minds. It should help prevent the erosion of a right by continuing "salami slicing" or, in more judicial language, "abrade" slippery slopes. As this chapter has shown, there is a great temptation for judges to elide the stages of a two-stage test; these are, presumably, people who would find the United States a more comfortable judicial environment. There is also a tendency to try to shortcut the application of principle, as with the dignity test or the use of specified and analogous categories, and move directly to the effect of, say, a discrimination on a litigant—a move towards a purer Franco-German proportionality test.

Cynics, or judicial realists, may argue that absolutely none of this matters, for it all comes out the same in the end, and we have been surveying nothing more than rival language games for describing decisions arrived at otherwise. It looks like this in part because no court can, or should, stick too closely to an ideal type. American scrutiny language crops up everywhere, because it is a basic idea, but many American critics of their own court long for a "proportionality orientation." Even were the "realism" true, it would not be fatal. The language of the courts becomes the language of other state actors, and language shapes decisions and revisions. American policemen may not like the "probable cause" test, and they may try to cheat on it. But before *Miranda* they had never heard of the phrase, and it could therefore have no controlling impact on their behaviour.[119] It is a seldom-noted fact about the judicial realist position that it only has much to say if it is assumed not only that judges do not really believe their own stories, but that the rest of the state does not either.

It would seem, then, that the position a court or a judge has on this spectrum is not only a useful shortcut description for a jurisprudential complex, but may well have behaviour consequences. Different sorts of litigants will thrive, and the state will be constrained in different ways, according to the point where the judiciary sit on such a spectrum.

[119] This does not mean a court's rule will necessarily be socially welcome, merely that it is likely to have an impact. See PG Cassell, "*Miranda*'s Negligible Effect on Law Enforcement: Some Skeptical Observations," 1997 20 *Harvard Journal of Law and Public Policy* 327–47; PG Cassell and R Fowles, "Handcuffing the Cops—a Thirty-Year Perspective on Miranda's Harmful Effects on Law Enforcement," 1997 50 *Stanford Law Review* 1055–1147. For a rival view about the necessity of such rules, see P Arenella, "*Miranda* Stories," 1996 20 *Harvard Journal of Law and Public Policy* 375–89.

CHAPTER EIGHT

Conclusions: Constitutional Jurists as Political Theorists

This book is intentionally, perhaps unavoidably, discursive. But a set of themes recurs in most chapters. In this concluding chapter I seek only to restate them, not to synthesise them, and certainly not to offer definitive answers to the questions they raise. The most important recurring themes, which overlap and interrelate, are probably the following:

- counter-majoritarian criticism, a judicial version of which is the sense of a duty of deference to legislatures;
- the role of nondiscrimination as a prime value, and the related theme of the increasing dominance of constitutions as value documents;
- the centrality of the idea of human dignity in the working out of rights;
- the role of legal culture and the beginnings of a development of "international common constitutional law";
- the role of constitutional courts as definers of democracy.

To a large extent these can all be contained in my broader theme: constitutional review is like writing political theory. The first part of this chapter elaborates that idea.

Constitutional Review and the Elaboration of Political Theory

This book started by raising the simple question of what exactly it is that constitutional courts do. The question concerns me primarily because I can find no answer that sits readily with the standard tripartite division of powers of government. As

I have tried to show by looking at a number of jurisdictions, such courts do a huge number of different things, probably too many to allow of any simple theoretical categorisation. Some critics have suggested that this characterisation is really only true of "new" or "recent" constitutional review. Even if the critics are right, it is the new courts and the new approaches that have been of concern to political scientists, and that they have largely failed to deal with. Nor have legal constitutional scholars done much better. One sign of this failure is recurring anxiety about the apparent problem for democracy presented by constitutional review bodies who regards themselves as entitled, or forced, to ignore majoritarian preferences in overturning parliamentary law. Because courts, when seen as part of the classic judicial branch, are not entitled to do this, it is sometimes argued that constitutional courts should not do so either. There may still be a problem of democratic legitimacy if one separates such constitutional review bodies out from the courts in general, but it is a different sort of problem, and a much subtler one. Though I do not think the problem, in either guise, is very important, I try to sketch an answer to the critics of active constitutional courts later in this chapter. For it seems to me that the richness of judicial activity on constitutional matters can only be handled if we cease to try to force constitutional courts into the classic trichotomy, and accept instead that they have come to exercise in some jurisdictions, and may come to exercise more widely, a new, fourth branch of power. Though there is no good label for this function, it could be called something like "articulation of values." Judges engaged in constitutional review act like political theorists, developing and explicating the value choices made, sometimes unconsciously, when the relevant constituent body set up the constitution.

What Makes Constitutional Interpretation Different?

To start, I briefly recapitulate the reasons constitutional interpretation is different in kind from statutory interpretation, or the incremental development of common law. These latter two activities are clearly the business of courts that, while involving judicial creativity, do not seem to worry those who oppose constitutional creativity. The fundamental difference between interpreting a statute and deciding whether a statute is constitutional or not can be stated quite simply. In the former case the court is entitled to query neither the purpose of the statute nor the means it embodies towards its end. The sole legitimate aim of the court is to decide what the statute does in fact cover. The intention of the parliament is everything, whether this is to be discovered only by textual analysis or also by consulting the legislative record. Of course this interpreting goes on against a rich background of assumptions, and of course the judge's values are involved in many ways, though that latter fact is not always openly recognized. Background assumptions naturally come from the dominant ideology. It is a presumption in English law, for example, that no statute can be read as imposing a tax or tax-like measure unless the language is crystal clear, but equally there is no limitation on the sort of tax that can be created, so long as the legislation creating it is clearly stated. Why this particular interpretative ban holds rather than others can only be explained by looking to core beliefs in British society about legitimate governmental activity. Statutory interpretation has moved a long way since the old method of using only the actual language, and seeking some meaning the words can convey without undue linguistic strain. Purposive or "teleological" interpretation happens everywhere, but the purpose is not itself challengeable, any more than the method.[1] A law can be as blunt and wide as Parliament writes, even if a narrower "test" or a more finally tuned end-state might in some way be preferable. Again, assumptions may enter in. Parliament will often be deemed not to have intended such bluntness or overinclusivity, but such an argument will always be presented as part of working out the intent, not as ruling it out of order. In a weaker sense this applies even to common-law creativity. Courts increasingly hold back from wide-ranging changes in common-law rules on the ground that any major changes must now be left to Parliament. Indeed parliamentary inaction will often be cited as a reason for not making some change. A judge may argue that the common-law rule in question has been around for a long time, Parliament could at any time have changed it, and Parliament's not having changed it is the equivalent of expressing a preference for leaving the rule as it is.[2]

This is very different from "reading down" a statute where a constitution can be taken into account. In the latter case the judge is not saying that a parliament can only have meant X—the judge is saying that the parliament can only be allowed to have meant X. Of course this is a simplified account. It omits the fact that judges frequently "cheat" and use the classic interpretative methodology precisely in order to impose external values on legislation because they lack, or prefer not to use, constitutional values.[3] The difference is between the "official" views of what a court does in a nonconstitutional role and how it acts in constitution review. It is partly because analysts have often tried to subsume constitutional interpretation under a form of statutory interpretation that much of the argument goes on.[4] The point is that just because ordinary courts in fact often break out from their proper function inside the standard division of powers does not mean that all court-like bodies that act in similar ways are equally illegitimately stepping out of their role. Instead we need to concentrate on the fact that constitutional courts cannot be seen as acting illegitimately when they act outside the restrictions of the judicial function, because they are not part of that functional machinery.

[1]A interesting view on interpretation is given in W Brugger, "Legal Interpretation, Schools of Jurisprudence, and Anthropology: Some Remarks from a German Point of View," 1994 42 *American Journal of Comparative Law* 2, 395–421. Bobbitt's work in *Constitutional Interpretation* on American constitutional interpretation helps make my point.

[2]See chapter 1 of Robertson, *Judicial Discretion*.

[3]In using this word *cheat* I am merely saying what many Law Lords said to me about statutory interpretation during interviews for my study of judicial discretion in the House of Lords. Robertson, *Judicial Discretion*.

[4]Even common-law courts are aware of the difference between constitutional and nonconstitutional interpretation. A good demonstration is the work of the English Privy Council in the 1970s and 1980s interpreting constitutions from the remnants of the Commonwealth that still used the English court as a supreme court. See especially the argument by Lord Wilberforce in *Minister of Home Affairs v Fisher*, AC 319 [1980] (Privy Council) on appeal from the Bermuda Court of Appeal.

Dworkin's Account of Constitutional Interpretation

One of the classic accounts of judicial reasoning is that given by Ronald Dworkin, who conjures up "a lawyer of superhuman skill, learning, patience and acumen, whom I shall call Hercules."[5] Hercules is used to make a variety of points about judging, particularly in the context of Dworkin's idea that law consists of principles rather than rules as understood by the positivist approach of previous English legal theorists such as H. L. Hart.[6] Here we can concentrate on only one small fragment of his Hercules, and only to use as a stepping stone. Dworkin gives an account of how Hercules might go about interpreting a statute so as to be guided by fundamental principles. He describes legislation in a particular way, as

> an event whose content is contested. [The judge] *constructs his political theory* as an argument about what the legislature has, on this occasion, done. The contrary argument, that it did not actually do what he said, is not a realistic piece of common sense, but a competitive claim about the true content of that contested event.[7] (Emphasis added)

It is this recognition that judicial argument is, or relies on, political theory that we need to take seriously. Others have found this a crucial part of Dworkin's approach (see where Choudhry argues that for Dworkin, "constitutional interpretation . . . becomes an exercise in applied political philosophy").[8] The way Dworkin works this out is directly relevant to any consideration about the true nature of judicial review. His argument depends on an extended analogy with the role of a referee in a game—in his example, chess.[9] Dworkin asks this question: suppose the rules of chess include a provision allowing the referee to stop a game, and give victory to one player, if the other intimidates him. What if one grandmaster continually smiles in an unnerving way at his opponent; does this count as intimidation? The only way for the referee to answer is to ponder on the character of the game. He will quickly arrive, for example, at the idea that it is an intellectual game, and not a game of chance, by comparing the implications of different characterisations against the known rules. Going further, chess cannot be intellectual in any sense

[5] R Dworkin, *Taking Rights Seriously* (London: Duckworth, 1977). The Hercules discussion appears in pages 105–30, but the whole of chapter 4, "Hard Cases," is germane. An interesting modern reflection on the Hercules model appears in Schlink, "Hercules in Germany." An article by the recently retired president of the South African Constitutional Court, Arthur Chaskalson, on Dworkin and the old South African legal system is also found in that volume: "From Wickedness to Equality: The Moral Transformation of South African Law," 2003 1 *International Journal of Constitutional Law* 4, 590–609.

[6] This debate had started earlier with Dworkin's first statement of his theory, R Dworkin, "The Model of Rules," 1967 35 *Chicago Law Review* 14–46. The debate has waged endlessly in legal philosophy, and this work is not intended as a contribution.

[7] Dworkin, *Taking Rights Seriously*, 109.

[8] S Choudhry, "Globalization in Search of Justification: Toward a Theory of Comparative Constitutional Interpretation," 1999 74 *Indiana Law Journal* 819–93, 844.

[9] This account is based on a more general discussion of mine on Dworkin in D Robertson, "Judicial Discretion, Legal Positivism, and Democratic Theory," in M Freeman and D Robertson, eds., *The Frontiers of Political Theory: Essays in a Revitalised Discipline* (Brighton: Harvester, 1980).

that involves physical grace, as ballet might be, because the rules do not penalise clumsily knocking over the board. This comparing of characterisations may not get one all the way: it might not allow one to decide between two types of intellectual game, one, like poker, where ability at psychological intimidation is part of the skill, another, like mathematics, where it is not. The referee, after this process of elimination, would be left finally having to decide by considering the notions of intellect itself and choosing one "which offers a deeper or more successful account of what intellect really is."[10]

The extension to judicial interpretation is direct. In place of the idea of the character of the game, the judge must create a general political theory where the statute is best justified. From that political theory and the statute the judge deduces the answer to the puzzle. Any judge who accepts the rules constitutive of the legal institution accepts the general political theory of his or her state. It should be noted that the political theories judges use are created inductively to justify the given material, the particular statute. The material a judge uses includes other statutes, the constitutional framework, or anything else germane. (So, for example, the French Conseil constitutionnel uses "the fundamental principles of republican law" to construct the *bloc de constitutionnalité.*) So the judge is neither taking some existent general ideology and solving the problem *de nove*, nor simply giving reign to his or her own preferences. The judge does not decide, for example, if bourgeois liberalism favours single-sex marriages, still less if he or she personally approves of such marriages. Instead a judge works out what form of marriage law can be justified given the legal gestalt, and if this form would allow or forbid same-sex marriages.

Dworkin's example is this: an American law forbids anyone from abducting or carrying away by any means another person, and makes it a federal crime so to do. A man converted a young girl to a freak religion and persuaded her to run away and consummate a "celestial marriage." Is this covered by the statute? Dworkin suggests the judge might work it out his way:

Question one: Why does *any* statute have the power to take away liberty?
Answer one: From democratic theory, legislatures are the right arena to make collective decisions about criminality. But the same constitutional doctrine imposes duties to act for the public good.
Question two: What interpretation of the statute best ties the language of it to the legislature's duties?
Answer two: The construction, not of some hypothesis about the legislator's minds but of a special political theory that justifies this statute in the light of their more general responsibilities, better than any alternative theory.
Question three: What principles and policies might properly have persuaded the legislature to enact that statute?
Answer three: Well, for example, not the policy of making all crimes federal, because that would deviate from known constitutional rules; but perhaps

[10] Dworkin, *Taking Rights Seriously*, 103.

either the desire to make all serious crimes federal, or to make all those involving possible crossing of state lines federal.

Question four: But which?

Answer four: Well, the statute sets such high penalties that only the policy of federalising serious crimes makes sense. Therefore the interpretation that appears justified by the general given features of the state is the one that frees the man.[11]

The details of Dworkin's theory are not clear, but the general outline is. A doctrine he calls the "thesis of political responsibility" requires a basic degree of consistency in legislation, so that constitutional principles and detailed statutes form a logical whole. An interpretation can be tried out against generalisations induced from these rules, until only one of the possible explanations fits. Of course it may not be possible to exhaust all alternative justifications for a statute this way. Discussing a statutory problem of religious liberty, Dworkin suggests that a judge might be left with two different versions, each equally in keeping with all other constitutional principles. Then only treating it as an issue in political philosophy, deciding for himself or herself which is the better definition of religious liberty, will yield the judge an answer.

This theory of interpretation genuinely does ignore legislative intent, by taking the legislature to have done an open-ended thing when it passed a statute. Dworkin's approach would similarly disbar any "original intent" theory of constitutional adjudication. The judge discovers what it is the legislature (or constituent assembly) has done, rather than trying to find out what it meant to do. Dworkin agrees, naturally, that any such account will be contestable. Dworkin is by no means the first legal theorist to make such an argument. Barak approvingly cites Gustav Radbruch, an early-twentieth-century German legal philosopher and member of the SPD, as arguing of statutes "that the interpreter may understand the statute better than the author of the statute, and that the statute is always wiser than its creator . . . the statute is a living creature; its interpretation must be dynamic." If this is true of a statute, it must be all the more true of a constitution. Certainly Barak's own views of the judicial role come close to mine in insisting on the creative role of the constitutional judge.[12]

But the approach is not absurdly far-fetched. There are traces of it already in modern judicial interpretation where the nature of other, not directly related, statutes constitute reasons for adopting a particular interpretation of a troublesome clause. Where statutory interpretation by constitutional courts exists, the question is when a statute that is not, under any reading, unconstitutional must nonetheless be read through constitutional spectacles. Several South African cases have involved this process, which might not be that different from the French Conseil constitutionnel's use of réserves d'interprétation.[13] In common law much progress

[11]Dworkin, *Taking Rights Seriously*, 107–8.

[12]Barak, *Judge in a Democracy*, 7.

[13]A good South African example is *Rail Commuters Action Group v Metrorail*, CCT 56/03 (South African Constitutional Court).

in the past has been made by drawing analogies from a rule contained in one set of precedents to a quite different area of law.[14]

Judicial creation of political theory by induction rests ultimately on one extremely strong assumption, that of the internal coherence and compatibility of statutes and constitutional rules. The analogy to chess might be thought to mislead, for chess has two characteristics lacking in a legal system. It is a *whole*, deliberately created as an entity, and has not developed over time by accretion and deletion of separate rules. However, even if this is a fair criticism of Dworkin's account of statutory interpretation, it would apply with less force to constitutional interpretation, which in most countries can be seen as the result of one initial deliberate act. Secondly, chess aims at one specific end. These two features mean that there is no danger of the rules and characteristics of chess conflicting—any such conflict inside the rules of chess would make the game unplayable. The political complex of statutes and rules is not a single creation, and it has no single identifiable aim. The preamble to the US constitution sets out a modest list of its aims:

> We the People of the United States, in Order to form a more perfect Union, establish Justice, insure domestic Tranquility, provide for the common defence, promote the general Welfare, and secure the Blessings of Liberty to ourselves and our Posterity, do ordain and establish this Constitution for the United States of America.

The constitution, though, consists not only of the original document, but of pieces of legislation passed at various times over two centuries. Even then it is an infinitely simpler complex than, for example, the body of English legislation, common law, and constitutional conventions, or perhaps the French *bloc de constitutionnalité*. There is no guarantee or likelihood that any political complex will be internally consistent. Indeed it is most certain that it will not be, because half the process of politics is of pursuing incompatible goals by optimisation, because maximisation is impossible. However when one turns to constitutional adjudication, a step Dworkin himself may not wish to take, the multiplicity of legitimate ends not only matters less for the theory, it may actually make judicial construction of political theory more necessary, indeed inevitable. And even if establishing justice, ensuring tranquillity, promoting the general welfare, and so forth, is underdefining, most modern constitutions commit their society to a small number of values, or to a broad goal. The South African conception of "transformative jurisprudence" or the German constitution's initial value statements narrow the range of possible answers to a theoretical quest much more, making the idea of finding a single account of "what the legislature has done" at least slightly more plausible. Even a concept like that of the "French republican tradition" is intellectually rich and coherent enough to help constitutional review judges.[15]

[14] Most classic accounts of legal reasoning stress this idea of reasoning by analogy, which in some ways is an older version of Dworkin's account. For example, EH Levi, *An Introduction to Legal Reasoning* (Chicago: University of Chicago Press, 1949).

[15] As an example of an analysis of French politics using the concept, see chapter 3 of A Cole and R Gino, *Redefining the French Republic* (Manchester: Manchester University Press, 2006).

Dworkin meant this argument to deal with the vexed question of whether or not judges have to exercise discretion, and he was primarily concerned not with constitutional interpretation but with statutory interpretation. The concern here is rather different. Except in some special refined philosophical sense, there can be no argument about whether judges do, and must, exercise discretion. Inevitably they do. Nor is statutory interpretation a very good analogue to constitutional interpretation—that is partly the point of this section—but there are obvious parallels. I want simply to plunder some of the ideas, especially that of the analogy of the referee, and the idea of constructing the meaning by seeking an overall consistency with relevant matters, combined with the notion that in constructing what the constituent assembly has done, the judge is writing political theory. There are important ways in which the Dworkinian approach fails to model institutional reality. Some critics worry that, while Dworkin is thinking of a single judge, in the real world such decisions are made by multimember courts by majority rule. (This may not be apparent where a single "opinion of the court" is issued, but is always true.) Thus over any sets of similar cases incoherence may set in as differing majorities, even of the same group of judges, come to different internal bargains—swing voters amongst the judiciary may have excessive influence. The real world can be even less fitting to the model where, as in the United Kingdom, but to some extent elsewhere, decisions are made by random panels drawn from the court. Two similar cases heard within a short time may be decided by two nonoverlapping groups. Secondly, high courts always have to remember that after they speak, lower courts will deal with the potentially large numbers of cases deemed to be governed by their original decision. Thus the way they craft an opinion has something to do with the best way to control and discipline these lower courts in the future, and that may moderate their ideal version of constitutional truth. A broader version of the same point is that courts have to keep an eye on the problem of "compliance" by other agencies and actors.

These points do not go against Dworkin himself because he can be seen as advising the individual judge how to think. They do tell somewhat against my attempt to use a Dworkinian model as both a description of, and a standard for, judicial review. It is partly an empirical matter of judicial culture and role expectations, partly an empirical matter of broader political culture. A system where neither precedent (*res judicata*) nor comity constrains judges to behave responsibly, and where the legitimate authority of the court does not deter other agencies from ignoring it, is probably a broken system anyway. To the extent that the US Supreme Court is subject to these problems—and the critics with these views are most often American—to that extent it is probably not the model of judicial review best emulated, nor the one empirically most applicable to comparative study.

The Judge as Political Theorist

As already noted, some will object to the very first step here, the idea that a constitution, like a chess game, has a purpose, or at least purposes. It is easiest simply to accept, for the time being, that national constitutional discourses vary, and that in some the idea of a purpose is not applicable. Or rather that only structural matters about who can do what can always be seen as constituting the purposes of a constitution. Most constitutions will have a slight extension to encompass a bill of rights, this often, however, being a list of highly individuated and specific things no part of the political system can do. At least some constitutions are much more than this, and can usefully be regarded as purposive. This distinction is to be taken as valid throughout this discussion—judges by their arguments can do much to transfer constitutions from one category to the other. But the argument for the judge as political theorist is more easily set out in the context of undoubtedly "purposive" constitutions. In this category one can include, with little chance of serious disagreement, the South African constitution, the German constitution, and some of those influenced by German thought in Eastern Europe.

The reason the constitutions that are unarguably "purposive" are so is that they are all, in one way or another, what South African writers have begun to call "transformatory" constitutions. Given the centrality of certain values and the often explicit reference to social goals in constitutional documents like these, it is simply not the case that the constitutions can be seen as neutral about legislation, or indeed, truly neutral about much of private law. To see them as just there to allow Kelsenian "negative legislation" when governments threaten specific rights is to miss the point. Peoples' rights claims are rather the triggers for constitutional shaping of the state's actions. While states under such constitutions may pursue a variety of goals, they may do so only in ways that are compliant with core values like dignity and equality. Such rights, especially the dignity rights, not only preclude certain things been done at all, and forbid certain routes to otherwise acceptable ends, but are often seen as requiring values and principles to be enshrined in institutions and practices. Further, as the German courts would argue, the constitution does not only grant subjective rights, that is, give individuals personal claims, but rewrites the state to create a context where the value in question can flourish. When a constitution suffused by such an outlook is created, Dworkin's idea of future judicial reasoning as making arguments about what has been done is apt. The intentions of the original constitution makers, delegates to an assembly, drafters in a committee, and political parties coming together to create the new institutional matrix for their existence are irrelevant.

They are irrelevant because the public legitimating of the constitution is and has to be a legitimating of a document, not of the intentions of those who wrote it. The intentions, after all, will have been a mixture of base and noble, of private or sectional interests, and of political vision. But the claims made actually have little to do with intentions in any discoverable away. In 1949 the West German Länder ratified this statement.

> (1) The dignity of man is inviolable. To respect and protect it is the duty of all state authority. . . . Everyone has the right to the free development of his personality insofar as he does not violate the rights of others or offend against the constitutional order or the moral code.[16]

[16] Part of the first two articles of the German Basic Law of 1949.

Doubtless those involved in the vote had some very crude sense of what they were seeking, but it is quite impossible that they could have thought out even a tiny fraction of the contexts in which someone might look at the state and ask, "Is what is going on really respectful of human dignity, is this practise really going to lead to free development of anyone's personality?" In the cases of the East European former Communist dictatorships, there can be no doubt that the constitution makers did *intend* that, for example Poland "be a democratic state ruled by law and implementing the principles of social justice," and that the Czech Republic be "a sovereign, unified, and democratic law-observing state, based on the respect for the rights and freedoms of the individual and citizen." We can be sure the constitution makers wanted the rule of law, because they had suffered for so long from its absence. But what exactly the rule of law might entail in any particular circumstance would have been beyond their ken, would have been something to be worked out later.

Constitution makers do not just automatically write in generalities, despite knowing exactly and in detail what they want. Where recent experience points clearly to specifics, they mention them. The first clause of the South African constitution of 1996 is an interesting mixture of general and specific:

> The Republic of South Africa is one, sovereign, democratic state founded on the following values:
>
> a. Human dignity, the achievement of equality and the advancement of human rights and freedoms.
> b. Nonracialism and nonsexism.
> c. Supremacy of the constitution and the rule of law.
> d. Universal adult suffrage, a national common voters roll, regular elections and a multi-party system of democratic government, to ensure accountability, responsiveness and openness.

Not only are two specific fundamental values picked out in subsection b, but one very clear and entirely pragmatic requirement, "a national common voters roll," is accorded the same status—and all of these come after the primacy of the much less specified "Human dignity." One hint to the fact that constitutions are intended to be worked out in detail later is the way most modern constitutions make no pretence that their bill of rights sections contain absolutes. Unlike the US Bill of Rights, the grandfather constitution whose politics have so influenced all our thinking, later constitutions contain explicit clauses allowing but constraining the restriction of rights. This is to admit that some deeply held value may well turn out to be impractical of full attainment, but in ways utterly unforeseeable.

There is one form of this constraint on rights abrogation that particularly helps this argument. The German Basic Law, in Article 19, provides rules limiting the constitutionality of infringements on basic rights: "Insofar as under this Basic Law a basic right may be restricted by or pursuant to a law . . ."; "In no case may a basic right be infringed upon in its essential content." This idea of there being an, as yet unspecified, "essential content" is replicated, almost in the same language, elsewhere. The idea appeared in the interim postapartheid South African constitution, where Section 1(b) of the limitations clause contained the prohibition that any statute limiting rights "shall not negate the essential content of the right in question." In Hungary laws may not "impose any limitations on the essential contents and meaning of fundamental rights." In Poland, "Such limitations shall not violate the essence of freedoms and rights."

The German court has made little use of their version, preferring to protect rights against legislative intrusion using other techniques, above all a simpler "proportionality test."[17] The South Africans actually removed this formulation when they moved to the final constitution in 1996, probably because the judiciary itself claimed it was too difficult to operate. It was discussed at some length in one of the early landmark cases, *Makwanyane*, the death penalty case where reference was made to the Hungarian court's use of the idea in its own early death penalty case.[18] Some of the judges did their best to avoid or postpone discussion of what "essential content" meant, and nearly all found it very difficult to apply. The most interesting comment was by the presiding judge, Chaskalson, who introduced the distinction between a subjective and objective right.

> If the essential content of the right not to be subjected to cruel, inhuman or degrading punishment is to be found in respect for life and dignity, the death sentence for murder, if viewed subjectively from the point of view of the convicted prisoner, clearly negates the essential content of the right. But if it is viewed objectively from the point of view of a constitutional norm that requires life and dignity to be protected, the punishment does not necessarily negate the essential content of the right. It has been argued before this Court that one of the purposes of such punishment is to protect the life and hence the dignity of innocent members of the public, and if it in fact does so, the punishment will not negate the constitutional norm.[19]

The most extended analysis is given by Ackerman, who insisted that the court should not decide what the concept meant at that stage in its history, saying amongst other things that

> Chaskalson P . . . has, without deciding, referred to two approaches which he describes as the "objective" and "subjective" determination of the essential content. Arguably, it is possible to consider a third angle which focuses on the distinction between the "essential content" of a right and some other content. This distinction might justify a relative approach to the determination of what is the essential content of a right by distinguishing the central core of the right from its peripheral outgrowth and subjecting "a law of general application" limiting an entrenched right, to the discipline of not invading the core, as distinct from the peripheral outgrowth. In this regard, there may conceivably be a difference between rights which are inherently capable of incremental invasion and those that are not. We have not heard proper

[17] The German experience is discussed in Currie, *Constitution of Germany*, especially p. 178.
[18] *S v Makwanyane and Another*, CCT 3/94 (South African Constitutional Court).
[19] *Makwanyane*, par. 133.

> argument on any of these distinctions which justify debate in the future in a proper case. I say no more.[20]

Others had less difficulty. For Mokgoro:

> The death penalty violates the essential content of the right to life embodied in Section 9, in that it extinguishes life itself. It instrumentalises the offender for the objectives of state policy. That is dehumanising. It is degrading and it violates the rights to respect for and protection of human dignity embodied in Section 10 of the Constitution.[21]

But it is instructive that this more easily reached judgement includes, in the same paragraph, a very strong statement of the nature of the constitution:

> Our new Constitution, unlike its dictatorial predecessor, is value-based. Among other things, it guarantees the protection of basic human rights, including the right to life and human dignity, two basic values supported by the spirit of *ubuntu* and protected in Sections 9 and 10 respectively.

Obviously we are not here concerned with whether or not the death penalty ought to have been outlawed in South Africa, or even whether it did violate the essential content of the right to life. The point of the quotations is to demonstrate that the framers of the constitution, like that of any "value-based" constitution, can be taken to have recognized that the content of the rights they stipulated could only be worked out, post hoc, and in a context. Furthermore those decisions seem inevitably to be connected to prior questions about why some right or another is valued at all. In other words, something rather like Dworkin's purpose of the game has to be constructed. It can come from one or more absolutely crucial rights seen as hierarchically superior; the Hungarian court's treatment of dignity as "a mother right" comes close to this. But even that did not avail the court when forced into a decision on whether the right to life and the right to dignity, which in the death penalty case it had treated as inescapably intertwined, were in conflict.[22]

Most probably the idea of an essential core cannot take a court very far. It may be better to treat it as simply offering constitutional jurists a trump card in argument. Certainly constitutions that use some other form of limitation clause do not negate the idea that the constitution is a political act recognising the need for future, more detailed political acts of instantiation. It is the very acceptance of the need for a limitation clause that makes this an inescapable way of looking at constitution making. Limitation clauses are double headed—they both recognise that no right can be absolute, and that no legislature can be absolute either—so the idea of an essential core is no more, nor less, than this acceptance. The more typical language of the Canadian Charter "guarantees the rights and freedoms set out in it subject only to such reasonable limits prescribed by law as can be demonstrably

[20] *Makwanyane*, 298.

[21] *Makwanyane*, par. 313.

[22] *Decision of 28th April 2003 on Physician Aided Termination of Life*, 22/2003 (IV.28) AB (Hungarian Constitutional Court).

justified in a free and democratic society." This raises at least as many questions as any concept of essential content, in part precisely because it does not suggest that there is anything that absolutely cannot be done. In fact it is far too open-ended, given that it says nothing about the justifications that may count, forcing the Dworkinian referee on the bench to work all the harder. What the Canadian court has done is to produce its own dignity-based political theory, even less textually based than in the countries so far mentioned. The problem is that "free" and "democratic" are not justifications, in the way that dignity might be; they are the framework within which proffered justifications must operate. It may be necessary to draft, as some Canadian judges have, a far more substantive theory of democracy than the casual reference in the text.

It is instructive, when thinking about justifications for imposing on rights, to consider the very much more specific versions set out in the European Convention on Human Rights, now incorporated into English constitutional law by the 1998 Human Rights Act. For example, the right to "respect for his private and family life, his home and his correspondence" is guaranteed subject only to such laws as are "necessary in a democratic society in the interests of national security, public safety or the economic well-being of the country, for the prevention of disorder or crime, for the protection of health or morals, or for the protection of the rights and freedoms of others." Similarly, the right to "freedom of thought, conscience and religion" can only be restricted where it is "necessary in a democratic society in the interests of public safety, for the protection of public order, health or morals, or the protection of the rights and freedoms of others." This European document is like neither the Canadian Charter, despite the references to democracy, nor the German / Hungarian / South African model, with its leading role for core values. It is intentionally much more prescriptive. Though national constitutions never spell out things in this way, an international treaty, such as the Convention, absolutely has to. The difference is fairly obvious: a country can face the inevitability of subsequent political acts of constitutional construction by a court, but an international agreement cannot conceive of such a thing. This is one of the reasons the European Court of Justice insisted from early on that EU law was not international law, but a wholly new legal phenomenon.

The sense of "political theory" used in this argument does not connote only traditional political philosophy, but comes much closer to the political scientist's idea of political theory. This embraces a sociological understanding of politics as well as normative preferences, and links the two via arguments about appropriate institutions—in this context, laws. An example from Australia demonstrates how little a blanket commitment to "democracy" fills out rules about rights limitation. The Australian constitution contains no bill of rights, but from time to time the High Court tries to deal with classical rights claims by "imputing" their necessity from the constitutionally prescribed structure of Australian politics.[23] In the realm

[23]This has always been controversial, and it is widely believed the High Court has returned to an "orthodoxy" that prohibits such judicial creativity after a bout of finding "implied rights" under Chief Justice Mason in the mid-1990s. However, the case I call on here is well post-*Mason* and yet still very much a development of implied rights. This and many other cases are described, through interviews

of speech rights, this started in 1992 in *Australian Capital Television Pty Ltd v The Commonwealth*, where a free speech right was held to be "implicit" in the system of competitive party electoral politics that underpinned democracy.[24] A series of similar cases followed until the court became anxious about the breadth of the doctrine and restricted it in 1997 in *Lange v Australian Broadcasting Corporation*.[25] The most recent case, *Coleman v Power*, where the doctrine seems to have developed more force, was in 2004.[26] In *Coleman* the High Court split in favour of Coleman, who had been convicted under a Queensland statute that banned the use of "threatening, abusive, or insulting words to any person" in a public place. While protesting against corruption Coleman had pushed a police officer, shouting, "This is Constable Brendan Power, a corrupt police officer."[27] Coleman claimed the Queensland statute offended against a freedom of expression right implicit in the constitution. To succeed, he had to show that the statue was not "reasonably appropriate and adapted to serve a legitimate end" in such a way as to be compatible with "the maintenance of the constitutionally prescribed system of representative and responsible government," which is a reformulation of the test defined in *Lange*.[28] What is most interesting here is the argument made by one of the dissenters, Justice Heydon, who would have upheld the statute. He saw it as an effort to improve the "civility" of the society by limiting abusive language in political discourse. This was given short shrift by the majority, who thought such a speech limitation incompatible with "representative and responsible government." Heydon saw a direct link between civility and democracy because, as he put it:

> In promoting civilised standards, [this law] not only improves the quality of communication on government and political matters . . . but it also increases the chance that those who might otherwise have been insulted, and those who might otherwise have heard the insults, will respond to the communications they have heard in a like manner and thereby enhance the quantity and quality of debate.

The majority instead thought such a limitation on speech far too wide, and incompatible with democracy in reality. Part of the argument was that Heydon sociologically (my word) misunderstood the nature of Australian political discourse. Heyden's argument was described as a "chronicle" that

> appears more like a description of an intellectual salon where civility always (or usually) prevails. . . . Australian politics has regularly included insult and

with judges, in a book that goes a long way to demonstrating my thesis of judges as political theorists, JL Pierce, *Inside the Mason Court Revolution: The High Court of Australia Transformed* (Durham, N.C.: Carolina Academic Press, 2006).

[24] *Australian Capital Television Pty Ltd v Commonwealth*, 177 CLR 106 (1992) (Australian High Court).

[25] *Lange v Australian Broadcasting Corporation*, 189 CLR 520 (1997) (Australian High Court).

[26] *Coleman v Power*, 220 CLR 1 (2004) (Australian High Court).

[27] The case is described in A Stone and S Evans, "Australia: Freedom of Speech and Insult in the High Court of Australia," 2006 4 *International Journal of Constitutional Law* 4, 677–88.

[28] Referred to in *Coleman v Power* by several justices; cf. pars. 93 and 196.

> emotion, calumny and invective, in its armoury of persuasion . . . the Constitution addresses the nation's representative government as it is practised.[29]

Whatever the truth may be about Australian political discourse, these arguments clearly demonstrate the way in which judges themselves have to construct rich theories of politics in interpreting constitutional restrictions on legislation. Most often these will be more implicit than explicit, and may indeed at times be partially unconscious. The theories are much more likely to be spelled out in cases like *Coleman* where democracy is at the centre of the issue itself, rather than being a background limiting factor on rights constraint. Such cases, however, are not rare, and do not comprise only classic speech cases. All cases dealing with media, as for example French and German cases on media pluralism, fall into this category. Even more obvious are issues arising in cases like the German decisions on party finance. More traditionally and obviously political theory is necessarily involved in many structural cases dealing with power allocation in constitutions. Cases dealing, for example, with separation of powers do not cease to require political theory simply because we have a ready-coined token concept in the very phrase *separation of powers*. Deciding whether a putative breach of the separation really *is* one requires a subtle understanding of how politics works, as well as a commitment to some ideal about how it should work, none of which is given just by the incantation of separation. When the South African Constitutional Court dealt with the certification of the constitution in 1996, it had to decide substantive and serious issues about whether the new form of upper chamber was compatible with the political aims of the original agreement on constitution building, and the court rejected the first version because it failed to satisfy the court's theoretical requirements.[30] Just as clearly calling for political theory was the detailed consideration of the nature of competitive party politics that court had to set out when deciding whether a statute allowing floor crossing was incompatible with the democratic aims of the electoral laws.[31] East European courts have on many occasions had to intervene to stop one house from trampling on the authority of the other. In each case substantive arguments of political theory have been needed.[32]

It is perhaps unnecessary to make the point about structural jurisprudence. It is mentioned largely to restate that the idea of political theory lying behind constitutional jurisprudence applies not only to litigation that is of the bills-of-rights

[29] *Coleman v Power*, at pars. 324 (Heyden) and 238–39 (Kirby). The quotations are taken from Stone and Evans, "Australia," section 1.4.

[30] *Certification of the Constitution of the Republic of South Africa*, CCT 23/96 (South African Constitutional Court), and *Certification of the Amended Text of the Constitution of the Republic of South Africa*, CCT 37/96 (South African Constitutional Court).

[31] *United Democratic Movement v The President of the Republic of South Africa*, CCT 23/02 (South African Constitutional Court).

[32] For example, *Decision of 22 June 2005—Role of Senate in Election Law*, Pl. US 13/05 (Czech Republic Constitutional Court), *Inequality in Competences of Sejm and Senate Committees in Respect of EU Proposals*, K24/04 (2005) (Polish Constitutional Tribunal), or, on a different topic, the intervention in electoral laws in *Decision of 27 April 1996 on Election Coalitions*, US 127/96 (Czech Republic Constitutional Court).

type. The intellectual problems are probably greater in this latter context because there is less consensus on what is meant by a richer conception of democracy, and because proportionality or essential core claims appear less obviously. But the activity is the same. In all the cases, the Dworkinian model of judicial decision-making applies: it is always a matter of deciding what the fundamental purpose of the constitutional settlement is, and seeking a reading of legislation that best accords with the answer.

Constitutional orders vary in the explicitness of their purpose; they vary in whether they even acknowledge core values. But one way or another, all constitutional orders in liberal democracies have come to accept at least one crucial value, and it is one that by its very nature often forces judges into very refined and detailed exercises of Dworkinian refereeing.

General Themes

The Problem of (Non)Discrimination

One reason constitutional courts and constitutional interpretation have come to be so important in the modern world may be that constitutions themselves play a newly important role as a result of wide social and political change. Although the "end of ideology / end of history" thesis is probably exaggerated and oversimplified, it is the case that modern liberal democracies have become much less attached to widely held and overarching moral codes.[33] The famous English case *Donoghue v Stevenson* from 1932 uses the New Testament story of the Good Samaritan as the core of the justification for an extensive reinterpretation of the duty of care in the tort of negligence. Such a reference today would be largely meaningless to even an educated legal elite. Where not unintelligible, it would be offensive for imposing the concepts and language of one religious tradition on a secular society. This is an extreme example, but it is generally true that secularisation in Western societies has progressed so far that no general knowledge of, let alone acquiescence to, Christianity is available as an overarching provider of arguments to those required to make binding value judgements, whether they be politicians or judges. Nor, however, are any of the other familiar sources of moral unity much more useful.[34] Patriotism as a simple commitment more or less on the order of "my country right or wrong" has gone, and "wrapping it in the flag" is a derisive criticism of political arguments that seek to rely on it. Nor has it been replaced effectively with appeals

[33] F Fukuyama, *The End of History and the Last Man* (New York: Simon & Schuster, 2006), exemplifies this approach, but similar implications can be drawn from much political sociology of the modern West—above all from the work on postmaterialism, best summarised in R Inglehart and C Weltzel, *Modernization, Cultural Change and Democracy* (Cambridge: Cambridge University Press, 2005).

[34] It might be argued that this is an excessively Western-oriented view. There is a body of Islamic jurisprudence, and the refusal to distinguish in a Western manner between church and state allows it to have a potentially unifying force, as well as providing solid legal protection for a version of positive welfare and a form of dignity jurisprudence, even if cast in terms the West finds repellent.

to “national” values of something like “the British way of life” because of ethnic pluralism. Social mobility and widespread effective education have removed any sense of social and political deference to leadership. Even the subcultural power of class-related ideology has faded, and appeals to class solidarity do politicians precious little good. Most sociologists would agree that there are few if any general “value producing” ideological appeals left available for solving legal and constitutional, or even more broadly constitutional, problems.[35]

This may incidentally be an explanation for an often noted phenomenon in Western parliaments that some critics of constitutional review have seized on. This is the idea that politics has become judicialized, so that members of parliaments seek to use “unconstitutionality” as a prime argument against government policies they oppose. Critics like Stone Sweet put this down to a “chilling effect” of constitutional courts overstepping their roles.[36] It is more likely, however, to be a consequence of the lack of any other reference frame that can be used in the hope that all members of society will share the parliamentarian’s opposition to the policy. He or she cannot attack the government for being unpatriotic, unchristian, nor even for preferring the interests of one social class to another—or not with much hope that it will be a rallying cry. He or she can cry “Unconstitutional!” with at least some hope that the constitution will now function as the flag used to.

Constitutions are very nearly all we have left, and one value permeates most if not all modern liberal constitutions—the value, it is almost the “default value,” of equality—or not exactly equality, but nondiscrimination. Not only is nondiscrimination one of the most potent modern common values, it is one that is itself peculiarly affected by the vanishing of other society-wide value frames. This is because one thing such frames did was in fact to legitimize discrimination. Acceptance of an ethnically based national culture meant governments need not worry much if a policy was implemented in a way that failed to be ethnically neutral in its costs. Male domination and superior status in society, buttressed by religious as well as secular traditions, similarly meant governments need not concern themselves about at least indirect sexual discrimination. A simpler example will make the point—as long as Canadian society was characterised by widespread acceptance of Christian morality, no government needed to concern itself with the differential impact of a policy on dependents’ allowances on homosexuals or on nonmarried heterosexual couples. Now, as the cases show, it must strive to take care of such groups. A related reason for nondiscrimination becoming a, perhaps *the*, prime constitutional value is that it is a problem for which the standard democratic op-

[35] An interesting example of this concern is the remarkable change in attitude exhibited by Jürgen Habermas, perhaps the most distinguished European sociologist of law, at least from the intellectual Left. In a debate with the then Cardinal Ratzinger in 2004 he agreed with the future pope that a return to religion was needed to provide moral consensus in modern society. This is discussed with a translation of the debate is published in H de Vries and LE Sullivan, eds., *Political Theologies: Public Religions in a Post Secular World* (New York: Fordham University Press, 2006). See also A Marga, *La Sortie du relativisme* (Editura-Limes Cluj 2006), 103–212.

[36] See in particular Stone Sweet’s comments on the use of the charge of unconstitutionality in his analysis of the French parliament in *Birth of Judicial Politics*.

tion of trusting to the people as represented in parliament may not work. Perhaps the most famous, because apparently erudite legal citation in this field is in fact to a single footnote, in one US Supreme Court case from the 1930s. *Carolene Products v United States* in 1938 was otherwise a typical example of the Supreme Court deferring to Congress, very shortly after it gave up its intransigence over the New Deal. One footnote, in a part of the judgement where only four of the nine justices concurred, sowed the seed was of what was to become the doctrine of "heightened review," a crucial technique for controlling discriminatory legislation. The relevant part of the footnote identifies a political justification for possibly striking down some forms of discrimination in suggesting that on another occasion the court might need to consider

> whether legislation which restricts those political processes which can ordinarily be expected to bring about repeal of undesirable legislation, is to be subjected to more exacting judicial scrutiny under the general prohibitions of the Fourteenth Amendment than are most other types of legislation.

A particular problem that might prevent the political system working fairly was identified as where

> prejudice against discrete and insular minorities may be a special condition, which tends seriously to curtail the operation of those political processes ordinarily to be relied upon to protect minorities, and which may call for a correspondingly more searching judicial inquiry.[37]

This ultimately led to the sort of analyses in the United States discussed in chapter 7. It is quoted here to show how antidiscrimination jurisprudence may be central just because, more than in most areas of policy, it rests its justification for overturning "democratic" decisions on the grounds that majoritarianism is only one aspect of democracy. Majoritarianism may require for its own legitimacy another aspect—the commitment to equality.

There is one final reason that constitutional courts have been so busy with antidiscrimination jurisprudence in the last fifty years. This is because the state has become a major provider of benefits and a regulator in detail of much else that happens in society. In the United States much of the jurisprudence has been concerned with legislation that actively and intentionally discriminated because the majority did not believe some people, blacks, were equal. Later logically similar intentional racially targeted discrimination caused many constitutional problems because of positive discrimination. But these are not, in fact, typical of the cases coming before constitutional courts. Rather, cases typically concern what one might think of better as discrimination by oversight, or by indifference, or because of the need to ration state benefits. Or they arise because a perfectly legitimate "law of general

[37] *Carolene Products v United States*, 304 US 144 (1938) (US Supreme Court) at 144. The full story of the role this has played in American constitutional jurisprudence is given in F Gilman, "The Famous Footnote Four: A History of the *Carolene Products* Footnote," 2005 46 *South Texas Law Review* 163–245. The best article, and one that has much to say about legal writing and thought generally, is Balkin, "The Footnote."

application" unequally burdens some people.[38] If the state provided as little in the way of welfare and support as it did almost everywhere before 1945, there would simply be far fewer cases—a state that provides little discriminates little. Indeed the range of potential discrimination or rights denial that can arise because of the extent of state provisions is very broad. In 1981 Justice Rehnquist dissented in a case largely concerning religious rights, making this point. The plaintiff had left his job when he was redeployed to a part of the firm making armaments, claiming that as a Jehovah's Witness he could not, for religious reasons, work there. He claimed unemployment benefits but was denied because he was deemed to be voluntarily unemployed. The majority of the Supreme Court upheld his claim that such denial was a denial of First Amendment religious rights, and therefore discriminatory. In his dissent Rehnquist explicitly argued that the growth of welfare rights has caused much of the conflict over such alleged discrimination:

> The growth of social welfare legislation during the latter part of the 20th century has greatly magnified the potential for conflict between the two Clauses, since such legislation touches the individual at so many points in his life. . . . None of these developments could have been foreseen by those who framed and adopted the First Amendment. The First Amendment was adopted well before the growth of much social welfare legislation and at a time when the Federal Government was in a real sense considered a government of limited delegated powers. Indeed, the principal argument against adopting the Constitution without a "Bill of Rights" was not that such an enactment would be undesirable, but that it was unnecessary because of the limited nature of the Federal Government. So long as the Government enacts little social welfare legislation, as was the case in 1791, there are few occasions in which the two Clauses may conflict. . . . Because those who drafted and adopted the First Amendment could not have foreseen either the growth of social welfare legislation or the incorporation of the First Amendment into the Fourteenth Amendment, we simply do not know how they would view the scope of the two Clauses.[39]

One does not have to sympathize with Rehnquist's originalist methodology to take his point here. Even much more modern constitutions than that of America throw up more problems than could have been expected in this area because of the combination of extended government reach and reduced government choice of justificatory ideology.

Similarly the endless regulation, for example, of access to professions, inevitably throws up discrimination claims that would not arise were there no regulations.

[38] This is the claim typically found where religious rights are at stake, and where a "constitutional exemption" is called for. A pair of similar cases from different jurisdictions show the problem well. For the United States, *Employment Div., Dept. of Human Resources of Oregon v Smith*, 494 US 872 (1990) (US Supreme Court) and from South Africa, *Garreth Anver Prince v The President of the Law Society of the Cape of Good Hope*, 2002 (2) SA 794 (CC). An unsympathetic but rigorous analysis of the logic of such claims in given in B Barry, *Culture and Equality* (Cambridge: Polity, 2001).

[39] *Thomas v. Review Bd., Ind. Empl. Sec. Div.*, 450 US 707 (1981) (US Supreme Court).

Both Canada and South Africa, for example, had to deal with discriminatory provisions governing access to the legal profession very early in their antidiscrimination jurisprudence, while the German constitutional right to practise a profession has been rife with problems.

For all of these reasons the values either explicit or implicit in constitutional documents have forced courts to develop theories to control discriminatory decisions made in the drafting of statutes. And herein lies the real problem because, as noted in chapter 7, discrimination is at the heart of most legislation, indeed of governing. With most constitutional values that a court might wish to protect, the problem is simpler. In general governments are not supposed to censor newspapers or restrict religious activities. Censorship may be allowed in national emergencies, some religious practices may be abhorrent, but the general activity of governing does not involve censoring newspapers or ritual. There are some governmental activities where the essence of the activity is basically an affront to human rights. Such are day-to-day executive politics, like policing, which involve depriving people of liberty or security of the person, and may only be done with due safeguards. But these are largely matters of public-law control of the executive, rather than legislation. With state provision of services and goods (and extraction of costs via taxation) the heart of the policy is to discriminate: some are entitled to more, some to less health benefit, some must pay more tax than others. Furthermore, much policy now involves deliberate use of discrimination to guide and incentivate behaviour. Making drivers of large cars pay more road tax is legitimate, perhaps vital, yet it is inherently to discriminate against some people who have exercised their freedom to buy one rather than another car, both being legal products. Forbidding the purchase of alcohol or cigarettes to those under eighteen is laudable, but discriminates on age grounds in a way that is generally forbidden by some constitutions. Allowing women free entry to swimming baths at sixty when men have to wait until they are sixty-five discriminates on age and gender, however valid the purpose.[40]

Hence the problem: antidiscrimination jurisprudence requires two very different sorts of decision by a constitutional court, though they are so some extent interdependent. One question addresses the identities of those claiming to be discriminated against: What sort of human characteristics may legitimately be used to differentiate recipients of welfare, payers of taxes, acceptability for a profession, or obligations under general laws? The second type of question covers the method of discrimination: Is it generally apposite? Footnote 4 to *Carolene Products* provided a political theory to work out answers to the first sort of question. If a group identity was such as to weaken their political ability to defend themselves because they made up a "discreet and insular minority," then, probably, legislation damaging them might be unconstitutional. Enormous intellectual effort has gone into defining the groups that can expect to be protected in this way. If the court is

[40] *James v Eastleigh Borough Council*, 2 AC 751 [1990] (House of Lords). The fact that this case comes from the United Kingdom before the Human Rights Act makes my point about the generality of nondiscrimination as an issue.

not going to rely on the political vulnerability argument, it is not enough just to list such groups: the theory requires its own justification for protecting particular groups rather than others. This has been most obvious in the "dignity" approach, especially in Canada and South Africa. But as we have seen, this has not exactly been unproblematic. These questions can be similar to structural constitutional questions, and depend on the more "social science" aspects of political theorising. But they may, indeed usually do, also involve pure moral choice: it is inherently wrong to deprive someone of equal status because the person has characteristic X, but not if he or she has characteristic Y. It is wrong to deprive people of one sexual preference of a benefit granted to those of another preference, but not wrong to make the wealthy pay more than others. Approaches based on dignity tend to obfuscate this distinction, because the argument is often that picking out a group because of characteristic X will tend to lower their status in the eyes of society. This concerned radical critics of the South African Constitutional Court for some time. Yet in fact it is a sociological judgement whether this lowering of esteem will happen or not, and the claimant may in any case care little about such matters and simply want as much as another of the welfare pot. "Why me?" is the common question to which courts must craft an answer where legislatures have failed to.

Even where there appears to be no problem in the identity of the loser, that "Why me?" question forces a court to the other consideration: Is the discrimination necessary anyway? Is there not some other way for the government to achieve its ends? Or, given that any discrimination is worse than none, is the end actually worth any degree of unequal treatment by society? Chapter 7 discussed at great length the various tests courts have come up with to try to handle these and related questions. What is clear is that no test or analytic device can hide the fact that courts are indeed second-guessing governments and legislatures when they take up discrimination cases. One of the simplest cases to show what is going on in discrimination jurisprudence comes from France, a country with much less developed judicial methodology in this area. In 2000 the Conseil constitutionnel objected to one part of an annual finance law that proposed to award Corsican farmers a much greater support payment than farmers in mainland France.[41] The problem was not that Corsicans in general, or farmers in general, or even Corsican farmers were groups it was unfair to single out. The problem was that there was no reason given in the statute for their special treatment, no legislative theory to support this group of farmers rather than any other. In practice everyone knew it was an attempt to pacify potential separatist feelings on Corsica—it was pure group bargaining politics, the absolute opposite of what courts seek to do in applying a constitution. As such it had to be held unconstitutional. Later the government came up with a scheme for agricultural help that, while still giving Corsicans more than farmers in mainland France, did provide a rational justification, and the Council accepted that second version.

[41] *Loi de finances rectificative pour 2000*, 2000-441 DC (Conseil constitutionnel). This is discussed properly in chapter 4.

Much of the time all a court can do is to judge whether or not a legitimate end is rationally connected to a discrimination that does not seem avoidable, and is not too broadly or narrowly conceived, and that does not apply to groups seen as vulnerable, nor groups whose dignity might be fragile. This can be seen as an approach based on deference to the legislature, and it is indeed so described in many American studies. It is equally familiar in much administrative law, evoking perhaps the old English test of "Wednesbury rationality" under which only a decision that no rational policymaker could come to would count as *ultra vires* the enabling statute. It is interesting to note that since the passing of the Human Rights Act in the United Kingdom, even judicial opinion is swinging against the use of this old administrative law test:

> And I think that the day will come when it will be more widely recognised that [Wednesbury] was an unfortunately retrogressive decision in English administrative law, insofar as it suggested that there are degrees of unreasonableness and that only a very extreme degree can bring an administrative decision within the legitimate scope of judicial invalidation.[42]

But whether Wednesbury or some other test is used, they are merely a formula; the court still has to have some way of deciding those specific questions—and only a quite subtle theory, blending social science elements with normative preferences will do the job. We know much more about how courts think when they go in for complex, multistep tests than when they assert that a discrimination is or is not proportional to a policy aim. But we should not make the mistake of thinking that proportionality is just a very simple test. It is more a way of announcing the results of a complex balance. How that balance is determined is the job of a sometimes unarticulated analysis. What the courts are always doing is to examine the justification given by a government for a policy differentiation. A similar argument was alluded to in chapter 7, when Richard Pildes's argument was cited.[43] He takes a broader view, that "rights are not trumps," saying they essentially control only the reasons that will count as good for governmental action. A more restricted version is probably true in the special case of antidiscrimination jurisprudence. The court sifts amongst a variety of reasons for discrimination, accepting some, rejecting others. To do so it must have a theory, very probably of a Dworkinian nature, to do the sifting work.

Another thing the courts crucially do is to define the range over which discrimination will run the risk of being seen as unconstitutional. It is relatively seldom that a constitution does mandate a court to ensure equality per se. The European Convention on Human Rights, for example, contains no direct ban on discrimination; it forbids discrimination only in the protection of other, enumerated, rights. In Poland in 2001 the question arose as to whether a citizen could bring a consti-

[42] Lord Cooke in *R v Secretary of State for the Home Department, ex parte Daly*, 2 AC 532 [2001] (House of Lords), par. 32.

[43] RH Pildes, "Why Rights Are Not Trumps: Social Meanings, Expressive Harms, and Constitutionalism," 1998 27 *Journal of Legal Studies* 2, 725–63. But see also Waldron's criticism on this argument: J Waldron, "Pildes on Dworkin's Theory of Rights," 2000 29 *Journal of Legal Studies*, 301–9.

tutional complaint to the Constitutional Tribunal simply because his wartime experiences of forced labour within Poland had been treated as undeserving of compensation, while those deported elsewhere for forced labour were given statutory compensation.[44] Because there was no specific guaranteed right he could claim had been unequally protected, the general constitutional guarantee of equality of treatment was held not to apply. The case was controversial, with five dissents, and occurred after different panels of the tribunal had given different rulings on this general question in previous cases. Nonetheless, the majority ruled against the idea of an enforceable general right to equal treatment despite the constitution containing the apparently powerful promise in Article 32:

1. All persons shall be equal before the law. All persons shall have the right to equal treatment by public authorities.
2. No one shall be discriminated against in political, social or economic life for any reason whatsoever.

The tribunal's decision is in keeping with one powerful strand of constitutional thought, the claim that a general equality right is inchoate. It is this that has led the South African court to attach more importance to loss of dignity in discrimination cases than the equality per se. Such a decision, though in the Polish case it was made for ostensibly textual reasons of the structure of the constitution itself, is quite clearly deeply rooted in what can only be seen as political theory.

The best way to see constitutional courts in their antidiscrimination role is to regard them as fine-tuning legislation, or as creating a sieve through which all statutes that differentiate between citizens must pass, the better to ensure modern liberal societies live up to the egalitarian thrust in democratic ideals. This never can really be reduced to meaningful tests, even if the language of tests makes their decisions look more legal and less what they really are, an inspection of the reasons behind legislation. So perhaps the most apt analogy is indeed the Dworkinian idea of the referee. What decision, taking the whole nature of the state and its constitution, is most compatible with that whole? Such a description makes it virtually impossible for us to regard a constitutional review body as a court in any way that can intelligibly put it within the classic judicial function—for that would be to privilege one function over another, and to allow far too much power to nonconstitutional courts.

The Counter-majoritarian Criticism and the Value of Judicial Deference

There is an extensive, and often rather heated literature on the question of whether or not constitutional review is compatible with democracy. The debate seems largely inspired by American concerns, and by an American comprehension of democracy—perhaps by an American trust in popular electoral democracy that is not entirely shared elsewhere. This book does not enter this debate. These courts

[44] *Constitutional Complaint and the Principle of Equality*, SK10/01 (2001) (Polish Constitutional Tribunal).

exist, and if the last few decades suggest anything, it is that more such courts will develop, rather than that reliance on courts to interpret and uphold fundamental values will decrease. My concern has been to describe what they are and how they act, and to try to find some framework for understanding them and their place in modern liberal democracies. Some points in the debate still require brief attention, because the courts themselves have to work in an environment where criticisms of their legitimacy matter.

One preliminary point is that much of the criticism of constitutional courts seems to derive from their role in applying human rights, rather than the structural aspect, the policing of institutional boundaries. Kelsen, the great architect of constitutional courts, thought almost entirely of this second aspect, and disapproved of courts having the power to apply a bill of rights. The leading modern philosophical critic of constitutional review, Jeremy Waldron, also largely restricts himself to concerns with rights jurisprudence.[45] Certainly the idea of constitutional review for structural matters has been less politically controversial, though this is not to say that any specific decision of this sort is less contested than many in the field of individual rights. The German constitutional court today and its predecessor in the Weimar Republic are fully fledged courts, but there was a predecessor to both of them in the German idea of "constitutional" as opposed to "judicial" review in imperial Germany: this was handled by the parliamentary chamber, like the modern Bundesrat, where the states themselves were represented. As the empire was federal, this could not be avoided. Indeed Kommers goes as far as saying the necessity of what I call structural review was seen in the Holy Roman Empire.[46] The early British colonies of Canada and Australia uncontroversially had courts to impose structure when they gained national independence, especially for issues concerned with federalism. The courts in these two countries only became politically controversial when they started making rights decisions—the Canadians after the Charter, Australia most recently under the Mason court. The French Conseil constitutionnel, though from its beginning a breach with the "French republican tradition," was nonetheless put in place by de Gaulle with few fears that it was in itself a counter-majoritarian body.

Yet it is not clear that such decisions are inherently less dangerous to democracy when made by a court than are decisions about human rights. The only obvious difference is that structural policing requires a court-like body because otherwise the legislative and executive bodies would have no referee, nor would federal and state conflicts be soluble. The decisions are perhaps seen as somehow or other more automatic, less engaged with political values, though any such belief is mistaken. At its crudest one might well point to the US Supreme Court's decision on the presidential election in 2000 as an example.[47] More seriously the great initial structural decisions in countries like the United States and Australia have all been

[45] Jeremy Waldron has written widely on the matter. See in particular "A Rights Based Critique of Constitutional Rights," 1993 13 *Oxford Journal of Legal Studies* 18–51; and "Legislation, Authority, and Voting," 1996 84 *Georgia Law Journal* 2185–2215.

[46] Kommers, *Constitutional Jurisprudence*, 4–7.

[47] *Bush v Gore*, 531 US 98 (2000) (US Supreme Court).

hotly contested examples of constitution making, not of simple constitution applying. It is impossible to regard these foundational decisions as somehow or other "normal" law, as the mere application of the words of the constitutional document. Nor were they in any obvious way dependent on the constitutional court looking at the intent of the constituent power. In all such cases highly creative attempts had to be made to work out from first principles what the very general outline of the new states required as answers to very precise questions—in the US case, for example, whether or not the United States, as opposed to a state, could charter a bank. These decisions are not restricted to the early days of a new state. The Australian High Court was still trying to define the meaning of Section 92, which governs federal control of interstate commerce, as late as 1988. And it was the Mason court, one of the most activist in Australian constitutional history and the inventor of a prototype human rights jurisprudence, that handed down the most important decision on the matter.[48] We have seen how the German court, East European courts, and the South African Constitutional Court have had to think very deeply about the requirements of democracy in handling issues of party competition and powers of legislative houses. The truth is that though the structure-versus-rights dichotomy is a useful simplification, it is only that. Issues regarding the media, for example, are simultaneously structural questions about the requirements of a functional democratic politics and questions about individual speech rights.[49]

So if constitutional review is to be allowed at all, it is probably hopeless to restrict it. In the end the debate often seems to be about matters of trust—some trust "the people," some prefer to trust legal elites. One of Waldron's themes, to be found in several places in his writing, takes the form of a commentary on a passage of Aristotle, where the latter appears to advocate trusting the masses more than the wise.[50] Waldron calls this the "Doctrine of the Wisdom of the Multitude." Against Waldron one might cite almost any political science study of party competition or electoral behaviour. The latter would show the almost complete lack of an articulated and subtle ideology on the part of the mass of voters. The former would show the distortion of electoral preferences by the competitive drives of the parties to win elections. If that is too sweeping a criticism, one might just fall back onto footnote 4 to *Carolene Products*, but only after noting that the justices who backed it had no warrant to regard it as a very narrow or exceptional gateway for judicial review. Again in the alternative, one need not distrust political parties and electoral politics to undermine the special legitimacy of parliaments vis-à-vis courts. As Dimitrios Kyritsis has shown, the most one provides by letting parliaments decide

[48] *Cole v Whitefield*, 165 CLR 360 (1988) (Australian High Court).

[49] Even courts not noted as creative or activist have been creative and even radical on media matters. See the discussion of Italian constitutional jurisprudence in this area in G Mazzoleni, "The RAI: Restructuring and Reform," in C Mershon and G Pasquino, eds., *Italian Politics: Ending the First Republic* (Boulder, Colo.: Westview Press, 1995), or the general overview of the court in M Volcansek, *Constitutional Politics in Italy* (London: Macmillan, 2000).

[50] Several of the essays in his collection, J Waldron, *Law and Disagreement* (Oxford: Oxford University Press, 1999), involve this idea. His use of Aristotle is criticized in R Mulgan, "Debate: Aristotle, Ethical Diversity and Political Argument," 1999 7 *Journal of Political Philosophy* 2, 191–207.

constitutional issues rather than courts is to replace a handful of decision makers acting as trustees of the constitution with a few hundred doing so—and doing so in less than ideal conditions, given the inevitably conflictual nature of party politics.[51] As suggested earlier in this book, much of the power of the "democratic deficit" concern comes from comparing a rather ideal version of parliamentary democracy with a more "warts and all" view of courts, a point made forcibly as far as Eastern Europe goes by Kim Schepple.[52]

But is the debate entirely miscast by turning it into one of trust? Is it even conceptually possible for democratically elected parliaments to do the job needed? Courts very seldom make highly generalised decisions that X should, or Y should not, be a legally enforceable right. What they actually do is to decide whether a rights claim is properly made out. The job of the constitutional court is to tease out the meaning, "on the ground," of the general rights statements in the constitution. It is, after all, precisely because constituent assemblies are incapable of handling the details of rights, or of any sort of rule in a constitution, that we have constitutional review. It is often argued by exponents of judicial deference, including many judges, that courts are just not the right sort of institutions to make policy decisions. But are parliaments the right sort of institutions to balance rights, to work out what free speech or religious freedom actually requires in a highly concrete situation, replete with factual difficulties? Even *a priori* judicial review is unlike a parliamentary vote. The review body may have to deal with the constitutionality of a statutory clause in abstract, and most judges restricted to that limit wish they could instead hear more concrete cases, but that is still an intellectual exercise different from voting on the clause in a parliamentary chamber where the focus is on the efficiency of the policy, not its capacity to violate values enshrined in the constitution. Many of the most severe critics of courts that seem to be overstepping their role and trespassing on legislative prerogatives are judges themselves. There is no jurisdiction, certainly none covered here, where judges do not frequently use references to a duty to defer to parliament against their own colleagues. The trouble is that it is unusual to find one group of judges on a court that always defers and one that frequently trespasses. Instead the deference argument is wielded when it fits the result a judge wants. The same judge may wilfully trespass on another occasion, only to be reproved by an earlier trespasser now turned deferential. There is little difference, in fact, between constitutional law and "ordinary law" as far as a duty of deference is concerned. The problem is not in recognizing that both sorts of courts should restrict themselves within boundaries, but in finding anyway whatsoever to demarcate those boundaries. It was well put by an English judge some years ago in a purely commercial law case:

> There is . . . a second objection to the recognition of such a right. . . . This is that for your Lordships' House to recognise such a principle would overstep the boundary which we traditionally set for ourselves, separating the legiti-

[51] D Kyritsis, "Representation and Waldron's Objection to Judicial Review," 2006 26 *Oxford Journal of Legal Studies* 4, 733–51.

[52] Schepple, "Constitutional Negotiations."

> mate development of the law by the judges from legislation. It was strongly urged . . . that we would indeed be trespassing beyond that boundary if we were to accept the argument of [the plaintiff]. I feel bound however to say that, although I am well aware of the existence of the boundary, I am never quite sure where to find it. Its position seems to vary from case to case. Indeed, if it were to be as firmly and clearly drawn as some of our mentors would wish, I cannot help feeling that a number of leading cases in your Lordships' House would never have been decided the way they were. For example, the minority view would have prevailed in Donoghue v. Stevenson [1932] A.C. 562; our modern law of judicial review would have never developed from its old, ineffectual, origins; and Mareva injunctions would never have seen the light of day.[53]

The case involved the refusal of the tax authorities to refund overpayment of taxes by a company. It is a measure of how one might find the boundaries, and where they might legitimately be overstepped, that Lord Goff justifies changing the law in the following way:

> To that objection, however, there are two answers. The first is that the retention by the state of taxes unlawfully exacted is particularly obnoxious, because it is one of the most fundamental principles of our law—enshrined in a famous constitutional document, the Bill of Rights 1688—that taxes should not be levied without the authority of Parliament; and full effect can only be given to that principle if the return of taxes exacted under an unlawful demand can be enforced as a matter of right. The second is that, when the revenue makes a demand for tax, that demand is implicitly backed by the coercive powers of the state and may well entail (as in the present case) unpleasant economic and social consequences if the taxpayer does not pay.[54]

If a court can do what Parliament would more normally do in a context of commercial law because of the nature of state power, and because of ancient rights, there seems very little point in objecting to constitutional courts acting as they are warranted to act by the constitutions they enforce. Two of the five Law Lords hearing the case did feel that the boundary was too high to be stepped over and dissented, believing they could see the boundary and would not step over it. Both, in other cases, could make such a step. Another English judgement from the same time, the early 1990s, provides a judicial obiter too acute for present purposes not to be cited here. In *M v Home Office* first the Court of Appeal and then the House of Lords took the huge and unprecedented step of holding the home secretary himself in contempt of court for ignoring a High Court order not to deport someone.[55] This clash between the executive and the courts was only a matter of administrative law at the time, the Human Rights Act not yet being in existence. Not

[53] Lord Goff in *Woolwich Equitable Building Society v Inland Revenue Commissioners*, AC 70 [1993] (House of Lords) 90.

[54] *Woolwich*, 88.

[55] *M v Home Office* QB 270 [1992] (Court of Appeal); *In Re M*, 1 AC 377 [1994] (House of Lords).

surprisingly, counsel for the Home Office argued that it was beyond the powers of the courts to treat a senior member of the executive branch in this manner. Lord Justice Nolan, in the Court of Appeal, produced the following summary of the constitutional position:

> the proper constitutional relationship of the executive with the courts is that the courts will respect all acts of the executive within its lawful province, and that the executive will respect all decisions of the court as to what its lawful province is.[56]

This is precisely the problem of judicial deference, and the real power of the constitutional court. In the UK case, given that Parliament is supreme and can rewrite the constitution as it wishes, the legislature could in principle come to the aid of the executive if the court's decision on the extension of the latter's "lawful province" was too restrictive. But where a constitution can only be amended by a special procedure, the constitutional court is the only institution within the constitution that can do that job of defining its own, and the other institutions' "rightful provinces." In this special but crucial sense, constitutional courts not only are, but are logically required to be, supreme. To say a court fails to defer when it ought to do so is to make an external judgement about how the constitution might be amended. The duty of deference, the duty to obey the majoritarian institution, is no duty at all. At best such "duties" may be counsels of wisdom about not straining the temper of actors who just might decide to act unconstitutionally themselves by ignoring the legitimate commands of the constitution interpreter.

Human Dignity

We have seen throughout this book how central is the role played by the idea of human dignity. It may be nearly universal as a touchstone. Dignity is protected in constitutions as diverse as those of Andorra and Kazakhstan, as well as, inter alia, several of the American states, including Montana and Illinois. Though it is seldom noticed, dignity is a prime constitutional value in France as well, enshrined in the preamble to the 1946 constitution, and therefore part of the *bloc de constitutionnalité*.[57] Perhaps the most powerful example is that the beginning of a written constitution in Israel is often dated to the passing, in 1992, of the Basic Law: Human Dignity and Liberty.[58] As the chapters on Canada and South Africa show, a primary role for dignity is in the constitutional analysis of discrimination. In both countries there have been judicial attempts to regard unequal treatment as unacceptable where it might be seen to lower someone's human dignity. The equality these judges seek to protect is essentially equality of esteem. This has often been criticized by those who would prefer a more direct concentration on inequality

[56] *M v Home Office*, 39.

[57] See the Conseil's own semiofficial statement in Conseil constitutionnel, "Human Rights and Public Order," 2003 *Eighth Seminar of Constitutional Courts, Erevan, 2 to 5 October 2003*, www.conseil-constitutionnel.fr.

[58] A Barak, "Human Rights in Israel," 2006 39 *Israel Law Review* 12, 39–62.

itself, but the idea that dignity is a core value is less often opposed.[59] Sometimes, of course, dignity is very clearly specified in the constitutional text as a value to be upheld above all—we have seen the vital role it plays in Germany. If dignity is named in the core text, judicial work is certainly easier, though Canada is developing a powerful dignity-based theory of rights without this.[60]

Dignity is relatively seldom used as a freestanding value in the sense that one could go to a court and object to a piece of legislation on the grounds, simply, that it offended against human dignity, though it can be done, as in the Hungarian approach to the death penalty. As I demonstrated when discussing Hungarian constitutional argument, dignity standing alone can even clash with other prime values like the right to life, as it did in the case involving the putative right to assisted euthanasia. More often, though, dignity is used as a way of working out whether some other right has been breached sufficiently, or in such a specific way, as to involve an affront to dignity. It can thus be used not only in discrimination, but, for example, in free speech cases.[61] In practise dignity is usually combined with some other constitutional principle both to stress how serious the rights violation is, and to clarify why the legislation or government action counts as a breach of some right or other. It should not be ignored, though, that very frequently in human rights discourse "dignity" is just a label to characterise an otherwise perfectly workable issue. As I write, it is national "Stop Bullying At Work" day in the United Kingdom. One of the aims of the movement is to introduce legislation to control such behaviour, under the title of the Dignity in the Workplace Act. Bullying is bad, and should be illegal, but to characterise it as about dignity adds little to that bald statement.

Nonetheless dignity, or some similar intellectual workhorse, may well be essential to the development of the fully fledged sense of a constitution as a moral order, and a result of political theorizing. This is because questions of the meaning of a right, in any specific context, need to be answered in terms of a more overarching value. For example, why is freedom of speech valuable? The overarching value may be a system value in this instance, as with the Australian example earlier. But such a referent will not always work, as with the German case against Benetton's adverts, or indeed any "content based" speech restriction, to use the American term. Consider the following case that ended up in the European Court of Human Rights.[62] *Paris-Match* had published a photograph of the dead body of the prefect

[59] A recent article that surveys criticism of dignity within equality jurisprudence is E Grant, "Dignity and Equality," 2007 7 *Human Rights Law Review* 2, 299–329.

[60] For an argument, by a judge, about the problems of using dignity absent a main textual reference, see D Ullrich, "Concurring Visions: Human Dignity in the Canadian Charter of Rights and Freedoms and the Basic Law of the Federal Republic of Germany," 2003 3 *Global Jurist Frontiers* 1, http://www.bepress.com/gj/frontiers/vol3/iss1/art1.

[61] GE Carmi, "Dignity—the Enemy from Within: A Theoretical and Comparative Analysis of Human Dignity as a Free Speech Justification," 2007 9 *Journal of Constitutional Law* 4, 957–1001. Rather like the attacks on dignity as a basis in discrimination cases, the author here regards dignity as possibly restricting freedom of speech.

[62] *Hachette Filipacchi Associes v France*, Chamber Judgment (71111/01). (European Court of Human Rights). This was not a constitutional law case because the French constitution only allows abstract and prior constitutional testing. Anywhere else it would have been one.

of Corsica lying in the street where he had been assassinated, with the comment, "Sur ce trottoir d'Ajaccio, vendredi 6 février à 21 h 15, Claude Erignac, préfet de Corse, a écrit de son sang une page tragique de notre histoire." His family asked the French courts to force *Paris-Match* to publish a statement expressing their horror at the photograph's publication. The Paris Court of Appeal upheld the injunction the family had gained, in large part because the court believed the publication of the photograph had infringed human dignity. The ECHR held that the French law was perfectly in keeping with the European Convention on Human Rights, which states that freedom of the press can only be acceptable when it is "prescribed by law" within the meaning of Article 10(2) of the Convention. It also, of course, had to be proportionate and pass a host of other tests. The dignity test may not have been the only way of dealing with it, but some high-order value had to be brought in to decide whether the precious value of press freedom could be trumped in this case.

One problem with dignity as a prime value used to flesh out other rights is that it is so expansive a concept. Some examples go to an undeniable core intuitively obvious to almost anyone. Thus the German decision that a full life sentence with no hope of parole offended the protection of dignity works because anyone can grasp that reducing a prisoner to a vegetable state is to make him less than human, a paradigmatic sense of deprivation of human dignity. Anything that turns a person, even a dead person, into an object for use offends our instinct about dignity, which is why the French case works. But does dignity really help when the question is whether a state can pay one category of welfare claimants but not another, as in some of the Canadian cases? Unless dignity is given a very broad definition, it can do relatively little work for a court, but the more that is claimed to follow from a basic acceptance of dignity, the more it seems just to sum up a set of freestanding rights that are capable of independent justification. One can agree with Barak, for example, that

> Most central of all human rights is the right to dignity. It is the source from which all other human rights are derived. Dignity unites the other human rights into a whole.[63]

Yet this is sometimes no more than accepting that humans have, or strive to have, integrated moral codes. In the end an appeal to dignity is what positivist philosophers like T. D. Weldon used to call a "logical full stop"—it simply stops further argument.[64] This is perhaps apparent to Barak himself when he tells us, at the end of the relevant section of his discussion, how to derive a right to dignity in a constitution that does not mention it. One can derive a dignity right "through interpretation of the whole bill of rights, whereby human dignity either is implied by the overall structure of the rights or is developed from their 'penumbras.'"[65] The use of "penumbras" is of course a reference to the famous US case where the

[63] Barak, *Judge in a Democracy*, 85.

[64] TD Weldon, *Vocabulary of Politics* (London: Penguin, 1953).

[65] Barak, *Judge in a Democracy*, 88.

Supreme Court derived the otherwise invisible constitutional right to privacy. But *Griswold v Connecticut* is not necessarily amongst the most admired examples of American judicial craftsmanship.[66]

What the use of dignity may often really do is to provide a secular and non-ideological replacement for previous overarching values stemming from religion, partisan ideology, class interest or patriotism, for a world where, as I have argued throughout this book, only constitutionalism remains as a nondivisive appeal to back fundamental value choices. It is none the worse for that. All systems seem to need such an appeal, some concept into which can be packed, and from which can be derived, the rights needed for a society at a particular moment in time.

I have tried to show, for example, how the very idea of a "rule of law" functions in much the same way, though inevitably with a more legal cast to it. As used particularly in Eastern Europe the apparently procedural idea of the rule of law becomes highly substantive. Certain things just cannot be done within the coverage of the rule of law, and to do them at all is to act lawlessly. For socio-historical reasons that particular appeal works better in some societies than the appeal to dignity (though it should be noted that in Hungary, at least, both concepts are used to achieve much the same purposes). With both concepts the jurisprudential power comes largely from the horror of the past. Dignity gets its leverage from the shock of genocide and racism; the rule of law draws on the fear of arbitrary state power, especially under Soviet rule in the old Eastern Europe. I do not mean to suggest that safe Western liberal democracies have no such conceptual needs because their recent history has been less awful—but as yet the idea of a constitution as an encapsulation of a country's moral choices is less keen in such countries. Yet even in the United Kingdom one finds government departments praising the Human Rights Act for protecting human dignity. For example, the Department of Health website states,

> The Act modernises relationships between people, and between people and the State and embeds in a new way, values of fairness, respect for human dignity and inclusiveness in the heart of public services.[67]

Legal Culture

Legal culture as a theme is only lightly and occasionally touched on in this book. This is not because it is unimportant, but rather that it is so huge a topic that no proper treatment can be given. Yet in one sense the whole book is an exercise in the analysis of legal cultures. Each of the chapters on particular jurisdictions is an attempt to sketch the salient features of judicial argument, goals, and assumptions in those territories—and such things are core elements in legal culture. For example, the account of the Canadian experience is specifically a discussion of the welding

[66] *Griswold v Connecticut*, 381 US 479 (1965) (US Supreme Court).

[67] http://www.dh.gov.uk/en/Policyandguidance/Equalityandhumanrights/Humanrights/DH_4136018.

of a rights-based culture onto a common-law, parliamentary supremacy culture. One leading British human rights lawyer has singled this out as a potential problem in the United Kingdom's development of effective human rights protection. Murray Hunt is, inter alia, legal adviser to the Joint Parliamentary Committee on Human Rights. He points to several assumptions held by English judges and practitioners likely to reduce the impact of the 1998 Human Rights Act, amongst which are the dominance of private law modes of thought, the narrowness of English rules of interpretation, and a general executive mindedness amongst the judiciary and the continued "Diceyan" belief in the rightful supremacy of Parliament.[68]

As an example of a decision that shows where such attitudes can lead to a restriction on human rights expansion, one might consider the recent case of *YL v Birmingham City Council*.[69] YL is an old woman who has been placed in a residential care home, managed as a private sector business, put there by the Birmingham City Council. Her attempt to have the Human Rights Act applied to the home failed because the act was held not to apply to the private sector, even though in this case it would have applied had the city council itself owned and managed the home. The majority of the Law Lords refused to interpret the part of the act that refers to public authorities to include private establishments carrying out public authority functions, despite the clear intention of the government at the time the act was passed precisely to allow the courts to work out the details of that concept. All the courts below the Lords, and two of the five Law Lords who heard the appeal, were clear that the act should apply in such circumstances. The result was described by the chairman of the Disability Rights Commission as untenable:

> Many local authorities rely on care placements in the private sector. This ruling will cement a fundamental inequality in disabled and older people's rights—those in care homes run by local councils have legal rights to human dignity, those "contracted out" will not.[70]

It is very hard not to see the result as emanating from the concatenation of assumptions Hunt sees as part of English legal culture. I choose the case because the public opposition to the result included a statement by the chairman of Murray Hunt's committee, Andrew Dismore, MP, that "the decision was contrary to what parliament intended when the Human Rights Act was passed." He called on the government to back his private members' bill, "The Human Rights (meaning of public authority) bill." It is important to see that what is going on here is not just a matter of judges voting from their own ideological heart, but judges acting through a perception, as political science puts it, of "the logic of appropriateness." Their role conception as English lawyers tells them it is inappropriate to broaden the overage of the act to include areas of private law.[71] The case is closely analogous

[68] M Hunt, "The Human Rights Act and Legal Culture: The Judiciary and the Legal Profession," 1999 26 *Journal of Law and Society* 86–105.

[69] *YL (Appellant) v Birmingham City Council and Others (Respondents)*, UKHL 27 [2007] (House of Lords).

[70] *Guardian*, June 20, 2007.

[71] March and Olsen, "The Logic of Appropriateness."

to *Dolphin Deliveries*, the Canadian case discussed earlier where an attachment to traditional common-law methods of dispute resolution led the Canadian Supreme Court to close down the hope of "horizontal effect" for the Charter.[72] Role perceptions are very much part of a society's political, in this case legal, culture. Where one finds parliamentary opposition to a court *not* expanding its own authority and reach, there seems *prima facie* evidence of a very broadly powerful restraint on legal activity.

Exactly what legal culture is remains too widely disputed to allow of treatment here. One major article lists at least six components, each of them broad, ranging from the very basic (what is law and how does it relate to other socials norms), via the rather technical ("a theory of valid legal sources" and "a theory of argumentation"), to "a theory of legitimation of law" and "a common basic ideology."[73] Hunt relies on a definition given by Klare, whose comments on South African legal culture have been discussed earlier. Klare defines legal culture thus:

> I mean professional sensibilities, habits of mind, and intellectual reflexes: What are the characteristic rhetorical strategies deployed by participants in a given legal setting? What is their repertoire of recurring argumentative moves? What counts as a persuasive legal argument? What types of arguments, possibly valid in other types of discourse . . . are deemed outside the professional discourse of lawyers?[74]

This seems entirely adequate to catch the essence of legal culture seen from a largely sociological perspective. It is difficult to know whether it should be broadened to include matters of doctrine on the one hand, and perhaps structural aspects on the other. The rules or doctrine that a system has on matters like standing (who can bring a case) are not perhaps "cultural"; in the same way that ideas about "rhetorical strategy" are. However, it is clear that legal culture does not only inhabit the minds of lawyers. A system with easy access to courts via generous "standing" rules is one where the nonlawyer actors are likely to develop a greater interest in going to court because of wider experience. After all, the layman's conception of differences in what they might not realize are matters of legal culture would centre on questions like why Americans are so much more litigious than the Japanese, which in part is a matter of the ease of standing. Because there was a widespread fear that no one would take cases to constitutional courts in the new East European democracies, courts being so distrusted in the past, these countries tried to make access as open as possible. Attitudes to standing are a good way of summarising quickly a judge's overall attitude to constitutional review. As Barak says:

[72] *Retail, Wholesale and Department Store Union v Dolphin Delivery Ltd*, 2 SCR 573 (1986) (Canadian Supreme Court).

[73] M Van Hoecke and M Warrington, "Legal Cultures, Legal Paradigms and Legal Doctrine: Towards a New Model for Comparative Law," 1998 47 *International and Comparative Law Quarterly* 495–537.

[74] Klare, "Legal Culture," 146–88.

> How a judge applies the rules of standing is a litmus test for determining his approach to his judicial role . . . a judge who regards his judicial role as bridging the gap between law and society and protecting . . . democracy will tend to expand the rules of standing.[75]

If this is true of a single judge, how much more important must the rules on standing be for the overall legal culture?

At the other end of this spectrum are clearly structural matters that are nonetheless emanations of historical experience and expectations and have no necessity about them. The public law / private law distinction in most Western countries is a structural matter, reflected in professional training and career patterns, a matter of doctrine, and a characteristic of legal minds. Thus, while Germany does not have the common-law versus constitutional-law dichotomy, many of the more important German constitutional-law developments have been hotly opposed by private-law critics for trespassing. Were the members of the constitutional court part of a career hierarchy that overrepresented such lawyers, the constitutional jurisprudence of Germany might look very much less adventurous than it does. But this is precisely why Kelsen courts have always limited the number of ordinary court judges on the constitutional benches. It may be accident, but the three-person majority against extending the reach of the Human Rights Act were judges drawn from the Chancery and Commercial bars, while Lord Bingham, who opposed them, had been Master of the Roles with enormous public law experience. He was supported by Lady Hale, the first ever female Law Lord, a family and social welfare lawyer noted for her egalitarian views. Accident or not, judges cannot be expected to embrace legal ideas widely at variance with their whole professional formation. Nor can advocates be expected to transform their expectations of their roles, or of what counts as a good argument. As long as neither the judges nor the advocates in general welcome the development of constitutional rights protection, they will not build a client base that itself has any high hopes of legal protection for human rights.

For these reasons cultural explanations of constitutional reach and efficacy cannot stand alone, but require the intermix of both structural and doctrinal factors. And all of these factors can only have their effect through the much broader question of whether or not the underlying political values of the population, or its elites, believe both in the importance of rights, and the appropriateness of the court system to deliver them. It is often commented on that the home secretary who piloted the English Human Rights Act through Parliament, Jack Straw, heralded it as "a major step-change in the creation of a culture of rights and responsibilities in our society."[76] He has now become the lord chancellor and a member of a government that has been at loggerheads with the Law Lords many times in the last few years. That government is now suggesting a new bill that will stress the need for rights to be balanced against the government's needs, and is to point out that rights must be balanced by "duties."

[75] Barak, *Judge in a Democracy*, 192.

[76] Home Office News Release 153/99, May 18, 1999.

The Internationalisation of Constitutional Law

A note needs to be added to this brief discussion of legal culture, because variance in legal culture is often held to be relevant to the extent that courts in one country can use the law of another. I have shown that the courts of Canada and South Africa very frequently cite opinions by judges in other jurisdictions. Indeed, the extent of Canadian usage of foreign judgements might seem staggering. One study claims that between 1984 and 1994, 23 percent of all cases cited in the Canadian Supreme Court were from foreign jurisdictions—and not particularly from America, whose cases account for only 7 percent of all citations.[77] So too do the Eastern European courts cite foreign jurisprudence, particularly amongst themselves. There is a widespread belief indeed in something often called the "globalization" of constitutional law, or just of law in general.[78] This field of comparative law studies is wide and cannot even be summarised here. One common theme is noteworthy, though. This a serious doubt that "constitutional borrowings" can easily work because of the differences between national legal cultures. Good examples are Rosenkrantz's concern about Argentinean "borrowing" from the United States, and Osiatynsk's concern about culture-related "paradoxes."[79] The truth is that while an interesting argument can be made that such borrowings of ideas from abroad are theoretically problematic, judges just go on and do it. Theorists have tried to catalogue the different ways in which foreign legal material is used, in part to try to find justifications for this practise. It may be the American domination of the field that has led to this thrust to justify. Outside of America the judges themselves do not usually seem to think their practice requires justification, but the strong US distaste for referring to foreign law may lead academic critics to this search for justification. The main reason that use of foreign imports can be thought of as requiring a defence is that legal systems are seen as precisely that, "systems," in which all parts are interrelated. Thus incorporating an external element may mean it fails to blend or wed properly with the other elements. Thus Tushnet takes special effort to justify some borrowings against one understanding of the nature of a constitution, that it is "expressive," that a constitution is part of a nation's self-conscious identity. He attributes many of these ideas to Mary Ann Glendon, whom he quotes as saying that law "tells stories about the culture that helped to shape it and which it in turn helps to shape."[80] Clearly there

[77] Figures taken from SK Harding, "Comparative Reasoning and Judicial Review," 2003 28 *Yale Journal of International Law* 409–65.

[78] See for example: S Choudhry, *The Migration of Constitutional Ideas* (Cambridge: Cambridge University Press, 2006); M Tushnet, "The Possibilities of Comparative Constitutional Law," 1999 108 *Yale Law Journal* 6, 1225–1309; T Allen and B Anderson, "The Use of Comparative Law by Common Law Judges," 1994 23 *Anglo-American Law Review* 435–60; A-M Slaughter, "A Typology of Transjudicial Communication," 1994 99 *University of Richmond Law Review* 29–69; and A-M Slaughter, "Judicial Globalization," 2000 40 *Virginia Journal of International Law* 1103–25.

[79] Rosenkrantz, "Against Borrowings"; W Osiatynski, "Paradoxes of Constitutional Borrowing," 2003 1 *International Journal of Constitutional Law* 2, 244–68. The whole issue of the journal is dedicated to the use of foreign material in courts.

[80] The quote is taken from Tushnet, "Comparative Constitutional Law," referring to MA Glendon, "Rights in Twentieth Century Constitutions," 1992 59 *University of Chicago Law Review* 519–38.

may be problems incorporating parts of one country's private story into another one, but this is by no means an obvious way of characterising a constitution—as indeed Tushnet himself clearly thinks. If one sees a constitution, as I have argued, as a moral choice made by a society, rather than as a historical tradition of self-understanding, the problem is somewhat less.

In fact, judges are probably nearer to two of Tushnet's characterisations, overtly "functionalist" or exercising "bricolage." A functionalist approach says that all societies face some problems in common, and a court may well look to see how other jurisdictions have dealt with a problem new to the society they work in and, if suitable, use it to develop their own technique. A stronger version of functionalism is what Choudhry calls a "universalist" position. With universalism the claim is not just that such and such a technique works somewhere else so it may as well be used, but that the presence of a legal mechanism in several or all jurisdictions means it represents some transcendent legal or constitutional truth—the mechanism to be borrowed is not only useful, it is "right." There are perhaps hints of this in the way the South African Constitutional Court went about testing the validity of the interim constitution. Shorn of the moral aspect, it seems quite probable that judges do think in roughly functionalist ways, especially with the new and transformative constitutions where similarity of problems is probably more important by a long way than any sense of expressing a national legal culture. After all, if a court sees itself as in the business of change, this would be a more plausible way of looking at things.

Tushnet's third form of judicial borrowing, however, appeals as the most plausible way of characterising what we have seen in this book. Bricolage is a term he borrows from social anthropology, where it describes a culture made up of more or less intentional but quite unprincipled borrowing of bits and pieces from any other cultures the people are familiar with. Reading opinions where foreign judgements are referred to fits this image very well. A trawl is made through available legal resources to find examples of similar cases, and the ones that appeal are used to develop one's own approach. In part this is an attractive characterisation because one feature that is quite notable is that a court will often base its opinion in part on minority opinions in foreign courts. It is the legal idea, rather than the legal authority, that is being borrowed. Indeed it is appropriate to note, in common with Choudhry and Allen, that judges seldom actually take the result of a case and use it semi-authoritatively. Rather they muse on parts of opinions to strengthen their arguments and make sharper their perceptions of their own legal system and their own problems.[81]

Is bricolage or even functionalism compatible with the idea that legal cultures differ and are important constraints on court behaviour? From my point of view it hardly seems to be a problem, for one very obvious reason. A judicial ideology that frowns on the use of comparative law is likely to reflect a legal culture that is highly

[81] Choudhry, *Migration of Constitutional Ideas*; T Allen and B Anderson, "The Use of Comparative Law by Common Law Judges," 1994 23 *Anglo-American Law Review* 435–60, who follow him on the point, call this a "dialogic" use.

restrictive of the sort of constitutional jurisprudence I have described in this book. By the very nature of being interested in developing the role, power, and reach of constitutional review, a legal culture makes itself more likely to reach widely for legal ideas. Without wishing to make it definitional, I would tend to expect scepticism about the utility or legitimacy of looking at foreign law to mark a legal culture opposed to human rights development by courts. Certainly a judiciary leaning towards expressivism is likely to prefer slow incremental change from a historical set of precedents, while transforming courts are both in a hurry and minded to break with the past.

Final Note

Whatever legal theorists may argue, constitutional review by courts, or court-like bodies, is a major part of modern democracy, and probably an inescapable institution under any newly created or seriously modernized constitution. As is true throughout jurisprudence, there may be gaps between legal philosophy and what courts do. But this has never much affected judges. Much of the more interesting modern democratic theory stresses the deliberative aspect, values the idea of politics as discussion and debate. There is an old saw to the effect that "Politicians bargain, judges argue." Unless legislative politics changes enormously in liberal democracy, the institution most capable of carrying on an argument about constitutional values is the constitutional court.

CASES CITED

A and Others v Secretary of State for the Home Department; X and Another v Secretary of State for the Home Department. 3 All ER 169 [2005] (House of Lords).

Abortion Case No 1. 39 BVerfGE 1 (1975) (German Federal Constitutional Court).

Abortion Decision. 74-54 DC (Conseil constitutionnel).

Adarand Constructors, Inc. v Pena. 513 US 1108 (1995) (US Supreme Court).

Amax Potash Ltd. v Government of Saskatchewan. 2 SCR 576 (1977) (Canadian Supreme Court).

Amendment to the Definition of "Co-operation" within the Lustration Act. K44/02 (2003) (Polish Constitutional Tribunal).

Andrews v Law Society of British Columbia. 1 SCR 143 (Canadian Supreme Court).

Application of the European Arrest Warrant to Polish Citizens. P105 (2005) (Polish Constitutional Tribunal).

Asylum Rights Decision. 93-325 DC (Conseil constitutionnel).

Audio-Visual Communications. 82-141 (Conseil constitutionnel).

Australian Capital Television Pty Ltd v Commonwealth. 177 CLR 106 (1992) (Australian High Court).

Bank Guarantee Case. 89 BVerfGE 214 (1993) (German Federal Constitutional Court).

Bank of New South Wales v Commonwealth. 76 CLR 1 (1948) (Australian High Court).

Benes Decree. Pl. US 14/94 (Czech Republic Constitutional Court).

Benetton II. 1 BvR 426 (2003) (German Federal Constitutional Court).

Bio-Components in Gasoline and Diesel. K33/03 (2004) (Polish Constitutional Tribunal).

Bowers v Hardwick. 478 US 186 (1986) (US Supreme Court).

Brandenburg v Ohio. 395 US 444 (1969) (US Supreme Court).

Braunfeld v Brown. 366 US 599 (1961) (US Supreme Court).

Brief Vacatio Legis in Introducing the Requirement to Obtain a License for Cable Network Retransmission. K55/02 (Polish Constitutional Tribunal).

Bush v Gore. 531 US 98 (2000) (US Supreme Court).
Canada (A.G.) v City of Montreal. 2 SCR 770 (1978) (Canadian Supreme Court).
Carmichele v The Minister of Safety and Security. CCT 48/00 (South African Constitutional Court).
Carolene Products v United States. 304 US 144 (1938) (US Supreme Court).
Case and Another v Minister of Safety and Security and Others; Curtis v Minister of Safety and Security and Others. CCT 20/95 (South African Constitutional Court).
Certification of the Amended Text of the Constitution of the Republic of South Africa. CCT 37/96 (South African Constitutional Court).
Certification of the Constitution of the Republic of South Africa. CCT 23/96 (South African Constitutional Court).
Chamberlain v Surrey School District No. 36. 4 SCR 710 (2002) (Canadian Supreme Court).
Chaoulli v Quebec (Attorney General). 2005 SCR 35 (Canadian Supreme Court).
Chocolate Candy Case. 53 BVerfGE 135 (1980) (German Federal Constitutional Court).
City of Cleburne, Texas v Cleburne Living Center Inc. 473 US 432 (US Supreme Court).
City of Pretoria v Walker. CCT 8/97 (South African Constitutional Court).
Co-Determination Case. 50 BVerfGE 290 (1979) (German Federal Constitutional Court).
Cole v Whitefield. 165 CLR 360 (1988) (Australian High Court).
Coleman v Power. 220 CLR 1 (2004) (Australian High Court).
Commercial Agent Case. 81 BVerfGE 242 (1990) (German Federal Constitutional Court).
Committal Case. 22 BVerfGE 180 (German Federal Constitutional Court).
Communist Party Case. 5 BVerfGE 85 (1956) (German Federal Constitutional Court).
Compulsory Purchase of Shares Held by Minority Shareholders (Squeeze-Out). P25/02 (2005) (Polish Constitutional Tribunal).
Constitutional Complaint and the Principle of Equality. SK 10/01 (2001) (Polish Constitutional Tribunal).
Cooper v Aaron. 358 US 1 (1958) (US Supreme Court).
Dawood and Another v Minister of Home Affairs and Others. CCT 35/99 (South African Constitutional Court).
Decision of 4th December 2001 on Right of Reply. 57/2001 (XII.5) AB (Hungarian Constitutional Court).
Decision 23/1990 on Capital Punishment. (Hungarian Constitutional Court).
Decision Dated 30th January 1991 on Religious Instruction (K11/90). In Oniszczuk, *A Selection of the Polish Constitutional Tribunal's Jurisprudence from 1986 to 1999*.
Decision of 10th June 1992 on the Media. 37/1992 (VI.10) AB (Hungarian Constitutional Court).
Decision of 11th February 1992 (K. 14/91)—Pensions Laws. In Oniszczuk, *A Selection of the Polish Constitutional Tribunal's Jurisprudence from 1986 to 1999*.
Decision of 13th April 1991 on Use of Personal Data. Decision 15/1991 (Hungarian Constitutional Court).
Decision of 13th July 1993—Unemployment Benefits. In Oniszczuk, *A Selection of the Polish Constitutional Tribunal's Jurisprudence from 1986 to 1999*.
Decision of 13th October 1993 on War Crimes and on Crimes against Humanity. Decision 53/1993.
Decision of 17th December 1991 on the Regulation of Abortion. 64/1991 (Hungarian Constitutional Court).
Decision of 18th October 1995 on Financing of Political Parties and Inspection of Their Management. Pl. US 26/94 (Czech Republic Constitutional Court).

Decision of 19th January 2005—On Election Contribution. Pl. US 10/03 (Czech Republic Constitutional Court).
Decision of 19th June 1992 on Lustration. U/92 (Polish Constitutional Tribunal).
Decision of 2003 on Procedure of Parliamentary Investigative Committees. 50/2003 (XI.5) AB (Hungarian Constitutional Court).
Decision of 20th April 1991 Compensation Case II. 16/1991 (Hungarian Constitutional Court).
Decision of 21st December Regarding the Lawlessness of the Communist Regime. Pl. US 19/93 (Czech Republic Constitutional Court).
Decision of 22 June 1998 on Unemployment Assistance. 32/1998 (VI.25) AB (Hungarian Constitutional Court).
Decision of 22 June 2005—Role of Senate in Election Law. Pl. US 13/05 (Czech Republic Constitutional Court).
Decision of 25th February 1992 on Powers Ex Nunc. Decision 10/1992 (Hungarian Constitutional Court).
Decision of 25th January 2005 on Constitutionally Conforming Interpretation. III. US. 252/04 (Czech Republic Constitutional Court).
Decision of 26 November 1992 on Lustration. Pl. US 1/92 (Constitutional Court of the Czech and Slovak Federal Republic).
Decision of 26th June 2001 Czech National Bank. Pl. US 14/01 (Czech Republic Constitutional Court).
Decision of 26th March 2003 on Freedom of Conscience. Pl. US 42/02 (Czech Republic Constitutional Court).
Decision of 27 April 1996 on Election Coalitions. US 127/96 (Czech Republic Constitutional Court).
Decision of 28th April 2003 on Physician Aided Termination of Life. 22/2003 (IV.28) AB
Decision of 2nd April 1997 on the Principles of the Electoral System of the Czech Republic. Pl. US 25/96 (Czech Republic Constitutional Court).
Decision of 2nd April 1998 Binding Force of Constitutional Court Decisions. III. US 425/97 (Czech Republic Constitutional Court).
Decision of 30th June 1995 on Social Security Benefits. 43/1995 (Hungarian Constitutional Court).
Decision of 31st October 1990 on Capital Punishment. 23/1990 AB (Hungarian Constitutional Court).
Decision of 3d May 2006 European Arrest Warrant. Pl. US 66/04 (Czech Republic Constitutional Court).
Decision of 4th October 1990 Compensation Case I. 21/1990 (Hungarian Constitutional Court).
Decision of 5th March 1992 on Retroactive Criminal Legislation. 11/92 (Hungarian Constitutional Court).
Decision of 8th November 1991 on Legal Guardians and on the Family Act. Decision 57/1991 (Hungarian Constitutional Court).
Decision of 9 July 2003 on Territorial Self Government. Pl. US 5/03 (Czech Republic Constitutional Court).
Decision of 11th June 2003 on Judges' Salaries. Pl. US 11/02 (Czech Republic Constitutional Court).
Derbyshire CC v Times Newspapers Ltd. 1 All ER 1011 [1993] (House of Lords).
Divorce Decision. 2001 Neue Juristiche Wochenschrift 957 (German Federal Constitutional Court).

Doctors for Life International v The Speaker of the National Assembly. CCT 12/05 (South African Constitutional Court).
Du Plessis and Others v De Klerk and Another. CCT 8/95 (South African Constitutional Court).
Dunmore v Ontario (Attorney General). 3 SCR 1016 (2001) (Canadian Supreme Court).
Egan v Canada. 2 SCR 513 (1995) (Canadian Supreme Court).
Eldred et al v Ashcroft, Attorney General. 123 S. Ct. 769 (2003) (US Supreme Court).
Employment Div., Dept. of Human Resources of Oregon v Smith. 494 US 872 (1990) (US Supreme Court).
EU Treaty Decision. 92-312 DC (Conseil constitutionnel).
Finance Law Decision. 81-133 DC (Conseil constitutionnel).
Finance Law for 1984. 83-164 DC (Conseil constitutionnel).
Financial Markets Law. 89-260 DC 1989 (Conseil constitutionnel).
Fose v Minister of Safety and Security. CCT 14/96 (South African Constitutional Court).
Fullilove v Klutznick. 448 US 503 (1980) (US Supreme Court).
Garreth Anver Prince v The President of the Law Society of the Cape of Good Hope. (2) SA 794 (2002) (CC).
Gideon v Wainwright. 372 US 335 (1963) (US Supreme Court).
Glasenapp v Germany. 4/1984 (1986) (European Court of Human Rights).
Glycol Case. 1 BvR 558, 1428/91 (2002) (German Federal Constitutional Court).
Good News Club v Milford Central School. 533 US 98 (2001) (US Supreme Court).
Green Party Exclusion Case. 70 BVerfGE 324 (1986) (German Federal Constitutional Court).
Griswold v Connecticut. 381 US 479 (1965) (US Supreme Court).
Grootboom and Others v Government of the Republic of South Africa and Others. CCT 11/00 (South African Constitutional Court).
Groundwater Case. 58 BVerfGE 300 (1981) (German Federal Constitutional Court).
Grutter v Bollinger. 123 S. Ct. 2325 (2003) (US Supreme Court).
Hachette Filipacchi Associes v France. Chamber Judgment (71111/01) (European Court of Human Rights).
Halpern v Canada (Attorney General). 65 O.R. (3d) 161 (2003) (Ontario Court of Appeal).
Harksen v Lane NO. CCT 9/97 (South African Constitutional Court).
Heinrich Case. 11 BVerfGE 234 (German Federal Constitutional Court).
Hesse Election Result. 2 BvF 1/00 (2001) (German Federal Constitutional Court).
High Council of the Judiciary. 2001-455 DC (Conseil constitutionnel).
Hill et al. v Colorado. 530 US 703 (2000) (US Supreme Court).
Hunter v Southam Inc. 2 SCR 145 (1984) (Canadian Supreme Court).
Identity Control Law. 93-323 DC (1993) (Conseil constitutionnel).
Immigration Issues. 97-389 DC (1997) (Conseil constitutionnel).
Immigration Law Decision. 2 BvF 1/02 (2002) (German Federal Constitutional Court).
In Re M. 1 AC 377 [1994] (House of Lords).
Inequality in Competences of Sejm and Senate Committees in Respect of EU Proposals. K24/04 (2005) (Polish Constitutional Tribunal).
Insufficient Vacatio Legis When Introducing Higher Rate of Personal Income Tax. K48/04 (2005) (Polish Constitutional Tribunal).
Investment Aid I. 4 BVerfGE 7 (1954) (German Federal Constitutional Court).
James v Eastleigh Borough Council. 2 AC 751 [1990] (House of Lords).
Jordan v The State. CCT 31/01 (South African Constitutional Court).

Khosa and Others v Minister of Social Development and Others. CCT 12/03 (South African Constitutional Court).
Kindler v Canada (Minister of Justice). 2 SCR 779 (1991) (Canadian Supreme Court).
Korematsu v United States. 323 US 214 (1944) (US Supreme Court).
Lange v Australian Broadcasting Corporation. 189 CLR 520 (1997) (Australian High Court).
Law on New Caledonia. 85-197 DC 1985 (Conseil constitutionnel).
Lawlessness. Pl. US. 19/93 (Czech Republic Constitutional Court).
Lawrence v Texas. 539 US 558 (2003) (US Supreme Court).
Lebach Case. 35 BVerfGE 202 (1973) (German Federal Constitutional Court).
Life Imprisonment. 45 BVerfGE 187 (1977) (German Federal Constitutional Court).
Little Sisters Book and Art Emporium v Canada (Minister of Justice). 2 SCR 1120 (2000) (Canadian Supreme Court).
Lochner v New York. 198 US 45 (1905) (US Supreme Court).
Loi de finances rectificative pour 2000. 2000-441 DC (Conseil constitutionnel).
Loi de modernisation sociale. 2001-455 DC (2002) (Conseil constitutionnel).
Lüth. 7 BVerfGE 198 (1958).
M v Home Office. QB 270 [1992] (Court of Appeal).
Maastricht Case. 89 BVerfGE 155 (German Federal Constitutional Court).
Madsen v Women's Health Center, Inc. 114 S. Ct. 2516 (1994) (US Supreme Court).
Marbury v Madison. US 137 (1803) (US Supreme Court).
Matatiele Municipality v President of the Republic of South Africa. CCT 73/05 (South African Constitutional Court).
McKinney v University of Guelph. 3 SCR 229 (1990) (Canadian Supreme Court).
Minister of Health and Others v Treatment Action Campaign and Others. CCT 8/02 (South African Constitutional Court).
Minister of Home Affairs v Fisher. AC 319 [1980] (Privy Council).
Ministry of Home Affairs v Fourie. CCT 60/04 (South African Constitutional Court).
Miranda v Arizona. 384 US 436 (1966) (US Supreme Court).
Miron v Trudel. 2 SCR 418 (1995) (Canadian Supreme Court).
Modifications to the Composition and Functioning of the National Broadcasting Council. K4/06 (2006) (Polish Constitutional Tribunal).
N K v Minister of Safety and Security. CCT 52/04 (South African Constitutional Court).
National Coalition for Gay and Lesbian Equality v Minister of Justice. CCT 11/98 (South African Constitutional Court).
National Director of Public Prosecutions v Mohamed NO and Others. CCT 44/02 (South African Constitutional Court).
National Socialist Party v Village of Skokie. 432 US 43 (1977) (US Supreme Court).
National Unity Election Case. 82 BverfGE 322 (1990) (German Federal Constitutional Court).
Nationality Reform Law. 93-321 DC (1993) (Conseil constitutionnel).
Nationalizations. 81-132 DC (1982) (Conseil constitutionnel).
Nevada Department of Human Resources v Hibbs. 123 S. Ct. 1972 (2003) (US Supreme Court).
New York Times Co. v Sullivan. 376 US 254 (1964) (US Supreme Court).
Night Work Decision. 85 BVerfGE 191 (1992) (German Federal Constitutional Court).
Nudist Magazine Case. 30 BVerfGE 336 (German Federal Constitutional Court).
Numerus Clausus I Case. 33 BVerfGE 303 (1972) (German Federal Constitutional Court).
Osman v UK. 5 BHRC 293 (1998) (European Court of Human Rights).

Pacte Civil de Solidarité. 99-419 DC (1999) (Conseil constitutionnel).
Personal Contributions Case. 69 BVerfGE 272 (1985) (German Federal Constitutional Court).
Pharmaceutical Manufacturers of South Africa: In re Ex Parte President of the RSA. CCT 31/99 (South African Constitutional Court).
Pharmacy Case. 7 BVerfGE 377 (1958) (German Federal Constitutional Court).
PKK Case. 1 BvR 98/97 (2002) (German Federal Constitutional Court).
Plenum Party Case. 4 BVerfGE 27 (1954) (German Federal Constitutional Court).
Poland's Membership in the European Union (the Accession Treaty). K18/04 (2005) (Polish Constitutional Tribunal).
Premier of Kwazulu-Natal v President of the Republic of South Africa. CCT 36/95 (South African Constitutional Court).
President of the Republic of South Africa v Hugo. CCT 11/96 (South African Constitutional Court).
President of the Republic of South Africa v Modderklip Boerdery (PTY) Ltd. CCT 20/04 (South African Constitutional Court).
Press Case. 86-210 DC (1986) (Conseil constitutionnel).
Press Pluralism I. Decision 84-181 DC (1984) (Conseil constitutionnel).
Price and Salaries Freeze Decision. 82-143 DC (1982) (Conseil constitutionnel).
Prinsloo v Van Der Linde. CCT 4/96 (South African Constitutional Court).
Privatization Modification Law. 89-254 (1989) (Conseil constitutionnel).
Privatizations. 86-210 DC (Conseil constitutionnel).
Professional Education. 2004-494 DC (Conseil constitutionnel).
Public Prosecution of Offences Arising from Failure to Publish, Contrary to the Press Act, a Rectification or Response. K10/04 (2005) (Polish Constitutional Tribunal).
Quotas par sexe I. 82-146 DC (Conseil constitutionnel).
Quotas par sexe II. 98-407 DC (1999) (Conseil constitutionnel).
Quotas par Sexe III. 2000-429 DC (Conseil constitutionnel).
R v Big M Drug Mart Ltd. 1 SCR 295 (1985) (Canadian Supreme Court).
R v Butler. 1 SCR 452 (1992) (Canadian Supreme Court).
R v Oakes. 1 SCR 103 (1986) (Canadian Supreme Court).
R v Secretary of State for the Home Department, ex parte Daly. 2 AC 532 [2001] (House of Lords).
R v Secretary of State for the Home Department, ex parte Fire Brigades Union. 2 AC 513 [1995] (House of Lords).
R v Keegstra. 3 SCR 697 (1990) (Canadian Supreme Court).
R v Morgentaler. 1 SCR 30 (1988) (Canadian Supreme Court).
R v Pan. 2 SCR 344 (2001) (Canadian Supreme Court).
Radical Groups Case. 47 BVerfGE 198 (1978) (German Federal Constitutional Court).
Rail Commuters Action Group v Metrorail. CCT 56/03 (South African Constitutional Court).
RAV v City of St. Paul, Minnesota. 505 US 377 (1992) (US Supreme Court).
Re B.C. Motor Vehicle Act. 2 SCR 486 (1985) (Canadian Supreme Court).
"Recent Cases—Chaoulli v Quebec (Attorney General)" 2005 119 *Harvard Law Review* 2, 677–84.
Reference re Ng Extradition (Can.). 2 SCR 858 (1991) (Canadian Supreme Court).
Reference re Provincial Electoral Boundaries (Sask.). 2 SCR 158 (1991) (Canadian Supreme Court).

Reference re Remuneration of Judges of the Provincial Court of Prince Edward Island. 3 SCR 3 (1997) (Canadian Supreme Court).
Reference re Same-Sex Marriage. 3 SCR 698 (2004) (Canadian Supreme Court).
Reference re Secession of Quebec. 2 SCR 217 (1998) (Canadian Supreme Court).
Regina (Anderson) v Secretary of State for the Home Department. 1 AC 837 [2003] (House of Lords).
Religious Schools Funding Case. 75 BVerfGE 40 (German Federal Constitutional Court).
Relinquishing Ownership of Real Estate and Interests of Communes. K9/04 (2005) (Polish Constitutional Tribunal).
Retail, Wholesale and Department Store Union v Dolphin Delivery Ltd. 2 SCR 573 (1968) (Supreme Court of Canada).
Roe v Wade. 410 US 113 (1973) (US Supreme Court).
S v Baloyi (Minister of Justice and Another Intervening). CCT 29/99 (South African Constitutional Court).
S v Makwanyane and Another. CCT 3/94 (South African Constitutional Court).
S v Zuma. CCT 5/94 (South African Constitutional Court).
San Antonio School District v Rodriguez. 411 US 1 (1973) (US Supreme Court).
Sauvé v Canada (Attorney General). 2 SCR 438 (1993) (Canadian Supreme Court).
Sauvé v Canada (Chief Electoral Officer). 3 SCR 519 (2002) (Canadian Supreme Court).
Schachter v Canada 679. 2 SCR 679 (1992) (Canadian Supreme Court).
Schenck v United States. 249 US 47 (1919) (US Supreme Court).
Sécurité et Liberté. 81-127 DC (1981) (Conseil constitutionnel).
Shaik v Minister of Justice and Constitutional Development and Others. CCT 34/03 (South African Constitutional Court).
Shelley v Kraemer. 334 US 1 (1948) (US Supreme Court).
Slaughterhouse Case. 16 Wall (83 US) 36 (1873) (US Supreme Court).
Socialist Reich Party Case. 2 BVerfGE1 (1952) (German Federal Constitutional Court).
Soobramoney v Minister of Health (Kwazulu-Natal). CCT 32/97 (South African Constitutional Court).
South African National Defence Union v Minister of Defence. CCT 27/98 (South African Constitutional Court).
Statutory Prohibitions of Political Party Membership. K26/00 (Polish Constitutional Tribunal).
Tax Estimation Case. 73-51 DC (1973) (Conseil constitutionnel).
Thibaudeau v Canada. 2 SCR 627 (1995) (Canadian Supreme Court).
Thomas v Review Bd., Ind. Empl. Sec. Div. 450 US 707 (1981) (US Supreme Court).
United Democratic Movement v President (NO 2). 2003 (1) SA 495 (CC).
United Democratic Movement v The President of the Republic of South Africa. CCT 23/02 (South African Constitutional Court).
United States v Burns. 1 SCR 283 (2001) (Canadian Supreme Court).
University of Alabama v. Garrett. 531 US 356 (2001) (US Supreme Court).
US Department of Agriculture v Moreno. 413 US 528 (1973) (US Supreme Court).
US v Lee. 455 US 252 (1982) (US Supreme Court).
Vogt v Germany. 7/1994 (1994) (European Court of Human Rights).
Volks v Robinson. CCT 12/04 (South African Constitutional Court).
Woolwich Equitable Building Society v Inland Revenue Commissioners. AC 70 [1993] (House of Lords).
Wüppesahl Case. 80 BVerfGE 188 (1989) (German Federal Constitutional Court).

YL (Appellant) v Birmingham City Council and Others (Respondents). UKHL 27 [2007] (House of Lords).

Zondi v Member of the Executive Council for Traditional and Local Government Affairs. CCT 73/03 (South African Constitutional Court).

BIBLIOGRAPHY

HJ Abraham and BA Perry. *Freedom and the Court: Civil Rights and Liberties in the United States*. 8th ed. Lawrence: University of Kansas Press, 2003.

B Ackerman. "The Rise of World Constitutionalism." 1997 83 *Virginia Law Review* 4, 771–97.

———. *We the People*. Cambridge, Mass.: Belknap Press, 1991.

G Ajani. "By Chance and Prestige: Legal Transplants in Russia and Eastern Europe." 1995 43 *American Journal of Comparative Law* 1, 93–117.

M Albers. "Rethinking the Doctrinal System of Fundamental Rights: New Decisions of the Federal Constitutional Court." 2002 3 *German Law Journal* (e-journal) 11.

C Albertyn and B Goldblatt. "Development of an Indigenous Jurisprudence of Equality." 1998 14 *South African Journal on Human Rights* 248–76.

———. "Facing the Challenge of Transformation: Difficulties in the Development of an Indigenous Jurisprudence of Equality." 1998 14 *South African Journal on Human Rights* 248–76.

TA Aleinikoff. "Constitutional Law in the Age of Balancing." 1987 96 *Yale Law Review* 943.

GS Alexander. "Property as a Fundamental Constitutional Right? The German Example." 2003 88 *Cornell Law Review* 733.

R Alexy. *A Theory of Constitutional Rights*. Oxford: Oxford University Press, 2002.

T Allen and B Anderson. "The Use of Comparative Law by Common Law Judges." 1994 23 *Anglo-American Law Review* 435–60.

AR Amar. *The Bill of Rights*. New Haven: Yale University Press, 1998.

P Arenella. "Miranda Stories." 1996 20 *Harvard Journal of Law and Public Policy* 1996–97, 375–89.

N Arndt and R Nickel. "Federalism Revisited: Constitutional Court Strikes Down New Immigration Act for Formal Reasons." 2003 4 *German Law Journal* 2 (e-journal).

JM Atwood. "Constitutional Law—a New Level of Means-End Scrutiny Applied to Content-Neutral Injunctions That Limit Protected Speech." 1995 29 *Suffolk University Law Review* 6, 1189–98.

S Baer. "Equality: The Jurisprudence of the German Constitutional Court." 1999 5 *Columbia Journal of European Law* 249.

JM Balkin. "The Footnote." 1989 83 *Northwestern University Law Review* 1, 275–320.

———. "'Wrong the Day It Was Decided': Lochner and Constitutional Historicism." 2005 85 *Boston University Law Review* 677–726.

A Barak. "Human Rights in Israel." 2006 39 *Israel Law Review* 12, 39–62.

———. *The Judge in a Democracy*. Princeton: Princeton University Press, 2006.

———. "Response to *The Judge as Comparatist*: Comparison in Public Law." 2005 80 *Tulane Law Review* 195–202.

B Barreiro. "Judicial Review and Political Empowerment: Abortion in Spain." 1998 21 *West European Politics* 4, 147–62.

J Barrett. "Dignatio and the Human Body." 2005 21 *South African Journal on Human Rights* 4, 168–206.

B Barry. *Culture and Equality*. Cambridge: Polity, 2001.

M Battacharyya. "From Nondifferentiation to Factual Equality: Gender Equality Jurisprudence under the German Basic Law." 1996 21 *Brooklyn Journal of International Law* 915.

L Baum. "What Judges Want: Judge's Goals and Judicial Behaviour." 1994 47 *Political Research Quarterly* 3, 749–68.

CD Bavis. "*Vriend v. Alberta, Law v. Canada, Ontario v. M. and H.*: The Latest Steps on the Winding Path to Substantive Equality." 1999 37 *Alberta Law Review* 683.

D Beatty. "The Canadian Charter of Rights: Lessons and Laments." 1997 60 *Modern Law Review* 4, 481–98.

———. "A Conservative's Court: The Politicization of Law." 1991 41 *University of Toronto Law Journal* 147–67.

———. "The Forms and Limits of Constitutional Interpretation." 2001 49 *American Journal of Comparative Law* 79.

J Bell. *French Constitutional Law*. Oxford: Clarendon Press, 1992.

———. *French Legal Cultures*. London: Butterworths, 2001.

———. *Judiciaries within Europe*. Cambridge: Cambridge University Press, 2006.

———. *Policy Arguments in Judicial Decisions*. Oxford: Clarendon Press, 1983.

E Berger. "The Right to Education under the South African Constitution." 2003 103 *Columbia Law Review* 3, 614–61.

MN Berman. "Constitutional Decision Rules." 2004 90 *Virginia Law Review* 1–139.

DL Beschle. "Clearly Canadian? *Hill v. Colorado* and Free Speech Balancing in the United States and Canada." 2001 28 *Hastings Constitutional Law Quarterly* 187.

JM Bessette. *The Mild Voice of Reason: Deliberative Democracy and American National Government*. Chicago: University of Chicago Press, 1994.

P Beyer. "Constitutional Privilege and Constituting Pluralism: Religious Freedom in National, Global, and Legal Context." 2003 42 *Journal for the Scientific Study of Religion* 3, 333–39.

P Bienvenu. "Secession by Constitutional Means: Decision of the Supreme Court of Canada in the Quebec Secession Reference." 1999 21 *Hamline Journal of Public Law and Policy* 1–65.

D Bilchitz. "South Africa: Right to Health and Access to HIV/AIDS Drug Treatment." 2003 1 *International Journal of Constitutional Law* 3, 524–33.

———. "Towards a Reasonable Approach to the Minimum Core: Laying the Foundations for Future Socio-economic Rights Jurisprudence." 2003 19 *South African Journal on Human Rights* 1–26.

P Bobbitt. *Constitutional Interpretation*. Oxford: Blackwell, 1991.

WA Bogart. *Courts and Country: The Limits of Litigation and Social and Political Life of Canada*. Toronto: Oxford University Press, 1994.

D Bottos. "Keegstra and Andrews: A Commentary on Hate Propaganda and the Freedom of Expression." 1989 27 *Alberta Law Review* 13, 461–75.

J Boudéant. "Le Président du Conseil constitutionnel." 1987 *Revue de droit public* 443.

S Brenner and M Stier. "Retesting Segal and Spaeth's Stare Decisis Model." 1996 40 *American Journal of Political Science* 4, 1036–48.

G Brinkmann. "Militant Democracy and Radicals in the West German Civil Service." 1983 46 *Modern Law Review* 584–600.

W Brugger. "Legal Interpretation, Schools of Jurisprudence, and Anthropology: Some Remarks from a German Point of View." 1994 42 *American Journal of Comparative Law* 2, 395–421.

MF Brzezinski. *The Struggle for Constitutionalism in Poland*. St Antony's Series. Basingstoke: Macmillan, 2000.

MF Brzezinski and L Garlicki. "Judicial Review in Post-Communist Poland: The Emergence of a *Rechtsstaat*?" 1995 16 *Stanford Journal of International Law* 13–60.

B Bugaric. "Courts as Policy Makers: Lessons from Transition." 2001 42 *Harvard International Law Journal* 2001, 248–88.

MA Burnham. "Cultivating a Seedling Charter: South Africa's Court Grows Its Constitution." 1997 3 *Michigan Journal of Race and Law* 3.

P Butler. "Human Rights and Parliamentary Sovereignty in New Zealand." 2004 35 *Victoria University Wellington Law Review* 341–67.

RP Caldarone. "Precedent in Operation: A Comparison of the Judicial House of Lords and the US Supreme Court." 2004 *Public Law* 759–87.

G Campeau. "McKinney et ses Consequences Pour les Groupes Defavorises." 1992 8 *Journal of Law and Social Policy* 3, 229–53.

P Cancik. "Making Parliamentary Rights Effective—the Role of the Constitutional Courts in Germany." 2004. Conference paper in author's files.

GE Carmi. "Dignity—the Enemy from Within: A Theoretical and Comparative Analysis of Human Dignity as a Free Speech Justification." 2007 9 *Journal of Constitutional Law* 4, 957–1001.

PG Cassell. "*Miranda*'s Negligible Effect on Law Enforcement: Some Skeptical Observations." 1997 20 *Harvard Journal of Law and Public Policy* 327–47.

PG Cassell and R Fowles. "Handcuffing the Cops—a Thirty-Year Perspective on *Miranda*'s Harmful Effects on Law Enforcement." 1997 50 *Stanford Law Review* 1055–1147.

M Chanock. "A Post-Calvinist Catechism or a Post-Communist Manifesto? Intersecting Narratives in the South African Bill of Rights Debate." In P Alston, ed., *Promoting Human Rights through Bills of Rights*. Oxford: Oxford University Press, 1999.

A Chaskalson. "From Wickedness to Equality: The Moral Transformation of South African Law." 2003 1 *International Journal of Constitutional Law* 4, 590–609.

S Choudhry. "Globalization in Search of Justification: Toward a Theory of Comparative Constitutional Interpretation." 1999 74 *Indiana Law Journal* 819–93.

———. "The *Lochner* Era and Comparative Constitutionalism." 2004 2 *International Journal of Constitutional Law* 1, 1–55.

S Choudhry. *The Migration of Constitutional Ideas*. Cambridge: Cambridge University Press, 2006.

A Cole and R Gino. *Redefining the French Republic*. Manchester: Manchester University Press, 2006.

Conseil constitutionnel. "Human Rights and Public Order." 2003 *Eighth Seminar of Constitutional Courts, Erevan, 2 to 5 October 2003*.

M Coper. *Freedom of Interstate Trade under the Australian Constitution*. Sydney: Butterworths, 1983.

Council of Europe. "Opening Address, 10th Conference of European Constitutional Courts." In *Bulletin on Constitutional Case Law*. Budapest: Council of Europe, 1996.

S Cowan. "Can 'Dignity' Guide South Africa's Equality Jurisprudence?" 2001 17 *South African Journal on Human Rights* 34–58.

S Coyle. "Positivism, Idealism and the Rule of Law." 2006 26 *Oxford Journal of Legal Studies* 2, 257–88.

P Craig and G De Búrca, eds. *The Evolution of EU Law*. Oxford: Oxford University Press, 1999.

DP Currie. *The Constitution of the Federal Republic of Germany*. Chicago: University of Chicago Press, 1994.

D Davis. "Equality: The Majesty of Legoland Jurisprudence." 1999 116 *South African Law Journal* 398.

———. "The Shaping of a New Democracy within the Context of Tradition: Equality and the Respect for Diversity." In VC Jackson and M Tushnet, eds., *Defining the Field of Comparative Constitutional Law*. London: Praeger, 2002.

H de Vries and LE Sullivan, eds. *Political Theologies: Public Religions in a Post Secular World*. New York: Fordham University Press, 2006.

K Detterbeck. "Cartel Parties in Western Europe?" 2005 11 *Party Politics* 2, 173–91.

TR Draeger. "Property as a Fundamental Right in the United States and Germany: A Comparison of Takings Jurisprudence." 2001 14 *Transnational Lawyer* 363.

G Drago. *L'Execution des decisions du Conseil constitutionnel: L'effectivité du controle de constitutionalité des lois*. Paris: Economica, 1991.

EA Driedger. "The Meaning and Effect of the Canadian Bill of Rights: A Draftsman's Viewpoint." 1977 9 *Ottawa Law Review* 303–20.

M Du Plessis. "Between Apology and Utopia—the Constitutional Court and Public Opinion." 2002 18 *South African Journal on Human Rights* 1–40.

C Dupré. *Importing the Law in Post-Communist Transitions: The Hungarian Constitutional Court and the Right to Human Dignity*. Oxford: Hart, 2003.

N Duxbury. "Jerome Frank and the Legacy of Legal Realism." 1991 18 *Journal of Law and Society* 2, 175–205.

R Dworkin. "The Model of Rules." 1967 35 *Chicago Law Review* 14–46.

———. *Taking Rights Seriously*. London: Duckworth, 1977.

JH Ely. *Democracy and Distrust: A Theory of Judicial Review*. Cambridge: Harvard University Press, 1980.

L Epstein, J Knight, and AD Martin. "The Supreme Court as a Strategic National Policy Maker." 2001 50 *Emory Law Journal* 583–611.

A Eser and H-G Koch. *Abortion and the Law: From International Comparison to Legal Policy*. The Hague: TMC Asser Press, 2005.

SL Esquith. "Toward a Democratic Rule of Law: East and West." 1999 27 *Political Theory* 3, 334–56.

F Fabbrini. "Kelsen in Paris: France's Constitutional Reform and the Introduction of A Posteriori Constitutional Review." 2008 9 *German Law Journal* 10, 1298–1312.

A Fagan. "Dignity and Unfair Discrimination: A Value Misplaced and a Right Misunderstood." 1998 14 *South African Journal on Human Rights* 220–47.

RH Fallon. "Individual Rights and the Powers of Government." 1993 27 *Georgia Law Review* 343.

———. " 'The Rule of Law' as a Concept in Constitutional Discourse." 1997 97 *Columbia Law Review* 1.

———. "Implementing the Constitution." 1997 111 *Harvard Law Review* 54–152.

L Favoreu. "The Principle of Equality in the Jurisprudence of the Conseil Constitutionnel." 1992 21 *Capital University Law Review* 165–97.

———. "Sur l'introduction hypothétique du recours individuel direct devant le Conseil constitutionnel." 2001 10 *Cahiers du Conseil constitutionnel.*

L Favoreu and L Philip. *Les grandes décisions du Conseil constitutionnel.* 12th ed. Paris: Dalloz, 2003.

D Feldman. "Human Dignity as a Legal Value—Part I." 1999 *Public Law* 682–702.

BF Fitzgerald. "Proportionality and Australian Constitutionalism." 1993 12 *University of Tasmania Law Review* 265–322.

S Flemig. "Access to Justice—a Jurimetric Analysis of the Constitutional Complaint Admission to the German Federal Constitutional Court." MPhil, University of Oxford, 2008.

J Frank. *Law and the Modern Mind.* New York: Brentano, 1930.

S Friedman and S Mottiar. "A Rewarding Engagement? The Treatment Action Campaign and the Politics of HIV/AIDS." 2005 33 *Politics & Society* 4, 511–65.

F Fukuyama. *The End of History and the Last Man.* New York: Simon & Schuster, 2006.

MJ Gabriel. "Coming to Terms with the East German Border Guards Cases." 1999 38 *Columbia Journal of Transnational Law* 375–418.

B Galligan. *A Federal Republic: Australia's Constitutional System of Government.* Cambridge: Cambridge University Press, 1995.

———. *Politics of the High Court: A Study of the Judicial Branch of Government in Australia.* St. Lucia: University of Queensland Press, 1987.

G Garrett, RD Kelemen, and R Schulz. "The European Court of Justice, National Governments, and Legal Integration in the European Union." 1998 52 *International organization* 1, 149–76.

SG Gey. "The Political Economy of the Dormant Commerce Clause." 1989 1 *New York University Review of Law and Social Change* 17–97.

JL Gibson. "Judges' Role Orientations, Attitudes, and Decisions: An Interactive Model." 1978 72 *American Political Science Review* 3, 911–24.

JL Gibson and GA Caldeira. "Defenders of Democracy? Legitimacy, Popular Acceptance, and the South African Constitutional Court." 2003 65 *Journal of Politics* 1, 1–30.

———. "The Legal Cultures of Europe." 1996 30 *Law and Society Review* 1, 55–86.

JL Gibson, GA Caldeira, and VA Baird. "On the Legitimacy of National High Courts." 1998 92 *American Political Science Review* 2, 343–58.

F Gilman. "The Famous Footnote Four: A History of the *Carolene Products* Footnote." 2005 46 *South Texas Law Review* 163–245.

T Ginsburg. *Judicial Review in New Democracies: Constitutional Courts in Asian Cases.* Cambridge: Cambridge University Press, 2003.

T Ginsburg and T Moustafa, eds. *Rule by Law: The Politics of Courts in Authoritarian Regimes.* Cambridge: Cambridge University Press, 2008.

MA Glendon. "Rights in Twentieth Century Constitutions." 1992 59 *University of Chicago Law Review* 519–38.

F Goguel. *Cours constitutionnelles européennes et droits fondamentaux*. Paris: Economica, 1982.

J Goldsworthy. "Implications in Law, Language and the Constitution." In G Lindell, ed., *Future Directions in Australian Constitutional Law*. Sidney: Federation Press, 1994.

MD Goodman. "Human Dignity in Supreme Court Constitutional Jurisprudence." 2005 84 *Nebraska Law Review* 740–94.

M Graber. "Legal, Strategic, or Legal Strategy: Deciding to Decide during the Civil War and Reconstruction." In R Kahn and KI Kersch, eds., *The Supreme Court and American Political Development*. Lawrence: University Press of Kansas, 2006.

E Grant. "Dignity and Equality." 2007 7 *Human Rights Law Review* 2, 299–329.

O Gross and F Ní Aoláin. "From Discretion to Scrutiny: Revising the Application of the Margin of Appreciation Doctrine in the Context of Article 15 of the European Convention on Human Rights." 2001 23 *Human Rights Quarterly* 625–49.

C Guarnieri and P Pederzoli. *The Power of Judges: A Comparative Study of Courts and Democracy*. Oxford Socio-Legal Studies. Oxford: Oxford University Press, 2002.

G Gunther. "Foreword: In Search of Evolving Doctrine on a Changing Court: A Model for a Newer Equal Protection." 1972 86 *Harvard Law Review* 1.

SK Harding. "Comparative Reasoning and Judicial Review." 2003 28 *Yale Journal of International Law* 409–65.

HLA Hart. *The Concept of Law*. Oxford: Clarendon Press, 1972.

Y Hasebe. "Constitutional Borrowing and Political Theory." 2003 1 *International Journal of Comparative Law* 2, 224–43.

H Hausmaninger. "Judicial Referral of Constitutional Questions in Austria, Germany and Russia." 1997 12 *Tulane European and Civil Law Forum* 25.

AD Heard. "The Charter in the Supreme Court of Canada: The Importance of Which Judges Hear an Appeal." 1991 24 *Canadian Journal of Political Science / Revue canadienne de science politique* 2, 289–307.

M Herdegen. "Global Economy, Lean Budgets, and Public Needs." 2000 53 *Southern Methodist University Law Review* 543.

GL Heriot. "Strict Scrutiny, Public Opinion, and Affirmative Action on Campus: Should the Courts Find a Narrowly Tailored Solution to a Compelling Need in a Policy Most Americans Oppose?" 2003 40 *Harvard Journal on Legislation* 217.

D Herman. "The Good, the Bad, and the Smugly: Perspectives on the Canadian Charter of Rights and Freedoms." 1994 14 *Oxford Journal of Legal Studies* 4, 589–604.

R Hirschl. "Israel's 'Constitutional Revolution': The Legal Interpretation of Entrenched Civil Liberties in an Emerging Neo-liberal Economic Order." 1998 46 *American Journal of Comparative Law* 3, 427–52.

———. *Towards Juristocracy: The Origins and Consequences of the New Constitutionalism*. Cambridge: Harvard University Press, 2004.

P Hogg and AA Bushell. "The Charter Dialogue between Courts and Legislatures (or Perhaps the Charter of Rights Isn't Such a Bad Thing After All)." 1997 35 *Osgood Hall Law Journal* 75.

P Horowitz. "Law's Expression: The Promise and Perils of Judicial Opinion Writing in Canadian Constitutional Law." 2000 38 *Osgoode Hall Law Journal* 1, 101–42.

P Humphreys. "The Goal of Pluralism and the Ownership Rules for Private Broadcasting in Germany: Re-regulation or De-regulation?" 1998 16 *Yeshiva University Cardozo Arts & Entertainment Law Journal* 527.

M Hunt. "The Human Rights Act and Legal Culture: The Judiciary and the Legal Profession." 1999 26 *Journal of Law and Society* 86–105.

K Iles. "Limiting Socio-economic Rights: Beyond the Internal Limitations Clause." 2004 20 *South African Journal on Human Rights* 3, 448–65.

R Inglehart and C Weltzel. *Modernization, Cultural Change and Democracy*. Cambridge: Cambridge University Press, 2005.

VC Jackson. "Ambivalent Resistance and Comparative Constitutionalism: Opening Up the Conversation on 'Proportionality,' Rights and Federalism." 1999 1 *University of Pennsylvania Journal of Constitutional Law* 583–639.

DA Jacobs. "The Ban of Neo-Nazi Music: Germany Takes On the Neo-Nazis." 1993 34 *Harvard International Law Journal* 563.

J Jones. "'Common Constitutional Traditions': Can the Meaning of Human Dignity under German Law Guide the European Court of Justice?" 2004 *Public Law* 167–87.

RS Katz and P Mair. "Changing Models of Party Organizations and Party Democracy: The Emergence of the Cartel Party." 1995 1 *Party Politics* 5–28.

J Keeler. "Confrontations juridico-politiques: Le Conseil constitutionnel face au gouvernement socialiste comparé à la Cour Suprême face au New Deal." 1985 35 *Pouvoirs* 133–48.

KJ Keith. "Concerning Change: The Adoption and Implementation of the New Zealand Bill of Rights Act 1990." 2000 31 *Victoria University Wellington Law Review* 721–47.

JB Kelly. "The Charter of Rights and Freedoms and the Rebalancing of Liberal Constitutionalism in Canada, 1982–1997." 1999 37 *Osgoode Hall Law Journal* 625–79.

JB Kelly and M Murphy. "Confronting Judicial Supremacy: A Defence of Judicial Activism and the Supreme Court of Canada's Legal Rights Jurisprudence." 2001 16 *Canadian Journal of Law and Society* 3–28.

H Kelsen. "La Garantie Jurisdictionel de La Constitution." 1928 44 *Revue de droit public* 197.

———. "Judicial Review of Legislation: A Comparative Study of the Austrian and the American Constitution." 1942 4 *Journal of Politics* 2, 183–200.

———. *The Pure Theory of Law*. Berkeley: University of California Press, 1967.

J Kis. *Constitutional Democracy*. Budapest: Central European University, 2003.

KE Klare. "Legal Culture and Transformative Constitutionalism." 1998 14 *South African Journal on Human Rights* 146–88.

A Knapp and V Wright. *The Government and Politics of France*. 4th ed. London: Routledge, 2001.

DP Kommers. *The Constitutional Jurisprudence of the Federal Republic of Germany*. 2nd ed. Durham, N.C.: Duke University Press, 1997.

T Koopmans. *Courts and Political Institutions: A Comparative View*. Cambridge: Cambridge University Press, 2003.

RJ Krotoszynski Jr. "A Comparative Perspective on the First Amendment: Free Speech, Militant Democracy, and the Primacy of Dignity as a Preferred Constitutional Value in Germany." 2004 78 *Tulane Law Review* 1549.

Z Kuhn and J Kysela. "Nomination of Constitutional Justices in Post-Communist Countries: Trial, Error, Conflict in the Czech Republic." 2006 2 *European Constitutional Law Review* 2, 183–208.

J Kurczewski. "Parliament and the Political Class in the Constitutional Reconstruction of Poland: Two Constitutions in One." 2003 18 *International Sociology* 1, 162–80.

D Kyritsis. "Representation and Waldron's Objection to Judicial Review." 2006 26 *Oxford Journal of Legal Studies* 4, 733–51.

C L'Heureux-Dubé. "The Dissenting Opinion: Voice of the Future?" 2000 38 *Osgoode Hall Law Journal* 495–518.

———. "Realising Equality in the Twentieth Century: The Role of the Supreme Court of Canada in Comparative Perspective." 2003 1 *International Journal of Constitutional Law* 1, 35–57.

G Laforest. *Trudeau and the End of a Canadian Dream*. Montreal: McGill-Queen's University Press, 1995.

C Landfried. *Constitutional Review and Legislation: An International Comparison*. Baden-Baden: Nomos, 1989.

———. "Judicial Policy-Making in Germany: The Federal Constitutional Court." 1993 15 *West European Politics* 52–63.

M Larkin. *France since the Popular Front: Government and People 1936–1996*. 2nd ed. Oxford: Oxford University Press, 1997.

M Lasser. *Judicial Deliberations: A Comparative Analysis of Judicial Transparency and Legitimacy*. Oxford Studies in European Law. Oxford: Oxford University Press, 2004.

N LaViolette. "The Immutable Refugees: Sexual Orientation in *Canada (A.G.) v. Ward*." 1997 55 *University of Toronto Faculty of Law Review* 1, 1–41.

O Lepsius. "Human Dignity and the Downing of Aircraft: The German Federal Constitutional Court Strikes Down a Prominent Anti-terrorism Provision in the New Air-Transport Security Act." 2006 7 *German Law Journal* 9, 762–76.

EH Levi. *An Introduction to Legal Reasoning*. Chicago: University of Chicago Press, 1949.

A Lewis. *Gideon's Trumpet*. New York: Random House, 1966.

M Liu. "A Prophet with Honour: An Examination of the Gender Equality Jurisprudence of Madam Justice Claire L'Heureux-Dubé of the Supreme Court of Canada." 2000 25 *Queen's Law Journal* 417–78.

K Lowenstein. "Militant Democracy and Fundamental Rights." 1937 31 *American Political Science Review* 417.

F Luchaire. *Le Conseil constitutionnel*. 2nd ed. 4 vols. Paris: Economica, 1997–2002.

F Luchaire and G Conac. *La Constitution de la République française article par article*. Paris: Economica, 1987.

GR MacConaill. "*Nevada Department of Human Resources v. Hibbs*: Does Application of Section 5 Represent a Fundamental Change in the Immunity Abrogation Rules of New Federalism, or Have the Burdens Simply Shifted." 2004 109 *Penn State Law Review* 4, 831.

P Macklem. "Militant Democracy, Legal Pluralism, and the Paradox of Self-Determination." 2006 4 *International Journal of Constitutional Law* 3, 488–516.

P Maduna. "The Death Penalty and Human Rights." 1996 12 *South African Journal on Human Rights* 193–217.

EM Maltz. "The Court, the Academy, and the Constitution: A Comment on *Bowers v. Hardwick* and Its Critics." 1989 *Brigham Young University Law Review* 59–95.

D Manno. *Le Juge constitutionnel et la technique des "decisions interprétatives" en France et en Italie*. Paris: Economica; Aix-en-Provence: Presses universitaires d' Aix-Marseilles, 1998.

JG March and JP Olsen. "The Logic of Appropriateness." In M Moran, M Rein, and RE Goodin, eds., *Oxford Handbook of Public Policy*. Oxford: Oxford University Press, 2006.

A Marga. *La Sortie du relativisme*. Cluj: Editura-Limes, 2006.

BS Markesinis. *Always on the Same Path: Essays on Foreign Law and Comparative Methodology*. Oxford: Hart, 2001.

G Mazzoleni. "The RAI: Restructuring and Reform." In C Mershon and G Pasquino, eds., *Italian Politics: Ending the First Republic*. Boulder, Colo.: Westview Press, 1995.
AJ McAdams. *Judging the Past in Unified Germany*. Cambridge: Cambridge University Press, 2001.
P McCormick. "Blocs, Swarms, and Outliers: Conceptualizing Disagreement on the Modern Supreme Court of Canada." 2004 42 *Osgoode Hall Law Journal* 100–138.
E McWhinney. *Canada and the Constitution, 1979–82: Patriation and the Charter of Rights*. Toronto: University of Toronto Press, 1982.
———. "Judicial Restraint and the West German Constitutional Court." 1961 75 *Harvard Law Review* 1, 5–38.
F Mélin-Soucramanien. *Le Principe d'égalité dans la jurisprudence du Conseil constitutionnel*. Paris: Economica, 1997.
JH Merryman. *The Civil Law Tradition*. Stanford, Calif.: Stanford University Press, 1969.
FI Michelman. "The Constitution, Social Rights, and Liberal Political Justification." 2003 1 *International Journal of Constitutional Law* 1, 13–34.
RA Miller. "Lords of Democracy: The Judicialization of 'Pure Politics' in the United States and Germany." 2004 61 *Washington & Lee Law Review* 587.
S Mölders. "Case Note—the European Arrest Warrant in the German Federal Constitutional Court." 2006 7 *German Law Journal* 11.
PJ Monahan. "The Law and Politics of Quebec Secession." 1995 33 *Osgoode Hall Law Journal* 1, 33–67.
PJ Monahan and M Finkelstein. "The Charter of Rights and Public Policy in Canada." 1992 30 *Osgood Hall Law Journal* 501–46.
FL Morton. "The Charter Revolution and the Court Party." 1992 30 *Osgood Hall Law Journal* 628–52.
———. "Judicial Review in France: A Comparative Analysis." 36 *American Journal of Comparative Law* 1, 89–110.
D Moseneke. "The Fourth Bram Fischer Memorial Lecture: Transformative Adjudication." 22002 18 *South African Journal on Human Rights* 309–19.
Z Motala and C Ramaphosa. *Constitutional Law: Analysis and Cases*. Oxford: Oxford University Press, 2002.
R Mulgan. "Debate: Aristotle, Ethical Diversity and Political Argument." 1999 7 *Journal of Political Philosophy* 2, 191–207.
J O'Neil. "*Marbury v Madison* at 200: Revisionist Scholarship and the Legitimacy of American Judicial Review." 2002 *Modern Law Review* 792–83.
J Oniszczuk, ed. *A Selection of the Polish Constitutional Tribunal's Jurisprudence from 1986 to 1999*. Warsaw: Polish Constitutional Tribunal, 1999.
C Osborn. "Constitutional Scrutiny and Speech: Eroding the Bedrock Principles of the First Amendment." 1990 44 *Southwestern Law Journal* 1013–44.
W Osiatynski. "Paradoxes of Constitutional Borrowing." 2003 1 *International Journal of Constitutional Law* 2, 244–68.
A Pagden. "Human Rights, Natural Rights, and Europe's Imperial Legacy." 2003 31 *Political Theory* 171–99.
G Palmer. "The New Zealand Constitution and the Power of Courts." 2005 15 *Transnational Law and Contemporary Problems* 551–79.
G Pearson and M Salter. "Getting Public Law Back into a Critical Condition: The Rule of Law as a Source for Immanent Critique." 1999 8 *Social Legal Studies* 4, 483–508.
JM Pellicciotti. "The Constitutional Guarantee of Equal Protection in Canada and the United States: A Comparative Analysis of the Standards for Determining the Valid-

ity of Governmental Action." 1997 5 *Tulsa Journal of Comparative & International Law* 1.

X Philippe. *Le contrôle de proportionnalité dans les jurisprudences constitutionnelle et administrative françaises*. Science et droit administratifs. Paris: Economica and Presses universitaires d'Aix-Marseilles, 1990.

JL Pierce. *Inside the Mason Court Revolution: The High Court of Australia Transformed*. Durham, N.C.: Carolina Academic Press, 2006.

RH Pildes. "Why Rights Are Not Trumps: Social Meanings, Expressive Harms, and Constitutionalism." 1998 27 *Journal of Legal Studies* 2, 725–63.

I Pogany. "Constitutional Reform in Central and Eastern Europe: Hungary's Transition to Democracy." 1993 42 *International and Comparative Law Quarterly* 2, 332–55.

———. *Righting Wrongs in Eastern Europe*. Europe in Change. Manchester: Manchester University Press, 1997.

RA Posner. *How Judges Think*. Cambridge: Harvard University Press, 2008.

RC Post. "The Supreme Court, 2002 Term: Foreword: Fashioning the Legal Constitution: Culture, Courts, and Law." 2003 117 *Harvard Law Review* 4.

D Pothier. "Twenty Years of Labour Law and the Charter." 2002 40 *Osgood Hall Law Journal* 370–400.

M Poto. "The Principle of Proportionality in Comparative Perspective—Part II/II." 8 *German Law Journal* 9.

HK Prempeh. "*Marbury* in Africa: Judicial Review and the Challenge of Constitutionalism in Contemporary Africa." 2005 80 *Tulane Law Review* 1239–1323.

J Priban. *Dissidents of Law*. London: Ashgate, 2002.

———. "Moral and Political Legislation in Constitutional Justice: A Case Study of the Czech Constitutional Court." 2001 8 *Journal of East European Law* 1.

P Quint. "The Border Guard Trials and the East German Past—Seven Arguments." 2000 48 *American Journal of Comparative Law*.

A Rainer. "The Treaty on European Union and German Constitutional Law: The German Constitutional Court's Decision of October 12, 1993, on the Treaty of Maastricht." 1994 9 *Tulane European and Civil Law Forum* 91–145.

BG Ramcharan. *Judicial Protection of Economic, Social and Cultural Rights: Cases and Materials*. Raoul Wallenberg Institute Human Rights Library. Leiden: Martinus Nijhoff, 2005.

DG Réaume. "Discrimination and Dignity." 2003 63 *Louisiana Law Review* 645–95.

T Rensmann. "Procedural Fairness in a Militant Democracy: The 'Uprising of the Decent' Fails before the Federal Constitutional Court." 2003 4 *German Law Journal* (e-journal) 11.

J Rivero. "Les principes fondamenteau reconnus par les lois de la République: Une nouvelle catégorie constitutionnelle." 1972 *Revue de droit public* 265–81.

J Robert. *La Garde de la République: Le Conseil constitutionnel raconté par l'un de ses membres*. Paris: Plon 2000.

D Robertson. *Democratic Transitions and a Common Constitutional Law for Europe*. Oxford: Europaeum, 2001.

———. *A Dictionary of Human Rights*. London: Europa, 1997.

———. *Judicial Discretion in the House of Lords*. Oxford: Clarendon Press, 1998.

———. "Judicial Discretion, Legal Positivism, and Democratic Theory." In M Freeman and D Robertson, eds., *The Frontiers of Political Theory: Essays in a Revitalised Discipline*. Brighton: Harvester, 1980.

———. "The Role of Constitutional Courts in the New Eastern European Democracies." Public Lecture, Jagellonian University, Kraków, October 3, 2005.

———. "Thick Constitutional Readings: When Classic Distinctions Are Irrelevant." 2006 35 *Georgia Journal of International and Comparative Law* 277–331.

CJ Roederer. "The Constitutionally Inspired Approach to Vicarious Liability in Cases of Intentional Wrongful Acts by the Police: One Small Step in Restoring the Public's Trust in the South African Police Services." 2005 21 *South African Journal on Human Rights* 4.

———. "Post-matrix Legal Reasoning: Horizontality and the Rule of Values in South African Law." 2003 19 *South African Journal on Human Rights* 57–81.

JR Rogers and G Vanberg. "Judicial Advisory Opinions and Legislative Outcomes in Comparative Perspective." 2002 46 *American Journal of Political Science* 2, 379–97.

R Rogowski and T Gawron. *Constitutional Courts in Comparison: The U.S. Supreme Court and the German Federal Constitutional Court.* Oxford: Berghahn, 2002.

FR Romeu. "The Establishment of Constitutional Courts: A Study of 128 Democratic Constitutions." 2006 2 *Review of Law and Economics* 1, 104–35.

K Roosevelt. "Constitutional Calcification: How the Law Becomes What the Court Does." 2005 91 *Virginia Law Review* 1649–1710.

———. *The Myth of Judicial Activism: Making Sense of Supreme Court Decisions.* New Haven: Yale University Press, 2005.

M Rosenfeld. "Constitutional Adjudication in Europe and the United States: Paradoxes and Contrasts." 2004 2 *International Journal of Comparative Law* 4, 633–68.

CF Rosenkrantz. "Against Borrowings and Other Nonauthoritative Uses of Foreign Law." 2003 1 *International Journal of Constitutional Law* 2, 269–95.

D Rousseau. *Droit du contentieux constitutionnel.* 6th ed. Paris: Montchrestien, 2001.

———. *Sur le Conseil constitutionnel: La doctrine Badinter et la démocratie.* Paris: Descartes & Cie, 1997.

R Ruge. "Between Law and Necessity: The Federal Constitutional Court Confirms the Right of the Federal Government to Warn the Public." 2002 3 *German Law Journal* (e-journal) 12.

A Sachs. "The Creation of South Africa's Constitution." 1997 41 *New York Law School Law Review* 669.

M Sachs. "The Equality Rule before the German Federal Constitutional Court." 1998 *St Louis-Warsaw Transatlantic Law Journal* 139.

W Sadurski, A Czarnota, and M Krygier, eds. *Spreading Democracy and the Rule of Law? The Impact of EU Enlargement on the Rule of Law, Democracy and Constitutionalism in Post-Communist Legal Orders.* Dordrecht: Springer, 2006.

A Sajo. "How the Rule of Law Killed Hungarian Welfare Reform." 1996 *East European Constitutional Review* 31.

———. "On Old and New Battles: Obstacles to the Rule of Law in Eastern Europe." 1995 22 *Journal of Law and Society* 1, 97–104.

———. "Reading the Invisible Constitution: Judicial Review in Hungary." 1995 15 *Oxford Journal of Legal Studies* 2, 253–67.

J Sarkin. "The Drafting of South Africa's Final Constitution from a Human-Rights Perspective." 1999 47 *American Journal of Comparative Law* 1, 67–87.

O Schachter. "Human Dignity as a Normative Concept." 1983 77 *American Journal of International Law* 4, 848–54.

HM Scheb, TD Ungs, and AL Hayes. "Judicial Role Orientation, Attitudes and Decision Making: A Research Note." 1989 42 *Political Research Quarterly* 427–35.

KL Schepple. "Constitutional Negotiations: Political Contexts of Judicial Activism in Post-Soviet Europe." 2003 18 *International Sociology* 1, 219–38.

KL Schepple. "Round Table Constitution-Making Process and the Rule of Law: Panel II. Constitutional Courts and the Rule of Law." 1997 12 *American University Journal of International Law and Policy* 85–115.

B Schlink. "Hercules in Germany." 2003 1 *International Journal of Constitutional Law* 4, 610–20.

N Schofield. "Constitutions, Voting and Democracy: A Review." 2001 18 *Social Choice and Welfare* 3, 571–600.

G Schram. "Ideology and Politics: The *Rechtsstaat* Idea in West Germany." 1971 33 *Journal of Politics* 1, 133–57.

H Schwartz. *The Struggle for Constitutional Justice in Post-Communist Europe*. Chicago: University of Chicago Press, 2000.

TA Schweitzer. "Supreme Court Rules in Favor of Religious Club's Right to Meet on Public School Premises: Is This Good News for First Amendment Rights?" 2001 18 *Touro Law Review* 127.

JA Segal and HJ Spaeth. "The Influence of Stare Decisis on the Votes of United States Supreme Court Justices." 1996 40 *American Journal of Political Science* 4, 971–1003.

M Shapiro. "The European Court of Justice." In P Craig and G De Búrca, eds., *The Evolution of EU Law*. Oxford: Oxford University Press, 1999.

M Shapiro and A Stone Sweet. *On Law, Politics and Judicialization*. Oxford: Oxford University Press, 2002.

M Singer. "The Constitutional Court of the German Federal Republic: Jurisdiction over Individual Complaints." 1982 31 *International and Comparative Law Quarterly* 2, 331–56.

A-M Slaughter. "Judicial Globalization." 2000 40 *Virginia Journal of International Law* 1103–25.

———. "A Typology of Transjudicial Communication." 1994 99 *University of Richmond Law Review* 29–69.

C Smith. "Judicial Review of Parliamentary Legislation: Norway as a European Pioneer." 2000 *Public Law* 595–606.

———. "More Disagreement over Human Dignity: Federal Constitutional Court's Most Recent Benetton Advertising Decision." 2003 4 *German Law Journal* (e-journal) 6.

L Sólyom. "Opening Address, 10th Conference of European Constitutional Courts." In *Bulletin on Constitutional Case Law*. Budapest: Council of Europe, 1996.

———. "The Role of Constitutional Courts in the Transition to Democracy: With Special Reference to Hungary." 2003 18 *International Sociology* 1, 133–61.

L Sólyom and G Brunner. *Constitutional Judiciary in a New Democracy: The Hungarian Constitutional Court*. Ann Arbor: University of Michigan Press, 2000.

TA Sparling. "Judicial Bias Claims of Homosexual Persons in the Wake of *Lawrence v. Texas*." 2004 *Southern Texas Law Review* 255–309.

R Spitz. *The Politics of Transition: A Hidden History of South Africa's Negotiated Settlement*. Oxford: Hart, 2000.

C Sprigman and M Osborne. "Du Plessis Is *Not* Dead: South Africa's 1996 Constitution and the Application of the Bill of Rights to Private Disputes." 1999 15 *South African Journal on Human Rights* 25–51.

R Stith. "New Constitutional and Penal Theory in Spanish Abortion Law." 1987 35 *American Journal of Comparative Law* 3, 513–58.

A Stone. "Judging Socialist Reform: The Politics of Coordinate Construction in France and Germany." 1994 26 *Comparative Political Studies* 443–69.

A Stone and S Evans. "Australia: Freedom of Speech and Insult in the High Court of Australia." 2006 4 *International Journal of Constitutional Law* 4, 677–88.

A Stone Sweet. *The Birth of Judicial Politics in France: The Constitutional Council in Comparative Perspective*. Oxford: Oxford University Press, 1992.

———. "Constitutional Courts and Parliamentary Democracy." 2002 25 *West European Politics* 1, 77–100.

———. *Governing with Judges; Constitutional Politics in Europe*. Oxford: Oxford University Press, 2000.

BA Streeter III. "Co-determination in West Germany—through the Best (and Worst) of Times." 1982 58 *Chicago-Kent Law Review* 981.

RS Summers. "Principles of the Rule of Law." 1999 74 *Notre Dame Law Review* 1691–1711.

LB Tremblay. "The Legitimacy of Judicial Review: The Limits of Dialogue between Courts and Legislatures." 2005 3 *International Journal of Constitutional Law* 4, 617–48.

A Trochev. "Ukraine: Constitutional Court Invalidates Ban on Communist Party." 2003 1 *International Journal of Constitutional Law* 3, 534–40.

R Turner. "Traditionalism, Majoritarian Morality, and the Homosexual Sodomy Issue: The Journey from *Bowers* to *Lawrence*." 2004 53 *University of Kansas Law Review* 1–81.

M Tushnet. "The Issue of State Action / Horizontal Effect in Comparative Constitutional Law." 2003 1 *International Journal of Constitutional Law* 1, 79–98.

———. "The Possibilities of Comparative Constitutional Law." 1999 108 *Yale Law Journal* 6, 1225–1309.

———. "Scalia and the Dormant Commerce Clause: A Foolish Formalism." 1990 12 *Cardozo Law Review* 1717–43.

———. "United States: Supreme Court Rules on Affirmative Action." 2004 2 *International Journal of Constitutional Law* 1, 158–73.

D Ullrich. "Concurring Visions: Human Dignity in the Canadian Charter of Rights and Freedoms and the Basic Law of the Federal Republic of Germany." 2003 3 *Global Jurist Frontiers* 1.

J Van Der Walt. "Progressive Indirect Horizontal Application of the Bill of Rights: Towards a Co-operative Relation between Common-Law and Constitutional Jurisprudence." 2001 17 *South African Journal on Human Rights* 341–63.

M Van Hoecke and M Warrington. "Legal Cultures, Legal Paradigms and Legal Doctrine: Towards a New Model for Comparative Law." 1998 47 *International and Comparative Law Quarterly* 495–537.

G Vanberg. "Legislative-Judicial Relations: A Game-Theoretic Approach to Constitutional Review." 2001 45 *American Journal of Political Science* 2, 346–61.

———. *The Politics of Constitutional Review in Germany*. Cambridge: Cambridge University Press, 2005.

V Vigoriti. "Italy: The Constitutional Court." 1972 20 *American Journal of Comparative Law* 3, 404–14.

M Volcansek. *Constitutional Politics in Italy*. London: Macmillan, 2000.

E Volokh. "Freedom of Speech, Permissible Tailoring and Transcending Strict Scrutiny." 1995 44 *University of Pennsylvania Law Review* 2417–61.

J Waldron. *Law and Disagreement*. Oxford: Oxford University Press, 1999.

———. "Legislation, Authority, and Voting." 1996 84 *Georgia Law Journal* 2185–2215.

———. "Pildes on Dworkin's Theory of Rights." 2000 29 *Journal of Legal Studies* 301–9.

———. "A Rights Based Critique of Constitutional Rights." 1993 13 *Oxford Journal of Legal Studies* 18–51.

A Watson. *Legal Transplants: An Approach to Comparative law*. Athens: University of Georgia Press, 1993.

J Weinstein and T DeMarco. "Challenging Dissent: The Ontology and Logic of *Lawrence v. Texas*." 2003 10 *Cardozo Women's Law Journal* 423–67.

TD Weldon. *Vocabulary of Politics*. London: Penguin, 1953.

U Werner. "The Convergence of Abortion Regulations in Germany and the United States: A Critique of Glendon's Rights Talk Thesis." 1996 18 *Loyola of Los Angeles International and Comparative Law Journal* 571.

M Wesson. "Grootboom and Beyond: Re-assessing the Socio-economic Jurisprudence of the South African Constitutional Court." 2004 20 *South African Journal on Human Rights* 2, 284–308.

ME Wetstein, CL Ostberg, DR Songer, and SW Johnson. "Ideological Consistency and Attitudinal Conflict: A Comparative Analysis of the U.S. and Canadian Supreme Courts." 2009 42 *Comparative Political Studies* 6, 763–92.

D Wielsch. "Calibrating Liberty and Security: Federal Constitutional Court Rules on Freedom of Speech in PKK Case." 2002 3 *German Law Journal* (e-journal) 6.

B Wilson. "Constitutional Advocacy." 1992 24 *Ottawa Law Review* 265–75.

S Woolman and D David. "'The Last Laugh': *Du Plessis v De Klerk*, Classical Liberalism, Creole Liberalism and the Application of Fundamental Rights under the Interim and Final Constitution." 1996 12 *South African Journal on Human Rights* 361–404.

T Yarbrough. *Mr. Justice Black and His Critics*. Durham, N.C.: Duke University Press, 1988.

J Yoo. "Peeking Abroad? The Supreme Court's Use of Foreign Precedents in Constitutional Cases." 2003 26 *University of Hawaii Law Review* 385–404.

INDEX

Note: Tables are indicated by *t* following the page number.